KB186203

한국의 토익 수험자 여러분께,

토익 시험은 세계적인 직무 영어능력 평가 시험으로, 지난 40여 년간 비즈니스 현장에서 필요한
영어능력 평가의 기준을 제시해 왔습니다. 토익 시험 및 토익스피킹, 토익라이팅 시험은 세계에서 가장
널리 통용되는 영어능력 검증 시험으로, 160여 개국 14,000여 기관이 토익 성적을 의사결정에
활용하고 있습니다.

YBM은 한국의 토익 시험을 주관하는 ETS 독점 계약사입니다.

ETS는 한국 수험자들의 효과적인 토익 학습을 돕고자 YBM을 통하여 'ETS 토익 공식 교재'를 독점
출간하고 있습니다. 또한 'ETS 토익 공식 교재' 시리즈에 기출문항을 제공해 한국의 다른 교재들에 수록된
기출을 복제하거나 변형한 문항으로 인하여 발생할 수 있는 수험자들의 혼동을 방지하고 있습니다.

복제 및 변형 문항들은 토익 시험의 출제의도를 벗어날 수 있기 때문에 기출문항을 수록한 'ETS 토익
공식 교재'만큼 시험에 잘 대비할 수 없습니다.

'ETS 토익 공식 교재'를 통하여 수험자 여러분의 영어 소통을 위한 노력에 큰 성취가 있기를 바랍니다.

감사합니다.

Dear TOEIC Test Takers in Korea,

The TOEIC program is the global leader in English-language assessment for the workplace. It has set the
standard for assessing English-language skills needed in the workplace for more than 40 years. The TOEIC
tests are the most widely used English language assessments around the world, with 14,000+ organizations
across more than 160 countries trusting TOEIC scores to make decisions.

YBM is the ETS Country Master Distributor for the TOEIC program in Korea and so is the exclusive
distributor for TOEIC Korea.

To support effective learning for TOEIC test-takers in Korea, ETS has authorized YBM to publish the only
Official TOEIC prep books in Korea. These books contain actual TOEIC items to help prevent confusion
among Korean test-takers that might be caused by other prep book publishers' use of reproduced or
paraphrased items.

Reproduced or paraphrased items may fail to reflect the intent of actual TOEIC items and so will not
prepare test-takers as well as the actual items contained in the ETS TOEIC Official prep books published
by YBM.

We hope that these ETS TOEIC Official prep books enable you, as test-takers, to achieve great success in
your efforts to communicate effectively in English.

Thank you.

입문부터 실전까지 수준별 학습을 통해 최단기 목표점수 달성!

ETS TOEIC® 공식수험서
스마트 학습 지원

구글플레이, 앱스토어에서
ETS 토익기출 수험서 다운로드

구글플레이

앱스토어

ETS 토익 모바일 학습 플랫폼!

ETS® 토익기출 수험서 [어플]

교재 학습 지원
1. 교재 해설 강의
2. LC 음원 MP3
3. 교재/부록 모의고사 채점 및 분석
4. 단어 암기장

부가 서비스
1. 데일리 학습(토익 기출문제 풀이)
2. 토익 최신 경향 무료 특강
3. 토익 타이머

모의고사 결과 분석
1. 파트별/문항별 정답률
2. 파트별/유형별 취약점 리포트
3. 전체 응시자 점수 분포도

ETS TOEIC 공식카페 ▼

etstoeicbook.co.kr

ETS 토익 학습 전용 온라인 커뮤니티!

ETS TOEIC® Book [공식카페]

강사진의 학습 지원   토익 대표강사들의 학습 지원과 멘토링

교재 학습관 운영   교재별 학습게시판을 통해 무료 동영상
강의 등 학습 지원

학습 콘텐츠 제공   토익 학습 콘텐츠와 정기시험
예비특강 업데이트

www.ybmbooks.com에서도 무료 MP3를 다운로드 받을 수 있습니다.

ETS. TOEIC.

토익 정기시험
기출문제집 3
1000
READING

YBM

토익 정기시험
기출문제집 3
1000
READING

발행인   허문호
발행처   YBM

편집   윤경림, 허유정
디자인   이현숙
마케팅   전경진, 정연철, 박천산, 고영노, 박찬경, 김동진, 김윤하

초판발행 2021년 11월 22일
10쇄발행 2024년 4월 15일

신고일자 1964년 3월 28일
신고번호 제 300-1964-3호
주소   서울시 종로구 종로 104
전화   (02) 2000-0515 [구입문의] / (02) 2000-0345 [내용문의]
팩스   (02) 2285-1523
홈페이지 www.ybmbooks.com

ISBN   978-89-17-23854-9

ETS, the ETS logo, TOEIC and 토익 are registered trademarks of Educational Testing Service, Princeton, New Jersey, U.S.A., used in the Republic of Korea under license. Copyright © 2021 by Educational Testing Service, Princeton, New Jersey, U.S.A. All rights reserved. Reproduced under license for limited use by YBM. These materials are protected by United States Laws, International Copyright Laws and International Treaties. In the event of any discrepancy between this translation and official ETS materials, the terms of the official ETS materials will prevail. All items were created or reviewed by ETS. All item annotations and test-taking tips were reviewed by ETS.

서면에 의한 저자와 출판사의 허락 없이 내용의 일부 혹은 전부를 인용 및 복제하거나 발췌하는 것을 금합니다.
낙장 및 파본은 교환해 드립니다.
구입철회는 구매처 규정에 따라 교환 및 환불처리 됩니다.

토익® 정기시험 기출문제집 3

1000

READING

Preface

Dear test taker,

English-language proficiency has become a vital tool for success. It can help you excel in business, travel the world, and communicate effectively with friends and colleagues. The TOEIC® test measures your ability to function effectively in English in these types of situations. Because TOEIC scores are recognized around the world as evidence of your English-language proficiency, you will be able to confidently demonstrate your English skills to employers and begin your journey to success.

The test developers at ETS are excited to help you achieve your personal and professional goals through the use of the ETS® TOEIC® 정기시험 기출문제집 1000 Vol. 3. This book contains test questions taken from actual, official TOEIC tests. It also contains three tests that were developed by ETS to help prepare you for actual TOEIC tests. All these materials will help you become familiar with the TOEIC test's format and content. This book also contains detailed explanations of the question types and language points contained in the TOEIC test. These test questions and explanations have all been prepared by the same test specialists who develop the actual TOEIC test, so you can be confident that you will receive an authentic test-preparation experience.

Features of the ETS® TOEIC® 정기시험 기출문제집 1000 Vol. 3 include the following.

- Seven full-length actual tests plus three full-length tests of equal quality created by ETS for test preparation use, all accompanied by answer keys and official scripts
- Specific and easy to understand explanations for learners
- The very same ETS voice actors that you will hear in an official TOEIC test administration

By using the ETS® TOEIC® 정기시험 기출문제집 1000 Vol. 3. to prepare for the TOEIC test, you can be assured that you have a professionally prepared resource that will provide you with accurate guidance so that you are more familiar with the tasks, content, and format of the test and that will help you maximize your TOEIC test score. With your official TOEIC score certificate, you will be ready to show the world what you know!

We are delighted to assist you on your TOEIC journey with the ETS® TOEIC® 정기시험 기출문제집 1000 Vol. 3. and wish you the best of success.

최신 기출문제 전격 공개!

'출제기관이 독점 제공한' 기출문제가 담긴 유일한 교재!

이 책에는 정기시험 기출문제 7세트와 토익 예상문제 3세트가 수록되어 있다. 시험에 나온 토익 문제로
실전 감각을 키우고, 동일한 난이도의 예상문제로 시험에 확실하게 대비하자!

기출 포인트를 꿰뚫는 명쾌한 해설!

최신 출제 경향을 가장 정확하게 알 수 있는 기출문제를 풀고 출제포인트가 보이는 명쾌한 해설로
토익을 정복해 보자!

'ETS가 제공하는' 표준점수 환산표!

출제기관 ETS가 독점 제공하는 표준점수 환산표를 수록했다. 채점 후 환산표를 통해 자신의 실력이
어느 정도인지 가늠해 보자!

What is the TOEIC?

TOEIC은 어떤 시험인가요?

Test of English for International Communication(국제적 의사소통을 위한 영어 시험)의 약자로서, 영어가 모국어가 아닌 사람들이 일상생활 또는 비즈니스 현장에서 꼭 필요한 실용적 영어 구사 능력을 갖추었는가를 평가하는 시험이다.

시험 구성

구성	Part	내용		문항수	시간	배점
듣기(L/C)	1	사진 묘사		6	45분	495점
	2	질의 응답		25		
	3	짧은 대화		39		
	4	짧은 담화		30		
읽기(R/C)	5	단문 빈칸 채우기(문법/어휘)		30	75분	495점
	6	장문 빈칸 채우기		16		
	7	독해	단일 지문	29		
			이중 지문	10		
			삼중 지문	15		
Total	**7 Parts**			**200문항**	**120분**	**990점**

TOEIC 접수는 어떻게 하나요?

TOEIC 접수는 한국 토익 위원회 사이트(www.toeic.co.kr)에서 온라인 상으로만 접수가 가능하다. 사이트에서 매월 자세한 접수 일정과 시험 일정 등의 구체적 정보 확인이 가능하니, 미리 일정을 확인하여 접수하도록 한다.

시험장에 반드시 가져가야 할 준비물은요?

신분증 규정 신분증만 가능

(주민등록증, 운전면허증, 기간 만료 전의 여권, 공무원증 등)

필기구 연필, 지우개 (볼펜이나 사인펜은 사용 금지)

시험은 어떻게 진행되나요?

09:20	입실 (09:50 이후는 입실 불가)
09:30 – 09:45	답안지 작성에 관한 오리엔테이션
09:45 – 09:50	휴식
09:50 – 10:05	신분증 확인
10:05 – 10:10	문제지 배부 및 파본 확인
10:10 – 10:55	듣기 평가 (Listening Test)
10:55 – 12:10	독해 평가 (Reading Test)

TOEIC 성적 확인은 어떻게 하죠?

시험일로부터 약 10-11일 후 인터넷과 ARS(060-800-0515)로 성적을 확인할 수 있다. TOEIC 성적표는 우편이나 온라인으로 발급 받을 수 있다(시험 접수시, 양자 택일). 우편으로 발급 받을 경우는 성적 발표 후 대략 일주일이 소요되며, 온라인 발급을 선택하면 유효기간 내에 홈페이지에서 본인이 직접 1회에 한해 무료 출력할 수 있다. TOEIC 성적은 시험일로부터 2년간 유효하다.

TOEIC은 몇 점 만점인가요?

TOEIC 점수는 듣기 영역(LC) 점수, 읽기 영역(RC) 점수, 그리고 이 두 영역을 합계한 전체 점수 세 부분으로 구성된다. 각 부분의 점수는 5점 단위이며, 5점에서 495점에 걸쳐 주어지고, 전체 점수는 10점에서 990점까지이며, 만점은 990점이다. TOEIC 성적은 각 문제 유형의 난이도에 따른 점수 환산표에 의해 결정된다.

토익 경향 분석

1인 등장 사진
주어는 He/She, A man/woman 등이며 주로 앞부분에 나온다.

2인 이상 등장 사진
주어는 They, Some men/women/people, One of the men/women 등이며 주로 중간 부분에 나온다.

사물/배경 사진
주어는 A car, Some chairs 등이며 주로 뒷부분에 나온다.

사람 또는 사물 중심 사진
주어가 일부는 사람, 일부는 사물이며 주로 뒷부분에 나온다.

사람 또는
사물 중심 사진
33%

1인
등장 사진
33%

**PART 1
최신 출제 경향**

사물/
배경 사진
17%

2인 이상
등장 사진
17%

기타
10%

단순 현재
수동태
25%

**정답의
시제와 태**

현재 진행 능동태
65%

현재 진행 능동태
〈is/are + 현재분사〉 형태이며 주로 사람이 주어이다.

단순 현재 수동태
〈is/are + 과거분사〉 형태이며 주로 사물이 주어이다.

기타
〈is/are + being + 과거분사〉 형태의 현재 진행 수동태,
〈has/have + been + 과거 분사〉 형태의 현재 완료 수동태,
'타동사 + 목적어' 형태의 단순 현재 능동태, There is/are와
같은 단순 현재도 나온다.

평서문

질문이 아니라 객관적인 사실이나 화자의 의견 등을 나타내는 문장이다.

명령문

동사원형이나 Please 등으로 시작한다.

의문사 의문문

각 의문사마다 1~2개씩 나온다. 의문사가 단독으로 나오기도 하지만 What time ~?, How long ~?, Which room ~? 등에서처럼 다른 명사나 형용사와 같이 나오기도 한다.

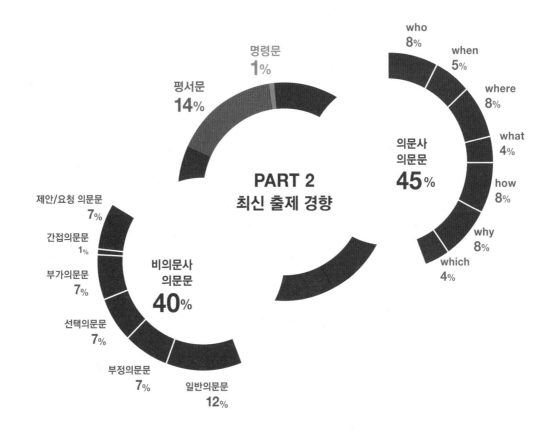

비의문사 의문문

일반(Yes/No) 의문문 적게 나올 때는 한두 개, 많이 나올 때는 서너 개씩 나오는 편이다.

부정의문문 Don't you ~?, Isn't he ~? 등으로 시작하는 문장이며 일반 긍정의문문보다는 약간 더 적게 나온다.

선택의문문 A or B 형태로 나오며 A와 B의 형태가 단어, 구, 절일 수 있다. 구나 절일 경우 문장이 길어져서 어려워진다.

부가의문문 ~ don't you?, ~ isn't he? 등으로 끝나는 문장이며, 일반 부정의문문과 비슷하다고 볼 수 있다.

간접의문문 의문사가 문장 처음 부분이 아니라 문장 중간에 들어 있다.

제안/요청 의문문 정보를 얻기보다는 상대방의 도움이나 동의 등을 얻기 위한 목적이 일반적이다.

| PART 3 | 짧은 대화 Short Conversations | 총 13대화문 39문제 (지문당 3문제) |

- 3인 대화의 경우 남자 화자 두 명과 여자 화자 한 명 또는 남자 화자 한 명과 여자 화자 두 명이 나온다. 따라서 문제에서는 2인 대화에서와 달리 the man이나 the woman이 아니라 the men이나 the women 또는 특정한 이름이 언급될 수 있다.

- 대화 & 시각 정보는 항상 파트의 뒷부분에 나온다.

- 시각 정보의 유형으로 chart, map, floor plan, schedule, table, weather forecast, directory, list, invoice, receipt, sign, packing slip 등 다양한 자료가 골고루 나온다.

2인 대화 &
시각 정보
23%

2인 대화
63%

PART 3
대화의 유형

3인 대화
14%

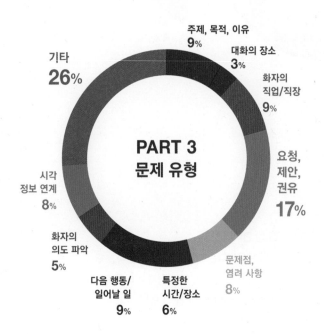

기타
26%

주제, 목적, 이유
9%

대화의 장소
3%

화자의
직업/직장
9%

PART 3
문제 유형

요청,
제안,
권유
17%

시각
정보 연계
8%

화자의
의도 파악
5%

다음 행동/
일어날 일
9%

특정한
시간/장소
6%

문제점,
염려 사항
8%

- 주제, 목적, 이유, 대화의 장소, 화자의 직업/직장 등과 관련된 문제는 주로 대화의 첫 번째 문제로 나오며 다음 행동/일어날 일 등과 관련된 문제는 주로 대화의 세 번째 문제로 나온다.

- 화자의 의도 파악 문제는 주로 2인 대화에 나오지만, 가끔 3인 대화에 나오기도 한다. 시각 정보 연계 대화에는 나오지 않고 있다.

- Part 3 안에서 화자의 의도 파악 문제는 2개가 나오고 시각 정보 연계 문제는 3개가 나온다.

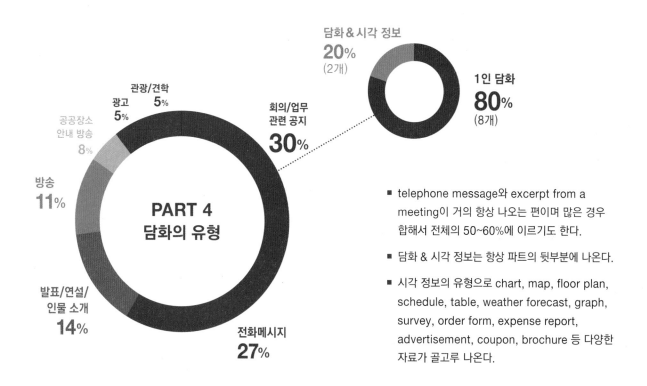

담화 & 시각 정보
20%
(2개)

관광/견학
5%

광고
5%

공공장소
안내 방송
8%

방송
11%

**PART 4
담화의 유형**

회의/업무
관련 공지
30%

1인 담화
80%
(8개)

발표/연설/
인물 소개
14%

전화메시지
27%

- telephone message와 excerpt from a meeting이 거의 항상 나오는 편이며 많은 경우 합해서 전체의 50~60%에 이르기도 한다.

- 담화 & 시각 정보는 항상 파트의 뒷부분에 나온다.

- 시각 정보의 유형으로 chart, map, floor plan, schedule, table, weather forecast, graph, survey, order form, expense report, advertisement, coupon, brochure 등 다양한 자료가 골고루 나온다.

- 문제 유형은 기본적으로 Part 3과 거의 비슷하다.

- 주제, 목적, 이유, 담화의 장소, 화자의 직업/직장 등과 관련된 문제는 주로 담화의 첫 번째 문제로 나오며 다음 행동/일어날 일 등과 관련된 문제는 주로 담화의 세 번째 문제로 나온다.

- Part 4 안에서 화자의 의도 파악 문제는 3개가 나오고 시각 정보 연계 문제는 2개가 나온다.

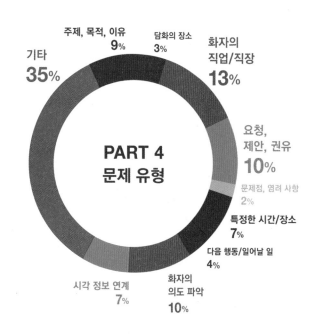

주제, 목적, 이유 **9%**

담화의 장소 **3%**

화자의
직업/직장
13%

기타
35%

**PART 4
문제 유형**

요청,
제안, 권유
10%

문제점, 염려 사항
2%

특정한 시간/장소
7%

다음 행동/일어날 일
4%

화자의
의도 파악
10%

시각 정보 연계
7%

토익 경향 분석

문법 문제

시제와 대명사와 관련된 문법 문제가 2개씩,
한정사와 분사와 관련된 문법 문제가 1개씩
나온다. 시제 문제의 경우 능동태/수동태나
수의 일치와 연계되기도 한다. 그 밖에 한정사,
능동태/수동태, 부정사, 동명사 등과 관련된
문법 문제가 나온다.

어휘 문제

동사, 명사, 형용사, 부사와 관련된
어휘 문제가 각각 2~3개씩 골고루
나온다. 전치사 어휘 문제는 3개씩
꾸준히 나오지만, 접속사나 어구와
관련된 어휘 문제는 나오지 않을 때도
있고 3개가 나올 때도 있다.

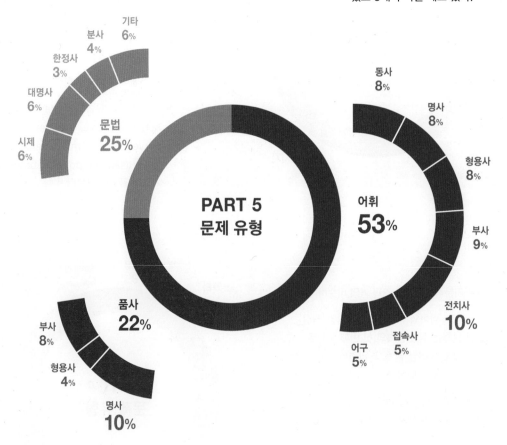

품사 문제

명사와 부사와 관련된 품사 문제가 2~3개
씩 나오며, 형용사와 관련된 품사 문제가
상대적으로 적은 편이다.

한 지문에 4문제가 나오며 평균적으로 어휘 문제가 2개, 품사나 문법 문제가 1개, 문맥에 맞는 문장 고르기 문제가 1개 들어간다. 문맥에 맞는 문장 고르기 문제를 제외하면 문제 유형은 기본적으로 파트 5와 거의 비슷하다.

어휘 문제

동사, 명사, 부사, 어구와 관련된 어휘 문제는 매번 1~2개씩 나온다. 부사 어휘 문제의 경우 therefore(그러므로)나 however(하지만)처럼 문맥의 흐름을 자연스럽게 연결해 주는 부사가 자주 나온다.

문맥에 맞는 문장 고르기

문맥에 맞는 문장 고르기 문제는 지문당 한 문제씩 나오는데, 나오는 위치의 확률은 4문제 중 두 번째 문제, 세 번째 문제, 네 번째 문제, 첫 번째 문제 순으로 높다.

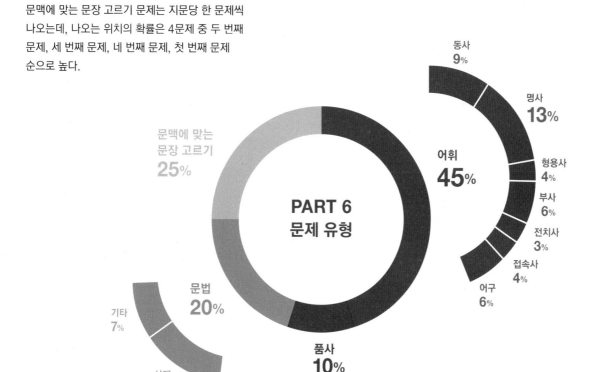

PART 6 문제 유형

- 문맥에 맞는 문장 고르기 **25%**
- 기타 **7%**
- 시제 **13%**
- 문법 **20%**
- 품사 **10%**
  - 부사 **2%**
  - 형용사 **4%**
  - 명사 **4%**
- 어휘 **45%**
  - 동사 **9%**
  - 명사 **13%**
  - 형용사 **4%**
  - 부사 **6%**
  - 전치사 **3%**
  - 접속사 **4%**
  - 어구 **6%**

문법 문제

문맥의 흐름과 밀접하게 관련이 있는 시제 문제가 2개 정도 나오며, 능동태/수동태나 수의 일치와 연계되기도 한다. 그 밖에 대명사, 능동태/수동태, 부정사, 접속사/전치사 등과 관련된 문법 문제가 나온다.

품사 문제

명사나 형용사 문제가 부사 문제보다 좀 더 자주 나온다.

PART 7 독해 Reading Comprehension

지문 유형	지문당 문제 수	지문 개수	비중 %
단일 지문	2문항	4개	약 15%
	3문항	3개	약 16%
	4문항	3개	약 22%
이중 지문	5문항	2개	약 19%
삼중 지문	5문항	3개	약 28%

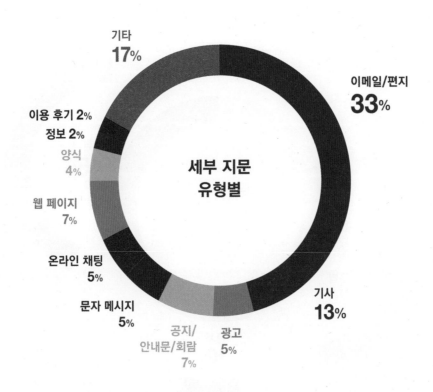

- 이메일/편지, 기사 유형 지문은 거의 항상 나오는 편이며 많은 경우 합해서 전체의 50~60%에 이르기도 한다.

- 기타 지문 유형으로 agenda, brochure, comment card, coupon, flyer, instructions, invitation, invoice, list, menu, page from a catalog, policy statement, report, schedule, survey, voucher 등 다양한 자료가 골고루 나온다.

(이중 지문과 삼중 지문 속의 지문들을 모두 낱개로 계산함 – 총 23지문)

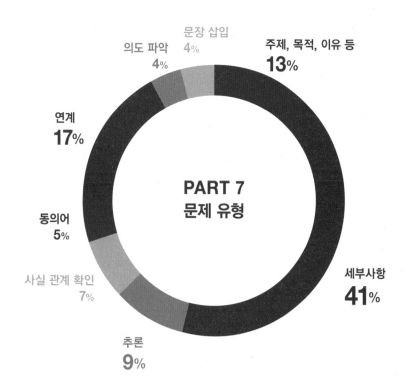

의도 파악
4%

문장 삽입
4%

주제, 목적, 이유 등
13%

연계
17%

PART 7
문제 유형

동의어
5%

사실 관계 확인
7%

추론
9%

세부사항
41%

■ 동의어 문제는 주로 이중 지문이나 삼중 지문에 나온다.

■ 연계 문제는 일반적으로 이중 지문에서 한 문제, 삼중 지문에서 두 문제가 나온다.

■ 의도 파악 문제는 문자 메시지(text-message chain)나 온라인 채팅(online chat discussion) 지문에서 출제되며 두 문제가 나온다.

■ 문장 삽입 문제는 주로 기사, 이메일, 편지, 회람 지문에서 출제되며 두 문제가 나온다.

점수 환산표 및 산출법

점수 환산표 이 책에 수록된 각 Test를 풀고 난 후, 맞은 개수를 세어 점수를 환산해 보세요.

LISTENING Raw Score (맞은 개수)	LISTENING Scaled Score (환산 점수)	READING Raw Score (맞은 개수)	READING Scaled Score (환산 점수)
96-100	475-495	96-100	460-495
91-95	435-495	91-95	425-490
86-90	405-470	86-90	400-465
81-85	370-450	81-85	375-440
76-80	345-420	76-80	340-415
71-75	320-390	71-75	310-390
66-70	290-360	66-70	285-370
61-65	265-335	61-65	255-340
56-60	240-310	56-60	230-310
51-55	215-280	51-55	200-275
46-50	190-255	46-50	170-245
41-45	160-230	41-45	140-215
36-40	130-205	36-40	115-180
31-35	105-175	31-35	95-150
26-30	85-145	26-30	75-120
21-25	60-115	21-25	60-95
16-20	30-90	16-20	45-75
11-15	5-70	11-15	30-55
6-10	5-60	6-10	10-40
1-5	5-50	1-5	5-30
0	5-35	0	5-15

점수 산출 방법 아래의 방식으로 점수를 산출할 수 있다.

STEP 1

자신의 답안을 수록된 정답과 대조하여 채점한다. 각 Section의 맞은 개수가 본인의 Section별 '실제 점수 (통계 처리하기 전의 점수, raw score)'이다. Listening Test와 Reading Test의 정답 수를 세어, 자신의 실제 점수를 아래의 해당란에 기록한다.

	맞은 개수	환산 점수대
LISTENING		
READING		
총점		

Section별 실제 점수가 그대로 Section별 TOEIC 점수가 되는 것은 아니다. TOEIC은 시행할 때마다 별도로 특정한 통계 처리 방법을 사용하며 이러한 실제 점수를 환산 점수(converted[scaled] score) 로 전환하게 된다. 이렇게 전환함으로써, 매번 시행될 때마다 문제는 달라지지만 그 점수가 갖는 의미는 같아지게 된다. 예를 들어 어느 한 시험에서 총점 550점의 성적으로 받는 실력이라면 다른 시험에서도 거의 550점대의 성적을 받게 되는 것이다.

▼

STEP 2

실제 점수를 위 표에 기록한 후 왼쪽 페이지의 점수 환산표를 보도록 한다. TOEIC이 시행될 때마다 대 개 이와 비슷한 형태의 표가 작성되는데, 여기 제시된 환산표는 본 교재에 수록된 Test용으로 개발된 것이다. 이 표를 사용하여 자신의 실제 점수를 환산 점수로 전환하도록 한다. 즉, 예를 들어 Listening Test의 실제 정답 수가 61~65개이면 환산 점수는 265점에서 335점 사이가 된다. 여기서 실제 정답 수 가 61개이면 환산 점수가 265점이고, 65개이면 환산 점수가 335점 임을 의미하는 것은 아니다. 본 책 의 Test를 위해 작성된 이 점수 환산표가 자신의 영어 실력이 어느 정도인지 대략적으로 파악하는 데 도 움이 되긴 하지만, 이 표가 실제 TOEIC 성적 산출에 그대로 사용된 적은 없다는 사실을 밝혀 둔다.

토익® 정기시험
기출문제집

RC

기출 TEST

01

READING TEST

In the Reading test, you will read a variety of texts and answer several different types of reading comprehension questions. The entire Reading test will last 75 minutes. There are three parts, and directions are given for each part. You are encouraged to answer as many questions as possible within the time allowed.

You must mark your answers on the separate answer sheet. Do not write your answers in your test book.

PART 5

Directions: A word or phrase is missing in each of the sentences below. Four answer choices are given below each sentence. Select the best answer to complete the sentence. Then mark the letter (A), (B), (C), or (D) on your answer sheet.

101. Mougey Fine Gifts is known for its large range of ------- goods.

(A) regional
(B) regionally
(C) region
(D) regions

102. Income levels are rising in the ------- and surrounding areas.

(A) family
(B) world
(C) company
(D) city

103. Since we had a recent rate change, expect ------- next electricity bill to be slightly lower.

(A) you
(B) yours
(C) yourself
(D) your

104. Hotel guests have a lovely view of the ocean ------- the south-facing windows.

(A) up
(B) except
(C) onto
(D) through

105. Mr. Kim would like ------- a meeting about the Jasper account as soon as possible.

(A) to arrange
(B) arranging
(C) having arranged
(D) arrangement

106. The factory is ------- located near the train station.

(A) regularly
(B) conveniently
(C) brightly
(D) collectively

107. Because of transportation ------- due to winter weather, some conference participants may arrive late.

(A) are delayed
(B) to delay
(C) delays
(D) had delayed

108. Proper maintenance of your heating equipment ensures that small issues can be fixed ------- they become big ones.

(A) as a result
(B) in addition
(C) although
(D) before

109. The information on the Web site of Croyell Decorators is ------- organized.

(A) clear
(B) clearing
(C) clearest
(D) clearly

110. The Copley Corporation is frequently ------- as a company that employs workers from all over the world.

(A) recognized
(B) permitted
(C) prepared
(D) controlled

111. Payments made ------- 4:00 P.M. will be processed on the following business day.

(A) later
(B) after
(C) than
(D) often

112. Greenfiddle Water Treatment hires engineers who have ------- mathematics skills.

(A) adjusted
(B) advanced
(C) eager
(D) faithful

113. After ------- the neighborhood, Mr. Park decided not to move his café to Thomasville.

(A) evaluation
(B) evaluate
(C) evaluating
(D) evaluated

114. The average precipitation in Campos ------- the past three years has been 22.7 centimeters.

(A) on
(B) for
(C) to
(D) under

115. Improving efficiency at Perwon Manufacturing will require a ------- revision of existing processes.

(A) create
(B) creativity
(C) creation
(D) creative

116. Conference attendees will share accommodations ------- they submit a special request for a single room.

(A) even
(B) unless
(C) similarly
(D) also

117. To receive -------, please be sure the appropriate box is checked on the magazine order form.

(A) renew
(B) renewed
(C) renewals
(D) to renew

118. Donations to the Natusi Wildlife Reserve rise when consumers feel ------- about the economy.

(A) careful
(B) helpful
(C) confident
(D) durable

119. When ------- applied, Tilda's Restorative Cream reduces the appearance of fine lines and wrinkles.

(A) consistent
(B) consist
(C) consistently
(D) consisting

120. The marketing director confirmed that the new software program would be ready to ------- by November 1.

(A) launch
(B) facilitate
(C) arise
(D) exert

GO ON TO THE NEXT PAGE

121. Satinesse Seat Covers will refund your order ------- you are not completely satisfied.

(A) if
(B) yet
(C) until
(D) neither

122. In the last five years, production at the Harris facility has almost doubled in -------.

(A) majority
(B) edition
(C) volume
(D) economy

123. Ms. Tsai will ------- the installation of the new workstations with the vendor.

(A) coordinated
(B) to coordinate
(C) coordination
(D) be coordinating

124. An upgrade in software would ------- increase the productivity of our administrative staff.

(A) significantly
(B) persuasively
(C) proficiently
(D) gladly

125. The Rustic Diner's chef does allow patrons to make menu -------.

(A) substituted
(B) substituting
(C) substitutions
(D) substitute

126. Ms. Rodriguez noted that it is important to ------- explicit policies regarding the use of company computers.

(A) inform
(B) succeed
(C) estimate
(D) establish

127. ------- Peura Insurance has located a larger office space, it will begin negotiating the rental agreement.

(A) Happily
(B) Now that
(C) Despite
(D) In fact

128. Mr. Tanaka's team worked ------- for months to secure a lucrative government contract.

(A) readily
(B) diligently
(C) curiously
(D) extremely

129. Though Sendark Agency's travel insurance can be purchased over the phone, most of ------- plans are bought online.

(A) whose
(B) his
(C) its
(D) this

130. Garstein Furniture specializes in functional products that are inexpensive ------- beautifully crafted.

(A) thus
(B) as well as
(C) at last
(D) accordingly

PART 6

Directions: Read the texts that follow. A word, phrase, or sentence is missing in parts of each text. Four answer choices for each question are given below the text. Select the best answer to complete the text. Then mark the letter (A), (B), (C), or (D) on your answer sheet.

Questions 131-134 refer to the following notice.

NOTICE

To continue providing the highest level of ------- to our corporate tenants, we have scheduled the
                                        131.

south lobby restrooms for maintenance this weekend, May 13 and May 14. ------- this time, the
                                                                         132.

restrooms will be out of order, so tenants and their guests should instead use the facilities in the

north lobby.

We ------- for any inconvenience this might cause. ------- .
    133.   134.

Denville Property Management Partners

---

131. (A) serve
    (B) served
    (C) server
    (D) service

132. (A) Along
    (B) During
    (C) Without
    (D) Between

133. (A) apologize
    (B) organize
    (C) realize
    (D) recognize

134. (A) If you would like to join our property management team, call us today.
    (B) Thank you for your patience while the main lobby is being painted.
    (C) Please do not attempt to access the north lobby on these days.
    (D) Questions or comments may be directed to the Management Office.

GO ON TO THE NEXT PAGE

Questions 135-138 refer to the following customer review.

I recently received a last-minute invitation to a formal dinner. I bought a suit and needed it

tailored as ------- as possible. A friend suggested that I use Antonio's Tailoring Shop in downtown
   135.

Auckland. When I met Antonio, he gave me his full attention ------- his shop was busy. He took
          136.

the time to listen to me and carefully noted all my measurements. He then explained all the

tailoring costs up front and assured me that he could have my suit ready in three days, but he

had it done in two! ------- .
     137.

Antonio has run his shop for over 30 years, and his experience really shows. He is a ------- tailor.
                  138.

I highly recommend him.

Jim Kestren, Auckland

135. (A) quickly
 (B) quicken
 (C) quickest
 (D) quickness

136. (A) as far as
 (B) even though
 (C) such as
 (D) whether

137. (A) Of course, the shop is busiest on
   Saturdays.
 (B) The suit fits me perfectly too.
 (C) I made another purchase.
 (D) He used to sell shirts.

138. (A) former
 (B) temporary
 (C) superb
 (D) best

Questions 139-142 refer to the following letter.

Dear Director Yoshida,

Thank you for your school's interest in visiting our farm next month. Please note that children must be at least six years old to visit and tour the farm. ------- . I have enclosed a list of the -------
　　　　　　　　　　　　　　　　　　　　　　　　　　　　　　　　　　　139.　　　　　　　　　　　　**140.**

activities available for our young visitors. Two of these ------- must be scheduled in advance.
　　　　　　　　　　　　　　　　　　　　　　　　　　　　141.

They are a cheese-making class and an introduction to beekeeping. Both are very popular with

our visitors.

Please let ------- know your selection by early next week. I look forward to welcoming your group
　　　　　　142.

soon!

Sincerely,

Annabel Romero, Coordinator
Merrytree Family Farm

---

139. (A) In the event of bad weather, the animals will be inside.
　　　(B) There are no exceptions to this policy.
　　　(C) Ones younger than that can find much to enjoy.
　　　(D) This fee includes lunch and a small souvenir.

140. (A) legal
　　　(B) artistic
　　　(C) athletic
　　　(D) educational

141. (A) events
　　　(B) plays
　　　(C) treatments
　　　(D) trips

142. (A) they
　　　(B) me
　　　(C) her
　　　(D) one

GO ON TO THE NEXT PAGE

To: Lakshmi Aiyar
From: info@healthonity.com
Date: February 8
Subject: Healthonity Dental

Dear Ms. Aiyar,

We, the dental health professionals of the Healthonity Dental Center, are ------- to introduce our
143.
just-opened practice. We aim to provide access to the largest team of dental specialists in the
region. On our Web site, you can see a comprehensive list of the procedures we offer. -------.
144.
The members of our practice share a passion for helping people maintain beautiful and healthy
smiles.

Contact our center today at 305-555-0121 ------- an initial evaluation. All first-time ------- will
145.   146.
benefit from a 50 percent discount on the cost through the end of the month.

Sincerely,

The Team at Healthonity Dental Center

143. (A) prouder
(B) proudly
(C) pride
(D) proud

144. (A) They include general and cosmetic
procedures.
(B) We have relocated from neighboring
Hillsborough.
(C) The Web site is a creation of A to Z
Host Builders.
(D) Several of them are surprisingly
expensive.

145. (A) scheduled
(B) to schedule
(C) scheduling
(D) being scheduled

146. (A) shoppers
(B) residents
(C) patients
(D) tenants

PART 7

Directions: In this part you will read a selection of texts, such as magazine and newspaper articles, e-mails, and instant messages. Each text or set of texts is followed by several questions. Select the best answer for each question and mark the letter (A), (B), (C), or (D) on your answer sheet.

Questions 147-148 refer to the following Web page.

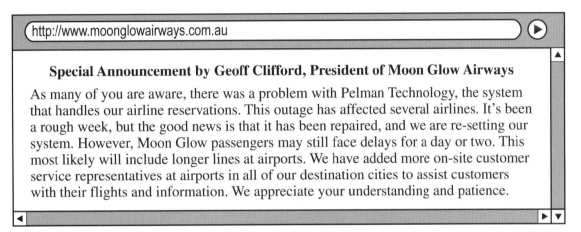

http://www.moonglowairways.com.au

Special Announcement by Geoff Clifford, President of Moon Glow Airways

As many of you are aware, there was a problem with Pelman Technology, the system that handles our airline reservations. This outage has affected several airlines. It's been a rough week, but the good news is that it has been repaired, and we are re-setting our system. However, Moon Glow passengers may still face delays for a day or two. This most likely will include longer lines at airports. We have added more on-site customer service representatives at airports in all of our destination cities to assist customers with their flights and information. We appreciate your understanding and patience.

147. What is the purpose of the announcement?

(A) To report on airport renovations
(B) To give an update on a technical problem
(C) To introduce a new reservation system
(D) To advertise airline routes to some new cities

148. According to Mr. Clifford, what has the airline temporarily increased?

(A) The number of flights available
(B) Dining options on flights
(C) Assistance for customers at airports
(D) Prices for international flights

GO ON TO THE NEXT PAGE

Questions 149-150 refer to the following job advertisement.

Video Captioners—Work from Home

Kiesel Video is seeking detail-oriented people to use our software to add text captions to a wide variety of video material, such as television programs, movies, and university lectures. We will provide free online training. Successful applicants must possess strong language skills and have a computer, a headset, and high-speed Internet access.

The position features:
• Flexible hours—you work as much or as little as you want.
• Choice of projects—we have work in many types of content.
• Good pay—our captioners earn $350 to $1,100 a week, depending on the assignment.

Apply today at www.kieselvideo.com/jobs

---

149. What are applicants for this position required to have?

(A) Experience in video production
(B) Certain pieces of equipment
(C) A university degree in language studies
(D) An office with a reception area

150. What is true about the job?

(A) It is a full-time position.
(B) It pays a fixed salary.
(C) It involves some foreign travel.
(D) It offers a choice of assignments.

Questions 151-152 refer to the following report.

February 1

SOFTWARE TESTING REPORT

Version of Software Program: Konserted 2.5
Testing Dates: January 10–12
Number of Participants: 8

Software Testing Overview: Participants were asked to complete a series of tasks testing the functionality of the revised Konserted interface. In task number 1, participants searched for a concert in a designated area. In task number 2, participants searched for new friends on the site. In task number 3, participants invited friends to a concert. In task number 4, participants posted concert reviews, photos, and videos.

Initial Findings: Task number 3 proved the most challenging, with three participants unable to complete it in under two minutes. A potential cause for this difficulty may be the choice of icons in the menu bar. Clearer, more intuitive icons could make this task easier to complete for participants.

151. What is true about the software testing?

(A) It included multiple versions of Konserted.
(B) It was done over several days.
(C) It required participants to complete a survey.
(D) It took place at a series of concerts.

152. What action was difficult for users to complete?

(A) Searching for an event
(B) Searching for friends
(C) Inviting friends to a performance
(D) Posting reviews to a Web site

Questions 153-155 refer to the following e-mail.

```
*E-mail*

To:        catiyeh@mymailroom.au
From:      achen@mutamark.au
Date:      1 July
Subject:   Mutamark conference
```

Dear Ms. Atiyeh,

To follow up on our phone conversation earlier today, I would like to extend to you a formal written invitation to speak at the eighth annual Mutamark conference, scheduled to take place this year from 17 to 20 September in Zagros. Because you drew a sizeable crowd when you appeared at the conference in the past, we will be making special arrangements for your visit this time. The Blue Room at the Debeljak Hotel holds only 120, so this year we are also booking the Koros Hall, which has a capacity of 270. We can offer you a 40-to-50-minute slot on the last day of the conference, when attendance should be at its peak. Please e-mail me to confirm your acceptance and to let me know more about your audiovisual requirements. We can provide overhead projection for still images if you will be using them again.

Very best regards,

Alex Chen, Conference Planning
Mutamark Headquarters, Melbourne

---

153. What is indicated about Ms. Atiyeh's previous appearance at Mutamark?

(A) It was very well attended.
(B) It was moved to a larger venue.
(C) It featured a musical performance.
(D) It took place at the Koros Hall.

154. How many people can the Koros Hall accommodate?

(A) 40
(B) 50
(C) 120
(D) 270

155. When will Ms. Atiyeh most likely appear at the Mutamark conference?

(A) On September 17
(B) On September 18
(C) On September 19
(D) On September 20

Monorail Coming to Sudbury

(4 Feb.)—Ottawa-based Saenger, Inc., has been selected by the city of Sudbury to build a monorail system that will connect the city's commercial district to the airport. — [1] —. Funding for the system is drawn from a combination of public agencies and private investors. — [2] —. Ticket sales for the monorail will also provide a new source of revenue for the city. — [3] —. Construction is slated to begin in early June and is expected to be completed within four years. — [4] —.

156. What kind of business most likely is Saenger, Inc.?

(A) A construction firm
(B) A real estate agency
(C) A cargo-handling company
(D) A financial services provider

157. What is indicated about the monorail?

(A) It needs more funding from investors.
(B) It will take years to finish.
(C) It was proposed by airport officials.
(D) It offers discounted tickets to city residents.

158. In which of the positions marked [1], [2], [3], and [4] does the following sentence best belong?

"Along the way, the line will stop at nine stations."

(A) [1]
(B) [2]
(C) [3]
(D) [4]

GO ON TO THE NEXT PAGE

Questions 159-160 refer to the following text-message chain.

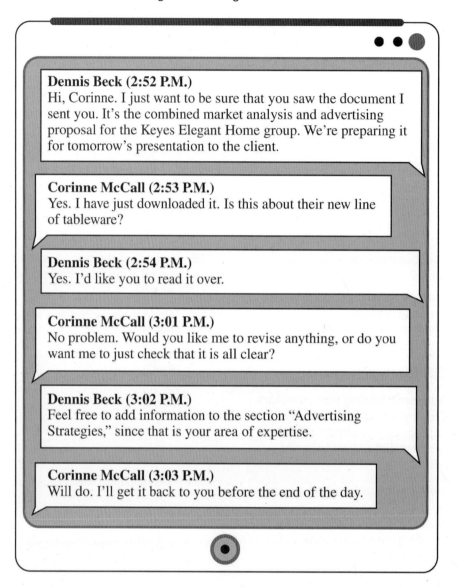

Dennis Beck (2:52 P.M.)
Hi, Corinne. I just want to be sure that you saw the document I sent you. It's the combined market analysis and advertising proposal for the Keyes Elegant Home group. We're preparing it for tomorrow's presentation to the client.

Corinne McCall (2:53 P.M.)
Yes. I have just downloaded it. Is this about their new line of tableware?

Dennis Beck (2:54 P.M.)
Yes. I'd like you to read it over.

Corinne McCall (3:01 P.M.)
No problem. Would you like me to revise anything, or do you want me to just check that it is all clear?

Dennis Beck (3:02 P.M.)
Feel free to add information to the section "Advertising Strategies," since that is your area of expertise.

Corinne McCall (3:03 P.M.)
Will do. I'll get it back to you before the end of the day.

159. At 3:01 P.M., what does Ms. McCall most likely mean when she writes, "No problem"?

(A) She did not have any issues logging on to her computer.
(B) She does not think a document has errors.
(C) She is willing to review a document.
(D) She has time to meet representatives from Keyes Elegant Home.

160. What type of work does Ms. McCall most likely do?

(A) Marketing
(B) Accounting
(C) Legal consulting
(D) Information technology services

Questions 161-164 refer to the following e-mail.

To:	Mara Renaldo <mrenaldo@viyamail.com>
From:	Lisa Yang <lyang@staffordsvillefair.org>
Date:	May 28
Subject:	RE: Staffordsville Craft Fair

Dear Ms. Renaldo,

Thank you for your interest in selling your handcrafted items at the annual Staffordsville Craft Fair. Please note that all applicants must submit a $25 application fee, whether or not they want to share a space with another applicant. Moreover, all applicants must submit a minimum of four photographs of their work in order to be considered as a vendor. — [1] —.

In addition to photographs, we ask that you submit a rough sketch showing how you would display your work. Since you propose to share a space with a friend, local potter Julia Berens, it would be helpful if your sketch could indicate how you are planning to use the space jointly. — [2] —.

Also, because we hold the fair rain or shine, all vendors must supply their own tenting to protect themselves and their wares from the possibility of rain. — [3] —.

Finally, please be aware that every year we receive far more applications from jewelry makers than we can accept. We hope that you will not be too discouraged if your work is not accepted this year, as you are applying for the first time. — [4] —.

Thanks again, and best of luck with your application,

Lisa Yang

161. What is suggested about the craft fair?

(A) It takes place in downtown Staffordsville.
(B) It is being held for the first time.
(C) It specializes in locally produced crafts.
(D) It will be held outdoors.

162. What is NOT mentioned as a requirement for selling at the craft fair?

(A) Sharing a space with another participant
(B) Paying a fee to participate
(C) Submitting images of the crafts
(D) Providing one's own tenting

163. What does Ms. Renaldo most likely sell?

(A) Sketches
(B) Photographs
(C) Pottery
(D) Jewelry

164. In which of the positions marked [1], [2], [3], and [4] does the following sentence best belong?

"Make sure they clearly represent the items you wish to offer for purchase at the event."

(A) [1]
(B) [2]
(C) [3]
(D) [4]

GO ON TO THE NEXT PAGE

SLEEP SOUNDLY SOLUTIONS

Thank you for choosing Sleep Soundly Solutions!

The updated control panel is linked to an integrated system that allows you to activate and disable all security systems in your home, including your Sleep Soundly motion sensor as well as your fire, smoke, and carbon monoxide detectors.

All Sleep Soundly residential alarm systems have been tested thoroughly to ensure the highest quality and sensitivity, so you can sleep soundly in the knowledge that your home is protected. We have also developed a new smartphone application that will notify you of any disturbances wherever you are. The app is available for download now.

Sleep Soundly control equipment is carefully manufactured for use with Sleep Soundly detectors and alarms. Using products manufactured by other companies may result in an alarm system that does not meet safety requirements for residential buildings or comply with local laws.

165. In what industry does Sleep Soundly Solutions operate?

(A) Real estate
(B) Life insurance
(C) Home security
(D) Furniture moving

166. What new product is being offered by Sleep Soundly Solutions?

(A) An outdoor motion sensor
(B) A smartphone application
(C) Home installation service
(D) Fire detection equipment

167. The word "meet" in paragraph 3, line 3, is closest in meaning to

(A) greet
(B) touch
(C) satisfy
(D) experience

Questions 168-171 refer to the following letter.

March 29

Dr. Maritza Geerlings
Poseidonstraat 392
Paramaribo
Suriname

Dear Dr. Geerlings,

I am writing to thank you for your years of service on the faculty of the Jamaican Agricultural Training Academy (JATA) and to let you know about some exciting developments. As you know, JATA was originally established as a vocational school for agriculture but now offers courses in a varied array of disciplines, including cybersecurity, electrical engineering, and health information management. Our student body, which for the first ten years consisted almost exclusively of locals, is now culturally diverse, with students from across the Americas and Europe. Today's students work with sophisticated equipment, much of which did not exist in our early days.

To reflect these and other significant changes that JATA has undergone over time, the Board of Trustees has approved a proposal by the Faculty Senate to rename the institution the Caribbean Academy of Science and Technology. As a result, a new institutional logo will be adopted. All students and faculty members, both current and former, are invited to participate in a logo design contest. Information about the contest will be forthcoming.

The renaming ceremony and the introduction of the new logo will take place at 11 A.M. on 1 June, the twentieth anniversary of the institution. We hope you will be able to join us.

Sincerely,

Audley Bartlett

Audley Bartlett
Vice President for Academic Affairs,
Jamaican Agricultural Training Academy

168. What is one purpose of the letter?

(A) To announce a name change
(B) To honor distinguished alumni
(C) To suggest revisions to a curriculum
(D) To list an individual's accomplishments

169. The word "established" in paragraph 1, line 3, is closest in meaning to

(A) affected
(B) founded
(C) confirmed
(D) settled

170. What is suggested about Dr. Geerlings?

(A) She plans to attend JATA's anniversary celebration.
(B) She has taught courses in cybersecurity.
(C) She can take part in JATA's logo design contest.
(D) She served on JATA's Board of Trustees.

171. What is NOT indicated about JATA in the letter?

(A) Its professors live on campus.
(B) Its students have access to modern equipment.
(C) It will be twenty years old on June 1.
(D) It is attended by international students.

GO ON TO THE NEXT PAGE

Ashley Montaine 8:54 A.M.: How did the interview with Mr. Erickson go?

Dan Campbell 8:55 A.M.: I really enjoyed meeting him. I think he'd be a great reporter here. He seems smart and organized, and his samples show that he's a great writer.

Ashley Montaine 8:57 A.M.: Brooke, can you contact Mr. Erickson to set up the next interview? Is that a problem?

Dan Campbell 8:58 A.M.: I'd really like to work with him. It is very important that he impress Mr. Peters.

Brooke Randolph 8:59 A.M.: Not at all.

Ashley Montaine 9:00 A.M.: Thanks. I also see that he has a varied work history. That will make him a well-rounded reporter.

Brooke Randolph 9:02 A.M.: When would you like to meet with him again?

Dan Campbell 9:03 A.M.: Ashley, I believe you will participate in the next interview. Note that Mr. Peters is probably going to ask why Mr. Erickson wants to transition from freelance writing to in-house news reporting. Also, Mr. Peters will want assurances that he's committed and will stick around for several years.

Ashley Montaine 9:04 A.M.: Brooke, Mr. Peters and I are both free Friday morning.

Brooke Randolph 9:06 A.M.: Great. I'll write an e-mail shortly.

172. For what type of company do the writers work?

(A) A book publisher
(B) A newspaper
(C) A film production company
(D) A job-placement firm

173. At 8:59 A.M., what does Ms. Randolph most likely mean when she writes, "Not at all"?

(A) She would like to participate in an interview.
(B) She does not think Mr. Erickson should be hired.
(C) She feels comfortable fulfilling a request.
(D) She has not read Mr. Erickson's writing.

174. What is indicated about Mr. Erickson?

(A) He has never been on a job interview before.
(B) He has held many different types of jobs.
(C) He is taking over Mr. Peters' position.
(D) He is a former colleague of Ms. Montaine.

175. According to the discussion, what is important to Mr. Peters about a new hire?

(A) Prior news reporting experience
(B) Ability to begin working immediately
(C) Communicating well with colleagues
(D) Staying with the company over the long term

GO ON TO THE NEXT PAGE ➤

Alberta Business Matters
April issue

Improve Your Office Environment Now!

Today's office environment, featuring numerous corridors, unexciting beige or white walls, and often rows of identical, windowless cubicles, might not inspire comfort, beauty, and energy. However, there are some easy, inexpensive ways to make your office space more inviting.

Air quality

- Add some green plants to the décor. Plants offer a natural filtration system, increasing oxygen levels. Nonflowering plants should be preferred, as they will not scatter pollen.
- A small, tabletop air purifier helps improve stale air and removes dust.

Light quality

- Take breaks and go outdoors. Even just five minutes before or after lunch break will provide your eyes with a respite from artificial light sources.
- Use desktop lamps with full-spectrum lightbulbs.
- Install double-glazed windows instead of blinds to reduce glare while maintaining natural light.

Stress relief

- Earplugs or noise-cancelling headphones can block distracting noise in an open office floor plan.
- Photographs of loved ones and places we have visited for vacation are reminders of our life away from the office. Select a few favorite pictures as important decorative elements.

Dear readers, if you have tips to add to this list, send them in and they will be published in next month's issue.

Alberta Business Matters

Letters to the Editor

It may interest your readers to know about the company I work for, called Moveable, Inc. We aspire to make dull offices more comfortable and convenient for workers, especially for today's on-the-move employees.

For example, say you work two days a week at your headquarters in Edmonton, and the rest of the week you are in a satellite office. Our "Can-Do Case" ensures that your favorite office supplies always travel with you. Our "Modular Décor Kit," weighing just 1.75 kg, contains a portable reading lamp, a miniature silk plant, and a folding photo frame with space for four pictures. Look us up online and follow us on social media, as we offer new items frequently!

Best,
Maria Testa

176. What is NOT recommended in the article?

(A) Using plants to decorate cubicles
(B) Walking outdoors during breaks
(C) Using a calming noise machine
(D) Decorating with personal photographs

177. Why are blinds mentioned?

(A) Because they are relatively expensive
(B) Because they block natural light
(C) Because they are hard to match to furniture
(D) Because they attract dust

178. What is indicated about the magazine?

(A) It is the only business publication in Alberta.
(B) Its publisher is hiring additional staff.
(C) Its editors would like to hear from readers.
(D) It is sponsored by a furniture company.

179. What is suggested about Ms. Testa?

(A) She is a professional writer.
(B) She is starting a new company.
(C) She travels frequently in her work.
(D) She read the previous issue of *Alberta Business Matters*.

180. What is suggested about Moveable, Inc.'s products?

(A) They are packable.
(B) They are affordable.
(C) They are available for a short time.
(D) They are made from recycled materials.

GO ON TO THE NEXT PAGE

← → ↻ 🏠 | http://www.Lloydtouringcompany.co.uk | ☆ ⋮

Choose one of Lloyd Touring Company's (LTC) most popular outings to see the best that London has to offer!

Tour 1: Full-day tour of the most popular tourist sites on one of our famous red double-decker buses. See the Changing of the Guard and conclude the day with a river cruise.

Tour 2: Full-day walking tour of London's best shopping areas. Explore London's famous department stores and wander along fashionable Bond and Oxford Streets.

Tour 3: Half-day tour on a red double-decker bus, including private tour of the Tower of London and lunch at a nearby café.

Tour 4: Half-day tour of Buckingham Palace, including the Changing of the Guard. Tour ends with a traditional fish-and-chips lunch.

Tour 5: Full-day walking tour featuring London's top highlights. Complete the day with a medieval banquet.

LTC's knowledgeable local staff members personally guide each one of our tours. Meals are not covered, except when noted in the tour description. Participants are responsible for meeting at chosen departure destination. LTC does not provide pickup from hotels. All tours can be upgraded for an additional fee to include an open-date ticket to the London Eye, London's famous observation wheel.

★★★★★
—**Ella Bouton**

Lloyd Touring Company Review

This was my first trip to London. I decided to see all the major tourist sites on my own, but I wanted someone to help me discover the most interesting places to shop in London. My LTC tour guide, Larissa, was wonderful. She is an avid shopper herself, and at the beginning of the tour, she tried to get to know the participants. She was able to guide everyone to the shops that they were most interested in. It was such a personalized tour! And it was a bonus that Larissa also speaks French. My daughter and I were visiting from Paris, and we appreciated being able to communicate in two languages. The tour was very reasonably priced, too. I would highly recommend it. The only unpleasant part of the tour was that Oxford Street was extremely crowded when we visited, and it was difficult to walk around easily.

181. How does Tour 1 differ from all the other tours?

(A) It uses a double-decker bus.
(B) It includes multiple meals at famous restaurants.
(C) It allows participants to see London from the water.
(D) It takes the entire day.

182. What is included in the cost of the tours?

(A) Transportation from hotels
(B) A tour guide
(C) Breakfast at a restaurant
(D) A ticket to the London Eye

183. What tour did Ms. Bouton most likely take?

(A) Tour 2
(B) Tour 3
(C) Tour 4
(D) Tour 5

184. What does the review suggest about Ms. Bouton?

(A) She prefers bus tours.
(B) She speaks French.
(C) She was on a business trip.
(D) She used LTC before.

185. Why was Ms. Bouton disappointed with the tour?

(A) It was expensive.
(B) It was disorganized.
(C) It was in a very crowded area.
(D) It was in an uninteresting part of the city.

GO ON TO THE NEXT PAGE

To:	Joseph Morgan <joseph.morgan@peltergraphics.com>
From:	administrator@costaseminars.org
Date:	May 31
Subject:	Book order

Dear Mr. Morgan,

Thank you for registering for Emilio Costa's seminar on June 11 at the Rothford Business Center. We are glad you took advantage of the opportunity for conference participants to purchase some of Emilio Costa's graphic-design books at a discounted price. The information below is a confirmation of your order. The books will be waiting for you at the check-in desk on the day of the seminar. Please note that we will accept any major credit card for payment. We are looking forward to seeing you on June 11.

Quantity	Title	Price	Discounted Price	Total Price
1	Perfected Figures: Making Data Visually Appealing	$22.00	$17.60	$17.60
1	Logos in the Information Age	$18.00	$14.40	$14.40
1	Branding Strategies in Graphic Design	$20.00	$16.00	$16.00
2	Best Practices in Web Design: A European Perspective	$28.00	$22.40	$44.80
			TOTAL DUE:	**$92.80**

Attention, Seminar Participants:

Unfortunately, we do not have copies of Emilio Costa's book *Branding Strategies in Graphic Design* with us today. For those of you who have ordered it, please give your mailing address to the volunteer at the check-in desk, and the book will be mailed to your home at no cost to you. We will charge your credit card upon shipment. We are sorry for the inconvenience.

```
*E-mail*
```

To:	roberta.tsu@peltergraphics.com
From:	joseph.morgan@peltergraphics.com
Date:	June 22
Sent:	Costa book

Dear Roberta,

I'm looking forward to finishing up our brochure design for Entchen Financial Consultants. Before we submit our final draft, I would like to rethink how we are presenting our data. Have you had a chance to look through the Costa book I showed you? He gives great advice on improving the clarity of financial information in marketing materials. Anyway, let's talk about it at lunch tomorrow.

Best,

Joseph

186. What most likely is the topic of the seminar on June 11 ?

(A) Financial consulting
(B) Graphic design
(C) Marketing strategies
(D) Business writing

187. What is suggested about Mr. Morgan?

(A) He attended the seminar with a coworker.
(B) He gave a presentation at the seminar.
(C) He received free shipping on a book purchase.
(D) He paid for some books in advance.

188. What is the purpose of the notice?

(A) To explain a problem
(B) To ask for volunteers
(C) To request payment
(D) To promote a book

189. According to the second e-mail, what does Mr. Morgan suggest changing?

(A) The deadline for submitting a project
(B) The content of a book review
(C) The time of a scheduled meeting
(D) The display of some information

190. How much did Mr. Morgan spend on the book he showed to Ms. Tsu?

(A) $17.60
(B) $14.40
(C) $16.00
(D) $22.40

GO ON TO THE NEXT PAGE

Anton Building

Clanton (12 October)—The planned renovation of the historic Anton Building by Jantuni Property Developers (JPD) is facing new delays. A JPD spokesperson says their negotiations with the city regarding a package of subsidies and tax incentives are ongoing and are proving somewhat contentious. According to the renovation plan, JPD must protect the historical integrity of the Anton Building while it creates a mixed-use interior, offering both office space and lower-level retail space. However, JPD's city permit to do the project is on hold pending the current negotiations.

This is making city revitalization advocates increasingly anxious. Aditi Yadav comments, "This plan to create useful space out of an empty decaying building will go a long way to restoring vibrancy to that area of the city. I sincerely hope that JPD does not back out. In creating their offer, the City Council should consider JPD's excellent record of beautifully restoring and maintaining several other historic buildings in Clanton."

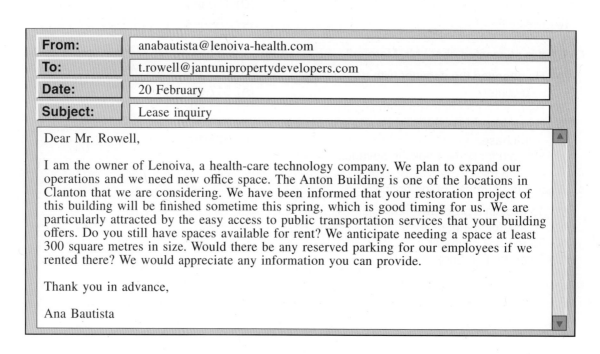

From:	anabautista@lenoiva-health.com
To:	t.rowell@jantunipropertydevelopers.com
Date:	20 February
Subject:	Lease inquiry

Dear Mr. Rowell,

I am the owner of Lenoiva, a health-care technology company. We plan to expand our operations and we need new office space. The Anton Building is one of the locations in Clanton that we are considering. We have been informed that your restoration project of this building will be finished sometime this spring, which is good timing for us. We are particularly attracted by the easy access to public transportation services that your building offers. Do you still have spaces available for rent? We anticipate needing a space at least 300 square metres in size. Would there be any reserved parking for our employees if we rented there? We would appreciate any information you can provide.

Thank you in advance,

Ana Bautista

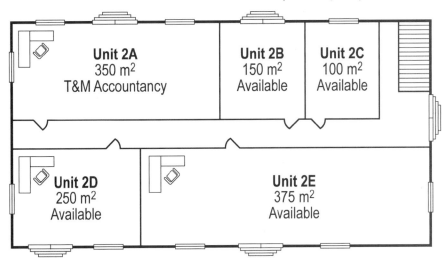

One Anton Place–2nd Floor Plan (office space)

Unit 2A
350 m²
T&M Accountancy

Unit 2B
150 m²
Available

Unit 2C
100 m²
Available

Unit 2D
250 m²
Available

Unit 2E
375 m²
Available

191. What is the purpose of the article?

(A) To report on the benefits of mixed-use buildings
(B) To provide an update on a project
(C) To encourage residents to apply for jobs
(D) To announce a change in city policy

192. What positive aspect of the Anton Building does Ms. Yadav mention?

(A) Its cost efficiency
(B) Its compliance with environmental standards
(C) The anticipated quality of the renovation work
(D) The large amount of retail space

193. What is suggested about JPD in Ms. Bautista's e-mail?

(A) It received the approval it was seeking.
(B) It has the only available office spaces for rent in Clanton.
(C) It has moved its main office to the Anton Building.
(D) It is a relatively new company.

194. What information about the building does Ms. Bautista request from Mr. Rowell?

(A) The distance to the nearest train station
(B) The other occupants' types of business
(C) The completion date of the renovation
(D) The availability of employee parking

195. What space would Lenoiva most likely choose to rent?

(A) Unit 2B
(B) Unit 2C
(C) Unit 2D
(D) Unit 2E

GO ON TO THE NEXT PAGE

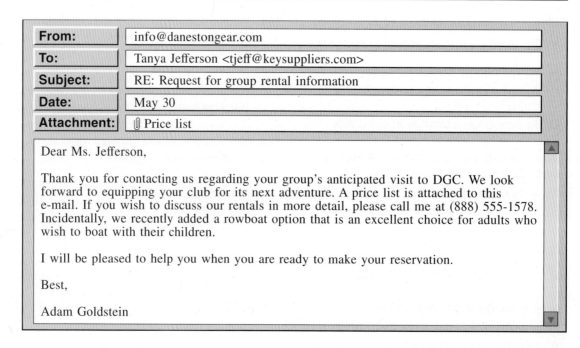

From:	Tanya Jefferson <tjeff@keysuppliers.com>
To:	info@danestongear.com
Subject:	Request for group rental information
Date:	May 29

Hello Daneston Gear Company (DGC),

I am the president of an activities club. This month, our 30 members intend to take a day trip to Daneston to go boating on the lake. Could you please send me information regarding your rates and offerings? We are most interested in renting boats that seat one person. Some time ago, I rented a kayak for myself from DGC, but this will be my first time renting from DGC for a group.

Thank you,

Tanya Jefferson

From:	info@danestongear.com
To:	Tanya Jefferson <tjeff@keysuppliers.com>
Subject:	RE: Request for group rental information
Date:	May 30
Attachment:	📎 Price list

Dear Ms. Jefferson,

Thank you for contacting us regarding your group's anticipated visit to DGC. We look forward to equipping your club for its next adventure. A price list is attached to this e-mail. If you wish to discuss our rentals in more detail, please call me at (888) 555-1578. Incidentally, we recently added a rowboat option that is an excellent choice for adults who wish to boat with their children.

I will be pleased to help you when you are ready to make your reservation.

Best,

Adam Goldstein

DGC Price list

	Boat type	Hourly rate	Additional 1/2 hour
Option 1	2-person canoe	$13	$8
Option 2	3-person canoe	$15	$8
Option 3	1-person kayak	$11	$8
Option 4	2-person kayak	$14	$8
Option 5	3- or 4-person rowboat (3 adults or 2 adults and 2 small children)	$13	$9

- We are open every day from April to October, 10:00 A.M. to 6:30 P.M.
- All boats must be returned by 6:15 P.M. on the day they are rented.
- Life jackets and paddles are included in the rental fee.
- Groups of ten or more qualify for a discount if they book at least one week in advance.

196. What does Ms. Jefferson mention in the first e-mail?

(A) She has used DGC's services before.
(B) She teaches a course in boating safety.
(C) She is a resident of Daneston.
(D) She owns her own kayak.

197. What rental option best meets Ms. Jefferson's needs?

(A) Option 1
(B) Option 2
(C) Option 3
(D) Option 4

198. What is the hourly rate of DGC's newest rental option?

(A) $11
(B) $13
(C) $14
(D) $15

199. What is indicated about DGC in the price list?

(A) It is open for business all year.
(B) It may close for the day if the weather is bad.
(C) It offers special rates for groups of ten or more.
(D) It accepts reservations on its Web site.

200. According to the price list, what is true about all boats?

(A) They can fit three adults.
(B) They can be rented overnight.
(C) They are suitable for small children.
(D) They are equipped with life jackets.

Stop! This is the end of the test. If you finish before time is called, you may go back to Parts 5, 6, and 7 and check your work.

토익˚ 정기시험
기출문제집

RC

기출 TEST

02

READING TEST

In the Reading test, you will read a variety of texts and answer several different types of reading comprehension questions. The entire Reading test will last 75 minutes. There are three parts, and directions are given for each part. You are encouraged to answer as many questions as possible within the time allowed.

You must mark your answers on the separate answer sheet. Do not write your answers in your test book.

PART 5

Directions: A word or phrase is missing in each of the sentences below. Four answer choices are given below each sentence. Select the best answer to complete the sentence. Then mark the letter (A), (B), (C), or (D) on your answer sheet.

101. Ms. Budrow was promoted after ------- group recorded the highest revenue growth for the year.

(A) her
(B) hers
(C) herself
(D) she

102. The community program features classes in photography, drawing, ------- other arts.

(A) yet
(B) but
(C) and
(D) thus

103. Glass containers must be ------- secured during transport.

(A) safely
(B) safe
(C) safety
(D) safer

104. This month's ------- figures have increased five percent over the last month.

(A) selling
(B) sold
(C) to sell
(D) sales

105. Summer interns may ------- either free company housing or a stipend of $2,000.

(A) choose
(B) wonder
(C) apply
(D) rent

106. If a client leaves a voice message, we will return the ------- promptly within one business day.

(A) extra
(B) effort
(C) signal
(D) call

107. The department's most ------- production unit will receive a bonus at the end of the quarter.

(A) effective
(B) effect
(C) effectively
(D) effecting

108. Al's Café will now be open on Sundays ------- the hours of 9 A.M. and 5 P.M.

(A) for
(B) between
(C) inside
(D) from

109. Mr. Liu will not be in the office this morning ------- he has a dentist appointment.

(A) following
(B) because
(C) including
(D) likewise

110. Ms. Trinacria's team is developing a kitchen faucet that can ------- respond to voice commands.

(A) reliably
(B) rely
(C) reliability
(D) reliable

111. So far this year, the Richmond City Orchestra has sold out ------- one of its concerts.

(A) complete
(B) total
(C) every
(D) entire

112. You must close the application before ------- the installation of the software update.

(A) to begin
(B) beginning
(C) must begin
(D) begins

113. The town's traffic committee urges motorists to drive ------- on Main Street.

(A) abundantly
(B) obviously
(C) rightfully
(D) cautiously

114. Eastington University just announced the ------- of all foods containing artificial preservatives from its cafeteria menu.

(A) eliminate
(B) eliminated
(C) elimination
(D) eliminates

115. Some commuters were late because of the weather, but the road closures affected an even ------- number.

(A) great
(B) greater
(C) greatest
(D) greatly

116. At each performance, dancer Clay Hastings displays a remarkable ------- to connect with his audience.

(A) degree
(B) function
(C) totality
(D) ability

117. Amand Corp.'s flexible work policy is ------- beneficial to the company as employee turnover is minimal.

(A) financially
(B) finances
(C) financial
(D) to finance

118. Ragini Kumari has published a book about the history of agricultural ------- in the region.

(A) practical
(B) practices
(C) practiced
(D) is practicing

119. Ms. Sanchez has ------- been promoted to office manager at Delbay Tech.

(A) anywhere
(B) soon
(C) recently
(D) when

120. Please reserve room 200 for Monday afternoon, since the workshop is expected to ------- several hours.

(A) occur
(B) start
(C) hold
(D) last

GO ON TO THE NEXT PAGE

121. Zachary Cho, president of the Canadian Florist Association, introduced the ------- speaker at the convention.

(A) opening
(B) expanded
(C) careful
(D) powered

122. The team ------- completes the online training first will receive a catered lunch.

(A) whichever
(B) it
(C) that
(D) either

123. Industry news and upcoming social events are ------- the items featured in the company newsletter.

(A) during
(B) among
(C) toward
(D) except

124. Many customers have remained faithful to Kristiansen Electronics ------- the years because of our excellent customer service.

(A) through
(B) even if
(C) prior to
(D) while

125. The release of the earnings report will ------- until the latest company figures are ready.

(A) delay
(B) have delayed
(C) be delayed
(D) be delaying

126. Assistant Director Melissa Arun works ------- the interns to monitor the quality of their work.

(A) across
(B) alongside
(C) against
(D) about

127. Ms. Fujita has postponed the team meeting until next week because everyone already has ------- to do this week.

(A) most
(B) enough
(C) neither
(D) which

128. Call Gislason Insurance today to speak to a ------- agent for a free quote.

(A) licensed
(B) maximum
(C) required
(D) former

129. Motorbike Unlimited's marketing campaign will begin ------- the terms of the contract are finalized.

(A) as well as
(B) other than
(C) rather than
(D) as soon as

130. ------- of planet Jupiter may provide scientists with long-awaited answers.

(A) Acceleration
(B) Intention
(C) Observation
(D) Provision

PART 6

Directions: Read the texts that follow. A word, phrase, or sentence is missing in parts of each text. Four answer choices for each question are given below the text. Select the best answer to complete the text. Then mark the letter (A), (B), (C), or (D) on your answer sheet.

Questions 131-134 refer to the following memo.

To: All staff
From: Leonard Villalobos, Vice President of Product Development
Date: August 27
Subject: Atzeret game (Product #DS8192)

Due to the results from our trial customer testing, we have decided to postpone the launch of the Atzeret video game. Customer surveys indicated that the game was less ------- than we
131.
anticipated. Over the next few months, the game development team will introduce several -------
132.
to make the product more attractive. ------- . If the changes are successful, we hope to launch the
133.
game by next January ------- February.
134.

131. (A) expensive
(B) repetitive
(C) appealing
(D) surprising

132. (A) modification
(B) modifies
(C) modifying
(D) modifications

133. (A) At that point, more tests will be conducted.
(B) The launch will be our biggest of the year.
(C) However, the surveys are not reliable.
(D) Team members must each sign the form.

134. (A) since
(B) or
(C) if
(D) later

GO ON TO THE NEXT PAGE

Questions 135-138 refer to the following e-mail.

To: Eva Linn, Lundtalk Industries
From: Technical Services
Date: January 15
Subject: Technical query

Dear Ms. Linn,

Thank you for contacting our technical department ------- your query. -------, our call got
                                                    135.   136.
disconnected when we were trying to reboot your system from our remote location. ------- .
                                                                                  137.
Therefore, please call us at your earliest convenience and refer to conversation ID #TECH12-
2020A to complete the system repair. We have prioritized your inquiry and look forward to helping

you ------- your computer to its full capabilities.
    138.

Sincerely,

Arthur Feldt
Technical Service Facilitator

135. (A) until
     (B) besides
     (C) into
     (D) with

136. (A) In other words
     (B) For this reason
     (C) For example
     (D) As you know

137. (A) We invite you to visit one of our
         computer repair centers in your area.
     (B) Unfortunately, we do not have a phone
         number at which we can reach you.
     (C) Thank you again for being one of our
         priority customers.
     (D) Please submit your check for the
         service fee promptly.

138. (A) restore
     (B) restoring
     (C) restored
     (D) restoration

For a limited time, the Uppercut Clothing Hanger Company is selling its highest quality hangers at huge discounts on wholesale orders. This special ------- is perfect for hotels, retailers, or
139.

anywhere hangers are used extensively. ------- of lacquered walnut wood, these hangers are not
140.

only durable, but also safe for the environment. ------- are strong enough to hold up to ten
141.

pounds. To order, visit www.uppercuthangerco.ca. Note that all orders require a 20 percent

deposit. ------- . Uppercut will cover all shipping and insurance costs.
142.

139. (A) clothing
(B) offer
(C) decoration
(D) performance

140. (A) Made
(B) Making
(C) To make
(D) They made

141. (A) Both
(B) They
(C) Fewer
(D) Theirs

142. (A) Our products make great gifts.
(B) While sturdy, wooden hangers are also heavy.
(C) Quality hangers are a great investment.
(D) The balance is due when the shipment is received.

From: mcrane@doodlemail.com
To: jkumar@baxterartsupplies.com
Date: October 14
Subject: Application
Attachment: Résumé

Dear Ms. Kumar,

I am writing in response to the advertisement posted in the window of Baxter Art Supplies. As a frequent visitor to your ------- , I have found it an invaluable source of inspiration over the years. I
143.
would be ------- to display my artwork. I would also enjoy running workshops to help inspire your
144.
customers.

I believe I would be well suited for this role because I am both enthusiastic and friendly.
------- , I have led successful workshops at various locations in the area. I have attached a copy
145.
of my résumé, which includes more details about these workshops. ------- . I look forward to
146.
hearing from you after you have reviewed my application and work.

Kind regards,

Melania Crane

143. (A) school
(B) house
(C) store
(D) museum

144. (A) thrilling
(B) thrill
(C) thrilled
(D) thrills

145. (A) In addition
(B) However
(C) In general
(D) Similarly

146. (A) I enjoyed the painting workshop last week.
(B) Samples of my art can be found at www.mcrane.com.
(C) I just started working with watercolors.
(D) For a price list, please contact me at 347-555-0101.

PART 7

Directions: In this part you will read a selection of texts, such as magazine and newspaper articles, e-mails, and instant messages. Each text or set of texts is followed by several questions. Select the best answer for each question and mark the letter (A), (B), (C), or (D) on your answer sheet.

Questions 147-148 refer to the following sign.

> ### WHAT'S GOING ON HERE?
> **Work in progress:** Commercial
> **Anticipated completion date:** March 1
>
> | **Owner** | **General Contractor** |
> |---|---|
> | Walker Booksellers | Matthiesen Builders |
> | 4634 Goosetown Drive | 4500 Smith Street |
> | Arden, NC | Raleigh, NC |
>
> **All work permits are on file with the Department of Planning.**
> To report a problem at this work site, call 919–555–0134.

147. Where would the sign most likely appear?

(A) Above a book display
(B) At a construction site
(C) On a residential building
(D) In a university classroom

148. Why should a reader of the sign call the phone number?

(A) To file a permit
(B) To apply for a job
(C) To confirm a date
(D) To report a problem

GO ON TO THE NEXT PAGE

On Saturday, August 1, the **Durhamtown Symphony Orchestra** will be giving a free educational performance at the Cardona Culture Center, 498 Mahogany Ave. Among other things, the musicians will discuss the origins and development of their instruments as well as some musical styles. Audience members will have an opportunity to ask questions. The event will conclude with the orchestra performing works by some of today's well-known musicians and song writers.

149. What is the purpose of the information?

(A) To announce a change of location
(B) To publicize an upcoming event
(C) To describe some instruments
(D) To review a performance

150. According to the information, what will the audience members be able to do?

(A) Sing along
(B) Request songs
(C) Talk to the musicians
(D) Sign up for music lessons

151. The word "conclude" in paragraph 1, line 6, is closest in meaning to

(A) raise
(B) decide
(C) believe
(D) finish

Questions 152-153 refer to the following online chat discussion.

          — ☐ X

Bonnie Ruiz 2:40 P.M.
Good morning; welcome to Ship With Us.

Nick Portier 2:41 P.M.
Hi. I'm Nick, and I'm having trouble getting into my account.

Bonnie Ruiz 2:42 P.M.
Hi, Nick. I'm happy to help. Have you tried resetting your password?

Nick Portier 2:43 P.M.
I have, and I'm still not able to get in. I need to send a large shipment of brochures and catalogs in the next 15 minutes, and I'm a little anxious.

Bonnie Ruiz 2:44 P.M.
Don't worry. I'm here to help! Your account number is X58292J, right? I can reset your account on my end.

Nick Portier 2:45 P.M.
That's it.

Bonnie Ruiz 2:46 P.M.
Great. I've sent a new password to the e-mail address associated with that account number, and you should receive it within the next two minutes. I'll stay available until I've heard from you to make sure that you've accessed your account.

Nick Portier 2:46 P.M.
Wonderful. Thanks!

---

152. What most likely is Ms. Ruiz' occupation?

(A) Bank teller
(B) Graphic designer
(C) Software developer
(D) Customer-support specialist

153. At 2:45 P.M., what does Mr. Portier most likely mean when he writes, "That's it"?

(A) A password has been changed.
(B) He is able to access his account.
(C) He has received Ms. Ruiz' e-mail.
(D) Ms. Ruiz has the information she needs.

GO ON TO THE NEXT PAGE ➤

Adnan's Auto Garage

5 Warner Place
Serving Manchester for 20 years!
Open Monday to Friday, 8 A.M. to 5 P.M.; Saturday, 9 A.M. to 1 P.M.

Adnan's Auto Garage is a full-service repair shop where customer service is our top priority! Our founder, Adnan Haddad, learned his skills as the head technician for a racing team. He and his staff of professional mechanics now service all makes and models of cars and trucks, both foreign and domestic. We'll keep your vehicle on the road!

We also sell used cars at competitive prices.
Interested in selling your car? Call us now!
0161 496 0437

154. What is indicated about Adnan's Auto Garage?

(A) It will move to a new location in Manchester.
(B) It has been in business for two decades.
(C) It offers evening hours once a week.
(D) It repairs locally manufactured cars only.

155. According to the advertisement, who is invited to call the phone number?

(A) Car owners
(B) Auto mechanics
(C) Race car technicians
(D) Truck drivers

Watford Shredding Day

Do you need to safely dispose of piles of confidential paperwork? Come to Watford Community Shredding Day on April 8 from 8:00 A.M. to 11:00 A.M.

A number of Security Too shredders will be conveniently located behind the Watford municipal parking garage. — [1] —. Bring any unneeded bank statements, tax documents, and bills. — [2] —. They will be securely shredded and recycled on the spot. Please note that the event is open to Watford Township residents only, and there is a five-kilo limit per household. — [3] —. Security Too representatives will be on hand to talk about ways to protect your private information.

Community Shredding Day is brought to you by radio station 82.9 WQYX and Security Too. — [4] —.

For more information, visit www.watfordtownship/shreddingday.org.

156. What is the purpose of the notice?

(A) To notify residents of a due date
(B) To promote a service
(C) To welcome a new business to town
(D) To advertise a contest

157. What will most likely happen on April 8 ?

(A) Paper will be recycled.
(B) A bank representative will meet clients.
(C) A new parking garage will open.
(D) An informational seminar will be offered.

158. In which of the positions marked [1], [2], [3], and [4] does the following sentence best belong?

"Simply drive up and drop them off."

(A) [1]
(B) [2]
(C) [3]
(D) [4]

GO ON TO THE NEXT PAGE

Questions 159-160 refer to the following e-mail.

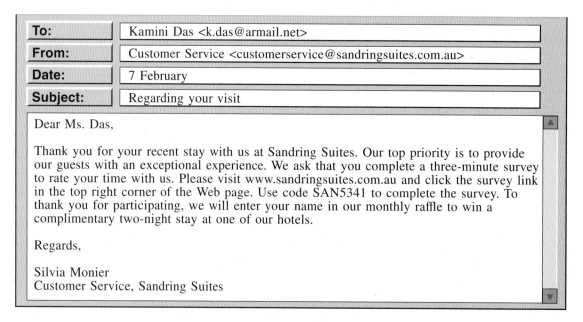

To:	Kamini Das <k.das@armail.net>
From:	Customer Service <customerservice@sandringsuites.com.au>
Date:	7 February
Subject:	Regarding your visit

Dear Ms. Das,

Thank you for your recent stay with us at Sandring Suites. Our top priority is to provide our guests with an exceptional experience. We ask that you complete a three-minute survey to rate your time with us. Please visit www.sandringsuites.com.au and click the survey link in the top right corner of the Web page. Use code SAN5341 to complete the survey. To thank you for participating, we will enter your name in our monthly raffle to win a complimentary two-night stay at one of our hotels.

Regards,

Silvia Monier
Customer Service, Sandring Suites

159. What is Ms. Das being asked to do?

(A) Confirm her contact information
(B) Provide some feedback
(C) Complete a purchase
(D) Renew a subscription

160. What does Ms. Monier indicate she will do for Ms. Das?

(A) Extend her hotel stay free of charge
(B) Assist her in using a Web site
(C) Give her a chance to win a prize
(D) Provide a discount code for a future hotel stay

AKBAR STORAGE COMPANY
227 Wexham Road, Bridgetown
Phone: 246-555-0147

Satisfying storage needs in Barbados for 30 years!

- Units are available in small, standard, and premium sizes to fit your storage needs.
- Your clean, dry storage unit is available to you around the clock.
- Our storage facility is monitored by high-quality security cameras, and each customer is given a pass code. Our secure electronic gate can be released only by entering this code.
- Our business office is open 9 A.M. to 6 P.M., Monday to Friday, and 9 A.M. to 2 P.M. on Saturday. Stop in to speak with one of our representatives.

And now, get 20 percent off with a twelve-month rental of our largest type of unit!

---

161. According to the advertisement, when can customers access their storage units?

(A) At any time
(B) Monday to Friday only
(C) On Saturday and Sunday only
(D) When accompanied by a security person

162. What do customers need to do in order to enter the facility?

(A) Purchase a day pass
(B) Be recognized by a security camera
(C) Enter an access code
(D) Show identification to a guard

163. How can customers receive a discount?

(A) By cutting back on their storage space by 20 percent
(B) By renting a premium-size unit for one year
(C) By showing the advertisement to a service representative
(D) By agreeing to rent a unit for a second year

GO ON TO THE NEXT PAGE

Questions 164-167 refer to the following article.

Gamer Arcades Joins Forces with Frankie's Burgers Franchises

LEEDS (9 July)—Gamer Arcades and fast-food franchise Frankie's Burgers have announced a new partnership, which will formally start at the beginning of August. At that time, all Gamer Arcades will introduce a Frankie's Burgers to their locations.

The president of Gamer Arcades, Allen Ingram, expressed his excitement about the possibilities of this strategic partnership.

"The outstanding quality of Frankie's Burgers will enhance customers' enjoyment of our arcades," said Mr. Ingram. "Until now, there have been no food options on the premises. With this partnership, however, customers will be able to take a break for a delicious meal and then get back to enjoying our state-of-the-art gaming centers."

This is not the first major change Mr. Ingram has made to the company since he took over from Justine Beckerman last November. A month after assuming the role of president, he brought virtual reality games to Gamer Arcades. Since that time, he has also expanded the company into Germany and Belgium, and he has launched several charity initiatives associated with Gamer Arcades.

164. When will the partnership become official?

(A) In July
(B) In August
(C) In November
(D) In December

165. What is indicated about Gamer Arcades' partnership with Frankie's Burgers?

(A) It was agreed upon after months of negotiation.
(B) It will not apply to all Gamer Arcades sites.
(C) It is waiting for shareholder approval.
(D) It is Gamer Arcades' first partnership with a restaurant.

166. According to the article, who is Ms. Beckerman?

(A) The president of a food supply company
(B) The owner of a Frankie's Burgers franchise
(C) The owner of a game manufacturing company
(D) The former president of Gamer Arcades

167. What did Mr. Ingram do first at Gamer Arcades?

(A) He introduced virtual reality games.
(B) He started several charity programs.
(C) He opened branches in Belgium.
(D) He moved the headquarters to Germany.

Questions 168-171 refer to the following letter.

25 May

Ms. Deborah Kiernan
Sonicboom Distribution Agency
84 Arthur Road
London N7 6DR

Dear Ms. Kiernan:

Earthsky Films International is seeking a distributor for our latest production, *Project Aerial*. Having premiered in April at the North Brabant Film Festival in Eindhoven, the Netherlands, the film received strong reviews from critics and was honored with the Diamond Pen Award for best screenplay. — [1] —.

Our film, *Project Aerial*, examines an exciting period in aviation history that began more than 150 years ago. The aviation industry owes its development to a number of brilliant and enterprising people. — [2] —. The film highlights the major innovators as well as those who were lesser known.

The two lead roles are played by Winston Halsey and Virgil Golding, figures that are familiar to international audiences. — [3] —. Mr. Golding is known for his role in, among others, *The Rigby Conspiracy*, and Mr. Halsey is recognized for his performance in *Whereabouts Unknown*.

If you are interested in marketing our film, I would be happy to e-mail you a secure link so that you can view it. — [4] —. I hope to hear from you soon.

Sincerely,

Jayesh Chaudhari, CEO
Earthsky Films International

168. What would Mr. Chaudhari like to do?

(A) Promote a museum exhibit about aviation
(B) Hire a manager for a new business
(C) Become a film festival judge
(D) Introduce a movie to a wider audience

169. What is stated about *Project Aerial* ?

(A) It was mostly filmed in the Netherlands.
(B) Its opening has been long awaited.
(C) It examines the early stages of an industry.
(D) It was financed by an airline company.

170. What is indicated about Mr. Halsey and Mr. Golding?

(A) They are well-known actors.
(B) They have trained as pilots.
(C) They researched aviation history.
(D) They have worked together on several films.

171. In which of the positions marked [1], [2], [3], and [4] does the following sentence best belong?

"Both have received critical acclaim over the years."

(A) [1]
(B) [2]
(C) [3]
(D) [4]

GO ON TO THE NEXT PAGE

Maria Andreou (9:06 A.M.) Good morning, Jakob and Sandra. I need help with the focus group with the photographers that is taking place on Thursday morning. I'm no longer available to lead it.

Jakob Wendt (9:09 A.M.) That's unfortunate. We need to follow up with that meeting to advise our client about what is important to potential customers.

Maria Andreou (9:10 A.M.) Exactly. So I would rather not have to reschedule. The client is expecting our report early next week. Would either of you be able to conduct the group instead of me?

Sandra Liu (9:12 A.M.) Sorry, Maria. I'm traveling out of town tomorrow for the marketing conference, and won't be back until Friday.

Jakob Wendt (9:15 A.M.) I've never led a focus group before, but I'm happy to do it.

Maria Andreou (9:17 A.M.) Great. I'll send you the participant consent form by e-mail. Remember that at the start of the group session, each participant will need to sign a copy.

Jakob Wendt (9:18 A.M.) OK. How many copies will be needed?

Sandra Liu (9:19 A.M.) Actually, there's no need. I have copies left over from another group I ran last Tuesday. They're still on my desk.

Jakob Wendt (9:20 A.M.) I'll stop by and pick them up later today.

Maria Andreou (9:21 A.M) Thank you both. This means we can meet and work on the advertising report for the client next Monday.

172. For what type of business do the writers most likely work?

(A) A market research agency
(B) A printing shop
(C) A software development firm
(D) A photography studio

173. When will the focus group with the photographers meet?

(A) On Monday
(B) On Tuesday
(C) On Thursday
(D) On Friday

174. What is indicated about Mr. Wendt?

(A) He would prefer to attend a conference.
(B) He works downstairs from Ms. Liu's office.
(C) He has never previously run a focus group.
(D) He is the most experienced member of the team.

175. At 9:19 A.M., what does Ms. Liu most likely mean when she writes, "there's no need"?

(A) She can cancel her business trip.
(B) Focus group participants will not complete consent forms.
(C) A focus group can be rescheduled.
(D) Mr. Wendt should not print any consent forms.

GO ON TO THE NEXT PAGE

Our Company	Our Products	Our Partners	Contact Us

Drymotic is pleased to announce that our revolutionary vacuum-microwave dehydration process is now being used by more than 30 companies in the food and pharmaceutical industries.

Here's how it works: Batches of raw organic materials, prepared in small pieces, are loaded into the machine's rotating drum. As the drum turns, moisture is removed from the pieces by microwave energy. The final moisture level can be preset by the operator. The dried pieces retain their color, taste, and nutrition, and are then ready for packaging. Drymotic machines produce better results in less time (and at lower cost) than freeze-drying and air-drying.

Drymotic machines are available in the following sizes:

Model Number	Power	Suggested use
G4200	10 kw	Testing new products
G4260	50 kw	Small-scale manufacturers
H4500	100 kw	Large-scale, high-volume manufacturers

E-mail

To:	customerservice@drymotic.com
From:	ovolterra@yambrett.com.au
Date:	6 May
Subject:	Malfunctioning unit

Dear Customer Service,

We purchased a Drymotic unit (product number: G4260, serial number: 01938207) last year for use with our line of instant stew mixes. We had no issues with the unit until the beginning of this month, when we began to notice an increase in processing time. We have followed the recommended cleaning schedule, so this problem cannot be caused by excess residue.

Please let me know if you have any suggestions for resolving this issue in a timely manner. I always prefer to handle minor repairs on my own, but if this issue persists, we may need to schedule a maintenance visit in the near future.

Best regards,

Olivia Volterra
Yambrett Corporation

176. What are Drymotic processors designed to do?

(A) Cut food into little pieces
(B) Preserve food by drying it
(C) Add moisture to organic material
(D) Improve a product's color and taste

177. On the Web page, the word "retain" in paragraph 2, line 4, is closest in meaning to

(A) remember
(B) support
(C) enhance
(D) keep

178. What is suggested about the Yambrett Corporation?

(A) It operates a high-volume dehydration machine.
(B) It produces packaged food on a small scale.
(C) It recently tested a new product.
(D) It was founded a year ago.

179. Why does Ms. Volterra write to Drymotic's customer service department?

(A) To schedule a maintenance visit
(B) To ask if a unit is covered by a warranty
(C) To obtain advice on making a repair
(D) To request a replacement for a machine

180. What problem has developed with the Yambrett Corporation's processor?

(A) It is operating more slowly.
(B) It is making more noise.
(C) It is using more power.
(D) It requires cleaning more often.

GO ON TO THE NEXT PAGE

Spotlight on Carl Ybor

GORE, New Zealand (2 May)—Architect Carl Ybor has created a name for himself by helping clients turn their trash into treasure. He has built dozens of houses in Gore composed almost entirely of reclaimed, recovered, or found materials.

"As much as possible, I like to use materials that are already available nearby," says Mr. Ybor. "It just takes some creativity, but that way nothing is wasted and houses can be built for a fraction of the price. Old fencing, discarded bottles, corks, mismatched bricks and tiles—nothing gets overlooked."

While Mr. Ybor is fully responsible for creating the design plans for the houses he builds, he always involves homeowners in the building process. With a waiting list of at least a year, Mr. Ybor is able to carefully select his clients. He works solely with homeowners who already know how to operate power tools and are willing to do some of the hands-on work themselves.

Some of his houses have been featured in magazines, travel shows, and online carpentry demonstrations. Mr. Ybor's Web site, featuring photos of his projects, can be found at yborhabitats.co.nz.

To:	contact@yborhabitats.co.nz
From:	c.holmes@hmail.net
Date:	4 May
Subject:	Proposal

Dear Mr. Ybor,

I just read an article about you. I was excited to learn about your services and how you work with the owners to create unique spaces. I have two projects I want to work on:

1. I want to add an extension to my current house, incorporating leftover materials I have from the patio that I had built a few years ago.

2. My roof needs to be replaced. I have researched ways to cut the cost, and one suggestion was to leave the existing roof intact and just install new metal sheeting on top. I like this idea!

Are you available and interested in doing this work? I would like to start as early as next month. I can pay half the money up front by credit card to secure an appointment.

Cynthia Holmes

181. What does the article state about the houses Mr. Ybor builds?

(A) They are large.
(B) They are expensive.
(C) They are located throughout New Zealand.
(D) They are built with used materials.

182. What does Mr. Ybor ask his clients to do?

(A) Replace old fencing
(B) Create decorative tiles
(C) Submit design plans
(D) Use power tools

183. According to the article, what can readers do on Mr. Ybor's Web site?

(A) Request a quote for his services
(B) View examples of his work
(C) Download some written instructions
(D) Read reviews from satisfied clients

184. What does Ms. Holmes want to do?

(A) Remove her old roof
(B) Replace the tiles in her patio
(C) Increase the size of her house
(D) Build a new house

185. What part of Ms. Holmes's proposal will Mr. Ybor most likely refuse?

(A) The starting date
(B) The suggested price
(C) The method of payment
(D) The choice of materials

To:	All CFA Staff
From:	Yung-Chien Chou
Date:	16 October
Subject:	Plans
Attachment:	📎 Agenda

Dear Colleagues,

Hagit Caspi will be visiting for a couple of days next week to interview for the position of executive vice president here at Cliff Feiring Associates (CFA). She is highly qualified, and her background in international finance makes her particularly well suited for this role. Please make every effort to welcome her.

It is important to the CFA leadership that everyone has the opportunity to get to know Ms. Caspi. As such, I am asking all of you to attend certain events with her. Please see the attached agenda, and add the events marked CFA to your calendar. More details will follow.

Best,

Yung-Chien Chou
CEO, Cliff Feiring Associates

Agenda for Hagit Caspi's Visit

Date	Time	Event	Invitees
23 October	9:00 A.M.	Breakfast at La Brunch	Board members
23 October	12:30 P.M.	Lunch in office	Department heads
23 October	3:00 P.M.	Question-and-answer session	CFA
23 October	7:00 P.M.	Dinner at Medium Hills Bistro	Board members
24 October	9:00 A.M.	Breakfast in office	CFA

To:	Yung-Chien Chou <chou@clifffeiring.ca>
From:	Hagit Caspi <hagit.caspi@volumel.co.il>
Date:	27 October
Subject:	Follow-up

Dear Mr. Chou,

Many thanks for hosting me last week. I truly enjoyed meeting everyone. I particularly appreciated my conversation with Mr. Georgopoulos at Medium Hills Bistro. He told me some amazing stories about CFA's history.

Again, I am sorry for not attending the event on the 24th. The weather was worrying, and I did not want to miss my flight to Tel Aviv.

Last but certainly not least, thank you for your offer, which I received this morning. I would be honoured to take on the role of executive vice president of CFA starting in January. The job description covers everything we discussed. The hours you noted for the position seem appropriate, and I am very pleased with the benefits. I look forward to working closely with you.

Most sincerely,

Hagit Caspi

186. What is a purpose of the first e-mail?

(A) To notify staff of an upcoming visit
(B) To advertise a job opening
(C) To recommend an employee for promotion
(D) To introduce a new colleague

187. What meal were all employees asked to add to their calendars?

(A) Breakfast on October 23
(B) Lunch on October 23
(C) Dinner on October 23
(D) Breakfast on October 24

188. What is one reason Ms. Caspi writes to Mr. Chou?

(A) To apologize for a delay
(B) To accept an offer
(C) To discuss air travel plans
(D) To ask for details about a job

189. Who most likely is Mr. Georgopoulos?

(A) A Medium Hills Bistro employee
(B) A board member
(C) A department head
(D) A worker in the human resources department

190. What does the second e-mail indicate about the job?

(A) It will begin in January.
(B) It will be based in Tel Aviv.
(C) It involves working overtime.
(D) It still needs a job description.

GO ON TO THE NEXT PAGE

TRIVESS (1 February)—Alacritum, Inc., has announced plans to build charging stations for electric vehicles along Highway 1. With over 400 stations across Asia already, Alacritum brings a wealth of experience to this large-scale undertaking. The Highway 1 stations, known as PRO stations, will provide vehicles with up to 200 kilowatts of power, achieving an 80 percent charge in 30 minutes. The system will periodically notify waiting drivers of the status of their battery charge by sending texts to their cell phones or other mobile devices. The company promises to provide motorists with clean, comfortable, brightly lit waiting facilities. A testing location will open at the beginning of next month in Logred.

PRO Stations: Proposed Distribution

Region	Number of Stations	Customers per Day
Elondell	26	9,220
Southern Borelvia	14	4,970
Western Borelvia	20	6,390
North Shore	10	3,560

To:	lhsiao@alacritum.com
From:	ctrigg@alacritum.com
Date:	15 March
Subject:	Meeting

Dear Mr. Hsiao,

Following the meeting with our community partners in Western Borelvia this week, I suggest adding air-conditioning to the waiting areas in that region because of the desert conditions there. Although the addition entails higher costs, it will ensure the comfort and safety of the customers. I have also learned firsthand that poor cell service along Highway 1 will make the wireless networks at most PRO stations unreliable, so we will need a technological solution for that as well. I will send a full report by the end of the week.

Chuck Trigg

191. What does the article indicate about Alacritum, Inc.?

(A) It operates 80 percent of the charging stations in Asia.
(B) It is moving its head office to Logred in February.
(C) It built 400 PRO stations along Highway 1.
(D) It will test a station site in March.

192. According to the chart, what region is expected to have the most customers?

(A) Elondell
(B) Southern Borelvia
(C) Western Borelvia
(D) North Shore

193. What is the main purpose of the e-mail?

(A) To negotiate costs
(B) To provide advice
(C) To explain why a delivery was late
(D) To suggest a new partnership

194. What system at PRO stations will require a technological solution?

(A) The cleaning system
(B) The food vending system
(C) The lighting system
(D) The text notification system

195. How many stations will need air-conditioned waiting areas?

(A) 10
(B) 14
(C) 20
(D) 26

GO ON TO THE NEXT PAGE

From:	cbeker@yourworkstyle.net
To:	lroytenberg@charlottes.com; ajordan@charlottes.com
Date:	January 27, 10:02 A.M.
Subject:	First draft of press release
Attachment:	📎 Press release draft

Dear Mr. Roytenberg and Ms. Jordan,

My first draft of the press release is attached. As we previously discussed by phone, my contract includes one additional half-hour meeting to discuss the project and any changes you would like me to make before I submit the press release to my contacts at *Pinetown Weekly*.

Please let me know if I can stop by this week. I would like to take photos of the space. I remember your mentioning that the historic architecture of the building would be a draw for customers.

In addition, I will need to get a direct quotation from either of you or from Chef Vaux. I know from working with *Pinetown Weekly* in the past that they will not run a piece like this without at least one quotation.

Best regards,

Cathy Beker

– DRAFT –

Charlotte's Opens for Business

Charlotte's, located at Avenue D and Oak Street, will open its doors on Friday, February 5. Owners Levon Roytenberg and Aubree Jordan are excited to welcome patrons for an aromatic cup of coffee or steaming espresso, specialty pastries, and savory café fare. Their aim is for Charlotte's to be a gathering place that indulges all the senses, where guests will be met with comfort and hospitality.

Award-winning executive chef Michel Vaux, most recently of Kahn's in Bloomington, has created an enticing menu featuring fresh-baked breads and grass-fed meats, with locally sourced vegetable dishes as accompaniments. Offerings will include breakfast and lunch selections. Chef Vaux will also bring to Charlotte's his elegant hot and cold beverages utilizing teas and herbal infusions.

From:	ajordan@charlottes.com
To:	cbeker@yourworkstyle.net
Cc:	lroytenberg@charlottes.com
Date:	January 28, 8:34 A.M.
Subject:	RE: First draft of press release

Hi Ms. Beker,

Mr. Roytenberg is in Boston for the next several days, and he has asked me to take the lead on the press release. I know you had asked to come by the site—are you available tomorrow, January 29, at 3:00 P.M.? I will be there all day decorating for the grand opening.

You have put together an excellent first draft. The only major problem I see is that you have mixed up the location of our corporate office and the café. The café is actually on the corner of Avenue C and Maple Street. Also, Mr. Roytenberg would like to include the operating hours, which are 8:00 A.M. to 4:00 P.M. daily. Please call Chef Vaux at 952-555-0133 for a quotation about specialty items on the menu.

All my best,

Aubree Jordan

196. Who most likely is Ms. Beker?

(A) An architect
(B) A freelance writer
(C) A professional chef
(D) An assistant to Mr. Roytenberg

197. According to the first e-mail, what must be added to the press release?

(A) A quotation
(B) A headline
(C) A contact's phone number
(D) A previously published photograph

198. What type of business is Charlotte's?

(A) A farm
(B) A catering service
(C) A café
(D) A supermarket chain

199. Why does Ms. Jordan invite Ms. Beker to visit Charlotte's on January 29 ?

(A) To sample a sandwich
(B) To help decorate for the grand opening
(C) To take pictures of a building
(D) To meet with Mr. Roytenberg

200. What is located on the corner of Avenue D and Oak Street?

(A) Ms. Beker's home office
(B) The headquarters of *Pinetown Weekly*
(C) Mr. Roytenberg's current residence
(D) A corporate office building

Stop! This is the end of the test. If you finish before time is called, you may go back to Parts 5, 6, and 7 and check your work.

토익® 정기시험
기출문제집

RC

기출 TEST

03

READING TEST

In the Reading test, you will read a variety of texts and answer several different types of reading comprehension questions. The entire Reading test will last 75 minutes. There are three parts, and directions are given for each part. You are encouraged to answer as many questions as possible within the time allowed.

You must mark your answers on the separate answer sheet. Do not write your answers in your test book.

PART 5

Directions: A word or phrase is missing in each of the sentences below. Four answer choices are given below each sentence. Select the best answer to complete the sentence. Then mark the letter (A), (B), (C), or (D) on your answer sheet.

101. Vantage Automotive Design has recently ------- with the Pallax Company.

(A) merge
(B) merger
(C) merged
(D) merging

102. Rain is predicted this weekend, ------- the office picnic will have to be postponed.

(A) so
(B) for
(C) but
(D) nor

103. Use an alternative shipping firm if Greer Freight is unable to expedite delivery of ------- order.

(A) you
(B) your
(C) yours
(D) yourselves

104. The cafeteria is featuring dishes ------- different regions of the world this week.

(A) over
(B) through
(C) into
(D) from

105. Ms. Patel is coming to Delhi today to visit possible ------- for her company's new warehouse.

(A) locating
(B) locations
(C) located
(D) locate

106. Clydeway, Inc., has grown dramatically ------- its beginnings as a small corner grocery store.

(A) since
(B) such
(C) except
(D) however

107. When booking a flight, it is wise to ------- the guidelines for luggage size on the airline's Web site.

(A) check
(B) close
(C) approve
(D) list

108. The melody is so ------- that the composer has simplified parts of it for live performances.

(A) direct
(B) complex
(C) favorable
(D) helpful

109. The test group found the illustrations in the appliance users' guide to be highly -------.

(A) inform
(B) information
(C) informatively
(D) informative

110. The directions for Masuda's do-it-yourself projects are comprehensive enough for ------- a novice builder.

(A) right
(B) soon
(C) how
(D) even

111. ------- of the two candidates for the position had the necessary qualifications.

(A) Neither
(B) Nobody
(C) None
(D) Nothing

112. The need for highly trained electricians in the construction ------- has grown rapidly in recent years.

(A) employment
(B) activity
(C) knowledge
(D) industry

113. Ms. Daly will prepare a marketing budget and propose ------- during the client meeting.

(A) those
(B) its
(C) it
(D) her

114. Mr. Silva asked sales staff to ------- travel expenditures to help cut costs.

(A) convince
(B) require
(C) decide
(D) limit

115. The city council will discuss certain policies, particularly those made ------- the previous administration.

(A) any
(B) by
(C) to
(D) and

116. Servers' tips are pooled at the end of each shift and divided evenly ------- the entire waitstaff.

(A) onto
(B) among
(C) beside
(D) about

117. Costpa Analytics Ltd. has made successful ------- in two emerging data companies.

(A) investments
(B) invested
(C) invest
(D) investor

118. Vallentrade manages clients' accounts more ------- than most other brokerage firms.

(A) conserves
(B) conservative
(C) conservatively
(D) conserving

119. The ideal operating temperature for the tablet computer is ------- 10 and 30 degrees Celsius.

(A) between
(B) above
(C) in
(D) off

120. Of the people who have publicly introduced ------- at the Carpentry Club meetings, about half are commercial contractors.

(A) their
(B) their own
(C) they
(D) themselves

GO ON TO THE NEXT PAGE

121. On Thursday, the technician will be on Sratus Road ------- two gas stoves.

(A) serviced
(B) service
(C) to service
(D) is servicing

122. The spreadsheet ------- data on retail sales during the fourth quarter is attached.

(A) contains
(B) contained
(C) containing
(D) containable

123. See our weekly promotional flyer for complete ------- of the discounted items.

(A) exchange
(B) support
(C) receipts
(D) descriptions

124. New salespeople are instructed to research the businesses of ------- customers before contacting them for the first time.

(A) total
(B) potential
(C) equal
(D) factual

125. If you use online banking, bills can be paid ------- it is most convenient.

(A) whenever
(B) simply
(C) accordingly
(D) quite

126. Our internship combines lectures with real-world projects to provide formal instruction ------- professional experience.

(A) above all
(B) as well as
(C) now that
(D) in order to

127. Employee ------- at Medmile Ventures include share options and scheduled raises.

(A) beneficial
(B) beneficially
(C) benefits
(D) benefited

128. City ------- hope to get the necessary permits to build a twenty-story office building on Minerva Street.

(A) agendas
(B) developers
(C) avenues
(D) boundaries

129. Compliance Department officers regularly monitor changes in the ------- framework.

(A) regulate
(B) regulates
(C) regulator
(D) regulatory

130. The X250 portable heater achieves the desirable ------- without reaching especially high temperatures.

(A) practices
(B) factors
(C) outcomes
(D) dimensions

PART 6

Directions: Read the texts that follow. A word, phrase, or sentence is missing in parts of each text. Four answer choices for each question are given below the text. Select the best answer to complete the text. Then mark the letter (A), (B), (C), or (D) on your answer sheet.

Questions 131-134 refer to the following information.

Thank you for shopping with Danforth Fashions online. Our quality-control team carefully inspects all products ------- packaging to ensure customer satisfaction. ------- . If not, we make exchanges
131.   **132.**
or returns easy. Simply contact us at service@danforthfashions.com if you need a different size, color, or pattern—or if you are dissatisfied for any reason. Your exchange ------- right away. To
                                                                                                        133.
return an item for a refund, use the prepaid return shipping label included with your order and send it back to us in its original packaging unused and undamaged. We issue refunds to the original method of payment, ------- the return shipping fee.
                                              134.

131. (A) in case
     (B) as much as
     (C) prior to
     (D) in keeping with

132. (A) We hope you are entirely pleased with
         your purchase.
     (B) We expect to be redesigning our Web
         site this summer.
     (C) We value all of our loyal customers.
     (D) We noticed that your billing address
         has changed.

133. (A) will be processed
     (B) was processed
     (C) is processing
     (D) to be processing

134. (A) past
     (B) above
     (C) aboard
     (D) minus

GO ON TO THE NEXT PAGE

Questions 135-138 refer to the following notice.

Attention, Alden-Apner Industries Employees:

Please remember that the switch to our new e-mail software will begin at 11:00 P.M. on Sunday, May 2. All ------- information in your account, including contacts and calendar events, will be
135.
moved to the new system by 4:00 A.M. on Monday, May 3. Though we are working diligently to anticipate and provide solutions for all potential issues, some employees may experience difficulty ------- attempting to log in to their accounts after the switch. In addition, there is a remote
136.
possibility that some information may be lost. ------- , be sure to back up any critical e-mail files as
137.
soon as possible. ------- . A training session will be scheduled next week to familiarize employees
138.
with key functions of the new software.

135. (A) existed
(B) existence
(C) to exist
(D) existing

136. (A) when
(B) plus
(C) already
(D) whose

137. (A) Previously
(B) Otherwise
(C) Even so
(D) For this reason

138. (A) The new software will be ordered this week.
(B) The current system will be reactivated in June.
(C) If you need assistance with this, please contact the IT department.
(D) In that case, you must complete the installation yourself.

Questions 139-142 refer to the following e-mail.

From: Hong Truong <htruong@jansenwebbfoundation.ca>
Sent: Friday, 16 November
To: Staff, Friends, and Stakeholders
Subject: JWF's new budget director

To the JWF team and our community partners:

------- . I just want to let you know that Sofia Vargas ------- as the Jansen-Webb Foundation's new
   139.   **140.**

budget director. Ms. Vargas has a strong background in fiscal ------- within the nonprofit sector.
                                                     141.

Ms. Vargas brings with her a wealth of experience in organizational finance, including most

recently at The Lawton Children's Centre in Winnipeg. Ms. Vargas started her employment with

us this morning, so please stop in and introduce ------- to her.
                                                       142.

Best,

Hong Truong
CEO, Jansen-Webb Foundation

139. (A) This is a request to be prompt.
(B) Thanks for the generous contribution.
(C) All are welcome here.
(D) I hope that all are well.

140. (A) is hiring
(B) will be hired
(C) has been hired
(D) is being hired

141. (A) referral
(B) administrator
(C) running
(D) management

142. (A) yourself
(B) him
(C) them
(D) ourselves

Questions 143-146 refer to the following flyer.

Jamaica National Tourist Organization Offers Free Cultural Passes

The Jamaica National Tourist Organization (JAMTO) announces an exciting new program that

provides free entry to a variety of cultural attractions. The program is sponsored by the JAMTO

------- the hotels and businesses listed on the back of this flyer. Together we ------- you to take
  143.   **144.**

advantage of some of the finest cultural and educational experiences that Jamaica has to offer.

------- attractions include the Caribbean National Gardens, Montego Bay Potters Gallery,
  145.

Jamaican Music Experience, and many others.

To obtain your pass, visit our Web site at www.jamto.org/freepass or stop by any JAMTO office.

One pass is valid for up to five people. ------- .
                                          146.

---

143. (A) despite
    (B) instead of
    (C) except for
    (D) along with

144. (A) invite
    (B) invited
    (C) may invite
    (D) were inviting

145. (A) Early
    (B) Past
    (C) Affordable
    (D) Participating

146. (A) Thank you for your order.
    (B) It can be used for three days.
    (C) The bus runs only on weekdays.
    (D) All major credit cards are accepted.

PART 7

Directions: In this part you will read a selection of texts, such as magazine and newspaper articles, e-mails, and instant messages. Each text or set of texts is followed by several questions. Select the best answer for each question and mark the letter (A), (B), (C), or (D) on your answer sheet.

Questions 147-148 refer to the following text-message chain.

Jun Kambayashi [10:12 A.M.] Rachel, it looks as if Mr. Tanaka's flight will be arriving 30 minutes earlier this afternoon. I'm on my way to pick him up.

Rachel Newman [10:13 A.M.] The staff are excited that he finally is going to be working with us here. Do you think the two of you have time to stop here in the office before the end of the workday?

Jun Kambayashi [10:14 A.M.] Probably. And I agree; Mr. Tanaka has done great work at our Chiba branch.

Rachel Newman [10:15 A.M.] So I've always heard. It would be nice for him to get a quick tour of the lab and meet some members of the team before our welcome dinner.

Jun Kambayashi [10:16 A.M.] Sounds good. Since flight schedules can be unpredictable, I'll keep you posted as I arrive at the airport.

Rachel Newman [10:17 A.M.] Perfect. See you later.

147. Who most likely is Mr. Tanaka?

(A) A new laboratory owner
(B) An important client
(C) A transferred staff member
(D) An airline pilot

148. At 10:16 A.M., what does Mr. Kambayashi mean when he writes, "Sounds good"?

(A) He is pleased with the dinner arrangements.
(B) He likes the idea of stopping by the office before dinner.
(C) He appreciates Mr. Tanaka's professional reputation.
(D) He is glad that team members have completed their work.

GO ON TO THE NEXT PAGE

Questions 149-150 refer to the following e-mail.

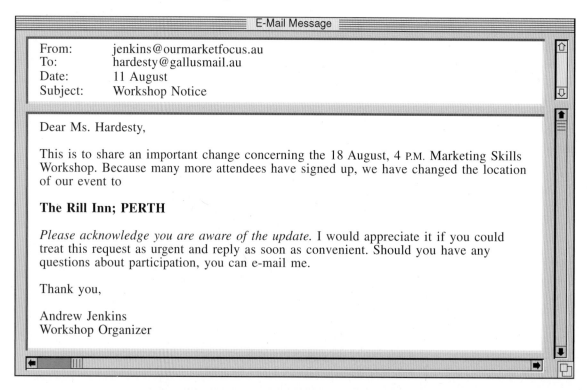

E-Mail Message

From: jenkins@ourmarketfocus.au
To: hardesty@gallusmail.au
Date: 11 August
Subject: Workshop Notice

Dear Ms. Hardesty,

This is to share an important change concerning the 18 August, 4 P.M. Marketing Skills Workshop. Because many more attendees have signed up, we have changed the location of our event to

The Rill Inn; PERTH

Please acknowledge you are aware of the update. I would appreciate it if you could treat this request as urgent and reply as soon as convenient. Should you have any questions about participation, you can e-mail me.

Thank you,

Andrew Jenkins
Workshop Organizer

149. What is the purpose of the e-mail?

(A) To cancel an event
(B) To announce a new venue
(C) To recruit new workshop presenters
(D) To request volunteers for a workshop

150. What is Ms. Hardesty asked to do?

(A) Share the notice with other attendees
(B) Choose a convenient time to meet
(C) Confirm receipt of the message
(D) Update her contact information

Virens

Come to Virens for the best televisions, phones, tablets, and more!

Grand Opening Celebration
featuring comedian and DJ Declan Gibb from radio station KYX 93.8

Saturday, October 2, 10:00 A.M.–8:00 P.M.
234 Morris Avenue, next to Mike's Pizza

Complimentary snacks from Sarah's Bakery—home of Sarah's delicious pastries!

Bring this ad for $5 off a purchase of $10 or more.
Valid throughout October.

---

151. What type of business is Virens?

(A) A pastry shop
(B) A radio station
(C) An electronics store
(D) A pizza restaurant

152. According to the advertisement, what will happen on October 2 ?

(A) Declan Gibb will perform at an event.
(B) Two businesses will move to new locations.
(C) A new product will be launched.
(D) A coupon will expire.

Questions 153-154 refer to the following Web page.

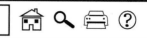

http://www.officenature.com

Want to boost the health and morale of your employees? Office Nature delivers a box filled with delicious food right to your break room.

We focus on the following.
- providing natural treats such as nuts, granola, and dried fruit
- working with local farmers to provide the freshest options
- reducing impact on the environment
- offering foods at reasonable prices

Just choose your selections and delivery day, and a fresh box of healthy food items will be brought automatically each week. First-time customers receive 10% off their order with code YUM.

153. For whom is the Web page most likely intended?

(A) Farmers
(B) Business owners
(C) Company employees
(D) Office Nature staff

154. What is indicated about Office Nature?

(A) It delivers healthy snacks.
(B) It offers weekly discounts.
(C) It makes its own baked goods.
(D) It grows its own fruit.

Spotlight on Geiger Travel

Wanting to combine his passion for exploring places and cultures with his career as a corporate travel consultant, Marcus Geiger founded Geiger Travel Management (GTM). Now, ten years later, the company has offices in the United States, Canada, and several South American nations. It crafts itineraries and facilitates travel and accommodation arrangements for business professionals.

GTM also offers its clients secure, high-speed computers, conference call systems, and file management software through an agreement with Balefire Electronics, located in Mumbai. "We owe a lot of our success to Balefire," says Mr. Geiger, "because their services enable our clients to work efficiently wherever they are."

Mr. Geiger is optimistic that further growth is on the horizon for GTM. Two additional businesses, Apura Airways, based in Paramaribo, Suriname, and the restaurant chain Triggerfish, headquartered in Bridgetown, Barbados, have agreed to enter into strategic partnerships with GTM in August. And looking to launch operations in Europe, the company is currently in discussions with Krokushaus AG, a hospitality company with locations throughout Germany.

For more information about Geiger Travel Management, visit www.gtm.com.

155. What is indicated about Mr. Geiger?

(A) He regularly goes to Mumbai for business.
(B) He has overseen the expansion of a business.
(C) He decided to become a travel writer ten years ago.
(D) He used to work for a hospitality company.

156. What service does GTM offer?

(A) Booking hotels for executives
(B) Leading cross-cultural training workshops
(C) Providing translation services at conferences
(D) Furnishing overseas branch offices

157. GTM does NOT have an agreement in place with which company?

(A) Balefire Electronics
(B) Apura Airways
(C) Triggerfish
(D) Krokushaus AG

GO ON TO THE NEXT PAGE

Questions 158-160 refer to the following press release.

FOR IMMEDIATE RELEASE   **Contact: Sherylin Stevens, sstevens@tearsoncorp.ca**

CALGARY (2 November)—Yves Vernier, the Chief Information Officer of the Tearson Corporation, announced on Monday that 200 robots will soon appear in Tearson's grocery stores. The robots, which are all named Bailey, will be used to locate areas where boxes or bottles have fallen and broken, spilling cereal, juice, or other substances onto the floor. The robots will report the spills so that the locations can be cleaned by store employees before they become safety hazards.

The robots were tested in Calgary, where Tearson's head office is located. During the eighteen-month pilot programme, store managers consistently gave the robots high marks. Although the robots have been used in the company's warehouses for several years, this will be their first time working in stores and interacting with customers. All Tearson stores should have the robots by the beginning of December.

For more information, visit Tearson Corporation at www.tearsoncorporation.ca.

---

158. What is the topic of the press release?

(A) The promotion of a company executive
(B) The use of technology in stores
(C) The launch of new product lines
(D) The relocation of a company's head office

159. What can Bailey do?

(A) Clean a mess on the floor
(B) Create labels for products
(C) Find areas that have spills
(D) Locate items for customers

160. What is suggested in the press release?

(A) A pilot program in Calgary was a success.
(B) Tearson stores will be renovated in December.
(C) A warehouse earned high marks for safety features.
(D) Managers will be hired in several stores.

From:	Helen Dietrich <hdietrich@morphospublishing.ca>
To:	Alia Cervantes <alia.cervantes@gotomail.ca>
Date:	3 March
Subject:	*Practical Gardening*

Dear Ms. Cervantes:

I am sorry to report that next month's issue of *Practical Gardening* will be our last. After 62 years of monthly issues, we at Morphos Publishing have decided that *Practical Gardening* will be among the periodicals that we must discontinue. We plan to redirect the resources gained through cost-cutting toward growing our book publishing and instructional video production businesses.

We are grateful for your support as a longtime subscriber to *Practical Gardening*. For the remainder of your subscription term, we hope you will allow us to instead send you *Flora Discovery*, our popular publication about wild plants. However, if you would rather have the balance of your subscription account refunded to you, please contact us at (822) 555-0127.

Sincerely,

Helen Dietrich
Subscription Manager, Morphos Publishing

161. What is the purpose of the e-mail?

(A) To apologize for a delay
(B) To promote a new product
(C) To announce a cancellation
(D) To address a billing error

162. What most likely is *Practical Gardening*?

(A) A film
(B) A book
(C) A Web site
(D) A magazine

163. The word "balance" in paragraph 2, line 4, is closest in meaning to

(A) amount remaining
(B) stability
(C) increase in cost
(D) production

Questions 164-167 refer to the following online chat discussion.

Lindsay Pokora (2:15 P.M.) Hello, Mr. Kopalinski. I need to place the monthly office supplies order. In addition to the regular items, can you let me know if anything extra is needed?

Craig Kopalinski (2:17 P.M.) Let me check with the other managers. Kaitlyn and Jeffrey, do you have any requests for office supplies in your departments?

Kaitlyn Daley (2:18 P.M.) Yes, we need more whiteboard markers.

Craig Kopalinski (2:19 P.M.) And how about accounting?

Jeffrey Carden (2:20 P.M.) Nothing here.

Lindsay Pokora (2:22 P.M.) Markers? I just checked our inventory and we still have a box in the supply room. Do you need a special kind?

Kaitlyn Daley (2:23 P.M.) No, just regular black markers. Three boxes should be enough. I tried some markers from the box we have, but they seem to have dried up. A group of new employees will be starting next week, and we'll need markers for the orientation and training sessions.

Craig Kopalinski (2:24 P.M.) OK. Lindsay, in addition to those markers, could you please order a new chair for the second-floor conference room to replace the one that is broken? You'll need to look up the model number. Thanks.

---

164. At 2:20 P.M., what does Mr. Carden most likely mean when he writes, "Nothing here"?

(A) He has not heard from Ms. Pokora.
(B) He does not need to place an order.
(C) He does not have extra markers.
(D) He has not checked the supply room.

165. What problem does Ms. Daley report?

(A) Some presentations are too long.
(B) Expenses in the office have increased.
(C) Some office supplies cannot be used.
(D) The conference room is not big enough.

166. In what department does Ms. Daley most likely work?

(A) Accounting
(B) Human Resources
(C) Purchasing
(D) Shipping

167. What will Ms. Pokora most likely do next?

(A) Locate some information
(B) Review a training document
(C) Conduct an orientation session
(D) Contact department managers

Questions 168-171 refer to the following e-mail.

To:	All staff
From:	Jan Merchant
Date:	October 15
Subject:	Reginald Carmen

Dear Colleagues,

It is my pleasure to welcome Reginald Carmen to Edmonton Engineering Consultants, LLC. — [1] —.

With his expertise in engineering and education, Dr. Carmen will be a valuable addition to our distinguished staff. — [2] —. Upon graduating from university, he spent six years designing telecommunications systems for AstroPart, Inc. He comes to us directly from the Glasse School of Engineering, where he spent the past nineteen years. While there, he served as a full-time professor for ten years, teaching advanced mathematics and various special courses in engineering. He was then appointed president of the school and served in that position for the remaining nine years of his tenure. — [3] —. During that time, he led the team that redesigned the school's electrical engineering curriculum. — [4] —.

Dr. Carmen's first day will be next Tuesday.

Jan Merchant, Director of Personnel

168. Why did Ms. Merchant send the e-mail?

(A) To announce that she is retiring
(B) To provide details about a new employee
(C) To welcome a distinguished guest presenter
(D) To publicize expansion into a new line of business

169. What is indicated about Dr. Carmen?

(A) He has experience designing communications systems.
(B) He worked as a consultant for Edmonton Engineering Consultants in the past.
(C) He mentored Ms. Merchant at another company.
(D) He graduated from the Glasse School of Engineering.

170. How long did Dr. Carmen teach at the Glasse School of Engineering?

(A) 6 years
(B) 9 years
(C) 10 years
(D) 19 years

171. In which of the positions marked [1], [2], [3], and [4] does the following sentence best belong?

"He is thus the perfect choice for redesigning our client training modules."

(A) [1]
(B) [2]
(C) [3]
(D) [4]

GO ON TO THE NEXT PAGE

Patrons See Big-City Art At Local Museum

No need to venture into the big city to see an impressive art collection. — [1] —.

Locals know Janford as a quiet town situated next to a forest that is popular with hikers. — [2] —. It is likewise home to Janford University and an unexpectedly outstanding museum. Considered one of the finest university art museums in the nation, the Janford University Art Museum (JUAM) houses over 94,000 pieces, with works dating from ancient times to the present. Due to the size of its collection, the museum regularly rotates the works on display. — [3] —. It also hosts temporary exhibitions featuring loans from other institutions.

Experts consider JUAM noteworthy as a home to a comprehensive collection of twentieth-century art. — [4] —. In particular, it holds the largest public collection of works by sculptor Robert Dabulis, with more than 50 of his pieces and an assortment of his sketches.

The museum offers free admission and is open daily from 10 A.M. to 5 P.M. On Friday evenings, the museum has extended hours until 10 P.M.

172. What does the review indicate about the town of Janford?

(A) It is in a peaceful setting.
(B) It is more than 100 years old.
(C) It has a thriving community of artists.
(D) It has a well-known school of forestry.

173. What is mentioned about the museum?

(A) Its main focus is on ancient art.
(B) It has received several national awards.
(C) Its location makes it difficult for tourists to find.
(D) It displays some items from its collection for only a limited time.

174. What is most likely true about Mr. Dabulis?

(A) He began his work as a painter.
(B) He created sculptures specifically for JUAM.
(C) He created art during the twentieth century.
(D) He studied art at Janford University.

175. In which of the positions marked [1], [2], [3], and [4] does the following sentence best belong?

"Art enthusiasts can find it right here in Janford."

(A) [1]
(B) [2]
(C) [3]
(D) [4]

GO ON TO THE NEXT PAGE

Ready Barn

Order #	#13565
Date:	June 3
Delivery:	24-hour Express Shipping
Shipping Address:	Helen Kang
	45 Skyrise Road
	Newten, NY 12039
Payment Method:	Credit Card–Jay Shim

Item Number	Description	Price
7563	Countertop Electric Grill	$49
7564	Egg Beater	$14
7565	Tea Kettle	$27
7566	Toaster	$56
7567	Cheese Grater	$16
	24-hour Express Shipping	$20
	TOTAL $182	

To:	customerservice@readybarn.com
From:	jayshim@silyex.com
Subject:	Order #13565
Date:	June 6

Hello,

I recently placed an order (#13565) with Ready Barn. The items I purchased are housewarming gifts for my niece, Helen Kang, who recently purchased a new home. Therefore, her address was provided as the delivery destination. I paid higher shipping fees for 24-hour delivery, as I wanted the items to arrive well ahead of the housewarming party being held tomorrow evening. Several days have passed, and my niece has yet to receive these items. I would appreciate it if you could find out what has happened and let me know when my niece can expect delivery. Also, I would like to ask you to return the money I paid for expedited shipping.

Additionally, I do not recognize item number 7564 that I was charged $14 for on my receipt. Please let me know how to send it back.

I am a longtime customer of Ready Barn, and I am usually very satisfied with your products and services. Please reply as soon as possible.

Sincerely,

Jay Shim

176. What most likely does Ready Barn specialize in?

(A) Kitchen equipment
(B) Party invitations
(C) Shipping supplies
(D) Large appliances

177. What is indicated about 45 Skyrise Road?

(A) It is Ready Barn's address.
(B) It is Mr. Shim's billing address.
(C) It is Ms. Kang's new address.
(D) It is Mr. Shim's former address.

178. What does Mr. Shim request in his e-mail?

(A) A discount
(B) A refund
(C) A receipt
(D) A gift list

179. What item did Mr. Shim not intend to buy?

(A) The cheese grater
(B) The grill
(C) The toaster
(D) The egg beater

180. According to the e-mail, what is true about Mr. Shim?

(A) He is satisfied with the items he purchased.
(B) He has shopped with Ready Barn before.
(C) He received his order on schedule.
(D) He prefers to shop through a catalog.

GO ON TO THE NEXT PAGE

Questions 181-185 refer to the following e-mail and boarding pass.

E-mail

To:	Yong-Sun Che <ysche@buztech.com>
From:	Ginny Redman <gredman@silvervaleair.com>
Subject:	RE: Seat problem
Date:	February 12
Attachment:	📎 Voucher

Dear Mr. Che:

Thank you for contacting us regarding your recent flight. We apologize for the discomfort you experienced during your flight because of the nonfunctioning air-conditioning vent above your seat.

We value you as a customer and want to make sure your experience with Silvervale Air is positive, so we have attached Voucher 789798 in the amount of $200. This may be applied to a future domestic flight with us. The voucher expires after twelve months.

Thank you for choosing Silvervale Air.

Sincerely,

Ginny Redman
Silvervale Air Customer Service

Passenger: Mr. Yong-Sun Che
Ticket number: 0272125899649
Confirmation code: CMOAAB

Flight	Departs	Arrives	Seat
Silvervale Air 29	Atlanta,GA(ATL) Mon.,May 6 11:43 A.M.	Los Angeles,CA(LAX) Mon.,May 6 1:35 P.M.	36D

Summary of airfare charges
Base fare	$259.54
Taxes and fees	$33.76
Voucher 789798	-$200.00
Total	$93.30

All passengers are entitled to travel with one complimentary carry-on and one checked bag.

---

181. Why did Ms. Redman e-mail Mr. Che?

(A) To update him on the repair of some equipment
(B) To announce changes to airfare pricing
(C) To assign him a new seat
(D) To offer him compensation

182. In the e-mail, the phrase "applied to" in paragraph 2, line 3, is closest in meaning to

(A) asked for
(B) used for
(C) dealt with
(D) kept with

183. What does Ms. Redman mention about Voucher 789798 ?

(A) It is valid for twelve months.
(B) It has not been mailed yet.
(C) It may be used for international flights.
(D) It cannot be transferred to another passenger.

184. What can be inferred from the boarding pass about Mr. Che?

(A) He redeemed the full value of a voucher.
(B) He paid an additional fee for an upgrade.
(C) He booked a round-trip flight.
(D) He is a frequent flyer on Silvervale Air.

185. What is indicated about Silvervale Air flight 29 ?

(A) It departs from Los Angeles.
(B) It arrives in the afternoon.
(C) Its passengers do not have assigned seats.
(D) Its passengers are allowed two free checked bags.

TEST 3

GO ON TO THE NEXT PAGE

Coffer Digital Management Steering Committee
Meeting Minutes
November 12

1. Re-pitch is ready to be pilot tested.

2. The pilot test will be carried out during the first quarter of the fiscal year, January 3–March 31.

3. Five existing clients will use the experimental version of Re-pitch during the pilot test. They will then take a survey to rate the software's effectiveness, ease of use, and affordability.

4. If the Re-pitch pilot is successful, a large dollar investment will be needed to design and run an extensive marketing campaign.

5. Our company president will explore potential funding sources for this campaign.

To:	sales@coffer.com
From:	tcao@ewest-taipei.com.tw
Date:	13 April
Subject:	Pilot test

Dear Coffer Digital,

I wanted to follow up after having just submitted our thoughts regarding your Re-pitch marketing software. You will find that our pilot-test feedback is overwhelmingly positive, which is why we would like to be notified immediately upon the rollout of this product. We are very eager to add Re-pitch to our permanent digital marketing efforts.

Sincerely,

Ting Cao, Director of Global Internet Marketing
Ewest Clothing Ltd., Taipei

Business Briefs

Coffer Digital closed a deal yesterday with GPZ Capital. GPZ will make a significant investment in Coffer Digital, enabling the funding of a new online marketing application called Re-pitch. This sales-boosting software works by generating a pop-up window that reminds online shoppers of products they have already viewed, after they have navigated away from the product page.

GPZ's knowledge of data and marketing has enabled them to make successful investments in three other software development firms in the past five years. Coffer Digital's strong company reputation and top-notch employees easily support GPZ's decision to invest. "Coffer Digital has a solid plan for distributing Re-pitch, so it was an easy decision to invest with them," said Jessica Gould, spokesperson for GPZ.

186. According to the meeting minutes, what is indicated about the pilot test?

(A) The testing period will last about three months.
(B) Problems identified during testing must be immediately reported.
(C) Running the test will be costly.
(D) The testing plan still needs the president's approval.

187. What did Mr. Cao do?

(A) He redesigned a Web site.
(B) He submitted an annual report.
(C) He completed a survey.
(D) He started a new business.

188. What does Mr. Cao request?

(A) To view the results of a test
(B) To participate in future testing
(C) To be notified when software is available for purchase
(D) To set up a marketing consultation appointment

189. According to the article, what does Re-pitch do?

(A) It tracks the sales of online retailers.
(B) It prevents pop-up windows in Internet browsers.
(C) It offers customers discounts on products.
(D) It displays products for online shoppers to consider buying.

190. How will Coffer Digital most likely use the funds from GPZ Capital?

(A) To purchase a smaller company
(B) To advertise a product
(C) To hire new employees
(D) To invest in new equipment

GO ON TO THE NEXT PAGE

TERMINAL C TO REOPEN

(May 23) Harrison City Airport's Terminal C will reopen to the public on June 1 following a two-year renovation project.

The project added eleven new gates, allowing the terminal to accommodate more flights. The three major airlines that used Terminal C before the renovation will now be back in operation there. Also at Terminal C will be newcomer Paik Airways, a regional carrier that is expanding its routes.

The terminal's new lobby features an efficient check-in process and a state-of-the-art baggage-handling system. Passengers will enjoy free Wi-Fi in the waiting area, which also contains shops and restaurants.

At one point during the renovations, it looked as if the construction team would miss its deadline. An environmental impact review conducted by the city questioned the placement of a parking lot. The planners solved the problem by moving the parking lot to the other side of the airport and instituting a shuttle bus service.

"Thanks to the cooperative efforts of all stakeholders, the project was completed by the deadline with no budget overage," said Arturo Benetti, the airport's chief operating officer. "The improvements to Terminal C will enable us to continue providing Harrison City with safe, comfortable air travel."

From:	Thomasina Yee <thomasina.yee@cooverbrothers.com>
To:	Sven Paulsen <sven.paulsen@cooverbrothers.com>
Date:	July 6
Subject:	Meeting with Slonim Company buyers

Hello, Sven,

I'm at the Harrison City Airport to catch the 3:30 flight home, but I want to give you a quick update. The meeting at Slonim went well. They are very pleased with Coover Brothers products and expect to double their orders next year. In fact, they offered to feature our bedroom and dining room sets at the upcoming Home and Garden Exposition. I'll give you all the details tomorrow.

Regards,

Thomasina

HARRISON CITY AIRPORT–TERMINAL C
DEPARTURES

Airline	Flight	Gate	Time	Destination	Status
Brightway	BR417	11	1:25	Detroit	ON TIME
Planet Z	PL700	3	2:06	Omaha	CANCELED
Paik	PA069	24	3:00	Cleveland	ON TIME
Windrover	WI645	6	3:30	Chicago	DELAYED

191. Why was it necessary to change the location of a parking lot?

(A) To reduce construction costs
(B) To protect the environment
(C) To make travel easier for passengers
(D) To provide spaces for large vehicles

192. What does Mr. Benetti emphasize about Terminal C?

(A) It is the only terminal with free Wi-Fi.
(B) It was designed by a famous architect.
(C) Its renovation was funded by the city.
(D) Its renovation was completed on time.

193. What products does Coover Brothers most likely manufacture?

(A) Furniture
(B) Clothing
(C) Kitchen appliances
(D) Gardening tools

194. What is implied about Brightway Airlines?

(A) It is an international carrier.
(B) It offers flights to Omaha.
(C) It used Terminal C before the renovation.
(D) It has a private waiting area for passengers.

195. What is suggested about Ms. Yee?

(A) She works in Omaha.
(B) She met with Mr. Benetti.
(C) Her flight departed late.
(D) Her luggage was lost.

GO ON TO THE NEXT PAGE

ZELL Exteriors

Zell Exteriors' metal roofing products offer many advantages over traditional roofing materials.

Benefit 1–Weather resistance:
Technology that provides greater protection from hail, wind, and rain

Benefit 2–Wide selection:
Large selection of panel types, trim options, and paint colors to choose from

Benefit 3–Satisfaction guarantee:
30-year warranty for added peace of mind

Benefit 4–Established reputation: Quality roofing from a trusted company

For questions about specific products or to request a quote from our sales staff, complete our online contact form. All our roofing panels are fabricated at one of our regional manufacturing facilities, precut to the necessary dimensions for your roof, and shipped to a branch near you. Our professional installers will then take it from there.

Name: Gus Keenan

E-mail: g.keenan@autoewrite.net

Phone: 555-0188

Comments:

I have been looking at various roofing materials, and the wide range of paint options makes your company my top choice. My shed building is an odd shade of purple, and I want to find a color that complements it. But I have a question. I would like the new metal roof to be placed on top of the old shingle roof I have. This would save money on time, labor, and disposal. Is that something you recommend? I have spent a lot of time reading online forums for professional contractors, and there are mixed opinions about this.

To:	g.keenan@autoewrite.net
From:	nshertz@zellexteriors.com
Date:	May 20
Subject:	Roofing Inquiry
Attachment:	⦚ Zell Exteriors catalog

Dear Mr. Keenan,

A sales representative will contact you by phone within 48 hours, but first please look over the attached product catalog. Here are the four basic roofing types that we offer:

SLP Snap Lock – Steel panels with a locking feature that enables rapid installation.

XM Panel – Aluminum panels with superior corrosion resistance. Ideal for wet climates.

QR Rigid – Low-cost panels that can be installed directly on top of an existing roof.

WT Panel – Our most durable commercial-grade steel. Available only in white and gray.

Thank you,

Nicola Shertz, Administrative Assistant, Zell Exteriors

196. What does the brochure mention about Zell Exteriors?

(A) It encourages people to visit a showroom.
(B) It schedules projects several months in advance.
(C) It requires an on-site inspection before installation.
(D) It custom cuts products prior to delivery.

197. Considering Mr. Keenan's comments, what listed benefit is probably most attractive to him?

(A) Benefit 1
(B) Benefit 2
(C) Benefit 3
(D) Benefit 4

198. What does the form indicate about Mr. Keenan?

(A) He has researched about roofing options.
(B) He made a mistake when installing some materials.
(C) He wants his project completed quickly.
(D) He is unhappy with a previous contractor.

199. What kind of roofing product will Mr. Keenan most likely select?

(A) SLP Snap Lock
(B) XM Panel
(C) QR Rigid
(D) WT Panel

200. What does Ms. Shertz tell Mr. Keenan?

(A) He can save money by not delaying a decision.
(B) He should look over a proposed contract.
(C) He will be called by a Zell representative.
(D) He ordered the wrong materials in the past.

Stop! This is the end of the test. If you finish before time is called, you may go back to Parts 5, 6, and 7 and check your work.

토익® 정기시험
기출문제집

RC

기출 TEST

04

READING TEST

In the Reading test, you will read a variety of texts and answer several different types of reading comprehension questions. The entire Reading test will last 75 minutes. There are three parts, and directions are given for each part. You are encouraged to answer as many questions as possible within the time allowed.

You must mark your answers on the separate answer sheet. Do not write your answers in your test book.

PART 5

Directions: A word or phrase is missing in each of the sentences below. Four answer choices are given below each sentence. Select the best answer to complete the sentence. Then mark the letter (A), (B), (C), or (D) on your answer sheet.

101. Mr. Akagi was unable to buy tickets for the concert because ------- was sold out.

(A) it
(B) others
(C) any
(D) they

102. Classes ------- using the new employee scheduling software will begin in December.

(A) at
(B) to
(C) by
(D) on

103. Hillsdale Fabrics' ------- collection of leathers was imported from Italy.

(A) diversity
(B) diversely
(C) diversify
(D) diverse

104. A ------- of four dental hygienists spoke about careers in their field.

(A) plan
(B) panel
(C) support
(D) version

105. Ardentine Realty is ------- seeking new rental properties for its portfolio.

(A) actively
(B) activate
(C) activity
(D) active

106. This Friday, Zone Fly Cameras invites the public to a free aerial photography -------.

(A) picture
(B) ticket
(C) action
(D) workshop

107. The Ambury Prize recognizes research that is notable for its ------- and innovation.

(A) creative
(B) creatively
(C) creativity
(D) creates

108. This year the harvest parade will ------- the village, beginning and ending at the town square.

(A) spin
(B) circle
(C) roll
(D) loosen

109. Questwiz, the library's newest database, ------- a wide range of resource materials.

(A) to contain
(B) contains
(C) container
(D) containing

110. After more than three years, the application for the new patent was ------- approved.

(A) already
(B) finally
(C) constantly
(D) exactly

111. The First Street Hotel has almost always been fully booked since it ------- last year.

(A) had renovated
(B) renovated
(C) was renovating
(D) was renovated

112. Departments should not spend an ------- amount of their budgets on office supplies.

(A) equal
(B) exciting
(C) excessive
(D) unknown

113. Maxwell Copies prints brochures on thick, glossy paper that was ------- selected for its quality and durability.

(A) caring
(B) careful
(C) carefully
(D) cares

114. ------- Mr. Kamau has worked for Mombasa Communications for two years, he has never taken time off.

(A) Although
(B) But
(C) Neither
(D) Yet

115. At the Morrighan Hotel, addressing customer feedback is of ------- importance.

(A) critique
(B) critic
(C) critically
(D) critical

116. Axofare's new computer program enables users to ------- organize and retrieve data.

(A) efficiently
(B) irreversibly
(C) vaguely
(D) especially

117. Trelmoni Corporation has just released its ------- of the global stock market.

(A) analysis
(B) analytical
(C) analyze
(D) analyzed

118. Liu's Foods is pleased to reveal the ------- product in its famous soup line: pumpkin soup.

(A) popularity of
(B) as popular as
(C) most popular
(D) popular than

119. The proposed city budget outlines various projects, ------- renovations of the Fessler Road fire station.

(A) these
(B) including
(C) even though
(D) always

120. The ------- opening of the new bakery had to be postponed when a pipe burst in the kitchen.

(A) scheduled
(B) maintained
(C) motivated
(D) experienced

GO ON TO THE NEXT PAGE

121. Two associates in the accounting department are being ------- for promotions.

    (A) consider
    (B) considerable
    (C) considered
    (D) consideration

122. ------- the rock band Captain Zino decided to offer free tickets to their concert, sales of their album have reached record numbers.

    (A) Since
    (B) Besides
    (C) As much as
    (D) Not only

123. ------- her interview, the committee agreed that Ms. Han was the best candidate for the supervisor job.

    (A) As in
    (B) Just as
    (C) Almost
    (D) After

124. After monitoring the Hasher Corporation's inventory control process ------- several days, the consultant identified the problem.

    (A) among
    (B) except
    (C) off
    (D) for

125. Crane operators must check that all moving parts of the machine are fastened ------- before use.

    (A) security
    (B) securely
    (C) secures
    (D) securing

126. Use this coupon to ------- a free quote for cloud storage services.

    (A) advertise
    (B) discount
    (C) develop
    (D) obtain

127. By testing the ------- of the vehicle in desert terrain, the designers proved that it works perfectly in harsh conditions.

    (A) enduring
    (B) endurance
    (C) endures
    (D) endure

128. The flashing yellow light serves as an ------- that the camera's battery needs to be charged.

    (A) example
    (B) allowance
    (C) alert
    (D) administration

129. Ms. Rosen did not say ------- about the plans for a new employee break room.

    (A) several
    (B) anything
    (C) each
    (D) someone

130. Revenue growth exceeding 2 percent was seen ------- all business segments this quarter.

    (A) across
    (B) into
    (C) prior to
    (D) above

PART 6

Directions: Read the texts that follow. A word, phrase, or sentence is missing in parts of each text. Four answer choices for each question are given below the text. Select the best answer to complete the text. Then mark the letter (A), (B), (C), or (D) on your answer sheet.

Questions 131-134 refer to the following e-mail.

To: Multiple Recipients
From: Gold Star Bank <information@goldstarbank.co.in>
Subject: Gold Star Bank App
Date: 15 July

Dear Customer:

Here at Gold Star Bank, we take our customers and their needs seriously. As some of you know,

we ------- technical difficulties with our mobile app. ------- . The trouble started on 14 July when our
　　131.　　　　　　　　　　　　　　　　　 132.

system went down because of a software bug. We expect the app to be up and running ------- the
　　　　　　　　　　　　　　　　　　　　　　　　　　　　　　　　　　　　 133.

next twenty-four hours. -------, banking transactions can be done at any of our branch locations,
　　　　　　　　　　 134.

and our automated cash machines are also working.

We apologize for any inconvenience.

Sincerely,

Ravi Chadda
Vice President of Customer Relations

---

131. (A) to experience
(B) experiencing
(C) had experienced
(D) are experiencing

132. (A) Our engineers are working on this
problem now.
(B) The new mobile app is easy to use,
and it is available for free.
(C) We have several openings for
customer service representatives.
(D) We are announcing the opening of a
new Gold Star Bank location.

133. (A) if
(B) within
(C) as long as
(D) above all

134. (A) Unusually
(B) Eventually
(C) In the meantime
(D) As an example

GO ON TO THE NEXT PAGE

Questions 135-138 refer to the following information.

Bethenie Industries guarantees that its products will function as ------- for at least one year from
135.
date of purchase. ------- . This ------- applies only to products sold at Bethenie Industries stores
136.   137.
and other licensed distributors. Products that are found to be defective may be shipped to our
address for repair or exchange. Please note that products that are being returned because of
damage should be shipped back to us, whenever possible, in their ------- packaging.
138.

135. (A) advertising
    (B) advertised
    (C) advertisement
    (D) advertises

136. (A) For certain products this period may be
       extended.
    (B) Bethenie Industries stores are located
       in three countries.
    (C) An electronic receipt was generated at
       that time.
    (D) Product samples are available in
       stores.

137. (A) agenda
    (B) sale
    (C) requirement
    (D) warranty

138. (A) originally
    (B) original
    (C) origin
    (D) originality

Healthy Foods Market has planned some exciting renovations in the coming weeks. During this time the store will remain open, but certain departments will be temporarily unavailable.

Beginning on August 3, the refrigerated and frozen-food sections of the store ------- to be under
139.
construction. ------- , food from these areas will be unavailable while work is being completed.
140.
Remodeling should be finished by August 9. Store managers are confident that the ------- days of
141.
inconvenience will be well worth it.

------- . At this event, there will be complimentary samples of some new food choices, including an
142.
expanded selection of nutritious, ready-to-eat lunch and dinner meals.

139. (A) schedules
(B) to be scheduled
(C) scheduling
(D) are scheduled

140. (A) However
(B) Therefore
(C) Besides
(D) Likewise

141. (A) few
(B) no
(C) less
(D) small

142. (A) The store must close for three days.
(B) Customers must park in the recently added parking area.
(C) Ice-cream products will be available during the remodeling.
(D) A special celebration will take place on August 12.

GO ON TO THE NEXT PAGE

VANCOUVER (3 February)—Poalesco unveiled its annual Plant Showcase today. According to Poalesco spokesman Nacio Roja, this ------- offering highlights the company's latest efforts in **143.** botanical research. Many of these efforts result from customer surveys designed to gain an understanding of common challenges. -------. This year, the company's specialized nurseries **144.** have turned out drought-hardy breeds, such as the Goldtone Apple Tree. These varietals can withstand extended dry conditions without sustaining damage. "Gardeners in desert ------- will **145.** appreciate the Goldtones in particular," noted Roja. "And ------- might also be interested in our **146.** new Q7 rose bushes, which thrive in a similar climate."

143. (A) daily
(B) weekly
(C) monthly
(D) yearly

144. (A) The company seeks out the most profitable sectors in agriculture.
(B) The company interviews researchers from across the world.
(C) The research and development team then works to develop varietals that address these difficulties.
(D) Their extensive research produces some of the most flavorful plants on the market.

145. (A) region
(B) regions
(C) regional
(D) regionally

146. (A) he
(B) she
(C) we
(D) they

PART 7

Directions: In this part you will read a selection of texts, such as magazine and newspaper articles, e-mails, and instant messages. Each text or set of texts is followed by several questions. Select the best answer for each question and mark the letter (A), (B), (C), or (D) on your answer sheet.

Questions 147-148 refer to the following advertisement.

> ### STAR FITNESS CLUB
> ### Grand Opening Event on 25 April
>
> Come and join us as we open our newest club in Summerlake City in our brand-new building located at 714 Shadow Road. Come and see our state-of-the-art equipment and meet our experienced fitness trainers and instructors while enjoying healthy refreshments.
>
> Special Offer: Take 20 percent off your first 3 months! The offer is for new members only and cannot be combined with any other offer. The offer is available at all Star Fitness locations and is good until 30 June.
>
> Visit www.starfitness.ca for more information, including a schedule of our fitness classes and club hours.

147. What is indicated about Star Fitness Club?

(A) It has just built a new facility.
(B) It provides refreshments with paid membership.
(C) It is currently selling its used exercise equipment.
(D) It is open seven days a week.

148. What is NOT mentioned about the special offer?

(A) It expires at the end of June.
(B) It can be used at any location.
(C) It includes sessions with a personal trainer.
(D) It is intended for new customers only.

GO ON TO THE NEXT PAGE

Questions 149-150 refer to the following note.

Westerly Hotel
295 Prudence Ave.
Atlanta, GA 30317

Dear Guest,

Welcome to Atlanta. We are pleased you have chosen the Westerly Hotel.

A complimentary breakfast is served daily from 6:00 A.M. to 10:30 A.M. in our dining area located in the lobby. Enjoy an array of selections including eggs, oatmeal, pastries, fresh fruit, cereal, juice, coffee, and tea. Please be aware, however, that on May 2 breakfast will be served in the Fin Restaurant, located on the third floor, to accommodate a private event.

Regards,

Malcolm Anderson, Manager
Westerly Hotel

149. What is a purpose of the note?

(A) To request feedback on a recent stay
(B) To inform a guest of a location change
(C) To invite a guest to a private event
(D) To announce the opening of a new hotel

150. What is stated about the breakfast?

(A) It is free of charge.
(B) It is not available on weekends.
(C) It will not be served on May 2.
(D) It will soon feature more selections.

Questions 151-152 refer to the following notice.

Things Are Happening with the Southeast Rail Line—Time to Get Involved!

Plans are moving forward with the renovations to the Southeast Rail Line. The changes will create a faster, more convenient, more reliable alternative to traveling on the area's congested roadways. Construction begins this September. Public meetings to solicit comments regarding design options for the new stations are scheduled for June, July, and August. Learn more about the meetings by visiting www.southeastrailproject.com/communityaffairs.

---

151. When will construction start on the project?

(A) In June
(B) In July
(C) In August
(D) In September

152. What will be discussed at the public meetings?

(A) The reduction of roadway traffic
(B) The source of construction materials
(C) The design of the train stations
(D) The schedule of the express trains

TEST 4

GO ON TO THE NEXT PAGE ▶

Questions 153-154 refer to the following text-message chain.

Lisa Dominguez (3:24 P.M.)
Hi, Travis. I'm at the market shopping for tomatoes, but none of them are ripe. Can you check to see if we have any frozen tomato sauce on hand from last week? Otherwise, I guess I could get some canned tomatoes.

Travis Farley (3:27 P.M.)
I'm afraid we are all out. Let me speak to the chef.

Lisa Dominguez (3:28 P.M.)
That would be great.

Travis Farley (3:32 P.M.)
She says that you can pick up red peppers instead. We will need to make a small change to the menu description, but the other ingredients can stay the same.

Lisa Dominguez (3:34 P.M.)
OK. I've got it. Thank you!

153. For what kind of business does Mr. Farley most likely work?

(A) A farm
(B) A grocery store
(C) A restaurant
(D) A delivery service

154. At 3:27 P.M., what does Mr. Farley mean when he writes, "I'm afraid we are all out"?

(A) Staff members have no more ideas.
(B) A deadline was missed.
(C) Employees have left the workplace.
(D) An item is not available.

Questions 155-157 refer to the following notice.

Attention, Members of the Belle Coffee Club:

— [1] —. Next week, Belle Coffee will debut our newest coffee creation, the Latte Slow Brew. — [2] —. Members of the Belle Coffee Club can get their first taste of this new treat at our flagship store at 200 Wellington Street. We invite you to stop by on January 12 and show your membership card for a complimentary cup of Latte Slow Brew and a pastry sample from our local partner, Yonge Confections. Choose from a variety of their fresh-baked muffins, including a flavour baked especially for Belle Coffee: the chocolate espresso muffin. — [3] —.

Rollout at our other Belle Coffee locations will follow over the next four weeks. To learn more, visit bellecoffee.ca. — [4] —.

Enjoy!

TEST 4

155. What will Belle Coffee do on January 12 ?

(A) Merge with Yonge Confections
(B) Open a second location
(C) Introduce a new product
(D) Start a membership program

156. According to the notice, what is available on the Web site?

(A) A coupon
(B) A recipe
(C) An application form
(D) A schedule

157. In which of the positions marked [1], [2], [3], and [4] does the following sentence best belong?

"Additional coffee products and pastries will be available for purchase."

(A) [1]
(B) [2]
(C) [3]
(D) [4]

Dalston Opera News

<u>**Season Tickets Now Available**</u>

Purchase your season tickets now at www.dalstonopera.com/seasontickets.

May 4–12: *Sigrun* (2 hours with 1 intermission)
July 6–14: *Le Lapin* (3 hours with 2 intermissions)
September 14–22: *The Shipmaster's Garden* (90 minutes with no intermission)
November 30–December 8: *Orkestia* (4 hours with 3 intermissions)

Performances will take place at the Saloudi Auditorium beginning promptly at 8:00 P.M.

<u>**Artist-in-Residence Series**</u>

Our rotating artist-in-residence program aims to bring new voices into the performances of our regular cast. Join us for a special series of noon matinee performances by these artists and help us celebrate the next generation of talent coming into the field of opera from around the globe. Each performance will feature a medley of opera favorites selected and performed by one of our artists-in-residence.

May 4: Diane Shimoda
July 6: Kalim Patton
September 14: Claudia Godin
November 30: Nicolai Souza

158. What opera will be performed without a break?

(A) *Sigrun*
(B) *Le Lapin*
(C) *The Shipmaster's Garden*
(D) *Orkestia*

159. What is probably true about the artists-in-residence?

(A) They are all from the Dalston area.
(B) They are younger than the regular performers.
(C) They are professionally trained as dancers.
(D) They are all well-known around the world.

160. Who most likely will perform in *Le Lapin* ?

(A) Ms. Shimoda
(B) Mr. Patton
(C) Ms. Godin
(D) Mr. Souza

Muelker Shipyard Undergoes Transformation

May 2—The Muelker Shipyard, a once-bustling ship manufacturing center, is being given a new role. A team of engineers is working to turn it into an open-air pedestrian mall with restaurants, a dozen retail businesses, and an outdoor patio that will feature live music performances.

Until June of last year, the city had planned to demolish the shipyard—a decision that caused a strong reaction from community members, especially former shipbuilders who viewed the site as a treasured industrial landmark. Wanting their labor to be remembered by future generations, many shipbuilders had etched their names on a wall near the entrance.

"In the peak of production, shipyard workers produced a naval ship in just a year," said lead engineer, Barney Enyart. "Then production gradually slowed, and the shipyard eventually closed. When this project is complete, the new complex will be enjoyed throughout the year, serving as a place for employment opportunities and recreation while the legacy of the site's past will endure."

161. What is NOT mentioned in the plans for the shipyard?

(A) Office spaces
(B) Entertainment
(C) A shopping section
(D) Eating establishments

162. What is suggested about the Muelker Shipyard?

(A) It will be featured in a video.
(B) It will have a monument to former workers.
(C) Local residents appreciate its history.
(D) A ship is currently being built there.

163. The word "serving" in paragraph 3, line 7, is closest in meaning to

(A) attending
(B) functioning
(C) distributing
(D) presenting

GO ON TO THE NEXT PAGE

Questions 164-167 refer to the following memo.

MEMO

To: Customer Service Team
From: Scott Davis, Director of Customer Service
Date: July 22

Today kicks off Harkness Clothiers' Customer Service Appreciation Week. I want to take this opportunity to thank you for your dedication and professionalism this year. — [1] —. Each one of you has delivered exceptional customer service. Management is proud of what you have achieved as a team. — [2] —. We understand that last year's merger with Sporting Clothes, Inc., was confusing and difficult at times. Your service stayed steady throughout the process and you provided a seamless transition for our clients. What a great accomplishment!

— [3] —. On Tuesday, starting at 8 A.M., everyone will be treated to a breakfast served with coffee, pastries, and fruit. On Wednesday, we will have a potluck lunch in the afternoon. On Thursday, we will host a team dinner at Mo's Bistro after work. On Friday, there will be contests after lunch where you can win prizes. — [4] —. I am excited about this week and hope you enjoy it.

---

164. Why did Mr. Davis write the memo?

(A) To ask employees to attend a training session
(B) To request that employees work overtime
(C) To provide details of a celebration
(D) To announce the end of a project

165. What is suggested about Harkness Clothiers?

(A) It has combined with another company.
(B) It gives awards to staff every year.
(C) It manufactures a line of waterproof clothes.
(D) It has a very small customer service team.

166. When will an event take place in the morning?

(A) On Tuesday
(B) On Wednesday
(C) On Thursday
(D) On Friday

167. In which of the positions marked [1], [2], [3], and [4] does the following sentence best belong?

"To show our appreciation, management is providing some opportunities to have fun this week."

(A) [1]
(B) [2]
(C) [3]
(D) [4]

Friends of the Chesterton Public Library
Book Sale

The Chesterton Public Library will host its annual book sale this weekend on the library's second floor. The hours are Saturday, November 16, 9:00 A.M. to 5:00 P.M., and Sunday, November 17, 12:00 noon to 5:00 P.M. A special preview sale for the Friends of Chesterton Public Library (FCPL), the library's volunteer support group, will be held on Friday, November 15, from 4:00 P.M. to 8:00 P.M.

The sale will include books that the library no longer lends, as well as books donated by the public. Proceeds will be used to develop a children's reading room.

We welcome donations of books for all ages, in all genres, in both paperback and hardcover. Please, note, however, that books that are torn or otherwise defaced will be rejected. Sorry, no magazines or journals, please. Donations for this event will be accepted through Friday, November 8, and can be dropped off at the front desk during the following times:

Monday to Thursday: 9:00 A.M. to 11:00 A.M.
Wednesday: 1:00 P.M. to 8:00 P.M.
Friday: 9:00 A.M. to 3:00 P.M.

Thank you for your support!

168. Who can attend the sale on Friday?

(A) Paid staff
(B) Volunteers
(C) Young children
(D) Financial donors

169. The word "welcome" in paragraph 3, line 1, is closest in meaning to

(A) accept
(B) greet
(C) honor
(D) satisfy

170. What is indicated about journals?

(A) They are located on the second floor.
(B) They will be sold to volunteers only.
(C) They cannot be borrowed.
(D) They cannot be donated.

171. When can donations be dropped off in the evening?

(A) On Monday
(B) On Wednesday
(C) On Thursday
(D) On Friday

GO ON TO THE NEXT PAGE

CHAT	X

Lily Park (4:03 P.M.) Hello, everyone. I just want to check in with you before the weekend. Kaz, how did your meeting with Blumfield Associates go?

Kaz Fedorowitz (4:10 P.M.) It could not have been better. They are purchasing 40 new laptops with a service agreement. I've got the signed contract in hand.

Lily Park (4:11 P.M.) Outstanding! Nice way to wrap up the week.

David Esposito (4:12 P.M.) Congratulations! This one puts you over the top. You are now the top salesperson for the third month in a row.

Danielle Becker (4:13 P.M.) That's great news, Kaz. By the way, if you can get all your receipts to me as soon as you are back in the office, you will get your travel reimbursement check early the following week.

Kaz Fedorowitz (4:14 P.M.) Are you sure about that? Didn't Michael Lim just land a big sale?

Lily Park (4:15 P.M.) Unfortunately, Michael's customers backed out at the last minute. They decided to lease computers and printers from another firm rather than purchase new equipment.

Kaz Fedorowitz (4:17 P.M.) That's too bad. And thanks for taking care of that, Danielle.

Danielle Becker (4:18 P.M.) My pleasure!

Lily Park (4:19 P.M.) Have a wonderful weekend, everyone.

172. In what type of business are the writers involved?

(A) Real estate
(B) Travel services
(C) Office technology
(D) Financial consulting

173. What most likely is Ms. Park's job title?

(A) Advertising specialist
(B) Director of human resources
(C) Bookkeeper
(D) Sales division manager

174. What is indicated about Mr. Lim?

(A) He was not able to complete a sale.
(B) He is currently away on business.
(C) He is a new member of the writers' department.
(D) He has just signed a contract.

175. At 4:18 P.M., what does Ms. Becker most likely mean when she writes, "My pleasure!"?

(A) She is happy to help in refunding some travel expenses.
(B) She is pleased to have successfully obtained a new client.
(C) She feels relieved that it is the end of the workweek.
(D) She is glad to have suggested leasing equipment.

GO ON TO THE NEXT PAGE

Get Business Cards Custom Made by You

Loretti Printing Co. is proud to announce loretticardprint.com, our new online platform for creating customized business cards. While our customers can still place orders in person, as they've done for nearly a decade, we now have a system that makes ordering business cards especially quick and easy. Choose from hundreds of easy-to-use templates, include your own text and images, and create professional-quality business cards within minutes.

We offer four different paper options:

Type	Description	Minimum Order
Matte-M1	Standard card stock, reduces glare	50 cards
Glossy-G4	Shiny, enhances colors and details	100 cards
Textured-T3	Unique grid-like pattern, interesting to the touch	100 cards
Metallic-M2	Extra shiny, unique, captures one's attention	200 cards

Contact us before placing an online order if you'd like us to send you a sample of each type of paper.

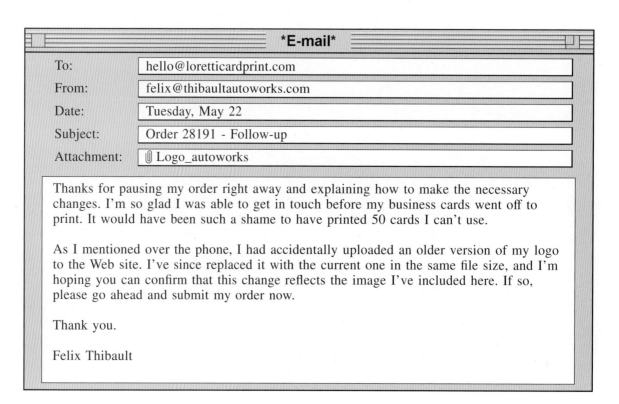

E-mail

To:	hello@loretticardprint.com
From:	felix@thibaultautoworks.com
Date:	Tuesday, May 22
Subject:	Order 28191 - Follow-up
Attachment:	📎 Logo_autoworks

Thanks for pausing my order right away and explaining how to make the necessary changes. I'm so glad I was able to get in touch before my business cards went off to print. It would have been such a shame to have printed 50 cards I can't use.

As I mentioned over the phone, I had accidentally uploaded an older version of my logo to the Web site. I've since replaced it with the current one in the same file size, and I'm hoping you can confirm that this change reflects the image I've included here. If so, please go ahead and submit my order now.

Thank you.

Felix Thibault

176. What is implied about Loretti Printing Co.?

(A) It has a physical retail location.
(B) It is merging with a card company.
(C) It is seeking experienced designers.
(D) It has expanded its paper selection.

177. According to the advertisement, what can customers do on the company's Web site?

(A) Give feedback about the company
(B) Design their own business cards
(C) Join a company mailing list
(D) Enter a code for a discount

178. What type of card stock did Mr. Thibault most likely order?

(A) Matte
(B) Glossy
(C) Textured
(D) Metallic

179. Why did Mr. Thibault replace the logo on his order?

(A) It was not aligned properly.
(B) It was an incorrect file size.
(C) It was for the wrong company.
(D) It was an outdated image.

180. In the e-mail, the word "reflects" in paragraph 2, line 3, is closest in meaning to

(A) returns
(B) matches
(C) considers
(D) shines

TEST 4

GO ON TO THE NEXT PAGE

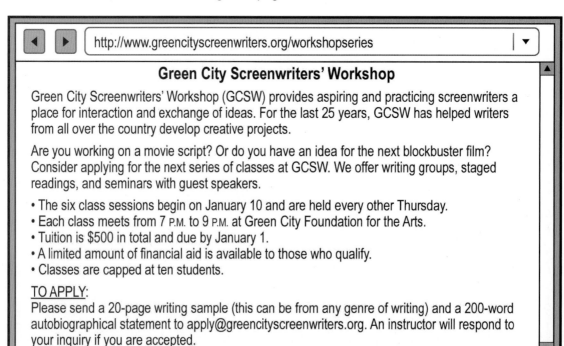

Green City Screenwriters' Workshop

Green City Screenwriters' Workshop (GCSW) provides aspiring and practicing screenwriters a place for interaction and exchange of ideas. For the last 25 years, GCSW has helped writers from all over the country develop creative projects.

Are you working on a movie script? Or do you have an idea for the next blockbuster film? Consider applying for the next series of classes at GCSW. We offer writing groups, staged readings, and seminars with guest speakers.

- The six class sessions begin on January 10 and are held every other Thursday.
- Each class meets from 7 P.M. to 9 P.M. at Green City Foundation for the Arts.
- Tuition is $500 in total and due by January 1.
- A limited amount of financial aid is available to those who qualify.
- Classes are capped at ten students.

TO APPLY:
Please send a 20-page writing sample (this can be from any genre of writing) and a 200-word autobiographical statement to apply@greencityscreenwriters.org. An instructor will respond to your inquiry if you are accepted.

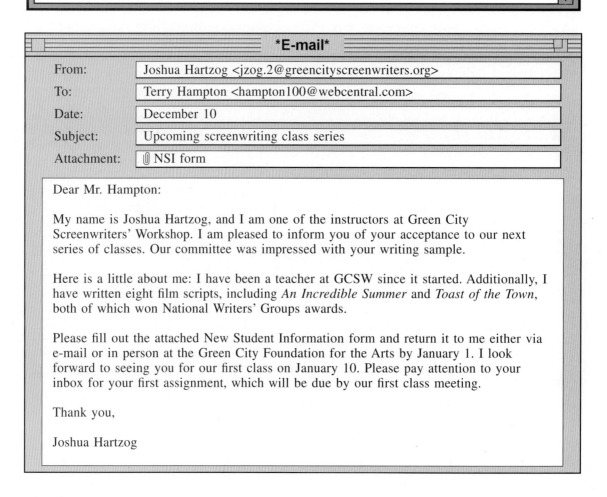

E-mail

From:	Joshua Hartzog <jzog.2@greencityscreenwriters.org>
To:	Terry Hampton <hampton100@webcentral.com>
Date:	December 10
Subject:	Upcoming screenwriting class series
Attachment:	📎 NSI form

Dear Mr. Hampton:

My name is Joshua Hartzog, and I am one of the instructors at Green City Screenwriters' Workshop. I am pleased to inform you of your acceptance to our next series of classes. Our committee was impressed with your writing sample.

Here is a little about me: I have been a teacher at GCSW since it started. Additionally, I have written eight film scripts, including *An Incredible Summer* and *Toast of the Town*, both of which won National Writers' Groups awards.

Please fill out the attached New Student Information form and return it to me either via e-mail or in person at the Green City Foundation for the Arts by January 1. I look forward to seeing you for our first class on January 10. Please pay attention to your inbox for your first assignment, which will be due by our first class meeting.

Thank you,

Joshua Hartzog

181. According to the Web page, what is true regarding the series of screenwriting classes?

(A) Morning classes are available.
(B) The deadline to apply is January 10.
(C) Class sizes are limited to ten students.
(D) Classes are held every weekday night.

182. What must be included with the application?

(A) A deposit on the tuition fee
(B) A brief personal history
(C) A proof of residency form
(D) Two published screenplays

183. What is the purpose of Mr. Hartzog's e-mail?

(A) To explain his numerous awards
(B) To outline the first class assignment
(C) To encourage a fellow writer to apply
(D) To respond to a student's application

184. What is indicated about Mr. Hartzog?

(A) He heads the application committee.
(B) He has taught at GCSW for 25 years.
(C) Eight of his screenplays have won awards.
(D) Three of his screenplays take place in Green City.

185. What is Mr. Hampton asked to do?

(A) Complete an attached form
(B) Send contact information
(C) Apply for financial aid
(D) Send a sample script

GO ON TO THE NEXT PAGE

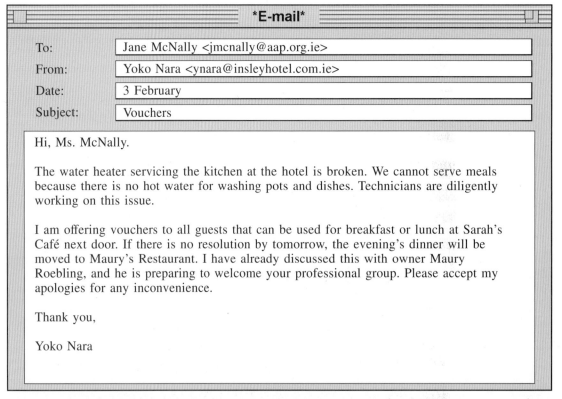

E-mail

To:	Jane McNally <jmcnally@aap.org.ie>
From:	Yoko Nara <ynara@insleyhotel.com.ie>
Date:	3 February
Subject:	Vouchers

Hi, Ms. McNally.

The water heater servicing the kitchen at the hotel is broken. We cannot serve meals because there is no hot water for washing pots and dishes. Technicians are diligently working on this issue.

I am offering vouchers to all guests that can be used for breakfast or lunch at Sarah's Café next door. If there is no resolution by tomorrow, the evening's dinner will be moved to Maury's Restaurant. I have already discussed this with owner Maury Roebling, and he is preparing to welcome your professional group. Please accept my apologies for any inconvenience.

Thank you,

Yoko Nara

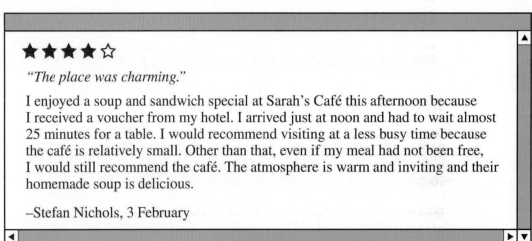

★★★★☆

"The place was charming."

I enjoyed a soup and sandwich special at Sarah's Café this afternoon because I received a voucher from my hotel. I arrived just at noon and had to wait almost 25 minutes for a table. I would recommend visiting at a less busy time because the café is relatively small. Other than that, even if my meal had not been free, I would still recommend the café. The atmosphere is warm and inviting and their homemade soup is delicious.

–Stefan Nichols, 3 February

Association of Accounting Professionals
Annual meeting–Scheduled events

https://www.app.org.ie/annualmeeting/schedule

Friday, 4 February

Guest speaker 5:30 P.M., Room 213, Insley Hotel	Mr. Ian Bagley, chief financial officer at Colford International, will discuss "Old Concerns and Current Trends in the Accounting Profession."
Networking dinner 7:00 P.M. Maury's Restaurant	Enjoy a gourmet dinner and relax with your colleagues at this popular eatery.

Saturday, 5 February

Job Fair 11:00 A.M. to 5:00 P.M.	Looking for a new opportunity? The job fair is for you. Meet with representatives from companies around the region. Bring copies of your résumé.
Tour of Dublin 1:00 P.M. to 4:00 P.M.	Visit some interesting sites in our host city. Wear comfortable shoes, as tour participants will cover approximately two miles.

186. Who most likely is Ms. McNally?

(A) A receptionist
(B) A banquet chef
(C) An event organizer
(D) A café owner

187. What problem is described in the e-mail?

(A) An event has been canceled.
(B) A hotel is closing.
(C) A repair bill was not paid on time.
(D) An industrial appliance is not working.

188. What can be concluded about Mr. Nichols?

(A) He did not enjoy a meal.
(B) He arrived 25 minutes late for a luncheon.
(C) He is a guest at the Insley Hotel.
(D) He is a frequent customer at a restaurant.

189. What does the event schedule indicate?

(A) Tour participants will travel on foot.
(B) Entertainment will be provided in the lobby.
(C) Attendees must register for the job fair.
(D) All activities take place in the afternoon.

190. What is suggested about the networking dinner?

(A) It will feature a talk by Mr. Bagley.
(B) It had to be postponed to a later time.
(C) It is intended for accounting students.
(D) It was moved from its original location.

GO ON TO THE NEXT PAGE

Questions 191-195 refer to the following Web page, e-mail, and form.

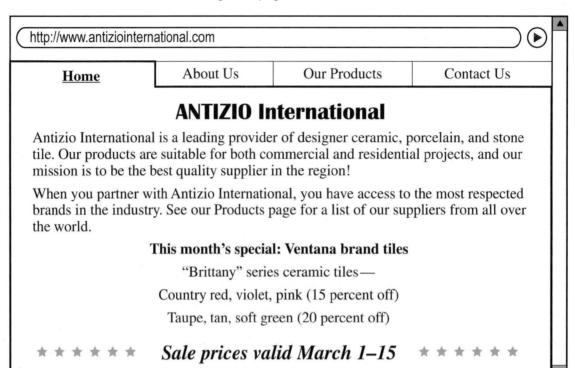

http://www.antiziointernational.com

| Home | About Us | Our Products | Contact Us |

ANTIZIO International

Antizio International is a leading provider of designer ceramic, porcelain, and stone tile. Our products are suitable for both commercial and residential projects, and our mission is to be the best quality supplier in the region!

When you partner with Antizio International, you have access to the most respected brands in the industry. See our Products page for a list of our suppliers from all over the world.

This month's special: Ventana brand tiles

"Brittany" series ceramic tiles—

Country red, violet, pink (15 percent off)

Taupe, tan, soft green (20 percent off)

★ ★ ★ ★ ★ ★ *Sale prices valid March 1–15* ★ ★ ★ ★ ★ ★

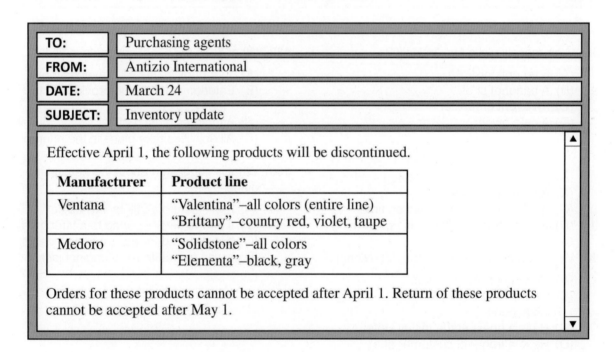

TO:	Purchasing agents
FROM:	Antizio International
DATE:	March 24
SUBJECT:	Inventory update

Effective April 1, the following products will be discontinued.

Manufacturer	Product line
Ventana	"Valentina"–all colors (entire line) "Brittany"–country red, violet, taupe
Medoro	"Solidstone"–all colors "Elementa"–black, gray

Orders for these products cannot be accepted after April 1. Return of these products cannot be accepted after May 1.

ANTIZIO International

~~ Merchandise Return ~~

Please review our return policy before submitting this form. Returns must be made within 60 days of purchase and must be in original, unused condition.

Return date: May 12

Customer name: William Lin, WKL Contractors, Inc.

Original invoice date: March 20

Item name: Medoro brand-"Elementa" tile

Color: Gray

Quantity: 20 boxes **Price/box:** $70

Reason for return: Actual color does not match catalog image.

Form of return requested: ☒ Refund ☐ Store credit

---

191. In what industry does Antizio International do business?

(A) Building materials
(B) Commercial advertising
(C) Computer manufacturing
(D) Fashion design

192. What advantage does Antizio International offer to clients?

(A) Its employees are bilingual.
(B) Its products have a good reputation.
(C) Its delivery fees are waived for frequent customers.
(D) Its payment plans are flexible.

193. What color of the Brittany product line can be ordered after April 1 ?

(A) Country red
(B) Violet
(C) Taupe
(D) Soft green

194. Why is Mr. Lin returning merchandise?

(A) He purchased more of the product than he needed.
(B) He is not pleased with the color of the product.
(C) The product sent to him was the wrong size.
(D) The product was damaged during shipping.

195. Why will Mr. Lin's refund request most likely be rejected?

(A) He bought an item that was custom designed.
(B) He failed to include proof of purchase.
(C) He returned a product after a deadline had expired.
(D) He forgot to ask for a return authorization number.

GO ON TO THE NEXT PAGE

E-mail

To:	All Staff
From:	Ronald Garrison
Date:	April 20
Subject:	Update

Dear Colleagues,

It's an exciting time here at Zikomo Solutions, and we have a lot to celebrate! Our company has shown tremendous growth over the past year. Just last month we exceeded our goals and conducted 25 customer service workshops for 18 different companies in the greater Groton area.

In response to our growth, we have added three new workshop presenters with significant customer service experience in their respective industries. Lisa Okoro will focus on the telemarketing industry. Caleb Patel will train those in fields related to medicine. And Alan Gorospe will specialize mainly in customer service for the technology industry. They will begin giving workshops during the first or second week of May. Please join me in welcoming these professionals to the Zikomo family.

Ronald Garrison
CEO, Zikomo Solutions

Zikomo Solutions
Tentative training schedule
Week of May 2

Course Name	Course Length	Date	Trainer	Location
Telephone Skills	Half Day	May 2	Lisa Okoro	Zikomo, Groton
Customer Service in a Digital World	Full Day	May 3	Alan Gorospe	Zikomo, Groton
Patient Relations for Hospital Professionals	Full Day	May 4	To Be Determined	Fitzer Medical Group, West Groton
Turn Tech Problems into Marketing Opportunities	Half Day	May 5	Alan Gorospe	Callipher Technologies, Fayetteville

```
┌──────────────────────────────────────────────────────────────────────┐
│                            *E-mail*                                    │
├──────────────────────────────────────────────────────────────────────┤
│  To:        Ronald Garrison <rgarrison@zikomosolutions.net>            │
│  From:      Jana Snyder <jsnyder@snyder.com>                           │
│  Date:      May 8                                                      │
│  Subject:   Recent workshops                                          │
├──────────────────────────────────────────────────────────────────────┤
│  Dear Mr. Garrison,                                                    │
│                                                                        │
│  Several of my employees from Snyder Goods attended Zikomo training    │
│  sessions on May 2 and 3. I wanted to provide feedback and ask a       │
│  question. I think the half-day session could be extended to a full    │
│  day, considering the interesting topic and skill of the excellent     │
│  presenter. Conversely, the full day, while interesting, would be      │
│  better condensed into a half day. Additionally, could you provide     │
│  more parking options? Spaces for participants were full, and a        │
│  number of our Snyder Goods employees had to park in an expensive      │
│  paid lot.                                                             │
│                                                                        │
│  Sincerely,                                                            │
│                                                                        │
│  Jana Snyder                                                           │
│  Snyder Goods                                                          │
└──────────────────────────────────────────────────────────────────────┘
```

196. What is the purpose of the first e-mail?

(A) To announce the hiring of new staff members
(B) To invite employees to a celebration
(C) To outline a plan for a company's growth
(D) To recognize high-performing employees

197. In what area does Zikomo Solutions specialize?

(A) Computer manufacturing
(B) Accounting
(C) Transportation
(D) Customer service

198. What does the schedule indicate about the workshops?

(A) Several are held on the same day.
(B) Some are held at Zikomo's office.
(C) They typically last a full day.
(D) They are usually filled to capacity.

199. Who is most qualified to lead the workshop on May 4 ?

(A) Mr. Garrison
(B) Ms. Okoro
(C) Mr. Patel
(D) Mr. Gorospe

200. What does Ms. Snyder suggest about her employees' training experience?

(A) The parking options were convenient.
(B) The May 2 session was too short.
(C) The topics were not interesting.
(D) The trainer arrived late.

Stop! This is the end of the test. If you finish before time is called, you may go back to Parts 5, 6, and 7 and check your work.

토익® 정기시험
기출문제집

RC

기출 TEST

05

READING TEST

In the Reading test, you will read a variety of texts and answer several different types of reading comprehension questions. The entire Reading test will last 75 minutes. There are three parts, and directions are given for each part. You are encouraged to answer as many questions as possible within the time allowed.

You must mark your answers on the separate answer sheet. Do not write your answers in your test book.

PART 5

Directions: A word or phrase is missing in each of the sentences below. Four answer choices are given below each sentence. Select the best answer to complete the sentence. Then mark the letter (A), (B), (C), or (D) on your answer sheet.

101. Ms. Abe will order supplies tomorrow, ------- tell her right away if you need anything.

    (A) than
    (B) wait
    (C) so
    (D) about

102. The Knysya Theater requests that all electronic devices be silenced ------- the play begins.

    (A) also
    (B) but
    (C) unless
    (D) before

103. ------- Human Resources if you have questions about taking time off from work.

    (A) Contacting
    (B) Contacted
    (C) Contacts
    (D) Contact

104. ------- eighty thousand people attended yesterday's soccer match.

    (A) Almost
    (B) More
    (C) Often
    (D) Enough

105. Online visitors report that our company's Web site is somewhat -------.

    (A) confuse
    (B) confuses
    (C) confusing
    (D) confusion

106. Traffic ------- are expected next week along Reimers Road.

    (A) drivers
    (B) crowds
    (C) delays
    (D) needs

107. Shaloub Hospital wants to hire several more ------- qualified laboratory workers.

    (A) higher
    (B) highest
    (C) high
    (D) highly

108. Whenever you are the ------- person to exit a room, please turn off the lights.

    (A) last
    (B) inside
    (C) finish
    (D) near

109. Following a brief ------- with the chief technician, Mr. Moore agreed to update the operations manual.

(A) converses
(B) conversation
(C) conversational
(D) conversationally

110. After record profits, Golden Shamrock Jewelry's stock price increased ------- our expectations.

(A) beside
(B) beyond
(C) behind
(D) between

111. We cannot ------- the filming of our documentary, *Morning after Night*, without sufficient funding.

(A) completely
(B) completion
(C) complete
(D) completing

112. Get to the station a few minutes early because Mr. Xu's train will arrive ------- at 7:00 P.M.

(A) carefully
(B) unexpectedly
(C) promptly
(D) clearly

113. ------- can be done to revise your order, since the merchandise has already shipped.

(A) Ours
(B) Nobody
(C) Others
(D) Nothing

114. Recent graduates tend to ------- workplaces where teamwork and collaboration are encouraged.

(A) think
(B) apply
(C) extend
(D) prefer

115. Zhang Cleaning takes great care to ensure that all its employees follow specific cleaning -------.

(A) proceeds
(B) procedures
(C) procedural
(D) proceeding

116. Mumbai Jewel is a widely acclaimed restaurant, mainly ------- its delicious buffet dinners.

(A) such as
(B) not only
(C) because of
(D) together with

117. Before a job interview, it is critical to prepare ------- for answering the most commonly asked questions.

(A) whose
(B) whichever
(C) theirs
(D) oneself

118. While it is not -------, staff are encouraged to read Joan Frantz's book *Balancing Work and Life*.

(A) required
(B) published
(C) limited
(D) guaranteed

119. It is ------- to bring sturdy boots to wear on the hike.

(A) advise
(B) advisor
(C) advisable
(D) advises

120. Nordel Park will open for the season once average daytime temperatures reach ------- 15 degrees.

(A) at least
(B) as of
(C) along with
(D) ahead of

GO ON TO THE NEXT PAGE

121. Before investing, Mr. Hwang will wait for greater ------- that Briomer Tech is fully committed to the project.

(A) assure
(B) assured
(C) assuredly
(D) assurance

122. Tralim Consulting's annual profits are expected to ------- exceed €5 million.

(A) exactly
(B) extremely
(C) eventually
(D) evenly

123. Although many factors contribute to a successful business, Mr. Lee thinks that keeping customers satisfied is the -------.

(A) essential
(B) most essential
(C) essentially
(D) more essentially

124. Ms. Alshammari took a full hour to ------- each of the budget changes during the staff meeting.

(A) detail
(B) attend
(C) respond
(D) comply

125. It is recommended that clients book the Desert Rose Ballroom for their event more than four months -------.

(A) over time
(B) in advance
(C) up to now
(D) far ahead

126. For a true understanding of our production levels, data from oil-drilling sites must be as ------- as possible.

(A) accurate
(B) optimistic
(C) exclusive
(D) competitive

127. Adopting advanced billing software would improve Narrin Group's fiscal-management process -------.

(A) substantial
(B) substantially
(C) more substantial
(D) substances

128. Thanks to the effective ------- of Drinkever's first beverage, last month's product launch was a success.

(A) service
(B) promotion
(C) response
(D) information

129. By this time next year, Grasswell Industries ------- two new plants in eastern Europe.

(A) opens
(B) will have opened
(C) is opening
(D) had opened

130. Please put an ------- supply of premium snack items on the carts for the next flight.

(A) absolute
(B) earned
(C) adequate
(D) energetic

PART 6

Directions: Read the texts that follow. A word, phrase, or sentence is missing in parts of each text. Four answer choices for each question are given below the text. Select the best answer to complete the text. Then mark the letter (A), (B), (C), or (D) on your answer sheet.

Questions 131-134 refer to the following article.

COPENHAGEN (25 May)—Odense Media announced today that initial sales of the latest version

of its tablet, Virtusonic, have ------- the company's expectations. Company spokesperson Kerstin
        131.

Vestergaard attributes the ------- sales to a number of factors. First, there is the tablet's high-
                    132.

quality case. ------- . In addition, the Virtusonic has an adaptive screen brightness feature. This
        133.

allows it to adjust automatically to less-than-ideal ------- conditions. Vestergaard believes that
                            134.

these characteristics make the Virtusonic a must-have for consumers.

131. (A) based
(B) surpassed
(C) invested
(D) progressed

132. (A) impress
(B) impressing
(C) impressive
(D) impressed

133. (A) Customers must consider what the
tablet will be used for.
(B) The Virtusonic will be available in other
colors next month.
(C) Check stores for the best deals on the
new device.
(D) The protective shell ensures the
durability of the device.

134. (A) lighting
(B) noise
(C) temperature
(D) wind

GO ON TO THE NEXT PAGE

Questions 135-138 refer to the following memo.

To: All employees
From: Marcus Sindhu, IT Director
Date: June 1
Subject: Web site maintenance

Please note that routine maintenance of the server will be performed this weekend, affecting the content of our company Web site. The server ------- down for approximately eight hours from 11 P.M.
135.
on Saturday, June 6, to 7 A.M. on Sunday, June 7. ------- this time, access to the Web site will
136.
be restricted, and e-mail delivery will be paused. ------- . Once the server is back up, please take
137.
some time to explore the ------- features on the Web site. These include a new scheduler and a
138.
more user-friendly search tool.

Your patience is greatly appreciated. Please direct any questions to me.

135. (A) is
(B) was
(C) will be
(D) had been

136. (A) During
(B) Despite
(C) Following
(D) Prior to

137. (A) The work will be done during business hours.
(B) A team of seven programmers will be hard at work.
(C) All Web site operations will resume on Sunday morning.
(D) Feel free to check your e-mail as needed.

138. (A) safety
(B) updated
(C) portable
(D) temporary

Small Business Costs: An Overview for Beginners

There are two main kinds of costs. Variable costs are one kind; they include staff wages or the cost of supplies. ------- costs are considered fixed. These include such things as rent payments and property taxes.
                    139.

A third kind of cost is called an opportunity cost. You incur an opportunity cost whenever you make a decision to do one specific thing ------- choosing some alternative option. This cost refers
                                             140.
to the lost opportunities you could have benefited from had you made a different choice. Careful consideration of potential opportunity costs is important. Ideally this should ------- decision
                                                                                    141.
making.

------- . You should consult a licensed accountant for a more complete understanding.
142.

---

139. (A) Any
  (B) Both
  (C) Other
  (D) Those

140. (A) except for
  (B) just as
  (C) rather than
  (D) only if

141. (A) eliminate
  (B) influence
  (C) replace
  (D) automate

142. (A) The number of employees is continuing to fluctuate.
  (B) A sales manager controls employee commissions.
  (C) The business used to have a larger inventory.
  (D) There are other types of business costs as well.

GO ON TO THE NEXT PAGE

Questions 143-146 refer to the following article.

Morlon Home Goods Set to Open

TISDALE (2 April)—Morlon Home Goods will open this Friday in a 130 square meter space on Waverly Road that was formerly ------- by Binkley's Market. The store features home décor items,
143.
such as lamps, wall art, and small furniture from around the globe, all at affordable prices.

"Morlon has a great variety of attractive items for the modern home. Our inventory changes

------- . Patrons like to stop in often to see what is new," said Naoko Sasaki, the chain's marketing
144.
director. This is the first Morlon in the local area. ------- . A grand opening ------- featuring free food,
145.   **146.**
giveaways, and discount coupons will be held on Saturday, 13 April from 10:00 A.M. to 6:00 P.M.

143. (A) occupation
     (B) occupied
     (C) occupy
     (D) occupying

144. (A) elsewhere
     (B) afterward
     (C) properly
     (D) frequently

145. (A) The company has fourteen other stores around the country.
     (B) Profits increased 25 percent since last quarter.
     (C) Morlon's biggest competitor is Country Home.
     (D) Binkley's Market went out of business earlier this year.

146. (A) celebrates
     (B) celebrating
     (C) celebrate
     (D) celebration

PART 7

Directions: In this part you will read a selection of texts, such as magazine and newspaper articles, e-mails, and instant messages. Each text or set of texts is followed by several questions. Select the best answer for each question and mark the letter (A), (B), (C), or (D) on your answer sheet.

Questions 147-148 refer to the following online advertisement.

147. What is the purpose of the advertisement?

(A) To promote a store opening
(B) To attract new customers
(C) To announce a new menu
(D) To report a Web site upgrade

148. What is available through the month of June?

(A) A diet analysis
(B) A sample recipe
(C) A free delivery
(D) A magazine subscription

GO ON TO THE NEXT PAGE

Questions 149-150 refer to the following e-mail.

To:	All Residents
From:	Dan Madsen
Date:	20 September
Subject:	Georgetown Marathon

To all Thompson Towers residents:

The 25th annual Georgetown Marathon will be held next Saturday. This year, for the first time, the race will turn off of River Street and proceed onto Elmont Avenue. So on Saturday, there will be nearly 5,000 registered contestants running along the stretch of road that provides the only access to our Thompson Towers parking garage entrance. Unsurprisingly, Elmont Avenue will be closed to all vehicle traffic between 7:00 A.M. and 10:45 A.M. This means that residents' cars will not be able to enter or exit our parking garage during this event. If you know that you will need to use your car during this period, we recommend that you make arrangements ahead of time for either leaving early or parking elsewhere.

For more information about the race, including maps, registration guidelines, and alternative parking locations, please go to www.georgetownmarathon.co.uk.

Sincerely yours,

Dan Madsen
Property Manager, Thompson Towers

149. What is the purpose of the e-mail?

(A) To encourage participation in a race
(B) To warn of an upcoming road closure
(C) To reschedule a tenant meeting
(D) To announce a construction plan

150. What is indicated about the Georgetown Marathon?

(A) It has close to 5,000 participants.
(B) It is being held for the first time.
(C) It starts on Elmont Avenue.
(D) It includes participants from Thompson Towers.

One reason that corrugated fiberboard has become such a popular material for shipping fresh vegetables and fruits is the ease of labeling the containers. Information such as the brand, size, and grade of the produce can be printed directly on the box after it has been formed. Although this method, known as "postprinting," is the most economical way of labeling fiberboard containers, it is limited to only one or two colors. Full-color graphics can be obtained by printing the information on the box before it has been formed. This method, known as "preprinting," costs about 15 percent more, but many supermarket managers prefer it because customers are attracted to the colorful displays, which leads to increased sales.

151. What is indicated about corrugated fiberboard boxes?

(A) They are easy to label.
(B) They hold more than other containers.
(C) They keep vegetables fresh.
(D) They are used less often than other types.

152. Why do store managers generally prefer boxes with full-color graphics?

(A) They can be cleaned and reused.
(B) They come in a wide variety of sizes.
(C) They are often requested by customers.
(D) They increase customers' purchases.

TEST 5

GO ON TO THE NEXT PAGE

ADMINISTRATIVE ASSISTANT

Position Summary:
Naidu Rai Electronics, one of the world's leading manufacturers in the telecommunications industry, is seeking a full-time administrative assistant in our Jaipur office.

Responsibilities:
1. Provide administrative support for members of the product design team, including travel and expense reports
2. Schedule appointments with prospective clients and designers
3. Maintain files, process documents, and compile reports

Required Qualifications/Education:
Senior school certificate mandatory; business school certification preferred

Skills:
1. Strong interpersonal skills
2. Strong organizational and planning skills
3. Software proficiency

To be considered, e-mail your résumé and cover letter to s.mohta@naiduraielec.in; candidates selected for an interview will be required to take a basic software proficiency test.

153. What is indicated about the job?

(A) It involves working with product designers.
(B) It requires frequent travel.
(C) It is a temporary position.
(D) It has been available for several months.

154. According to the advertisement, what must a person do to apply?

(A) Provide a client list
(B) Forward school transcripts
(C) Submit a résumé
(D) Send a reference letter

155. What will an applicant do at an interview?

(A) Answer a telephone call
(B) Take a computer test
(C) Submit a writing sample
(D) Compile a report

Questions 156-158 refer to the following Web page.

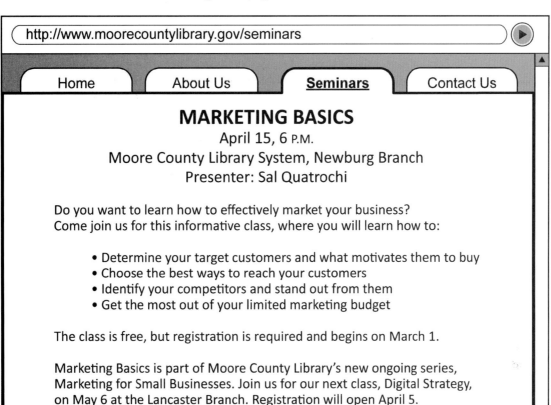

156. When will the Marketing Basics class take place?

(A) On March 1
(B) On April 5
(C) On April 15
(D) On May 6

157. What topic will NOT be covered in the Marketing Basics class?

(A) Identifying potential customers
(B) Showing how a business is different from its competitors
(C) Choosing a graphic designer to create advertisements
(D) Spending marketing money efficiently

158. What is indicated about the Marketing Basics class?

(A) It is taught by a marketing professor.
(B) It is one of several classes offered to business owners.
(C) It is designed for corporate executives.
(D) It will be offered again in the near future.

GO ON TO THE NEXT PAGE

Questions 159-161 refer to the following Web page.

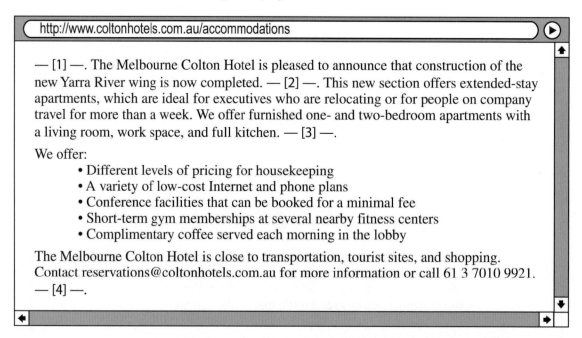

http://www.coltonhotels.com.au/accommodations

— [1] —. The Melbourne Colton Hotel is pleased to announce that construction of the new Yarra River wing is now completed. — [2] —. This new section offers extended-stay apartments, which are ideal for executives who are relocating or for people on company travel for more than a week. We offer furnished one- and two-bedroom apartments with a living room, work space, and full kitchen. — [3] —.

We offer:
- Different levels of pricing for housekeeping
- A variety of low-cost Internet and phone plans
- Conference facilities that can be booked for a minimal fee
- Short-term gym memberships at several nearby fitness centers
- Complimentary coffee served each morning in the lobby

The Melbourne Colton Hotel is close to transportation, tourist sites, and shopping. Contact reservations@coltonhotels.com.au for more information or call 61 3 7010 9921. — [4] —.

159. For whom is the information mainly intended?

(A) Business travelers
(B) Tourists
(C) Hotel staff members
(D) Construction workers

160. What does the hotel provide at no charge?

(A) Housekeeping
(B) Internet
(C) Conference rooms
(D) Coffee

161. In which of the positions marked [1], [2], [3], and [4] does the following sentence best belong?

"In addition, optional services are available for extended-stay guests."

(A) [1]
(B) [2]
(C) [3]
(D) [4]

Questions 162-163 refer to the following text-message chain.

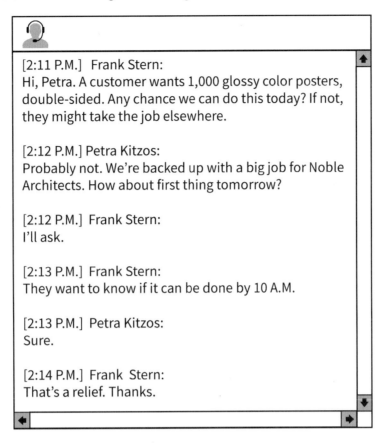

[2:11 P.M.] Frank Stern:
Hi, Petra. A customer wants 1,000 glossy color posters, double-sided. Any chance we can do this today? If not, they might take the job elsewhere.

[2:12 P.M.] Petra Kitzos:
Probably not. We're backed up with a big job for Noble Architects. How about first thing tomorrow?

[2:12 P.M.] Frank Stern:
I'll ask.

[2:13 P.M.] Frank Stern:
They want to know if it can be done by 10 A.M.

[2:13 P.M.] Petra Kitzos:
Sure.

[2:14 P.M.] Frank Stern:
That's a relief. Thanks.

162. Where do Mr. Stern and Ms. Kitzos most likely work?

(A) At a shipping store
(B) At an architecture firm
(C) At an accounting office
(D) At a print shop

163. At 2:14 P.M., what does Mr. Stern most likely mean when he writes, "That's a relief"?

(A) He is grateful to Ms. Kitzos for working overtime.
(B) He is no longer worried that his company might lose a client.
(C) He appreciates how quickly Ms. Kitzos responded.
(D) He is glad that he does not need to come in early in the morning.

GO ON TO THE NEXT PAGE

Houkcomm Eyes Downtown Roseville

(April 22)—Houkcomm, one of the state's leading telecommunications companies, will likely establish operations in Roseville. Houkcomm is reportedly looking to open a Roseville office as part of a new venture for the company: an expansion into the digital media industry. Houkcomm spokespeople have not offered any details on the plan, but two architects involved with the project confirmed that one proposed office building design would accommodate over 100 workers. The likely location for this soon-to-be constructed building, according to these sources, is a property adjacent to Behr Square in central Roseville.

164. What is Houkcomm planning to do in Roseville?

(A) Offer a new telephone service
(B) Lease space to subcontractors
(C) Relocate its headquarters
(D) Open a new business division

165. What is true about Houkcomm?

(A) It is the only telecommunications company in the state.
(B) It is currently leasing space in central Roseville.
(C) It has recently hired more than 100 new workers.
(D) It already has a major presence in the state.

166. How did the reporter most likely obtain information for the article?

(A) From a press release written by Houkcomm representatives
(B) By interviewing employees of a firm that is doing work for Houkcomm
(C) Through public documents and construction permits
(D) By attending a press conference in Roseville

167. According to the article, what is likely to happen soon?

(A) Construction will begin on a new building.
(B) All Behr Square residences will be purchased.
(C) Houkcomm will negotiate new supply contracts.
(D) Manufacturing jobs will increase in Roseville.

Questions 168-171 refer to the following e-mail.

From:	Takeshi Ishiguro
To:	All Sevastya employees
Subject:	Update
Date:	December 13

Dear Sevastya employees,

I am writing to give you an update on this year's sales so far. — [1] —. I am happy to report that currently our sales volume is up 20% from last year. This is due in part to the fact that we have been very successful in expanding our international reach.

— [2] —. In Brazil, sales increased 57%, which can be attributed to the Rio de Janeiro Fashion Show where our evening wear was featured. A similar trend emerged in Russia, where sales were up by 32%. — [3] —. There we anticipate sustained growth for the rest of the year, especially in our winter apparel line. We also saw sales growth in the United Arab Emirates (UAE), but growth was a modest 10% due to fierce competition. That said, in this market, sign-ups for our credit card were strong. Finally, in Korea, where we have had our most successful international market launch thus far, favorable news articles about our products drove very strong sales.

— [4] —. Thus, overall, it's been an excellent year so far. I am confident that our new program, which offers discounts to customers who invite others to shop with us, will begin to boost sales growth at all locations.

Sincerely,

Takeshi Ishiguro
Vice President of Sales

168. What kind of business is Sevastya?

(A) A travel agency
(B) A magazine publisher
(C) A clothing retailer
(D) A hotel chain

169. According to the e-mail, where was the company's product seen by an audience?

(A) In Brazil
(B) In Russia
(C) In the UAE
(D) In Korea

170. According to Mr. Ishiguro, what will likely bring increased business in the future?

(A) Television commercials
(B) An expanded credit card program
(C) Company-sponsored contests
(D) Referrals from customers

171. In which of the positions marked [1], [2], [3], and [4] does the following sentence best belong?

"Here are some figures from around the world."

(A) [1]
(B) [2]
(C) [3]
(D) [4]

GO ON TO THE NEXT PAGE

Lynda McCann (1:08 P.M.) Hello, Bernadette and Harrison. We urgently need to schedule a team meeting, so we can get working on our project.

Bernadette Ecco (1:10 P.M.) Sure. Are you wanting an all-marketing-staff meeting? Let me know if I can assist.

Lynda McCann (1:12 P.M.) No, I was thinking of the O'Neil project, so only the three of us who are on that team need to meet.

Bernadette Ecco (1:14 P.M.) Okay. I'm free either this Wednesday or Friday during the early afternoon.

Harrison Miller (1:15 P.M.) I thought I had been reassigned to the McMillan project instead.

Bernadette Ecco (1:17 P.M.) No, the final slot on that team was filled by Jacob Aikens, since he's worked on similar projects in the past, like the Greller project and the Allford project.

Harrison Miller (1:18 P.M.) Okay, I see.

Lynda McCann (1:19 P.M.) I'm available on Wednesday and Friday as well, but only before 3 P.M.; I'll be meeting with the sales team on Wednesday at 3 P.M. and the research team on Friday at 3:30 P.M.

Harrison Miller (1:21 P.M.) Wednesday won't work for me, but I could do Friday at 1 P.M.

Lynda McCann (1:23 P.M.) Sounds good! Bernadette?

Bernadette Ecco (1:23 P.M.) Perfect! I'll reserve the small conference room for us.

172. In what department do the writers most likely work?

(A) Sales
(B) Marketing
(C) Billing
(D) Research

173. To what project are the three writers assigned?

(A) The O'Neil project
(B) The McMillan project
(C) The Greller project
(D) The Allford project

174. At 1:18 P.M., what does Mr. Miller most likely mean when he writes, "Okay, I see"?

(A) He understands that he was not moved to another team.
(B) He recognizes that he did not come to a meeting on time.
(C) He accepts that he is not going to meet with a client.
(D) He acknowledges that he did not complete a task.

175. Why was the meeting scheduled for Friday rather than Wednesday?

(A) Ms. McCann has a commitment with another team on that day.
(B) Ms. Ecco's schedule is very busy this month.
(C) Mr. Miller is unavailable on Wednesday.
(D) A sales team will be using the conference room on Wednesday.

GO ON TO THE NEXT PAGE

Questions 176-180 refer to the following e-mail and Web page.

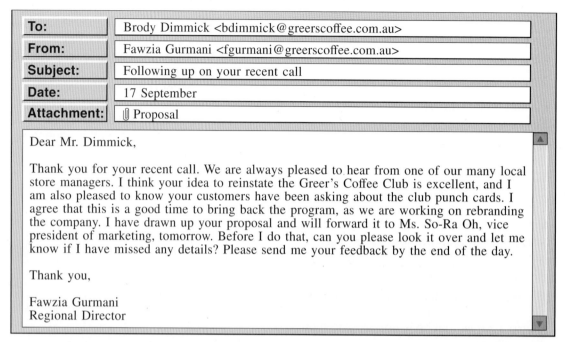

To:	Brody Dimmick <bdimmick@greerscoffee.com.au>
From:	Fawzia Gurmani <fgurmani@greerscoffee.com.au>
Subject:	Following up on your recent call
Date:	17 September
Attachment:	📎 Proposal

Dear Mr. Dimmick,

Thank you for your recent call. We are always pleased to hear from one of our many local store managers. I think your idea to reinstate the Greer's Coffee Club is excellent, and I am also pleased to know your customers have been asking about the club punch cards. I agree that this is a good time to bring back the program, as we are working on rebranding the company. I have drawn up your proposal and will forward it to Ms. So-Ra Oh, vice president of marketing, tomorrow. Before I do that, can you please look it over and let me know if I have missed any details? Please send me your feedback by the end of the day.

Thank you,

Fawzia Gurmani
Regional Director

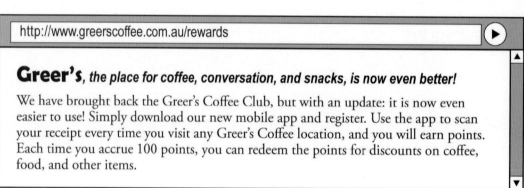

http://www.greerscoffee.com.au/rewards

Greer's, *the place for coffee, conversation, and snacks, is now even better!*

We have brought back the Greer's Coffee Club, but with an update: it is now even easier to use! Simply download our new mobile app and register. Use the app to scan your receipt every time you visit any Greer's Coffee location, and you will earn points. Each time you accrue 100 points, you can redeem the points for discounts on coffee, food, and other items.

176. Why did Ms. Gurmani send the e-mail?

(A) To welcome a new employee
(B) To describe how to join a club
(C) To invite Mr. Dimmick to a meeting
(D) To confirm the details of a proposal

177. Who is Mr. Dimmick?

(A) A new supplier
(B) A store manager
(C) A vice president
(D) A regional director

178. What does Ms. Gurmani suggest about Greer's Coffee?

(A) It has had a coffee club before.
(B) It is a new company.
(C) It hired a marketing consultant.
(D) It is launching a new coffee flavor.

179. What does the Web page suggest about Greer's Coffee Club?

(A) It allows customers to place orders online.
(B) It no longer requires the use of a punch card.
(C) It is no longer offered at all locations.
(D) It requires customers to make a monthly purchase.

180. On the Web page, the word "redeem" in paragraph 1, line 4, is closest in meaning to

(A) trade in
(B) pay off
(C) set free
(D) win over

GO ON TO THE NEXT PAGE

Job Posted: April 10

Seeking: Highly Experienced Finance Director

Employer: Vimaxo Financial Services (VFS)

Duties include:

• Setting annual financial targets

• Managing the duties of accounting staff

• Overseeing investments and cash flow

• Developing sound financial strategies

Prerequisites:

• 5 years of experience as a finance director

• A university degree in economics or similar field

• Excellent communication skills

• Outstanding analytical skills

To apply: Send application and supporting documents to our director of Human Resources, Celeste Zomorodi, at zomorodi.c@vfs.com by May 15. We aim to hire the ideal applicant by June 21 and have him/her begin work on July 1.

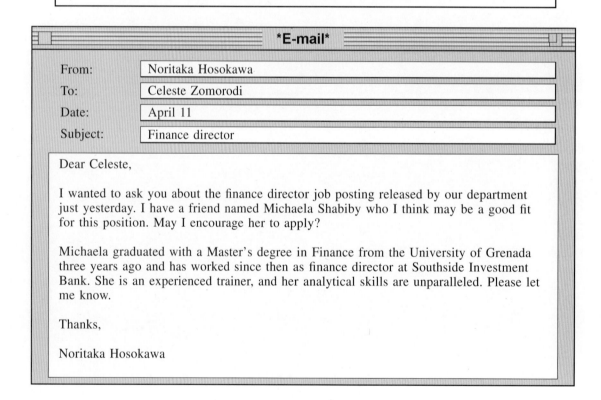

E-mail

From:	Noritaka Hosokawa
To:	Celeste Zomorodi
Date:	April 11
Subject:	Finance director

Dear Celeste,

I wanted to ask you about the finance director job posting released by our department just yesterday. I have a friend named Michaela Shabiby who I think may be a good fit for this position. May I encourage her to apply?

Michaela graduated with a Master's degree in Finance from the University of Grenada three years ago and has worked since then as finance director at Southside Investment Bank. She is an experienced trainer, and her analytical skills are unparalleled. Please let me know.

Thanks,

Noritaka Hosokawa

181. According to the job advertisement, what will be one responsibility of the successful candidate?

(A) Reviewing tax policies
(B) Overseeing financial planning
(C) Evaluating promotional campaigns
(D) Meeting with fund-raising coordinators

182. When is the job application deadline?

(A) April 10
(B) May 15
(C) June 21
(D) July 1

183. What most likely is true about Mr. Hosokawa and Ms. Zomorodi?

(A) They met at university.
(B) They are friends of Ms. Shabiby's.
(C) They work in Human Resources.
(D) They have known each other since childhood.

184. In the e-mail, the word "fit" in paragraph 1, line 2, is closest in meaning to

(A) agreement
(B) success
(C) match
(D) preparation

185. From Ms. Zomorodi's description, what position requirement might Ms. Shabiby NOT meet?

(A) Job-related experience
(B) A university degree
(C) Good communication skills
(D) Outstanding analytical skills

GO ON TO THE NEXT PAGE

Questions 186-190 refer to the following Web page, survey response, and memo.

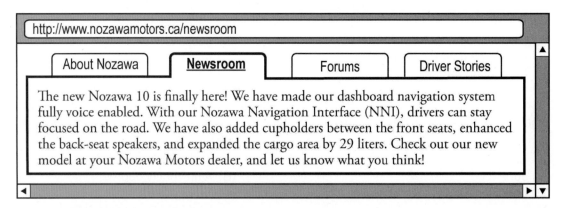

http://www.nozawamotors.ca/newsroom

| About Nozawa | **Newsroom** | Forums | Driver Stories |

The new Nozawa 10 is finally here! We have made our dashboard navigation system fully voice enabled. With our Nozawa Navigation Interface (NNI), drivers can stay focused on the road. We have also added cupholders between the front seats, enhanced the back-seat speakers, and expanded the cargo area by 29 liters. Check out our new model at your Nozawa Motors dealer, and let us know what you think!

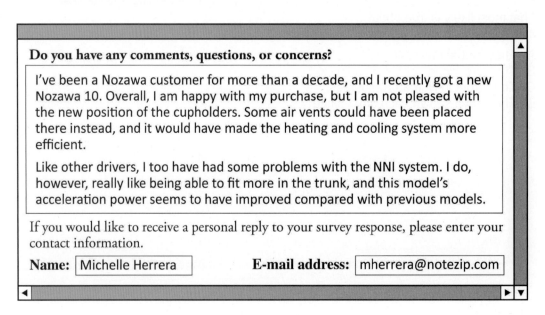

Do you have any comments, questions, or concerns?

I've been a Nozawa customer for more than a decade, and I recently got a new Nozawa 10. Overall, I am happy with my purchase, but I am not pleased with the new position of the cupholders. Some air vents could have been placed there instead, and it would have made the heating and cooling system more efficient.

Like other drivers, I too have had some problems with the NNI system. I do, however, really like being able to fit more in the trunk, and this model's acceleration power seems to have improved compared with previous models.

If you would like to receive a personal reply to your survey response, please enter your contact information.

Name: Michelle Herrera   **E-mail address:** mherrera@notezip.com

MEMO

From: Tabitha Marks
To: Nozawa Service Center Managers
Subject: New release

We received negative customer feedback about the new Nozawa 10 model's NNI system. In response we have just released a new NNI software update that fixes the bugs. Please begin installing this update immediately to all current year Nozawa 10s that are brought to your shops for servicing. You can expect an increase in Nozawa 10s being brought in for service as we will be notifying all owners that this update is available.

186. What is the purpose of the Web page?

(A) To describe recent consumer research
(B) To explain delays to a product release
(C) To announce updates to a vehicle
(D) To report on a vehicle usability test

187. According to the Web page, what is bigger in the new Nozawa 10 ?

(A) The storage space
(B) The steering wheel
(C) The engine
(D) The mirrors

188. What does Ms. Herrera indicate in the survey response?

(A) She contacted the district manager.
(B) She plans to have the dealership repair her vehicle.
(C) She has recently been promoted to a new position.
(D) She has driven more than one Nozawa vehicle.

189. Where in the vehicle would Ms. Herrera prefer to have air vents?

(A) Near the rear seats
(B) Between the front seats
(C) Next to the display screen
(D) On the dashboard

190. What needs to be corrected?

(A) The vehicle service records
(B) A navigation device
(C) Customer contact information
(D) The stereo system

GO ON TO THE NEXT PAGE

Pink Begonia Farms

Pink Begonia Farms is your one-stop shop for all your plant-related needs. Whether you are a landscape professional, a backyard gardener, or a houseplant enthusiast, we have just about everything you need! Some seeds, fertilizer, and equipment can be ordered online, but please come visit our nursery in person for a much larger selection.

Our sizable facility is divided into four distinct sections as follows:

• <u>North Gate</u>
– indoor houseplants, tropical plants, exotics

• <u>South Gate</u>
– plants and landscaping products sold in bulk quantities at wholesale prices

• <u>East Gate</u>
– local landscape plants that grow well in our area and require little maintenance

• <u>West Gate</u>
– herbs, vegetable plants, fruit and nut trees, and other edibles

Attention Pink Begonia Farms Customers!

We are changing to new ownership on April 1. Several other changes will follow, most notably renovation work that will cause the area where we service our bulk-order customers to be closed from April 1 through May 5.

Also, we would kindly request that if you use our baskets or wagons to move your purchased items to your car, please do not leave them in the middle of the parking area. Thanks!

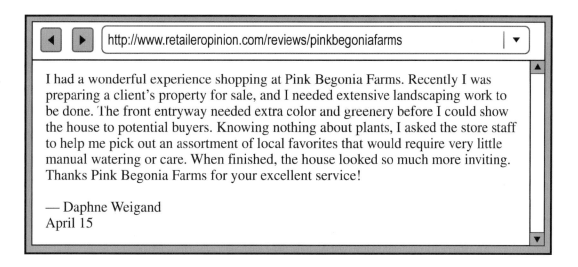

http://www.retaileropinion.com/reviews/pinkbegoniafarms

I had a wonderful experience shopping at Pink Begonia Farms. Recently I was preparing a client's property for sale, and I needed extensive landscaping work to be done. The front entryway needed extra color and greenery before I could show the house to potential buyers. Knowing nothing about plants, I asked the store staff to help me pick out an assortment of local favorites that would require very little manual watering or care. When finished, the house looked so much more inviting. Thanks Pink Begonia Farms for your excellent service!

— Daphne Weigand
April 15

191. What does the Web site mention about the online store?

(A) It offers specials on a seasonal basis.
(B) It is scheduled to be launched in April.
(C) It features the most popular plants on its home page.
(D) It offers fewer items for sale than the physical store does.

192. What does the notice suggest about Pink Begonia Farms?

(A) It provides containers for transporting plants.
(B) Its name will be changed soon.
(C) Its parking area is under construction.
(D) It will no longer allow discounted items to be returned.

193. What area of Pink Begonia Farms will reopen in May?

(A) North Gate
(B) South Gate
(C) East Gate
(D) West Gate

194. What most likely is Ms. Weigand's job?

(A) Landscaper
(B) Event planner
(C) Real estate agent
(D) Nursery worker

195. What is implied about Ms. Weigand?

(A) She has flowers delivered on a regular basis.
(B) She learned of the store through one of her clients.
(C) She plans to buy a house in the near future.
(D) She shopped in the East Gate section of the nursery.

GO ON TO THE NEXT PAGE

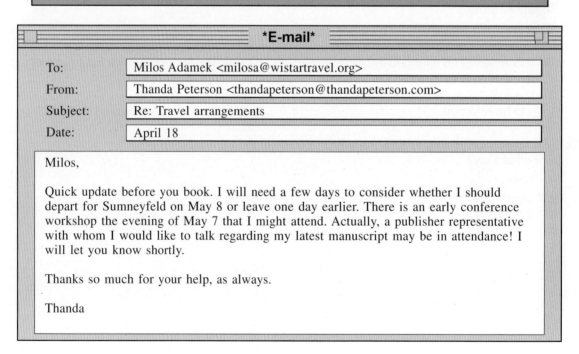

To:	Thanda Peterson <thandapeterson@thandapeterson.com>
From:	Milos Adamek <milosa@wistartravel.org>
Subject:	Travel arrangements
Date:	April 17

Hello Thanda,

I hope you are well. I looked into available flights from Concord to Sumneyfeld for your writers' conference and discovered that discount carrier Alterr Airlines offers daily direct service on that route. The tentative itinerary would be:

> Concord depart: Friday, May 8, 8:50 A.M.
> Sumneyfeld arrive: Friday, May 8, 11:05 A.M.
>
> Sumneyfeld depart: Monday, May 11, 1:20 P.M
> Concord arrive: Monday, May 11, 3:35 P.M.

I will book this as soon as you confirm. Keep in mind on your return trip that the Sumneyfeld Airport is advising passengers to arrive a full two hours before departure because of extensive renovations being done there.

By the way, you might be interested in an excellent Peruvian lunch place near the Sumneyfeld Airport. Just let me know and I will give you the name.

Best,
Milos

E-mail

To:	Milos Adamek <milosa@wistartravel.org>
From:	Thanda Peterson <thandapeterson@thandapeterson.com>
Subject:	Re: Travel arrangements
Date:	April 18

Milos,

Quick update before you book. I will need a few days to consider whether I should depart for Sumneyfeld on May 8 or leave one day earlier. There is an early conference workshop the evening of May 7 that I might attend. Actually, a publisher representative with whom I would like to talk regarding my latest manuscript may be in attendance! I will let you know shortly.

Thanks so much for your help, as always.

Thanda

| Sumneyfeld Quick Taxi |
| 555–0194 |

| Date: May 7 |
| From: Sumneyfeld Airport |
| To: Peru Dreaming Café, 98 Treetop Avenue |
| Pickup: 11:55 A.M. |
| Drop off: 12:04 P.M. |
| Distance: 1.2 miles |
| Total: $8.00 |
| Payment type: [X] credit card   [ ] cash |
| Name on Credit Card: Thanda Peterson |
| Credit Card Number: xxxx xxxx xxxx 5523 |

196. What is indicated about the Sumneyfeld Airport?

(A) It is very near Ms. Peterson's hotel.
(B) It has new check-in staff.
(C) It is undergoing construction work.
(D) It often has delayed flight departures.

197. What is suggested about Ms. Peterson?

(A) She frequently flies on Alterr Airlines.
(B) She has visited Sumneyfeld in the past.
(C) She often goes on business trips for her company.
(D) She has used Mr. Adamek's services before.

198. Who most likely is Ms. Peterson?

(A) A news journalist
(B) A travel-magazine writer
(C) A food critic
(D) A book author

199. What did Ms. Peterson most likely do in response to advice?

(A) She visited a restaurant.
(B) She took advantage of a free shuttle service.
(C) She met with a representative.
(D) She changed airlines.

200. What can be concluded about Ms. Peterson based on the receipt?

(A) She paid in cash for transportation.
(B) She arrived at the airport later than recommended.
(C) She rode a bus to the conference venue.
(D) She decided to attend an extra conference event.

Stop! This is the end of the test. If you finish before time is called, you may go back to Parts 5, 6, and 7 and check your work.

토익® 정기시험
기출문제집

RC

기출 TEST

06

READING TEST

In the Reading test, you will read a variety of texts and answer several different types of reading comprehension questions. The entire Reading test will last 75 minutes. There are three parts, and directions are given for each part. You are encouraged to answer as many questions as possible within the time allowed.

You must mark your answers on the separate answer sheet. Do not write your answers in your test book.

PART 5

Directions: A word or phrase is missing in each of the sentences below. Four answer choices are given below each sentence. Select the best answer to complete the sentence. Then mark the letter (A), (B), (C), or (D) on your answer sheet.

---

101. Chef Daniels impresses customers with ------- sophisticated entrées.

(A) his
(B) him
(C) himself
(D) he

102. Oil production ------- 5 percent from January to February.

(A) drop
(B) to drop
(C) dropping
(D) dropped

103. Ms. Ito has ------- suggestions to resolve the computer problems.

(A) help
(B) helper
(C) helped
(D) helpful

104. The Vidorn Hotel ------- to construct a fountain in the front entryway.

(A) matches
(B) plans
(C) tells
(D) praises

105. The schedule of events for the music ------- will be posted on Friday.

(A) festival
(B) situation
(C) instrument
(D) issue

106. When processing a medical leave request, the attending physician must fill out a form -------.

(A) completes
(B) completed
(C) completely
(D) completeness

107. Many fashion stylists ------- their online portfolios on a regular basis.

(A) dress
(B) invite
(C) range
(D) update

108. All flights were delayed three hours because of a heavy blanket of -------.

(A) fog
(B) fogger
(C) foggy
(D) fogged

109. The Northwick Orchestra will perform later this month ------- Reverbury Hall.

(A) at
(B) up
(C) on
(D) of

110. Only staff ------- based in the Toronto office may reserve the conference room.

(A) possibly
(B) currently
(C) immediately
(D) exactly

111. ------- of the employees have placed their order for a new standing desk.

(A) Any
(B) Several
(C) Another
(D) Either

112. Betsy Riley will seek support from ------- volunteers for our revised museum tours.

(A) former
(B) following
(C) entire
(D) gradual

113. Casorama customers receive store ------- instead of a cash refund upon returning an item.

(A) acceptance
(B) training
(C) preference
(D) credit

114. Our factory in Mannheim was upgraded last year, but the loading dock ------- needs work.

(A) such
(B) very
(C) still
(D) even

115. The recently ------- mayor said she plans to address the town's traffic problems soon.

(A) electing
(B) election
(C) elected
(D) elects

116. Mr. Kim's research reveals that types of hay differ ------- in their nutritional content.

(A) significant
(B) signify
(C) significance
(D) significantly

117. Let us extend our warmest welcome ------- Mr. Lam Keong Wu, our new vice president of marketing.

(A) to
(B) under
(C) against
(D) in

118. The latest polling shows increased public ------- for the stadium renovation project.

(A) approve
(B) approval
(C) approving
(D) approvingly

119. Oshka Landscape Supply revenue is highly ------- on seasonal sales.

(A) extensive
(B) dependent
(C) accessible
(D) insightful

120. Tourism in Cork has slowed in recent weeks ------- the unseasonably cold weather.

(A) as long as
(B) in case of
(C) because of
(D) except for

GO ON TO THE NEXT PAGE

TEST 6

121. The Aznet Foundation is offering three $5,000 grants to entrepreneurs with the most ------- business ideas.

(A) imagine
(B) imagining
(C) imaginative
(D) imagination

122. Based on her ------- performance, Ms. Soares is likely to do quite well in the 50-meter race.

(A) neither
(B) past
(C) apart
(D) twice

123. The manual provides a basic ------- of the R25100 camera's primary features.

(A) overview
(B) adviser
(C) challenge
(D) instance

124. Be sure to ------- the wireless Internet option on your company mobile phone to avoid additional data fees.

(A) return
(B) pull
(C) enable
(D) inflate

125. The CEO of True Home Estates ------- hires agents who have overcome obstacles in their lives.

(A) soon
(B) most
(C) enough
(D) always

126. To receive payment, vendors must submit an invoice online ------- twenty business days of finishing a project.

(A) whether
(B) whose
(C) within
(D) while

127. ------- opening a bakery, Mr. Laxalt had worked in the food industry for fifteen years.

(A) Prior to
(B) Although
(C) Then
(D) If

128. Investors' initial fears were calmed by the ------- sales report issued this week.

(A) remote
(B) attentive
(C) reassuring
(D) restful

129. One distinctive aspect of the painter Chapin Kurek's portrait style is her almost comic ------- of facial features.

(A) exaggerate
(B) exaggerated
(C) exaggeratedly
(D) exaggeration

130. Ramirez Instruments ------- high-quality acoustic guitars for over a century.

(A) to be designed
(B) has been designing
(C) was designed
(D) is designing

PART 6

Directions: Read the texts that follow. A word, phrase, or sentence is missing in parts of each text. Four answer choices for each question are given below the text. Select the best answer to complete the text. Then mark the letter (A), (B), (C), or (D) on your answer sheet.

Questions 131-134 refer to the following letter.

9 October

Eva Archer, Owner
Archer Café
40 Thorpe Street
Port Fairy VIC 3284

Dear Ms. Archer:

An inspection of your restaurant was conducted on 16 September by ------- of the Department of
                                                                                                131.
Health and Safety. ------- . The purpose of the inspection was to confirm that your business is in
                    132.
compliance with all local regulations and that all ------- permits are up-to-date. The Department
                                                   133.
has determined that all regulations are being followed ------- . Therefore, no further action is
                                                        134.
required on your part.

Sincerely,

Oliver Wu
Department of Health and Safety

---

131. (A) represents
   (B) representative
   (C) representatives
   (D) representations

132. (A) Such visits are conducted once a year.
   (B) The restaurant will be closed for inspection.
   (C) Regulations are posted on our Web site.
   (D) The department opens at 9:00 A.M.

133. (A) meaningful
   (B) fortunate
   (C) persistent
   (D) necessary

134. (A) potentially
   (B) satisfactorily
   (C) inconsistently
   (D) temporarily

GO ON TO THE NEXT PAGE

Questions 135-138 refer to the following e-mail.

To: Certain Boutique <info@certainboutique.co.uk>
From: Premium Thai Candles <orders@prethaican.com>
Date: October 28
Subject: Order status

Dear Customer,

We are delighted ------- you as a customer of Premium Thai Candles. Your wholesale order for 40
                    135.

boxes of candles is being processed. ------- .
                                      136.

Most of your order is currently in stock and will arrive in the United Kingdom within ten days.

------- , please be advised that the rose-scented candles are on back order. They will be available
137.

three weeks from now, and we will ship them as soon as possible.

We sincerely hope that you are happy with your ------- order as a new customer of Premium Thai
                                                138.

Candles.

Best,

Samaraya Sharma

135. (A) welcome
     (B) welcomed
     (C) will welcome
     (D) to welcome

136. (A) Save now on this limited-time offer.
     (B) Thank you for the purchase.
     (C) We have other boxes, too.
     (D) Our Web site is now available.

137. (A) However
     (B) Given that
     (C) As you can imagine
     (D) At that point

138. (A) proper
     (B) usual
     (C) initial
     (D) rapid

Questions 139-142 refer to the following article.

GREENWAY (December 15)—The country's employment rose by over 40,000 jobs during

October and November, ------- government statistics just released. The biggest increase was in
            139.

the retail sector, with 9,000 new jobs created. The service sector came in ------- in overall activity
                                                                      140.

with 8,400 added jobs. Professional and business services gained jobs as well. Health services

and education each saw strong gains with 4,200 jobs. ------- . By company size, medium-sized
                                                    141.

businesses of 50 to 499 employees hired the most workers. Large businesses of 500 or more

employees hired 12,000 workers. "The job market remains robust, and we ------- it to continue,"
                                                                  142.

said economist Keisha Hou.

139. (A) because
     (B) whereas
     (C) according to
     (D) instead of

140. (A) last
     (B) second
     (C) primary
     (D) best

141. (A) Utilities stocks rose about 5 percent on
         average.
     (B) However, a new car manufacturing
         plant will open next month.
     (C) The only sector with zero growth was
         agriculture.
     (D) College enrollment increased by only 4
         percent.

142. (A) expect
     (B) expecting
     (C) expected
     (D) expectant

GO ON TO THE NEXT PAGE

Questions 143-146 refer to the following notice.

Loffler Mobile Banking

In the coming weeks, Loffler Bank will be making upgrades to its mobile application to provide a more secure and user-friendly experience. Customers will now be able to view all their Loffler accounts simultaneously and enjoy ------- security through a fingerprint identification scan. ------- ,
143.   144.
users may now customize their online dashboard to track their expenses and budgets.

Changes can prove to be challenging for individuals, particularly in light of rapid technological advancement. ------- . Therefore, should you ever need assistance ------- any of the features of
145.   146.
our app, call us at 555-0133 or visit us online at www.lofflerbank.com/faq.

---

143. (A) enhance
     (B) enhanced
     (C) enhancing
     (D) enhancement

144. (A) Additionally
     (B) Consequently
     (C) Ultimately
     (D) Conversely

145. (A) The new security measures aim to fix
         this problem.
     (B) We will be monitoring this development
         closely.
     (C) Our team members are well aware of
         this fact.
     (D) We sincerely apologize for this
         mistake.

146. (A) over
     (B) for
     (C) by
     (D) with

Directions: In this part you will read a selection of texts, such as magazine and newspaper articles, e-mails, and instant messages. Each text or set of texts is followed by several questions. Select the best answer for each question and mark the letter (A), (B), (C), or (D) on your answer sheet.

Questions 147-148 refer to the following advertisement.

Kendricks Appliances Sale
March 5 and 6

This event is our way of saying thank you to our friends and neighbors for welcoming our new business to the South Waterfront neighborhood one year ago. Members of the community who live east of Broad Avenue and west of Riverside Avenue are invited to stop in and claim an additional discount on selected merchandise this weekend. Just remember to bring proof of residency.

147. What is being advertised?

(A) The recent relocation of a business
(B) The grand opening of a branch store
(C) A special promotion for local residents
(D) The introduction of new product brands

148. What is indicated about Kendricks Appliances?

(A) It has been in business for one year.
(B) It has a store on Broad Avenue.
(C) Its delivery service is limited to South Waterfront.
(D) Its hours are extended on the weekend.

GO ON TO THE NEXT PAGE

MEMO

To: All Eastland Regional Hospital staff
From: Patrick Menzales
Date: February 1
Subject: Referrals

Eastland Regional Hospital is planning to hire more registered nurses, x-ray technicians, and cafeteria and housekeeping staff. We will be holding a hiring and information event on Wednesday, February 27, from 2 P.M. to 5 P.M. in the Winkler Auditorium. If you have friends or family interested in working here, this is a great opportunity for them to find out about open positions. There is no fee for entry. It is not necessary to make an appointment.

As a valued employee, you will receive a bonus if you refer a candidate who is hired and whose employment lasts at least three months. Ask the candidate to include your name on the application in the space labeled "referred by." The bonus will be added to your paycheck.

Please contact me if you have any questions.

149. What is indicated about the hiring and information event?

(A) It will be held in the cafeteria.
(B) An admission fee will be charged.
(C) It will take place in the afternoon.
(D) Attendees will be asked to register in advance.

150. What does Mr. Menzales encourage employees to do?

(A) Volunteer to lead a project
(B) Refer applicants for employment
(C) Earn a bonus by working overtime
(D) Apply for a better-paying position

Meeting of the Chelmsbury Civic Association
Where: Alvar Madsen Community Center, 4141 Hoover Road
When: Tuesday, June 14, 7:00 P.M.–8:30 P.M.

Agenda
- Introduce new neighbors
- Update on road construction
- Election of vice president
- Refreshments

Please note:
We are currently collecting dues for the year. The dues are $25.
If you have not yet paid your dues, please do so. You may pay at
the meeting, or you may send your payment to Bob Robsen at
595 Shelton Drive.

We hope to see you at the meeting!

Susan Wolfe, President, Chelmsbury Civic Association
784 Harmony Drive

151. What is stated about the upcoming
meeting?

(A) It will be held on Harmony Drive.
(B) It will include voting for an office.
(C) It will be led by Mr. Robsen.
(D) It will have a speaker from the local
community center.

152. What is true about Mr. Robsen?

(A) He is the vice president of the
association.
(B) He forgot to pay his membership fee.
(C) He provides refreshments at meetings.
(D) He collects association members' dues.

Questions 153-154 refer to the following text-message chain.

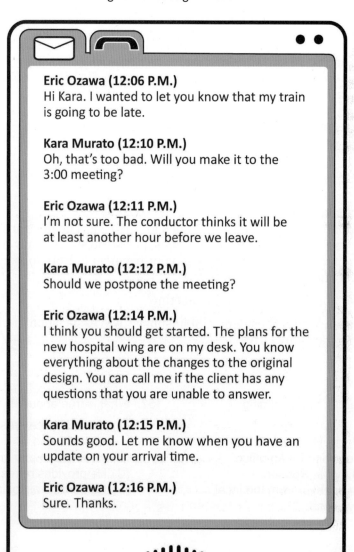

Eric Ozawa (12:06 P.M.)
Hi Kara. I wanted to let you know that my train is going to be late.

Kara Murato (12:10 P.M.)
Oh, that's too bad. Will you make it to the 3:00 meeting?

Eric Ozawa (12:11 P.M.)
I'm not sure. The conductor thinks it will be at least another hour before we leave.

Kara Murato (12:12 P.M.)
Should we postpone the meeting?

Eric Ozawa (12:14 P.M.)
I think you should get started. The plans for the new hospital wing are on my desk. You know everything about the changes to the original design. You can call me if the client has any questions that you are unable to answer.

Kara Murato (12:15 P.M.)
Sounds good. Let me know when you have an update on your arrival time.

Eric Ozawa (12:16 P.M.)
Sure. Thanks.

153. Why does Mr. Ozawa contact Ms. Murato?

(A) To introduce her to a new client
(B) To inform her of a delay
(C) To ask her to book a train ticket
(D) To thank her for changing a project's deadline

154. At 12:15 P.M., what does Ms. Murato most likely mean when she writes, "Sounds good"?

(A) She will contact Mr. Ozawa if she has questions.
(B) She will attend a meeting by phone.
(C) She will drive Mr. Ozawa to the station.
(D) She will reschedule a consultation.

Questions 155-157 refer to the following e-mail.

```
┌─────────────────────────────────────────────────────────────────┐
│                           *E-mail*                                │
├─────────────────────────────────────────────────────────────────┤
│  From:      noreply@vacationsiteseer.com                          │
│  To:        vneuman@gzetmail.com                                  │
│  Date:      July 16, 2:52 P.M.                                    │
│  Subject:   Your upcoming trip                                    │
├─────────────────────────────────────────────────────────────────┤
│  Mr. Neuman:                                                      │
│                                                                   │
│  Your trip to Milan is only a week away. — [1] —. Your room at    │
│  the Classico Hotel has been confirmed. Check-in is on July 23    │
│  at 2 P.M., and checkout is on July 28 at 11 A.M. There is no     │
│  need to pay now, as payment is not required until you have       │
│  checked out. — [2] —.                                            │
│                                                                   │
│  We urge you to plan ahead regarding car rentals. As a Vacation   │
│  Siteseer customer, you are entitled to a discount of 20% if you  │
│  book your car now. Our car rental partners are offering this     │
│  special deal only until July 20, so do not wait. — [3] —.        │
│                                                                   │
│  Thank you for choosing Vacation Siteseer to book your stay in    │
│  Milan. — [4] —.                                                  │
│                                                                   │
│  Enjoy your journey!                                              │
│                                                                   │
│  Vacation Siteseer Team                                           │
└─────────────────────────────────────────────────────────────────┘
```

155. When will Mr. Neuman begin his stay in Milan?

(A) On July 16
(B) On July 20
(C) On July 23
(D) On July 28

156. What offer is included in the e-mail?

(A) A car rental discount
(B) Late checkout times
(C) A hotel room upgrade
(D) Free sightseeing tours

157. In which of the positions marked [1], [2], [3], and [4] does the following sentence best belong?

"Explore your options on our Web site and make a reservation today."

(A) [1]
(B) [2]
(C) [3]
(D) [4]

GO ON TO THE NEXT PAGE

Craverton Returns to Business as Usual
—Brianna Wible, Staff Reporter

A power outage yesterday caused a number of businesses and area attractions in downtown Craverton to close. The cause of the outage is still unknown, but the early morning's stormy weather most likely played a part. — [1] —.

Sung Min Nam, who was leading a tour of some of the historic sites downtown, changed his itinerary. "Fortunately, I know the area well," Mr. Nam said. "I led the group back to the bus, and we headed to a different part of the city to discover alternative sites, such as Grantwood Park and Holtrop Tower." — [2] —.

For the Craverton Art Museum, the outage did not make a difference in earnings because its galleries are closed to the public on Tuesdays. — [3] —. Craverton University canceled its classes, but generators powered residence halls and cafeterias. Power was restored to most area businesses by late yesterday afternoon. — [4] —. And today Craverton returned to business as usual.

158. What is the main topic of the article?

(A) Reasons to move to Craverton
(B) An unexpected situation in Craverton
(C) Reliable weather forecasting sources
(D) Possible sites for a tourist attraction

159. Who most likely is Mr. Nam?

(A) A reporter
(B) A professor
(C) An art historian
(D) A tour guide

160. What does the article mention about the Craverton Art Museum?

(A) It did not lose money yesterday.
(B) It is located near downtown Craverton.
(C) It is open to visitors on Tuesdays.
(D) It will be starting a series of art classes.

161. In which of the positions marked [1], [2], [3], and [4] does the following sentence best belong?

"However, staff members did get the day off."

(A) [1]
(B) [2]
(C) [3]
(D) [4]

Questions 162-165 refer to the following text-message chain.

Isabelle Porter (8:15 A.M.): Hi. Our new intern, Mila Erben, arrives tomorrow. Do you have any tasks for Mila to start on?

Omar Shirani (8:16 A.M.): I'm really sorry. I was out of the office last week at the JNTD Convention. Can I get back to you later today?

Rico Alvarez (8:16 A.M.): I don't have anything for Mila right now.

Isabelle Porter (8:17 A.M.): I'm confused. Your department manager mentioned that your team would greatly benefit from having an intern. Can you work together to find something for her to do?

Omar Shirani (8:17 A.M.): Can you remind us what she's studying at the university?

Isabelle Porter (8:18 A.M.): Accounting. Her résumé says she'd like to become an auditor.

Rico Alvarez (8:19 A.M.): Well, I might have a few tasks, although they may be a bit dull.

Isabelle Porter (8:20 A.M.): That will do. And I might have some documents for her to copy. That ought to be enough for Mila's first week. But I'd appreciate it if you could meet with your team by Thursday and organize additional tasks for Mila for next week.

162. What is suggested about Ms. Erben?

(A) She is an accountant.
(B) She is a department manager.
(C) She is a convention planner.
(D) She is a student.

163. What did Mr. Shirani do last week?

(A) Attend a convention
(B) Work at a branch office
(C) Take a vacation
(D) Start a new job

164. At 8:20 A.M., what does Ms. Porter most likely mean when she writes, "That will do"?

(A) She will complete a project by herself.
(B) She thinks the work will take two weeks to do.
(C) She agrees with the idea Mr. Alvarez proposed.
(D) She will give Mr. Shirani more information later.

165. What does Ms. Porter ask the writers to do before Thursday?

(A) Hire an intern
(B) Copy documents
(C) Send her an e-mail
(D) Plan a set of tasks

GO ON TO THE NEXT PAGE

```
========================== *E-mail* ==========================

From:       Vera Fernandez

To:         Carla Rosa

Sent:       June 07, 12:47 P.M.

Subject:    Initiatives for distance learning
```

Dear Ms. Rosa,

I am contacting you on behalf of the Dolina Foundation. Our mission is to promote the use of distance-learning platforms in rural areas and communities that are isolated geographically. We do so through a network of partners in the technology industry. We would be honored to have your company join our network.

At 2:00 P.M. on June 25, Dolina is sponsoring a presentation entitled "Distance Learning in Rural Libraries." The presentation will be given online as a webinar, using some of the technologies our partners have developed. Jay Ralston, the foundation's director of systems integration, will describe technologies being used to support academic and vocational education programs. In addition, five librarians will discuss how they offer a variety of education programs in their regions using technologies developed and delivered by our business partners. To register for the webinar, and to learn more about our foundation's projects, visit our Web site at www.dolinafoundation.org.

Feel free to contact me if you have any questions. We hope that you will consider our invitation.

With kind regards,

Vera Fernandez, Outreach Coordinator

166. What does the Dolina Foundation do?

(A) Sell software to schools
(B) Print textbooks used in schools
(C) Use technology to support learning
(D) Build libraries in large cities

167. What is Ms. Rosa asked to do?

(A) Approve a grant
(B) Participate in a webinar
(C) Apply for a job opening
(D) Visit some libraries

168. Who most likely is Ms. Fernandez?

(A) A student in a foundation program
(B) An executive at a technology firm
(C) A researcher at a rural library
(D) An employee of the foundation

Questions 169-171 refer to the following letter.

29 July

Shari MacCauley
103 Easton Lane
Tomintoul, Ballindalloch AB37 9EX

Dear Ms. MacCauley,

It was a privilege to stay in your home during the week of 22 July as part of the Scottish Connections home exchange program.

The location was the perfect setting for our family gathering. My daughter and son-in-law relished the peace and quiet of the village, while their children enjoyed playing in the wide-open space behind your home. And my husband was quite pleased with the large-screen television set in the living room.

It was very thoughtful of you to provide so many extra blankets. We did not expect it to be so cold at night in July.

As I said in the note I left on your dining room table on 25 July, the day of my wedding anniversary party, the lid of your food processor cracked as we were preparing our meal. We ordered a replacement lid that same day, which should be delivered to your home soon, assuming it hasn't been already. I sincerely apologize for the mishap.

I hope that you and your friends enjoyed our apartment here in Aberdeen just as much as we enjoyed your mountain home. If so, we hope you will be willing to exchange homes with us again in the future.

Sincerely,

Clara Brinwall

Clara Brinwall

169. What is a purpose of the letter?

(A) To explain a family tradition
(B) To confirm that a package was received
(C) To express appreciation for a house
(D) To outline the benefits of taking vacation

170. What happened on July 25 ?

(A) An item was damaged.
(B) An order was delivered.
(C) An event was catered.
(D) A wedding was held.

171. What is suggested about Ms. MacCauley?

(A) She heads the home exchange program.
(B) She lives in a mountainous area.
(C) She is a relative of Ms. Brinwall's.
(D) She plans to move to Aberdeen.

GO ON TO THE NEXT PAGE

Questions 172-175 refer to the following e-mail.

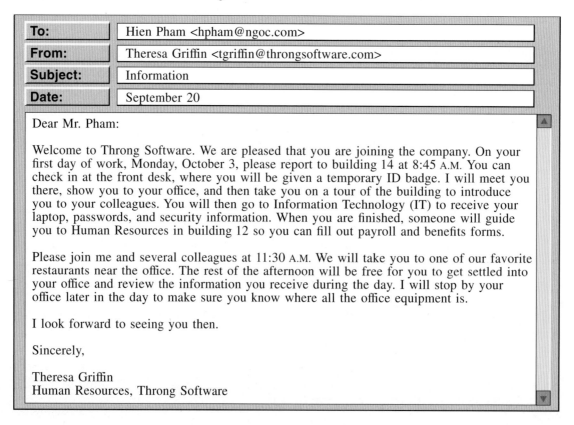

To: Hien Pham <hpham@ngoc.com>

From: Theresa Griffin <tgriffin@throngsoftware.com>

Subject: Information

Date: September 20

Dear Mr. Pham:

Welcome to Throng Software. We are pleased that you are joining the company. On your first day of work, Monday, October 3, please report to building 14 at 8:45 A.M. You can check in at the front desk, where you will be given a temporary ID badge. I will meet you there, show you to your office, and then take you on a tour of the building to introduce you to your colleagues. You will then go to Information Technology (IT) to receive your laptop, passwords, and security information. When you are finished, someone will guide you to Human Resources in building 12 so you can fill out payroll and benefits forms.

Please join me and several colleagues at 11:30 A.M. We will take you to one of our favorite restaurants near the office. The rest of the afternoon will be free for you to get settled into your office and review the information you receive during the day. I will stop by your office later in the day to make sure you know where all the office equipment is.

I look forward to seeing you then.

Sincerely,

Theresa Griffin
Human Resources, Throng Software

172. What will happen on October 3 ?

(A) New laptops will be issued to employees.
(B) A luncheon will be held in the cafeteria.
(C) Tours of a renovated building will be given.
(D) A new employee will start work.

173. Where will Mr. Pham complete some documents?

(A) In building 12
(B) In building 14
(C) In his office
(D) In the IT office

174. The word "rest" in paragraph 2, line 2, is closest in meaning to

(A) majority
(B) remainder
(C) break
(D) purpose

175. What will Mr. Pham do in the afternoon?

(A) Test some equipment
(B) Visit Ms. Griffin's office
(C) Review some project proposals
(D) Learn where equipment is located

GO ON TO THE NEXT PAGE

Calbo Cuts

★★★☆☆

My visit to Calbo Cuts as a first-time customer was disappointing. When I arrived, the sign on the door said "Walk-ins welcome," but the receptionist bluntly told me that I would need to wait about an hour for my haircut, even though only one other customer was in the shop and three stylists were there. The quality of the work was fine; the haircut was fairly priced at just $15, and I was happy with my standard men's cut. The stylist, though, cut my hair without saying a word. I understand that not everyone likes to make small talk, but I found my stylist's total silence to be rude. When she finished my haircut, she removed the haircutting cape without even offering to blow-dry my hair.

– Martin Silver, Bishopville

Calbo Cuts · 678 Seventh Street · Lamar, South Carolina · 29069

Martin Silver
51 Oak Street
Bishopville, South Carolina 29010

Dear Mr. Silver,

Thank you for taking the time to leave us a review. We always try to provide the best service available. If you feel that any of our staff were unaccommodating or unprofessional, then I would like to hear more details regarding your complaint. Feel free to call me directly at 803-555-0110.

At Calbo Cuts, we are serious about earning your continued business. I would be happy to schedule an appointment for you for a haircut and blow-dry with Marissa Lopez, as I believe she can provide you with the haircut experience you are looking for. In addition, on your next visit to Calbo Cuts, we would like to offer you a complimentary bottle of our all-natural shampoo, one of our best-selling products. We hope you will come back to Calbo Cuts in the future whenever you need a trim.

Best regards,

Jenna Makowski

Jenna Makowski
Owner, Calbo Cuts

176. According to the review, what is suggested about Mr. Silver?

(A) He was late for an appointment.
(B) He did not ask for a standard haircut.
(C) He has been to Calbo Cuts only once.
(D) He did not see a sign on the door.

177. What aspect of his experience at Calbo Cuts disappointed Mr. Silver?

(A) The price
(B) The location
(C) The shop hours
(D) The customer service

178. Why did Ms. Makowski suggest that Mr. Silver contact her?

(A) To change an appointment
(B) To provide additional details
(C) To arrange a personal meeting
(D) To update contact information

179. What is suggested about Ms. Lopez?

(A) She takes a full hour to give a haircut.
(B) She does not accept walk-in customers.
(C) She is now the most popular stylist.
(D) She enjoys talking to customers.

180. What will Mr. Silver receive for free on his next visit to Calbo Cuts?

(A) A bottle of shampoo
(B) A haircut
(C) A blow-dry
(D) A new product

GO ON TO THE NEXT PAGE

Business Happenings

By Harriet Mellors

LONDON (1 April)—It is often hard for managers or team leaders to learn the best way to give feedback to employees and colleagues. Samia Bishara's new book, *Facts on Feedback* (Fox Mill Press), offers advice on this subject. Ms. Bishara is an expert consultant on company management problems and solutions. She advises managers to give facts and reactions, rather than advice and criticism.

Ms. Bishara will be speaking at Stonecliff Bookstore on Monday, 6 April at 2:00 P.M. For more details, visit www.stonecliff.co.uk.

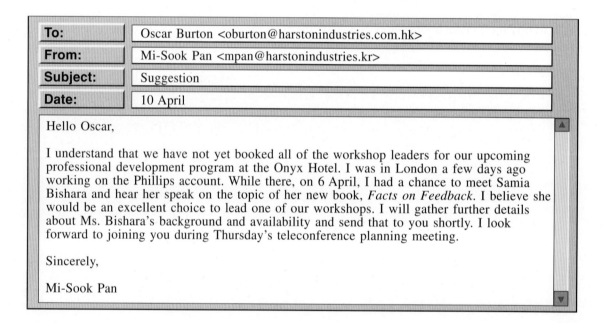

To:	Oscar Burton <oburton@harstonindustries.com.hk>
From:	Mi-Sook Pan <mpan@harstonindustries.kr>
Subject:	Suggestion
Date:	10 April

Hello Oscar,

I understand that we have not yet booked all of the workshop leaders for our upcoming professional development program at the Onyx Hotel. I was in London a few days ago working on the Phillips account. While there, on 6 April, I had a chance to meet Samia Bishara and hear her speak on the topic of her new book, *Facts on Feedback*. I believe she would be an excellent choice to lead one of our workshops. I will gather further details about Ms. Bishara's background and availability and send that to you shortly. I look forward to joining you during Thursday's teleconference planning meeting.

Sincerely,

Mi-Sook Pan

181. In the article, the word "hard" in paragraph 1, line 1, is closest in meaning to

(A) durable
(B) difficult
(C) solid
(D) true

182. What is a purpose of the article?

(A) To announce an upcoming event
(B) To report on a new book publisher
(C) To advertise a consultant's services
(D) To promote a new bookstore

183. What is suggested about Ms. Pan in the e-mail?

(A) She has returned from a business trip.
(B) She is interested in writing a book.
(C) She is not able to attend an event.
(D) She plans to move to London.

184. Where did Ms. Pan most likely meet Ms. Bishara?

(A) At a hotel
(B) At a planning meeting
(C) At an accounting office
(D) At a bookstore

185. What does Ms. Pan plan to give to Mr. Burton?

(A) A budget proposal
(B) A conference program
(C) Some information about a business consultant
(D) Documents related to the Phillips account

GO ON TO THE NEXT PAGE

Questions 186-190 refer to the following e-mails and Web page.

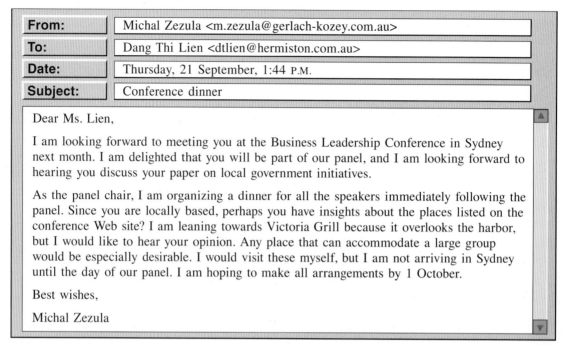

From:	Michal Zezula <m.zezula@gerlach-kozey.com.au>
To:	Dang Thi Lien <dtlien@hermiston.com.au>
Date:	Thursday, 21 September, 1:44 P.M.
Subject:	Conference dinner

Dear Ms. Lien,

I am looking forward to meeting you at the Business Leadership Conference in Sydney next month. I am delighted that you will be part of our panel, and I am looking forward to hearing you discuss your paper on local government initiatives.

As the panel chair, I am organizing a dinner for all the speakers immediately following the panel. Since you are locally based, perhaps you have insights about the places listed on the conference Web site? I am leaning towards Victoria Grill because it overlooks the harbor, but I would like to hear your opinion. Any place that can accommodate a large group would be especially desirable. I would visit these myself, but I am not arriving in Sydney until the day of our panel. I am hoping to make all arrangements by 1 October.

Best wishes,

Michal Zezula

http://www.blcsydney.com.au/thingstodo

| Schedule | Accommodations | Map | Contacts | **Things to Do** |

Restaurant Recommendations

All of these restaurants are located within walking distance of the conference site. Given the anticipated activity, reservations are recommended, especially for large groups.

- **Bombay Palace:** Contemporary Indian cuisine. Large menu with several vegetarian options. Price: Moderate.

- **Victoria Grill:** Innovative Australian cooking. Located on the top floor of the Hesiod Building, overlooking the spectacular Sydney Harbor. Price: Expensive.

- **Amir's Kitchen:** Lebanese cuisine with a modern flair. Private rooms available; ideal for parties and group events. Price: Inexpensive.

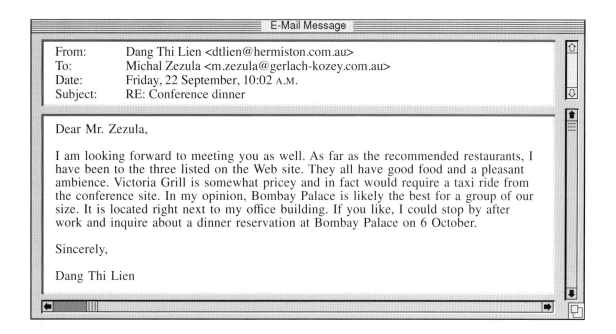

From: Dang Thi Lien <dtlien@hermiston.com.au>
To: Michal Zezula <m.zezula@gerlach-kozey.com.au>
Date: Friday, 22 September, 10:02 A.M.
Subject: RE: Conference dinner

Dear Mr. Zezula,

I am looking forward to meeting you as well. As far as the recommended restaurants, I have been to the three listed on the Web site. They all have good food and a pleasant ambience. Victoria Grill is somewhat pricey and in fact would require a taxi ride from the conference site. In my opinion, Bombay Palace is likely the best for a group of our size. It is located right next to my office building. If you like, I could stop by after work and inquire about a dinner reservation at Bombay Palace on 6 October.

Sincerely,

Dang Thi Lien

186. What is the purpose of the first e-mail?

(A) To request advice about an event
(B) To give information about tourist sites
(C) To propose a topic for a paper
(D) To invite business leaders to a conference

187. What is Ms. Lien's role in the conference?

(A) Chairing a panel
(B) Giving a presentation
(C) Contacting catering companies
(D) Staffing an information desk

188. Why is Mr. Zezula interested in dining at Victoria Grill?

(A) It offers vegetarian options.
(B) It offers private rooms.
(C) It is open relatively late.
(D) It has an attractive view.

189. When is the panel scheduled to take place?

(A) On September 21
(B) On September 22
(C) On October 1
(D) On October 6

190. What information on the conference Web site does Ms. Lien think is inaccurate?

(A) Bombay Palace's ability to host large groups
(B) Victoria Grill's distance from the conference site
(C) The price of food at the restaurants
(D) The need to make dinner reservations

GO ON TO THE NEXT PAGE

Questions 191-195 refer to the following e-mail, product information, and invoice.

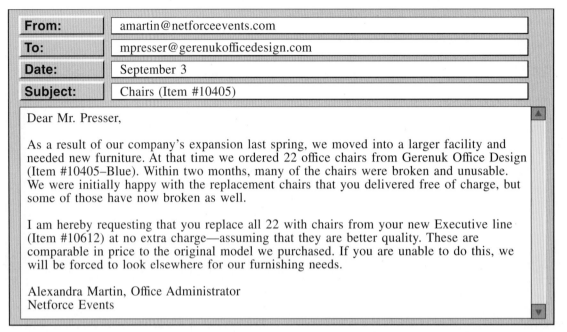

From:	amartin@netforceevents.com
To:	mpresser@gerenukofficedesign.com
Date:	September 3
Subject:	Chairs (Item #10405)

Dear Mr. Presser,

As a result of our company's expansion last spring, we moved into a larger facility and needed new furniture. At that time we ordered 22 office chairs from Gerenuk Office Design (Item #10405–Blue). Within two months, many of the chairs were broken and unusable. We were initially happy with the replacement chairs that you delivered free of charge, but some of those have now broken as well.

I am hereby requesting that you replace all 22 with chairs from your new Executive line (Item #10612) at no extra charge—assuming that they are better quality. These are comparable in price to the original model we purchased. If you are unable to do this, we will be forced to look elsewhere for our furnishing needs.

Alexandra Martin, Office Administrator
Netforce Events

http://www.hansons-office.com/ergonomic-task-chair

HANSON'S: YOUR ONE-STOP SHOP FOR OFFICE SUPPLIES

| Home | **Products** | Customer Help | About Us |

Ergonomic Task Chair
The Ergonomic Task Chair is our best-selling swivel model. It is specially designed to promote good posture and avoid discomfort, and therefore it is perfect for those long workdays at the office. Best of all, it is built to last and comes with a lifetime warranty. The model is available in four attractive colors.
$159 per unit

- Black, Item Code 429BL
- Blue, Item Code 469BB
- Green, Item Code 490GN
- Red, Item Code 459RD

HANSON'S: YOUR ONE-STOP SHOP FOR OFFICE SUPPLIES

INVOICE

Client: Netforce Events
Address: 342 Collard Boulevard, Hampton, ME
Date: September 10

Item	Quantity	Unit Price	Total
Ergonomic Task Chair, Item 490GN	22	$159.00	$3,498.00

Subtotal	**$3,498.00**
Discount for first-time customers	−$159.00
Total	**$3,339.00**

Please contact customerhelp@hansons-office.com if you have any questions.

---

191. What is true about Netforce Events?

(A) It recently moved into another building.
(B) It manufactures furniture.
(C) It has just opened a new store.
(D) It was founded last spring.

192. What is the purpose of the e-mail?

(A) To complain about available chair colors
(B) To request that some chairs be repaired
(C) To place an office stationery order
(D) To ask that some furniture be replaced

193. What is stated about the Ergonomic Task Chair?

(A) It is reasonably priced.
(B) It is a popular model.
(C) It comes with a limited warranty.
(D) It is made from a washable fabric.

194. What is implied about Gerenuk Office Design?

(A) It offers a discount for first-time customers.
(B) It did not agree to Ms. Martin's request.
(C) Its Executive chairs sell out quickly.
(D) It is under new management.

195. What color are the chairs Netforce Events ordered from Hanson's?

(A) Black
(B) Blue
(C) Green
(D) Red

GO ON TO THE NEXT PAGE

KLOOF PHOTOGRAPHY EVENT

On 21 November, all Kloof employees are invited to a celebration to commemorate our first five years in business. Please attend our company picnic featuring a traditional braai as well as live music and competitive games. The company will provide meats fresh off the grill prepared in the traditional braai style. Beverages will also be provided. In exchange, we ask that attendees either plan to bring a side dish to share or volunteer to join the setup crew. To make the event run smoothly, we will need at least two people to help with setup.

Our gathering will convene from 1 to 8 P.M. on the patio of our headquarters building. If you plan to attend, please open the sign-up sheet saved on the company drive and indicate there how you will contribute. Employees are welcome to bring a guest, so long as they indicate their intention to do so. Any questions may be directed to our events coordinator, Noxolo Nwosu, at nnwosu@kloofphoto.sa.

Kloof Photography Sign-Up Sheet

Name	Side dish	Bringing a guest?
Mason Kivundu	sweet corn	No
Clara Singh	potato salad	Yes
Karl Williams	garlic bread	Yes
Said Diallo	jollof rice	Yes
Sekou Lombard		Yes
Patricia Williamson	drinks	Yes

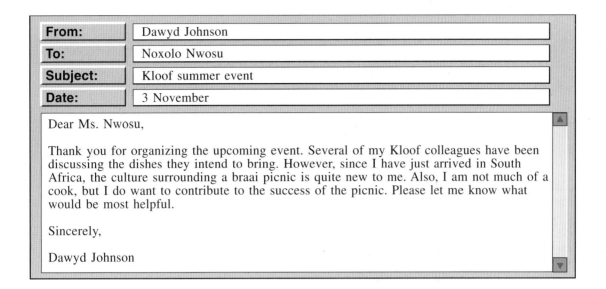

From:	Dawyd Johnson
To:	Noxolo Nwosu
Subject:	Kloof summer event
Date:	3 November

Dear Ms. Nwosu,

Thank you for organizing the upcoming event. Several of my Kloof colleagues have been discussing the dishes they intend to bring. However, since I have just arrived in South Africa, the culture surrounding a braai picnic is quite new to me. Also, I am not much of a cook, but I do want to contribute to the success of the picnic. Please let me know what would be most helpful.

Sincerely,

Dawyd Johnson

196. What is the reason for the event?

(A) To promote a product
(B) To celebrate a store opening
(C) To welcome a new company president
(D) To mark a company anniversary

197. According to the notice, where will the event be held?

(A) At a park
(B) Near an office building
(C) At a retail store
(D) On a sports field

198. Based on the information in the chart, what mistake did Ms. Williamson make?

(A) She did not sign up to bring anything.
(B) She did not confirm her intention to attend.
(C) She plans to bring something that the company will provide.
(D) She intends to bring more guests than are permitted.

199. What will Ms. Nwosu most likely encourage Mr. Johnson to do?

(A) Help with setting up
(B) Bring some meat
(C) Assist with grilling
(D) Lead one of the games

200. What does the e-mail suggest about Mr. Johnson?

(A) He is not a beginner photographer.
(B) He enjoys cooking.
(C) He is not from South Africa.
(D) He prefers indoor events.

TEST 6

Stop! This is the end of the test. If you finish before time is called, you may go back to Parts 5, 6, and 7 and check your work.

토익˚ 정기시험
기출문제집

RC

기출 TEST

07

READING TEST

In the Reading test, you will read a variety of texts and answer several different types of reading comprehension questions. The entire Reading test will last 75 minutes. There are three parts, and directions are given for each part. You are encouraged to answer as many questions as possible within the time allowed.

You must mark your answers on the separate answer sheet. Do not write your answers in your test book.

PART 5

Directions: A word or phrase is missing in each of the sentences below. Four answer choices are given below each sentence. Select the best answer to complete the sentence. Then mark the letter (A), (B), (C), or (D) on your answer sheet.

101. Please direct all questions about ------- recent order to the customer care center.

   (A) yours
   (B) your
   (C) yourself
   (D) you

102. Ms. Wu was the ------- of the contest, and she may collect her prize next week.

   (A) partner
   (B) member
   (C) player
   (D) winner

103. For a ------- time, Marco Bank is offering first-time customers a $100 bonus when they open an account.

   (A) limits
   (B) limiting
   (C) limit
   (D) limited

104. A ------- greenhouse donated several potted plants to beautify the lobby of the city hall.

   (A) potential
   (B) local
   (C) main
   (D) future

105. The attached document shows how to report any ------- incurred during business travel.

   (A) expenses
   (B) expensed
   (C) expensively
   (D) expensive

106. Nonmembers may use the gym if they pay a daily admission ------- and sign a guest waiver.

   (A) fee
   (B) income
   (C) salary
   (D) money

107. Sharik Pharmaceuticals will host a company picnic for ------- employees at Hain Park.

   (A) them
   (B) its
   (C) itself
   (D) themselves

108. Call Bowton Chimney for a complete inspection and cleaning ------- winter starts.

   (A) now that
   (B) even though
   (C) before
   (D) since

109. Ikeda Real Estate Group now ------- text messages to update clients about properties of interest.

(A) uses
(B) users
(C) useful
(D) using

110. According to our records, you are ------- for your annual checkup at Dr. Barell's office.

(A) willing
(B) helpful
(C) concerned
(D) overdue

111. The employee help desk will be moved to room 530 ------- the Human Resources offices are being renovated.

(A) opposite
(B) that
(C) while
(D) anywhere

112. Bray Farm Mart is located ------- Elm Road, near its intersection with Wye Lane.

(A) about
(B) inside
(C) beneath
(D) along

113. Our office offers ------- hours to provide our customers with additional flexibility.

(A) extending
(B) extends
(C) extend
(D) extended

114. The Arraneo Group has created an online ------- specifically to encourage sales among young people.

(A) promotion
(B) price
(C) contact
(D) volume

115. Corracar Ltd. is ------- looking for new ways to expand its transportation network.

(A) continued
(B) continuation
(C) continual
(D) continually

116. Employees may bring their lunch to the meeting and enjoy it ------- the presentation.

(A) in case
(B) during
(C) into
(D) although

117. The merchandise at Logan's Clothing requires ------- at the beginning of each season.

(A) reorganize
(B) reorganization
(C) reorganizes
(D) reorganized

118. Interns must complete and return the new hire ------- by their first day of work.

(A) background
(B) management
(C) publication
(D) paperwork

119. Weekday dining at Jake's Downtown Bistro is by reservation only ------- the high volume of customers.

(A) regarding
(B) as
(C) in
(D) due to

120. Should anyone need to ------- with Ms. De Sola, be sure to do so prior to today's meeting.

(A) reflect
(B) arrange
(C) regard
(D) consult

GO ON TO THE NEXT PAGE

121. Mr. Lau looks forward to meeting the ------- students at the Career Day event.

(A) ambitious
(B) ambition
(C) ambitiously
(D) ambitions

122. Please ------- daily spending records, since online balance statements may not reflect recent account activity.

(A) kept
(B) keep
(C) keeps
(D) keeping

123. Mr. Bhatt ------- promotes people within the company, but he recently went outside of the organization to replace the Facilities Director.

(A) later
(B) forgetfully
(C) together
(D) normally

124. The National Health Agency's latest report ------- that recently adopted health-care regulations have been successful.

(A) concludes
(B) concluding
(C) conclusion
(D) to conclude

125. ------- who wants to attend the luncheon next week must tell Ms. Hasegawa by noon tomorrow.

(A) Anyone
(B) Some
(C) Those
(D) Other

126. Once orders are processed by the sales office, they are ------- within 48 hours.

(A) committed
(B) positioned
(C) filled
(D) occurred

127. Profits at Talhee Beverage Co. rose about 4 percent last year, according to new figures ------- by the company.

(A) to release
(B) releasing
(C) released
(D) have released

128. ------- the CEO and the CFO are authorized to sign checks over $10,000.

(A) Each
(B) Either
(C) Both
(D) Whoever

129. There are multiple reasons ------- cost to negotiate a new agreement.

(A) also
(B) besides
(C) indeed
(D) yet

130. Editors at Benchley Press are skilled at reading texts ------- to correct errors and polish the prose.

(A) sensibly
(B) perfectly
(C) tightly
(D) closely

PART 6

Directions: Read the texts that follow. A word, phrase, or sentence is missing in parts of each text. Four answer choices for each question are given below the text. Select the best answer to complete the text. Then mark the letter (A), (B), (C), or (D) on your answer sheet.

Questions 131-134 refer to the following e-mail.

To: All employees <staff@TFF.com>
From: Walter C. Handy <wchandy@TFF.com>
Subject: Sales Incentive Program
Date: 15 November

Dear TFF Sales Team,

I am writing to introduce you to a new, double-incentive program for the fourth quarter of this

year! In addition to our standard cash bonus plan, sales associates will now have the opportunity

------- tickets to concerts, sporting events, and theater performances. This extra incentive is
131.

designed to help make this our greatest sales year ever. ------- .
132.

More ------- will be provided in the next few days. ------- , if you have any questions about this
133.   **134.**

program, contact the Human Resources Department.

To our continued success,

Walter C. Handy, CEO

131. (A) to earn
     (B) earning
     (C) earner
     (D) having earned

132. (A) The fiscal year ends in October.
     (B) I am confident that we can achieve this
         goal.
     (C) Attendance at the event is mandatory.
     (D) TFF is looking to renovate its offices
         next year.

133. (A) supplies
     (B) details
     (C) products
     (D) receipts

134. (A) Similarly
     (B) Therefore
     (C) Above all
     (D) In the meantime

GO ON TO THE NEXT PAGE

Questions 135-138 refer to the following information.

Accountarium: The quarterly magazine for accountants

Call for Submissions

Our fourth and final edition of the year will include a feature on accountants who have made a career shift. The financial service ------- that accountants gain are in demand even by those
135.
seeking to hire for positions outside of finance. ------- , many professional accountants have been
136.
persuaded to take on other roles.

If you have made such a change in careers, we would like to hear about it. In no more than 800 words, describe your background in accounting and explain ------- it is useful in your new
137.
profession. Send this as an attachment to features@accountarium.com. ------- . We regret that
138.
any submissions received after this date cannot be considered.

---

135. (A) industry
     (B) skills
     (C) needs
     (D) fields

136. (A) Nevertheless
     (B) Once again
     (C) In addition
     (D) Consequently

137. (A) what
     (B) whose
     (C) how
     (D) which

138. (A) The deadline for submissions is October 15.
     (B) We hire accountants at all stages of their careers.
     (C) This credential is widely recognized.
     (D) We thank you for your response received today.

For months, Yi Zhang, owner of Zhang Office Supplies, had been searching for a way to increase

------- . Then, by sheer chance, he heard about an approach called Voice of the Customer (VOC).
139.

"When I called Hsing Market Research I was really intrigued as the method was presented to me.

The representative I spoke with convinced me to give ------- a try." Mr. Zhang learned that VOC
140.

uses market research as an aid to designing targeted advertisements. Using the method, he first

determined ------- what potential customers are concerned about and what they want when
141.

shopping for office supplies. Then he used candid quotes from the people who participated in his

market research to create advertisements for his Web site. ------- . "Thanks to VOC," he says,
142.

smiling, "my customer base has expanded like never before."

139. (A) production
(B) capacity
(C) sales
(D) wages

140. (A) anyone
(B) it
(C) mine
(D) those

141. (A) exactly
(B) exact
(C) exacting
(D) exactness

142. (A) He has been in business for eleven years.
(B) He also used them in direct e-mail campaigns.
(C) He also owns a local supermarket.
(D) He plans to move to a smaller building.

TEST 7

Questions 143-146 refer to the following notice.

To help reduce traffic congestion and make parking easier, Newgrange Township will provide free bus rides to and from this year's Newgrange County Fair. ------- will be available from Friday,
143.
June 5, to Sunday, June 7. Planned pickup locations include the Rhinesberg Elementary School on Route 38 and the Newgrange Municipal Building on Main Street.

Buses going to the fair will depart from these locations hourly from 8 A.M. to 5 P.M. Buses -------
144.
the fairgrounds on the half hour, from 8:30 A.M. to 7:30 P.M. Please note that children under the age of 16 must be accompanied by an adult. ------- .
145.

The Newgrange County Fair Committee thanks our generous sponsors for providing buses and ------- this year. We hope you will join us at the Newgrange County Fair!
146.

143. (A) Refreshments
(B) Information
(C) Transportation
(D) Entertainment

144. (A) will leave
(B) have left
(C) leaving
(D) left

145. (A) Thank you for coming to this year's auto show.
(B) There will be an increase in the cost of the service.
(C) We hope you enjoyed your stay at the hotel.
(D) No food or drinks are permitted on the buses.

146. (A) driven
(B) drivers
(C) drivable
(D) drive

PART 7

Directions: In this part you will read a selection of texts, such as magazine and newspaper articles, e-mails, and instant messages. Each text or set of texts is followed by several questions. Select the best answer for each question and mark the letter (A), (B), (C), or (D) on your answer sheet.

Questions 147-148 refer to the following e-mail.

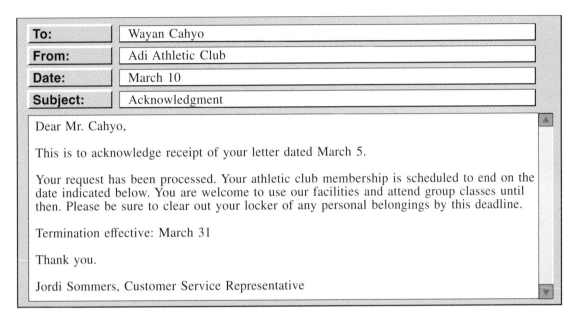

To:	Wayan Cahyo
From:	Adi Athletic Club
Date:	March 10
Subject:	Acknowledgment

Dear Mr. Cahyo,

This is to acknowledge receipt of your letter dated March 5.

Your request has been processed. Your athletic club membership is scheduled to end on the date indicated below. You are welcome to use our facilities and attend group classes until then. Please be sure to clear out your locker of any personal belongings by this deadline.

Termination effective: March 31

Thank you.

Jordi Sommers, Customer Service Representative

147. What is the purpose of the e-mail?

(A) To correct some information
(B) To offer a membership discount
(C) To promote a new group class
(D) To confirm a cancellation

148. What must Mr. Cahyo do by March 31 ?

(A) Mail a check
(B) Empty a locker
(C) Write to an instructor
(D) Call Mr. Sommers

GO ON TO THE NEXT PAGE

Questions 149-150 refer to the following notice.

NOTICE

On Monday, 23 September, Constellation Internet Service will install a new, state-of-the-art system here at Bluestone Tower. Internet service will be down for much of the day. This means that residents will not be able to access the building's wireless network, nor will it be possible for them to contact our management or maintenance staff by e-mail. Those who require access to the Internet between 9:00 A.M. and 5:00 P.M. on 23 September will need to make other arrangements. I apologize for the inconvenience.

Claire Cho
Property Manager, Bluestone Tower

---

149. For whom is the notice intended?

(A) Construction crews
(B) Internet providers
(C) Building residents
(D) Maintenance workers

150. What does the notice suggest will happen at 5:00 P.M. on September 23 ?

(A) A new Web site will be launched.
(B) A new service charge will take effect.
(C) Access to a building will be restricted.
(D) Internet service will be restored.

To:	a.thompson@pepperfam.com
From:	customerservice@dixons_clothing.com
Date:	November 4, 11:31 A.M.
Subject:	Your recent order

Dear Mr. Thompson,

Our records show that your Dixon's Clothing order number 5409281 has been delivered.

Item: Canvas Rain-Resistant Jacket (Men's): $ 85.00
Shipping Fee: $ 4.50
                                      Total: $ 89.50

It's important to us to know that you're happy with your item. Therefore, if you have any questions, comments, or concerns about it, call us at 555-0142, Monday through Friday between 8:00 A.M. and 7:00 P.M., and Saturday and Sunday between 10:00 A.M. and 5:00 P.M. You can also e-mail us at customerservice@dixons_clothing.com. We look forward to serving you again.

Sincerely,

Customer Service Department
Dixon's Clothing

151. What is a purpose of the e-mail?

(A) To notify a customer of a late delivery
(B) To confirm a request for an exchange
(C) To request payment for an order
(D) To tell a customer how to give feedback

152. What is indicated about Dixon's Clothing?

(A) It has several store locations.
(B) It offers free shipping.
(C) Its customer service representatives are available daily.
(D) Its Web site features product reviews from customers.

TEST 7

GO ON TO THE NEXT PAGE

Questions 153-154 refer to the following text-message chain.

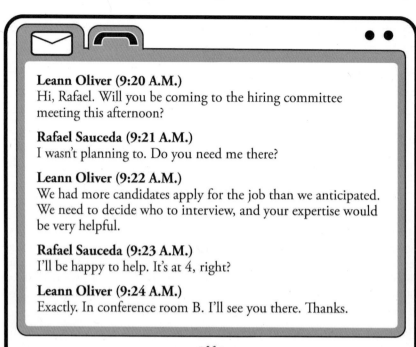

Leann Oliver (9:20 A.M.)
Hi, Rafael. Will you be coming to the hiring committee meeting this afternoon?

Rafael Sauceda (9:21 A.M.)
I wasn't planning to. Do you need me there?

Leann Oliver (9:22 A.M.)
We had more candidates apply for the job than we anticipated. We need to decide who to interview, and your expertise would be very helpful.

Rafael Sauceda (9:23 A.M.)
I'll be happy to help. It's at 4, right?

Leann Oliver (9:24 A.M.)
Exactly. In conference room B. I'll see you there. Thanks.

153. What is the purpose of the meeting mentioned by Ms. Oliver?

(A) To interview a candidate for an open position
(B) To approve a job announcement
(C) To consider applicants for a job
(D) To select members for a hiring committee

154. At 9:24 A.M., what does Ms. Oliver most likely mean when she writes, "Exactly"?

(A) The meeting room is on the fourth floor.
(B) The meeting is scheduled for 4:00 P.M.
(C) Four people will attend the meeting.
(D) The committee will meet four times.

Manufacturer Celebrates Milestone

MINNEAPOLIS (August 13)—Lindgren Machinery, a manufacturer of precision machine parts, recently celebrated the one hundredth anniversary of its founding. The company was started by Jona Lindgren, who began his career as an apprentice at a metal parts firm in Sweden. He eventually immigrated to the United States and settled in the outskirts of the city of Minneapolis. Mr. Lindgren established a modest enterprise that grew, generating most of its revenue from the production of custom machine parts.

Thirty years ago, Lindgren Machinery was purchased by James Wallin. Today, the firm continues as a family-owned and family-directed operation. In recent years, current president and CEO Mary Wallin has gradually assumed the leadership role from her father.

Lindgren Machinery makes parts for airplanes, exercise equipment, and health-care devices. According to Ms. Wallin, the company is planning to expand its facility and add capacity as its product list grows and diversifies.

155. What is the main purpose of the article?

(A) To announce job openings at a company
(B) To tell about the relocation of a company
(C) To summarize the history of a company
(D) To describe successful manufacturing strategies

156. The word "assumed" in paragraph 2, line 6, is closest in meaning to

(A) undertaken
(B) pretended
(C) thought
(D) attempted

157. What is currently true about Lindgren Machinery?

(A) It is training new management.
(B) It has recently moved its headquarters.
(C) It is the largest employer in the city.
(D) It is a family-operated business.

GO ON TO THE NEXT PAGE

Questions 158-160 refer to the following e-mail.

E-mail

From:	Reservations <reservations@panticohotels.com>
To:	Roger Underhill <runderhill@monthpress.com>
Date:	10 February
Subject:	Pantico Lisbon

Dear Mr. Underhill:

Thank you for booking your reservation with the Pantico Hotel Group. We are looking forward to your upcoming stay with us in Lisbon from 8 March through 12 March.

We are proud to offer a range of services, including a 24-hour coffee shop, a fitness center, and a business lounge. There is also a parking area for guests who wish to travel by car. However, the Pantico Lisbon is well situated and is within walking distance to many fine shopping, entertainment, and dining options. We also have convenient access to public transportation, and airport transfers can be booked for a fee.

To learn more about us, please visit our Web site, www.panticohotels.com/lisbon. A calendar with details about upcoming events, both at our hotel and in the surrounding area, can be found there.

If you have any questions or concerns, please feel free to respond directly to this e-mail.

All the best,

Branca Lopes
Pantico Lisbon Hotel

---

158. What is the main purpose of the e-mail?

(A) To request a change to a room reservation
(B) To introduce a new hotel employee
(C) To provide a description of hotel amenities
(D) To obtain feedback from a recent customer

159. What does the hotel offer its guests?

(A) Complimentary airport shuttle service
(B) A parking facility
(C) Meal vouchers for area restaurants
(D) Guided city tours

160. According to the e-mail, what will Mr. Underhill be able to find on a Web site?

(A) Information about some events
(B) Maps of the local area
(C) A list of staff members
(D) A detailed receipt

Questions 161-163 refer to the following letter.

November 23

Matteo Fernandez
5196 Revol St.
Laketon, CA 97999

Dear Mr. Fernandez,

We are writing to notify you that your license as described below will expire at the end of the year. — [1] —.

License Type: Motorcycle

License Number: 297461

Expiration: December 31

State law requires all motor vehicle licenses to be renewed periodically. The fees are $20 for boat and snowmobile licenses, $30 for motorcycle licenses, $40 for car licenses, and $50 for truck licenses. — [2] —. Check our Web site regarding further requirements for truck licenses, as well as fees for other types of vehicle licenses: www.motorvehiclelicense.net.

It is quick and easy to renew online. — [3] —. You can also renew by mail. If you choose this option, please send a copy of this notice along with payment to your local Motor Vehicle License office. — [4] —.

Sincerely,

Betty Tsai

Betty Tsai
Administrator, Motor Vehicle Licenses

161. What is the purpose of the letter?

(A) To explain the reasons for a fee increase
(B) To provide the status of a license
(C) To schedule a meeting in Laketon
(D) To update a user's identification number

162. According to the letter, how much does Mr. Fernandez need to pay?

(A) $20
(B) $30
(C) $40
(D) $50

163. In which of the positions marked [1], [2], [3], and [4] does the following sentence best belong?

"To do so, please visit our Web site."

(A) [1]
(B) [2]
(C) [3]
(D) [4]

GO ON TO THE NEXT PAGE

Questions 164-167 refer to the following online chat discussion.

⊕▸⊕

David Tham [8:04 A.M.] Hello, Kelly and Jonathan. Have we confirmed who will be arriving from Hong Kong next week?

Kelly Cromwell [8:05 A.M.] The Hong Kong office is sending Sara Wang and Neha Agarwal. Others can call in if needed.

David Tham [8:07 A.M.] Where will Sara and Neha be working when they arrive?

Kelly Cromwell [8:09 A.M.] They'll be set up in conference room B. Otherwise, they can use the empty desks located near Michael Klein in Human Resources.

Jonathan Li [8:11 A.M.] Hold on. Actually, there are going to be three. Lillian Zhang is coming, too.

David Tham [8:12 A.M.] We will need another work space then. I'd like to keep them together. Maybe there's a spare office in Accounting?

Kelly Cromwell [8:13 A.M.] Why is Ms. Zhang coming? I thought it was just the marketing team.

Jonathan Li [8:14 A.M.] The packaging designers have been working closely with Marketing on this project.

Kelly Cromwell [8:17 A.M.] Got it. I'll take care of it. I'll send a final schedule to you before lunch. Jonathan, please update the list of call-in participants' names and numbers and send it to all of us.

---

164. Who will be visiting from the Hong Kong office?

(A) Mr. Tham
(B) Ms. Cromwell
(C) Ms. Agarwal
(D) Mr. Klein

165. At 8:11 A.M., what does Mr. Li most likely mean when he writes, "there are going to be three"?

(A) An additional visitor is arriving.
(B) Another conference room is available.
(C) The Accounting Department has several open work spaces.
(D) The schedule will include one more day of meetings.

166. Who most likely is Ms. Zhang?

(A) An accountant
(B) A human resources representative
(C) A marketing specialist
(D) A package designer

167. What does Ms. Cromwell ask Mr. Li to do?

(A) Print a meeting schedule
(B) Prepare a list of contacts
(C) Distribute a lunch menu
(D) Assign visitors to offices

Questions 168-171 refer to the following information.

Request for Proposal

Purpose
The City of New Langston is seeking proposals for the manufacture and installation of electronic signage at bus stops throughout the city. New Langston plans to deploy new electronic signs that display real-time arrival information to bus riders.

Background
Currently, New Langston's bus stops are marked by simple metal signs displaying only the location of the stop and the lines that stop at the location. Cities around the world have begun to incorporate real-time arrival information into bus stop signage. Electronic signs are proving to be very popular with riders, and studies show that the introduction of such signage has contributed to increased ridership in numerous cities.

Project Description
The successful bidder will provide New Langston with up to 350 electronic signs. The signs must be powered by solar energy and have a battery backup allowing them to operate at night, on cloudy days, and in all weather conditions. The signs must have a reliability factor of at least 99 percent. The signs must display at least three and no more than five lines of text, and be connected to the Internet in order to provide real-time information to bus riders.

Please submit detailed bids outlining costs by 11:59 p.m. on May 31 to the City of New Langston Regional Council at regionalcouncil@cityofnewlangston.gov.

---

168. What is the purpose of the information?

(A) To detail a city's public transportation issues
(B) To solicit bids for a city project
(C) To outline the history of bus ridership
(D) To encourage environmental responsibility

169. What is indicated about the proposed signs?

(A) They would look exactly like the current bus stop signs in New Langston.
(B) They would be manufactured by a company in New Langston.
(C) They would inform riders about the arrival of the next bus.
(D) They would need to be programmed only once a month.

170. According to the information, what has been the result of installing the signs in other cities?

(A) Increased use of public transportation
(B) Higher bus fares
(C) Improved lighting at bus stops
(D) More on-time bus arrivals

171. What is NOT a requirement for the new signs?

(A) They must be powered by solar energy.
(B) They must operate in the rain.
(C) They must be reliable.
(D) They must display information in color.

GO ON TO THE NEXT PAGE

Junior Project Manager

Traskin Public Relations
Seattle, WA

Traskin Public Relations is a marketing and public relations firm focusing on the hospitality industry. We are based in Seattle and have been in business for more than twenty years. To keep up with our recent rapid expansion, Traskin is now seeking a new junior project manager. — [1] —. This is an opportunity to be trained in valuable strategic and creative processes. This training program served as the starting point for several of our current senior project managers. Traskin offers all employees competitive compensation and benefits. — [2] —.

Responsibilities include coordinating with managers and clients, scheduling meetings and presentations, and managing budgets. — [3] —. Additionally, the successful applicant will create weekly e-mail updates for internal teammates and clients.

Qualifications include a minimum of two years' management experience at a similar agency, knowledge of project management software, and excellent organizational skills. — [4] —.

Upload résumé and cover letter to careers@traskinpr.com.

---

172. What is indicated about Traskin Public Relations?

(A) It is a new company.
(B) It has international offices.
(C) It focuses on Web site development.
(D) It is growing in size.

173. What is suggested about the job being advertised?

(A) It offers travel opportunities.
(B) It requires experience in training new employees.
(C) It may lead to a promotion.
(D) It is a temporary position.

174. What is one responsibility of the job?

(A) Sending updates regularly
(B) Leading weekly team meetings
(C) Conducting market research
(D) Assigning tasks to team members

175. In which of the positions marked [1], [2], [3], and [4] does the following sentence best belong?

"Experience preparing budgets is a plus."

(A) [1]
(B) [2]
(C) [3]
(D) [4]

GO ON TO THE NEXT PAGE

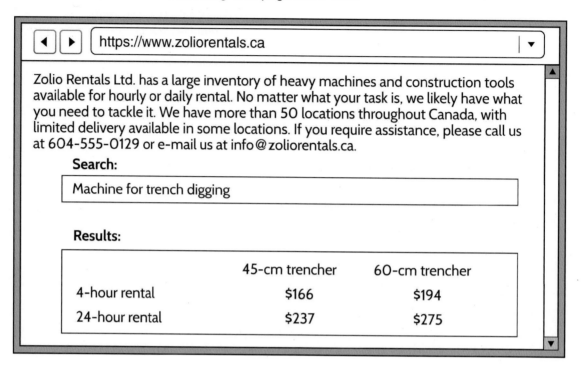

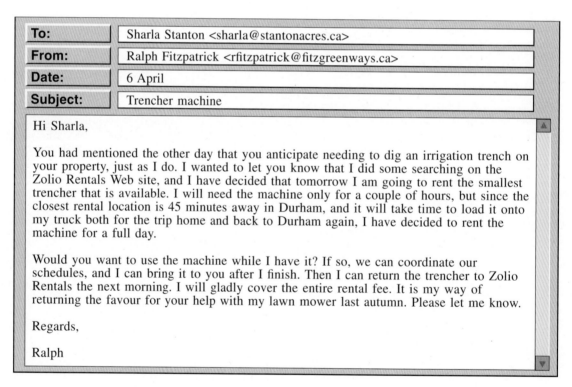

176. What does the Web page state about Zolio Rentals?

(A) It is expanding its inventory.
(B) It is training new customer-service associates.
(C) It can deliver equipment to certain areas.
(D) It recently opened branch locations.

177. Why did Mr. Fitzpatrick send the e-mail?

(A) To make an offer of assistance
(B) To apologize for an oversight
(C) To ask for feedback on a product
(D) To postpone a project

178. In the e-mail, the word "cover" in paragraph 2, line 3, is closest in meaning to

(A) report on
(B) protect
(C) conceal
(D) pay for

179. What does the e-mail suggest about Mr. Fitzpatrick?

(A) His family is planning to relocate to Durham.
(B) He worked as an irrigation consultant for many years.
(C) He regularly rents equipment from Zolio Rentals.
(D) His property is close to Ms. Stanton's property.

180. How much will Mr. Fitzpatrick most likely spend at Zolio Rentals?

(A) $166
(B) $194
(C) $237
(D) $275

GO ON TO THE NEXT PAGE

Welinaras Corporation to Move R&D Division

PUNE (12 March)—Welinaras Corporation, the health technology company headquartered in Pune, announced today that its Research and Development (R&D) Division will be based in Mumbai effective 1 May. "Mumbai has the business climate, facilities, and creative talent we need to help push our production forward," said Mr. Ram Jadhav, who became the company's third president last month. Currently, the company has offices in two other Indian cities, namely New Delhi and Hyderabad.

Welinaras Corporation is the manufacturer of high-quality technological equipment. Its product that is most in demand and, thus, profitable, is called *Vigilant*. Invented by Mr. Jadhav, and available across India, the device is intended for people with health problems. A key feature is its ability to regularly gather and update data about the patient's condition, information that might be crucial in emergencies.

Welinaras Corporation

Job title: Senior Research and Development Engineer
Listing date: 23 March
Apply by: 25 April

Responsible for designing and testing wearable health-monitoring devices.

EDUCATION AND SKILLS:

- Graduate degree in biomedical engineering
- Minimum of five years' experience developing medical devices and conducting clinical trials
- Minimum of three years' experience in managing research teams
- Excellent written and oral communication skills
- Ability to work collaboratively in a global, multicultural environment

Candidate must attend a preliminary training course on 25 May, prior to starting work on 8 June.

181. What is stated about Mr. Jadhav?

    (A) He created one of the company's products.

    (B) He is the founder of Welinaras Corporation.

    (C) He used to be in charge of the R&D Division.

    (D) He has been company president for three years.

182. What is indicated about *Vigilant*?

    (A) It is sold internationally.

    (B) It collects information.

    (C) It is inexpensive.

    (D) It is a new product.

183. Where will the chosen candidate most likely work?

    (A) In Pune

    (B) In Mumbai

    (C) In New Delhi

    (D) In Hyderabad

184. When is the application deadline?

    (A) In March

    (B) In April

    (C) In May

    (D) In June

185. What is one requirement of the position?

    (A) Having published scholarly articles

    (B) Having provided medical care

    (C) Having managerial experience

    (D) Having worked abroad

GO ON TO THE NEXT PAGE

Questions 186-190 refer to the following e-mails and schedule.

To:	All Library Members
From:	Ada County Library
Date:	March 20
Subject:	Upcoming lectures
Attachment:	📎 Spring_schedule

Dear Ada County Library members:

Our long-awaited spring lecture schedule has been finalized. We expect an excellent turnout for these lectures. A highlight is a presentation on Arabic poetry translation, presented by a lecturer who will make her first visit to Ada County Library.

Access to library events is always free and is on a first-come, first-served basis, so please plan accordingly, especially for events in our two smallest venues, the Helms Room, which seats 35, and the Avery Room, which has only 20 computer stations.

Ada County Library
Spring Lecture Schedule

Featured Topic	Guest Lecturer	Date and Time	Location
Idaho Literature	Yvonne Briggs	April 10, 4–6 P.M.	Helms Room
Arabic Poetry Translation	Carole Elgin	April 17, 3–5 P.M.	Stokes Room
Effective Résumé Design	Marc D'Angelo	April 24, 3–5 P.M.	Avery Room
History of the Dictionary	Jax Morrison	May 8, 4–6 P.M.	Stokes Room
Philosophical Nonfiction	Darla Weiss	May 15, 3–5 P.M.	Fredricks Room
Programming as a Skill	Alissa Reynolds	May 22, 4–6 P.M.	Avery Room

To:	Mary Carlton <mcarlton@adacountylibrary.org>
From:	Jax Morrison <jmorrison@bookpress.com>
Date:	April 3
Subject:	Scheduled library event

Dear Ms. Carlton,

I am writing to let you know that my planned event at the library on May 8 will need to be rescheduled, as I will be away for business that week. I have already prepared some exciting materials that I think library patrons will really enjoy, so I am still interested in giving the lecture. It is currently scheduled to take place in the Stokes Room, which is the perfect size for the crowd I hope to draw. It also has all the necessary technology for my lecture, so I would still like to use that room.

I apologize for the inconvenience of needing to reschedule, but I appreciate your help in getting this event rebooked, as I am excited to present my topic.

Best,

Jax Morrison

186. What venue seats only twenty people?

(A) The Helms Room
(B) The Stokes Room
(C) The Avery Room
(D) The Fredricks Room

187. Who is highlighted as a new speaker at Ada County Library?

(A) Ms. Briggs
(B) Ms. Elgin
(C) Ms. Weiss
(D) Ms. Reynolds

188. What most likely is Ms. Carlton's job?

(A) University lecturer
(B) Computer programmer
(C) Event coordinator
(D) Travel agent

189. What event will need to be rescheduled?

(A) Idaho Literature
(B) History of the Dictionary
(C) Philosophical Nonfiction
(D) Programming as a Skill

190. What is indicated about Mr. Morrison?

(A) He has not yet begun to prepare for his lecture.
(B) He will visit the library on May 8.
(C) He is not required to travel for his job.
(D) He plans to utilize technology in his presentation.

TEST 7

GO ON TO THE NEXT PAGE

Questions 191-195 refer to the following Web page and e-mails.

http://www.crfoundation.org/volunteer

River Advocates

The Central River Foundation coordinates water-monitoring operations at various sites along the Central River and its tributaries. The foundation would like to train individuals in area communities to conduct periodic water-quality tests.

If interested in becoming a river advocate, contact us at www.crfoundation.org.

Requirements:
- ▶ Reliable transportation is essential; we work in relatively remote areas.
- ▶ Attention to detail and the ability to take precise measurements
- ▶ Availability to conduct testing at least once every four weeks to detect any changes in water quality

To:	Janis Gutierrez, Mitch Gregory, Mary Connors, Ross Howard
From:	Clare Schroeder <cschroeder@crfoundation.org>
Subject:	Training
Date:	May 5

Thank you for your interest in participating as a river advocate for the Central River Foundation.

A training session has been scheduled at Clifford Park on Saturday, May 8, from 9:00 A.M. to 12 noon. During the training you will practice using the sample kits and be introduced to your mentors. You will leave with your first assignments and a certificate of completion. Then your mentor will accompany you on your first one-hour assignment. This will prepare you to work independently afterwards.

Although we will be training at Clifford Park, you will usually be working at other sites. Please see your individual testing sites below.

Water Testing Site	Volunteer
Sutton Bridge	Janis Gutierrez
Bradford Bend	Mitch Gregory
Alderwick Cove	Mary Connors
Tanner Park	Ross Howard

I look forward to seeing you all on Saturday!

Clare Schroeder

To:	Susan Lim
From:	Mary Connors
Date:	May 13
Subject:	Site visit

Hi Susan,

I'm supposed to complete my first water testing on May 20. Are you available to meet me there to help me do it correctly? I'm available any time between 3:00 P.M. and 6:00 P.M. I looked up the site online, and it looks like we will have to park about half a kilometer away from the river and then walk to the site. Ms. Schroeder mentioned that it will add about 30 minutes to our trip.

Also, do you have an extra water-testing kit? It looks like mine is missing a few pieces. Can we use one of yours until I can get my supplies replaced?

Thanks,

Mary

191. What are the volunteer river advocates responsible for?

(A) Monitoring changes in water quality
(B) Promoting water conservation practices
(C) Keeping the riverbanks clean
(D) Leading educational tours of rivers and creeks

192. What is implied about the recipients of the first e-mail?

(A) They will be sharing a vehicle.
(B) They have helped to recruit volunteers.
(C) They have committed to being available once a month.
(D) They will enter records into a computer system.

193. What does the first e-mail indicate about the training?

(A) It will be held at the Central River Foundation building.
(B) It will take place in the morning.
(C) It will last for one hour.
(D) It will take place at multiple sites.

194. Where will Ms. Lim most likely meet Ms. Connors?

(A) At Sutton Bridge
(B) At Bradford Bend
(C) At Alderwick Cove
(D) At Tanner Park

195. In the second e-mail, what does Ms. Connors ask Ms. Lim to do?

(A) Give her a ride
(B) Contact Ms. Schroeder
(C) Arrive 30 minutes early
(D) Bring a water-testing kit

GO ON TO THE NEXT PAGE

Questions 196-200 refer to the following e-mails and Web page.

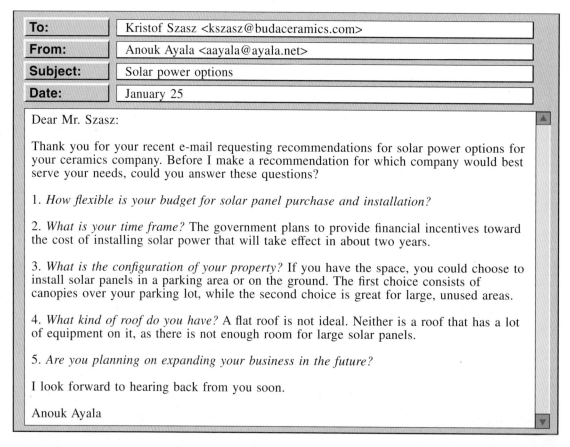

To: Kristof Szasz <kszasz@budaceramics.com>
From: Anouk Ayala <aayala@ayala.net>
Subject: Solar power options
Date: January 25

Dear Mr. Szasz:

Thank you for your recent e-mail requesting recommendations for solar power options for your ceramics company. Before I make a recommendation for which company would best serve your needs, could you answer these questions?

1. *How flexible is your budget for solar panel purchase and installation?*

2. *What is your time frame?* The government plans to provide financial incentives toward the cost of installing solar power that will take effect in about two years.

3. *What is the configuration of your property?* If you have the space, you could choose to install solar panels in a parking area or on the ground. The first choice consists of canopies over your parking lot, while the second choice is great for large, unused areas.

4. *What kind of roof do you have?* A flat roof is not ideal. Neither is a roof that has a lot of equipment on it, as there is not enough room for large solar panels.

5. *Are you planning on expanding your business in the future?*

I look forward to hearing back from you soon.

Anouk Ayala

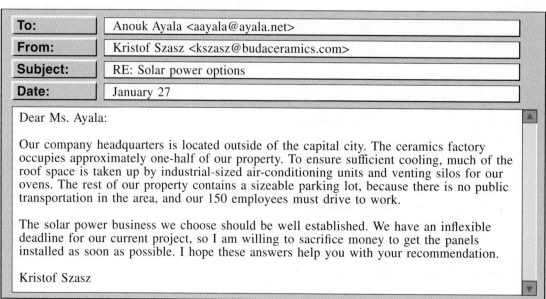

To: Anouk Ayala <aayala@ayala.net>
From: Kristof Szasz <kszasz@budaceramics.com>
Subject: RE: Solar power options
Date: January 27

Dear Ms. Ayala:

Our company headquarters is located outside of the capital city. The ceramics factory occupies approximately one-half of our property. To ensure sufficient cooling, much of the roof space is taken up by industrial-sized air-conditioning units and venting silos for our ovens. The rest of our property contains a sizeable parking lot, because there is no public transportation in the area, and our 150 employees must drive to work.

The solar power business we choose should be well established. We have an inflexible deadline for our current project, so I am willing to sacrifice money to get the panels installed as soon as possible. I hope these answers help you with your recommendation.

Kristof Szasz

Based on a recent customer survey, these four solar power companies in the capital city area are rated the most successful.

Company	Specialty	Comments
AKX Solar	Rooftop	Very low cost; a very stable company
Sun365	All types	Superior quality; very thorough; but a bit slow
Beranek Systems	Parking areas	Fast turnaround; but quite expensive
Plutosolar	Ground installation	Cannot begin until March

196. What most likely is Ms. Ayala's job?

(A) Technical consultant
(B) Factory supervisor
(C) Magazine writer
(D) Maintenance worker

197. What does Ms. Ayala indicate about solar power?

(A) Many government buildings are equipped with solar panels.
(B) Solar businesses overseas are growing extremely fast.
(C) Rooftop panels provide the most energy efficiency.
(D) Delaying installation of solar panels for two years would lower costs.

198. Which of Ms. Ayala's questions does Mr. Szasz fail to answer?

(A) Number 1
(B) Number 3
(C) Number 4
(D) Number 5

199. According to the second e-mail, what is suggested about the ceramics factory?

(A) It is situated far from the road.
(B) It requires extensive cooling.
(C) It is located on a public transportation route.
(D) It recently moved to the capital city area.

200. What company will Ms. Ayala most likely recommend?

(A) AKX Solar
(B) Sun365
(C) Beranek Systems
(D) Plutosolar

Stop! This is the end of the test. If you finish before time is called, you may go back to Parts 5, 6, and 7 and check your work.

TEST 7

토익® 정기시험
기출문제집

RC

ETS TEST

08

READING TEST

In the Reading test, you will read a variety of texts and answer several different types of reading comprehension questions. The entire Reading test will last 75 minutes. There are three parts, and directions are given for each part. You are encouraged to answer as many questions as possible within the time allowed.

You must mark your answers on the separate answer sheet. Do not write your answers in your test book.

PART 5

Directions: A word or phrase is missing in each of the sentences below. Four answer choices are given below each sentence. Select the best answer to complete the sentence. Then mark the letter (A), (B), (C), or (D) on your answer sheet.

101. Mr. Pierce requested that all employees meet in ------- office at noon.

(A) himself
(B) his
(C) him
(D) he

102. We greatly appreciate your ------- in preparing your office for the upcoming move.

(A) cooperates
(B) cooperated
(C) cooperation
(D) cooperate

103. Employees who ------- to contribute to the company picnic should contact Mr. Liu.

(A) require
(B) supply
(C) wish
(D) express

104. Ms. Ngo will make the awards announcement ------- the luncheon next week.

(A) up
(B) onto
(C) off
(D) at

105. As of October 1, Ms. Givens will be planning our department's travel -------.

(A) budgeted
(B) budget
(C) budgetary
(D) budgeter

106. Job applicants are ------- encouraged to submit a work portfolio and a résumé.

(A) rapidly
(B) strongly
(C) nearly
(D) tightly

107. Join us for dinner on Friday ------- Mr. Yi's promotion to Vice President of Marketing.

(A) to celebrate
(B) celebrates
(C) will celebrate
(D) celebrated

108. The ------- of 21 tools ordered will be delivered to the Abby Street warehouse this afternoon.

(A) set
(B) room
(C) fit
(D) power

109. Galaxy Health Club offers a 20 percent discount for all classes ------- November.

(A) entire
(B) during
(C) while
(D) ever

110. ------- the printer cartridge was installed correctly, it leaked some ink.

(A) Although
(B) So
(C) If
(D) However

111. Ms. Chu will explain how the factory workers can protect ------- equipment from damage.

(A) theirs
(B) them
(C) themselves
(D) their

112. Promotional ideas for violinist Zelina Ortiz will be ------- by the publicity team next month.

(A) escorted
(B) tutored
(C) discussed
(D) subscribed

113. *Giffords Global Investors Magazine* experienced its highest numbers in ------- sales in the last quarter.

(A) digits
(B) digital
(C) digit
(D) digitize

114. A new barbershop is opening ------- the neighborhood already has three others.

(A) among
(B) that
(C) prior to
(D) even though

115. Now that Rocker Guitar School is a ------- enterprise, it can afford to hire additional teachers.

(A) musical
(B) profitable
(C) compact
(D) long

116. The renovated office building did not look the way Ms. Garcia ------- it would.

(A) imagine
(B) imagining
(C) imagined
(D) imagination

117. Arsov Consulting advised us to wait until the ------- to ship the new line of sweaters.

(A) summer
(B) year
(C) hours
(D) weather

118. The heads of ------- department in the company must attend the training session in Kolkata.

(A) its
(B) each
(C) most
(D) several

119. Vurk Ltd., manufacturer of industrial sewing machines, is ------- to introduce a line of home products soon.

(A) applied
(B) expected
(C) inquired
(D) objected

120. Reception desk personnel are thoroughly trained to answer any ------- that hotel guests may have.

(A) questioner
(B) questioned
(C) questions
(D) questionable

GO ON TO THE NEXT PAGE

121. Wyckshire Mobile's unlimited talk, text, and data plan is priced ------- at £50.00 per month.

(A) promptly
(B) reasonably
(C) partially
(D) loyally

122. Khaab Staffers announced its acquisition of an international database of ------- 5,000 companies sorted by location or industry.

(A) many
(B) beside
(C) wide
(D) over

123. The presence of several eagle nests makes Hilltop Grove a favorite site for ------- bird watchers.

(A) enthusiastic
(B) affordable
(C) elaborate
(D) comparable

124. The general manager has implemented a system to fill online orders of costume jewelry lines more -------.

(A) quick
(B) quickest
(C) quicker
(D) quickly

125. Quillet Motors has been working ------- the goal of reducing its factory emissions by 25 percent since last year.

(A) after
(B) across
(C) opposite
(D) toward

126. Gribson & Kim's ------- brand identity accurately conveys the company's image and values.

(A) powers
(B) powered
(C) powerful
(D) powerfully

127. The city council approved Remco's application to build a shopping center ------- opposition from local residents.

(A) in spite of
(B) in order that
(C) even so
(D) on the contrary

128. Marliet Marketing can help any business ------- its products through multimedia advertising packages.

(A) promote
(B) promoted
(C) promotable
(D) promoter

129. Local reporters sought ------- with the department manager who found old property records in the city hall basement.

(A) permits
(B) materials
(C) conditions
(D) interviews

130. To appeal to younger consumers throughout Asia, the sportswear company is shifting its marketing tactics -------.

(A) drama
(B) dramatic
(C) dramatically
(D) more dramatic

PART 6

Directions: Read the texts that follow. A word, phrase, or sentence is missing in parts of each text. Four answer choices for each question are given below the text. Select the best answer to complete the text. Then mark the letter (A), (B), (C), or (D) on your answer sheet.

Questions 131-134 refer to the following information.

Welcome to Dining-Ticket, the online service that delivers high-quality, delicious meals to your

------- . To start ------- Dining-Ticket, simply enter your location to view your local delivery options.
   131.   132.

Next, filter the information by your desired price range, cuisine type, or by the restaurant name.

Then, track your order as it is transported by a Dining-Ticket delivery person. ------- . To enjoy
               133.

your favorite restaurant fare from the ------- of your own home, try Dining-Ticket today!
          134.

131. (A) doorstep
(B) station
(C) program
(D) market

132. (A) usage
(B) using
(C) usable
(D) users

133. (A) Additional delivery staff are being recruited now.
(B) Your order will be ready for in-store pickup within one hour.
(C) Our training is thorough and fast.
(D) It's as easy as that.

134. (A) comforted
(B) comforting
(C) comfortable
(D) comfort

GO ON TO THE NEXT PAGE

To: Rashida Willis <rwillis@pintaur.net>

From: Customer Accounts <accounts@stauntonnaturalgas.com>

Date: August 4

Subject: Paperless billing

Dear Ms. Willis,

Thank you for selecting the paperless billing ------- for your Staunton Natural Gas account.
135.

------- on August 20, you will receive your monthly statement electronically. To ensure receipt of
136.

your bill, please add our e-mail address to your list of contacts. At any time you may

------- to traditional paper billing by selecting it in your account settings.
137.

------- . Your bill will still be due on the first of each month.
138.

Sincerely,

Staunton Natural Gas

---

135. (A) value
(B) degree
(C) project
(D) option

136. (A) Until
(B) Only
(C) Beginning
(D) Even

137. (A) return
(B) returnable
(C) to return
(D) returning

138. (A) The account balance is now overdue.
(B) Nothing else about your billing process has changed.
(C) A company representative will contact you soon.
(D) The account will be closed on the final day of the month.

Questions 139-142 refer to the following memo.

To: Red Division Sales Team Members
From: Matias Gama, Director
Subject: Information
Date: 22 November
Attachment: Third-quarter results

Let me commend all of you on your outstanding work this past quarter! See for yourselves in the attached report, which provides all the details. ------- , there's always room for growth. That's why
139.
we're launching a new ------- program. It will be provided by an outside agency that has carefully
140.
------- our needs. Although the learning modules will be offered across the organization, they are
141.
scheduled to begin in our division. ------- . In the meantime, please carry on with your good work.
142.

139. (A) Similarly
(B) In that case
(C) Nevertheless
(D) Even if

140. (A) radio
(B) exercise
(C) training
(D) benefits

141. (A) analyzed
(B) analyzing
(C) to analyze
(D) been analyzed

142. (A) This was our best quarter ever!
(B) I will let you know the dates soon.
(C) Our clients are very pleased as well.
(D) Registration is now full.

TEST 8

GO ON TO THE NEXT PAGE

Questions 143-146 refer to the following e-mail.

From: Joanna Markian
To: All management staff
Subject: Meeting with Adacorp leadership
Date: 11 January

Dear Credulux colleagues,

Please be advised that our Wednesday Board of Directors meeting will focus on the ------- **143.** company merger with Adacorp Ltd. We will be joined by Adacorp's CEO and several managers as well as members of both companies' legal teams. ------- . **144.**

The purpose of this meeting is to clarify the timeline of the merger process. ------- with questions **145.** for our Board of Directors will be given ample time to ask them. ------- , I would like to request that **146.** all nonurgent agenda items be saved for our management team meeting in early February.

Sincerely,

Joanna Markian

---

143. (A) selected
　　 (B) upcoming
　　 (C) occasional
　　 (D) assorted

144. (A) Please plan to attend this meeting in person.
　　 (B) Interns will report on their experience at Adacorp.
　　 (C) Instead, we will extend the meeting by one hour.
　　 (D) You will soon be notified of the new law.

145. (A) Each other
　　 (B) Yours
　　 (C) Anyone
　　 (D) Whoever

146. (A) On the contrary
　　 (B) For this reason
　　 (C) Soon after
　　 (D) For example

PART 7

Directions: In this part you will read a selection of texts, such as magazine and newspaper articles, e-mails, and instant messages. Each text or set of texts is followed by several questions. Select the best answer for each question and mark the letter (A), (B), (C), or (D) on your answer sheet.

Questions 147-148 refer to the following information.

Smith County Transportation Department
Current Postings

Bridge Inspector (BI9253)—Take your career to new heights as a bridge inspector in beautiful Smith County, known for its spectacular and varied landscape! The geography of our county is large and hilly, necessitating the use of our many bridges and tunnels by residents and tourists alike. The position involves assessing the condition of existing bridges, tunnels, culverts, and related road signs as well as proposing and overseeing repairs. We offer competitive salaries with excellent benefits. For details on requirements and how to apply, please visit www.smithcounty.gov/jobs. The deadline is January 15.

---

147. What does the information suggest about Smith County?

(A) Its population is growing rapidly.
(B) Its tunnel system requires modernization.
(C) It is an attractive place to live and visit.
(D) It is currently building many new highways.

148. According to the information, what is one duty of the bridge inspector?

(A) Supervising maintenance work
(B) Planning new bridges
(C) Collecting bridge and tunnel tolls
(D) Designing traffic signs

GO ON TO THE NEXT PAGE

Questions 149-150 refer to the following notice.

Thank you for purchasing tickets for a tour of the historic Walton Steamship. If you need to cancel or change your appointment, please be aware of our cancellation policy. Cancellations up to one day before the scheduled tour will receive a refund of 50% per ticket. Canceling on the same day or failing to appear at the time of your scheduled tour will result in no refund. All refunds will be credited to the card used to purchase the tickets.

Please note that tours are conducted both inside the ship and outside on deck. Tours are rarely canceled due to weather. Please wear appropriate clothing in case we experience cold or wet weather.

149. For whom is the notice most likely intended?

(A) Current ticket holders
(B) Steamship crew members
(C) Customer service representatives
(D) Tour guides in training

150. What does the notice recommend people do?

(A) Update their contact information
(B) Print historical reference materials
(C) Dress to spend time outdoors
(D) Arrive early on the day of the tour

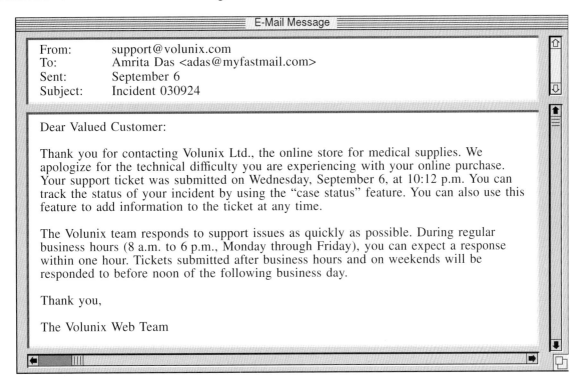

151. What problem is Ms. Das most likely experiencing?

(A) Her firm's Web site is not accessible.
(B) Her computer needs a system update.
(C) She has not received a refund.
(D) She is unable to buy an item.

152. What is indicated about a support ticket?

(A) It was submitted incorrectly.
(B) It was submitted after business hours.
(C) It was resolved in one hour.
(D) It was addressed by a Volunix supervisor.

GO ON TO THE NEXT PAGE

To:	Mary Lim <mlim412@mailhouz.com>
From:	George Siskos <gsiskos@crehcorp.com>
Date:	September 24
Subject:	Referral from Joe Argento
Attachment:	📎 Information

Hello Ms. Lim,

I am George Siskos, Recruiting Manager at Crehcorp Ltd. We are currently looking to hire an accounting clerk, and Joe Argento recommended you. From what Joe told me, your background makes you a good fit for the role (posting attached). If you are interested in learning more about Crehcorp and the position, I will be happy to provide further information. Let me know when you are available to talk, and I will give you a call.

I look forward to hearing back from you!

George Siskos

153. What is the purpose of the e-mail?

(A) To advertise for Crehcorp
(B) To request a reference
(C) To recruit an employee
(D) To announce a promotion

154. What does Mr. Siskos attach?

(A) A job description
(B) A financial report
(C) A conference invitation
(D) A link to driving directions

155. What is Ms. Lim asked to do?

(A) Visit Crehcorp's Web site
(B) Contact Mr. Argento
(C) Mail a résumé
(D) Respond to the e-mail

Questions 156-157 refer to the following text-message chain.

Francis Chang [4:32 P.M.]
Hi, Connie. I'm putting together the schedule for the summer. Will you still be able to teach the Friday afternoon workshops twice a month? We could take turns, and I would take the other two Fridays.

Connie Kehoe [4:39 P.M.]
Thanks for getting in touch, Francis. I'd still like to be involved, but I'll be busier this summer. I'm coordinating a volleyball league.

Francis Chang [4:40 P.M.]
Well, OK. I guess I could cover the workshops three Fridays a month.

Connie Kehoe [4:42 P.M.]
That would be perfect. That will give me enough time for my other obligation.

Francis Chang [4:43 P.M.]
The other thing is, this summer we want to focus on painting with watercolors, rather than basic drawing.

Connie Kehoe [4:44 P.M.]
I'll look over some old lesson plans, but that should be fine. Also, let's get together soon to work on a budget for the class materials.

156. At 4:42 P.M., what does Ms. Kehoe mean when she writes, "That would be perfect"?

(A) She is looking forward to summer.
(B) She thinks a workshop will be popular.
(C) She is happy with a proposed schedule.
(D) She is glad that Mr. Chang will be hired.

157. What type of workshop is being planned?

(A) Art
(B) Personal finance
(C) Travel
(D) Customer service

GO ON TO THE NEXT PAGE

Questions 158-160 refer to the following letter.

May 15

Mr. Roger Lang, Executive Director
Parker Solutions Foundation
40 Northside Drive, Suite 500
Portland, OR 97215

Dear Mr. Lang:

The purpose of this letter is to invite you, on behalf of the board of directors, to be the keynote speaker at the International Green Solutions Research Institute (IGSRI) Conference. — [1] —. It will be held at the Fairview Conference Center in Saint Louis, Missouri, from December 3 to 5. You were recommended by a number of my colleagues. — [2] —.

Professor Suzanne Benedetto will deliver the opening speech on the morning of December 3. A draft program will be sent to you in two weeks to give you an idea of the topics that will be highlighted at the conference.

We expect attendance this year to be the highest ever, around 2,500 delegates and 40 speakers. — [3] —. This includes a large contingent from our newest chapter in Geneva. — [4] —.

I hope to contact you in a week to follow up and answer any questions you may have.

Yours sincerely,

Brian Morgan
Brian Morgan

158. Why was the letter to Mr. Lang written?

(A) To request a recommendation letter from him
(B) To ask him to evaluate some conference topics
(C) To congratulate him for receiving an award
(D) To ask him to participate in a conference

159. In what city will the IGSRI Conference be held?

(A) Portland
(B) Fairview
(C) Saint Louis
(D) Geneva

160. In which of the positions marked [1], [2], [3], and [4] does the following sentence best belong?

"They spoke highly of your expertise."

(A) [1]
(B) [2]
(C) [3]
(D) [4]

Questions 161-163 refer to the following Web page.

---

www.sergeyparksandrec.gov/survey

Welcome!

You have been directed to this survey through a page on the Scrgey Parks and Recreation Department's Web site, from one of Ecology Alive's most recent online newsletters, or from a friend's social media page. Regardless of how you got here, we appreciate your taking the time to complete it.

This survey aims to help local wildlife organizations find practical approaches to attracting a dedicated and reliable volunteer base. The survey takes about 15 minutes to complete, and your participation is completely optional. If you do not wish to answer a particular question, you can move on to the next one.

If you have any questions regarding how this survey will be used, please contact Stefan McHann at stefan_mchann@sergeyparksandrec.gov.

Survey #4123

Name: Kenshawn Odeyemi

---

161. What is indicated about the survey?

(A) It was recently modified.
(B) It can be accessed from multiple online sources.
(C) It requires an hour to complete.
(D) It is being sent only to university students.

162. What is the purpose of the survey?

(A) To find ways to recruit volunteers
(B) To evaluate an organization's strengths
(C) To assess an area's wildlife populations
(D) To determine important leadership traits

163. What is suggested about the survey respondents?

(A) They can skip some of the questions.
(B) They must subscribe to Ecology Alive.
(C) They will be paid for their participation.
(D) They will receive an additional survey from Mr. McHann.

TEST 8

GO ON TO THE NEXT PAGE

Questions 164-167 refer to the following notice.

December 1

Attention, All Employees:

Beginning on January 1, Barkley-Stephens Corporation (BSC) will transition to a security system that uses integrated ID badges. Until now, BSC employees have used traditional identification cards that security personnel checked at entrances to the building. They simply compared the badge photograph with the employee's appearance. The new system will be more technologically advanced, integrating ID badge information with various access points around our facility.

Integrated ID badges allow employees entry only to areas of the building that are permitted to them. Moreover, the badges create an electronic record of who has entered which areas of the building and when. In the case of temporary employees, badges will be disabled when their tenure ends.

New photographs of all staff will be taken in mid-December, when everyone will be asked to fill out a brief form to complete badge processing.

164. What is the purpose of the notice?

(A) To ask employees to submit information
(B) To encourage greater use of the facilities
(C) To discuss renovations to a building
(D) To announce security system changes

165. The word "points" in paragraph 1, line 6, is closest in meaning to

(A) purposes
(B) details
(C) places
(D) moments

166. What is a stated advantage of the new ID badges?

(A) They fit conveniently into a pocket.
(B) They allow access to additional areas of a building.
(C) They are more durable than the older ID cards.
(D) They can track an employee's location on-site.

167. According to the notice, what feature of the current IDs will be updated?

(A) The photo
(B) The company logo
(C) The shape
(D) The employee's job title

Questions **168-171** refer to the following online chat discussion.

Franklin Smith (7:51 A.M.)
Good morning, Josephine and Carl. Is either one of you at the office yet? My train is running late and I want to make sure everything is set up for our 8:30 A.M. workshop.

Josephine Mallian (7:56 A.M.)
I'm walking in now. What can I do to help, Franklin?

Carl Domingo (7:57 A.M.)
I'll be there in about ten minutes. Are you talking about the workshop in the Aster Room? Because there is another workshop taking place in Obell Hall too.

Franklin Smith (7:59 A.M.)
Yes, the one in the Aster Room—the Savvy Steel sales workshop. I would appreciate it if you would rearrange the seats into a circle, turn on the projector, and run through the presentation slides I sent last night, just to make sure that everything, including the audio, is working.

Carl Domingo (8:02 A.M.)
Got it. I actually set the chairs up last night.

Josephine Mallian (8:04 A.M.)
Thanks, Carl. Would you mind printing out fifteen copies of the agenda while I take care of the rest?

Carl Domingo (8:05 A.M.)
Sure. I'll get it done as soon as possible.

Franklin Smith (8:07 A.M.)
Thank you both. My train is arriving now. I think I'll make it in time.

Josephine Mallian (8:08 A.M.)
No problem, Franklin. We will also make sure there is plenty of coffee for you!

168. Why did Mr. Smith send the first message?

(A) To extend an invitation
(B) To request some help
(C) To apologize for a mistake
(D) To confirm a travel reservation

169. What is suggested about the Savvy Steel meeting?

(A) It is being moved to a different location.
(B) It is one of two meetings taking place on the same day.
(C) It will include a presentation by Ms. Mallian.
(D) It will start later than planned.

170. At 8:02 A.M., what does Mr. Domingo most likely mean when he writes, "Got it"?

(A) He will check some equipment.
(B) He will unlock the Aster Room.
(C) He will bring some more chairs.
(D) He will revise the meeting's agenda.

171. What is Mr. Domingo asked to do?

(A) Bring coffee to his coworkers
(B) Make changes to some slides
(C) Meet Mr. Smith at the station
(D) Make some copies

GO ON TO THE NEXT PAGE

Foxtail Airlines

July 30

Ms. Gina Carracia
General Manager
Obsidian Villa
1121 Marine Boulevard
Seattle, WA 98101

Dear Ms. Carracia:

My name is Isaac Bolton, and I am Director of Marketing at Foxtail Airlines.
— [1] —. I am writing to share a marketing idea with you that would be beneficial
for both our companies. Our crew members who fly into Seattle have stayed at
Obsidian Villa several times in the past. They report that the rooms are consistently
comfortable and clean and that the staff is friendly and efficient. — [2] —. However,
there is often no vacancy at your excellent establishment, and so our crews must stay
elsewhere. We have arrangements with hotels in several cities around the world in
which rooms are reserved for our crews in advance. Foxtail Airlines advertises for
these hotels in our in-flight magazine at a significant discount. — [3] —. We would
like to develop a similar partnership with Obsidian Villa.

To give you an idea of the advertising possibilities we offer, our graphic design team
has created four potential advertisements. They are enclosed with this letter.
— [4] —. I hope these samples demonstrate how enthusiastic we are about promoting
Obsidian Villa to the over three million passengers who fly with us every year. If you
are interested in exploring this idea further, please contact me by phone at
546-555-0182 or by e-mail at i.r.bolton@foxtailairlines.com. I hope to have the
opportunity to work with you.

Sincerely,

Isaac Bolton

Isaac Bolton, Director of Marketing
Foxtail Airlines

Enclosures

172. What is the purpose of the letter?

    (A) To introduce a product
    (B) To make a reservation
    (C) To propose a new partnership
    (D) To announce a promotion

173. What is indicated about Obsidian Villa?

    (A) It usually has rooms available.
    (B) It recently hired additional managers.
    (C) It has three million customers a year.
    (D) It provides good customer service.

174. What did Mr. Bolton send with the letter?

    (A) Sample advertisements
    (B) An in-flight magazine
    (C) Airline tickets
    (D) A client's itinerary

175. In which of the positions marked [1], [2], [3], and [4] does the following sentence best belong?

"I have read numerous positive reviews that say the same."

    (A) [1]
    (B) [2]
    (C) [3]
    (D) [4]

TEST 8

GO ON TO THE NEXT PAGE

Monthly Reading Series at the Spotted Cat Bookstore
June Schedule

Saturday, June 2   Brian Stenick, author of *Into the Sea: Collected Poems*
Sunday, June 3   David Callander, author of *The Mastery of Comfort*
Monday, June 11   Nina Brown, author of *Family Threads*
Wednesday, June 13   Bernice Sandene, author of *Retroactive: A History of Athletic Wear*

Readings begin at 7:00 P.M., and there is a reception with light refreshments afterward.

If you are a published writer interested in reading for our series this July, please submit a five-page example of your work as an attachment to readings@spottedcatbooks.com. With your writing sample, send a one-paragraph biography. Your bio should mention your education and artist residencies, publications, readings, and lectures, if applicable. The series welcomes both well-established and emerging writers.

From:	Jo Ann Rodcliff <jrodcliff@weeklycourier.com>
To:	David Callander <dcallander@elwyn.edu>
Date:	May 16
Subject:	Reading

Dear Professor Callander,

I heard that you and Professor Sandene are reading at the Spotted Cat in a few weeks. How exciting! I am hoping to attend both readings and am looking forward to seeing you both again.

Since graduating from Elwyn University last year, I've been working for the *Weekly Courier* as an arts and culture columnist. Mostly, I write reviews on art shows, concerts, and other cultural events around the city. I also write profiles and book reviews. I would like to ask whether I may feature you and your book in my next column. The column will be published the day before your reading.

I was fascinated by your book, and it would be my pleasure to review it in the *Weekly Courier.* Are you available for a phone call tomorrow? Of course, I would prefer to interview you in person, but I'm out of town on assignment until next week. Please let me know if you are interested.

Sincerely,

Jo Ann Rodcliff

176. What is stated about the reading series?

(A) It is held once a month.
(B) It features both new and well-known writers.
(C) It requires a ticket to attend.
(D) It highlights recently published books.

177. What should writers send to the bookstore?

(A) Information about their background
(B) A book they would like to read to customers
(C) The location at which they prefer to lecture
(D) A signed contract

178. Why did Ms. Rodcliff write the e-mail?

(A) To introduce herself to a new client
(B) To describe her experience to a potential employer
(C) To arrange an interview as part of her work
(D) To schedule a visit to a university

179. On what date does Ms. Rodcliff hope to hear Professor Sandene read?

(A) June 2
(B) June 3
(C) June 11
(D) June 13

180. What book does Ms. Rodcliff want to review in her column?

(A) *Into the Sea: Collected Poems*
(B) *The Mastery of Comfort*
(C) *Family Threads*
(D) *Retroactive: A History of Athletic Wear*

GO ON TO THE NEXT PAGE

TEST 8

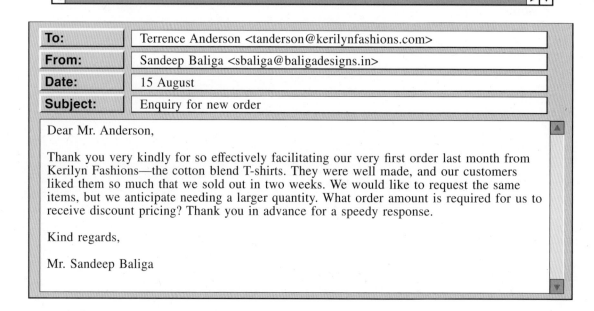

Kerilyn Fashions—Exceptional Apparel for Your Company's Brand

Are you an apparel retailer seeking products that you can rebrand as your own? We offer shirts, pants, shoes, and fashion accessories as a business-to-business wholesaler. Shop our extensive catalog and choose products for your customer base. We will badge the products in your order with sewn-in labels carrying your company's branded logo. Your order will arrive in three to four weeks. Kerilyn Fashions saves you time in product production so that your merchandise gets to market quickly. And we offer fresh, new designs every season; sample items can be sent to you upon request.

We extend discounts on large orders. We ship anywhere in the world, with charges that are based on the weight of the order.

Merchandise is nonrefundable, and a credit will be issued for any items that arrive damaged. To get started with your first order, you are invited to set up an online account. You will be assigned an account manager who will contact you within 24 hours and facilitate your first and future orders.

To:	Terrence Anderson <tanderson@kerilynfashions.com>
From:	Sandeep Baliga <sbaliga@baligadesigns.in>
Date:	15 August
Subject:	Enquiry for new order

Dear Mr. Anderson,

Thank you very kindly for so effectively facilitating our very first order last month from Kerilyn Fashions—the cotton blend T-shirts. They were well made, and our customers liked them so much that we sold out in two weeks. We would like to request the same items, but we anticipate needing a larger quantity. What order amount is required for us to receive discount pricing? Thank you in advance for a speedy response.

Kind regards,

Mr. Sandeep Baliga

181. What is indicated about Kerilyn Fashions?

(A) It is a family-run company.
(B) It offers overnight shipping.
(C) Its prices are competitive.
(D) Its product selection is updated regularly.

182. What is NOT a stated advantage of Kerilyn Fashions' service?

(A) It can provide sample products to examine in advance of ordering.
(B) Shipping charges are waived on large orders.
(C) Merchandise arrives at a client's business prelabeled.
(D) It assigns special managers to assist new clients.

183. Who most likely is Mr. Anderson?

(A) A fashion model
(B) A fashion designer
(C) An account manager
(D) An office supervisor

184. In the e-mail, the word "anticipate" in paragraph 1, line 4, is closest in meaning to

(A) expect
(B) prevent
(C) look forward to
(D) depend on

185. What is mentioned by Mr. Baliga?

(A) His firm is planning to open branch locations.
(B) His stock of T-shirts was too large.
(C) He ordered T-shirts in several colors.
(D) He believes Kerilyn Fashions' goods are of high quality.

GO ON TO THE NEXT PAGE

BETH'S SECONDHAND FURNITURE
Hold Rules

1. Purchased merchandise can be held for 7 days.
2. Merchandise unclaimed after 7 days will be returned to inventory and resold.
3. We are not responsible for damage to items that are awaiting collection.
4. We will provide delivery services for large furniture on request. Large furniture is considered 25 kg or heavier.
5. All sales are final.

RECEIPT
BETH'S SECONDHAND FURNITURE

Item Number: 39235

Receipt Number: 47712

Weight: 18 kg

Date of Purchase: 8 August

Customer Name: Edward Hasegawa

Total: $135.00

Payment Method: Credit Card

Note: Please hold for pickup.

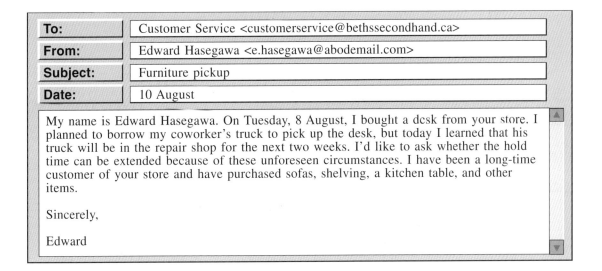

To:	Customer Service <customerservice@bethssecondhand.ca>
From:	Edward Hasegawa <e.hasegawa@abodemail.com>
Subject:	Furniture pickup
Date:	10 August

My name is Edward Hasegawa. On Tuesday, 8 August, I bought a desk from your store. I planned to borrow my coworker's truck to pick up the desk, but today I learned that his truck will be in the repair shop for the next two weeks. I'd like to ask whether the hold time can be extended because of these unforeseen circumstances. I have been a long-time customer of your store and have purchased sofas, shelving, a kitchen table, and other items.

Sincerely,

Edward

186. According to the sign, what happens to unclaimed furniture?

(A) It is made available for sale again.
(B) It is donated to a local charity.
(C) It is promptly disposed of.
(D) It is moved to long-term storage.

187. What is suggested about Beth's Secondhand Furniture?

(A) It is under new management.
(B) It does not accept returns.
(C) It is a nonprofit business.
(D) It is opening another location.

188. What is indicated about Mr. Hasegawa's purchase?

(A) It cost less than $100.
(B) It must be picked up within two days.
(C) It had a reduced price because of damage.
(D) It is not considered large furniture.

189. What most likely is item number 39235 ?

(A) A couch
(B) A desk
(C) A shelving unit
(D) A table

190. What is the purpose of the e-mail?

(A) To schedule a delivery time
(B) To confirm a purchase amount
(C) To request an extension for a hold
(D) To ask about making an item exchange

GO ON TO THE NEXT PAGE

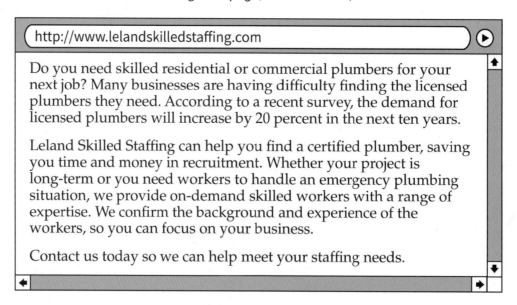

http://www.lelandskilledstaffing.com

Do you need skilled residential or commercial plumbers for your next job? Many businesses are having difficulty finding the licensed plumbers they need. According to a recent survey, the demand for licensed plumbers will increase by 20 percent in the next ten years.

Leland Skilled Staffing can help you find a certified plumber, saving you time and money in recruitment. Whether your project is long-term or you need workers to handle an emergency plumbing situation, we provide on-demand skilled workers with a range of expertise. We confirm the background and experience of the workers, so you can focus on your business.

Contact us today so we can help meet your staffing needs.

LICENSED PLUMBER
Huang Services
Job Title: *Residential Plumber*

Position Summary: Full-time position available at newest location in Springfield. Perform work in both new construction and existing homes, which includes servicing, repairing, and replacing plumbing, fixtures, and gas pipes.

Position Requirements: Plumbing license; 3 years' experience; driver's license; ability to use modern technology.

Pay Scale: $50,000–$90,000, depending on experience. Paid time off.

Work Hours: Vary according to seasonal needs. Some evening work required.

Send résumé to s.huang@huangservices.com. We will contact those who pass a thorough background check to schedule an interview.

To:	info@lelandskilledstaffing.com
From:	s.huang@huangservices.com
Date:	April 15
Subject:	Staff needed

To Whom It May Concern,

I am writing because I am seeking a residential plumber for my business. I have had a job advertisement posted for a while now but have not had success in finding the right candidate. We require that the candidate have a plumbing license and will accept two years of experience. The candidate will also need a driver's license and be available to occasionally work evening hours. Could you please send me a list of people who would be able to start on Monday, May 5? My business will begin installing the plumbing in a new housing development in the area on that day.

Regards,

Stephanie Huang

191. According to the Web page, what is expected to increase?

(A) The time for training
(B) The price of equipment
(C) The cost of labor
(D) The need for skilled plumbers

192. What does the advertisement suggest about Huang Services?

(A) It has been in business for three years.
(B) It is closed during certain seasons.
(C) It has only part-time work available.
(D) It has more than one location.

193. What do Leland Skilled Staffing and Huang Services have in common?

(A) They were both founded by Ms. Huang.
(B) They are located in Springfield.
(C) They verify workers' qualifications.
(D) They specialize in commercial plumbing.

194. What does Ms. Huang mention about a job posting?

(A) It was not successful.
(B) It will soon be deleted.
(C) It did not contain the correct information.
(D) It was posted on a popular Web site.

195. What has changed about the position at Huang Services?

(A) The starting salary
(B) The number of licenses needed
(C) The work hours
(D) The required years of experience

GO ON TO THE NEXT PAGE

Questions 196-200 refer to the following article, schedule, and e-mail.

New Conference Scholarships from Wenford Technologies

(Jan. 2)—Wenford Technologies, an industry leader in Internet services, has announced that it will offer six scholarships to qualified candidates to attend the Breakthroughs in Computer Science Conference in Newark, New Jersey, from April 21 to 23. To encourage a greater global perspective among conference participants, two individuals each from Latin America, Africa, and Asia will be selected as scholarship recipients.

"We believe that a variety of perspectives is what helps our industry grow and thrive," explained Wenford Technologies' CEO Dale Kelvin. "To this end, we would like to extend this opportunity to professionals from certain geographic regions."

Applicants must be employed full-time in computer science for a period of between one and five years in order to be eligible. For more information about the scholarships, visit wenfordtech.com/scholarships.

Breakthroughs in Computer Science Conference
Preliminary Schedule, April 21–23

Below is an outline of activities for the conference. Each day will follow the same format. A final schedule with speakers' names and their affiliations will be available two months prior to the event.

8:30 A.M.–9:00 A.M.	Continental breakfast—Food will be available in the reception hall.
9:00 A.M.–9:30 A.M.	Announcements
9:40 A.M.–Noon	Presentations
Noon–1:00 P.M.	Lunch break—Conference attendees will be on their own. There are many reasonably priced dining establishments within walking distance of the conference venue.
1:00 P.M.–4:00 P.M.	Workshops
4:00 P.M.–5:15 P.M.	Panel discussions and session evaluations

To:	Cindy Connelly <cconnelly@wenfordtech.com>
From:	Adamu Adebayo <aadebayo@spmail.co.za>
Date:	3 February
Subject:	Scholarship thanks

Dear Ms. Connelly,

Sincere thanks to Wenford Technologies for supporting my attendance at the Breakthroughs conference. It is an exciting opportunity for me, and I am really looking forward to learning from others in the same field who work in different parts of the world.

I would like to mention that I lead a daily client conference call at 2:30 P.M. (the time in Johannesburg) that I am unable to cancel. This task would start at 9:30 A.M. in Newark, and it will require my attention for 30 minutes or so. Otherwise, I hope to participate fully in all conference proceedings. Please let me know if there is any information you might still need from me.

Best regards,

Adamu Adebayo

196. What does Wenford Technologies want to promote with the scholarships?

(A) Rapid growth
(B) Collaborative work
(C) Diverse perspectives
(D) Innovative problem-solving

197. According to the article, what is expected of scholarship applicants?

(A) They must respond to an online survey.
(B) They should propose workshop topics.
(C) They must select conference sessions in advance.
(D) They should be at an early stage of their careers.

198. What does the schedule suggest about the conference?

(A) It will provide a catered lunch each day.
(B) It is still finalizing some details.
(C) It relies on volunteers to lead discussions.
(D) It will vary in format each day.

199. What can be concluded about Mr. Adebayo?

(A) He works in the field of computer science.
(B) He received a job offer from Wenford Technologies.
(C) He hopes to acquire some international clients.
(D) He completed his professional training in Newark.

200. During which part of the conference will Mr. Adebayo be absent each day?

(A) Breakfast
(B) Announcements
(C) Presentations
(D) Panel discussions

Stop! This is the end of the test. If you finish before time is called, you may go back to Parts 5, 6, and 7 and check your work.

토익®정기시험
기출문제집

RC

ETS TEST

09

In the Reading test, you will read a variety of texts and answer several different types of reading comprehension questions. The entire Reading test will last 75 minutes. There are three parts, and directions are given for each part. You are encouraged to answer as many questions as possible within the time allowed.

You must mark your answers on the separate answer sheet. Do not write your answers in your test book.

PART 5

Directions: A word or phrase is missing in each of the sentences below. Four answer choices are given below each sentence. Select the best answer to complete the sentence. Then mark the letter (A), (B), (C), or (D) on your answer sheet.

---

101. There is coffee in the break room for anyone who ------- a cup before the meeting.

(A) want
(B) wants
(C) wanting
(D) to want

102. Each Ready Wear suitcase comes ------- a ten-year warranty.

(A) if
(B) with
(C) so
(D) upon

103. Mr. O'Sullivan oversaw the electrical work in the new apartment building ------- the river.

(A) into
(B) as
(C) to
(D) by

104. For questions about your hotel reservation, please telephone ------- booking department at 555-0109.

(A) we
(B) us
(C) our
(D) ourselves

105. Janet Rhodes was commended for ------- defending the company's reputation.

(A) assertively
(B) assert
(C) assertive
(D) assertion

106. A second order for 500 recycled paper cups ------- last week.

(A) was placed
(B) was placing
(C) to place
(D) placed

107. One of the ------- for the position is three years of customer service experience.

(A) associates
(B) requirements
(C) tips
(D) assistants

108. ------- will receive a weekly e-mail reminding them to approve time sheets.

(A) Supervises
(B) Supervisory
(C) Supervisors
(D) Supervising

109. As of next week, the hotel chain Contempo Inns will be ------- new management.
(A) across
(B) under
(C) beside
(D) near

110. Managers can access information about ------- staff members by contacting Human Resources.
(A) whose
(B) while
(C) their
(D) much

111. After eighteen years in business, Chu Home Health Services remains committed to customer -------.
(A) satisfaction
(B) production
(C) energy
(D) opportunity

112. The obstetrics nurses ------- are working under Dorothy Caramella will now be working for Pierre Cocteau.
(A) they
(B) who
(C) when
(D) these

113. Visitor parking is ------- behind the office complex on Mayfield Avenue.
(A) adjusted
(B) visual
(C) available
(D) urgent

114. Among other -------, purchasing departments negotiate contracts to procure goods at the best possible prices.
(A) tasks
(B) task
(C) tasking
(D) tasked

115. The community swimming pool will be constructed ------- three separate stages.
(A) for
(B) far
(C) in
(D) at

116. The Lanaiya 7 laptop ------- its debut at the annual Delbar Tech Summit.
(A) made
(B) knew
(C) heard
(D) drew

117. Enjoy one month free when you start your company on Rooster's e-mail ------- Web hosting service.
(A) then
(B) yet
(C) but
(D) and

118. The bridge project bids turned out to be ------- higher than expected.
(A) considering
(B) consider
(C) consideration
(D) considerably

119. Contract negotiations are now close ------- to completion to sign the deal by Thursday.
(A) already
(B) quite
(C) such
(D) enough

120. Filber Woodworking reminds customers that direct sunlight will cause ------- damage to furniture.
(A) lasting
(B) lasts
(C) last
(D) lastly

GO ON TO THE NEXT PAGE

121. ------- employees wishing to take time off must submit the request two weeks in advance.

   (A) Each
   (B) All
   (C) Every
   (D) Total

122. Bronco Building Equipment uses data to make ------- decisions and plot future operations.

   (A) strategized
   (B) strategic
   (C) strategize
   (D) strategically

123. In addition to the evening concert series, Centennial Park will ------- be hosting several events for children this summer.

   (A) nevertheless
   (B) although
   (C) consequently
   (D) also

124. Because ------- spaces in the mall now have tenants, foot traffic has increased greatly.

   (A) that much
   (B) after which
   (C) in case
   (D) so many

125. Complete the form carefully to ensure the ------- processing of your application.

   (A) rapidly
   (B) more rapidly
   (C) most rapid
   (D) rapidity

126. Changes to the Top Fizz soft-drink formulation failed to ------- to consumers.

   (A) remain
   (B) result
   (C) appreciate
   (D) appeal

127. The Liu Supermarket ------- that Jennifer Chan will take over as CEO next month came as a surprise.

   (A) announced
   (B) announcement
   (C) announcing
   (D) announcer

128. ------- extensive renovations, Main Vault Bank will temporarily relocate to 1450 Barrister Avenue.

   (A) If only
   (B) Since
   (C) Due to
   (D) Though

129. Donell and Franklyn Investments promises incomparable loyalty and ------- to its clients.

   (A) transparent
   (B) transparency
   (C) transparencies
   (D) transparently

130. The ------- who work for ARF Recordings seek out talented but unknown musicians who are hoping to record a first album.

   (A) authors
   (B) announcers
   (C) dancers
   (D) agents

PART 6

Directions: Read the texts that follow. A word, phrase, or sentence is missing in parts of each text. Four answer choices for each question are given below the text. Select the best answer to complete the text. Then mark the letter (A), (B), (C), or (D) on your answer sheet.

Questions 131-134 refer to the following notice.

Notice of Public Meeting

The Fallberg City Library will hold its monthly board meeting on August 19 at 6 P.M. Members of the community are encouraged to ------- . The agenda, ------- available on the library's Web site,
        131.   132.
includes an information session about the proposed library building on the city's east side.

Project Manager Andre Cazal will share design concepts for the building. ------- , he will lead a
                                                                            133.
discussion about how construction should be funded. There will be a period for public comment

following the regular agenda items. ------- .
                                     134.

131. (A) write
     (B) attend
     (C) donate
     (D) volunteer

132. (A) be
     (B) being
     (C) which is
     (D) what can be

133. (A) In addition
     (B) As a result
     (C) As mentioned
     (D) In the meantime

134. (A) New board members will be appointed in September.
     (B) The main branch will remain closed until further notice.
     (C) The project has been canceled due to a lack of public funding.
     (D) Attendees will have an opportunity to share feedback at that time.

GO ON TO THE NEXT PAGE

Questions 135-138 refer to the following e-mail.

To: All Sales Associates
From: Dean Verdoorn
Date: June 27
Subject: Store improvement

It is very important to us at V and J Camping Supplies that we work together as a unit. Teamwork not only improves productivity but also leads to increased satisfaction for customers and employees. ------- , we will be combining a team-building exercise with an in-store improvement
135.
plan that we believe will make employees, management, and customers happy.

We will be redesigning the walls in our stores to look like trees with hollow spaces -------
136.
products can be displayed. These outdoor-themed shelves are actually easy-to-assemble modular wall units. Associates ------- the task to work cooperatively in teams to assemble them.
137.
------- . When it is completed, we will stock the shelves and have a fun grand reopening event for
138.
customers.

More information will be forthcoming.

Dean Verdoorn
Buildings Director

135. (A) For that reason
(B) For instance
(C) Unfortunately
(D) On the other hand

136. (A) for
(B) that
(C) whatever
(D) where

137. (A) are giving
(B) were given
(C) have to give
(D) will be given

138. (A) Customers have been informed.
(B) This project should take one day.
(C) An announcement will be made soon.
(D) These units are available in several colors.

Questions 139-142 refer to the following e-mail.

To: Donald Haroway <dharoway@indomail.co.nz>
From: Fix-It Plumbing
Date: 4 August
Subject: Service request

Mr. Haroway,

This e-mail serves as confirmation that Fix-It Plumbing will be able to ------- a gas line at your
139.
residence at 458 Heron Street. We ------- Bradley Burns, a certified and licensed master plumber,
140.
to do this on Monday, 10 August, between 10:00 A.M. and 11:00 A.M. It should take about an hour

to put in the line. ------- .
141.

Should you need to cancel the ------- , please contact us right away. This is a particularly busy
142.
time of year, and our schedules are quite full.

Elna Dlamini
Fix-It Plumbing

139. (A) fill
 (B) install
 (C) inspect
 (D) examine

140. (A) would have sent
 (B) were sending
 (C) sent
 (D) will send

141. (A) Then your gas stove will be ready to
 use.
 (B) Mr. Evans worked in your area last
 week.
 (C) Please call us by 9:30 A.M. the day
 before.
 (D) We do this job better than our
 competitors.

142. (A) subscription
 (B) membership
 (C) celebration
 (D) appointment

GO ON TO THE NEXT PAGE

Questions 143-146 refer to the following e-mail.

To: Store Managers
From: Alain Mareau
Date: 4 October
Subject: Recycling Initiative

Hello All,

As one of Australia's top electronics retailers, we always ------- to maintain our standing as an
                                                          143.
industry leader. Earlier this year, we began testing a new program that allowed our customers to

bring their used electronic devices to our stores for recycling. In exchange they received

discounts on their purchases. The initiative exceeded our expectations. ------- .
                                                                        144.

In late November, all store managers will be sent ------- instructions on how to collect items and
                                                   145.

send them to our recycling partner. ------- , we will be announcing the program to the public via
                                     146.

social media and print ads beginning in mid-November.

Please anticipate further updates and instructions on this exciting initiative.

Sincerely,

Alain Mareau
Vice President, Product Development

143. (A) seek
     (B) imply
     (C) predict
     (D) remember

144. (A) Electronics recycling is helpful for the
         environment.
     (B) Thus we are expanding this program to
         all our locations later this year.
     (C) Several customers had unfortunately
         failed to retain their receipts.
     (D) Businesses across the country already
         recycle many materials.

145. (A) detail
     (B) details
     (C) detailed
     (D) detailing

146. (A) Instead
     (B) Additionally
     (C) However
     (D) For example

PART 7

Directions: In this part you will read a selection of texts, such as magazine and newspaper articles, e-mails, and instant messages. Each text or set of texts is followed by several questions. Select the best answer for each question and mark the letter (A), (B), (C), or (D) on your answer sheet.

Questions 147-148 refer to the following advertisement.

Wayne Rental Available

A sparkling two-bedroom, one-bath apartment is available in the village of Wayne, fifteen miles from the center of Bowling Green. Situated in a mid-rise building that is ten years old, the apartment is convenient to shops and cafés and within walking distance of the train station. The oven and dishwasher have just been replaced, and a fresh tile countertop has been installed in the kitchen. A new washer and dryer set is next to the pantry. The monthly rent is $950, including utilities. Sign a one-year lease and you can move in as early as August 1. Call (419) 555-0145 to arrange a tour.

---

147. What is suggested about the apartment building?

(A) It is under new management.
(B) It has a large parking area.
(C) It is close to public transportation.
(D) It was constructed one year ago.

148. What is NOT mentioned as a new appliance?

(A) A refrigerator
(B) A clothes dryer
(C) An oven
(D) A dishwasher

GO ON TO THE NEXT PAGE

Questions 149-150 refer to the following notice.

We appreciate your purchase from Drapes-A-Lot!

For issues regarding payment, exchanges, and returns, please contact your nearest Drapes-A-Lot retailer. For help with damaged or missing parts, instructions for do-it-yourself installation, or questions about your product, call Drapes-A-Lot customer support at (713) 555-0101. Representatives are available to answer questions Monday through Friday, 9:00 A.M. to 5:00 P.M. Before calling, please have the following information ready: your name and phone number, the purchase order number, and where you made your purchase.

---

149. What does the notice suggest about Drapes-A-Lot?

(A) It does not offer installation service.
(B) It does not accept returns.
(C) It provides online customer support.
(D) It recently opened retail stores.

150. According to the notice, what information is necessary when contacting customer support?

(A) The serial number of the product
(B) The store location where the product was bought
(C) The credit card number used to make the purchase
(D) The e-mail address of the customer

Questions 151-152 refer to the following text-message chain.

Keith Odom (10:15 A.M.) We're almost finished trimming the bushes and trees around the lobby entrance. We'll trim everything in the back garden after lunch. While we're in the front, though, we're going to weed the flower beds.

Rebecca Truesdell (10:18 A.M.) I thought they were cleaned up earlier this week.

Keith Odom (10:20 A.M.) Remember it rained. We couldn't get to the weeding on Wednesday.

Rebecca Truesdell (10:25 A.M.) That's right. Yes, please finish out front first. We have two large parties scheduled for tomorrow, so we want the hotel entrance and grounds to look good.

Keith Odom (10:27 A.M.) Okay. This should not take more than an hour or so.

Rebecca Truesdell (10:28 A.M.) Let me know when you're finished in the back garden. We're expecting the delivery of some new patio furniture later this afternoon, and that will be set up as soon as it arrives.

151. Who most likely is Mr. Odom?

(A) A hotel manager
(B) An event planner
(C) A building inspector
(D) A groundskeeper

152. At 10:25 A.M., what does Ms. Truesdell most likely mean when she writes, "That's right"?

(A) She requested that some trees be trimmed.
(B) She confirmed the guest reservations.
(C) She remembered why a job was not done.
(D) She understood why some furniture had not been delivered.

GO ON TO THE NEXT PAGE

Questions 153-154 refer to the following advertisement.

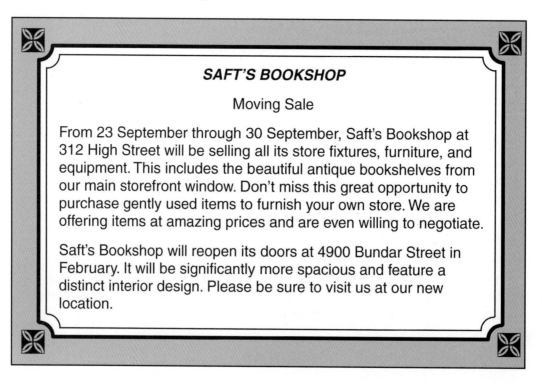

SAFT'S BOOKSHOP

Moving Sale

From 23 September through 30 September, Saft's Bookshop at 312 High Street will be selling all its store fixtures, furniture, and equipment. This includes the beautiful antique bookshelves from our main storefront window. Don't miss this great opportunity to purchase gently used items to furnish your own store. We are offering items at amazing prices and are even willing to negotiate.

Saft's Bookshop will reopen its doors at 4900 Bundar Street in February. It will be significantly more spacious and feature a distinct interior design. Please be sure to visit us at our new location.

153. What is indicated about antique bookshelves?

(A) They will be moved to a location on Bundar Street.
(B) They have been on display in a shop window.
(C) They are in poor condition.
(D) They were built by a famous designer.

154. What is suggested about the new Saft's Bookshop?

(A) It will be on the same street as the current location.
(B) It will be open seven days a week.
(C) It will be larger than the old shop.
(D) It will retain most of its staff.

Questions 155-157 refer to the following newsletter.

Birch Hill Center for the Arts Committee
Supporters' Newsletter

The committee has been hard at work this year! We are close to reaching our goal of building a community arts center that will serve all the people of our lovely town of Birch Hill. Here is what we have accomplished so far.

- In January, we completed a community survey about what activities to offer in the new Birch Hill Center for the Arts.
- In February, we completed a feasibility report and narrowed the potential building sites to three possibilities.
- In April, we submitted our project budget proposal to the city council for approval.
- In May, we interviewed several candidates for the managing director position.

During the next two months, we will:

- Select our new managing director
- Choose the location for the center
- Complete the construction blueprints
- Finalize the construction budget and timeline
- Draft our events calendar

And this fall, we should begin construction on the Birch Hill Center for the Arts!

As always, we welcome your input on the process. Please send questions or comments to our committee at project@bhca.org. If you are interested in serving on the committee, please call 952-555-0128.

---

155. When did the committee send a proposed budget to the city?

(A) In January
(B) In February
(C) In April
(D) In May

156. Where did the committee gather information about what activities to offer?

(A) From a survey
(B) From a report
(C) From a proposal
(D) From personal interviews

157. What is someone who wants to join the committee directed to do?

(A) Complete a questionnaire
(B) Send an e-mail
(C) Visit a Web site
(D) Make a phone call

TEST 9

GO ON TO THE NEXT PAGE

Patton Advertising Is Hiring Now!

We are seeking motivated, enthusiastic individuals to join us in our design, finance, and IT departments. Previous experience in the advertising sector is useful but not required.

Our Work
Here at Patton, we've designed advertisements and created marketing strategies for a wide range of clients. This work has included designing logos and Web sites, as well as creating ads for local radio and a national billboard. Under the leadership of CEO Amie Adesina, we're looking to expand in new directions and tackle even more exciting projects.

Some Employee Comments

• "In my first six months as a designer at Patton, I've already had the chance to work with several clients and even lead my own team. The work isn't always easy, but if you enjoy a fast-paced, challenging environment, you'll really thrive here." *Thomas Kuti*

• "I've been working as a legal consultant at Patton for just under a year now, and I've enjoyed every moment. There's a fantastic working culture, with generous employee benefits including a gym membership and paid time off for volunteering. It's the best company I've ever worked for." *Sabina Hussain*

Visit our Web site www.pattonads.com/careers to see vacancies and apply for jobs.

---

158. The word "sector" in paragraph 1, line 2, is closest in meaning to

(A) portion
(B) industry
(C) region
(D) operation

159. What is Mr. Kuti's job?

(A) Designer
(B) Lawyer
(C) IT technician
(D) CEO

160. What is true about both Mr. Kuti and Ms. Hussain?

(A) They enjoy volunteering in their spare time.
(B) They think everyone would enjoy working at Patton.
(C) They are team leaders in their departments.
(D) They have worked at Patton for less than a year.

Questions 161-163 refer to the following letter.

31 July

Dr. Shamalie Mowatt
Cornwall University Hospital
22-28 Victoria Avenue
Kingston 6

Dear Dr. Mowatt,

It is a pleasure to recommend Mr. Renaldo Silva for your nursing programme.
— [1] —. Mr. Silva has served as an assistant to our two on-site registered nurses
at Summer Camp West, four days a week for the past two summers. The young
campers here have grown quite fond of Mr. Silva. They appreciate his kind but
dedicated approach to wellness. — [2] —. He is patient and nurturing, and I am
confident that he will succeed in a nursing programme such as yours.

As a nurse myself for more than three decades, I have worked with young
professionals in various settings, including large hospitals, small clinics, schools,
and, for the past several years, exclusively at Summer Camp West. — [3] —.
I therefore strongly believe that Mr. Silva will be an active and successful
programme participant.

— [4] —. If you have any questions about Mr. Silva, please feel free to call me at
(876) 555-0140.

Yours sincerely,

Benita Oliveira
Benita Oliveira

161. Who most likely is Dr. Mowatt?

(A) The owner of a summer camp
(B) The director of a training program
(C) A candidate for a health-care position
(D) A professor of human biology

162. What is indicated about Ms. Oliveira?

(A) Her child attends Summer Camp West.
(B) She has been employed in health care
    for over 30 years.
(C) She works at Summer Camp West four
    days a week.
(D) She supervises nursing staff at a
    hospital.

163. In which of the positions marked [1], [2], [3],
and [4] does the following sentence best
belong?

"As such, I can attest to Mr. Silva's
professionalism and his compassion for
those in his care."

(A) [1]
(B) [2]
(C) [3]
(D) [4]

GO ON TO THE NEXT PAGE

Questions 164-167 refer to the following document.

Sky-High Roofing

Workers doing construction or repair work on roofs face multiple potential hazards. Ladders, skylights, and physical exposure to the natural elements involve risks. Stay safe by using commonsense practices. Follow these guidelines.

Dress for safety.
- Wear long-sleeved shirts, even in warm weather, and keep your wrist cuffs buttoned
- Wear long pants without cuffs, as they can snag on roofing material and catch debris
- Wear work boots that cover the ankles, and replace boots when the soles show excessive wear

Use personal protective equipment.
- Wear gloves that cover the wrists, making sure there is no gap between the top of the gloves and the bottom of the sleeve cuffs
- Use protective eyewear

Begin the day right.
- Review the work plan with all members of the team
- Check the condition of ladders and all safety equipment

I confirm that I have reviewed and understood these guidelines.

Signature: _____ Date: _____

---

164. For whom is the document most likely intended?

(A) Ladder manufacturers
(B) Clothing designers
(C) Home inspectors
(D) Roof installers

165. The word "practices" in paragraph 1, line 3, is closest in meaning to

(A) regular actions
(B) physical exercises
(C) professional businesses
(D) performance rehearsals

166. What is indicated in the document?

(A) Sky-High Roofing specializes in solar panel installation.
(B) Homeowners are responsible for marking hazardous areas.
(C) Clothing that covers the arms and the legs is essential.
(D) Roofers must attend a company workshop.

167. What is NOT mentioned in the document as a safety measure?

(A) Using safety glasses
(B) Using earmuffs
(C) Wearing sturdy footwear
(D) Performing equipment checks

Public Works Challenge

CARBERRY (April 15)—From its inception, the Carberry Public Works Building has met with little appreciation from the public. When architects unveiled the blueprints for the structure, longtime residents argued that its bright colors and angular shapes did not blend well with Carberry's distinctive redbrick buildings. Local concerns even sparked the creation of a social media group, whose members urged residents to voice their opinions at town council meetings and in other public forums. — [1] —.

In the end, a more conservative version of the original building design was drafted and the grand opening was planned for April 28. — [2] —. However, the owners of nearby buildings started to report drainage issues caused by significant water runoff.

"When the property was an open field with grass and trees, excess rainwater was quickly absorbed into the ground," explains Trudy Molina, owner of the Axios Office Building. "Now water pools up and floods adjacent parking areas during heavy rains." — [3] —.

According to town manager Bert Montiel, the unfortunate result of the building project was unforeseen, and construction engineers are working swiftly to correct the issue before the Public Works Building opens. — [4] —. A team has begun the installation of additional gutters and connecting drains to divert the water to the neighborhood's underground sewer system. The work should be completed in time to celebrate the building's opening in late May.

---

168. What was the subject of initial complaints about the Carberry Public Works Building?

(A) Its size
(B) Its design
(C) Its location
(D) Its purpose

169. What is suggested about the town of Carberry?

(A) It is postponing an event.
(B) It is seeking a new town manager.
(C) It has multiple projects for next year.
(D) It has fewer residents than nearby towns.

170. How will the town address Ms. Molina's concerns?

(A) By improving the signage at the Axios Office Building
(B) By reimbursing her for a utility bill
(C) By directing water away from an area
(D) By expanding a building's parking area

171. In which of the positions marked [1], [2], [3], and [4] does the following sentence best belong?

"Dozens of people did just that."

(A) [1]
(B) [2]
(C) [3]
(D) [4]

GO ON TO THE NEXT PAGE

Questions 172-175 refer to the following online chat discussion.

Reese, Tamara [1:30 P.M.] Thank you for contacting Green City Tours. How may I assist you?

Chambers, Curtis [1:32 P.M.] Hello. I am writing about Yorke Corporation's upcoming trip to Vancouver. I believe that Green City Tours has arranged for all meals to be included for the participants. Is that correct?

Reese, Tamara [1:33 P.M.] No, the terms of the contract specifically state that "Participants will be hosted to both a welcome reception and a farewell dinner. All other meals are to be covered at the participants' own expense during the program." Please let me know if there are any more questions you have about this trip.

Chambers, Curtis [1:35 P.M.] That's disappointing! Our previous employee trips have included all meals. Could I be connected with a supervisor? I'm quite certain that this option should have been included in the contract.

Diaz, Marta [1:37 P.M.] Good afternoon, Mr. Chambers. I apologize for any misunderstanding concerning Yorke Corporation's contract terms with Green City Tours. The contract was created in accordance with the requests of Franklin Wang, your company's CFO. It was his stipulation that intervening meals not be included. We could make recommendations for some other dining options.

Chambers, Curtis [1:40 P.M.]
That's OK. Thank you both for your assistance. I'm going to consult with Mr. Wang about the situation. I may be in touch with you again soon.

172. Why does Mr. Chambers contact Green City Tours?

(A) To plan a trip for new employees
(B) To question a credit card charge
(C) To inquire about the details of a trip
(D) To provide emergency contact information

173. At 1:35 P.M., what does Mr. Chambers most likely mean when he writes, "That's disappointing"?

(A) He does not agree with the restaurant recommendations.
(B) He is frustrated with being unable to attend the trip.
(C) He does not think Ms. Reese can answer his question.
(D) He does not like some contract terms.

174. What most likely is Ms. Diaz' job?

(A) Customer service manager
(B) Vancouver city administrator
(C) Travel blog writer
(D) Hotel concierge

175. What will Mr. Chambers do next?

(A) Prepare a welcome speech
(B) Research a historical site
(C) Speak with a colleague
(D) Sample some food items

GO ON TO THE NEXT PAGE

To:	Nadja Burton <manager_publicaffairs@jaspertonintlairport.com>
From:	Ron Hylton <rhylton@cityofjasperton.gov>
Date:	October 3
Subject:	Ribbon-cutting ceremony

Hello, Ms. Burton,

I am sorry to tell you that, because of an unexpected scheduling conflict, Mayor Blau must cancel her appearance at next week's event. The mayor is proud to have played a part in negotiating a noise-reduction agreement between Jasperton International Airport and nearby homeowners, and she regrets that she will not be there to celebrate. The city council chairperson will take her place.

By the way, we heard the good news about Arovion Air—congratulations! A lot of people traveling to East Asia on business will be happy to take advantage of this.

Regards,

Ron Hylton, Communications Director
Office of the Mayor

Airport and City Leaders to Celebrate Project Completion

JASPERTON (October 5)—A ribbon-cutting ceremony will be held at Jasperton International Airport on October 12. The event will mark the completion of the extension of airport runway 15. City council chairperson Rosalie Colman and airport director Norris Yuan will gather with other invited guests to cut the ribbon at 9:30 A.M.

The runway extension project, which began five months ago, was not without controversy. Complaints by groups of homeowners concerned about noise pollution eventually led to the construction of concrete noise barriers that were not a part of the initial project plan.

The extension of runway 15 ushers in a new era for travel in the region. The runway is now long enough to accommodate the wide-body aircraft that can travel lengthy international routes. At least one long-haul carrier is already preparing to fly nonstop from Jasperton to East Asia.

176. Why most likely was the e-mail written?

(A) To give notification of a change in plans
(B) To issue an invitation
(C) To modify a flight reservation
(D) To summarize a recent meeting

177. How did Mayor Blau support a project?

(A) She helped obtain some construction permits.
(B) She helped two groups reach an agreement.
(C) She established a relationship with an overseas airline.
(D) She negotiated with the city council for increased funding.

178. What is being publicized in the article?

(A) The dedication of a new airport
(B) The appointment of an airport director
(C) The design of a new wide-body aircraft
(D) The opening of an extended runway

179. What is suggested about Arovion Air?

(A) It is under new management.
(B) It is popular for its low ticket prices.
(C) It will provide long-distance flights.
(D) It recently relocated its headquarters.

180. Who most likely will represent Jasperton's mayor at a ceremony?

(A) Ms. Burton
(B) Ms. Colman
(C) Mr. Hylton
(D) Mr. Yuan

GO ON TO THE NEXT PAGE

December 2

Paul Reggar, Manager
Pelder Opticians
930 Main Street
Tamisville VT 05003

Dear Mr. Reggar,

I recently visited your store and was unable to find eyeglass frames that were the right size for me. Ms. Morgan waited on me and was very helpful, but you had virtually no adult styles that fit my small, narrow face. I hope that in the future you will have more petite frames for women.

I found a pretty pair of glasses online at Your Best Frames that are a petite size. I plan to purchase them this week. If I buy the frames, could I have them shipped directly to your store for you to make and insert the lenses? I look forward to hearing back from you promptly.

Sincerely,

Stephanie Potts

Stephanie Potts

YOUR BEST FRAMES
www.yourbestframes.com

Date:	December 5
Customer:	Stephanie Potts 201 Broad Street, Tamisville VT 05003
Ship to:	Manager, Pelder Opticians RE: Order for S. Potts 930 Main Street, Tamisville VT 05003
Order number:	28734T2 Order details: 1 pair women's frames by Sue Lane Color/Style: Black/Petite frame 9374-87
Price:	$127.00 Credit card: LANA Bank **** **** **** 7872
Processed by:	Simon Gyula
Notes:	Ship directly to Pelder Opticians, per Ms. Potts. Expected delivery by December 12. Paid in full.

181. What is the purpose of the letter?

    (A) To ask how to return a product
    (B) To inquire about a repair
    (C) To make a special request
    (D) To ask about a shipping date

182. Where does Ms. Morgan work?

    (A) At a shipping company
    (B) At a retail clothing store
    (C) At an optician's shop
    (D) At a credit card company

183. What is suggested about Pelder Opticians?

    (A) It is located on Broad Street.
    (B) It has a large selection of petite
        eyewear.
    (C) It has an online store that sells frames.
    (D) It will insert lenses into frames bought
        elsewhere.

184. To whom is Your Best Frames shipping a package?

    (A) Mr. Reggar
    (B) Ms. Potts
    (C) Ms. Lane
    (D) Mr. Gyula

185. What is indicated about the order?

    (A) It was submitted on December 2.
    (B) It is expected to arrive by December 5.
    (C) It has already been paid for.
    (D) It contains an extra pair of frames.

GO ON TO THE NEXT PAGE

Questions 186-190 refer to the following Web page, schedule, and letter.

http://www.milfordjanitorialservice.com

Milford Janitorial Service

956 Meadowvale Road, Milford, Connecticut 06460

Let Milford Janitorial Service (MJS) help you showcase your workplace in its best light. Using top-rated cleaning products, MJS serves large and small businesses based on their specific needs and schedule. Our professionally certified staff delivers quality, stress-free cleaning services seven days a week. Interested? Here is the process.

1. Contact MJS with your request, describing how we can best serve you.

2. We will visit your place of business for a free consultation.

3. We contact you with recommendations and a cost estimate within 72 hours.

4. You review our estimate and if satisfied, you sign our contract.

Milford Janitorial Service (MJS)
Assignment schedule for the evening of Monday, June 10

Location	Details	Team
Hallender Office Supply	Dusting and vacuuming	Silver Team
Shoreside Bank	Window cleaning	Blue Team*
Larimar Café	Restroom cleaning	Green Team
Powder's Laundromat	Floor cleaning and polishing	Gold Team*
J. Mallery Accounting	Dusting and vacuuming	Silver Team

*Note that beginning next month, the Blue Team and the Gold Team will switch cleaning roles.

Irene's Formal Wear • 1800 Canopy Lane • Milford, Connecticut 06461

June 17

Milford Janitorial Service
956 Meadowvale Road
Milford, Connecticut 06460

Hello,

Your company was referred to me by a customer of mine. I have a specific need,
requiring professional floor cleaning and polishing in the large lobby of my business.
It is important that the lobby is always sparkling. I would like this service provided
weekly, beginning on July 1. Looking forward to hearing from you soon.

Sincerely,

Irene Nogueira

Irene Nogueira
Irene's Formal Wear

---

186. What is indicated about MJS?

(A) It is under new management.
(B) It is renewing its annual contracts.
(C) It specializes in residential cleaning.
(D) It provides services every day of the
week.

187. For whom is the schedule intended?

(A) Clients of MJS
(B) Cleaning product suppliers
(C) Employees of MJS
(D) Job seekers

188. Where will the Silver Team be on June 10 ?

(A) Shoreside Bank
(B) Larimar Café
(C) Powder's Laundromat
(D) J. Mallery Accounting

189. What will an MJS representative most likely
do next in response to the letter?

(A) Call Irene's Formal Wear to provide
references
(B) Make a visit to Irene's Formal Wear
(C) E-mail an estimate to Ms. Nogueira
(D) Send a contract to Ms. Nogueira

190. Which team will most likely be assigned to
work at Irene's Formal Wear in July?

(A) The Silver Team
(B) The Blue Team
(C) The Green Team
(D) The Gold Team

GO ON TO THE NEXT PAGE

TEST 9

Deelish Barbecue Catering Menu

BBQ and Fixings Buffet: $17.95 per person
Choose two meats and two side dishes.
      Meats: Beef, chicken, pork, sausage
      Sides: Green beans and onions, potato salad, macaroni and cheese, baked beans
Comes with salad, drink (soft drink, coffee, or tea), and bread (cornbread or dinner roll).

Extra sides available by the pound
$6.50: Green beans and onions
$6.00: Potato salad
$5.00: Macaroni and cheese
$4.00: Baked beans

Breakfast Buffet (priced per person)
Choice A ($8.95): Assorted pastries and fresh fruit plus drink (coffee, tea, milk, or fruit juice)
Choice B ($10.95): Pancakes with syrup and all of Choice A
Choice C ($13.95): Assorted omelets and all of Choice A

Contact our events manager with any questions or issues with your order.

INVOICE
Deelish Barbecue Catering

Item	Unit Cost	Quantity	Amount
BBQ and Fixings Buffet	$17.95	30	$538.50
Extra side	$6.00	3	$18.00
Delivery charge			$20.00
(Order to be delivered June 23)			
Breakfast Choice C	$13.95	30	$418.50
Delivery charge			$20.00
(Order to be delivered June 24)			
Subtotal			$1,015.00
Tasting fee			$14.00
Sales tax (6%)			$61.74
Total Due Now			**$1,090.74**

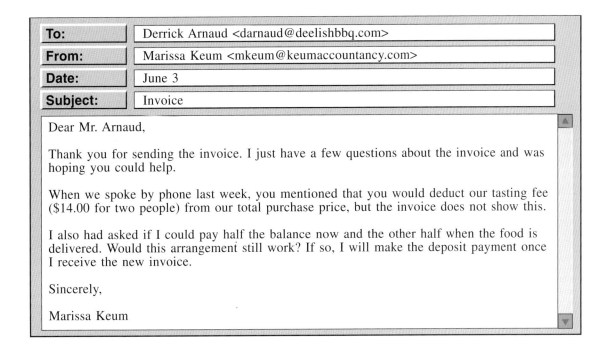

To:	Derrick Arnaud <darnaud@deelishbbq.com>
From:	Marissa Keum <mkeum@keumaccountancy.com>
Date:	June 3
Subject:	Invoice

Dear Mr. Arnaud,

Thank you for sending the invoice. I just have a few questions about the invoice and was hoping you could help.

When we spoke by phone last week, you mentioned that you would deduct our tasting fee ($14.00 for two people) from our total purchase price, but the invoice does not show this.

I also had asked if I could pay half the balance now and the other half when the food is delivered. Would this arrangement still work? If so, I will make the deposit payment once I receive the new invoice.

Sincerely,

Marissa Keum

191. According to the menu, what item is NOT included with the BBQ and Fixings Buffet?

(A) Salad
(B) Drink
(C) Bread
(D) Fruit

192. According to the invoice, why is the customer being charged twice for delivery?

(A) The deliveries will occur on separate days.
(B) The deliveries will be made outside the usual delivery area.
(C) Deelish Barbecue made a mistake in the charges.
(D) The customer made an error in payment.

193. What extra side item did Ms. Keum purchase?

(A) Green beans and onions
(B) Potato salad
(C) Macaroni and cheese
(D) Baked beans

194. Who most likely is Mr. Arnaud?

(A) A catering supervisor
(B) A customer
(C) A restaurant owner
(D) A food critic

195. Based on the e-mail, what does Ms. Keum expect Mr. Arnaud to do next?

(A) Call her to review the order
(B) Reschedule a delivery
(C) Send her a new invoice
(D) Provide tasting samples

GO ON TO THE NEXT PAGE

Clareton Business Digest

(February 8)—Many companies, especially those that sell mid-priced apparel brands, have embraced an interesting strategy. Instead of focusing on local and regional markets for their products, they purposely diversify their retail locations. For example, instead of opening ten stores across East Asia, the companies may opt to limit locations in East Asia to only a few, while adding new ones in Latin America or the Middle East.

As Chester Mau, a marketing consultant, explained, "This approach serves as a buffer against economic downturns or periods of slower growth in any one geographical area."

Some of the companies already pursuing this strategy include Charisma Fashions and The Baby's Closet. With its planned April move into the Latin American market, Lolo Sportswear will follow suit.

FOR IMMEDIATE RELEASE
June 13

Contact: Maura Keele, mkeele@lolosportswear.com

(Clareton)—Lolo Sportswear announced today that Joseph Chakata will become its new chief executive officer. Mr. Chakata will assume responsibilities in July. He previously served as CEO for eight years at the leading fashion design firm Colorspright, Inc.

Mr. Chakata will replace Shirley Alden, who founded Lolo Sportswear and then served as its CEO for eighteen years. Remarked Ms. Alden, "I am pleased to be leaving Lolo Sportswear in such capable hands. The company is ready for its next big chapter." The leadership transition comes after the successful launch in April of the company's first overseas stores. An additional expansion is planned for the end of the year.

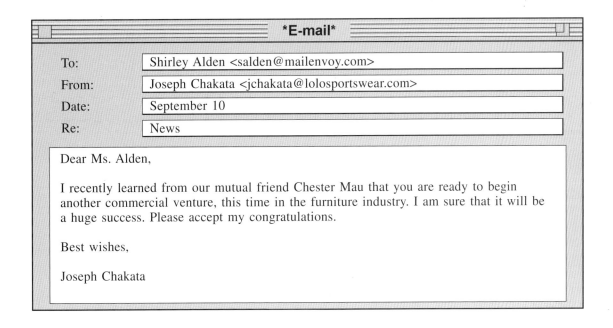

E-mail

To:	Shirley Alden <salden@mailenvoy.com>
From:	Joseph Chakata <jchakata@lolosportswear.com>
Date:	September 10
Re:	News

Dear Ms. Alden,

I recently learned from our mutual friend Chester Mau that you are ready to begin another commercial venture, this time in the furniture industry. I am sure that it will be a huge success. Please accept my congratulations.

Best wishes,

Joseph Chakata

---

196. Why should a company use the business strategy described in the article?

(A) To fill leadership positions more quickly
(B) To increase a brand's visibility
(C) To create a more diverse workforce
(D) To avoid dependence on a single region

197. In what month did Lolo Sportswear's leadership change?

(A) April
(B) June
(C) July
(D) December

198. What is suggested about Mr. Chakata?

(A) He is a fashion designer.
(B) He lives in the Middle East.
(C) He recently graduated from business school.
(D) He will oversee businesses in Latin America.

199. According to the press release, who is Ms. Alden?

(A) The founder of a successful company
(B) A marketing consultant
(C) A human resources specialist
(D) The owner of a business publication

200. What is implied about Ms. Alden?

(A) Her retirement in East Asia has been enjoyable.
(B) Her latest venture is in an industry that is new to her.
(C) She has previously invested in Colorspright, Inc.
(D) She has asked Mr. Chakata for advice.

Stop! This is the end of the test. If you finish before time is called, you may go back to Parts 5, 6, and 7 and check your work.

TEST 9

토익® 정기시험
기출문제집

RC

ETS TEST

10

READING TEST

In the Reading test, you will read a variety of texts and answer several different types of reading comprehension questions. The entire Reading test will last 75 minutes. There are three parts, and directions are given for each part. You are encouraged to answer as many questions as possible within the time allowed.

You must mark your answers on the separate answer sheet. Do not write your answers in your test book.

PART 5

Directions: A word or phrase is missing in each of the sentences below. Four answer choices are given below each sentence. Select the best answer to complete the sentence. Then mark the letter (A), (B), (C), or (D) on your answer sheet.

101. A ------- salesperson assisted Ms. Han with choosing a new computer.

(A) help
(B) helpfully
(C) helpful
(D) helped

102. Author Daniel Aiduk ------- gives talks at national writing conferences.

(A) gradually
(B) longer
(C) together
(D) regularly

103. Mr. Kohl has a great deal of ------- performing cost analysis tasks.

(A) experience
(B) experienced
(C) experiencing
(D) experiencer

104. To make an -------, clients can click on "Schedule" at the top right corner of the home page.

(A) example
(B) option
(C) individual
(D) appointment

105. The used coffee grounds should be disposed of at the end of ------- business day.

(A) now
(B) each
(C) whose
(D) and

106. Our company's efforts to hire new workers have intensified ------- so many employees have recently retired.

(A) because
(B) although
(C) instead
(D) unless

107. The occurrence of heavy rains during the month of May is fairly -------.

(A) predict
(B) predicts
(C) predicting
(D) predictable

108. Remind customers to return their rental car ------- a full tank of fuel.

(A) with
(B) from
(C) except
(D) toward

109. ------- the winter season, Serina Builders will once again offer roof installations and repairs.

(A) Such as
(B) Moreover
(C) After
(D) Whereas

110. The lights in the cinema ------- before a movie begins.

(A) dim
(B) dimming
(C) dimmer
(D) dims

111. When scheduling a meeting, please be ------- of colleagues in other time zones.

(A) significant
(B) mindful
(C) exclusive
(D) serious

112. Greentrim's product sales rose ------- following the introduction of its new shipping policy.

(A) sharp
(B) sharper
(C) sharply
(D) sharpest

113. Please ------- Hearnshaw for all your home appliance needs.

(A) assemble
(B) balance
(C) share
(D) consider

114. Monday will be the best day for ------- to clean the carpet in the lobby.

(A) we
(B) us
(C) ours
(D) ourselves

115. Hikers, ------- to explore the newly opened trails, have been visiting Millar Nature Reserve in record numbers.

(A) tender
(B) bright
(C) vast
(D) eager

116. KOHW ------- Jenae Johnson will be promoted to news anchor when Dana Wagner retires.

(A) reporter
(B) reporting
(C) to report
(D) will report

117. Residents ------- raised concerns about the project's impact on traffic congestion.

(A) extremely
(B) unlikely
(C) densely
(D) primarily

118. ------- your Fromo grocery order is placed before 10:00 A.M., it will be delivered the same day.

(A) That
(B) Such
(C) As long as
(D) In spite of

119. The finance department will be ------- a lunch-and-learn session on Wednesday.

(A) contacting
(B) collecting
(C) meeting
(D) holding

120. ------- clothing must be worn by all personnel entering the construction zone.

(A) Protective
(B) Protecting
(C) Protect
(D) Protects

GO ON TO THE NEXT PAGE

121. At the Star Elite membership level, most flight changes can be made ------- incurring a rebooking fee.

(A) along
(B) without
(C) until
(D) inside

122. Any letter ------- sensitive information should be sent using a courier service.

(A) contains
(B) containing
(C) will contain
(D) has contained

123. Abelos Café sources its vegetables and fruit from local farms ------- possible.

(A) anyhow
(B) whenever
(C) once
(D) very

124. Demand for the Waterlace running shoes was so high that the store owner set a ------- of two pairs per customer.

(A) limit
(B) price
(C) supply
(D) procedure

125. The new security camera adjusts ------- in such a way that it can record quality video at night.

(A) himself
(B) oneself
(C) itself
(D) herself

126. Contact Ms. Meyer if you would like a hard copy of the budget analysis ------- during the president's presentation.

(A) occurred
(B) mentioned
(C) learned
(D) served

127. Saul's Pizzeria changed its menu options after receiving ------- negative customer feedback.

(A) increase
(B) increases
(C) to increase
(D) increasingly

128. Topticolor produces devices intended for use by ------- photographers.

(A) visible
(B) eventual
(C) amateur
(D) necessary

129. The study of consumer behavior will be repeated in order to ensure the ------- of the results.

(A) rely
(B) relies
(C) reliable
(D) reliability

130. Check e-mail ------- throughout the day to make sure important client communications are not overlooked.

(A) artificially
(B) periodically
(C) reluctantly
(D) simultaneously

PART 6

Directions: Read the texts that follow. A word, phrase, or sentence is missing in parts of each text. Four answer choices for each question are given below the text. Select the best answer to complete the text. Then mark the letter (A), (B), (C), or (D) on your answer sheet.

Questions 131-134 refer to the following notice.

Hemel Bookstore is seeking temporary store associates ------- the upcoming holiday season.
131.

Duties will include greeting customers and answering questions. ------- . In addition, associates
132.

will shelve, clean, and organize merchandise. We want to hire friendly and ------- candidates. To
133.

apply, please fill out an online job application at www.hemelbookstore.com/application. The

------- is October 21.
134.

131. (A) about
(B) on
(C) to
(D) for

132. (A) The job also involves processing sales transactions.
(B) We stay open until midnight during the holidays.
(C) Our bookstore carries art supplies as well.
(D) The café is on the first floor of the store.

133. (A) energetic
(B) energy
(C) energize
(D) energizer

134. (A) celebration
(B) release
(C) deadline
(D) meeting

GO ON TO THE NEXT PAGE

Fishing Village to Become Bustling Port

DODOMA (14 April)—The unassuming town of Kikole, on the Tanzanian coast, is set to become a fully equipped port after an increase in ------- in the region. The government has recently
135.
designated the area as a business district. This ------- attract new businesses and further spur
136.
economic growth. One firm, Marina International Shipping, has already announced plans to open a hub there. ------- .
137.

A number of government officials have recently expressed opposition to the plan. ------- , with the
138.
needed finances already secured, it seems certain that the project will move forward.

---

135. (A) security
     (B) tourism
     (C) investment
     (D) fishing

136. (A) is meant to
     (B) means to
     (C) meaning to
     (D) is meant for

137. (A) Some believe it would be better to
         make improvements to other ports.
     (B) The Tanzanian government has
         promised to fund the new port.
     (C) Developers hope to complete Kikole's
         transformation within ten years.
     (D) This would be the shipping company's
         first major presence in East Africa.

138. (A) Nonetheless
     (B) Therefore
     (C) In case
     (D) Equally as

Mark your calendars for this year's Family Fun Fair at Delray! Join us from June 20 to June 26

for seven days of summer fun. You will find not only fantastic food, rides, and games,

------- exciting shows for all ages. And make sure not to miss our newest -------. The Crazy
139.   **140.**

Cowboy Train is a thrilling journey through the Wild West!

This year's shows include the Bicycle Circus, the Dinosaur Show, and Walter the Magician.

Please note that all basic admission ticket holders will need to pay additional fees to gain

entrance to shows. -------.
                           141.

We also ------- a VIP Family Fun pass for $95. This pass provides free admission to all shows
       142.

plus unlimited free amusement rides.

---

139. (A) if only
(B) or else
(C) so that
(D) but also

140. (A) shop
(B) member
(C) attraction
(D) refreshment

141. (A) There are over twenty different food
vendors at the fair.
(B) There is an age requirement for most
rides at the fair.
(C) Refer to the entertainment schedule for
show times and prices.
(D) Visit our Web site to see whether you
are eligible.

142. (A) offer
(B) offered
(C) were offering
(D) will be offered

TEST 10

Brightman Heating and Cooling

16 Primrose Way

Sydney NSW 2146

(02) 5550 8899

www.brightmanheatingandcooling.com.au

15 May

Alia Bajpa

422 Hudson St.

Sydney NSW 2000

Dear Ms. Bajpa:

We have some important news to share with you. We ------- to retire and close the company after **143.**

40 years in the business. ------- , we want to make sure that you do not experience any disruption **144.**

to your service. For that reason, we have arranged for Kondo's Heating and Air to begin providing

service to you effective on 1 June. I'm certain you will be pleased with ------- service. **145.**

Kondo's is a wonderful company with experienced, highly skilled technicians. ------- . If you have **146.**

any questions, please do not hesitate to call.

Sincerely,

Nathaniel and Constance Brightman

143. (A) decide
(B) were deciding
(C) could decide
(D) have decided

144. (A) Similarly
(B) However
(C) In general
(D) At that time

145. (A) our
(B) their
(C) whose
(D) his

146. (A) Building a strong customer base can take years.
(B) We will be holding a grand reopening event.
(C) You should be receiving a letter from them soon.
(D) Many jobs in heating and air-conditioning are available.

PART 7

Directions: In this part you will read a selection of texts, such as magazine and newspaper articles, e-mails, and instant messages. Each text or set of texts is followed by several questions. Select the best answer for each question and mark the letter (A), (B), (C), or (D) on your answer sheet.

Questions 147-148 refer to the following text-message chain.

> **Brycen Bodine [1:07 P.M.]**
> Hi, Avichai. I finished the upholstery on the sofa and chairs for Ms. Levin. They look great! It's such a nice fabric. Which order should I work on next?
>
> **Avichai Rosen [1:14 P.M.]**
> Glad to hear it. I promised the Chens their dining chairs by Saturday. By the way, the Metropolitan Design Show on June 14 has been postponed to July 7.
>
> **Brycen Bodine [1:19 P.M.]**
> Oh, then I can't make it.
>
> **Avichai Rosen [1:22 P.M.]**
> That's too bad. I'll need at least two employees to come help. We'll be showing our office desks and bookshelves.
>
> **Brycen Bodine [1:24 P.M.]**
> I'll ask Rita and Tom if they are available on that day. Unfortunately, I have a family commitment out of town that day. I'll get started on the Chens' order now.
>
> **Avichai Rosen [1:25 P.M.]**
> Sounds good. Thank you!

147. What will Mr. Bodine most likely work on next?

(A) A sofa
(B) An office desk
(C) A bookshelf
(D) A set of chairs

148. At 1:19 P.M., what does Mr. Bodine mean when he writes, "I can't make it"?

(A) He will not be seeing Rita or Tom.
(B) He will not be able to attend an event.
(C) He will not be able to meet a deadline.
(D) He does not know how to build a piece of furniture.

GO ON TO THE NEXT PAGE ➤

TEST 10

Thank you for downloading the Spumoni mobile phone app!

At your current basic membership level, your ability to save recipes is limited to five per day. If you would like the freedom to save unlimited recipes daily, automatically generate shopping lists, create weekly meal plans, and track nutritional data, you can become a premium member for just $2.99 a month.

Many users find this small fee to be money well spent, as the premium features save them time and enable them to make healthier meal choices. Visit our "PM Community" Web page to view real testimonials from our premium members.

149. What does the notice encourage users to do?

(A) Share their own recipes
(B) Submit their own testimonials
(C) Upgrade their membership status
(D) Download a recent software update

150. According to the notice, why should users go to a Web page?

(A) To take a virtual tour
(B) To see a sample meal plan
(C) To compare ingredients from similar recipes
(D) To find out about people's experiences

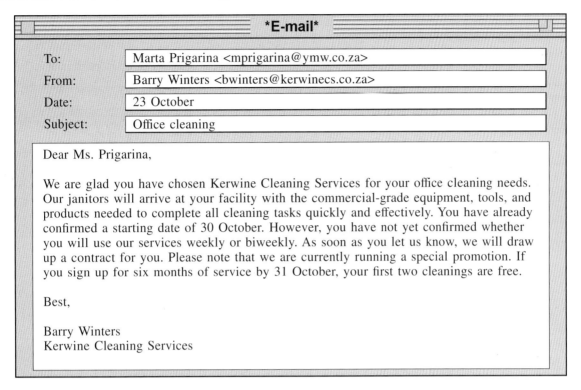

151. What does Mr. Winters ask Ms. Prigarina to confirm?

(A) How often to clean her office
(B) When he should arrive at her facility
(C) Where her office is located
(D) What products she prefers

152. How can Ms. Prigarina receive two free cleanings?

(A) By prepaying for services
(B) By signing a contract for six months
(C) By changing her starting date
(D) By using a discount code

Questions 153-154 refer to the following e-mail.

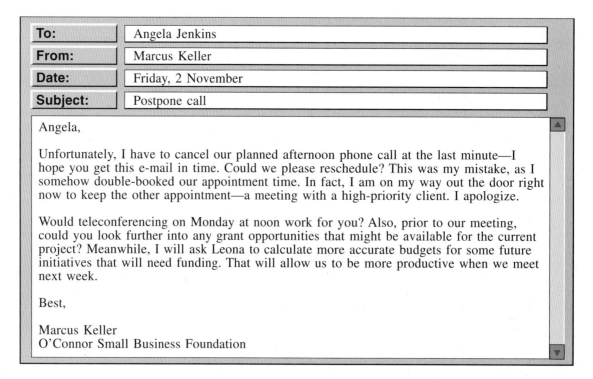

To:	Angela Jenkins
From:	Marcus Keller
Date:	Friday, 2 November
Subject:	Postpone call

Angela,

Unfortunately, I have to cancel our planned afternoon phone call at the last minute—I hope you get this e-mail in time. Could we please reschedule? This was my mistake, as I somehow double-booked our appointment time. In fact, I am on my way out the door right now to keep the other appointment—a meeting with a high-priority client. I apologize.

Would teleconferencing on Monday at noon work for you? Also, prior to our meeting, could you look further into any grant opportunities that might be available for the current project? Meanwhile, I will ask Leona to calculate more accurate budgets for some future initiatives that will need funding. That will allow us to be more productive when we meet next week.

Best,

Marcus Keller
O'Connor Small Business Foundation

153. Why does Mr. Keller say he cannot meet as planned?

(A) He anticipates a late return from a trip.
(B) He has no new information to report.
(C) He decided to take the afternoon off.
(D) He discovered a scheduling conflict.

154. What will most likely be done before the meeting?

(A) More financial information will be gathered.
(B) The meeting location will be changed.
(C) Another person will be invited to attend.
(D) A marketing plan will be modified.

Questions 155-157 refer to the following comment card.

Gracio Store Comment Card

Gracio Store is seeking to make your visit with us a better experience. Tell us about your visit to our store today so we can improve the way we serve you. And each week, one comment card will be drawn from those submitted to earn the customer a $50 store coupon!

Customer name: Huy Nguyen

E-mail contact: hnguyen@brightmail.co.nz

Date: 4 May

Reason for your visit today: Shopping for a gift

Comment: I was shopping for a friend's birthday. Ms. Davie, a sales associate in Accessories, greeted me and asked me questions to narrow down my gift search. She even offered to hold some of my bags so that I could shop more easily. She directed me to a colourful display of silk scarves and told me about the various places they were produced. The one I chose ended up in my planned price range too.

---

155. What is indicated about Gracio Store?

(A) It has recently opened.
(B) It is training new sales associates.
(C) It wants to improve its customer service.
(D) It has organized a competition.

156. The word "drawn" in paragraph 1, line 3, is closest in meaning to

(A) sketched
(B) picked
(C) attracted
(D) described

157. What does Mr. Nguyen write about his experience?

(A) He bought several different accessories.
(B) It took him a long time to find a gift.
(C) A manager answered his questions.
(D) He was able to stay within his gift budget.

Questions 158-160 refer to the following e-mail.

From:	lcho@cuvacorporatetraining.com
To:	all_staff@cuvacorporatetraining.com
Date:	Monday, April 12, 10:53 A.M.
Subject:	Special notice

Dear colleagues,

Please be advised that the Customer Security System (CSS) installed on your computer will be automatically updated this weekend. Specifically, the update will be taking place from midnight, Saturday, April 17, to midnight, Sunday, April 18. — [1] —. Your device will restart after the update has been completed.

The purpose of the update is twofold. First, it will increase the security of our client information. Moreover, it will improve overall system performance. — [2] —. As a result, you should notice improved processing speeds and less unplanned system downtime.

Please note that following the update there will be a change in the appearance of the CSS log-in screen, but this change will not affect the log-in procedures.

The tech support team will be available to answer any questions you may have before and after the update. — [3] —. By Thursday, you will receive a link to a training video with explanations of the new features that will become available with the update. — [4] —.

Best regards,

Leana Cho
Manager, Technical Support Team

---

158. Why was the e-mail sent?

(A) To motivate employees to increase their performance
(B) To instruct employees how to install a computer program update
(C) To obtain feedback about some new security procedures
(D) To alert employees about upcoming changes to some software

159. According to the e-mail, what will employees experience after April 18 ?

(A) Better quality Web cameras
(B) A different CSS log-in screen
(C) Faster technical support service
(D) More comfortable keyboards

160. In which of the positions marked [1], [2], [3], and [4] does the following sentence best belong?

"During this period, some functions will be limited or unavailable."

(A) [1]
(B) [2]
(C) [3]
(D) [4]

https://www.electronicsplusexpress.com/returns

Electronics Plus Express Return Policy

All returns require prior authorization. Please call during business hours (Monday–Friday 9:00 A.M. to 7:00 P.M. and weekends 10:00 A.M. to 5:00 P.M.) or e-mail Customer Service with your return request to receive a return authorization code.

Defective merchandise may be returned within 30 days of purchase date. Any new merchandise may be returned within 14 days of purchase date. The original box and packaging materials must be included. If you need to return the item by post, the store will issue and e-mail a postage-paid shipping label for you to print at home and attach to your parcel. The cost of your item will be refunded once it has been received.

Customer Service contact information is as follows:

Phone: 1-800-555-0176
E-mail: cs@electronicsplusexpress.com

161. For whom is the information most likely intended?

(A) Customers of Electronics Plus Express
(B) Customer service representatives
(C) Repair technicians
(D) Shipping department employees

162. What is indicated about all returns?

(A) They are only received at store locations.
(B) They cannot be processed on weekends.
(C) They require an authorization code.
(D) They are not accepted after 14 days.

163. What is mentioned about return shipping fees?

(A) They are calculated based on the weight of the package.
(B) They are listed on the company's Web site.
(C) They will be refunded to the customer within 30 days.
(D) They are paid for by the company.

GO ON TO THE NEXT PAGE

Questions 164-167 refer to the following online chat discussion.

Kelli Wethers [2:15 P.M.] Hi, Mr. Easton. I want to remind you about the dinner meeting with your client, Mr. Kasai, at the Magnolia Grill this evening. Mr. Kasai will be coming directly from the airport. Anna Kwon from our marketing department will be joining both of you.

Adam Easton [2:31 P.M.] Thanks, Ms. Wethers. It occurs to me, if he is coming straight from the airport, what will he do with his luggage?

Kelli Wethers [2:33 P.M.] Don't worry. Kyle Friedman is picking Mr. Kasai up at the airport and dropping the bags off at the hotel. I'm adding Kyle to this message now in case you two need to communicate.

Adam Easton [2:34 P.M.] Sounds great. I can drive Mr. Kasai back to his hotel following our meeting. It would be a nice gesture for such a key client.

Kyle Friedman [2:36 P.M.] Heading to the airport soon, Ms. Wethers. Just text me later if I need to know anything more.

Kelli Wethers [2:40 P.M.] Good idea, Mr. Easton. A taxi for after the dinner will not be necessary then.

164. What is the purpose of the online chat discussion?

(A) To review arrangements for a client visit
(B) To choose a location for a company celebration
(C) To give invitations to a dinner event
(D) To arrange a taxi for some traveling colleagues

165. Who will go to the airport?

(A) Ms. Wethers
(B) Mr. Easton
(C) Mr. Friedman
(D) Ms. Kwon

166. What is indicated about Mr. Kasai?

(A) He prefers to dine at the Magnolia Grill.
(B) He is an important customer.
(C) He wants to get to his hotel on time.
(D) He is confused about driving directions.

167. At 2:40 P.M., what does Ms. Wethers most likely mean when she writes, "Good idea, Mr. Easton"?

(A) She thinks that a dinner meeting should be informal.
(B) She believes that a hotel selection is appropriate.
(C) She does not think that a client has a driver's license.
(D) She agrees that a client should be offered a ride to a hotel.

To:	staff@rindersbusiness.co.ke
From:	dcloeten@rindersbusiness.co.ke
Subject:	Information
Date:	25 October

Dear Rinders Staff:

Our company is growing, and I am pleased to welcome new staff members! Those in our Nairobi office will get to know Mary Gichuki very well. She will be the new office manager there, beginning on 1 November. Some of you met her last week when she visited the office. She will be replacing David Alberts.

Anila Pillai will also be a new face in our Nairobi office. Ms. Pillai will be an administrative assistant, and she will greet visitors, answer the phone, and perform office duties. She will work on Wednesdays, Thursdays, and Fridays from 10:00 A.M. to 3:00 P.M.

Mark Karunga, who has worked in the Nairobi office for the past fifteen years, is being promoted to senior accountant and will work in our new Mombasa office beginning on 15 November.

I will soon be sending another e-mail alerting you to more new faces in our offices since we are still hiring personnel for the Mombasa location. We hope to have all positions filled there before the grand opening in November.

Sincerely,

Deborah Cloeten
Vice President
Rinders Business Systems

168. What is the main purpose of the e-mail?

(A) To describe some staff changes
(B) To discuss some new office procedures
(C) To contrast two company locations
(D) To report on recent office visitors

169. Who will be working part-time at Rinders Business Systems?

(A) Ms. Gichuki
(B) Mr. Alberts
(C) Ms. Pillai
(D) Ms. Cloeten

170. What is NOT indicated about Mr. Karunga?

(A) He is an accountant.
(B) He is a recent hire.
(C) He is being promoted.
(D) He is being transferred.

171. What does Ms. Cloeten indicate about the Mombasa location?

(A) It is her new workplace.
(B) It has not yet opened.
(C) It is fully staffed.
(D) It is larger than the Nairobi office.

GO ON TO THE NEXT PAGE

http://www.finnertontheater.com/aboutus

The Finnerton Theater

The Finnerton Theater is Grenville's premier cinema for independent movies, documentaries, and film classics. — [1] —. Locally owned and operated for over 50 years, the theater retains its strong connection to the city. Once a top entertainment destination, it later persisted through years of economic stagnation and urban decline. — [2] —. An anchor for neighborhood revitalization and growth, the Finnerton Theater now serves as the backbone of the city's thriving Riverside Arts District.

In the last half century, the Finnerton Theater has become a destination for film lovers from throughout the region. Attendees from cities as far away as Nesterport and Belmere come regularly to enjoy the theater's unique ambiance. Over the theater's history, more than 1,000 movies have been screened and dozens of others have premiered. — [3] —. The Finnerton Theater has hosted events with critically acclaimed directors and served as the stage for renowned public speakers. In the past decade, it has served as the host for the Greater Cincinnati Film Festival, the Midwest Documentary Fest, and the annual Clearacre Conference, which is sponsored by the city's largest employer, Clearacre Tech. Five years ago, the theater was added to the state's register of historic places.

To this day, filmgoers continue to frequent the Finnerton Theater whenever film releases are screened. — [4] —. And despite the ever-increasing popularity of online film-streaming services, ticket sales at the Finnerton Theater have risen continuously since its listing in the state's register. It is a true cultural gem and a source of civic pride for local residents.

172. What is the purpose of the Web page?

    (A) To announce an upcoming film festival
    (B) To discuss the opening of a new theater
    (C) To promote a recent film release
    (D) To profile a local movie theater

173. In what city is the Finnerton Theater located?

    (A) Grenville
    (B) Nesterport
    (C) Belmere
    (D) Cincinnati

174. What is indicated about the Finnerton Theater?

    (A) It will move to a new building soon.
    (B) It has expanded its concession menu.
    (C) It is where a yearly conference is held.
    (D) It is the city's largest employer.

175. In which of the positions marked [1], [2], [3], and [4] does the following sentence best belong?

    "Amid a changing cityscape, it continued to evolve with the neighborhood around it."

    (A) [1]
    (B) [2]
    (C) [3]
    (D) [4]

GO ON TO THE NEXT PAGE

TEST 10

Here at Hapler's Landscape Company, we believe that landscape design does not have to be challenging. Our goal is to design unique, beautiful gardens that meet our clients' specifications and require minimal care once they have been planted. We also care deeply about reducing air, soil, and water pollution. For more information about how we achieve this, visit haplers.co.uk.

Our process is implemented in four phases. This is how it works:

Phase 1 – One of our consultants will call you and discuss your goals and vision for your property.

Phase 2 – We will conduct a thorough survey of your land to collect information on water level, elevation, soil type, and sun patterns. Note that we work on many projects at once and may not complete the survey until up to a month after your initial consultation call.

Phase 3 – Our design specialists will present you with a proposed design to suit your existing landscape. We will discuss adjustments until you are satisfied with every aspect of the plan.

Phase 4 – We will implement the design per approved project specifications.

Are you ready to get this process started and watch your land change before your eyes? Contact Hapler's at 01632 960255.

To:	melinda_grotenhuis@charmail.net.uk
From:	martin.sampsell@haplers.co.uk
Date:	22 February
Subject:	Proposal
Attachment:	🔗 haplers-draft1.org

Dear Ms. Grotenhuis,

I have attached an initial draft of a landscape design for you to consider. In our property walk-through, you indicated where you want to have a walkway from the parking area to your office. However, we are proposing something slightly different for you to consider. Experience has taught us to make pathways in commercial settings as direct as possible. Otherwise, people often walk through the grass anyway. You also mentioned wanting year-round flowers, so we have incorporated a variety of native plants with different blooming seasons into the design.

Please give me a call once you've had a chance to look at this design and I'll walk you through the details.

Martin Sampsell

176. What does the brochure indicate about the company's designs?

(A) They are colorful.
(B) They are easy to maintain.
(C) They make use of vacant areas.
(D) They incorporate old structures.

177. Why are readers directed to Hapler's Web site?

(A) To understand its environmental practices
(B) To view its staff's credentials
(C) To explore design ideas
(D) To view testimonials from previous clients

178. What is indicated about Hapler's?

(A) It provides services to multiple clients at the same time.
(B) It bills all of its clients on an hourly basis.
(C) It works with residential clients only.
(D) It is recommended by most of its clients.

179. At which phase of the process is Ms. Grotenhuis' project?

(A) Phase 1
(B) Phase 2
(C) Phase 3
(D) Phase 4

180. Why does Mr. Sampsell suggest changing the location of a pathway?

(A) To avoid a potential hazard
(B) To provide the most efficient option
(C) To take advantage of the shade available
(D) To show the most attractive side of a building

GO ON TO THE NEXT PAGE

Questions 181-185 refer to the following notice and e-mail.

Merenville Regional Bus Authority
Notice to the Public

In response to its recently conducted passenger survey, the Merenville Regional Bus Authority (MRBA) will be adjusting its Saturday and Sunday service between Merenville Central Station (MCS) and Louberg. The following schedule changes will be in effect as of May 1.

- Bus 36, in service on Saturdays only, will be departing MCS every hour on the hour, with the first departure scheduled for 6:00 A.M. and the last to take place at midnight. This adjustment is intended to provide passengers with more departure options.

- Bus 47, which runs on both days, will now be departing MCS at 7:00 A.M. in addition to its regularly scheduled departure times of 12:15 P.M. and 6:15 P.M.

- Bus 51, which runs on both days, will continue to have three departures from MCS. However, they are now scheduled to take place at 7:30 A.M., 1:30 P.M., and 4:30 P.M.

- Bus 65, in service on Sundays only, will now be departing MCS at 10:00 A.M. instead of 8:00 A.M. Departures scheduled for 1:00 P.M., 3:00 P.M., and 5:00 P.M. remain unchanged.

To:	Adriano Martinez <amartinez@mrba.com>
From:	Claire Brunkhorst <cbrunkhorst@mrba.com>
Date:	May 14
Re:	Switch shift request

Hi Adriano,

Regarding your request, I can take over your late-night bus driving shift on Saturday, May 22. I realize that I'll have to be alert, so I'll make sure to get plenty of rest.

In return, could you possibly take over my day shift on Tuesday, May 25? A friend of mine, who works for the same Chicago-based company that I used to work for, will be visiting me that day.

Thanks in advance for your assistance.

Claire Brunkhorst, MRBA Associate

181. What is the purpose of the notice?

(A) To introduce a new bus route
(B) To report on the closing of a bus station
(C) To announce transportation-service improvements
(D) To invite comments about proposed schedule changes

182. What is suggested in the notice about Bus 47 ?

(A) It has new stops on its route.
(B) It has the earliest departure time.
(C) It used to depart only in the afternoon.
(D) It is in service on only one day of the week.

183. What bus will Ms. Brunkhorst most likely drive on May 22 ?

(A) Bus 36
(B) Bus 47
(C) Bus 51
(D) Bus 65

184. In the e-mail, the word "realize" in paragraph 1, line 2, is closest in meaning to

(A) earn
(B) comprehend
(C) exchange
(D) achieve

185. What does Ms. Brunkhorst indicate in the e-mail?

(A) She plans to take a new job in Chicago.
(B) She does not have time to visit Mr. Martinez.
(C) She prefers to work the early shift on Tuesday.
(D) She would like to spend time with an old friend.

GO ON TO THE NEXT PAGE

Quick Fix Workshops

Join Hagerstown residents at the community center on January 15 for our Quick Fix workshop series. There is sure to be at least one topic that will interest you. For example, you might learn how to economize financially without inhibiting your lifestyle or to discover ways of reducing your impact on the environment by living smarter. Alternatively, by attending a workshop, you may find inspiration for improving the health and well-being of your family. Our own Grant Cardwell, prominent and long-time Hagerstown resident, will be leading a session on weatherizing your home. Arrive early to secure a seat for that one since nearly everyone is eager to learn how to trim their heating and cooling bills.

Registration is not required, although we will record attendance. For questions, contact Mike Greenly at m.greenly@hagerstown.gov.

Quick Fix Workshop Series - Schedule

10:00 A.M.	**Weatherization** – Make your home more energy efficient by learning from an expert from the Marion County Regional Weatherization Initiative (MCRWI). **Save Water and Your Wallet** – Find out about the Hagerstown water supply and get tips for limiting consumption and reducing your monthly water utility bills.
11:00 A.M.	**DIY Personal Care Products** – Make your own everyday personal care products, such as deodorant, soap, and skin moisturizer.
1:00 P.M.	**Creating Natural Spaces** – Grow native plants and learn about nurturing the local ecosystem. Help build a naturally sustainable habitat right in your own garden or yard.
2:00 P.M.	**A New Year, a Healthier You** – See demonstrations on creating delicious and healthy meals for your family. Samples will be provided. **Essential Maintenance** – Keep your vehicle in top driving condition despite harsh winter weather.

To:	Mike Greenly
From:	Antonio Perkins
Date:	January 12
Subject:	Inquiry

Dear Mr. Greenly,

I recently moved to Hagerstown, and I am interested in learning about the native vegetation in the area. I have a lot of experience growing trees and plants in my former hometown, but the varieties that grow here are completely different. A neighbor mentioned that there would be a session related to gardening, but do any of the workshops address my specific interest in learning about the native flora and fauna?

Sincerely,

Antonio Perkins

186. According to the flyer, what topic will be addressed in the workshops?

(A) Beautifying a home
(B) Saving money
(C) Caring for pets
(D) Using city recycling services

187. What is most likely true about Mr. Cardwell?

(A) He is a professional weather forecaster.
(B) He is a member of the MCRWI organization.
(C) He is a university professor.
(D) He is in charge of organizing the Quick Fix workshop series.

188. At what time is a session offered about working on cars?

(A) 10:00 A.M.
(B) 11:00 A.M.
(C) 1:00 P.M.
(D) 2:00 P.M.

189. What does Mr. Perkins want information about?

(A) Event topics
(B) Event registration
(C) Event location
(D) Event scheduling

190. What workshop will Mr. Perkins likely attend?

(A) Weatherization
(B) DIY Personal Care Products
(C) Creating Natural Spaces
(D) Essential Maintenance

GO ON TO THE NEXT PAGE

TEST 10

E-mail

To:	Rowan's Playland management staff
From:	Henry Louis
Date:	12 April
Subject:	Update

Dear All,

It was a pleasure to see everyone at yesterday's management meeting. Please note that we will not be able to meet the next two Mondays, since I will be out of town. That means we will not meet again until next month. If there is an urgent issue that needs attention in the meantime, please contact Lydia Chang.

For now, we will move forward with plans for installing a climbing wall in the Runabout Room. Kelly Mulgrew has agreed to send us the names of some companies that can do the work, along with their availability and prices.

Tom Holden will research a new vendor for the sandwiches and snacks we sell at the Little Engineer Café.

Thank you,

Henry Louis
Rowan's Playland

CLIMBING WALL OPTIONS

Company	Total Cost	Earliest Installation Date
Rick's Walls of Fun	$1450	29 May
Climbing Walls Galore	$1300	18 May
Pru's Climbing Walls	$1350	3 June
Wethersfield Walls and Playgrounds	$1450	10 June

Note: Rick's, Pru's and Wethersfield offer green and black climbing walls. Climbing Walls Galore offers many colors and mix-and-match options.

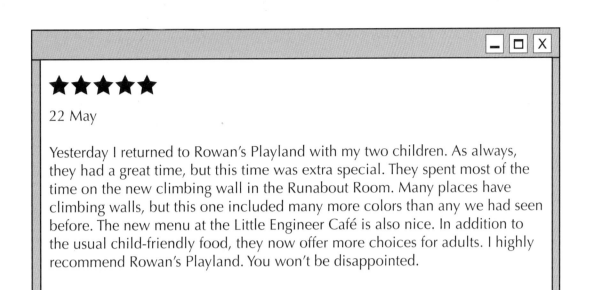

★★★★★

22 May

Yesterday I returned to Rowan's Playland with my two children. As always, they had a great time, but this time was extra special. They spent most of the time on the new climbing wall in the Runabout Room. Many places have climbing walls, but this one included many more colors than any we had seen before. The new menu at the Little Engineer Café is also nice. In addition to the usual child-friendly food, they now offer more choices for adults. I highly recommend Rowan's Playland. You won't be disappointed.

John Rawlston
East Lindstrom Village

191. According to the e-mail, how often do management meetings usually take place?

(A) Twice a week
(B) Once a week
(C) Twice a month
(D) Once a month

192. What does the e-mail indicate about the Runabout Room?

(A) It will undergo some changes.
(B) It will be hosting a special event.
(C) It was recently opened.
(D) It was featured in a recent publication.

193. Who most likely created the chart?

(A) Mr. Louis
(B) Ms. Chang
(C) Ms. Mulgrew
(D) Mr. Holden

194. According to the online review, what is true about the café?

(A) Its prices have been reduced.
(B) Its hours have been extended.
(C) Its menu includes new items.
(D) Its interior was redecorated.

195. What company most likely installed the climbing wall at Rowan's Playland?

(A) Rick's Walls of Fun
(B) Climbing Walls Galore
(C) Pru's Climbing Walls
(D) Wethersfield Walls and Playgrounds

GO ON TO THE NEXT PAGE

Questions 196-200 refer to the following brochure, chart, and e-mail.

Dublin in the Sun

with Donovan Tour Operators

The following tours run from 1 April to 30 August. Please visit our headquarters or phone us at +353 22 455 0827 for tour start times each day.

Dublin Castle—3 hours, €15 per person
Guided tour of Dublin's thirteenth-century castle led by experts in its history. Price includes entry to the castle. Starts and finishes at the castle's main visitor entrance.

Secrets of Dublin—2 hours, €12 per person
Walking tour around Dublin. Discover its untold stories. Starts and finishes at Donovan's headquarters.

Garden of Ireland—5 hours, €30 per person
Half-day excursion to the mountains south of Dublin and the old city of Kilkenny. Starts and finishes at Gardiner Street Coach Station.

Galway Mini Cruise—9 hours, €70 per person
Full-day excursion to the Atlantic coast for a mini cruise beside the magnificent Cliffs of Moher. Includes lunch. Starts and finishes at Gardiner Street Coach Station.

Donovan Tour Operators: July Summary				
Tour Name	Tours per day	Average profit per tour (€)	Average profit per day (€)	Average customer review (/5)
Dublin Castle	8	41	328	4.8
Secrets of Dublin	6	58	348	3.3
Garden of Ireland	2	124	248	4.5
Galway Mini Cruise	1	-297	-297	4.6

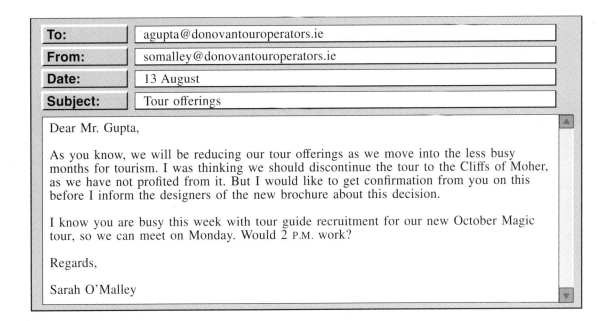

To:	agupta@donovantouroperators.ie
From:	somalley@donovantouroperators.ie
Date:	13 August
Subject:	Tour offerings

Dear Mr. Gupta,

As you know, we will be reducing our tour offerings as we move into the less busy months for tourism. I was thinking we should discontinue the tour to the Cliffs of Moher, as we have not profited from it. But I would like to get confirmation from you on this before I inform the designers of the new brochure about this decision.

I know you are busy this week with tour guide recruitment for our new October Magic tour, so we can meet on Monday. Would 2 P.M. work?

Regards,

Sarah O'Malley

196. According to the brochure, what do all of the tours have in common?

(A) They last the same number of hours.
(B) They start from the same place.
(C) They are offered during the same months.
(D) They cost the same per person.

197. What does the chart indicate about the Dublin Castle tour?

(A) It is the most highly rated.
(B) It runs less often than the Secrets of Dublin tour.
(C) It makes the most profit per day of all the tours.
(D) It makes more profit per tour than the Garden of Ireland tour.

198. How many tours to Kilkenny does Donovan Tour Operators run each day?

(A) One
(B) Two
(C) Six
(D) Eight

199. What is the purpose of the e-mail?

(A) To place an order for brochures
(B) To explain policies to a new tour guide
(C) To schedule a meeting with a colleague
(D) To respond to a customer complaint

200. According to Ms. O'Malley, what tour will most likely be discontinued?

(A) Dublin Castle
(B) Secrets of Dublin
(C) Garden of Ireland
(D) Galway Mini Cruise

Stop! This is the end of the test. If you finish before time is called, you may go back to Parts 5, 6, and 7 and check your work.

TEST 10

ANSWER SHEET

ETS® TOEIC® 토익 정기시험 기출문제집

수험번호

응시일자 : 20　　　년　　　월　　　일

성명 | 한글
한자
영자

Test 01 (Part 5~7)

Test 02 (Part 5~7)

ANSWER SHEET

ETS® TOEIC® 토익 정기시험 기출문제집

수험번호

응시일자 : 20   년   월   일

성명 한글
한자
영자

Test 03 (Part 5~7)

101 102 103 104 105 106 107 108 109 110 111 112 113 114 115 116 117 118 119 120
121 122 123 124 125 126 127 128 129 130 131 132 133 134 135 136 137 138 139 140
141 142 143 144 145 146 147 148 149 150 151 152 153 154 155 156 157 158 159 160
161 162 163 164 165 166 167 168 169 170 171 172 173 174 175 176 177 178 179 180
181 182 183 184 185 186 187 188 189 190 191 192 193 194 195 196 197 198 199 200

Test 04 (Part 5~7)

101 102 103 104 105 106 107 108 109 110 111 112 113 114 115 116 117 118 119 120
121 122 123 124 125 126 127 128 129 130 131 132 133 134 135 136 137 138 139 140
141 142 143 144 145 146 147 148 149 150 151 152 153 154 155 156 157 158 159 160
161 162 163 164 165 166 167 168 169 170 171 172 173 174 175 176 177 178 179 180
181 182 183 184 185 186 187 188 189 190 191 192 193 194 195 196 197 198 199 200

ANSWER SHEET

ETS® TOEIC® 토익 정기시험 기출문제집

성명	한글
	한자
	영자

수험번호

응시일자 : 20   년   월   일

Test 05 (Part 5~7)

(Answer bubbles for questions 101–200, options A B C D)

Test 06 (Part 5~7)

(Answer bubbles for questions 101–200, options A B C D)

ANSWER SHEET

ETS® TOEIC® 토익 정기시험 기출문제집

수험번호

응시일자 : 20   년   월   일

성명 한글 / 한자 / 영자

Test 07 (Part 5~7)

101–200 answer bubbles (a b c d)

Test 08 (Part 5~7)

101–200 answer bubbles (a b c d)

ANSWER SHEET

ETS® TOEIC 토익® 정기시험 기출문제집

수험번호

응시일자 : 20   년   월   일

| 한글 |
| 한자 |
| 영자 |

성명

Test 09 (Part 5~7)

101	102	103	104	105	106	107	108	109	110	111	112	113	114	115	116	117	118	119	120
121	122	123	124	125	126	127	128	129	130	131	132	133	134	135	136	137	138	139	140
141	142	143	144	145	146	147	148	149	150	151	152	153	154	155	156	157	158	159	160
161	162	163	164	165	166	167	168	169	170	171	172	173	174	175	176	177	178	179	180
181	182	183	184	185	186	187	188	189	190	191	192	193	194	195	196	197	198	199	200

Test 10 (Part 5~7)

101	102	103	104	105	106	107	108	109	110	111	112	113	114	115	116	117	118	119	120
121	122	123	124	125	126	127	128	129	130	131	132	133	134	135	136	137	138	139	140
141	142	143	144	145	146	147	148	149	150	151	152	153	154	155	156	157	158	159	160
161	162	163	164	165	166	167	168	169	170	171	172	173	174	175	176	177	178	179	180
181	182	183	184	185	186	187	188	189	190	191	192	193	194	195	196	197	198	199	200

토익® 정기시험
기출문제집 3
1000
READING

정답 및 해설

기출 TEST 1

101 (A)	**102** (D)	**103** (D)	**104** (D)	**105** (A)
106 (B)	**107** (C)	**108** (D)	**109** (D)	**110** (A)
111 (B)	**112** (B)	**113** (C)	**114** (B)	**115** (D)
116 (B)	**117** (C)	**118** (C)	**119** (C)	**120** (A)
121 (A)	**122** (C)	**123** (D)	**124** (A)	**125** (C)
126 (D)	**127** (B)	**128** (B)	**129** (C)	**130** (B)
131 (D)	**132** (B)	**133** (A)	**134** (D)	**135** (A)
136 (B)	**137** (B)	**138** (C)	**139** (B)	**140** (D)
141 (A)	**142** (B)	**143** (D)	**144** (A)	**145** (B)
146 (C)	**147** (B)	**148** (C)	**149** (B)	**150** (D)
151 (B)	**152** (C)	**153** (A)	**154** (D)	**155** (D)
156 (A)	**157** (B)	**158** (C)	**159** (C)	**160** (A)
161 (D)	**162** (A)	**163** (D)	**164** (A)	**165** (C)
166 (B)	**167** (C)	**168** (A)	**169** (B)	**170** (C)
171 (A)	**172** (B)	**173** (C)	**174** (B)	**175** (D)
176 (C)	**177** (B)	**178** (C)	**179** (D)	**180** (A)
181 (C)	**182** (B)	**183** (A)	**184** (D)	**185** (C)
186 (B)	**187** (C)	**188** (A)	**189** (D)	**190** (A)
191 (B)	**192** (C)	**193** (D)	**194** (D)	**195** (D)
196 (A)	**197** (C)	**198** (B)	**199** (C)	**200** (D)

PART 5

101 형용사 자리 _ 명사 수식

해설 빈칸에는 명사 goods를 수식하는 형용사 또는 goods와 복합명사를 이루는 명사가 들어갈 수 있다. 문맥상 '지역의 제품, 지역산 제품'이라는 내용이 되어야 하므로, 형용사인 (A) regional(지역의)이 정답이다. (C) region과 (D) regions는 '지역'을 의미하기 때문에 goods와 복합명사를 이룰 수 없고, (B) regionally는 부사로 품사상 빈칸에 들어갈 수 없다.

번역 모우기 파인 기프트는 폭넓은 지역산 제품으로 잘 알려져 있다.

어휘 known for 잘 알려진, 유명한   a range of 다양한, 광범위한

102 명사 어휘

해설 등위접속사 and가 빈칸과 인근 지역(surrounding areas)을 연결하고 있으므로, 빈칸에도 지역을 나타내는 단어가 들어가야 한다. 따라서 area와 성격 및 규모가 비슷한 (D) city(도시)가 정답이다.

번역 그 도시 및 인근 지역에서 소득 수준이 증가하고 있다.

어휘 income 소득, 수입   surrounding 인근의, 주위의

103 인칭대명사의 격 _ 소유격

해설 명사구 next electricity bill을 한정 수식하는 자리이다. 형용사

next 앞에 올 수 있는 것은 소유격이므로, (D) your가 정답이다.

번역 최근 요금 변동이 있었으니 귀하의 다음 번 전기 요금이 약간 감소할 것으로 예상하세요.

어휘 recent 최근의   rate 요금   electricity bill 전기 요금   slightly 약간

104 전치사 어휘

해설 the south-facing windows와 어울리는 전치사를 선택해야 한다. 남향 창문을 통해 전망을 즐길 수 있다는 내용이 되어야 하므로, '~을 통해'라는 의미의 (D) through가 정답이다.

번역 호텔 투숙객들은 남향 창문을 통해 멋진 바다 풍경을 볼 수 있다.

어휘 view 전망, 풍경   south-facing 남향의   except ~를 제외하고

105 to부정사

해설 동사 would like 다음에는 to부정사나 명사가 올 수 있는데, 빈칸 뒤에 명사 a meeting이 있으므로 빈칸에는 이를 목적어로 취할 수 있는 to부정사가 들어가야 한다. 따라서 (A) to arrange가 정답이다. (B) arranging과 (C) having arranged는 동명사, (D) arrangement는 명사로 구조상 빈칸에 들어갈 수 없다.

번역 김 씨는 가능한 한 빨리 재스퍼 사 거래에 관한 회의를 잡고 싶어 한다.

어휘 account 고객(사), 거래 (관계), 계정   arrange 마련하다, 주선하다, 준비하다

106 부사 어휘

해설 공장의 입지조건(located near the train station)을 적절히 묘사하는 부사를 선택해야 한다. 따라서 '편리하게'라는 의미의 (B) conveniently가 정답이다. conveniently(편리한 위치에)/ideally(이상적인 위치에)/strategically(전략적인 위치에) located는 빈출 표현이므로 암기해 두자.

번역 공장은 기차역 근처의 편리한 위치에 있다.

어휘 regularly 규칙적으로, 정기적으로   brightly 밝게   collectively 집합적으로, 총괄하여

107 명사 자리 _ 전치사의 목적어 _ 복합명사

해설 transportation과 함께 복합명사를 이루어 전치사 Because of의 목적어 역할을 하는 명사 자리이다. 따라서 보기 중 명사로 쓰일 수 있는 (C) delays(지연, 연착)가 정답이다. (B) to delay는 앞에 온 명사를 수식할 수는 있지만, 빈칸 뒤에 목적어가 없으며 의미상으로도 어색하므로 오답이다. (A) are delayed와 (D) had delayed는 본동사이므로 구조상 빈칸에 들어갈 수 없다.

번역 겨울 날씨로 인한 교통편 지연으로 회의 참가자들 중 일부가 늦게 도착할 지도 모른다.

어휘 transportation 교통(편), 운송   due to ~때문에   conference 회의   participant 참가자   delay 지연시키다

108 접속사 자리 _ 어휘

해설　두 개의 완전한 절을 이어주는 접속사 자리로, 보기에서 부사절 접속사인 (C) although와 (D) before 중 하나를 선택해야 한다. 문맥상 시점을 나타내는 접속사가 빈칸에 들어가서 '작은 문제들(small issues)이 커지기 전에 해결되게끔 해준다'라는 내용이 되어야 자연스럽다. 따라서 (D) before가 정답이 된다. (A) as a result와 (B) in addition은 (접속)부사로 절과 절을 연결할 수 없다.

번역　난방기기를 적절하게 유지 관리하면 작은 문제들은 커지기 전에 분명 해결될 수 있다.

어휘　proper 적절한　maintenance 유지 관리　ensure 반드시 ~하게 하다, 보장하다　as a result 결과적으로　in addition 게다가

109 부사 자리 _ 동사 수식

해설　be동사 is와 과거분사 organized 사이에서 동사를 수식하는 부사 자리이므로, (D) clearly(명확하게)가 정답이다. (A) clear는 형용사/동사, (B) clearing은 동명사/현재분사, (C) clearest는 형용사의 최상급으로 품사상 빈칸에 들어갈 수 없다.

번역　크로엘 데코레이터즈의 웹사이트에 있는 정보는 명확하게 정리되어 있다.

어휘　organize 정리하다, 체계화하다

110 동사 어휘 _ 과거분사

해설　전치사 as와 어울려 쓰이는 과거분사를 선택해야 한다. 주어인 The Copley Corporation이 회사로서 받는 평가를 설명하는 문장이므로, be동사 및 as와 함께 '~로 알려져 있다, ~로 인정받다'라는 의미를 완성하는 (A) recognized가 정답이다.

번역　코플리 사는 전 세계에서 직원들을 고용하는 회사로 흔히 알려져 있다.

어휘　frequently 흔히, 자주　employ 고용하다　recognized 알려진, 인정받는　permitted 허가된　prepared 준비된　controlled 통제된

111 전치사 자리 _ 어휘

해설　Payments부터 4:00 P.M.까지가 주어, will be processed가 동사인 문장이다. 따라서 빈칸에는 과거분사 made와 시간 표현을 적절히 연결해주는 전치사가 들어가야 하므로, (B) after가 정답이다. 참고로, (A) later가 비교급 부사로 쓰일 경우 전치사 (C) than과 결합하여 '오후 4시보다 더 늦게'라는 의미로 쓰일 수 있으나, 각자 단독으로 빈칸에 들어갈 수는 없다.

번역　오후 4시 이후 이뤄진 결제 건은 다음 영업일에 처리될 것이다.

어휘　payment 결제 (건), 지불(금)　process 처리하다　following 다음의　business day 영업일

112 형용사 어휘

해설　고용(hires)의 대상이 되는 기술자들(engineers)이 갖추어야 할 수

학 실력(mathematics skills) 수준을 나타내는 형용사가 필요하다. 따라서 '고급의, 상급의'라는 의미의 (B) advanced가 정답이다.

번역　그린피들 워터 트리트먼트는 고급 수학 실력을 갖춘 기술자를 채용한다.

어휘　adjusted 조정된, 조절된　eager 열렬한, 간절히 바라는　faithful 충실한, 신의 있는

113 동명사

해설　명사 the neighborhood를 목적어로 취하는 동시에 전치사 After의 목적어 역할을 하는 자리이다. 따라서 빈칸에는 동명사가 들어가야 하므로, (C) evaluating이 정답이다. (A) evaluation은 명사로 After의 목적어 역할을 할 수는 있지만, the neighborhood를 목적어로 취할 수 없으므로 오답이다. (B) evaluate는 동사, (D) evaluated는 동사/과거분사로 품사상 빈칸에 들어갈 수 없다.

번역　박 씨는 인근 지역을 평가한 후 자신의 카페를 토마스빌로 옮기지 않기로 결정했다.

어휘　neighborhood 인근 (지역)　evaluation 평가　evaluate 평가하다

114 전치사 어휘

해설　기간을 나타내는 명사구 the past three years를 목적어로 취하는 전치사 자리이다. 따라서 '~동안'이라는 뜻으로 현재완료 시제(has been)와 어울려 쓰이는 (B) for가 정답이다.

번역　지난 3년간 캠포스의 평균 강수량은 22.7센티미터였다.

어휘　average 평균(의)　precipitation 강수량

115 형용사 자리 _ 명사 수식

해설　빈칸에는 명사 revision을 수식하는 형용사 또는 revision과 복합명사를 이루는 명사가 들어갈 수 있다. 문맥상 효율성 제고(Improving efficiency)에 필요한(require) 절차 수정 방식을 묘사하는 형용사가 필요하므로, (D) creative(창의적인)가 정답이다. (A) create는 동사로 품사상 빈칸에 들어갈 수 없고, (B) creativity는 '창의력', (C) creation은 '창작'이라는 뜻으로 revision과 복합명사를 이루기엔 어색하다.

번역　퍼원 매뉴팩처링에서 효율성을 제고하려면 기존 절차를 창의적으로 바꾸는 일이 필요하다.

어휘　improve 향상시키다　efficiency 효율성　require 필요로 하다, 요구하다　revision 수정, 변경　existing 기존의

116 접속사 자리

해설　빈칸은 두 개의 완전한 절을 이어주는 접속사 자리이다. 따라서 보기 중 부사절 접속사인 (B) unless(~하지 않는 한)가 정답이다. (A) even은 형용사/부사/동사, (C) similarly와 (D) also는 부사로 절과 절을 연결할 수 없다.

번역　회의 참석자들은 1인실 특별 요청서를 제출하지 않는 한 숙소를 공유하게 될 것이다.

어휘 **attendee** 참석자 **accommodation** 숙소 **submit** 제출하다 **request** 요청 **even** 평평한, 고른; 심지어; 평평하게 하다 **similarly** 마찬가지로

117 명사 자리 _ to부정사의 목적어

해설 to부정사 To receive의 목적어 역할을 하는 명사 자리이다. 따라서 (C) renewals(갱신, 기한 연장)가 정답이다. (A) renew는 동사, (B) renewed는 동사/과거분사, (D) to renew는 to부정사로 구조상 빈칸에 들어갈 수 없다.

번역 갱신을 하시려면 반드시 잡지 주문서의 알맞은 칸에 표시해 주십시오.

어휘 **appropriate** 적절한, 알맞은 **order form** 주문서 **renewal** 갱신, (기한의) 연장

118 형용사 어휘

해설 빈칸을 포함한 절은 기부금이 증가하는(Donations ~ rise) 경우를 나타낸다. 따라서 빈칸에는 경제(economy)에 대한 소비자의 긍정적인 판단을 나타내는 형용사가 들어가야 자연스러우므로, '신뢰하는, 좋을 거라 확신하는'이라는 의미의 (C) confident가 정답이다.

번역 소비자들이 경제상황에 대해 확신하게 되면 나투시 야생동물 보호구역으로 가는 기부금이 증가한다.

어휘 **donation** 기부(금) **reserve** 보호구역 **economy** 경제 (상황) **careful** 주의하는 **helpful** 도움이 되는 **durable** 내구성이 있는

119 부사 자리 _ 과거분사 수식

해설 부사절 접속사 When 뒤에는 완전한 절 또는 분사구문이 올 수 있는데, 주절의 주어 Tilda's Restorative Cream과 동사 apply(~을 바르다, 도포하다)의 의미로 보아 applied(도포되는)가 과거분사로 쓰였음을 알 수 있다. 따라서 빈칸에는 applied를 수식하는 부사가 들어가야 하므로, (C) consistently(지속적으로)가 정답이다. (A) consistent는 형용사, (B) consist는 동사, (D) consisting은 동명사/현재분사로 품사상 빈칸에 들어갈 수 없다.

번역 틸다 재생크림은 지속적으로 바르면 잔주름 생성을 감소시켜 준다.

어휘 **restorative** 복원하는 **reduce** 줄이다 **appearance** (없던 것의) 출현, 나타남 **fine** 가는, 촘촘한 **wrinkle** 주름

120 동사 어휘

해설 새 소프트웨어 프로그램(new software program)이 무엇을 할 준비가 된 것인지 설명하는 동사가 필요하다. 따라서 '출시하다'라는 뜻의 (A) launch가 정답이다. 참고로, launch는 타동사이지만 앞에 형용사 ready가 쓰였기 때문에 to be launched로 쓰일 필요가 없다. 주어인 소프트웨어 프로그램이 launch의 "의미상" 목적어(=ready to launch the new software program)라고 보면 된다. 이와 같은 구조가 가능한 형용사로는 ready, easy, difficult, impossible 등이 있다.

번역 마케팅 담당자는 새 소프트웨어 프로그램이 11월 1일까지 출시 준비가 될 것이라고 확인해 주었다.

어휘 **confirm** 확인해 주다, 확정하다 **facilitate** 가능하게 하다 **arise** 발생하다, 생기다 **exert** 가하다, 행사하다

121 접속사 자리 _ 어휘

해설 두 개의 완전한 절을 연결해 주는 접속사 자리로, 보기에서 (A) if, (B) yet, (C) until 중 하나를 선택해야 한다. 주문품에 완전히 만족하지 못하는 것(you are not completely satisfied)은 환불(refund)을 해주는 경우에 해당하므로, '만일 ~하면'이라는 의미의 (A) if가 정답이다.

번역 새티니스 시트 커버는 귀하가 전적으로 만족하지 못하실 경우 주문 제품을 환불해 드립니다.

어휘 **refund** 환불해 주다 **completely** 전적으로, 완전히

122 명사 어휘

해설 빈칸에는 생산(production)이 두 배로 늘어날 수 있는(has doubled) 부분이나 측면을 나타내는 명사가 들어가야 한다. 따라서 '양, 용량'이라는 의미의 (C) volume이 정답이다. double in size/number/price 등의 표현도 알아두는 것이 좋다.

번역 지난 5년 간, 해리스 시설의 생산 물량은 거의 두 배가 됐다.

어휘 **production** 생산 **facility** 시설 **double** 두 배가 되다 **majority** 다수 **edition** 판, 호 **economy** 경제 (상황)

123 조동사 + 동사원형

해설 조동사 will과 결합해 명사 the installation을 목적어로 취하는 자리로, 능동태 동사원형이 들어가야 한다. 따라서 동사원형 be로 시작하는 (D) be coordinating이 정답이다.

번역 차이 씨는 판매업체와 새 워크스테이션 설치 작업을 조율할 것이다.

어휘 **installation** 설치 **workstation** 워크스테이션(단말기), 사무실 컴퓨터, 작업 장소 **vendor** 판매업체 **coordinate** 조정[조율]하다, 편성하다

124 부사 어휘

해설 동사 increase를 수식하는 부사 자리이므로, 증가의 폭이나 속도를 나타내는 단어가 들어가야 자연스럽다. 따라서 '상당히, 크게'라는 의미의 (A) significantly가 정답이다. increase와 같은 증감동사와 잘 어울리는 부사로는 considerably/dramatically(상당히/크게), slightly(약간), rapidly(빠르게), steadily(꾸준히) 등이 있다.

번역 소프트웨어 업그레이드는 우리 행정 직원들의 생산성을 크게 높일 것이다.

어휘 **productivity** 생산성 **administrative** 행정상의, 관리상의 **persuasively** 설득력 있게 **proficiently** 능숙하게 **gladly** 기쁘게, 기꺼이

125 명사 자리 _ to부정사의 목적어 _ 복합명사

해설 가산명사 menu 앞에 한정사가 없으므로, 빈칸에는 menu와 함께 복합명사를 이루어 to make의 목적어 역할을 하는 복수명사 또는 불가산명사가 들어가야 한다. 주방장이 고객의 메뉴 대체 요청(특정 재료 변경 등의 요구)을 들어준다는 내용이 되어야 자연스러우므로, '대체'라는 뜻의 복수 가산명사 (C) substitutions가 정답이다. menu substitution은 고정 표현이므로 암기해 두는 것이 좋다. (D) substitute는 가산명사로 '대리자, 대체물'을 뜻하며, 동사로 쓰일 경우 '대체하다'를 의미하므로 의미상 정답이 될 수 없다.

번역 러스틱 다이너의 주방장은 고객이 메뉴 대체를 하게끔 허용한다.

어휘 allow 허용[허락]하다   patron 고객, 후원자

126 동사 어휘

해설 가주어 it의 진주어 역할을 하는 to부정사의 동사원형 자리로, 명사구 explicit policies를 목적어로 취한다. 따라서 '명확한 정책'과 어울리는 단어를 선택해야 하므로, '수립하다, 제정하다'라는 의미의 (D) establish가 정답이다. 참고로, policy는 implement(시행하다), introduce(도입하다) 등의 동사와도 자주 쓰인다. (A) inform이 '알리다'라는 의미로 쓰일 경우, 정보를 제공받는 대상을 목적어로 취하므로 빈칸에는 들어갈 수 없다.

번역 로드리게즈 씨는 회사 컴퓨터 사용에 관해 명확한 정책을 수립하는 것이 중요하다고 말했다.

어휘 note 말하다   explicit 명확한, 분명한   regarding ~에 관한   succeed 성공하다, 뒤를 잇다   estimate 추산하다

127 접속사 자리

해설 빈칸 뒤 완전한 절(Peura Insurance has located a larger office space)을 이끄는 접속사 자리이므로, 부사절 접속사 (B) Now that(~이기 때문에)이 정답이다. (A) Happily와 (D) In fact는 부사, (C) Despite는 전치사로 절을 이끌 수 없다.

번역 프라 보험사는 더 큰 사무 공간을 찾았기 때문에 임대 계약을 협상하기 시작할 것이다.

어휘 insurance 보험   negotiate 협상하다   rental agreement 임대 계약   despite ~에도 불구하고

128 부사 어휘

해설 자동사 worked를 수식하는 부사 자리로, 수익성 높은 정부 계약을 따기 위해(to secure a lucrative government contract) 어떻게 일했는지 묘사하는 단어가 필요하다. 따라서 '열심히, 부지런히'라는 의미의 (B) diligently가 정답이다.

번역 다나카 씨의 팀은 수익성 높은 정부 계약을 따기 위해 몇 달간 열심히 일했다.

어휘 secure 얻어내다, 획득하다   lucrative 수익성이 높은   contract 계약   readily 손쉽게, 순조롭게   curiously 궁금한 듯이, 기이하게   extremely 극도로

129 소유격 대명사 어휘

해설 전치사 of의 목적어 역할을 하는 명사 plans를 한정 수식하는 자리이다. 여행 보험 상품은 센다크 에이전시가 제공하는 것이므로, Sendark Agency's를 대신하는 (C) its가 정답이다. 문두에 부사절 접속사 Though가 이미 있기 때문에, 접속사 역할을 하는 소유격 관계대명사 (A) whose는 구조상 빈칸에 들어갈 수 없다. (B) his는 가리킬만한 대상이 앞에 언급되지 않았고, (D) this는 plans와 수가 일치하지 않으므로 오답이다.

번역 센다크 에이전시의 여행 보험은 전화로 구입 가능하지만, 대부분의 상품이 온라인으로 구매된다.

어휘 purchase 구입하다   plan (보험 등의) 상품, 요금제

130 상관접속사

해설 빈칸이 관계사절의 선행사(functional products)를 보충 설명하는 inexpensive와 beautifully crafted 사이에 있으므로, 빈칸에는 이 둘을 연결하는 등위/상관접속사가 들어가야 한다. 따라서 (B) as well as(~뿐만 아니라)가 정답이다. (A) thus, (C) at last, (D) accordingly는 부사로 품사상 빈칸에 들어갈 수 없다.

번역 가스타인 가구는 비싸지 않을 뿐만 아니라 아름답게 제작된 기능성 제품을 전문으로 한다.

어휘 specialize in ~을 전문으로 하다   functional 기능적인   craft 공들여 만들다   thus 그러므로   at last 마침내   accordingly 그에 맞춰

PART 6

131-134 공지

> **공지**
>
> 기업 임차인분들께 최상의 **131 서비스**를 계속 제공해 드리기 위해, 당사는 이번 주말인 5월 13일과 5월 14일에 남쪽 로비 화장실 보수 공사 일정을 잡았습니다. 이 기간 **132 동안** 해당 화장실들은 작동이 되지 않을 것입니다. 따라서 임차인 및 방문객은 북쪽 로비 시설을 대신 이용해야 합니다.
>
> 불편을 드려 **133 죄송합니다.** **134 문의사항이나** 의견은 관리사무실로 전달하시면 됩니다.
>
> 덴빌 부동산 관리 회사

어휘 corporate 회사의, 기업의   tenant 임차인, 세입자   maintenance 유지보수   out of order 작동되지 않는, 고장 난   facility 시설   inconvenience 불편   property 부동산, 건물   Partners 합자 회사

131 명사 자리 _ 전치사의 목적어

해설 전치사 of의 목적어 역할을 하는 명사 자리인데, 전치사 of와 빈칸 사

이에 한정사가 없으므로, 빈칸에는 복수명사 또는 불가산명사가 들어가야 한다. 따라서 (D) service(서비스)가 정답이다. (C) server는 단수 가산명사, (A) serve는 동사, (B) served는 동사/과거분사로 구조상 빈칸에 들어갈 수 없다.

132 전치사 어휘

해설 빈칸의 목적어 역할을 하는 this time은 앞 문장에 언급된 '이번 주말인 5월 13일과 5월 14일(this weekend, May 13 and May 14)'을 대신한다. 따라서 빈칸에는 기간 명사와 어울려 쓰이는 전치사가 들어가야 하므로, '~ 동안'이라는 의미의 (B) During이 정답이다. 참고로, (D) Between은 「between A and B」 구조로 쓰여 '(특정 시점) 사이에'라는 뜻을 나타낼 수 있다.

133 동사 어휘

해설 불편함을 야기한 것(for any inconvenience)에 대해 회사에서 취하는 행위를 나타내는 동사가 들어가야 한다. 따라서 '사과하다'라는 의미의 (A) apologize가 정답이다. 참고로, (C) realize와 (D) recognize는 타동사로 구조상으로도 빈칸에 들어갈 수 없다.

어휘 organize 조직하다, 단결하다 realize 깨닫다 recognize 알아보다, 인정하다

134 문맥에 맞는 문장 고르기

번역 (A) 저희 부동산 관리팀에 입사하고 싶으시면 오늘 전화해 주십시오.
(B) 메인 로비에 페인트칠이 되는 동안 양해해 주시면 감사하겠습니다.
(C) 해당 일자에는 북쪽 로비에 가지 마십시오.
(D) 문의사항이나 의견은 관리사무실로 전달하시면 됩니다.

해설 빈칸 앞 문장에서 보수 공사로 인한 불편에 대해 사과(We apologize for any inconvenience this might cause)했으므로, 빈칸에는 보수 공사와 관련된 추가 설명 또는 공지를 마무리하는 문장이 들어가야 자연스럽다. 따라서 문의사항이나 의견(Questions or comments)을 보낼 곳을 언급한 (D)가 정답이다. 참고로, 첫 번째 단락에서 공사 장소는 남쪽 로비 화장실(the south lobby restrooms)이라고 밝혔고, 임차인 및 방문객이 북쪽 로비 시설을 대신 이용해야 한다(tenants and their guests should instead use the facilities in the north lobby)고 했으므로, (B)와 (C)는 정답이 될 수 없다.

어휘 patience 참을성, 인내력 attempt 시도하다 access 이용하다, 접근하다 direct 보내다

135-138 고객 후기

최근에 저는 정찬 날짜에 임박해서 초대를 받은 적이 있습니다. 정장을 구입했고 가능한 한 135빨리 맞춤 수선을 해야 했어요. 한 친구가 오클랜드 시내에 있는 안토니오 양복점을 이용해 보라고 제안했습니다. 안토니오 씨를 만났을 때, 매장이 바쁜 136했지만 저에게 오롯이 집중해서 응대해 주셨어요. 시간을 내어 이야기를 들어주고 제 치수를 전부 꼼꼼하게 적으셨습니다. 그리고는 모든 수선 비용을 미리 설명하고 제 정장을 3일 후에 준비해 놓을 수 있다고 확약해 주셨습니다. 그런데 이틀만에 완료하셨어요! 137정장이 저에게 아주 잘 맞기도 합니다.

안토니오 씨는 30년 이상 매장을 운영하셨는데, 그 경력이 확연히 드러납니다. 138최고의 재단사예요! 강력 추천합니다.

짐 케스트렌, 오클랜드

어휘 last-minute 마지막 순간의, 막바지의 formal 정중한, 격식을 차린 tailor 맞추다 attention 주목, 집중 measurement 치수 up front 미리, 선불로 assure 확언하다, 확약하다 highly recommend 적극 추천하다

135 원급 부사 자리 _ 동사 수식

해설 as와 as possible 사이에서 과거분사 tailored를 수식하는 원급 부사 자리이다. 따라서 (A) quickly가 정답이다. (B) quicken(재촉하다)은 동사, (C) quickest는 최상급 형용사/(비격식체) 부사, (D) quickness(빠름)는 명사로 구조상 빈칸에 들어갈 수 없다.

136 접속사 자리 _ 어휘

해설 두 개의 완전한 절을 이어주는 접속사 자리로, 보기에서 (A) as far as와 (B) even though 중 하나를 선택해야 한다. 매장이 바쁜(his shop was busy) 와중에 집중해서 응대하는 것(he gave me his full attention)은 예상 밖의 상황이라고 볼 수 있으므로, 양보/대조의 부사절 접속사 (B) even though(비록 ~일지라도)가 정답이다. (D) whether는 or (not)과 결합해야만 부사절 접속사로 쓰일 수 있고, (C) such as는 전치사이므로 빈칸에 들어가 절을 이끌 수 없다.

어휘 as far as ~하는 한 such as ~와 같은 whether ~이든 (아니든)

137 문맥에 맞는 문장 고르기

번역 (A) 물론 매장은 매주 토요일에 가장 붐빕니다.
(B) 정장이 저에게 아주 잘 맞기도 합니다.
(C) 또 하나 구입했습니다.
(D) 그는 예전에 셔츠를 판매하곤 했습니다.

해설 빈칸 앞 문장에서는 안토니오 씨가 수선 작업을 빠르게 완료한 것(He ~ assured me that he could have my suit ready in three days, but he had it done in two!)에 대해 칭찬했고, 뒤 문단에서는 안토니오 씨의 경력 및 능력을 언급하며 그를 추천했다. 따라서 빈칸에도 안토니오 씨를 칭찬하는 내용이나 추천하는 이유가 들어가야 자연스러우므로, 수선이 완벽하게 되었다는 것을 말해주는 (B)가 정답이다.

어휘 fit perfectly 꼭 맞다 purchase 구입

138 형용사 어휘

해설 뒤에서 안토니오 씨를 강력 추천한다(I highly recommend him)고 했으므로, 추천할 만한 재단사(tailor)의 특징을 묘사하는 형용사가 필요하다. 따라서 '최상의, 대단히 훌륭한'이라는 의미의 (C) superb가 정답이다. (D) best는 형용사 good의 최상급 표현으로 빈칸에 들어가려면 앞에 정관사 the가 와야 한다.

어휘 former 이전의 temporary 임시의

139-142 편지

요시다 실장님께,

귀하의 학교에서 다음 달 저희 농장을 방문하고자 관심을 보여주신 점 감사합니다. 농장을 방문하고 견학하려면 어린이는 최소 6세 이상이어야 함을 알려드립니다. ¹³⁹**본 방침에 예외는 없습니다.** 어린 방문객들이 참여할 수 있는 ¹⁴⁰**교육** 활동 목록을 동봉해 드렸습니다. 이 ¹⁴¹**행사들** 중 두 가지는 미리 일정을 잡아야 하는데, 바로 치즈 만들기 수업과 양봉 입문입니다. 두 가지 모두 방문객들 사이에 인기가 매우 높습니다.

다음 주 초까지 선택하신 내용을 ¹⁴²**저에게** 알려주세요. 곧 귀하의 단체를 맞이할 수 있길 바랍니다!

애너벨 로메로, 진행 담당자
메리트리 가족 농장

어휘 at least 최소한 enclose 동봉하다 activity 활동
available 이용 가능한 in advance 미리 introduction 입문,
소개 beekeeping 양봉 selection 선택(한 것) look forward
to 고대하다

139 문맥에 맞는 문장 고르기

번역 (A) 날씨가 좋지 않을 경우 동물은 내부에 있을 것입니다.
      (B) 본 방침에 예외는 없습니다.
      (C) 이보다 어린 아이들이 즐길 거리가 많습니다.
      (D) 해당 요금에는 점심식사 및 작은 기념품이 포함됩니다.

해설 빈칸 앞 문장에서는 농장 방문 및 견학이 허용되는 최소 연령 (children must be at least six years old to visit and tour the farm)을, 뒤 문장에서는 어린 방문객들이 참여할만한 활동 목록 (a list of the ~ activities available for our young visitors)을 언급했다. 따라서 빈칸에는 나이 제한이나 농장 방문에 관한 설명이 들어가야 자연스러우므로, 최소 연령 관련 방침의 예외 유무를 밝힌 (B)가 정답이다.

어휘 in the event of 만약 ~하면 exception 예외 policy 정책,
      방침 souvenir 기념품

140 형용사 어휘

해설 activities를 수식하는 형용사 자리로, 어린 방문객들이 참여할만한 (available for our young visitors) 활동의 성격을 나타내는 단어가 들어가야 한다. 뒤에서 치즈 만들기 수업(a cheese-making class)과 양봉 입문(an introduction to beekeeping)을 예시로 들고 있으므로, 교육용 활동임을 알 수 있다. 따라서 '교육의, 교육적인' 이라는 의미의 (D) educational이 정답이다.

어휘 legal 법률에 관련된 artistic 예술의 athletic 육상의, 탄탄한

141 명사 어휘

해설 these -------가 앞에서 언급된 어린 방문객들을 위한 활동 (activities)을 가리키므로, activities와 유사한 단어가 빈칸에 들어

가야 한다. 따라서 '행사'라는 의미의 (A) events가 정답이다.

어휘 play 연극 treatment 치료 trip 여행

142 대명사 어휘

해설 「let + 목적어 + 목적격 보어(know your selection)」 구조에서 let의 목적어 역할을 하는 자리이다. 최종 선택 사항을 자신에게 알려달라고 요청하는 내용이므로, (B) me가 정답이다.

143-146 이메일

수신: 락쉬미 아이야르
발신: info@healthonity.com
날짜: 2월 8일
제목: 헬소니티 치과

아이야르 씨께,

저희 헬소니티 치과의 치아 건강 전문가들은 새롭게 문을 연 병원을 소개하게 되어 ¹⁴³**기쁩니다.** 저희는 지역 내에서 가장 큰 규모의 치의학 전문가팀을 만나실 수 있는 기회를 드리고자 합니다. 웹사이트에서 저희가 제공하는 시술이 총망라된 목록을 확인하실 수 있습니다. ¹⁴⁴**여기에는 일반 및 미용 시술이 포함됩니다.** 저희 병원의 직원들은 사람들이 아름답고 건강한 미소를 유지할 수 있도록 돕겠다는 열정을 함께하고 있습니다.

최초 검진 ¹⁴⁵**일정을 잡으시려면,** 오늘 저희 병원 305-555-0121번으로 연락하세요. 초진 ¹⁴⁶**환자는** 누구나 해당 월말까지의 비용에서 50퍼센트 할인 혜택을 받으실 수 있습니다.

헬소니티 치과팀

어휘 dental 치아의, 치과의 practice (의사, 변호사 등 전문직 종사자의) 사무실, 업무 aim to ~를 목표로 하다 specialist 전문가 comprehensive 종합적인, 포괄적인 procedure 시술, 수술 initial 처음의 evaluation 평가, 검사 benefit 혜택을 받다

143 형용사 자리 _ 주격 보어

해설 be동사 are와 결합해 주어 We를 보충 설명하는 보어 자리로, to introduce our just-opened practice의 수식을 받는다. '소개하게 되어 기쁘다'라는 내용이 되어야 자연스러우므로, 형용사인 (D) proud(자랑스러워하는, 기뻐하는)가 정답이다. (A) prouder는 비교급 형용사로 앞에 couldn't be(더할 나위 없이 ~하다)가 쓰이거나 문맥상 비교 대상이 있어야 한다. (C) pride는 명사로 주격 보어 역할을 할 수는 있지만 We와 동격 관계를 이루지 않으므로 빈칸에 적절하지 않다. (B) proudly는 부사로 품사상 빈칸에 들어갈 수 없다.

144 문맥에 맞는 문장 고르기

번역 (A) 여기에는 일반 및 미용 시술이 포함됩니다.
      (B) 저희는 인근의 힐스버러에서 이전했습니다.
      (C) 웹사이트는 A to Z 호스트 빌더스에서 만들었습니다.
      (D) 이들 중 몇 개는 놀랄 만큼 비쌉니다.

해설 빈칸 앞 문장에서는 병원에서 제공하는 시술 목록 확인 방법을 안내(On our Web site, you can see a comprehensive list of the procedures we offer)했고, 뒤 문장에서는 시술을 통해 사람들을 도와주고자 하는 병원 직원들의 사명(The members of our practice share a passion for helping people ~ smiles)을 언급했다. 따라서 시술의 예시를 든 (A)가 빈칸에 들어가야 가장 자연스럽다. 참고로, 여기서 They는 the procedures we offer를 가리킨다. 일종의 광고성 이메일인데 시술 비용이 굉장히 비싸다며 부정적인 측면을 시사하는 것은 적절치 않으므로 (D)는 정답이 될 수 없다.

어휘 cosmetic 미용의 relocate 이전하다 surprisingly 놀랄 만큼

145 to부정사

해설 빈칸 앞에는 완전한 명령문(Contact our center today at 305-555-0121)이, 뒤에는 명사구 an initial evaluation이 왔으므로, 빈칸에는 an initial evaluation을 목적어로 취하면서 앞에 온 명령문을 수식할 수 있는 준동사가 들어가야 한다. 최초 검진 일정을 잡는 것은 병원에 연락하는 목적이라고 볼 수 있다. 따라서 '일정을 잡기 위해'라는 의미로 부사적 역할을 하는 to부정사 (B) to schedule이 정답이다.

146 명사 어휘

해설 동사 will benefit의 주어 역할을 하는 명사 자리로, All first-time의 수식을 받는다. 문맥상 병원 검진 예약을 하고 할인 혜택을 받는 대상이 빈칸에 들어가야 하므로, '환자'라는 의미의 (C) patients가 정답이다.

어휘 shopper 쇼핑객 resident 거주민 tenant 세입자, 임차인

PART 7

147-148 웹페이지

http://www.moonglowairways.com.au

문글로우 항공 제프 클리포드 회장의 특별 공지

[147]여러분 다수가 알고 계신 대로, 저희 항공사 예약 처리 시스템인 펠먼 테크놀로지에 문제가 있었습니다. 이번 시스템 정지는 여러 항공사에 영향을 미쳤습니다. 힘든 한 주였지만 수리가 끝났고 시스템을 재설정하고 있다는 좋은 소식이 있습니다. 그러나 문글로우 승객들은 하루 이틀간 더 지연을 겪게 될 수도 있습니다. 여기에는 아마 공항에서의 대기열이 길어진 것도 포함될 것입니다. [148]저희가 취항하는 모든 도시의 공항에 고객의 항공편과 정보에 관해 도움을 드릴 현장 고객 서비스 담당자들을 추가로 투입했습니다. 너그러이 양해해 주시면 감사하겠습니다.

어휘 announcement 발표, 공지 be aware 알다 reservation 예약 outage 정전, 정지 affect 영향을 미치다 passenger 승객 face 겪다, 마주치다 most likely 아마, 필시 on-site 현장의 representative 대표, 대리인 destination 목적지 appreciate 감사하다

147 주제 / 목적

번역 공지의 목적은?
(A) 공항 보수 공사를 알리기 위해
(B) 기술적인 문제에 대한 새로운 소식을 전하기 위해
(C) 새 예약 시스템을 소개하기 위해
(D) 일부 새로운 도시로의 항공 노선을 광고하기 위해

해설 초반부에서 항공사 예약 처리 시스템에 문제가 있었다(there was a problem with ~ the system that handles our airline reservations)고 한 후, 처리 상황에 대한 설명을 이어가고 있다. 따라서 (B)가 정답이다.

어휘 renovation 보수, 개조 advertise 광고하다

148 세부 사항

번역 클리포드 씨에 따르면, 항공사는 임시로 무엇을 증가시켰는가?
(A) 이용 가능한 항공편 수
(B) 기내식 선택 메뉴
(C) 공항 고객 지원
(D) 국제선 항공편 가격

해설 후반부를 보면 문글로우 항공사가 취항하는 모든 도시의 공항에 고객의 항공편과 정보에 관해 도움을 줄 현장 고객 서비스 담당자들을 추가로 투입했다(We have added more on-site customer service representatives ~ to assist customers with their flights and information)고 되어 있다. 따라서 (C)가 정답이다.

어휘 temporarily 임시로 available 이용 가능한 assistance 도움

▶▶ Paraphrasing 지문의 for a day or two
→ 질문의 temporarily
지문의 added → 질문의 increased
지문의 more on-site customer service representatives ~ to assist customers
→ 정답의 Assistance for customers

149-150 구인광고

동영상 자막 작업자 - 재택근무

키셀 비디오는 저희 소프트웨어를 사용해 TV 프로그램, 영화, 대학 강의 등 광범위한 동영상 자료에 자막을 삽입할 꼼꼼한 분을 찾고 있습니다. 당사에서 무료 온라인 교육을 제공해 드립니다. [149]선발될 지원자는 뛰어난 언어 구사력과 컴퓨터, 헤드셋, 초고속 인터넷 등을 갖추고 있어야 합니다.

해당 직책에는 다음 사항이 포함됩니다.
• 유연한 근무시간 - 원하는 만큼 일하실 수 있습니다.
• [150]프로젝트 선택권 - 많은 유형의 콘텐츠 작업이 있습니다.
• 뛰어난 보수 - 저희 자막 작업자들은 과업에 따라 주당 350달러에서 1,100달러까지 받습니다.

오늘 www.kieselvideo.com/jobs에서 지원하세요.

어휘 work from home 재택근무하다 seek 찾다 detail-oriented 꼼꼼한 a wide variety of 매우 광범위한, 다양한 material 자료 applicant 지원자 possess 소유하다, 지니다 feature ~를 특징으로 하다, 특별히 포함하다 flexible 유연한, 융통성 있는 depending on ~에 따라 assignment 과업, 과제, 배정 apply 지원하다

149 세부 사항

번역 해당 직책 지원자들은 무엇을 갖춰야 하는가?

(A) 동영상 제작 경험
(B) 특정 장비
(C) 어문학사 학위
(D) 리셉션 공간을 갖춘 사무실

해설 첫 번째 단락에서 선발될 지원자는 컴퓨터, 헤드셋 등을 갖추고 있어야 한다(Successful applicants must ~ have a computer, a headset, and high-speed Internet access)고 했으므로, (B)가 정답이다. 뛰어난 언어 구사력을 갖춰야 한다(Successful applicants must possess strong language skills)고 했지만 어문학사 학위가 필수 요건은 아니므로, (C)는 정답이 될 수 없다.

어휘 production 제작 equipment 장비 university degree 학사 학위

▸▸ Paraphrasing 지문의 must ~ have
→ 질문의 are ~ required to have

지문의 a computer, a headset
→ 정답의 Certain pieces of equipment

150 사실 관계 확인

번역 직책에 대해 사실인 것은?

(A) 정규직이다.
(B) 고정급을 받는다.
(C) 외국 출장이 있다.
(D) 과업 선택권이 있다.

해설 직책에 대해 설명한 두 번째 항목에서 프로젝트 선택권(Choice of projects)이 있다고 했으므로, (D)가 정답이다. 자막 작업자들이 주당 350달러에서 1,100달러까지 받는다(our captioners earn $350 to $1,100 a week)고 했으므로 (B)는 명백한 오답이다.

어휘 fixed 고정된, 변함없는 involve 수반하다

▸▸ Paraphrasing 지문의 Choice of projects
→ 정답의 a choice of assignments

151-152 보고서

2월 1일
소프트웨어 테스트 보고서

소프트웨어 프로그램 버전: 콘서티드 2.5
[151] 테스트 일자: 1월 10-12일

참가자 수: 8명

소프트웨어 테스트 개요: 참가자들에게 개정된 콘서티드 인터페이스의 기능을 시험하는 일련의 과제를 완수하도록 요청했다. 1번 과제에서 참가자들은 지정된 지역 내에서 콘서트를 검색했다. 2번 과제에서 참가자들은 현장에서 새로운 친구들을 검색했다. [152] 3번 과제에서 참가자들은 친구들을 콘서트로 초대했다. 4번 과제에서 참가자들은 콘서트 후기, 사진, 동영상을 게시물로 올렸다.

초기 결과: [152] 3번 과제는 3명의 참가자가 2분 이내에 과제를 완료하지 못하면서 가장 어려운 과제로 드러났다. 이러한 어려움에 대한 잠재적 원인은 메뉴 바의 아이콘 선택일 수 있다. 더 명확하고 직관적인 아이콘은 참가자들이 해당 과제를 더 쉽게 완수할 수 있도록 해 줄 것이다.

어휘 overview 개요 complete 완수하다 functionality 기능, 기능성 designated 지정된 post 게시하다 initial 처음의 findings 조사 결과 challenging 힘든, 어려운 potential 잠재적인, 가능성 있는 intuitive 직관적인, 이해하기 쉬운

151 사실 관계 확인

번역 소프트웨어 테스트에 대해 맞는 것은?

(A) 여러 버전의 콘서티드가 포함됐다.
(B) 며칠에 걸쳐 진행됐다.
(C) 참가자들에게 설문을 작성하도록 요구했다.
(D) 여러 콘서트에서 진행됐다.

해설 상단의 테스트 일자(Testing Dates: January 10-12)를 보면 며칠에 걸쳐 진행되었음을 알 수 있다. 따라서 (B)가 정답이다.

어휘 multiple 많은, 다수의 complete a survey 설문을 작성하다 take place 일어나다, 열리다

▸▸ Paraphrasing 지문의 January 10-12
→ 정답의 over several days

152 세부 사항

번역 사용자들은 어떤 활동을 완료하기가 어려웠는가?

(A) 행사 검색
(B) 친구 검색
(C) 공연에 친구들 초대
(D) 웹사이트에 후기 게시

해설 초기 결과(Initial Findings)에서 3번 과제가 가장 어려운 것으로 드러났다(Task number 3 proved the most challenging)고 했는데, 소프트웨어 테스트 개요(Software Testing Overview)를 보면 3번 과제는 친구들을 콘서트로 초대하는 것(In task number 3, participants invited friends to a concert)으로 설명되어 있다. 따라서 (C)가 정답이다.

어휘 performance 공연

> ▸▸ Paraphrasing 지문의 **proved the most challenging, with three participants unable to complete**
> → 질문의 **was difficult for users to complete**
>
> 지문의 **to a concert**
> → 정답의 **to a performance**

153-155 이메일

수신: catiyeh@mymailroom.au
발신: achen@mutamark.au
날짜: 7월 1일
제목: 무타마크 회의

아티예 씨께,

¹⁵⁵오늘 아까 전화로 나눴던 대화에 이어, 올해 9월 17일부터 20일까지 자그로스에서 열릴 제8회 무타마크 연례회의에서 연설해 주십사 정식 초청장을 보내 드리고자 합니다. ¹⁵³예전에 회의에 나와 주셨을 때 상당 수의 관객을 끌었기 때문에 이번 방문을 위해 특별 준비를 하려고 합니다. ^{153/154}드벨자크 호텔 블루룸은 120명만 수용할 수 있어서 올해는 수용 인원이 270명인 코로스홀도 예약할 예정입니다. ¹⁵⁵귀하께 회의 마지막날 40-50분 정도의 시간을 드릴 수 있습니다. 이 날은 참석률이 가장 높을 겁니다. 저에게 이메일로 수락 여부를 확정해 주시고 시청각 관련 필요 사항에 대해 알려주시기 바랍니다. 스틸 이미지를 다시 이용하실 경우 저희가 오버헤드 프로젝션을 제공해 드릴 수 있습니다.

알렉스 첸, 회의 기획 담당
무타마크 본사, 멜버른

어휘   follow up on ~에 덧붙이다, 후속 조치를 하다   extend an invitation 초대장을 보내다, 초대하다   formal 공식적인, 정식의   take place 열리다   sizeable 상당한   arrangement 준비   hold 수용하다   capacity 수용력   attendance 참석률, 참석자 수   acceptance 수락   audiovisual 시청각의   requirement 요건, 필요한 사항   overhead projection 사용자 뒤에 있는 화면에 화상을 투영시키는 것   still image 스틸 이미지, 정지 화상

153 사실 관계 확인

번역   아티예 씨가 예전에 무타마크에 참석했던 일에 대해 알 수 있는 것은?

(A) 참석자가 매우 많았다.
(B) 더 큰 장소로 옮겼다.
(C) 음악 공연이 있었다.
(D) 코로스홀에서 열렸다.

해설   초반부에서 아티예 씨가 예전에 회의에 나왔을 때 상당한 수의 관객을 끌었다(Because you drew a sizeable crowd when you appeared at the conference in the past)고 했으므로, (A)가 정답이다. 중반부에서 지난번과 달리 올해는 수용 인원이 270명인 코로스홀을 예약할 것(this year we are also booking the Koros Hall, which has a capacity of 270)이라고 했으므로, (B)와 (D)는 정답이 될 수 없다.

어휘   appearance 나타남, 등장, 출연   well attended 참석자가 많은, 참석률이 높은   venue 장소

> ▸▸ Paraphrasing 지문의 **you appeared ~ in the past**
> → 질문의 **Ms. Atiyeh's previous appearance**
>
> 지문의 **drew a sizeable crowd**
> → 정답의 **very well attended**

154 세부 사항

번역   코로스홀은 몇 명을 수용할 수 있는가?

(A) 40명
(B) 50명
(C) 120명
(D) 270명

해설   중반부에서 코로스홀의 수용 인원이 270명(the Koros Hall, which has a capacity of 270)이라고 했으므로, (D)가 정답이다.

> ▸▸ Paraphrasing 지문의 **has a capacity of**
> → 질문의 **accommodate**

155 추론 / 암시

번역   아티예 씨는 언제 무타마크 회의에 등장하겠는가?

(A) 9월 17일
(B) 9월 18일
(C) 9월 19일
(D) 9월 20일

해설   중반부에서 아티예 씨에게 회의 마지막날 40-50분 정도의 시간을 줄 수 있다(We can offer you a 40-to-50-minute slot on the last day of the conference)고 했는데, 초반부를 보면 회의가 9월 17일부터 20일까지 열릴 예정(the eighth annual Mutamark conference, scheduled to take place this year from 17 to 20 September)이라고 쓰여 있다. 따라서 아티예 씨가 마지막 날인 9월 20일 회의에서 연설할 것이라고 추론할 수 있으므로, (D)가 정답이다.

156-158 기사

서드베리에 모노레일이 온다

(2월 4일) — ^{156/158}오타와에 본사를 둔 샌저 주식회사가 서드베리 시의 상업지구와 공항을 연결할 모노레일 시스템 건설 업체로 선정됐다. 길을 따라, 노선은 9개의 정류장에서 정차할 예정이다. 시스템을 위한 자금은 공공기관과 개인 투자자들의 합작으로 조성된다. 모노레일 탑승권 판매도 시에 새로운 수입원을 제공할 것이다. ¹⁵⁷공사는 6월 초에 시작될 예정이며 4년 이내에 완료될 것으로 예상된다.

어휘   commercial 상업의   district 지구   draw funding 자금을 끌어내다   combination 조합, 합작   investor 투자자   revenue 수입, 수익   be slated to ~할 예정이다   complete 완료하다

156 추론 / 암시

번역 샌저 주식회사는 어떤 종류의 업체이겠는가?

(A) 건설회사
(B) 부동산 중개업체
(C) 화물 취급업체
(D) 금융 서비스 제공업체

해설 초반부에서 샌저 주식회사가 모노레일 시스템을 건설할 업체로 선정됐다(Saenger, Inc., has been selected ~ to build a monorail system)고 했으므로, 건설회사임을 추론할 수 있다. 따라서 (A)가 정답이다.

157 사실 관계 확인

번역 모노레일에 대해 알 수 있는 것은?

(A) 투자자들에게 자금을 더 받아야 한다.
(B) 완공하는 데 몇 년이 걸릴 것이다.
(C) 공항 관계자들에 의해 제안됐다.
(D) 시민들에게 할인 탑승권을 제공한다.

해설 후반부에서 공사는 4년 이내에 완료될 것으로 예상된다(Construction ~ is expected to be completed within four years)고 했으므로, (B)가 정답이다.

어휘 propose 제안하다 discount 할인하다 resident 거주민

> ▸▸ Paraphrasing 지문의 be completed within four years
> → 정답의 take years to finish

158 문장 삽입

번역 [1], [2], [3], [4]로 표시된 곳 중에서 다음 문장이 가장 적합한 곳은?

"길을 따라, 노선은 9개의 정류장에서 정차할 예정이다."

(A) [1]
(B) [2]
(C) [3]
(D) [4]

해설 주어인 노선(the line)이 가리키는 대상이 앞에서 먼저 언급되어야 한다. [1] 앞에서 시의 상업지구와 공항을 연결할 모노레일 시스템 건설(to build a monorail system that will connect the city's commercial district to the airport) 소식을 전하며 우회적으로 노선을 밝혔으므로, (A)가 정답이다.

159-160 문자 메시지

데니스 벡 (오후 2시 52분)

안녕하세요, 코린. 제가 보낸 문서를 보셨는지 확인하고 싶어서요. 키스 엘리건트 홈 그룹을 위한 시장 분석과 광고 제안서가 결합된 문서입니다. 내일 고객 발표를 위해 준비하고 있거든요.

코린 맥콜 (오후 2시 53분)

네. 방금 다운로드했어요. 그들의 새로운 식기류 제품에 관한 것인가요?

데니스 벡 (오후 2시 54분)

네. 159읽어봐 주셨으면 합니다.

코린 맥콜 (오후 3시 1분)

문제 없어요. 제가 수정했으면 하세요, 아니면 모두 명확한지 확인만 했으면 하세요?

데니스 벡 (오후 3시 2분)

160'광고 전략' 부분은 당신 전문 분야이니 자유롭게 정보를 추가해 주세요.

코린 맥콜 (오후 3시 3분)

그럴게요. 오늘 퇴근 시간 전까지 돌려드릴게요.

어휘 combined 결합된 analysis 분석 advertising 광고 proposal 제안(서) presentation 발표 revise 변경하다, 수정하다 strategy 전략 expertise 전문 지식

159 의도 파악

번역 오후 3시 1분에 맥콜 씨가 "문제 없어요"라고 쓸 때, 그 의도는 무엇인가?

(A) 컴퓨터에 로그인하는 데 아무런 문제도 없었다.
(B) 문서에 오류가 있다고 생각하지 않는다.
(C) 문서를 기꺼이 검토할 것이다.
(D) 키스 엘리건트 홈 담당자들을 만날 시간이 있다.

해설 벡 씨가 오후 2시 54분 메시지에서 자신이 보낸 문서를 읽어봐 주면 좋겠다(I'd like you to read it over)며 도움을 요청하자, 이에 대해 문제되지 않는다고 응답한 것이다. 즉, 벡 씨의 문서 검토 요청을 수락한다는 의미이므로, (C)가 정답이다.

어휘 be willing to 기꺼이 ~하다 review 검토하다 representative 대표, 대리인

> ▸▸ Paraphrasing 지문의 read it over
> → 정답의 review a document

160 추론 / 암시

번역 맥콜 씨는 어떤 종류의 일을 하겠는가?

(A) 마케팅
(B) 회계
(C) 법률 자문
(D) 정보기술 서비스

해설 벡 씨가 오후 3시 2분 메시지에서 광고 전략(Advertising Strategies)이 맥콜 씨의 전문 분야(that is your area of expertise)임을 언급했으므로, (A)가 정답이다.

161-164 이메일

수신: 마라 레날도 ⟨mrenaldo@viyamail.com⟩
발신: 리사 양 ⟨lyang@staffordsvillefair.org⟩
날짜: 5월 28일
제목: 회신: 스태포즈빌 공예박람회

레날도 씨께,

스태포즈빌 연례 공예박람회에서 귀하의 수공예 제품을 판매하는 데 관심을 보여주셔서 감사합니다. **162(B)다른 신청자와 공간 공유를 희망하는지 여부와 관계없이, 모든 신청자는 25달러의 신청비를 내야 함을 알려드립니다.** **162(C)/164아울러, 판매자로 채택되기 위해서는 최소 4장의 작품 사진을 제출해야 합니다.** 그것들이 행사에서 판매하고자 내놓는 제품을 명확히 보여줄 수 있도록 하십시오.

사진과 더불어 작품을 어떻게 전시할 것인지 보여주는 대강의 스케치를 제출해 주십시오. 귀하가 지역 도예가인 친구 줄리아 베렌스와 공간을 함께 쓰고 싶다고 제안하셨으므로, 해당 공간을 공동으로 어떻게 사용할 계획인지 스케치에 표시되어 있으면 도움이 될 것 같습니다.

161/162(D)또한 날씨에 관계없이 박람회를 열기 때문에 모든 판매자는 본인과 물품이 비에 젖지 않도록 보호할 천막을 각자 구비해야 합니다.

163마지막으로 저희는 매년 수용할 수 있는 것보다 훨씬 많은 보석 제작자들의 신청을 받고 있습니다. 귀하의 작품이 올해 뽑히지 않더라도 처음 신청하시는 것이니 너무 실망하지 않으셨으면 합니다.

다시 한번 감사 드리며, 신청에 행운이 따르길 바랍니다.

리사 양

어휘 fair 박람회 handcrafted 수공예품인 annual 연례의 applicant 신청자, 지원자 submit 제출하다 moreover 게다가 consider (채택 대상으로) 고려하다 vendor 판매자[업체] in addition to ~에 더하여, ~ 이외에 propose 제안하다 potter 도예가 indicate 나타내다 jointly 공동으로 rain or shine 날씨에 관계없이 supply 제공하다, 공급하다 ware 상품, 용품 possibility 가능성 be aware 알다 discouraged 낙담한

161 추론 / 암시

번역 공예박람회에 대해 암시된 것은?

(A) 스태포즈빌 시내에서 열린다.
(B) 최초로 열리는 것이다.
(C) 지역에서 만든 공예품을 전문으로 한다.
(D) 야외에서 열릴 것이다.

해설 세 번째 단락에서 날씨에 관계없이 박람회를 열기 때문에 비가 올 경우 물품이 젖지 않도록 보호할 천막을 각자 구비해야 한다(because we hold the fair rain or shine, all vendors must supply their own tenting to protect ~ from the possibility of rain)고 했다. 따라서 박람회가 야외에서 열린다고 추론할 수 있으므로, (D)가 정답이다.

어휘 specialize in ~를 전문으로 하다

162 사실 관계 확인

번역 공예박람회 판매를 위한 조건으로 언급되지 않은 것은?

(A) 다른 참가자와 공간 함께 쓰기
(B) 참가비 내기
(C) 공예품 사진 제출하기
(D) 각자의 천막 제공하기

해설 첫 번째 단락의 '모든 신청자는 25달러의 신청비를 내야 한다(all applicants must submit a $25 application fee)'에서 (B)를, '모든 신청자는 최소 4장의 작품 사진을 제출해야 한다(all applicants must submit a minimum of four photographs of their work)'에서 (C)를, 세 번째 단락의 '모든 판매자는 각자 천막을 구비해야 한다(all vendors must supply their own tenting)'에서 (D)를 확인할 수 있다. 따라서 선택 사항(whether or not they want to share a space with another applicant)에 해당하는 (A)가 정답이다.

> **▸▸ Paraphrasing**   지문의 **submit a $25 application fee**
> → 보기 **(B)의 Paying a fee**
> 지문의 **photographs of their work**
> → 보기 **(C)의 images of the crafts**
> 지문의 **supply their own tenting**
> → 보기 **(D)의 Providing one's own tenting**

163 추론 / 암시

번역 레날도 씨는 무엇을 판매하겠는가?

(A) 스케치
(B) 사진
(C) 도자기
(D) 보석

해설 네 번째 단락에서 매년 박람회에서 수용할 수 있는 것보다 훨씬 더 많은 보석 제작자들의 신청을 받고 있다(every year we receive far more applications from jewelry makers)고 한 후, 레날도 씨의 작품이 올해 뽑히지 않을 가능성(if your work is not accepted this year)을 언급했다. 따라서 레날도 씨도 보석 제작자라고 추론할 수 있으므로, (D)가 정답이다.

164 문장 삽입

번역 [1], [2], [3], [4]로 표시된 곳 중에서 다음 문장이 가장 적합한 곳은?

"그것들이 행사에서 판매하고자 내놓는 제품을 명확히 보여줄 수 있도록 하십시오."

(A) [1]
(B) [2]
(C) [3]
(D) [4]

해설 주어진 문장의 '그것들', 즉 제품을 보여주어야 하는 것이 앞에서 먼저 언급되어야 한다. [1] 앞에서 박람회 판매자로 채택되려면 작품 사진을 제출해야 한다(all applicants must submit a minimum of four photographs of their work)고 했으므로, 이 뒤에 주어진 문장이 들어가야 자연스럽다. 따라서 (A)가 정답이다.

어휘 represent 보여주다, 제시하다

165-167 정보문

슬립 사운들리 솔루션즈
슬립 사운들리 솔루션즈를 선택해 주셔서 감사합니다!

---

¹⁶⁵업데이트된 제어판은 슬립 사운들리 동작 센서와 화재, 연기, 일산화탄소 감지기를 비롯해 귀하의 가정에 있는 모든 보안 시스템을 활성화, 비활성화할 수 있도록 하는 통합 시스템으로 연결됩니다.

슬립 사운들리의 모든 주거 경보 시스템은 최상의 품질과 감도를 보장하게끔 철저한 시험을 거쳤습니다. 따라서 귀하의 주거지가 보호받고 있다는 사실에 안심하며 푹 주무실 수 있습니다. ¹⁶⁶또한 어디에 계시든 소란이 발생하면 알려드리는 새로운 스마트폰 앱을 개발했습니다. 해당 앱은 지금 바로 다운로드 가능합니다.

슬립 사운들리의 제어 장치는 슬립 사운들리의 탐지기 및 경보기에 쓸 수 있도록 세밀하게 제작되었습니다. 다른 업체에서 제조한 제품을 사용하시면 경보 장치가 주거용 건물 안전 요건이나 지역 법규에 ¹⁶⁷맞지 않는 결과를 초래할 수 있습니다.

어휘 control panel 제어판 integrated 통합된 activate 활성화하다 security 보안 carbon monoxide 일산화탄소 detector 탐지기 residential 주거의 thoroughly 철저히, 완전히 sensitivity 감도, 민감도 in the knowledge that ~임을 알고 안심하는[자신하는] develop 개발하다 disturbance 방해, 교란, 소란 manufacture 제조하다 requirement 요구사항, 요건 comply with ~를 준수하다

---

165 세부 사항

번역 슬립 사운들리 솔루션즈는 어떤 업계에서 영업하고 있는가?

(A) 부동산
(B) 생명보험
(C) 주택 보안
(D) 가구 이사

해설 첫 번째 단락에서 업데이트된 제어판이 슬립 사운들리 동작 센서를 비롯해 가정에 있는 모든 보안 시스템을 활성화, 비활성화할 수 있도록 하는 통합 시스템으로 연결된다(The updated control panel ~ allows you to activate and disable all security systems in your home, including your Sleep Soundly motion sensor)고 했으므로, 슬립 사운들리 솔루션즈가 주택 보안 관련 업체임을 알 수 있다. 따라서 (C)가 정답이다.

166 세부 사항

번역 슬립 사운들리 솔루션즈는 어떤 신제품을 제공하고 있는가?

(A) 옥외 동작 센서
(B) 스마트폰 앱
(C) 주택 설치 서비스
(D) 화재 감지 장치

해설 두 번째 단락에서 새로운 스마트폰 앱을 개발했다(We have also developed a new smartphone application)고 한 후, 지금 바로 다운로드 가능하다(The app is available for download now)고 덧붙였다. 따라서 (B)가 정답이다.

어휘 installation 설치 detection 탐지, 감지

▸▸ **Paraphrasing** 지문의 **is available ~ now**
→ 질문의 **is being offered**

---

167 동의어 찾기

번역 세 번째 단락, 세 번째 줄에 쓰인 'meet'과 의미가 가장 가까운 단어는?

(A) 인사하다
(B) 만지다
(C) 충족시키다
(D) 경험하다

해설 'meet'을 포함한 부분은 '주거용 건물 안전 요건에 맞지 않는 경보 장치(an alarm system that does not meet safety requirements for residential buildings)'라는 의미로 해석되는데, 여기서 meet은 '맞다, 충족시키다'라는 뜻으로 쓰였다. 따라서 '충족시키다, 채우다'라는 의미의 (C) satisfy가 정답이다.

168-171 편지

3월 29일

마리차 기어링스 박사
포세이돈 가 392번지
파라마리보
수리남

기어링스 박사님께,

^{168/170}자메이카 농업 교육 아카데미(JATA)의 교수로 수년간 재직해 주신 것에 대해 감사를 표하고 몇 가지 흥미로운 진행상황을 알려드리고자 편지를 씁니다. 아시다시피, JATA는 원래 농업 직업학교로 ¹⁶⁹세워졌지만 현재는 사이버 보안, 전기공학, 보건정보 관리 등 다양한 학문의 강좌를 제공하고 있습니다. ^{171(D)}처음 10년간 거의 지역 출신으로만 구성되었던 학생층은 이제 북·남미와 유럽 등지에서 온 학생들로 문화적 다양성을 띠고 있습니다. ^{171(B)}요즘 학생들은 고도로 발달한 기기를 사용하며, 그 중 대다수는 초기에는 없었던 것들입니다.

¹⁶⁸JATA가 지난 시간 동안 겪은 이러한 변화 및 기타 중요한 변화를 반영하기 위해, 이사회는 기관 이름을 캐리비안 과학 기술 아카데미로 변경하자는 교수협의회의 제안서를 승인했습니다. 따라서 새로운 기관 로고가 채택될 예정입니다. ¹⁷⁰현재와 과거의 모든 학생 및 교수진은 로고 디자인 경연에 참가할 수 있습니다. 경연 관련 정보는 곧 발표할 것입니다.

^{171(C)}명칭 변경 기념식 및 새 로고 소개가 기관 20주년 기념일인 6월 1일 오전 11시에 열릴 예정입니다. 함께해 주시기 바랍니다.

오드리 바틀렛
교무처 부처장
자메이카 농업 교육 아카데미

어휘 faculty 교수진 agricultural 농업의 originally 원래 establish 설립하다 vocational 직업과 관련된 an array of 다수의 varied 다양한 discipline 지식 분야, 학과목 management 관리 exclusively 오로지 culturally 문화적으로 diverse 다양한 sophisticated 정교한, 고도로 발달한 reflect 반영하다, 나타내다 significant 중요한 undergo 겪다 Board of Trustees 이사회 approve 승인하다

Faculty Senate 교수협의회 institution 기관 adopt 채택하다 former 이전의 forthcoming 곧 있을, 다가오는 take place 열리다

168 주제 / 목적

번역 편지를 쓴 한 가지 목적은?

(A) 명칭 변경을 알리려고
(B) 성공한 동문을 기리려고
(C) 교육과정 변경을 제안하려고
(D) 개인의 업적을 열거하려고

해설 첫 번째 단락에서 자메이카 농업 교육 아카데미에서 일어나고 있는 몇 가지 흥미로운 상황을 알려주기 위해 편지를 쓴다(I am writing ~ to let you know about some exciting developments)고 한 후, 두 번째 단락에서 이사회가 기관 이름을 캐리비안 과학 기술 아카데미로 변경하자는 교수협의회의 제안서를 승인했다(the Board of Trustees has approved a proposal by the Faculty Senate to rename the institution the Caribbean Academy of Science and Technology)고 했다. 따라서 편지를 쓴 목적 중 하나가 명칭 변경 소식을 알리는 것이라고 볼 수 있으므로, (A)가 정답이다.

어휘 distinguished 유명한, 성공한 alumni 졸업생들 revision 수정, 변경 individual 개인 accomplishment 성취, 업적

> ▸▸ **Paraphrasing** 지문의 **rename**
> → 정답의 **a name change**

169 동의어 찾기

번역 첫 번째 단락, 세 번째 줄에 쓰인 'established'와 의미가 가장 가까운 단어는?

(A) 영향을 받은
(B) 설립된
(C) 확정된
(D) 안정적인

해설 'established'를 포함한 부분은 'JATA는 원래 농업 직업학교로 세워졌다(JATA was originally established as a vocational school for agriculture)'라는 의미로 해석되는데, 여기서 established는 '세워진, 설립된'이라는 뜻으로 쓰였다. 따라서 '설립된'이라는 의미의 (B) founded가 정답이다.

170 추론 / 암시

번역 기어링스 박사에 대해 암시된 것은?

(A) JATA의 기념 행사에 참석할 계획이다.
(B) 사이버 보안 강좌를 가르쳤다.
(C) JATA의 로고 디자인 경연에 참가할 수 있다.
(D) JATA의 이사회에 있었다.

해설 첫 번째 단락에서 기어링스 박사가 자메이카 농업 교육 아카데미 교수로 재직해 왔다(your years of service on the faculty of the Jamaican Agricultural Training Academy)고 했는데, 두 번째 단락을 보면 모든 학생 및 교수진이 기관의 새 로고 디자인 경연

에 참가할 수 있다(All students and faculty members ~ are invited to participate in a logo design contest)고 쓰여 있다. 따라서 기어링스 박사도 로고 디자인 경연에 참가할 자격이 있다고 추론할 수 있으므로, (C)가 정답이다.

어휘 celebration 기념 행사, 기념 take part in ~에 참가하다

> ▸▸ **Paraphrasing** 지문의 **participate in** → 정답의 **take part in**

171 사실 관계 확인

번역 편지에서 JATA에 대해 명시되지 않은 것은?

(A) 교수들이 캠퍼스에 상주한다.
(B) 학생들이 현대식 기기를 쓸 수 있다.
(C) 6월 1일이면 20주년이 된다.
(D) 외국 학생들이 다닌다.

해설 첫 번째 단락의 '요즘 학생들은 고도로 발달한 기기를 사용하며, 그 중 대다수는 초기에는 없었던 것이다(Today's students work with sophisticated equipment, much of which did not exist in our early days)'에서 (B)를, 세 번째 단락의 '기관 20주년 기념일인 6월 1일(on 1 June, the twentieth anniversary of the institution)'에서 (C)를, 첫 번째 단락의 '이제 북·남미와 유럽 등지에서 온 학생들로 문화적 다양성을 띠고 있다(Our student body ~ is now culturally diverse, with students from across the Americas and Europe)'에서 (D)를 확인할 수 있다. 따라서 언급되지 않은 (A)가 정답이다.

어휘 have access to ~에 접근할 수 있다 attend 다니다, 참석하다

> ▸▸ **Paraphrasing** 지문의 **work with sophisticated equipment, much of which did not exist in our early days** → 보기 (B)의 **have access to modern equipment**
> 지문의 **the twentieth anniversary** → 보기 (C)의 **twenty years old**
> 지문의 **students from across the Americas and Europe** → 보기 (D)의 **international students**

172-175 온라인 채팅

애슐리 몬테인 (오전 8시 54분): 에릭슨 씨 면접은 어떻게 됐나요?

댄 캠벨 (오전 8시 55분): 정말 좋았습니다. ¹⁷²이곳에서 훌륭한 기자가 될 수 있을 거라고 봅니다. 똑똑하고 체계적인 분 같아요. 견본을 보니 글을 매우 잘 쓰더군요.

애슐리 몬테인 (오전 8시 57분): ¹⁷³브룩, 에릭슨 씨에게 연락해서 다음 면접을 잡아 주시겠어요? 문제가 될까요?

댄 캠벨 (오전 8시 58분): 정말 함께 일하고 싶어요. 피터스 씨에게 좋은 인상을 주는 것이 중요할 텐데요.

브룩 랜돌프 (오전 8시 59분): 아닙니다.

애슐리 몬테인 (오전 9시): 고맙습니다. ¹⁷⁴다양한 업무 경력도 있는 걸로 알고 있어요. 이로 인해 다재다능한 기자가 될 수 있겠죠.

브룩 랜돌프 (오전 9시 2분): 언제 다시 보기를 원하세요?

댄 캠벨 (오전 9시 3분): 애슐리, 다음 면접 때 당신도 참여하시는 걸로 아는데요. 피터스 씨는 아마 에릭슨 씨가 프리랜서 작가에서 회사 소속 뉴스 기자로 전향하고 싶어 하는 이유를 물어볼 거예요. **175**그리고 에릭슨 씨가 헌신적인 자세로 몇 년간 근무할 거라는 확약을 원할 겁니다.

애슐리 몬테인 (오전 9시 4분): 브룩, 피터스 씨와 저는 둘 다 금요일 오전에 시간이 돼요.

브룩 랜돌프 (오전 9시 6분): 좋습니다. 제가 곧 이메일을 쓸게요.

어휘 **organized** 정돈된, 체계적인 **varied** 다양한
well-rounded 다재다능한 **probably** 아마 **transition** 이행
assurance 확약, 장담, 자신감 **committed** 헌신적인, 열정적인
shortly 곧

172 세부 사항

번역 채팅 참여자들은 어떤 종류의 업체에서 일하는가?

(A) 출판사
(B) 신문사
(C) 영화제작사
(D) 취업 알선업체

해설 캠벨 씨가 오전 8시 55분 메시지에서 면접자인 에릭슨 씨가 훌륭한 기자가 될 수 있을 거라고 본다(he'd be a great reporter here)며 글도 잘 쓴다고 평가했다. 따라서 채팅 참여자들이 신문사에서 일하고 있다고 볼 수 있으므로, (B)가 정답이다.

173 의도 파악

번역 오전 8시 59분에 랜돌프 씨가 "아닙니다"라고 쓸 때, 그 의도는 무엇인가?

(A) 면접에 참여하고 싶다.
(B) 에릭슨 씨가 채용될 것으로 생각하지 않는다.
(C) 요청사항을 처리하는 것을 수월하게 여긴다.
(D) 에릭슨 씨의 글을 읽은 적이 없다.

해설 몬테인 씨가 오전 8시 57분 메시지에서 에릭슨 씨에게 연락해서 다음 면접을 잡아달라(can you contact Mr. Erickson to set up the next interview?)고 랜돌프 씨에게 요청한 후, 문제가 되는지(Is that a problem?) 확인했다. 이에 대해 랜돌프 씨가 '아닙니다(Not at all)'라고 응답한 것이므로, 요청을 처리하는 데 문제가 없다는 의도로 쓴 메시지라고 볼 수 있다. 따라서 (C)가 정답이다.

어휘 **fulfill a request** 요청을 들어주다

174 사실 관계 확인

번역 에릭슨 씨에 대해 명시된 것은?

(A) 전에 면접을 본 적이 없다.
(B) 다양한 종류의 직업을 가졌다.
(C) 피터스 씨의 후임이 될 것이다.
(D) 몬테인 씨의 이전 동료다.

해설 몬테인 씨가 오전 9시 메시지에서 에릭슨 씨에게는 다양한 업무 경력도 있다(he has a varied work history)고 했으므로, (B)가 정답이다.

어휘 **former** 이전의 **colleague** 동료

▸▸ Paraphrasing 지문의 **has a varied work history**
→ 정답의 **has held many different types of jobs**

175 세부 사항

번역 논의에 따르면, 신입사원의 어떤 면이 피터스 씨에게 중요한가?

(A) 이전의 뉴스 보도 경력
(B) 바로 일을 시작할 수 있는 능력
(C) 동료와의 원활한 의사소통
(D) 회사 장기 근속

해설 캠벨 씨가 오전 9시 3분 메시지에서 피터스 씨는 에릭슨 씨가 헌신적인 자세로 몇 년간 근무할 거라는 확약을 원한다(Mr. Peters will want assurances that he ~ will stick around for several years)고 했다. 따라서 피터스 씨가 장기 근속을 중시한다는 것을 알 수 있으므로, (D)가 정답이다.

어휘 **prior** 이전의 **immediately** 바로, 즉시 **long term** 장기간

▸▸ Paraphrasing 지문의 **stick around for several years**
→ 정답의 **Staying ~ over the long term**

176-180 기사 + 편지

앨버타 비즈니스 매터스
4월호

여러분의 사무 환경을 지금 바로 개선하세요!

오늘날 사무 환경은 수많은 복도, 따분한 베이지색 또는 흰색 벽, 대부분 똑같은 모양으로 줄지어 늘어선 창문 없는 작은 방들이 특징으로, 편안함, 아름다움, 에너지를 불어넣지 못합니다. 하지만 당신의 사무 공간을 더욱 매력적으로 만들 쉽고 저렴한 방법이 존재합니다.

공기 질

- **176(A)**장식으로 녹색 식물을 들여놓으세요. 식물은 천연 여과 체계를 제공해 산소도를 높여줍니다. 꽃이 피지 않는 식물이 꽃가루를 흩날리지 않아 더 좋습니다.
- 탁상용 소형 공기청정기는 탁한 공기를 개선하고 먼지를 제거합니다.

광질

- **176(B)**잠시 휴식을 취하고 밖으로 나가세요. 점심시간 전이나 후 5분만으로도 인공 광원으로부터 벗어나 눈에 잠시 휴식을 제공할 수 있습니다.
- 풀 스펙트럼 전구를 사용한 책상용 램프를 사용하세요.
- **177**블라인드 대신 이중창을 설치해 자연광을 유지하면서 눈부심을 줄여보세요.

스트레스 해소
- 귀마개 또는 소음 차단 헤드폰은 개방된 사무실 구조에서 주의를 산만하게 하는 소음을 차단할 수 있습니다.
- 176 (D) 사랑하는 사람이나 휴가 때 방문한 장소 등의 사진은 사무실과 별개인 우리의 생활을 상기시켜 줍니다. 중요한 장식 요소로 좋아하는 사진을 몇 장 골라보세요.

178/179 독자 여러분, 목록에 덧붙일 방법이 있다면 저희에게 보내주세요. 다음 달 호에 실릴 것입니다.

어휘 environment 환경 numerous 수많은 corridor 복도 identical 동일한, 똑같은 cubicle 작은 방 inviting 유혹적인 filtration 여과 scatter 뿌리다 pollen 꽃가루 purifier 정화기 stale 신선하지 않은 take a break 휴식을 취하다 respite 한숨 돌리기, 일시적인 중단 artificial 인공적인 full-spectrum 모든 파장의 (자연광에 가까운) install 설치하다 double-glazed 이중 유리를 끼운 glare 환한 빛, 눈부심 noise-cancelling 소음 차단의 distracting 산만하게 하는 floor plan 평면 배치도 decorative 장식의 element 요소

앨버타 비즈니스 매터스
편집자께 드리는 편지

179 귀사의 독자들이 제가 일하는 무버블 주식회사에 대해 알면 흥미로워할 것 같습니다. 저희는 근무자들, 특히 오늘날 이동이 많은 직원들을 위해 지루한 사무실을 더욱 편안하고 편리한 곳으로 만들고자 합니다.

일례로, 에드먼턴에 있는 본사에서 1주일에 이틀 일하고 나머지 요일은 지사에서 일하는 걸로 생각해 보죠. 180 저희의 '캔두 케이스'는 좋아하는 사무용품을 항상 가지고 다닐 수 있도록 해 줍니다. 무게가 1.75kg 밖에 안 되는 '모듈라 데코 키트'는 휴대용 독서등, 소형 조화, 4장의 사진을 넣을 공간이 있는 접이식 사진 액자가 들어있습니다. 신상품을 자주 선보이고 있으니, 온라인으로 당사를 찾아보시고 SNS에서 팔로우하세요!

마리아 테스타

어휘 letter to the editor 편집자에게 보내는 편지, (잡지/신문 등의) 독자란 interest 흥미를 끌다 aspire 열망하다 dull 지루한 on-the-move 이리저리 이동하는, 매우 분주한 comfortable 편안한 convenient 편리한 headquarters 본사, 본부 satellite office 지국, 지사 ensure 보장하다, ~하게 하다 office supply 사무용품 contain 포함하다 portable 휴대용의 silk plant 조화 folding 접이식의 frequently 자주

---

176 사실 관계 확인

번역 기사에서 권장되지 않는 것은?
(A) 식물을 이용해 작은 방 장식하기
(B) 휴식 시간 동안 바깥에 나가서 걷기
(C) 잔잔한 소음 기계 사용하기
(D) 개인 사진으로 장식하기

해설 공기 질(Air quality) 항목에서 사무실 장식으로 녹색 식물을 들여

놓으라(Add some green plants to the décor)고 했고, 광질(Light quality) 항목에서는 잠시 휴식을 취하고 밖으로 나가라(Take breaks and go outdoors)고 권했습니다. 또한 스트레스 해소(Stress relief)를 위해 개인의 삶을 상기시켜주는 사진을 몇 장 골라보라(Photographs of loved ones and placed ~ as important decorative elements)고 했으므로, (A), (B), (D)는 권장 사항임을 확인할 수 있다. 따라서 언급되지 않은 (C)가 정답이다.

> ▶▶ Paraphrasing
> 지문의 Add some green plants to the décor
> → 보기 (A)의 Using plants to decorate cubicles
> 지문의 Take breaks and go outdoors
> → 보기 (B)의 Walking outdoors during breaks
> 지문의 Select a few favorite pictures as important decorative elements
> → 보기 (D)의 Decorating with personal photographs

---

177 세부 사항

번역 블라인드를 언급한 이유는?
(A) 상대적으로 비싸기 때문
(B) 자연광을 차단하기 때문
(C) 가구와 매치하기 어렵기 때문
(D) 먼지를 끌어당기기 때문

해설 기사의 광질(Light quality) 항목에서 블라인드 대신 이중창을 설치해 자연광을 유지하면서 눈부심을 줄여보라(Install double-glazed windows instead of blinds to reduce glare while maintaining natural light)고 권장했다. 즉, 블라인드로는 자연광을 받지 못한다는 것을 설명한 것이므로, (B)가 정답이다.

어휘 relatively 비교적, 상대적으로

---

178 사실 관계 확인

번역 잡지에 대해 알 수 있는 것은?
(A) 앨버타의 유일한 비즈니스 출판물이다.
(B) 출판사는 직원을 추가 채용하고 있다.
(C) 편집자들은 독자의 의견을 듣고 싶어 한다.
(D) 가구 회사가 후원한다.

해설 기사의 마지막 부분에서 독자에게 사무 환경 개선 방법 목록에 덧붙일 팁이 있다면 보내달라(if you have tips to add to this list, send them in)고 요청했으므로, (C)가 정답이다.

어휘 publication 출판물 additional 추가의 sponsor 후원하다

---

179 연계

번역 테스타 씨에 대해 암시된 것은?
(A) 전문 작가다.
(B) 새로운 회사를 연다.
(C) 출장을 자주 다닌다.
(D) 〈앨버타 비즈니스 매터스〉 이전 호를 읽었다.

해설 편지의 첫 번째 단락에서 테스터 씨는 자신이 일하는 회사에 대해 〈앨버타 비즈니스 매터스〉의 독자들이 알면 흥미로워할 것 같다(It may interest your readers to know about the company I work for)고 한 후, 사무실 개선에 적합한 자사의 제품들을 소개했다. 기사의 마지막 부분을 보면 사무 환경 개선 방법 목록에 덧붙일 팁이 있다면 보내달라(if you have tips to add to this list, send them in)며 다음 달 호에 실릴 것(they will be published in the next month's issue)이라고 되어 있다. 따라서 테스터 씨가 〈앨버타 비즈니스 매터스〉의 이전 호에 나온 사무 환경 개선 방법 기사를 읽고 나서 해당 편지를 쓴 것임을 추론할 수 있으므로, (D)가 정답이다.

어휘 professional 전문적인 frequently 자주 previous 이전의

180 추론 / 암시

번역 무버블 주식회사의 제품에 대해 암시된 것은?

(A) 짐을 꾸리기에 쉽다.
(B) 가격이 적당하다.
(C) 단기간 동안 이용 가능하다.
(D) 재활용된 원료로 만들었다.

해설 편지의 두 번째 단락에서 무버블 주식회사의 '캔두 케이스(ensures that your favorite office supplies always travel with you)'와 '모듈라 데코 키트(weighing just 1.75 kg, contains a portable reading lamp ~ four pictures)'가 소개되었는데, 두 제품 모두 이동 시 휴대가 가능하다고 볼 수 있다. 따라서 (A)가 정답이다.

어휘 packable 짐 꾸리기 쉬운 affordable 가격이 알맞은

▸▸ Paraphrasing 지문의 travel with you/weighing just 1.75kg, contains a portable reading lamp ~ pictures → 정답의 packable

181-185 웹페이지 + 후기

http://www.Lloydtouringcompany.co.uk

런던 최고의 볼거리를 감상할 수 있는 로이드 투어 컴퍼니(LTC)의 최고 인기 여행 상품 중 하나를 선택해 보세요!

투어 1: 유명한 빨간색 이층버스에서 최고 인기 명소를 둘러보는 전일 투어입니다. 근위병 교대식을 감상하고 181**강 크루즈로 하루를 마무리하세요.**

183**투어 2: 런던 최고의 쇼핑 구역을 도보로 둘러보는 전일 투어입니다.** 런던의 유명 백화점을 둘러보고 유행의 첨단을 걷는 본드 가와 옥스포드 가를 거닐어 보세요.

투어 3: 빨간색 이층버스에서 이뤄지는 반일 투어입니다. 런던 타워 개인 투어와 인근 카페에서의 점심식사가 포함됩니다.

투어 4: 버킹엄 궁전 반일 투어로, 근위병 교대식이 포함됩니다. 전통음식인 피시 앤 칩스 점심식사로 투어가 종료됩니다.

투어 5: 런던 최고 명소들이 포함된 전일 도보 투어입니다. 중세식 연회로 일정을 마무리하세요.

182**해박한 LTC 현지 직원들이 모든 투어마다 개인적으로 가이드해 드립니다.** 투어 설명에 명시된 경우를 제외하고 식사는 포함되지 않습니다. 선택된 출발 장소로 와서 만나야 할 책임은 참가자에게 있습니다. LTC는 호텔 픽업 서비스를 제공해 드리지 않습니다. 모든 투어에 추가 요금을 지불하면 런던의 유명한 대관람차인 런던아이의 날짜 무관 이용권을 포함하도록 업그레이드해 드립니다.

어휘 outing 여행, 야유회 conclude 끝내다, 마치다 wander 거닐다, 돌아다니다 nearby 인근의 traditional 전통적인 medieval 중세의 banquet 연회 knowledgeable 아는 것이 많은 description 설명, 서술 departure 출발 destination 목적지 additional 추가의 open-date 날짜가 지정되지 않은 observation wheel 관람차

★★★★★

-엘라 부통

로이드 투어 컴퍼니 후기

런던으로 처음 간 여행이었어요. 183**모든 주요 관광 명소를 혼자서 돌아보기로 결심했지만, 런던에서 쇼핑하기에 가장 좋은 곳을 찾는 데 도와줄 사람이 필요했습니다.** LTC 투어 가이드 라리사는 훌륭했어요. 본인이 쇼핑을 아주 좋아했거든요. 투어 초반에 라리사는 참가자들에 대해 알려고 노력했어요. 그래서 모두가 가장 관심 있어 하는 매장으로 데려갈 수 있었죠. 정말 개인 맞춤형 투어였어요! 184**라리사가 프랑스어도 구사하는 건 덤으로 얻은 이득이었습니다.** 제 딸과 저는 파리에서 와서, 두 개 언어로 의사소통을 할 수 있는 점에 감사했죠. 투어는 가격도 매우 적당했습니다. 적극 추천해요. 185**단 한 가지 아쉬운 점은 우리가 옥스포드 가에 갔을 때 너무 붐벼서 쉽게 돌아다니기가 어려웠다는 겁니다.**

어휘 discover 발견하다, 찾다 avid 열렬한 personalized 개인 맞춤형의 appreciate 감사하다 reasonably 합리적으로, 타당하게 extremely 극도로, 극히

181 세부 사항

번역 투어 1은 다른 투어들과 어떻게 다른가?

(A) 이층버스를 이용한다.
(B) 유명 레스토랑에서의 식사가 여러 번 포함되어 있다.
(C) 참가자들이 강에서 런던을 바라볼 수 있다.
(D) 하루 종일 걸린다.

해설 강 크루즈로 하루를 마무리하는 것(conclude the day with a river cruise)은 투어 1에서만 이용 가능하므로, (C)가 정답이다. 이층버스 (red double-decker bus)는 투어 1과 3에서 이용 가능하고, 투어 1, 2, 5 모두 전일 투어(Full-day tour)이므로, (A)와 (D)는 정답이 될 수 없다.

어휘 multiple 다수의 entire 전체의

▸▸ Paraphrasing 지문의 with a river cruise → 정답의 to see ~ from the water

182 사실 관계 확인

번역 투어 비용에 포함된 것은?

(A) 호텔에서 출발하는 교통편
(B) 투어 가이드
(C) 음식점에서 아침식사
(D) 런던아이 이용권

해설 웹페이지의 마지막 단락에서 해박한 LTC 현지 직원들이 모든 투어마다 개인적으로 가이드한다(LTC's knowledgeable local staff members personally guide each one of our tours)고 한 후 별도의 추가 비용을 언급하지 않았다. 따라서 투어 가이드가 비용에 포함되어 있다고 볼 수 있으므로, (B)가 정답이다. 투어에 포함된 식사 외의 식사는 포함되지 않고(Meals are not covered, except ~ description), 호텔 픽업 서비스는 제공되지 않으며(LTC does not provide pickup from hotels), 추가 요금을 지불하면 런던아이 이용권을 포함하도록 업그레이드해준다(All tours can be upgraded for an additional fee to include an open-date ticket to the London Eye)고 했으므로, (A), (C), (D)는 정답이 될 수 없다.

어휘 transportation 교통편, 운송

183 연계

번역 부통 씨는 어떤 투어를 선택했겠는가?

(A) 투어 2
(B) 투어 3
(C) 투어 4
(D) 투어 5

해설 후기의 초반부에서 부통 씨는 런던에서 쇼핑하기에 가장 좋은 곳을 찾는 데 도와줄 사람이 필요해서(I wanted someone to help me discover the most interesting places to shop in London) 투어를 이용했다고 했다. 웹페이지에 나열된 투어 종류를 보면, 런던 최고의 쇼핑 구역을 도보로 둘러보는(Full-day walking tour of London's best shopping areas) 투어 2가 부통 씨의 요구에 가장 부합한다. 따라서 (A)가 정답이다.

184 추론 / 암시

번역 후기에서 부통 씨에 대해 암시된 것은?

(A) 버스 투어를 선호한다.
(B) 프랑스어를 구사한다.
(C) 출장 중이었다.
(D) LTC를 전에 이용한 적이 있다.

해설 후기의 중반부에서 부통 씨는 투어 가이드인 라리사가 프랑스어도 구사하는 건 덤으로 얻은 이득이었다(it was a bonus that Larissa also speaks French)고 한 후, 자신과 딸이 파리에서 와서 두 개 언어로 의사소통을 할 수 있는 점에 감사했다(My daughter and I were visiting from Paris, and we appreciated being able to communicate in two languages)고 했다. 따라서 부통 씨가 프랑스어를 구사한다고 추론할 수 있으므로, (B)가 정답이다.

어휘 business trip 출장

185 세부 사항

번역 부통 씨가 투어에 실망한 이유는?

(A) 비용이 높았다.
(B) 체계가 없었다.
(C) 매우 붐비는 장소에서 이뤄졌다.
(D) 도시에서 흥미롭지 않은 곳에서 이뤄졌다.

해설 후기의 후반부에서 부통 씨가 단 한 가지 아쉬운 점(The only unpleasant part of the tour)으로 옥스포드 가에 갔을 때 너무 붐벼서 쉽게 돌아다니기 어려웠던 점(Oxford Street was extremely crowded when we visited, and it was difficult to walk around easily)을 언급했다. 따라서 (C)가 정답이다.

어휘 disorganized 체계적이지 않은

▸▸ **Paraphrasing**　　지문의 **unpleasant**
　　　　　　　　　　　→ 질문의 **disappointed**

186-190 이메일 + 공지 + 이메일

수신: 조셉 모건 〈joseph.morgan@peltergraphics.com〉
발신: administrator@costaseminars.org
날짜: 5월 31일
제목: 도서 주문

모건 씨께,

[186]6월 11일 로스포드 비즈니스 센터에서 열릴 에밀리오 코스타 세미나에 신청해 주셔서 감사합니다. [186/190]회의 참가자들이 에밀리오 코스타의 그래픽디자인 도서를 할인된 가격으로 구입할 수 있는 기회를 귀하께서도 이용하셔서 기쁩니다. 아래의 정보는 귀하의 주문 확인입니다. [187]책은 세미나 당일 체크인 데스크에 있을 것입니다. 모든 주요 신용카드로 결제 가능합니다. 6월 11일에 뵙게 되기를 고대합니다.

수량	제목	가격	할인가	총 금액
1	[190]완벽해진 수치: 데이터를 시각적으로 멋지게 꾸미기	22달러	[190]17.60달러	[190]17.60달러
1	정보화 시대의 로고	18달러	14.40달러	14.40달러
1	[187]그래픽 디자인에서의 브랜딩 전략	20달러	16달러	16달러
2	웹디자인 모범 관례: 유럽식 관점	28달러	22.40달러	44.80달러

총액: 92.80달러

어휘 order 주문　register for 등록하다, 신청하다　take advantage of 이용하다　opportunity 기회　purchase 구입하다　at a discounted price 할인된 가격으로　accept 수용하다, 받아 주다　look forward to 고대하다　figures 수치　visually 시각적으로　strategy 전략　practice 관례, 관행　perspective 관점, 시각

188 세미나 참가자들에게 알립니다.

187/188 아쉽게도 오늘 에밀리오 코스타의 도서 〈그래픽 디자인에서의 브랜딩 전략〉 재고가 없습니다. **187** 주문하신 분께서는 체크인 데스크의 자원봉사자에게 우편주소를 알려주시기 바랍니다. 그러면 댁으로 책을 무료 배송해 드리겠습니다. 신용카드 청구는 배송 시 이뤄질 예정입니다. 불편을 드려 죄송합니다.

어휘   mailing address 우편주소   at no cost 무료로   charge 청구하다   inconvenience 불편

수신: roberta.tsu@peltergraphics.com
발신: joseph.morgan@peltergraphics.com
날짜: 6월 22일
제목: 코스타 도서

로버타에게,

엔트첸 파이낸셜 컨설턴트의 안내책자 디자인을 마무리하기를 고대하고 있습니다. **189** 저희 최종 안을 제출하기 전 데이터 제시 방법을 재고하고 싶습니다. **190** 혹시 제가 보여드린 코스타의 저서를 한 번 살펴보셨는지요? 그는 마케팅 자료에서 재무 정보의 명확성을 향상시키는 방법에 관해 훌륭한 조언을 하고 있습니다. 아무튼 내일 점심식사 때 이야기 나누시죠.

조셉

어휘   submit 제출하다   draft 원고, 초안   present 보여주다, 나타내다   clarity 명확성   financial 금융의, 재무의   material 자료

186 추론 / 암시

번역   6월 11일 세미나의 주제는 무엇이겠는가?

(A) 재무 컨설팅
(B) 그래픽 디자인
(C) 마케팅 전략
(D) 업무용 글쓰기

해설   첫 번째 이메일의 초반부에서 모건 씨가 6월 11일에 열릴 에밀리오 코스타 세미나에 신청한 것(registering for Emilio Costa's seminar on June 11)과 에밀리오 코스타가 여러 그래픽 디자인 도서(graphic-design books)를 집필한 사람임을 확인할 수 있다. 따라서 이 세미나의 주제가 그래픽 디자인 관련이라고 추론할 수 있으므로, (B)가 정답이다.

187 연계

번역   모건 씨에 대해 암시된 것은?

(A) 동료와 함께 세미나에 참석했다.
(B) 세미나에서 발표를 했다.
(C) 책 구입 시 무료 배송을 받았다.
(D) 일부 책들에 대해 미리 결제했다.

해설   첫 번째 이메일에서 모건 씨가 주문한 책들은 세미나 당일 체크인 데스크에서 찾아가면 된다고 했는데, 세미나 참석자들을 대상으로 한 공지를 보면 〈그래픽 디자인에서의 브랜딩 전략〉 재고가 오늘 없다(we do not have ~ Branding Strategies in Graphic Design with us today)며 주문한 사람에게 집으로 책을 무료 배송해 주겠다(For those of you who have ordered it, ~ the book will be mailed to your home at no cost to you)고 쓰여 있다. 첫 번째 이메일의 표에서 모건 씨도 해당 책을 주문했음을 확인할 수 있으므로, 그가 무료로 배송받았을 것으로 추론할 수 있다. 따라서 (C)가 정답이다.

어휘   give a presentation 발표하다   free shipping 무료 배송   in advance 미리

▸▸ Paraphrasing   지문의 will be mailed to your home at no cost → 정답의 free shipping

188 주제 / 목적

번역   공지의 목적은?

(A) 문제를 설명하려고
(B) 자원봉사자를 찾으려고
(C) 결제를 요청하려고
(D) 책을 홍보하려고

해설   초반부에서 에밀리오 코스타의 도서가 오늘 없다(we do not have copies of Emilio Costa's book ~ with us today)며 추후 해당 도서를 구매한 사람들에게 무료로 배송해 주겠다는 해결책을 제시하고 있다. 따라서 문제를 설명하기 위한 공지라고 볼 수 있으므로, (A)가 정답이다.

어휘   request 요청하다   promote 홍보하다

189 세부 사항

번역   두 번째 이메일에 따르면, 모건 씨는 무엇을 변경하자고 제안하는가?

(A) 프로젝트 제출 마감 기한
(B) 책 후기 내용
(C) 예정된 회의 시간
(D) 정보 배열

해설   두 번째 이메일의 초반부에서 모건 씨가 데이터 제시 방법을 재고하고 싶다(I would like to rethink how we are presenting our data)고 제안했으므로, (D)가 정답이다.

▸▸ Paraphrasing   지문의 would like to rethink
→ 질문의 suggest changing
지문의 how we are presenting our data
→ 정답의 The display of some information

190 연계

번역   모건 씨는 추 씨에게 보여준 책에 대해 얼마를 지불했는가?

(A) 17.60달러
(B) 14.40달러
(C) 16달러
(D) 22.40달러

해설 두 번째 이메일의 중반부에서 모건 씨는 추 씨에게 자신이 보여 준 코스타 도서를 살펴봤는지(Have you had a chance to look through the Costa book I showed you?) 물은 후, 마케팅 자료에서 재무 정보의 명확성을 향상시키는 방법(improving the clarity of financial information in marketing materials)에 대해 조언하는 책이라고 덧붙였다. 첫 번째 이메일의 표를 보면 해당 도서가 〈완벽해진 수치: 데이터를 시각적으로 멋지게 꾸미기(Perfect Figures: Making Data Visually Appealing)〉이며, 모건 씨가 할인가인 17.60달러에 구입했음을 확인할 수 있다. 따라서 (A)가 정답이다.

191-195 기사 + 이메일 + 배치도

안톤 빌딩

클랜튼 (10월 12일) - ¹⁹¹**잰투니 부동산 개발업체(JPD)의 역사적인 안톤 빌딩 보수 공사가 다시 지연된다.** JPD 대변인은 보조금 및 감세 조치와 관련해 시와의 협상이 진행 중이나 다소 논쟁의 여지가 있다고 설명한다. 보수 계획에 따르면, JPD는 사무 공간과 저층 소매 공간을 제공해 다용도로 이용될 실내를 조성하는 동시에 안톤 빌딩의 역사적인 모습을 온전히 보전해야 한다. ¹⁹³**그러나 JPD에게 발급될 시의 프로젝트 진행 허가서는 현재 협상을 기다리는 동안 보류 중이다.**

이로 인해 도시 재활성화 지지자들은 점점 더 염려하고 있다. 아디티 야다브는 "퇴락하고 있는 빈 건물을 유용한 공간으로 조성하려는 이 계획은 해당 지역이 활력을 되찾는 데 큰 기여를 할 것입니다. JPD가 철회하지 않기를 진심으로 바랍니다. ¹⁹²**시 의회는 제안 시 JPD가 클랜튼의 다른 역사적 건물 여러 곳을 아름답게 복원하고 유지한 훌륭한 기록을 고려해야 할 것입니다."**

어휘 renovation 보수, 개조 spokesperson 대변인 negotiation 협상 regarding ~와 관련하여 subsidy 보조금 tax incentive 감세 조치 ongoing 진행 중인 somewhat 다소 contentious 논쟁거리가 있는 integrity 온전함, 완전한 상태 mixed-use 다목적 이용의 retail 소매(의) permit 허가증 be on hold 보류 중이다 pending ~를 기다리는 동안 revitalization 재활성화 advocate 지지자, 옹호자 increasingly 점점 더 anxious 불안해하는, 염려하는 decay 퇴락하다 go a long way to(wards) ~에 도움이 되다 restore 되찾다 vibrancy 활력

발신: anabautista@lenoiva-health.com
수신: t.rowell@jantunipropertydevelopers.com
날짜: 2월 20일
제목: 임대 문의

로웰 씨께,

¹⁹⁵**저는 의료기술 업체인 르노이바의 소유주입니다.** 사업체를 확장할 계획이라 새 사무 공간이 필요합니다. 안톤 빌딩은 클랜튼에서 저희가 고려하고 있는 장소 중 한 곳인데요. ¹⁹³**귀사의 안톤 빌딩 복원 프로젝트가 올 봄 즈음 완료될 예정이라는 이야기를 들었습니다.** 저희에게는 적절한 시점입니다. 건물에서 대중교통 서비스를 쉽게 이용할 수 있다는 점에 특히 끌렸는데요. 아직 임대 가능한 공간이 있습니까? ¹⁹⁵**면적**

이 최소 300제곱미터인 공간이 필요할 것으로 예상됩니다. ¹⁹⁴**임대를 하게 되면 직원들을 위해 따로 마련된 주차 공간이 있나요?** 어떤 정보라도 주시면 감사하겠습니다.

미리 감사 드립니다.

애나 바티스타

어휘 lease 임대 inquiry 문의 expand 확장하다 restoration 복원, 회복 particularly 특히 public transportation 대중교통 anticipate 예상하다, 기대하다 at least 최소 reserved 지정된 in advance 미리

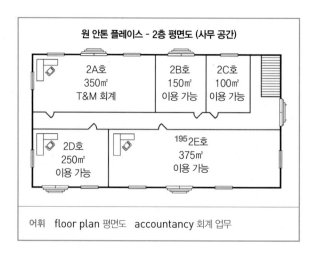

원 안톤 플레이스 - 2층 평면도 (사무 공간)

| 2A호 350m² T&M 회계 | 2B호 150m² 이용 가능 | 2C호 100m² 이용 가능 |

| 2D호 250m² 이용 가능 | ¹⁹⁵2E호 375m² 이용 가능 |

어휘 floor plan 평면도 accountancy 회계 업무

---

191 주제 / 목적

번역 기사의 목적은?
(A) 다용도 건물의 이점을 보도하려고
(B) 프로젝트의 최근 소식을 전하려고
(C) 주민들이 일자리에 지원하도록 독려하려고
(D) 시 정책의 변경사항을 알리려고

해설 첫 번째 단락에서 잰투니 부동산 개발업체의 안톤 빌딩 보수 공사가 다시 지연된다(The planned renovation of the historic Anton Building by Jantuni Property Developers ~ is facing new delays)고 한 후, 프로젝트 지연 상황에 대한 설명을 이어가고 있다. 따라서 (B)가 정답이다.

어휘 encourage 격려하다, 권장하다 policy 정책

192 사실 관계 확인

번역 야다브 씨는 안톤 빌딩의 긍정적인 측면 중 어떤 것을 언급하는가?
(A) 비용 효율성
(B) 환경 기준 준수
(C) 보수 공사의 예상되는 품질
(D) 대규모 소매 공간

해설 기사의 두 번째 단락에서 야다브 씨는 시 의회에서 안톤 빌딩 보수 공사 프로젝트 제안을 할 때 JPD가 클랜튼의 다른 역사적 건물 여러 곳을 아름답게 복원하고 유지한 훌륭한 기록을 고려해야 할 것 (the City Council should consider JPD's excellent record of beautifully restoring and maintaining several other historic buildings in Clanton)이라고 했다. 즉, JPD가 안톤 빌딩에 진행할 보수 공사의 품질에 대해 긍정적으로 예상했다고 볼 수 있으므로, (C)가 정답이다.

어휘 cost efficiency 비용 효율성 compliance 준수 environmental 환경의 standard 기준, 표준

> ▸ Paraphrasing 지문의 excellent record of beautifully restoring and maintaining several other historic buildings
> → 정답의 The anticipated quality of the renovation work

193 연계

번역 바티스타 씨의 이메일에서 JPD에 대해 암시된 것은?

(A) 요청했던 승인을 받았다.
(B) 클랜튼에서 유일하게 임대 가능한 사무 공간을 보유하고 있다.
(C) 안톤 빌딩으로 본사를 이전했다.
(D) 비교적 신생 업체다.

해설 2월 20일에 발송된 이메일의 중반부에서 바티스타 씨가 JPD의 안톤 빌딩 복원 프로젝트가 올 봄 즈음 완료될 예정이라는 이야기를 들었다(We have been informed that your restoration project of this building will be finished sometime this spring)고 했는데, 이전 해 10월 12일에 작성된 기사의 첫 번째 단락을 보면 JPD에게 발급될 시의 프로젝트 진행 허가서는 보류 중(JPD's city permit to do the project is on hold)이라고 되어 있다. 따라서 그 이후 JPD가 허가서 승인을 받아 프로젝트를 진행하는 중이라고 추론할 수 있으므로, (A)가 정답이다.

어휘 approval 승인 available 이용 가능한 relatively 비교적, 상대적으로

> ▸ Paraphrasing 지문의 permit → 정답의 approval

194 세부 사항

번역 바티스타 씨는 로웰 씨에게 건물에 대한 어떤 정보를 요청하는가?

(A) 가장 가까운 기차역까지 거리
(B) 다른 사용업체의 업종
(C) 보수 완공일자
(D) 직원 주차공간 이용 가능성

해설 이메일의 후반부에서 사무실을 임대하게 되면 직원들을 위해 따로 마련된 주차 공간이 있는지(Would there be any reserved parking for our employees if we rented there?)를 문의했으므로, (D)가 정답이다.

어휘 occupant 사용자 completion 완료, 완공

> ▸ Paraphrasing 지문의 any reserved parking for our employees
> → 정답의 The availability of employee parking

195 연계

번역 르노이바는 어떤 공간을 임대하겠는가?

(A) 2B호
(B) 2C호
(C) 2D호
(D) 2E호

해설 이메일의 후반부에서 르노이바는 면적이 최소 300제곱미터인 공간이 필요할 것으로 예상한다(We anticipate needing a space at least 300 square metres in size)고 했는데, 배치도를 보면 이용 가능한(Available) 공간 중 300제곱미터 이상인 곳이 2E호임을 확인할 수 있다. 따라서 (D)가 정답이다.

196-200 이메일 + 이메일 + 가격표

발신: 타냐 제퍼슨 〈tjeff@keysuppliers.com〉
수신: info@danestongear.com
제목: 단체 대여 정보 요청
날짜: 5월 29일

데인스톤 기어 컴퍼니(DGC) 귀하,

저는 동호회 회장입니다. 이번 달에 저희 회원 30명이 호수에서 배를 타기 위해 데인스톤으로 당일치기 여행을 가려고 합니다. 귀사의 요금과 서비스에 관한 정보를 보내주시겠습니까? **197 1인용 보트 대여에 가장 관심이 있습니다. 196 얼마 전에 DGC에서 제가 탈 카약을 대여한 적이 있습니다만, 단체로 DGC에서 대여하는 것은 이번이 처음입니다.**

미리 감사드리며,

타냐 제퍼슨

어휘 request 요청 intend 의도하다, 생각하다 regarding ~에 관하여 rate 요금 offering (사람들이 사용하거나 즐기도록) 내놓은 것

발신: info@danestonegear.com
수신: 타냐 제퍼슨 〈tjeff@keysuppliers.com〉
제목: 회신: 단체 대여 정보 요청
날짜: 5월 30일
첨부: ⬀ 가격표

제퍼슨 씨께,

계획하고 계신 DGC로의 단체 여행 건으로 연락 주셔서 감사합니다. 동호회의 다음 모험을 위해 준비해 드릴 수 있기를 고대합니다. 이메일에 가격표가 첨부되어 있습니다. 저희 대여 제품에 관해 더 자세히 이야기를 나누고 싶으시다면 (888) 555-1578로 전화해 주십시오. **198 그리고 최근 자녀와 함께 보트를 타고 싶어 하는 성인들에게 안성맞춤인 노 젓는 보트를 새롭게 추가했습니다.**

예약 준비가 되시면 기꺼이 도와드리겠습니다.

애덤 골드스타인

어휘 anticipate 예상하다, 기대하다 look forward to 고대하다 equip 준비를 해 주다 attach 첨부하다 incidentally 그건 그렇고, 그리고 recently 최근 make a reservation 예약하다

DGC 가격표

	보트 유형	시간당 요금	30분 추가요금
선택사항 1	2인용 카누	13달러	8달러
선택사항 2	3인용 카누	15달러	8달러
197 선택사항 3	197 1인용 카약	11달러	8달러
선택사항 4	2인용 카약	14달러	8달러
선택사항 5	3/4인용 노 젓는 보트 (198 성인 3인 또는 성인 2인과 아동 2인)	198 13달러	9달러

- 4월부터 10월까지 매일 오전 10시-오후 6시 30분까지 영업합니다.
- 모든 보트는 대여 당일 오후 6시 15분까지 반납해야 합니다.
- 200 구명조끼와 노는 대여료에 포함됩니다.
- 199 10인 이상 단체는 최소 1주일 전 예약 시 할인을 받을 수 있습니다.

어휘 hourly rate 시간당 요금 paddle (배 젓는) 노 qualify for ~의 자격을 얻다 in advance 미리

196 사실 관계 확인

번역 제퍼슨 씨가 첫 번째 이메일에서 언급한 것은?

(A) 이전에 DGC의 서비스를 이용한 적이 있다.
(B) 보트 안전 강의를 한다.
(C) 데인스톤 주민이다.
(D) 자기 소유의 카약이 있다.

해설 첫 번째 이메일의 후반부에서 제퍼슨 씨가 얼마 전에 DGC에서 자신이 탈 카약을 대여한 적이 있다(Some time ago, I rented a kayak for myself from DGC)고 했으므로, (A)가 정답이다.

어휘 resident 거주자

197 연계

번역 제퍼슨 씨의 요구사항에 가장 알맞은 대여 제품은?

(A) 선택사항 1번
(B) 선택사항 2번
(C) 선택사항 3번
(D) 선택사항 4번

해설 첫 번째 이메일의 중반부에서 제퍼슨 씨가 1인용 보트 대여에 가장 관심이 있다(We are most interested in renting boats that seat one person)고 했는데, 가격표에 나온 선택사항 중 제퍼슨 씨의 요구에 부합하는 것은 1인용 카약(1-person kayak)뿐이다. 따라서 (C)가 정답이다.

어휘 meet one's needs ~의 요구사항을 충족시키다

198 연계

번역 DGC의 새로운 대여 제품에 대한 시간당 요금은?

(A) 11달러
(B) 13달러
(C) 14달러
(D) 15달러

해설 두 번째 이메일의 후반부에서 DGC가 최근 자녀와 함께 보트를 타고 싶어 하는 성인들에게 안성맞춤인 노 젓는 보트를 새롭게 추가했다(we recently added a rowboat option that is an excellent choice for adults who wish to boat with their children)고 했다. 가격표를 보면 성인과 아동이 함께(2 adults and 2 small children) 이용할 수 있는 노 젓는 보트의 시간당 요금(Hourly rate)이 13달러임을 확인할 수 있다. 따라서 (B)가 정답이다.

▸▸ Paraphrasing 지문의 recently added a rowboat option → 질문의 newest rental option

199 사실 관계 확인

번역 가격표에서 DGC에 대해 명시된 것은?

(A) 연중 내내 영업한다.
(B) 날씨가 좋지 않은 날은 문을 닫는다.
(C) 10인 이상 단체에게 특별 요금을 제공한다.
(D) 웹사이트로 예약을 받는다.

해설 가격표 아래에 있는 설명에서 10인 이상 단체는 최소 1주일 전 예약 시 할인을 받을 수 있다(Groups of ten or more qualify for a discount if they book at least one week in advance)고 했으므로, (C)가 정답이다. 4월부터 10월까지 문을 연다(We are open every day from April to October)고 했으므로 (A)는 명백한 오답이고, (B)와 (D)는 언급되지 않았다.

어휘 accept 받아 주다

▸▸ Paraphrasing 지문의 a discount → 정답의 special rates

200 사실 관계 확인

번역 가격표에 따르면, 모든 보트에 대해 사실인 것은?

(A) 성인 3인에게 적합하다.
(B) 하룻밤 동안 대여 가능하다.
(C) 어린 아동에게 적합하다.
(D) 구명조끼를 갖추고 있다.

해설 가격표 아래에 있는 설명에서 구명조끼와 노는 대여료에 포함된다(Life jackets and paddles are included in the rental fee)고 했으므로, (D)가 정답이다. 모든 보트는 대여 당일 오후 6시 15분까지 반납해야 한다(All boats must be returned by 6:15 P.M. on the day they are rented)고 했고, 성인 3인에게는 2번과 5번 옵션이, 어린 아동에게는 5번 옵션이 적합하므로, (A), (B), (C)는 정답이 될 수 없다.

어휘 suitable 적합한, 알맞은 be equipped with ~를 갖추다

기출 TEST 2

101 (A)	**102** (C)	**103** (A)	**104** (D)	**105** (A)
106 (D)	**107** (A)	**108** (B)	**109** (B)	**110** (A)
111 (C)	**112** (B)	**113** (D)	**114** (C)	**115** (B)
116 (D)	**117** (A)	**118** (B)	**119** (C)	**120** (D)
121 (A)	**122** (C)	**123** (B)	**124** (A)	**125** (C)
126 (B)	**127** (B)	**128** (A)	**129** (D)	**130** (C)
131 (C)	**132** (D)	**133** (A)	**134** (B)	**135** (D)
136 (D)	**137** (B)	**138** (A)	**139** (B)	**140** (A)
141 (B)	**142** (D)	**143** (C)	**144** (C)	**145** (A)
146 (B)	**147** (B)	**148** (D)	**149** (B)	**150** (C)
151 (D)	**152** (D)	**153** (C)	**154** (B)	**155** (A)
156 (B)	**157** (A)	**158** (B)	**159** (B)	**160** (C)
161 (A)	**162** (C)	**163** (B)	**164** (B)	**165** (D)
166 (D)	**167** (A)	**168** (D)	**169** (C)	**170** (A)
171 (C)	**172** (A)	**173** (C)	**174** (D)	**175** (D)
176 (B)	**177** (D)	**178** (B)	**179** (C)	**180** (A)
181 (D)	**182** (D)	**183** (B)	**184** (D)	**185** (B)
186 (A)	**187** (D)	**188** (C)	**189** (B)	**190** (A)
191 (D)	**192** (A)	**193** (B)	**194** (D)	**195** (C)
196 (B)	**197** (A)	**198** (C)	**199** (C)	**200** (D)

PART 5

101 인칭대명사의 격 _ 소유격

해설 after가 이끄는 절의 주어인 group을 한정 수식하는 자리이다. 따라서 소유격 인칭대명사 (A) her가 정답이다.

번역 버드로우 씨는 자신의 그룹이 그 해 가장 높은 수익 성장을 기록한 이후 승진됐다.

어휘 promote 승진시키다 revenue 수익, 수입 growth 성장

102 등위접속사 _ 어휘

해설 빈칸은 세 개의 명사구(photography, drawing, other arts)를 연결해주는 등위접속사 자리이다. '사진 촬영', '그림', '기타 예술'은 강좌(classes)의 내용을 순서대로 나열한 것이므로, (C) and가 정답이다. (D) thus는 '따라서, 이와 같이'라는 의미의 부사로, 구조상으로도 빈칸에 들어갈 수 없다.

번역 지역공동체 프로그램에는 사진 촬영, 그림 및 기타 예술 강좌가 포함된다.

어휘 feature (특별히) 포함하다, ~가 특징이다

103 부사 자리 _ 동사 수식

해설 be동사와 과거분사 secured 사이에서 동사를 수식하는 부사 자리이므로, (A) safely(안전하게)가 정답이다. (B) safe와 (D) safer는 형용사, (C) safety는 명사로 품사상 빈칸에 들어갈 수 없다.

번역 유리 용기는 운송 중에 안전하게 보관해야 한다.

어휘 container 용기 secure 안전하게 지키다 transport 운송, 수송

104 명사 자리 _ 복합명사

해설 빈칸이 소유격 This month's와 명사 figures 사이에 있으므로, 빈칸에는 figures를 수식하는 형용사 또는 figures와 복합명사를 이루는 명사가 들어갈 수 있다. 5퍼센트 증가한(have increased) 것은 '판매 수치'라고 보아야 자연스러우므로, (D) sales가 정답이다. 참고로, sale은 복수형으로 쓰여 복합 명사를 이루는 경우가 많다. sales figures(판매 수치), sales target(판매 목표치), sales representative(영업 직원), sales performance(매출 실적) 등의 빈출 표현은 암기해 두는 것이 좋다.

번역 이번 달 판매 수치는 지난달보다 5퍼센트 상승했다.

어휘 figure 수치 increase 증가하다, 늘다

105 동사 어휘

해설 빈칸의 목적어 either free company housing or a stipend of $2,000(무료 사택 혹은 2,000달러의 급여)는 인턴이 고를 수 있는 선택 사항을 나타낸다. 따라서 '선택하다, 고르다'라는 의미의 (A) choose가 정답이다. 참고로, (C) apply가 '~를 신청하다'라는 뜻으로 쓰이려면 전치사 for가 있어야 한다.

번역 하계 인턴은 무료 사택이나 2,000달러의 급여 중 하나를 선택할 수 있다.

어휘 company housing 사택 stipend 급여, 생활비 보조금 wonder 궁금해 하다 apply 적용하다, 응용하다 rent 대여하다

106 명사 어휘

해설 빈칸을 포함한 절은 고객이 음성 메시지를 남긴 경우(If a client leaves a voice message)에 하는 후속 조치를 나타내고 있다. 따라서 return과 어울려 쓰여 '회신 전화를 주다'라는 의미를 나타내는 (D) call이 정답이다.

번역 고객이 음성 메시지를 남길 경우, 영업일 기준 1일 이내에 신속하게 회신 전화를 드립니다.

어휘 promptly 지체 없이, 신속하게 extra 여분의 것 effort 노력, 활동 signal 신호

107 형용사 자리 _ 명사 수식 _ 최상급

해설 최상급 표현 most와 결합하여 복합명사 production unit을 수식하는 형용사 자리이므로, (A) effective가 정답이다. 여기서 The department's most effective production unit은 '부서에서 가장 좋은 결과를 낸 생산팀'이라는 의미를 나타낸다. (B) effect는 명사/동사, (C) effectively는 부사로 품사상 빈칸에 들어갈 수 없다. (D) effecting은 현재분사로 '~을 초래하는'이라는 뜻을 나타내므로 빈칸에는 적절하지 않다.

번역 | 부서에서 가장 좋은 결과를 낸 생산팀은 분기 말에 보너스를 받을 예정이다.

어휘 | department 부서   production 생산   unit 단체, 과   quarter 분기   effective 효과적인, 좋은 결과를 내는   effect 효과; (어떤 결과를) 초래하다

108 전치사 어휘

해설 | 빈칸 뒤에 오는 the hours of 9 A.M. and 5 P.M.은 특정 시간 사이의 범위를 나타낸다. 따라서 '~ 사이'라는 의미의 (B) between이 정답이다. 참고로, (A) for 뒤에는 범위가 아닌 하나의 기간(eg. for (숫자) hours, for the hours they work)을 명시하는 명사구가 와야 한다.

번역 | 알 카페는 이제 매주 일요일 오전 9시부터 오후 5시까지 문을 열 것이다.

109 부사절 접속사 자리

해설 | 빈칸 뒤 완전한 절(he has a dentist appointment)을 이끄는 접속사 자리로, 해당 절은 리우 씨가 사무실을 비울 이유를 나타낸다. 따라서 '~ 때문에'라는 의미의 부사절 접속사 (B) because가 정답이다. (A) following과 (C) including은 분사형 전치사, (D) likewise는 부사로 절을 이끄는 자리에 들어갈 수 없다.

번역 | 리우 씨는 오늘 아침 치과 예약이 있어서 사무실에 없을 것이다.

어휘 | dentist 치과   appointment 약속   likewise 똑같이, 비슷하게

110 부사 자리 _ 동사 수식

해설 | 조동사 can과 동사원형 respond 사이에서 동사를 수식하는 부사 자리이므로, (A) reliably(믿음직하게, 제대로)가 정답이다. (B) rely는 동사, (C) reliability는 명사, (D) reliable은 형용사로 품사상 빈칸에 들어갈 수 없다.

번역 | 트리나크리아 씨의 팀은 음성 명령에 제대로 반응할 수 있는 주방 수전을 개발하고 있다.

어휘 | develop 개발하다   faucet 수전   respond to ~에 반응하다   command 명령   rely 신뢰하다   reliability 신뢰도   reliable 믿을 수 있는

111 형용사 어휘

해설 | 모든 콘서트를 매진시켰다(sold out)는 내용의 문장인데, 단수 대명사 one 뒤에 「of+한정사+복수명사(of its concerts)」가 왔으므로 '한 묶음으로 보는 전체'가 아닌 '~의 하나하나 다/각각 다'의 개념이 되어야 한다. 따라서 (C) every가 정답이다. 참고로, 이때 every와 one은 반드시 띄어 써야 한다. (A) complete는 '완전한, 완료된', (B) total은 '전체의, 완전한', (D) entire는 '전체의, 온'이라는 의미로 모두 '전체'를 나타내므로, one of its concerts와 쓰일 수 없다.

번역 | 리치몬드 시립 교향악단은 올해 들어 지금까지 모든 음악회 입장권을 매진시켰다.

어휘 | sell out 매진시키다, 매진되다

112 동명사 자리

해설 | 전치사 before의 목적어 역할을 하는 동시에, 명사구 the installation of the software update를 목적어로 취하는 자리이다. 따라서 빈칸에는 동명사가 들어가야 하므로, (B) beginning이 정답이다.

번역 | 소프트웨어 업데이트 설치를 시작하기 전에 애플리케이션을 종료해야 합니다.

어휘 | installation 설치

113 부사 어휘

해설 | 빈칸에는 권장(urges)되는 운전(to drive) 방식을 적절히 묘사하는 부사가 들어가야 한다. 따라서 '조심스럽게, 주의하여'라는 의미의 (D) cautiously가 정답이다.

번역 | 시 교통위원회는 운전자들에게 메인 가에서 조심스럽게 운전할 것을 권고한다.

어휘 | committee 위원회   urge 강력히 권고하다   abundantly 충분하게, 풍부하게   obviously 분명하게   rightfully 마땅히, 정당하게

114 명사 자리 _ 동사의 목적어

해설 | 동사 announced의 목적어 역할을 하는 자리로, 정관사 the의 한정 수식을 받는다. 따라서 보기 중 명사인 (C) elimination(제거, 배제)이 정답이다. (A) eliminate와 (D) eliminates는 동사, (B) eliminated는 동사/과거분사로 품사상 빈칸에 들어갈 수 없다.

번역 | 이스팅턴 대학교는 구내 식당 메뉴에서 인공 방부제를 함유한 모든 음식을 없애겠다고 발표했다.

어휘 | contain 포함하다, 함유하다   artificial 인공적인   preservative 방부제   eliminate 없애다, 제거하다

115 형용사 자리 _ 명사 수식 _ 비교급

해설 | 빈칸에는 비교급 강조 부사 even의 수식을 받는 동시에 명사 number를 수식하는 비교급 형용사가 들어가야 한다. 따라서 (B) greater가 정답이다.

번역 | 날씨로 인해 일부 통근자들이 지각했지만, 도로 폐쇄는 훨씬 더 많은 수의 사람들에게 영향을 주었다.

어휘 | commuter 통근자   closure 폐쇄   affect 영향을 미치다

116 명사 어휘

해설 | 빈칸은 동사 displays의 목적어 역할을 하는 명사 자리로, remarkable과 to connect with his audience의 수식을 받는다. '관객과 공감대를 형성하는 것'은 무용수가 보여주는 뛰어난 능력이라고 볼 수 있으므로, (D) ability(능력, 재능)가 정답이다. 참고로, ability는 to부정사의 수식을 받는 경우가 많다.

번역 | 무용수인 클레이 헤이스팅스는 매 공연마다 관객과 소통하는 놀라운 능력을 보여준다.

어휘 performance 공연 remarkable 놀랄 만한 connect with ~와 소통하다, 공감대를 형성하다 degree 정도 function 기능 totality 전체, 총액

117 부사 자리 _ 형용사 수식

해설 빈칸 없이도 「주어(Amand Corp.'s flexible work policy)+동사(is)+보어(beneficial to the company)」 구조를 이루는 완전한 문장이다. 따라서 빈칸에는 형용사 beneficial을 수식하는 부사가 들어가야 하므로, (A) financially(재정적으로, 재무상)가 정답이다. (B) finances는 명사/동사, (C) financial은 형용사, (D) to finance는 to부정사로 구조상 빈칸에 들어갈 수 없다.

번역 아만드 사의 탄력 근무 정책은 직원 이직률을 최소화하므로 회사에 재무상 이익이 된다.

어휘 flexible work 탄력[유연] 근무(제) beneficial 유익한, 이로운 employee turnover 직원 이직률 minimal 아주 적은, 최소의

118 명사 자리 _ 전치사의 목적어

해설 빈칸은 전치사 of의 목적어 역할을 하는 명사 자리로, 형용사 agricultural의 수식을 받는다. 따라서 명사인 (B) practices(관행, 관례)가 정답이다. 참고로 practice는 '연습하다, 실습하다'라는 의미의 동사로도 쓰일 수 있다. (A) practical은 형용사, (C) practiced는 동사/과거분사, (D) is practicing은 동사로 품사상 빈칸에 들어갈 수 없다.

번역 라기니 쿠마리는 지역의 농업 관행 역사에 관한 책을 출판했다.

어휘 publish 출판하다 agricultural 농업의 practical 실용적인

119 부사 자리 _ 어휘

해설 빈칸이 has와 been promoted 사이에 있으므로, 현재완료 시제와 어울려 쓰이는 부사가 들어가야 한다. 따라서 '최근에'라는 의미의 (C) recently가 정답이다. 참고로, (B) soon은 '(현재 시점을 기준으로) 곧, (과거 특정 시점을 기준으로) 얼마 지나지 않아'라는 뜻으로 현재완료와 어울려 쓰이지 않는다.

번역 산체스 씨는 최근 델베이 테크에서 사무실 관리자로 승진했다.

어휘 promote 승진시키다

120 동사 어휘

해설 기간을 나타내는 several hours와 어울리는 동사를 선택해야 하므로, '계속되다, 지속하다'라는 의미의 (D) last가 정답이다. 참고로, last와 several hours 사이에 for가 생략되었다고 볼 수 있으며, last가 타동사로 쓰일 경우 「last+사람 목적어+기간」의 구조로 쓰이기도 한다.

번역 워크숍이 몇 시간 동안 계속될 것으로 예상되니, 월요일 오후로 200호실을 예약해 주세요.

어휘 reserve 예약하다 be expected to ~할 것으로 예상되다 occur 발생하다 hold 잡다, 보류하다

121 형용사 어휘

해설 speaker를 적절히 수식하는 형용사를 선택해야 한다. 문맥상 소개(introduced)의 대상은 '개회 연사'이므로, '시작의, 첫 부분의'라는 뜻의 (A) opening이 정답이다.

번역 캐나다 플로리스트 협회 회장인 재커리 조는 대회에서 개회 연사를 소개했다.

어휘 association 협회 convention 대회 expanded 확대된 careful 주의 깊은 powered 동력의, 힘이 있는

122 관계대명사 _ 주격

해설 The team이 주어, will receive가 동사인 문장으로, 빈칸에는 불완전한 절(completes the online training first)을 이끌어 The team을 수식하는 관계대명사가 들어가야 한다. 따라서 주격 관계대명사로 쓰일 수 있는 (C) that이 정답이다. (A) whichever는 대명사로 쓰일 경우 '어느 쪽이든 ~한 것(anything which/that), 누구든 ~한 사람(anyone who/that)'이라는 뜻을 나타내며 자체적으로 명사를 내포하고 있어 앞에 나온 명사를 수식하는 자리에 들어갈 수 없다.

번역 온라인 교육을 가장 먼저 완료한 팀은 출장 요리 점심 식사를 제공받을 것이다.

어휘 complete 완료하다

123 전치사 어휘

해설 '업계 뉴스와 앞으로 있을 사교 행사(Industry news and upcoming social events)'는 소식지에 포함될 내용들이(the items)이라고 할 수 있으므로, '(셋 이상의 대상) 중에'라는 의미의 전치사 (B) among이 정답이다. 「among+복수명사」는 빈출 표현이므로 암기해 두는 것이 좋다.

번역 회사 소식지에 특집으로 포함될 내용 중에는 업계 뉴스와 앞으로 있을 사교 행사가 있다.

어휘 upcoming 앞으로 있을, 곧 다가올 feature 특별히 포함하다, ~를 특징으로 하다

124 전치사 자리 _ 어휘

해설 명사구 the years를 목적어로 취하는 전치사 자리로, 보기에서 (A) through와 (C) prior to 중 하나를 선택해야 한다. the years가 기간을 나타내며 앞에 현재완료 시제(have remained)가 쓰였으므로, '(기간) 동안 내내'라는 의미의 (A) through가 정답이 된다. (C) prior to는 '~전에'라는 뜻으로 뒤에 특정 시점을 나타내는 명사가 와야 한다. (B) even if와 (D) while은 부사절 접속사이므로 빈칸에 들어갈 수 없다.

번역 크리스티안센 일렉트로닉스는 뛰어난 고객 서비스 덕분에 수년간 많은 고객들이 충성 고객으로 남아 있다.

어휘 faithful 충실한, 신의 있는

125 동사 어형 _ 태

해설 주어 The release of the earnings report(수익 보고서의 발표)는 연기되는 대상이므로, delay가 수동태로 쓰여야 한다. 따라서 (C) be delayed가 정답이다. (A) delay, (B) have delayed, (D) be delaying은 모두 능동태 동사 형태이므로 빈칸에 들어갈 수 없다. 참고로, delay는 주어가 사람일 경우 자동사로 쓰일 수도 있다.

번역 수익 보고서 발표는 회사의 최근 수치가 준비될 때까지 연기될 예정이다.

어휘 release 공개, 발표 earnings 수익 figures 수치 delay 연기하다

126 전치사 어휘

해설 동사 works와 명사 the interns를 적절히 이어주는 전치사를 선택해야 한다. 업무의 질을 감독하기 위해(to monitor the quality of their work) 인턴 곁에서 함께 일한다는 내용이 되어야 자연스러우므로, '~ 곁에서, ~와 함께'라는 의미의 전치사 (B) alongside가 정답이다. 참고로, alongside는 부사로도 쓰일 수 있다.

번역 멜리사 에이런 부팀장은 인턴들이 하는 업무의 질을 감독하기 위해 그들 곁에서 함께 일한다.

어휘 against ~에 대항하여

127 대명사 어휘

해설 빈칸을 포함한 부사절(because ~ this week)이 팀 회의를 연기한 이유를 설명하고 있으므로, 모두가 이미(already) 해야 할 일이 있다는 내용이 되어야 자연스럽다. 따라서 '충분한 양'이라는 의미의 (B) enough가 정답이다. 참고로, enough는 형용사와 부사로도 쓰일 수 있다. (A) most는 '대부분의 것'이나 '가장 많은 것'을 나타내므로 문맥상 어색하다.

번역 모두에게 이번 주에 할 일이 이미 충분히 있었기 때문에 후지타 씨는 팀 회의를 다음 주까지 연기했다.

어휘 postpone 연기하다

128 형용사 어휘

해설 보험료에 관해 상담해 줄 직원(agent)을 적절히 묘사하는 형용사를 선택해야 한다. 따라서 '면허를 소지한, 허가를 받은'이라는 의미의 (A) licensed가 정답이다.

번역 오늘 기술라손 보험사에 전화해서 면허를 소지한 상담원에게 무료 견적을 달라고 말하세요.

어휘 insurance 보험 quote 견적 maximum 최대의 required 요구되는 former 이전의

129 접속사 자리 _ 어휘

해설 두 개의 완전한 절을 이어주는 접속사 자리이다. 계약 조건 마무리(the terms of the contract are finalized)는 마케팅 캠페인 시작(Motorbike Unlimited's marketing campaign will begin)

의 전제 조건이므로, '~하자마자, ~하는 대로'라는 의미의 부사절 접속사 (D) as soon as가 정답이다. 참고로, 시간 부사절의 현재 동사 are finalized는 미래를 나타낸다. (A) as well as(~뿐만 아니라 ~도), (B) other than(~를 제외하고), (C) rather than(~라기 보다는)은 상관접속사로 쓰일 수 있지만 두 개의 완전한 절을 이어주는 역할을 할 수 없다.

번역 모터바이크 언리미티드의 마케팅 캠페인은 계약 조건이 마무리되면 바로 시작될 것이다.

어휘 terms 조건 contract 계약 finalize 완결하다, 마무리하다

130 명사 어휘

해설 빈칸을 포함한 주어는 과학자들이 해답을 얻을 수 있는 방법을 나타내며, 빈칸에는 행성(planet Jupiter)에 할 만한 행위를 나타내는 단어가 들어가야 한다. 따라서 '관찰'이라는 의미의 (C) Observation이 정답이다.

번역 목성 관찰은 과학자들에게 오래 기다려 온 해답을 제공할 것이다.

어휘 planet 행성 Jupiter 목성 long-awaited 오래 기다리던 acceleration 가속 intention 의도 provision 제공

PART 6

131-134 회람

수신: 전 직원
발신: 레오나르드 빌라로보스, 제품개발 부사장
날짜: 8월 27일
제목: 앗제렛 게임 (제품 #DS8192)

고객 시범 테스트 결과 때문에 앗제렛 비디오 게임 출시를 연기하기로 결정했습니다. 고객 설문조사는 게임이 우리 예상보다 덜 **131 흥미롭다**는 사실을 보여줍니다. 앞으로 몇 달 동안 게임 개발팀은 제품을 더 매력적이게 만들 수 있도록 몇 가지 **132 수정**을 시도할 예정입니다. **133 그때 테스트를 더 실시할 것입니다.** 변화가 성공적이라면 다음 1월 **134 또는** 2월에 게임을 출시하고자 합니다.

어휘 development 개발 due to ~ 때문에 trial 시험적인; 시험 postpone 연기하다 launch 출시, 개시 indicate 나타내다, 보여주다 anticipate 예상하다 attractive 멋진, 매력적인

131 형용사 어휘

해설 주어인 the game을 적절히 묘사하는 형용사를 선택해야 한다. 앞 문장에서 고객 시범 테스트 결과 비디오 게임 출시를 연기하기로(to postpone the launch) 결정했다고 했으므로, 빈칸을 포함한 부분은 부정적인 결과를 나타내야 문맥상 자연스럽다. 따라서 less와 함께 '덜 매력적인, 덜 흥미로운'이라는 의미를 완성하는 (C) appealing이 정답이다.

어휘 expensive 값 비싼 repetitive 반복적인 surprising 놀라운

132 명사 자리 _ 동사의 목적어 _ 수 일치

해설 동사구 will introduce의 목적어 역할을 하는 명사 자리로, 빈칸을 수식하는 several과 수가 일치하는 복수명사가 들어가야 한다. 따라서 (D) modifications(수정, 변경)가 정답이다. (B) modifies는 동사, (C) modifying은 동명사/현재분사로 품사상 빈칸에 들어갈 수 없다.

어휘 modify 수정하다, 변경하다

133 문맥에 맞는 문장 고르기

번역 (A) 그때 테스트를 더 실시할 것입니다.
(B) 출시는 올해 최대 규모일 것입니다.
(C) 그러나 설문조사는 믿을 수 없습니다.
(D) 팀원들은 각각 서식에 서명해야 합니다.

해설 빈칸 앞 문장에서 게임 개발팀이 몇 가지 수정을 시도할 예정(the game development team will introduce several modifications)이라고 했고, 뒤에서는 이 작업이 성공적일 경우를 가정하고 있다. 따라서 빈칸에도 수정 작업과 관련된 내용이 들어가야 자연스러우므로, 수정 후 결과를 알아보는 단계, 즉 추가 테스트 단계를 언급한 (A)가 정답이다.

어휘 conduct 실시하다 reliable 믿을 수 있는, 믿을 만한

134 등위접속사

해설 전치사 by의 목적어 역할을 하는 next January와 February는 게임 출시(launch) 일정으로 제시된 선택 사항이다. 따라서 '또는, 혹은'이라는 의미의 등위접속사 (B) or가 정답이다.

135-138 이메일

수신: 에바 린, 룬드토크 인더스트리즈
발신: 기술 서비스
날짜: 1월 15일
제목: 기술 문의

린 씨께,

저희 기술 부서에 문의 건**135으로** 연락해주셔서 감사합니다. **136아시다시피**, 저희 원격 지점에서 귀하의 시스템을 다시 시작하려고 했을 때 전화가 끊겼습니다. **137안타깝게도 연락 드릴 수 있는 전화번호가 저희에게 없습니다.** 그러니 가급적 빨리 전화 주셔서 대화 아이디 #TECH12-2020A를 말씀하시고 시스템 수리를 완료하십시오. 귀하의 문의를 우선적으로 처리하기로 하였으며, 컴퓨터가 완전한 기능을 다할 수 있게 **138복구되도록** 도와드리기를 고대합니다.

아서 펠트
기술 서비스 지원 전문가

어휘 technical 기술의, 기술과 관련된 query 문의 disconnected 연결이 끊어진 remote 원격의, 멀리 떨어진 therefore 그러므로 at your earliest convenience 가급적 빨리 refer to 언급하다 prioritize 우선적으로 처리하다 look

forward to ~를 고대하다 capability 기능, 능력 facilitator 촉진자, 지원 전문가

135 전치사 어휘

해설 빈칸 뒤 명사구 your query를 목적어로 취하는 전치사 자리이다. 문의 사항(query)은 기술 부서에 연락하는 사유이므로, '~와 함께, ~을 가지고'라는 의미의 (D) with가 정답이다.

136 접속부사

해설 빈칸 앞 문장에서 연락 주어 감사하다(Thank you for contacting our technical department)고 했는데, 뒤에서는 원격 지원 중 전화가 끊어졌다(our call got disconnected)며 함께 알고 있는 문제를 언급했다. 따라서 '아시다시피'라는 의미의 (D) As you know가 정답이다. 앞서 한 말을 바꿔 말하거나, 이유에 따른 결과를 설명하거나, 예시를 든 것이 아니므로 (A), (B), (C)는 오답이다.

어휘 in other words 다시 말하자면 for this reason 이러한 이유로 for example 예를 들면

137 문맥에 맞는 문장 고르기

번역 (A) 귀하의 지역에 있는 저희 컴퓨터 수리센터 중 한 곳을 방문하시면 됩니다.
(B) 안타깝게도 연락 드릴 수 있는 전화번호가 저희에게 없습니다.
(C) 저희 우수 고객이 되어 주셔서 다시 한번 감사 드립니다.
(D) 서비스 요금 지불을 위해 즉시 수표를 보내주십시오.

해설 빈칸 앞 문장에서 전화가 끊어졌다(our call got disconnected)는 문제점을 언급했는데, 뒤 문장에서 인과관계를 연결해 주는 Therefore로 시작한 후, 가급적 빨리 전화를 달라(please call us at your earliest convenience)고 요청하고 있다. 따라서 빈칸에는 직접 전화하지 않고 린 씨에게 전화를 요청하는 사유가 들어가야 자연스러우므로, (B)가 정답이다.

어휘 priority 우선 (사항) submit 제출하다 promptly 신속하게, 즉시

138 원형부정사(동사원형) _ 목적격 보어

해설 빈칸은 「helping+목적어(you)+목적격 보어」의 구조에서 you의 행위를 보충 설명하는 목적격 보어에 해당하며, your computer를 목적어로 취한다. 준사역동사 help는 to부정사 또는 원형부정사(동사원형)를 목적격 보어로 취하므로, (A) restore가 정답이다.

어휘 restore 복원하다, 회복시키다 restoration 복원

139-142 웹페이지

한시적으로, 어퍼컷 클로딩 행어 사에서 최고급 품질의 옷걸이를 대량 주문할 경우 파격적으로 할인해 드립니다. 본 특별 **139할인**은 호텔, 소매점이나 옷걸이가 많이 쓰이는 곳이면 어디든 안성맞춤일 겁니다. 옻칠한 호두나무로 **140만든** 옷걸이는 내구성이 좋을 뿐 아니라 환경에도

안전합니다. **141그것들은** 10파운드에 달하는 무게까지 견딜 수 있을 만큼 튼튼합니다. 주문하시려면 www.uppercuthangerco.ca를 방문하세요. 모든 주문 건에 대해 20퍼센트의 보증금을 내셔야 합니다. **142잔금은 배송 받으실 때 지불하시면 됩니다.** 어퍼컷에서 모든 배송비와 보험료를 부담합니다.

> 어휘 limited 한정된, 제한된 discount 할인 wholesale 도매의, 대량의 retailer 소매점 extensively 널리, 광범위하게 lacquered 옻칠한 durable 내구성이 있는 environment 환경 hold up 견디다 require 필요로 하다, 요구하다 deposit 착수금, 보증금 insurance 보험

139 명사 어휘

해설 This special -------은 앞서 언급된 파격 할인(at huge discounts on wholesale orders)을 가리킨다. 따라서 빈칸에도 유사한 의미의 명사가 들어가야 자연스러우므로, '할인 (혜택)'이라는 뜻으로 쓰일 수 있는 (B) offer가 정답이다.

어휘 clothing 의류 decoration 장식 performance 공연, 실적

140 분사구문

해설 빈칸은 전치사구 of lacquered walnut wood와 함께 콤마 뒤에 오는 절을 수식한다. 따라서 빈칸에는 부사 역할을 할 수 있는 to부정사나 분사가 들어갈 수 있는데, 타동사 make 뒤에 of가 오려면 수동태로 쓰여야 하므로, 과거분사 (A) Made가 정답이다. Be made of는 '~로 만들어지다'라는 뜻을 나타내며, 분사구문으로 쓰일 경우 Being made of에서 Being은 보통 생략된다.

141 대명사 어휘

해설 앞 문장에서 옷걸이(these hangers)의 장점(not only durable, but also safe for the environment)을 언급했는데, 빈칸을 포함한 문장에서도 또 다른 장점(strong enough to hold up to ten pounds)을 추가로 기술하고 있다. 따라서 빈칸에는 these hangers를 대신하는 대명사가 들어가야 하므로, (B) They가 정답이다.

142 문맥에 맞는 문장 고르기

번역 (A) 저희 제품은 좋은 선물이 됩니다.
(B) 나무 옷걸이는 견고한 반면 무겁기도 합니다.
(C) 품질 좋은 옷걸이는 훌륭한 투자입니다.
(D) 잔금은 배송 받으실 때 지불하시면 됩니다.

해설 빈칸 앞 문장에서는 고객이 주문 시 지불해야 하는 보증금(all orders require a 20 percent deposit)을, 뒤 문장에서는 어퍼컷에서 부담하는 배송비와 보험료(Uppercut will cover all shipping and insurance costs)를 언급했다. 따라서 빈칸에도 주문 관련 비용에 대한 설명이 들어가야 자연스러우므로, 잔금 지불 시점을 안내한 (D)가 정답이다. deposit과 연관된 단어인 balance가 결정적인 힌트가 된다.

어휘 sturdy 견고한, 튼튼한 investment 투자 balance 잔액, 잔금 due (돈을) 지불해야 하는

143-146 이메일

> 발신: mcrane@doodlemail.com
> 수신: jkumar@baxterartsupplies.com
> 날짜: 10월 14일
> 제목: 지원
> 첨부: ⬂ 이력서
>
> 쿠마르 씨께,
>
> 박스터 미술용품점 창문에 게시된 광고를 보고 이메일을 씁니다. 귀하의 **143매장** 단골 고객으로서, 그곳은 수년간 귀중한 영감의 원천이 되었다고 생각합니다. 제 미술품을 전시하면 **144정말 좋을** 것 같습니다. 고객들에게 영감을 불어넣을 워크숍도 진행하고 싶고요.
>
> 이러한 역할에 제가 잘 맞을 거라고 확신합니다. 열정적이고 친절하기 때문이지요. **145게다가** 지역 내 다양한 장소에서 워크숍을 성공적으로 진행한 바 있습니다. 제 이력서를 첨부했는데, 해당 워크숍들에 대한 세부사항이 포함되어 있습니다. **146제 작품 견본은 www.mcrane. com에서 찾아보실 수 있습니다.** 지원서와 작품을 검토해 보시고 나서 제게 연락 주시면 좋겠습니다.
>
> 멜라니아 크레인

> 어휘 application 지원 in response to ~에 응하여 advertisement 광고 frequent 빈번한, 자주 다니는 invaluable 귀중한 inspiration 영감 inspire 영감을 주다 well suited for ~에 적절한 enthusiastic 열정적인 attach 첨부하다 look forward to -ing ~하기를 고대하다

143 명사 어휘

해설 수신자인 쿠마르 씨의 이메일 주소로 미루어 보아, 앞 문장에서 언급된 박스터 미술용품점(Baxter Art Supplies)이 그녀의 가게임을 알 수 있다. 따라서 미술용품점을 가리키는 단어가 빈칸에 들어가야 하므로, (C) store가 정답이다.

144 형용사 자리 _ 과거분사

해설 주어인 I를 보충 설명하는 주격 보어 자리로, 문맥상 사람이 느끼는 감정을 나타내는 형용사가 들어가야 자연스럽다. 따라서 과거분사 (C) thrilled(신이 난, 흥분된)가 정답이다. (A) thrilling은 감정을 유발하는 대상(a thrilling experience)을 묘사할 때 쓰인다.

어휘 thrilling 황홀한, 짜릿한

145 접속부사

해설 앞 문장에서는 자신이 역할에 잘 맞는 이유(I would be well suited for this role because I am both enthusiastic and friendly)를, 빈칸 뒤에서는 역할과 관련된 자신의 경험(I have led successful workshops at various locations in the area)을 언급했다. 즉, 본인이 업무에 적합한 이유를 추가적으로 설명한 것이므로, '게다가, 또한'이라는 의미의 (A) In addition이 정답이다.

어휘 however 그러나　in general 보통, 대개　similarly 마찬가지로, 유사하게

146 문맥에 맞는 문장 고르기

번역 (A) 지난주 그림 워크숍이 아주 좋았습니다.
(B) 제 작품 견본은 www.mcrane.com에서 찾아보실 수 있습니다.
(C) 이제 막 수채화 물감으로 작업하기 시작했습니다.
(D) 가격 목록은 347-555-0101로 연락 주십시오.

해설 빈칸 앞 문장에서는 이력서를 첨부했다(I have attached a copy of my résumé)고만 했는데, 뒤 문장에서는 지원서와 작품을 검토해 보고(after you have reviewed my application and work) 연락을 주면 좋겠다고 했다. 따라서 앞 문장에서는 언급되지 않았던 작품(work)과 관련된 내용이 빈칸에 들어가야 하므로, 작품 견본을 볼 수 있는 방법을 설명한 (B)가 정답이다.

어휘 watercolor 수채화 물감, 수채화

PART 7

147-148 표지판

여기에서 무슨 일이 벌어지고 있나요?[147]
진행 중인 작업: 상업용[147]
예상 완공 일자: 3월 1일

소유주　　　　**종합 건설업체**
월커 서점　　　　매티슨 빌더스
구즈타운 길 4634번지　스미스 가 4500번지
아덴, 노스캐롤라이나　롤리, 노스캐롤라이나

모든 작업 허가서는 기획부서에서 보관하고 있습니다.
작업 현장에서 발생한 문제는 919-555-0134로 전화해[148]
알려주십시오.

어휘 in progress 진행 중인　commercial 상업의　anticipate 예상하다　completion 완공, 완료　general contractor 종합 건설업자　permit 허가증　on file 보관되어 있는

147 추론 / 암시

번역 표지판은 어디에 있겠는가?
(A) 도서 전시대 위
(B) 공사 현장
(C) 주거용 건물
(D) 대학교 강의실

해설 상단을 보면 표지판이 있는 장소(HERE)에서 현재 상업용 건물(Walker Booksellers) 공사 작업이 진행 중(Work in progress: Commercial)임을 알 수 있다. 따라서 표지판이 상업용 건설 현장에

있다고 추론할 수 있으므로, (B)가 정답이다.

어휘 construction 공사　residential 주거의

148 세부 사항

번역 표지판을 읽는 사람이 해당 전화번호로 전화해야 하는 이유는?
(A) 허가서를 보관하려고
(B) 일자리에 지원하려고
(C) 날짜를 확정하려고
(D) 문제점을 알리려고

해설 하단에서 작업 현장에서 발생한 문제는 919-555-0134로 전화해 알려달라(To report a problem at this work site, call 919-555-0134)고 요청하고 있으므로, (D)가 정답이다.

어휘 apply for 지원하다　confirm 확인하다, 확정하다

149-151 정보

8월 1일 토요일, 더럼타운 교향악단이 마호가니 가 498번지에 있[149]는 카도나 문화센터에서 교육적인 공연을 무료로 제공한다. 그 중에서도, 음악가들이 악기의 기원과 발달뿐만 아니라 몇몇 음악 양식에[150]대해서도 이야기할 예정이다. 청중은 질문할 기회가 있을 것이다. 행사는 오늘날 잘 알려진 음악가와 작곡가들의 작품을 교향악단이 연주하며 막을 내린다.[151]

어휘 educational 교육적인　performance 공연　origin 기원 development 발달　instrument 악기　opportunity 기회 conclude with ~로 마무리짓다

149 주제 / 목적

번역 정보의 목적은?
(A) 장소 변경을 알리기 위해
(B) 앞으로 있을 행사를 알리기 위해
(C) 악기를 묘사하기 위해
(D) 공연을 평가하기 위해

해설 첫 번째 문장에서 8월 1일 토요일에 더럼타운 교향악단이 카도나 문화센터에서 교육적인 공연을 무료로 제공한다(the Durhamtown Symphony Orchestra will be giving a free educational performance)고 한 후, 공연 관련 추가 설명을 이어가고 있다. 따라서 행사를 홍보하기 위한 글이라고 볼 수 있으므로, (B)가 정답이다.

어휘 announce 알리다, 발표하다　publicize 알리다, 광고하다 upcoming 앞으로 있을, 곧 다가오는　describe 묘사하다, 서술하다

▸▸ Paraphrasing　지문의 **free educational performance**
→ 정답의 **event**

150 세부 사항

번역   정보에 따르면, 청중들은 무엇을 할 수 있는가?

    (A) 노래를 따라 부르기
    (B) 노래 신청하기
    (C) 음악가들에게 이야기하기
    (D) 음악 수업 신청하기

해설   중반부를 보면 음악가들이 악기와 음악 양식에 대해 이야기하고 청중은 질문할 기회를 갖게 된다(Audience members will have an opportunity to ask questions)고 나와 있다. 따라서 (C)가 정답이다.

어휘   sign up for ~를 신청하다

> ▸▸ Paraphrasing   지문의 **have an opportunity to**
> → 질문의 **be able to**
> 지문의 **ask questions** → 정답의 **talk**

151 동의어 찾기

번역   첫 번째 단락, 여섯 번째 줄에 쓰인 "conclude"와 의미가 가장 가까운 단어는?

    (A) 들어올리다
    (B) 결정하다
    (C) 믿다
    (D) 끝마치다

해설   'conclude'를 포함한 부분은 '행사는 교향악단이 연주하며 막을 내린다(The event will conclude with the orchestra performing works)'는 의미로 해석되는데, 여기서 conclude는 '막을 내리다, 끝나다'라는 뜻으로 쓰였다. 따라서 '끝마치다, 완료하다'라는 의미의 (D) finish가 정답이다.

152-153 온라인 채팅

보니 루이즈 오후 2시 40분

안녕하세요. ¹⁵²쉽 위드 어스에 오신 것을 환영합니다.

닉 포티어 오후 2시 41분

안녕하세요. 닉이라고 해요. ¹⁵²제 계정에 접속하는 데 문제가 있어요.

보니 루이즈 오후 2시 42분

안녕하세요, 닉. ¹⁵²기꺼이 도와드리겠습니다. 비밀번호를 재설정해 보셨나요?

닉 포티어 오후 2시 43분

네, 그런데 여전히 안 돼요. 15분 후에 책자와 카탈로그를 대량으로 보내야 해서 조금 염려스럽군요.

보니 루이즈 오후 2시 44분

걱정 마세요. 제가 도와드릴 거니까요! ¹⁵³계정번호가 X58292J죠, 그렇죠? 제 쪽에서 계정을 리셋할 수 있습니다.

닉 포티어 오후 2시 45분

맞습니다.

보니 루이즈 오후 2시 46분

좋습니다. 해당 계정번호에 연동된 이메일 주소로 새 비밀번호를 보냈으니 앞으로 2분 이내에 받으실 겁니다. 계정에 접속하셨다는 말씀을 들을 때까지 이대로 있겠습니다.

닉 포티어 오후 2시 46분

좋아요. 감사합니다!

어휘   account 계정   shipment 수송   anxious 염려스러운, 걱정되는   on one's end ~의 쪽에서   associated with ~와 연동된, 관련된   available 이용할 수 있는   access 접속하다

152 추론 / 암시

번역   루이즈 씨의 직업은 무엇이겠는가?

    (A) 은행 창구 직원
    (B) 그래픽 디자이너
    (C) 소프트웨어 개발자
    (D) 고객 지원 전문가

해설   루이즈 씨가 오후 2시 40분 메시지에서 포티어 씨에게 쉽 위드 어스에 온 것을 환영한다(welcome to Ship With Us)고 한 후, 포티어 씨가 계정에 접속이 안된다고 하자 도와주겠다(I'm happy to help)고 했다. 따라서 루이즈 씨가 고객 응대 업무를 한다고 볼 수 있으므로, (D)가 정답이다.

153 의도 파악

번역   오후 2시 45분에 포티어 씨가 "맞습니다"라고 쓸 때, 그 의도는 무엇인가?

    (A) 비밀번호가 변경됐다.
    (B) 자신의 계정에 접속할 수 있다.
    (C) 루이즈 씨의 이메일을 받았다.
    (D) 루이즈 씨가 자신이 필요로 하는 정보를 가지고 있다.

해설   루이즈 씨가 오후 2시 44분 메시지에서 계정번호를 확인(Your account number is X58292J, right?)했는데, 이에 대해 포티어 씨가 '맞습니다(That's it)'라고 응답한 것이다. 즉, 루이즈 씨에게 계정 리셋에 필요한 정보(=포티어 씨의 계정번호)가 있음을 확인해 준 것이므로, (D)가 정답이다. 이 메시지 이후에 루이즈 씨가 새 비밀번호를 이메일로 보냈으므로, (A), (B), (C)는 오답이다.

154-155 광고

아드난 자동차 정비소

워너 플레이스 5번지
¹⁵⁴**20년간 맨체스터에서 서비스 제공!**

영업시간: 월-금요일 오전 8시-오후 5시; 토요일 오전 9시-오후 1시

아드난 자동차 정비소는 고객 서비스를 최우선으로 여기는 종합 서비스 수리점입니다! 창업자인 아드난 하다드는 레이싱팀의 수석 기술자로 근무하며 기량을 익혔습니다. 그와 전문 정비사 직원들이 수입이든 국산

이든 상관없이 모든 브랜드 및 모델의 자동차와 트럭을 점검해 드립니다. 귀하의 차량이 잘 주행할 수 있도록 해 드리겠습니다!

아울러 중고차를 경쟁력 있는 가격에 판매합니다.
155차량을 팔고 싶으신가요? 그럼 저희에게 전화하세요!
0161 496 0437

어휘 garage 차고, 정비소 repair 수리 priority 우선 (사항) mechanic 정비공 service 서비스를 제공하다 make 제조사, 브랜드 foreign 외국의, 수입의 domestic 국내의 competitive 경쟁력 있는

154 사실 관계 확인

번역 아드난 자동차 정비소에 대해 알 수 있는 것은?
(A) 맨체스터 내 새로운 장소로 이전할 예정이다.
(B) 20년간 영업해 왔다.
(C) 1주일에 한 번 저녁에 영업을 한다.
(D) 지역에서 제조된 차량만 수리한다.

해설 상단에서 20년간 맨체스터에서 서비스를 제공해 오고 있다(Serving Manchester for 20 years!)고 광고하고 있으므로, (B)가 정답이다. 참고로, 주중에는 오후 5시까지, 토요일에는 오후 1시까지 영업(Open Monday to Friday, 8 A.M. to 5 P.M.; Saturday, 9 A.M. to 1 P.M.)하며, 수입이든 국산이든 상관없이 모든 브랜드 및 모델의 차량(all makes and models of cars and trucks, both foreign and domestic)을 점검한다고 했으므로, (C)와 (D)는 오답이다. 언급되지 않은 (A)는 정답이 될 수 없다.

어휘 in business 사업을 하는 locally 지역[현지]에서 manufacture 제조하다

▶▶Paraphrasing 지문의 Serving ~ for 20 years!
→ 정답의 has been in business for two decades

155 세부 사항

번역 광고에서 누구에게 해당 전화번호로 전화하라고 유도하는가?
(A) 자동차 소유주
(B) 자동차 정비공
(C) 경주용 차량 기술자
(D) 트럭 운전사

해설 하단에서 현재 소유하고 있는 차량을 팔고 싶다면(Interested in selling your car?) 전화하라(Call us now!)고 했으므로, 광고 대상이 차량 소유주임을 알 수 있다. 따라서 (A)가 정답이다.

156-158 공지

왓포드 서류 파쇄의 날

156수북이 쌓인 기밀 문서를 안전하게 폐기해야 합니까? 156/157**4월 8일 오전 8시부터 11시까지 열리는 '왓포드 커뮤니티 서류 파쇄의 날'에 오세요.**

수많은 시큐리티 투 문서 파쇄기가 왓포드 시립 주차장 건물 뒤편의 편리한 장소에 놓여 있습니다. 158**불필요한 입출금 내역서, 세무 서류, 청구서 등을 모두 가져오세요.** 157차로 와서 그것들을 내려놓기만 하시면 됩니다. 157현장에서 안전하게 파쇄되어 재활용될 것입니다. 본 행사는 왓포드 타운십 거주민에게만 개방되며 가구당 5킬로그램의 한도가 있음을 알려드립니다. 시큐리티 투 담당자들이 상주하여 여러분의 개인 정보를 보호할 수 있는 방법에 관해 이야기해 드립니다.

'커뮤니티 파쇄의 날'은 라디오 방송국 82.9 WQYX와 시큐리티 투가 함께 합니다.

더 자세한 정보를 원하시면 www.watfordtownship/shredding day.org를 확인하세요.

어휘 shredding (종이, 문서를) 파쇄하다 dispose of 없애다, 처리하다 confidential 기밀의 be conveniently located 편리한 위치에 있다 bank statement 입출금 내역서 tax 세금 securely 안전하게 recycle 재활용하다 resident 거주민 household 가구 representative 직원 on hand (도움 등을) 구할 수 있는, 가까이에 있는 protect 보호하다 private information 개인 정보

156 주제 / 목적

번역 공지의 목적은?
(A) 거주민들에게 만기일을 알려주려고
(B) 서비스를 홍보하려고
(C) 시에 새로 들어온 업체를 환영하려고
(D) 대회를 광고하려고

해설 첫 번째 단락에서 기밀 문서를 폐기해야 하는 사람은 4월 8일에 열리는 '왓포드 커뮤니티 서류 파쇄의 날'에 오라(Come to Watford Community Shredding Day on April 8)고 한 후, 파쇄기 제공 서비스에 대한 설명을 이어가고 있다. 따라서 이를 홍보하기 위한 공지라고 볼 수 있으므로, (B)가 정답이다.

어휘 due date 만기일 promote 홍보하다 advertise 광고하다

157 추론 / 암시

번역 4월 8일에 어떤 일이 일어나겠는가?
(A) 종이가 재활용될 것이다.
(B) 은행 담당자가 고객들을 만날 것이다.
(C) 새로운 주차장 건물이 문을 열 것이다.
(D) 안내 세미나가 제공될 것이다.

해설 질문에 언급된 4월 8일은 서류 파쇄 행사가 있는 날인데, 두 번째 단락을 보면 폐지들이 현장에서 안전하게 파쇄되어 재활용된다(They will be securely shredded and recycled on the spot)고 나와 있다. 따라서 이날 파쇄된 종이가 재활용된다고 추론할 수 있으므로, (A)가 정답이다.

어휘 informational 정보를 제공하는

158 문장 삽입

번역 [1], [2], [3], [4]로 표시된 곳 중에서 다음 문장이 가장 적합한 곳은?

"차로 와서 그것들을 내려놓기만 하시면 됩니다."

(A) [1]
(B) [2]
(C) [3]
(D) [4]

해설 주어진 문장의 '그것들(them)'이 가리키는 대상, 즉, 차로 운반해 와서 놓고 갈 것들이 앞에서 먼저 언급되어야 한다. [2] 앞에서 불필요한 입출금 내역서, 세무 서류, 청구서 등을 모두 가져오라(Bring any unneeded bank statements, tax documents, and bills)고 했고, 뒤에서는 처리 과정을 설명했으므로, 이 사이에 해당 문장이 들어가야 자연스럽다. 따라서 (B)가 정답이다.

159-160 이메일

수신: 카미니 다스 〈k.das@armail.net〉
발신: 고객 서비스 〈customerservice@sandringsuites.com.au〉
날짜: 2월 7일
제목: 방문 관련

다스 씨께,

최근 샌드링 스위트에 투숙해 주셔서 감사합니다. 저희는 고객에게 특별한 경험을 선사해 드리는 것을 최우선으로 여깁니다. ¹⁵⁹저희 호텔에서 보내신 시간을 평가하는 3분짜리 설문조사에 응답해 주셨으면 합니다. www.sandringsuites.com.au를 방문하셔서 웹페이지 상단 오른쪽 구석에 있는 설문조사 링크를 클릭하십시오. 코드 SAN5341을 입력하시고 설문을 완료하시면 됩니다. ¹⁶⁰참여해 주신 것에 대한 감사의 의미로, 저희 호텔 중 한 곳에서의 2박 무료 숙박권을 얻을 수 있는 월간 경품 추첨에 귀하의 성함을 등록하겠습니다.

실비아 모니어
고객 서비스, 샌드링 스위트

어휘 regarding ~에 관해 priority 우선 (사항) exceptional 이례적으로 우수한, 특출한 complete a survey 설문에 응하다 raffle 경품 추첨 (행사) complimentary 무료의

159 세부 사항

번역 다스 씨는 무엇을 하라고 요청받는가?

(A) 연락처 확인
(B) 피드백 제공
(C) 구매 완료
(D) 구독 연장

해설 이메일의 초반부에서 다스 씨에게 호텔에서 보낸 시간을 평가하는 3분짜리 설문조사에 응답해달라(We ask that you complete a three-minute survey to rate your time with us)고 요청했으므로, (B)가 정답이다.

어휘 purchase 구입, 구매 renew 갱신하다, 연장하다 subscription 구독

▸▸ Paraphrasing 지문의 complete a three-minute survey to rate your time with us
→ 정답의 Provide some feedback

160 세부 사항

번역 모니어 씨는 다스 씨를 위해 무엇을 하겠다고 말하는가?

(A) 호텔 투숙 무료로 연장하기
(B) 웹사이트 이용 도와주기
(C) 경품에 당첨될 기회 제공하기
(D) 향후 호텔 투숙에 쓸 할인 코드 제공하기

해설 이메일의 후반부에서 모니어 씨는 샌드링 스위트 호텔 2박 무료 숙박권을 얻을 수 있는 월간 경품 추첨에 다스 씨의 이름을 등록하겠다(we will enter your name in our monthly raffle to win a complimentary two-night stay at one of our hotels)고 했다. 따라서 (C)가 정답이다.

어휘 extend 연장하다 free of charge 무료로 win a prize 상을 타다, 복권에 당첨되다

▸▸ Paraphrasing 지문의 enter your name in our monthly raffle to win a complimentary two-night stay → 정답의 Give her a chance to win a prize

161-163 광고

악바르 보관 업체
웩스햄 로 227번지, 브리지타운
전화번호: 246-555-0147

30년간 바베이도스에서 저장 공간이 필요하신 분들께 만족스러운 서비스를 제공해 드리고 있습니다!

- 귀하의 니즈에 맞춰 소형, 표준형, 프리미엄 크기의 단위로 창고 이용이 가능합니다.
- ¹⁶¹청결하고 습기 없는 창고를 24시간 내내 이용할 수 있습니다.
- ¹⁶²보관 시설은 고성능 보안 카메라로 감시되며, 각 고객에게는 비밀번호가 부여됩니다. 이 비밀번호를 입력해야만 보안 전자 출입문이 열립니다.
- 저희 사무실은 월-금요일 오전 9시-오후 6시, 토요일 오전 9시-오후 2시까지 운영됩니다. 저희 직원과 이야기하시려면 잠시 들러주십시오.

¹⁶³지금 가장 큰 창고를 12개월간 대여하고 20퍼센트 할인을 받아보세요!

어휘 storage 저장 (공간) satisfy 충족시키다 needs (소비자의) 니즈, 요구 available 이용 가능한 around the clock 24시간 내내 facility 시설 pass code 암호, 비밀번호 secure 안전한, 보안이 철저한 release (제한하고 있던 것을 사용할 수 있도록) 풀다 representative 직원

161 세부 사항

번역 광고에 따르면, 고객은 언제 자신의 창고를 이용할 수 있는가?

(A) 언제든지
(B) 월–금요일에만
(C) 토–일요일에만
(D) 보안 담당자와 동반 시에만

해설 두 번째 항목에서 창고를 24시간 내내 이용할 수 있다(Your ~ storage unit is available to you around the clock)고 했으므로, (A)가 정답이다.

어휘 access 접근하다, 들어가다, 이용하다 accompany 동반하다, 동행하다

▸▸ Paraphrasing 지문의 Your ~ storage unit is available → 질문의 access their storage units

지문의 around the clock → 정답의 At any time

162 세부 사항

번역 고객은 시설 출입을 위해 무엇을 해야 하는가?

(A) 일일 출입증 구입
(B) 보안 카메라 인식
(C) 출입 코드 입력
(D) 경비원에게 신분증 제시

해설 세 번째 항목에서 각 고객에게 비밀번호가 부여된다(each customer is given a pass code)고 한 후, 비밀번호를 입력해야만 보안 전자 출입문이 열린다(Our secure electronic gate can be released only by entering this code)고 했다. 따라서 (C)가 정답이다.

어휘 pass 출입증, 통행증 recognize 인식하다 identification 신분증명서, 신원 확인

▸▸ Paraphrasing 지문의 pass code → 정답의 access code

163 세부 사항

번역 고객은 어떻게 할인을 받을 수 있는가?

(A) 저장 공간을 20퍼센트 줄여서
(B) 1년간 프리미엄 크기의 공간을 대여해서
(C) 서비스 직원에게 광고를 보여줘서
(D) 저장소를 1년 더 대여하는 데 동의해서

해설 하단에서 가장 큰 창고를 12개월 대여하고 20퍼센트 할인을 받아보라(get 20 percent off with a twelve-month rental of our largest type of unit)고 권하고 있으므로, (B)가 정답이다.

▸▸ Paraphrasing 지문의 get 20 percent off → 질문의 receive a discount

지문의 a twelve-month rental of our largest type of unit → 정답의 renting a premium-size unit for one year

164-167 기사

게이머 아케이즈, 프랭키 버거스 체인점과 제휴에 나서

리즈 (7월 9일) - 164게이머 아케이즈와 패스트푸드 체인점 프랭키 버거스가 새로운 협력 관계를 발표했으며, 공식적으로 8월 초에 시작된다. 해당 시점이 되면 게이머 아케이즈 전 지점에 프랭키 버거스가 들어올 예정이다.

166게이머 아케이즈의 앨런 잉그램 회장은 금번 전략적 제휴가 가져올 기회에 대한 기대감을 드러냈다.

"프랭키 버거스의 뛰어난 품질은 저희 아케이즈 고객의 즐거움을 한층 더 높일 것입니다."라고 잉그램 씨가 말했다. "165지금까지 구내에 식당이 있던 적은 없었습니다. 하지만 이번 제휴를 통해 고객들은 맛있는 식사를 하며 잠시 휴식을 취하고 나서, 다시 최신식 게임 센터로 돌아가 즐거운 시간을 보낼 수 있습니다."

166/167지난 11월 저스틴 벡커맨 씨의 자리를 이어받은 이후, 잉그램 씨가 회사에 일으킨 중요한 변화 중 이번 제휴가 처음은 아니다. 166/167그는 회장직을 맡고 나서 한 달 뒤, 게이머 아케이즈에 가상현실 게임을 들여왔다. 이후 독일과 벨기에로 사세를 확장하기도 했으며 게이머 아케이즈와 연관된 여러 자선 활동을 시작했다.

어휘 join forces with ~와 협력[제휴]하다 formally 공식적으로 express 표현하다 possibility 기회, 가능성 strategic 전략적인 outstanding 뛰어난, 두드러진 enhance 높이다, 향상시키다 premises 부지, 구내 take a break 휴식을 취하다 state-of-the-art 최신(식)의 take over from ~로부터 이어받다 assume (역할 등을) 맡다 virtual reality 가상현실 expand 확장시키다 charity 자선 initiative 계획, (특정 목적을 이루고자 하는) 활동 associated with ~와 관련된

164 세부 사항

번역 제휴는 언제 공식화되는가?

(A) 7월
(B) 8월
(C) 11월
(D) 12월

해설 첫 번째 단락에서 게이머 아케이즈와 패스트푸드 체인점 프랭키 버거스의 새로운 제휴(a new partnership)가 8월 초에 공식적으로 시작된다(which will formally start at the beginning of August)고 했다. 따라서 (B)가 정답이다.

어휘 official 공식적인

▸▸ Paraphrasing 지문의 formally start → 질문의 become official

165 사실 관계 확인

번역 게이머 아케이즈와 프랭키 버거스의 제휴에 대해 명시된 것은?

(A) 수 개월의 협상 끝에 합의를 이뤘다.
(B) 게이머 아케이즈 전 지점에 적용되지는 않을 것이다.
(C) 주주 승인을 기다리고 있다.
(D) 게이머 아케이즈가 음식점과 맺은 첫 번째 제휴이다.

해설 세 번째 단락에 나온 잉그램 씨의 인터뷰 내용을 보면, 지금까지 게이머 아케이즈 구내에 식당이 있던 적은 없었다(Until now, there have been no food options on the premises)고 되어 있다. 따라서 음식점과 맺은 첫 번째 제휴임을 알 수 있으므로, (D)가 정답이다.

어휘 negotiation 협상 apply to ~에 적용되다 shareholder 주주 approval 승인

> ▸▸ Paraphrasing   지문의 there have been no food options on the premises
> → 정답의 Gamer Arcades' first partnership with a restaurant

166 세부 사항

번역 기사에 따르면, 벡커맨 씨는 누구인가?

(A) 식품 공급업체 회장
(B) 프랭키 버거스 체인점 소유주
(C) 게임 제조업체 소유주
(D) 게이머 아케이즈 전 회장

해설 마지막 단락의 첫 문장에서 잉그램 씨가 벡커맨 씨의 자리를 이어받았다(he took over from Justine Beckerman)고 했는데, 그 다음 부분을 보면 잉그램 씨가 회장직(A month after assuming the role of president)을 맡아 게이머 아케이즈를 이끌어 오고 있음을 알 수 있다. 즉, 백커맨 씨는 게이머 아케이즈의 전 회장인 것이므로, (D)가 정답이다.

어휘 supply 공급 manufacturing 제조 former 이전의

167 세부 사항

번역 잉그램 씨가 게이머 아케이즈에서 처음 한 일은?

(A) 가상현실 게임을 도입했다.
(B) 여러 개의 자선 프로그램을 시작했다.
(C) 벨기에에 지점을 열었다.
(D) 독일로 본사를 이전했다.

해설 마지막 단락을 보면, 프랭키 버거스와의 제휴는 잉그램 씨가 회장직을 맡고 나서 일으킨 첫 번째 중요한 변화가 아니라(not the first major change)고 되어 있다. 그가 처음 일으킨 변화는 취임 한 달 뒤 게이머 아케이즈에 가상현실 게임을 들여온 것(he brought virtual reality games to Gamer Arcades)이므로, (A)가 정답이다. 자선 활동을 시작하고 사세를 확장한 것은 그 다음의 일이므로, (B), (C)는 정답이 될 수 없다.

어휘 branch 지점 headquarters 본사, 본부

> ▸▸ Paraphrasing   지문의 brought → 정답의 introduced

168-171 편지

5월 25일

드보라 키어난 씨
소닉붐 배급 대행사
아서 로 84번지
런던 N7 6DR

키어난 씨께,

168 어스스카이 필름 인터내셔널에서는 당사의 최신작인 〈항공 프로젝트〉의 배급사를 찾고 있습니다. 지난 4월 네덜란드 에인트호벤에서 열렸던 북 브라반트 영화제에서 개봉된 이 영화는 평론가들에게서 호평을 받았으며, 다이아몬드 펜 어워드의 최우수 각본상을 수상하는 영예를 안았습니다.

169 저희 영화 〈항공 프로젝트〉는 150년도 더 전에 시작된 항공 역사의 흥미로운 시기를 살펴봅니다. 항공 산업의 발전은 뛰어나고 진취적인 수많은 사람들 덕분입니다. 이 영화는 혁신을 이룬 주요 인물뿐만 아니라 덜 알려진 사람들까지도 조명합니다.

170/171 두 주인공 역은 전 세계 관객들에게 친숙한 윈스턴 할시와 버질 골딩이 맡았습니다. 둘 다 수년간 평론가들의 찬사를 받아왔습니다. 골딩 씨는 여러 영화 중에서도 〈릭비 음모론〉에서 맡은 역할로 잘 알려져 있고, 할시 씨는 〈소재 불명〉에서의 연기로 인정받고 있습니다.

저희 영화 마케팅에 관심이 있으시다면, 감상하실 수 있도록 보안 링크를 이메일로 보내드리겠습니다. 빠른 시일 내에 답변 주시기를 바랍니다.

자예쉬 차우드하리, CEO
어스스카이 필름 인터내셔널

어휘 distribution 유통, 배급, 배포 production 작품 aerial 항공의 premier(e) 개봉[초연]하다, 시사회를 하다 critic 비평가, 평론가 be honored with ~의 영예를 안다, 수상하다 screenplay 영화 대본, 각본 aviation 항공 industry 산업 owe ~ 덕분이다, 빚지다 enterprising 진취적인 highlight 강조하다 innovator 혁신자 figure 인물 familiar 친숙한 audience 청중, 관중 recognize 인정하다 performance 연기

168 세부 사항

번역 차우드하리 씨는 무엇을 하고 싶어하는가?

(A) 항공 관련 박물관 전시회 홍보하기
(B) 새 사업체 관리자 채용하기
(C) 영화제 심사위원 되기
(D) 더 많은 관객들에게 영화 소개하기

해설 첫 번째 단락에서 회사가 제작한 최신작의 배급사를 찾고 있다(Earthsky Films International is seeking a distributor for our latest production)고 했으므로, 배급사를 통해 영화를 더 많은 관객들에게 소개하고 싶어 한다는 것을 알 수 있다. 따라서 (D)가 정답이다.

어휘 promote 홍보하다 exhibit 전시 judge 심사위원, 판사

169 사실 관계 확인

번역 〈항공 프로젝트〉에 대해 알 수 있는 것은?

(A) 네덜란드에서 주로 촬영했다.
(B) 개봉을 오래 기다렸다.
(C) 어떤 업계의 초창기를 살펴본다.
(D) 항공사에서 자금을 댔다.

해설 두 번째 단락에서 〈항공 프로젝트〉가 150년도 더 전에 시작된 항공 역사의 흥미로운 시기를 살펴본다(Project Aerial, examines an exciting period in aviation history that began more than 150 years ago)고 했으므로, 항공 산업의 초창기를 다루고 있음을 알 수 있다. 따라서 (C)가 정답이다.

어휘 long awaited 오래 기다렸던 stage 단계 finance 자금을 대다

> ▸▸ **Paraphrasing** 지문의 an exciting period in aviation history that began more than 150 years ago → 정답의 the early stages of an industry

170 사실 관계 확인

번역 할시 씨와 골딩 씨에 대해 명시된 것은?

(A) 잘 알려진 배우들이다.
(B) 항공기 조종사 훈련을 받았다.
(C) 항공 역사를 연구했다.
(D) 여러 영화 작품에서 함께 연기했다.

해설 세 번째 단락에서 할시 씨와 골딩 씨가 전 세계 관객들에게 친숙한 인물(Winston Halsey and Virgil Golding, figures that are familiar to international audiences)이라고 했으므로, (A)가 정답이다.

어휘 research 연구하다

> ▸▸ **Paraphrasing** 지문의 figures that are familiar to international audiences → 정답의 well-known actors

171 문장 삽입

번역 [1], [2], [3], [4]로 표시된 곳 중에서 다음 문장이 가장 적합한 곳은?

"둘 다 수년간 평론가들의 찬사를 받아왔습니다."

(A) [1]
(B) [2]
(C) [3]
(D) [4]

해설 평론가들의 찬사를 받을 만한 두 명의 사람(Both)이 누구인지 앞에서 먼저 언급되어야 한다. [3] 앞에서 할시 씨와 골딩 씨가 전 세계 관객들에게 친숙한 인물(Winston Halsey and Virgil Golding, figures that are familiar to international audiences)이라며 Both가 가리키는 대상을 구체적으로 밝혔으므로, (C)가 정답이다.

어휘 critical 비평가의, 비평적인 acclaim 찬사

172-175 온라인 채팅

마리아 안드레우 (오전 9시 6분) 안녕하세요, 제이콥, 산드라. 172/173목요일 아침에 열릴 사진작가 포커스 그룹 회의에 도움이 필요해요. 제가 더 이상 진행할 수가 없어서요.

제이콥 웬트 (오전 9시 9분) 안타깝네요. 172잠재 고객에게 중요한 요소에 대해 의뢰인에게 자문해 주려면 저 회의를 들어가서 제대로 진행되는지 확인해야 하는데요.

마리아 안드레우 (오전 9시 10분) 맞아요. 그래서 일정을 바꾸지 않으려고 해요. 의뢰인이 보고서를 다음 주 초로 예상하고 있잖아요. 둘 중 한 분이 저 대신 그룹을 이끌어 주실 수 없을까요?

산드라 리우 (오전 9시 12분) 미안해요, 마리아. 저는 내일 마케팅 회의 때문에 외부로 출장을 가서 금요일까지는 못 올 거예요.

제이콥 웬트 (오전 9시 15분) 174포커스 그룹을 이끌어 본 적이 없긴 하지만, 제가 하겠습니다.

마리아 안드레우 (오전 9시 17분) 좋아요. 제가 이메일로 참가자 동의서를 보내드릴게요. 그룹 시간을 시작할 때 모든 참가자가 각자 동의서에 서명을 해야 해요.

제이콥 웬트 (오전 9시 18분) 네. 175사본이 몇 장이나 필요할까요?

산드라 리우 (오전 9시 19분) 사실 필요 없어요. 175지난 화요일에 진행했던 다른 그룹 회의에서 남은 사본이 있거든요. 아직 제 책상에 있어요.

제이콥 웬트 (오전 9시 20분) 제가 오늘 들러서 가져갈게요.

마리아 안드레우 (오전 9시 21분) 두 분 모두 감사합니다. 그럼 다음 주 월요일에 만나서 의뢰인을 위한 광고 보고서 작업을 할 수 있겠군요.

어휘 focus group 포커스 그룹 (시장 조사를 위해 각 계층을 대표하도록 뽑은 소수의 사람들로 이뤄진 그룹), 또는 그 회의 take place 열리다, 개최되다 no longer 더 이상 ~ 아닌 available ~할 여건이 되는 follow up with (회의 등에) 참석해서 제대로 진행되는지 확인하다, 후속 조치를 하다 potential 잠재적인 expect 기대하다, 예상하다 reschedule 일정을 변경하다 conduct 지휘하다, 이끌다 conference 회의 participant 참가자 consent form 동의서 actually 사실

172 추론 / 암시

번역 채팅에 참여한 사람들은 어떤 유형의 업체에서 일하겠는가?

(A) 시장조사 대행사
(B) 인쇄소
(C) 소프트웨어 개발업체
(D) 촬영 스튜디오

해설 안드레우 씨의 오전 9시 6분 메시지에서 사진작가 포커스 그룹 회의(the focus group with the photographers)가, 웬트 씨의 9시 9분 메시지에서 의뢰인에게 해주는 자문 업무(to advise our client about what is important to potential customers)가 언급되었다. 따라서 채팅 참가자들이 포커스 그룹을 대상으로 한 조사 결과를 바탕으로 의뢰인에게 조언을 제공하는 시장조사 대행사에서 일한다고 추론할 수 있으므로, (A)가 정답이다.

173 세부 사항

번역 사진작가들과 함께 하는 포커스 그룹 회의는 언제 진행될 예정인가?

(A) 월요일
(B) 화요일
(C) 목요일
(D) 금요일

해설 안드레우 씨의 오전 9시 6분 메시지를 보면, 사진작가가 포커스 그룹 회의가 목요일 오전(the focus group with the photographers that is taking place on Thursday morning)에 열릴 예정임을 알 수 있다. 따라서 (C)가 정답이다.

174 사실 관계 확인

번역 웬트 씨에 대해 알 수 있는 것은?

(A) 회의에 참석하는 것을 좋아한다.
(B) 리우 씨 사무실 아래층에서 근무한다.
(C) 전에 포커스 그룹을 이끌어 본 적이 없다.
(D) 팀에서 경험이 가장 많은 팀원이다.

해설 웬트 씨가 오전 9시 15분 메시지에서 자신이 포커스 그룹을 이끌어 본 적이 없다(I've never led a focus group before)고 했으므로, (C)가 정답이다.

어휘 previously 이전에   experienced 숙련된, 경험이 풍부한

> ▸▸ **Paraphrasing**   지문의 **never led a focus group before**
> → 정답의 **never previously run a focus group**

175 의도 파악

번역 오전 9시 19분에 리우 씨가 "필요 없어요"라고 쓸 때, 그 의도는 무엇인가?

(A) 자신의 출장을 취소할 수 있다.
(B) 포커스 그룹 참가자들은 동의서를 작성하지 않을 것이다.
(C) 포커스 그룹 회의 일정을 변경할 수 있다.
(D) 웬트 씨는 동의서를 출력할 필요가 없다.

해설 웬트 씨가 오전 9시 18분 메시지에서 참가자 동의서 사본이 몇 장이나 필요할지(How many copies will be needed?) 물었는데, 이에 대해 리우 씨가 '필요 없어요(there's no need)'라고 응답한 것이다. 이후 지난 화요일에 진행했던 다른 그룹 회의에서 남은 사본이 있다(I have copies left over from another group I ran last Tuesday)고 덧붙였으므로, (D)가 정답이다.

어휘 business trip 출장   complete a form 서식을 작성하다

176-180 웹페이지 + 이메일

회사	**제품**	협력업체	연락처

드라이모틱은 당사의 혁신적인 진공 극초단파 건조 공정이 식품 및 제약 업계에 있는 30개 이상 업체들에서 사용되고 있음을 자랑스럽게 알려드립니다.

[176]작동 방식은 이렇습니다. 작은 조각으로 준비한 유기농 원재료의 여러 분량을 기계의 회전통에 넣습니다. 통이 돌아가면 극초단파 에너지에 의해 조각에 있던 수분이 제거됩니다. 최종 수분 수치는 작동자가 미리 맞출 수 있습니다. 건조된 조각들은 색상, 맛, 영양을 그대로 [177]유지하며, 그러고 나서 포장만 하면 됩니다. 드라이모틱 기계는 동결건조 및 공기건조보다 더 짧은 시간에 (더 적은 비용으로) 더 나은 결과물을 얻습니다.

드라이모틱 기계는 아래와 같은 크기로 이용 가능합니다.

모델번호	전력	추천 용도
G4200	10킬로와트	신제품 시험
[178]G4260	50킬로와트	[178]소규모 제조업체
H4500	100킬로와트	대규모 대용량 제조업체

어휘 announce 알리다, 발표하다   revolutionary 혁명적인 vacuum 진공의   microwave 극초단파   dehydration 탈수, 건조   pharmaceutical 제약의   batch 한 회분, 집단   organic 유기농의   rotating 회전하는   preset 미리 설정하다   operator 조작하는 사람   retain 유지하다   nutrition 영양   packaging 포장   freeze-drying 동결건조   suggest 제안[추천]하다

수신: customerservice@drymotic.com
발신: ovolterra@yambrett.com.au
날짜: 5월 6일
제목: 기계 오작동

고객 서비스 담당자께,

[178]작년에 저희의 즉석 스튜 가루 제품에 쓰려고 드라이모틱 기계 (제품 번호: G4260, 일련번호: 01938207)를 구입했습니다. [179/180]이번 달 초까지는 기계에 문제가 없었는데, 그때 처리 시간이 길어졌다는 걸 알게 됐어요. 권고되는 청소 일정을 따라왔으니, 이 문제가 과도한 잔여물 때문일 리는 없습니다.

[179]이 문제를 제때 해결하기 위한 제안사항이 있다면 알려 주세요. 경미한 수리는 제가 직접 처리하는 편을 늘 선호하긴 합니다만, 이 문제가 계속되면 머지않아 유지보수 방문 일정을 잡아야 할 지도 모르겠습니다.

올리비아 볼테라
얌브렛 사

어휘 malfunction (기계 등이) 제대로 작동하지 않다   instant 즉석의   notice 알다   processing 처리   recommend 권고하다, 추천하다   excess 초과의   residue 잔여물   resolve 해결하다   in a timely manner 적기에, 제때   persist 계속되다 maintenance 유지보수

176 세부 사항

번역 드라이모틱 가공 처리용 기계는 무엇을 하도록 고안되었는가?

(A) 식품을 작은 조각으로 자르기
(B) 식품을 건조시켜 보존하기
(C) 유기농 재료에 수분 더하기
(D) 제품의 색과 맛 향상시키기

해설 웹페이지의 첫 번째 단락에서 작은 조각으로 준비한 유기농 원재료의 여러 분량을 기계의 회전통에 넣고(Batches of raw organic materials ~ are loaded into the machine's rotating drum) 돌리면 조각에서 수분이 제거된다(As the drum turns, moisture is removed from the pieces)며 기계의 작동법(how it works)을 설명하고 있다. 따라서 식품 건조 기기임을 알 수 있으므로, (B)가 정답이다.

어휘 processor 가공 처리용 기계 preserve 보존하다

> ▸ Paraphrasing 지문의 moisture is removed from the pieces → 정답의 drying it

177 동의어 찾기

번역 웹페이지 두 번째 단락, 네 번째 줄에 쓰인 "retain"과 의미가 가장 가까운 단어는?

(A) 기억하다
(B) 지원하다
(C) 향상시키다
(D) 유지하다

해설 'retain'을 포함한 부분은 '색상, 맛, 영양을 그대로 유지한다(The dried pieces retain their color, taste, and nutrition)'라는 의미로 해석되는데, 여기서 retain은 '그대로 유지하다, 간직하다'라는 뜻으로 쓰였다. 따라서 (D) keep이 정답이다.

178 연계

번역 얌브렛 사에 대해 암시된 것은?

(A) 대용량 건조 기계를 운용한다.
(B) 소규모로 포장 식품을 생산한다.
(C) 최근 신제품을 시험했다.
(D) 1년 전에 설립됐다.

해설 이메일의 첫 번째 단락에서 얌브렛 사가 즉석 스튜 가루 제품에 쓰려고 드라이모틱 기계(제품번호: G4260, 일련번호: 01938207)를 구입했다(We purchased a Drymotic unit (product number: G4260, serial number: 01938207) ~ for use with our line of instant stew mixes)고 했는데, 웹페이지의 표를 보면 회사가 구입한 G4260은 소규모 제조업체(Small-scale manufacturers)에 적합한 제품이라고 나와 있다. 따라서 얌브렛 사가 소규모 포장 식품을 생산하는 업체라고 추론할 수 있으므로, (B)가 정답이다.

어휘 found 설립하다

179 주제 / 목적

번역 볼테라 씨가 드라이모틱 고객 서비스 부서에 이메일을 쓴 이유는?

(A) 유지보수 일정을 잡으려고
(B) 기계에 품질보증이 적용되는지 물어보려고
(C) 수리하는 데 조언을 구하려고
(D) 기계 교체를 요청하려고

해설 이메일의 첫 번째 단락에서 기계의 가공 처리 시간이 길어졌다(we began to notice an increase in processing time)는 문제점을 언급한 후, 두 번째 단락에서 이 문제를 해결하기 위한 제안사

항이 있다면 알려달라(Please let me know if you have any suggestions for resolving this issue)고 요청했다. 따라서 수리 관련 조언을 구하는 이메일이라고 볼 수 있으므로, (C)가 정답이다.

어휘 warranty 품질보증(서) obtain 구하다, 얻다 replacement 교체

> ▸ Paraphrasing 지문의 any suggestions for resolving this issue → 정답의 advice on making a repair

180 세부 사항

번역 얌브렛 사의 가공 처리 기계에 어떤 문제가 생겼는가?

(A) 더 느리게 작동한다.
(B) 소음이 더 많이 난다.
(C) 전력을 더 많이 소모한다.
(D) 청소를 더 자주 해야 한다.

해설 이메일의 첫 번째 단락에서 가공 처리 시간이 길어졌다(we began to notice an increase in processing time)는 문제점을 밝혔으므로, (A)가 정답이다.

> ▸ Paraphrasing 지문의 an increase in processing time → 정답의 operating more slowly

181-185 기사 + 이메일

칼 이버, 스포트라이트를 받다

고어, 뉴질랜드 (5월 2일) - 건축가 칼 이버는 의뢰인들이 쓰레기를 보물로 바꿀 수 있도록 도와주며 이름을 떨치게 되었다. **181그는 거의 대부분 재생되거나 복구된, 혹은 일상 생활에서 볼 수 있는 자재로만 이루어진 수십 채의 주택을 고어에 지었다.**

"가능한 한, 이미 근처에서 구할 수 있는 자재를 사용하고 싶습니다." 이버 씨가 말한다. "창의력이 좀 필요할 뿐이고, 그렇게 하면 아무 것도 낭비되지 않고, 매우 저렴한 비용으로 집을 지을 수 있죠. 낡은 울타리, 버려진 병, 코르크, 어울리지 않는 벽돌과 타일 등 무엇도 그냥 보고 지나칠 것이 없습니다."

이버 씨는 건축하는 집의 디자인 설계안 작성을 전적으로 도맡아 하지만, 건축 과정에 집주인들을 항상 참여시킨다. **185최소 1년에 이르는 대기 목록을 가지고 있어, 이버 씨는 자신의 고객을 신중하게 선택할 수 있다. 182전동 공구 사용법을 이미 알고 있고 스스로 직접 작업해 볼 의향이 있는 집주인하고만 작업을 진행한다.**

그가 지은 집 중 일부는 잡지, 여행 프로그램, 온라인 목공 시연 등에서 다뤄졌다. **183이버 씨의 프로젝트 사진이 담긴 그의 웹사이트 주소는 yborhabitats.co.nz이다.**

어휘 architect 건축가 treasure 보물 dozens of 수십의 composed of ~로 구성된 entirely 전부, 전적으로 reclaimed 재생된 recovered 복구된 found 일상 생활에서 볼 수 있는 (예술이나 건축 등 다른 용도로 사용하는) material 자재, 재료 creativity 창의성 for a fraction of the price 매우 적은 비용으로 discard 버리다, 폐기하다 mismatch 어울리지 않다

overlook 간과하다, 지나치다 involve 참여시키다 solely 오로지
power tool 전동 공구 hands-on work 직접 해보는 작업
feature 특집으로 다루다, 특별히 포함하다 carpentry 목공일
demonstration 시연

수신: contact@yborhabitats.co.nz
발신: c.holmes@hmail.net
날짜: 5월 4일
제목: 제안

이버 씨께,

귀하에 관한 기사를 막 읽었습니다. 귀하의 서비스와 독특한 공간을 만들어 내기 위해 집주인들과 협력하는 방식을 알게 되어 흥미로웠습니다. 제가 진행하고 싶은 두 개의 프로젝트가 있습니다.

1. ¹⁸⁴**몇 년 전 지은 테라스에 쓰고 남은 자재들을 포함시켜 현재 집을 증축하고 싶습니다.**

2. 지붕을 교체해야 합니다. 비용을 줄일 방법을 찾아봤는데, 기존 지붕을 그대로 놔두고 그 위에 새로운 금속판을 설치하는 안이 있었습니다. 저는 이 아이디어가 좋습니다!

작업을 하실 시간과 의향이 있으십니까? ¹⁸⁵**다음 달에는 시작하고 싶은데요.** 예약을 위해 비용의 절반을 신용카드로 선지급할 수 있습니다.

신시아 홈즈

어휘 proposal 제안 unique 독특한 extension 확대, 증축된 건물 current 현재의 incorporate 포함시키다 leftover 남은 patio 파티오, 야외 테라스 replace 교체하다 cut the cost 비용을 줄이다 suggestion 제안 existing 기존의 intact 온전한 install 설치하다 sheeting 얇은 판 up front 선불로 appointment 예약, 약속

181 사실 관계 확인

번역 기사에서 이버 씨가 짓는 집에 대해 명시된 것은?

(A) 규모가 크다.
(B) 값이 비싸다.
(C) 뉴질랜드 전역에 있다.
(D) 중고 자재로 짓는다.

해설 기사의 첫 번째 단락에서 이버 씨가 거의 대부분 재생되거나 복구된, 혹은 일상 생활에서 볼 수 있는 자재들로만 이루어진 수십 채의 주택(houses ~ composed almost entirely of reclaimed, recovered, or found materials)을 지었다고 했으므로, 중고 자재로 집을 짓는다는 것을 알 수 있다. 따라서 (D)가 정답이다.

▸▸ Paraphrasing 지문의 **reclaimed, recovered, or found materials** → 정답의 **used materials**

182 세부 사항

번역 이버 씨는 고객들에게 무엇을 하라고 요청하는가?

(A) 낡은 울타리 교체
(B) 장식용 타일 제작
(C) 디자인 설계안 제출
(D) 전동 공구 사용

해설 기사의 세 번째 단락에서 이버 씨가 전동 공구 사용법을 이미 알고 있는 집주인하고만 작업을 진행한다(He works solely with homeowners who already know how to operate power tools ~ themselves)고 했으므로, (D)가 정답이다.

어휘 decorative 장식용의 submit 제출하다

▸▸ Paraphrasing 지문의 **operate power tools** → 정답의 **Use power tools**

183 세부 사항

번역 기사에 따르면, 독자들은 이버 씨의 웹사이트에서 무엇을 할 수 있는가?

(A) 서비스 견적 요청
(B) 작업 예시 확인
(C) 설명 문서 다운로드
(D) 만족한 고객들이 작성한 후기 읽기

해설 기사의 마지막 단락에서 이버 씨의 웹사이트에 그가 이전에 했던 프로젝트 사진이 있다(featuring photos of his projects)고 했으므로, (B)가 정답이다.

어휘 quote 견적 instructions 설명, 지시

▸▸ Paraphrasing 지문의 **photos of his projects** → 정답의 **examples of his work**

184 세부 사항

번역 홈즈 씨는 무엇을 하고 싶어하는가?

(A) 오래된 지붕 철거
(B) 테라스 타일 교체
(C) 주택 규모 확장
(D) 신규 주택 건축

해설 이메일의 두 번째 단락을 보면 홈즈 씨가 진행하고 싶은 작업을 설명하고 있다. 1번 항목에서 현재 집을 증축하고 싶다(I want to add an extension to my current house)고 했으므로, (C)가 정답이다. 2번 항목에서 지붕을 교체해야 한다(My roof needs to be replaced)고는 했으나, 곧이어 기존 지붕을 그대로 놔두고 그 위에 새로운 금속판을 설치하는 안이 좋다고 했으므로, (A)는 정답이 될 수 없다.

어휘 remove 없애다, 제거하다

▸▸ Paraphrasing 지문의 **add an extension to my current house** → 정답의 **Increase the size of her house**

185 연계

번역 홈즈 씨 제안의 어떤 부분 때문에 이버 씨가 거절하겠는가?

(A) 시작 일자
(B) 제안된 가격
(C) 지불 방식
(D) 자재 선택

해설 이메일의 마지막 단락에서 홈즈 씨가 다음 달에는 작업을 시작하고 싶다(I would like to start as early as next month)고 했는데, 기사의 세 번째 단락을 보면 이버 씨에게 최소 1년에 이르는 대기 목록이 있다(With a waiting list of at least a year)고 나와 있다. 따라서 촉박한 작업 시작 일자가 거절의 사유가 될 것이라고 추론할 수 있으므로, (A)가 정답이다.

186-190 이메일 + 일정 + 이메일

수신: CFA 전 직원
발신: 융첸 추
날짜: 10월 16일
제목: 계획
첨부: ⌀ 일정

직원 여러분께,

186하기트 카스피 씨가 이곳 클리프 페이링 어소시에이츠(CFA)의 부사장 직책 면접을 위해 다음 주 이틀간 방문할 예정입니다. 그녀는 훌륭한 자질을 갖췄으며, 국제 금융 분야에서의 경력을 갖춰 해당 직책에 특히 적합합니다. 부디 그녀를 적극 환영해 주시기 바랍니다.

모두가 카스피 씨를 알아가는 기회를 갖는 것이 CFA 지도부에게는 중요한 일입니다. 그래서 여러분 모두가 카스피 씨와 함께 하는 특정 행사들에 참석해 주시기를 요청합니다. **187첨부한 일정을 확인해 주시고, CFA라고 표시된 행사를 여러분의 일정표에 추가하십시오.** 더 자세한 내용은 계속 알려드리겠습니다.

융첸 추
CEO, 클리프 페이링 어소시에이츠

어휘 agenda 일정, 안건 colleague 동료, 함께 일하는 직원 executive vice president 부사장 Associates 합자 회사 qualified 자격을 갖춘 background 배경 finance 금융, 재무 particularly 특히 well(-)suited 적합한 make every effort to ~하는 데 온갖 노력을 다하다 opportunity 기회 attach 첨부하다 marked 표시된

하기트 카스피 방문 일정

날짜	시간	행사	초청객
10월 23일	오전 9시	라 브런치에서 아침 식사	이사회 임원
10월 23일	오후 12시 30분	사무실에서 점심 식사	부서장
10월 23일	오후 3시	질의응답 시간	CFA
10월 23일	오후 7시	189미디엄 힐즈 비스트로에서 저녁 식사	189이사회 임원
18710월 24일	오전 9시	187사무실에서 아침 식사	187CFA

어휘 board 이사회

수신: 융첸 추 〈chou@clifffeiring.ca〉
발신: 하기트 카스피 〈hagit.caspi@volumel.co.il〉
날짜: 10월 27일
제목: 후속 이메일

추 씨께,

지난주에 초대해 주셔서 감사합니다. 모두를 만날 수 있어 정말 좋았습니다. **189특히 미디엄 힐즈 비스트로에서 조고풀로스 씨와 나눈 대화에 감사했어요.** CFA의 역사에 관해 멋진 이야기들을 들려주셨답니다.

24일 행사에 참석하지 못한 것에 대해 다시 한번 사과의 말씀 드려요. 날씨가 걱정됐고, 텔아비브로 가는 비행기를 놓치고 싶지 않았습니다.

188마지막으로, 제안해 주신 내용 감사합니다. 오늘 아침에 전달받았어요. **188/1901월부터 CFA 부사장직을 맡을 수 있어 영광입니다.** 직무기술서에 함께 논의했던 모든 내용이 포함되어 있더군요. 해당 직책에 대해 언급하신 시간도 적절해 보이며 혜택도 매우 만족스럽습니다. 긴밀히 협력하게 되기를 고대합니다.

하기트 카스피

어휘 follow-up 후속조치, 후속편 appreciate 감사하다 last but not least 마지막으로 (하지만 똑같이 중요한) hono(u)red 영광으로 생각하는 take on 맡다 job description 직무기술서 appropriate 적절한 benefit 혜택, 복리후생

186 주제 / 목적

번역 첫 번째 이메일을 쓴 목적은?

(A) 앞으로 있을 방문을 직원들에게 알리려고
(B) 구인 광고를 하려고
(C) 승진 대상으로 직원을 추천하려고
(D) 새로운 동료를 소개하려고

해설 첫 번째 이메일의 첫 단락에서 하기트 카스피 씨가 클리프 페이링 어소시에이츠(CFA)의 부사장 직책 면접을 위해 다음 주 이틀간 방문할 예정(Hagit Caspi will be visiting for a couple of days next week to interview for the position of executive vice president)이라고 한 후, 해당 일정과 관련된 추가 설명을 이어가고 있다. 따라서 (A)가 정답이다.

어휘 notify 알리다 job opening 구인 promotion 승진

187 연계

번역 전 직원은 어떤 식사를 일정표에 추가하라고 요청받았는가?

(A) 10월 23일 아침 식사
(B) 10월 23일 점심 식사
(C) 10월 23일 저녁 식사
(D) 10월 24일 아침 식사

해설 첫 번째 이메일의 두 번째 단락에서 추 씨는 전 직원들에게 CFA라고 표시된 행사를 각자의 일정표에 추가하라(add the events marked CFA to your calendar)고 요청했다. 일정에서 CFA가 표기된 식사 행사(Breakfast in office)는 10월 24일 오전 9시에 열릴 예정이므로, (D)가 정답이다.

188 주제 / 목적

번역 카스피 씨가 추 씨에게 편지를 쓴 이유는?

(A) 지연을 사과하려고
(B) 제안을 수락하려고
(C) 항공 여행 계획을 의논하려고
(D) 직책에 대한 세부사항을 요청하려고

해설 두 번째 이메일의 세 번째 단락에서 부사장직 제안에 감사를 표하고 (thank you for your offer ~ to take on the role of executive vice president of CFA) 있다. 따라서 제안의 수락을 알리는 이메일임을 알 수 있으므로, (B)가 정답이다.

어휘 apologize 사과하다 delay 지연 accept 수락하다

189 연계

번역 조고풀로스 씨는 누구이겠는가?

(A) 미디엄 힐즈 비스트로 직원
(B) 이사회 임원
(C) 부서장
(D) 인사부서 직원

해설 두 번째 이메일의 첫 번째 단락에서 카스피 씨는 미디엄 힐즈 비스트로에서 조고풀로스 씨와 나눈 대화(my conversation with Mr. Georgopoulos at Medium Hills Bistro)를 언급하며 그로부터 CFA의 역사를 들었다고 했다. 일정을 보면 미디엄 힐즈 비스트로에서의 저녁 식사 행사(Dinner at Medium Hills Bistro)에 초대받은 사람들은(Invitees) 이사회 임원(Board members)이라고 나와 있으므로, 조고풀로스 씨가 CFA 이사회 임원임을 추론할 수 있다. 따라서 (B)가 정답이다.

190 사실 관계 확인

번역 두 번째 이메일에서 해당 직책에 대해 명시한 것은?

(A) 1월에 시작할 것이다.
(B) 텔아비브에 근거지를 둘 것이다.
(C) 초과 근무를 포함한다.
(D) 여전히 직무기술서가 필요하다.

해설 두 번째 이메일의 세 번째 단락에서 1월부터 CFA 부사장직을 맡을 수 있어 영광(I would be honoured to take on the role of executive vice president of CFA starting in January)이라고

했으므로, (A)가 정답이다. 참고로, 직무기술서에 함께 논의했던 모든 내용이 포함되어 있다(The job description covers everything we discussed)고 했으므로 (D)는 정답이 될 수 없다.

어휘 involve 수반하다 work overtime 초과 근무하다

191-195 기사 + 도표 + 이메일

트라이베스 (191**2월 1일**) – 알라크리텀 주식회사는 1번 고속도로를 따라 전기차 충전소를 지을 계획을 발표했다. 이미 아시아 전역에 400개 이상의 충전소를 보유한 알라크리텀은 풍부한 경험을 활용해 이 대규모 작업에 착수한다. PRO 충전소라고도 알려진 1번 고속도로 충전소는 최대 200킬로와트의 전력을 제공하며 30분에 80퍼센트까지 충전이 되게끔 할 예정이다. 194**해당 시스템은 대기 중인 운전자들에게 휴대전화나 다른 모바일 기기로 문자메시지를 보내 배터리 충전 상태를 주기적으로 알려줄 것이다.** 알라크리텀은 운전자들에게 청결하고 편안하며 환한 대기 시설을 제공할 것을 약속하고 있다. 191**시범 운영 사업소가 다음 달 초 로그레드에 문을 열 예정이다.**

어휘 charging 충전 electric vehicle 전기차 bring A to B A를 B에 가져오다, 활용하다 a wealth of 풍부한 undertaking 작업, 프로젝트 up to ~까지 periodically 주기적으로, 정기적으로 notify 알리다 device 기기 motorist 운전자 status 상황

PRO 충전소: 제안 분포도

지역	충전소 개수	일일 고객 수
192엘론델	26	192**9,220**
서던 보렐비아	14	4,970
195웨스턴 보렐비아	19520	6,390
노스 쇼어	10	3,560

어휘 distribution 분포 region 지역

수신: lhsiao@alacritum.com
발신: ctrigg@alacritum.com
날짜: 3월 15일
제목: 회의

샤오 씨께,

193/195**이번 주 웨스턴 보렐비아 지역 협력단체와의 회의 결과에 따라, 그곳의 사막 환경을 고려하여 해당 지역 대기실에 냉방 장치를 추가할 것을 제안합니다.** 추가 시 더 큰 비용이 들겠지만 고객의 안락함과 안전을 보장할 수 있을 것입니다. 193/194**또한 제가 직접 겪어보니, 1번 고속도로의 열악한 모바일 네트워크 연결 서비스가 PRO 충전소 대부분의 무선 네트워크를 불안정하게 만들어 버릴 듯 합니다.** 그러므로 이에 대한 기술적 해결방안도 필요할 겁니다. 이번 주가 끝나기 전에 상세 보고서를 보내드리겠습니다.

척 트리그

어휘 condition 조건 entail (비용 등을) 들게 하다, 수반하다 ensure 보장하다 comfort 편안함, 안락함 firsthand 직접 cell service (모바일) 네트워크 연결 서비스 unreliable 신뢰할 수 없는, 불안정한

191 사실 관계 확인

번역 기사에서 알라크리텀 주식회사에 대해 명시한 것은?

(A) 아시아 내 충전소의 80퍼센트를 운영하고 있다.
(B) 2월에 본사를 로그레드로 이전한다.
(C) 1번 고속도로를 따라 400개의 PRO 충전소를 지었다.
(D) 3월에 충전소를 시범 운영할 예정이다.

해설 기사 후반부에서 시범 운영 사업소가 다음 달 초 로그레드에 문을 열 예정(A testing location will open at the beginning of next month in Logred)이라고 했는데, 기사 작성일이 2월 1일이므로 3월에 시범 운영할 예정임을 알 수 있다. 따라서 (D)가 정답이다.

어휘 operate 운영하다

192 세부 사항

번역 도표에 따르면, 어떤 지역에 고객이 가장 많을 것으로 예상되는가?

(A) 엘론델
(B) 서던 보렐비아
(C) 웨스턴 보렐비아
(D) 노스 쇼어

해설 도표를 보면 일일 고객 수(Customers per Day)가 가장 많을 것으로 예상되는 곳은 엘론델(Elondell)이므로, (A)가 정답이다.

193 주제 / 목적

번역 이메일을 쓴 목적은?

(A) 비용을 협상하려고
(B) 조언하려고
(C) 배송 지연 이유를 설명하려고
(D) 새 협력 관계를 제안하려고

해설 이메일 전반에서 지역 대기실에 냉방 장치를 추가할 것(adding air-conditioning to the waiting areas in that region)과 네트워크 서비스 문제에 대한 기술적 해결방안을 마련할 것(we will need a technological solution)을 제안하고 있다. 따라서 (B)가 정답이다.

어휘 negotiate 협상하다 explain 설명하다 suggest 제안하다

194 연계

번역 PRO 충전소의 어떤 시스템에 기술적 해결방안이 필요한가?

(A) 청소 시스템
(B) 식품 자동판매 시스템
(C) 조명 시스템
(D) 문자메시지 알림 시스템

해설 이메일의 중반부에서 트리그 씨는 1번 고속도로의 열악한 모바일 네트워크 연결 서비스가 PRO 충전소 대부분의 무선 네트워크를 불안정하게 만들어(poor cell service ~ will make the wireless networks at most PRO stations unreliable) 버릴 듯 하니 이에 대한 기술적 해결방안을 준비하자고 제안했다. 기사 중반부를 보면, 대기 중인 운전자들에게 휴대전화나 다른 모바일 기기로 문자메시지를 보내 충전 상태를 주기적으로 알려준다(The system will periodically notify waiting drivers ~ by sending texts to their cell phones or other mobile devices)고 되어 있으므로, 이 알림 시스템에 기술적 해결방안이 필요함을 알 수 있다. 따라서 (D)가 정답이다.

어휘 vending 자동판매, 판매 notification 알림, 통지

195 연계

번역 대기실 냉방 장치가 필요한 충전소는 몇 개인가?

(A) 10개
(B) 14개
(C) 20개
(D) 26개

해설 이메일의 초반부에서 웨스턴 보렐비아 지역 협력단체와의 회의 결과에 따라 해당 지역 대기실에 냉방 장치를 추가할 것을 제안한다(Following the meeting with our community partners in Western Borelvia ~ I suggest adding air-conditioning to the waiting areas in that region)고 했는데, 도표를 보면 웨스턴 보렐비아 지역에 지을 예정인 충전소는 20개라고 되어 있다. 따라서 (C)가 정답이다.

196-200 이메일 + 보도자료 + 이메일

발신: cbeker@yourworkstyle.net
수신: lroytenberg@charlottes.com; ajordan@charlottes.com
날짜: 1월 27일 오전 10시 2분
제목: 보도자료 초안
첨부: 🔗 보도자료 초안

로이텐버그 씨, 조던 씨께

196 보도자료 초안을 첨부했습니다. 일전에 전화로 논의했던 것처럼, 제 계약서에는 〈파인타운 위클리〉 담당자에게 보도자료를 제출하기 전에, 해당 프로젝트에 대해 논의하는 30분짜리 회의 1회와 두 분께서 수정을 원하는 사항을 반영하는 업무가 포함되어 있습니다.

이번 주에 들러도 되는지 알려주세요. 199 해당 공간을 사진에 담고 싶습니다. 건물의 역사적인 건축 양식이 고객에게 인기 있을 거라고 말씀하신 걸 기억하고 있거든요.

197 아울러 두 분 중 한 분이나 보 셰프님의 말씀을 직접 인용해야 할 것 같습니다. 예전에 〈파인타운 위클리〉와 일하면서 알게 된 사실인데, 인용구가 한 개도 없다면 이런 종류의 기사를 싣지 않을 겁니다.

캐시 베커

어휘 draft 초안 press release 보도자료 previously 이전에 contract 계약(서) additional 추가의 submit 제출하다

contact 담당자, 인맥　mention 언급하다　architecture 건축술, 건축 양식　quotation 인용(구)　run (신문, 잡지 등에) 싣다　piece 글, 기사

-초안-

샬롯츠가 문을 열다

[200] D 가와 오크 가 모퉁이에 위치한 샬롯츠가 2월 5일 금요일 문을 연다. [198] 소유주인 레본 로이텐버그 씨와 오브리 조던 씨는 향긋한 커피, 김이 모락모락 나는 에스프레소, 특선 제과류, 맛있는 카페 음식 등을 찾는 고객들을 맞을 생각에 들떠 있다. 이들의 목표는 샬롯츠가 오감을 만족시키는 모임 장소가 되어, 고객들에게 편안함과 친절한 서비스를 선사하는 것이다.

가장 최근 블루밍턴의 칸즈에서 근무했으며 수상 경력이 있는 수석 셰프 미첼 보 씨는 갓 구워낸 빵과 목초육에, 현지에서 재배한 채소를 곁들인 매력적인 메뉴를 개발했다. 제공되는 메뉴는 아침 및 점심 식사다. 보 셰프는 차와 허브 추출물을 활용한 품격 있는 냉, 온음료도 샬롯츠에 들여올 예정이다.

어휘　patron 고객, 후원자　aromatic 향이 좋은　specialty 전문 음식　savory 맛이 좋은　gathering 모임　indulge 마음껏 하다, (욕구, 관심 등을) 채우다　hospitality 환대　award-winning 상을 받은　enticing 매력적인, 유혹적인　accompaniment 반찬, 곁들이는 것　beverage 음료　infusion 혼합물, 추출물

발신: ajordan@charlottes.com
수신: cbeker@yourworkstyle.net
참조: lroytenberg@charlottes.com
날짜: 1월 28일 오전 8시 34분
제목: 회신: 보도자료 초안

베커 씨께,

로이텐버그 씨가 앞으로 며칠간 보스턴에 있을 거라서 저에게 보도자료 건을 맡아 달라고 부탁했어요. [199] 현장에 오고 싶다고 말씀하셨죠. 내일 1월 29일 오후 3시에 시간이 되시나요? 저는 개업식을 위해 장식을 하며 그곳에 하루 종일 있을 겁니다.

훌륭한 초안을 작성해서 보내주셨는데요. [200] 제가 봤을 때 딱 한 가지 문제점은 저희 회사 사무실과 카페 위치를 혼동하신 것입니다. 사실 카페는 C 가와 메이플 가 모퉁이에 있어요. 아울러, 로이텐버그 씨는 영업 시간을 포함하고 싶어합니다. 매일 오전 8시부터 오후 4시까지예요. 보 셰프님께 952-555-0133으로 전화하셔서 특선 메뉴에 대한 인용구를 받아보세요.

오브리 조던

어휘　take the lead 주도권을 잡다　available 시간이 되는　decorate 장식하다　put together 만들어 내다, 작성하다　mix up 혼동하다　corporate 회사의　actually 사실　operating hours 영업시간

---

196 추론 / 암시

번역　베커 씨는 누구이겠는가?
(A) 건축가
(B) 프리랜서 작가
(C) 전문 요리사
(D) 로이텐버그 씨의 비서

해설　첫 번째 이메일의 첫 단락에서 베커 씨는 보도자료 초안(My first draft of the press release)을 첨부했다고 하며 〈파인타운 위클리〉 담당자에게 제출하기 전에 로이텐버그 씨와 조던 씨가 원하는 수정 사항을 반영하기로 되어있다는 본인의 계약서 내용(my contract includes ~ any changes you would like me to make before I submit the press release to my contacts at *Pinetown Weekly*)을 언급했다. 따라서 그녀가 프리랜서 작가라고 추론할 수 있으므로, (B)가 정답이다.

197 세부 사항

번역　첫 번째 이메일에 따르면, 보도자료에 무엇을 추가해야 하는가?
(A) 인용구
(B) 헤드라인
(C) 인맥의 전화번호
(D) 이전에 게재된 사진

해설　첫 번째 이메일의 세 번째 단락에서 로이텐버그 씨, 조던 씨, 혹은 보 셰프의 말을 직접 인용해야 할 것 같다고 한 후, 〈파인타운 위클리〉가 인용구가 없는 기사를 싣지 않는다(they will not run a piece like this without at least one quotation)고 덧붙였다. 따라서 (A)가 정답이다.

어휘　publish 출판하다, 게재하다

198 세부 사항

번역　샬롯츠는 어떤 유형의 업체인가?
(A) 농장
(B) 케이터링 서비스
(C) 카페
(D) 슈퍼마켓 체인점

해설　보도자료의 첫 번째 단락에서 샬롯츠의 소유주들이 향긋한 커피, 김이 모락모락 나는 에스프레소, 특선 제과류, 맛있는 카페 음식 등을 찾는 고객들을 맞을 생각에 들떠 있다(Owners ~ to welcome patrons for an aromatic cup of coffee or steaming espresso, specialty pastries, and savory café fare)고 했으므로, 샬롯츠가 카페임을 알 수 있다. 따라서 (C)가 정답이다.

199 연계

번역　조던 씨가 베커 씨를 1월 29일에 샬롯츠로 초청한 이유는?
(A) 샌드위치를 시식하게 하려고
(B) 개업식 장식을 도와달라고 하려고
(C) 건물 사진을 찍을 수 있게 하려고
(D) 로이텐버그 씨와 만나게 하려고

해설 두 번째 이메일의 첫 번째 단락에서 조던 씨는 베커 씨가 일전에 카페에 방문하고 싶다고 했던 것을 언급하며 1월 29일에 올 수 있는지(are you available ~ January 29 ~ ?) 물었다. 첫 번째 이메일의 두 번째 단락을 보면, 베커 씨가 해당 장소를 사진에 담고 싶다(I would like to take photos of the space)고 했던 것을 확인할 수 있다. 따라서 베커 씨이 사진 촬영 요청을 수락하기 위한 초청임을 알 수 있으므로, (C)가 정답이다.

어휘 sample 시식하다

> ▸▸ Paraphrasing 지문의 take photos of the space
> → 정답의 take pictures of a building

200 연계

번역 D 가와 오크 가 모퉁이에 위치한 것은?

(A) 베커 씨의 재택근무 사무실
(B) 〈파인타운 위클리〉 본사
(C) 로이텐버그 씨의 현재 거주지
(D) 회사 사무실 건물

해설 보도자료의 첫 번째 단락을 보면 샬롯츠가 D 가와 오크 가 모퉁이에 위치해 있다(located at Avenue D and Oak Street)고 쓰여 있다. 하지만 두 번째 이메일의 두 번째 단락에서 조던 씨는 베커 씨가 회사 사무실과 카페 위치를 혼동(you have mixed up the location of our corporate office and the café)했다고 지적하며 올바른 카페 위치를 알려 주었다. 즉, D 가와 오크 가 모퉁이에 있는 것은 카페가 아닌 회사 사무실이므로, (D)가 정답이다.

어휘 headquarters 본사 current 현재의 residence 거주지

101 (C)	102 (A)	103 (B)	104 (D)	105 (B)
106 (A)	107 (A)	108 (B)	109 (D)	110 (D)
111 (A)	112 (D)	113 (C)	114 (D)	115 (B)
116 (B)	117 (A)	118 (C)	119 (A)	120 (D)
121 (C)	122 (C)	123 (D)	124 (B)	125 (A)
126 (B)	127 (C)	128 (B)	129 (D)	130 (C)
131 (C)	132 (A)	133 (A)	134 (D)	135 (D)
136 (A)	137 (D)	138 (C)	139 (D)	140 (C)
141 (D)	142 (A)	143 (D)	144 (A)	145 (D)
146 (B)	147 (C)	148 (C)	149 (B)	150 (D)
151 (C)	152 (D)	153 (C)	154 (C)	155 (B)
156 (A)	157 (D)	158 (B)	159 (C)	160 (A)
161 (C)	162 (D)	163 (A)	164 (B)	165 (C)
166 (B)	167 (A)	168 (C)	169 (A)	170 (C)
171 (D)	172 (D)	173 (D)	174 (C)	175 (A)
176 (A)	177 (C)	178 (B)	179 (D)	180 (B)
181 (D)	182 (B)	183 (A)	184 (A)	185 (B)
186 (A)	187 (C)	188 (C)	189 (D)	190 (B)
191 (B)	192 (D)	193 (C)	194 (C)	195 (C)
196 (D)	197 (B)	198 (A)	199 (C)	200 (C)

PART 5

101 동사 어형 _ 현재완료

해설 빈칸은 has와 함께 현재완료 동사를 이루는 과거분사 자리이다. 따라서 (C) merged가 정답이다. 부사 recently가 현재완료와 자주 쓰인다는 것을 알아두면 좋다. (A) merge는 동사원형, (B) merger는 가산명사, (D) merging은 동명사/현재분사로 구조상 빈칸에 들어갈 수 없다.

번역 밴티지 오토모티브 디자인은 최근 팔랙스 사와 합병했다.

어휘 recently 최근 merge 합병하다

102 접속사 어휘

해설 빈칸 앞에서 주말에 비가 올 것으로 예보되고 있다(Rain is predicted this weekend)고 했고, 뒤에서 이를 근거로 회사 야유회를 미뤄야 한다(the office picnic will have to be postponed)고 판단하고 있다. 따라서 '그래서'라는 의미의 (A) so가 정답이다. 참고로, (B) for가 등위접속사로 쓰일 경우, for 뒤에 원인을 설명하는 절이 와야 한다. (D) nor는 앞에 부정문이 와야 하고, 뒤에는 주어와 동사가 도치된 절이 와야 한다.

번역 이번 주말에 비가 올 것으로 예보되고 있어서, 회사 야유회는 연기되어야 할 것이다.

어휘 predict 예측하다, 예보하다 postpone 연기하다

103 인칭대명사의 격 _ 소유격

해설 전치사 of의 목적어 역할을 하는 명사 order를 한정 수식하는 자리이다. 따라서 소유격 인칭대명사 (B) your가 정답이다.

번역 그리어 화물이 귀하의 주문 배송을 신속히 처리할 수 없다면, 대체 가능한 다른 배송업체를 이용하십시오.

어휘 alternative 대안이 되는, 대체 가능한 expedite 더 신속히 처리하다

104 전치사 어휘

해설 명사구 different regions를 목적어로 취해 dishes를 수식하는 전치사 자리이다. '다양한 지역'은 요리들(dishes)의 출처라고 볼 수 있으므로, '~로부터, ~출신의'라는 의미의 (D) from이 정답이다.

번역 이번 주에 카페테리아에서 전 세계 다양한 지역의 요리들을 특별히 선보인다.

어휘 feature 특별히 포함하다, 선보이다

105 명사 자리 _ to부정사의 목적어

해설 형용사 possible의 수식을 받으며 to visit의 목적어 역할을 하는 명사 자리이다. 따라서 방문할 곳을 나타내는 (B) locations(장소)가 정답이다. (A) locating은 동명사/현재분사, (C) located는 동사/과거분사, (D) locate는 동사로 빈칸에 들어갈 수 없다.

번역 파텔 씨는 회사의 새 창고로 쓰일 수 있는 장소들을 방문하기 위해 오늘 델리에 올 것이다.

어휘 warehouse 창고 locate ~의 위치를 찾다, (특정 위치에) 두다

106 전치사 자리 _ 어휘

해설 명사구 its beginnings를 목적어로 취하는 전치사 자리이다. 앞에 현재완료 동사(has grown)가 있으므로, 과거 시점(its beginnings)부터 현재까지의 시간을 나타내는 단어가 들어가야 자연스럽다. 따라서 '~이래로'라는 의미의 (A) since가 정답이다. 참고로, since는 부사절 접속사나 부사로도 쓰일 수 있다. (C) except는 '~을 제외하고'라는 뜻으로 문맥상 어색하며, (B) such는 한정사/대명사/부사, (D) however는 부사/부사절 접속사로 빈칸에 들어갈 수 없다.

번역 클라이드웨이 주식회사는 작고 구석진 식료품점으로 시작한 이래로 급속히 성장해 왔다.

어휘 dramatically 급속히, 극적으로 grocery 식료품

107 동사 어휘

해설 가주어 it의 진주어 역할을 하는 to부정사의 동사원형 자리로, 목적어인 the guidelines for luggage size와 어울리는 타동사를 선택해야 한다. 항공편 예약 시(When booking a flight) 수하물 크기 지침은 확인해 보는 게 좋다는 내용이 되어야 자연스럽다. 따라서 '확인하다, 알아보다'라는 의미의 (A) check가 정답이다.

번역 항공편을 예약할 때 해당 항공사 웹사이트에서 수하물 크기 지침을 확인하는 것이 현명하다.

어휘 book 예약하다 guideline 지침 luggage 수하물 approve
승인하다 list 열거하다, 기재하다

108 형용사 어휘

해설 '너무 ~해서 ~하다'라는 의미의 「so + 형용사 + that + 주어 동사」
구문으로, 곡의 일부를 단순화한(has simplified) 이유를 나타내
는 형용사가 빈칸에 들어가야 한다. 따라서 '복잡한'이라는 의미의
(B) complex가 정답이다.

번역 곡이 너무 복잡해서 작곡가는 라이브 공연을 위해 일부를 간단하게 만
들었다.

어휘 composer 작곡가 simplify 간소화하다, 간단하게 만들다
direct 직접적인 favorable 호의적인 helpful 도움이 되는

109 형용사 자리

해설 「주어(The test group) + 동사(found) + 목적어(the illustrations
in the appliance users' guide) + 목적격 보어(to be highly
-------)」 구조의 5형식 문장이다. 따라서 빈칸에는 to be의 보어 역
할을 하며 부사 highly의 수식을 받는 형용사가 들어가야 하므로,
(D) informative(유익한, 유용한)가 정답이다. (A) inform은 동사,
(B) information은 명사, (C) informatively는 부사로 품사상 빈칸
에 들어갈 수 없다.

번역 체험단은 기기 사용설명서에 나오는 삽화들이 매우 유익하다고 여
겼다.

어휘 illustration 삽화 appliance 기기

110 부사 어휘

해설 a novice builder를 적절히 강조하는 부사를 선택해야 한다. DIY(셀
프) 작업에 대한 설명서(directions)가 초보자도 보고 따라할 수 있을
만큼 충분히 포괄적이고 상세하다(comprehensive enough)는 내
용이 되어야 자연스럽다. 따라서 '~조차, ~도'라는 의미의 (D) even
이 정답이다.

번역 마스다의 DIY 작업에 대한 설명서는 초보 건축가에게도 충분히 포괄
적이고 상세하다.

어휘 directions 설명(서) comprehensive 포괄적인, 상세한
novice 초보자

111 대명사 어휘

해설 동사 had의 주어 역할을 하는 자리로, 전치사구 of the two
candidates의 수식을 받는다. 숫자 two와 어울리며 사람을 대신
하는 대명사가 필요하므로, '둘 중 어느 누구도 아니다'라는 의미의
(A) Neither가 정답이다. (B) Nobody는 no one과 같은 뜻으로 뒤
에 of 없이 단독으로 쓰이고, (C) None은 of와 쓰일 경우 뒤에 셋 이
상의 복수명사나 불가산명사, 혹은 대명사가 와야 한다.

번역 그 직책 지원자 두 명 중 어느 누구도 필요한 자격을 갖추지 못했다.

어휘 candidate 지원자, 후보자 qualification 자격

112 명사 어휘

해설 빈칸에는 construction과 함께 복합명사를 이루어 전치사 in의 목적
어 역할을 하는 단어가 들어가야 한다. 인력에 대한 수요(need)가 증
가(has grown)할 만한 곳은 분야나 업계이므로, (D) industry가 정
답이다.

번역 최근 몇 년간 건설업계에서는 고도로 훈련된 전기 기사에 대한 수요가
빠르게 증가했다.

어휘 electrician 전기 기사 construction 건설 rapidly 빠르게
employment 고용 activity 활동 knowledge 지식

113 인칭대명사의 격 _ 목적격 _ 수 일치

해설 동사원형 propose의 목적어 역할을 하는 자리이다. 제안의 대상은
앞서 언급된 마케팅 예산안(a marketing budget)이므로, 3인칭 단
수 대명사 (C) it이 정답이다.

번역 데일리 씨는 마케팅 예산을 준비해서 이를 고객 회의에서 제안할 예정
이다.

어휘 budget 예산 propose 제안하다

114 동사 어휘

해설 「asked + 목적어(sales staff) + 목적격 보어(to ------- travel
expenditures)」 구조에서 목적격 보어에 해당하는 동사로, 출장 경
비와 관련하여 영업사원들에게 요구되는 행위를 나타낸다. 비용 절감
에 일조하기(to help cut costs) 위해서는 출장 경비를 줄여야 하므
로, '제한하다, 한정하다'라는 의미의 (D) limit가 정답이다.

번역 실바 씨는 영업사원들에게 비용 절감에 일조하는 차원에서 출장 경비
를 제한하라고 요청했다.

어휘 expenditure 경비, 지출 convince 납득시키다, 확신시키다
require 요청하다 decide 결정하다

115 전치사 자리 _ 어휘

해설 명사구 the previous administration을 목적어로 취하는 전치사
자리이다. 빈칸 앞 과거분사 made가 수식하는 those는 policies를
대신하며, 이전 행정부(the previous administration)는 해당 정책
을 만든 주체라고 보는 것이 타당하다. 따라서 '~에 의하여'라는 의미
의 (B) by가 정답이다. (A) any는 대명사/한정사, (D) and는 등위접
속사로 구조상 빈칸에 들어갈 수 없다.

번역 시 의회는 특정 정책들, 특히 이전 행정부가 만든 것들을 논의할 것
이다.

어휘 city council 시 의회 discuss 논의하다 policy 정책
particularly 특히 previous 이전의 administration 행정부

116 전치사 어휘

해설 동사구 (are) divided evenly와 명사구 the entire waitstaff를 적
절히 연결하는 전치사를 선택해야 한다. 팁은 식당 종업원 전체를 대
상으로 분배되는 것이므로, '(셋 이상의) 사이에서, ~의 사이에서 분

배하여'라는 의미의 (B) among이 정답이다. 「among＋복수명사」와 「among＋집합명사(eg. staff, crowd)」는 빈출 표현이므로 암기해 두자.

번역 서빙 직원들의 팁은 매 교대 근무가 끝나갈 때 모아서 전 종업원들 사이에 똑같이 나눈다.

어휘 pool 모으다 divide 나누다 evenly 고르게, 균등하게 entire 전체의

117 명사 자리 _ 어휘

해설 형용사 successful의 수식을 받으면서 동사 has made의 목적어 역할을 하는 명사 자리로, 보기에서 (A) investments(투자)와 (D) investor(투자자) 중 하나를 선택해야 한다. 빈칸 뒤 전치사 in과 함께 '~에 성공적인 투자를 했다'라는 내용을 완성해야 하므로, (A) investments가 정답이 된다. 가산명사 (D) investor는 앞에 한 정사가 붙거나 복수형으로 쓰여야 하며, (B) invested는 동사/과거분사, (C) invest는 동사로 품사상 빈칸에 들어갈 수 없다.

번역 코스트파 애널리틱스 주식회사는 신흥 데이터 업체 두 곳에 성공적으로 투자했다.

어휘 emerging 최근 생겨난, 신흥의 investment 투자 investor 투자자

118 부사 자리 _ 동사 수식 _ 비교급

해설 비교급 표현을 없애고 보면 「주어(Vallentrade)＋동사(manages)＋목적어(clients' accounts)」 구조의 완전한 절이 남는다. 즉, 빈칸에는 동사 manages를 수식하는 부사가 들어가야 하므로, (C) conservatively(보수적으로)가 정답이다. (A) conserves는 동사, (B) conservative는 형용사, (D) conserving은 동명사/현재분사로 품사상 빈칸에 들어갈 수 없다.

번역 밸런트레이드는 대부분의 다른 종합 증권회사보다 더 보수적으로 고객들의 계좌를 관리한다.

어휘 account 계정, 계좌 brokerage firm 종합 증권회사 conserve 보존하다 conservative 보수적인 conservatively 보수적으로

119 전치사 어휘

해설 빈칸에는 and와 어울려 쓰여 범위(10 and 30 degrees Celsius)를 나타내는 전치사가 들어가야 하므로, '~ 사이에'라는 의미의 (A) between이 정답이다.

번역 태블릿 컴퓨터가 작동하기에 이상적인 온도는 섭씨 10-30도 사이다.

어휘 ideal 이상적인 temperature 온도

120 재귀대명사

해설 who가 이끄는 관계사절에서 동사 have introduced의 목적어 역할을 하는 자리이다. 관계사절의 주어인 who는 선행사 people을 대신하고, 소개의 대상은 사람들 자신이 되어야 문맥상 자연스럽다. 따라서 재귀대명사 (D) themselves가 정답이다.

번역 목공 클럽 회의에서 공개적으로 자신을 소개한 사람들 중에서 절반 정도가 상업시설 도급업자다.

어휘 publicly 공개적으로 carpentry 목공(품) commercial 상업의, 상업적인 contractor 도급업자, 계약자

121 to부정사

해설 앞에 완전한 절(the technician will be on Status Road)이 왔고 뒤에는 명사구(two gas stoves)가 있으므로 빈칸에 또 다른 동사가 들어갈 수는 없다. 따라서 two gas stoves를 목적어로 취하면서 앞에 온 절을 수식하는 to부정사 (C) to service가 정답이다. 여기서 to service는 부사적 용법으로 쓰여 목적을 나타낸다. (A) serviced는 동사/과거분사, (B) service는 동사/명사, (D) is servicing은 현재 진행 동사 형태로 품사상 빈칸에 들어갈 수 없다.

번역 목요일에 기술자가 두 대의 가스 난로를 점검해 주러 스라투스 로에 올 것이다.

어휘 technician 기술자 service (기계 등을) 점검하다, 정비하다; 서비스, 용역

122 현재분사

해설 The spreadsheet부터 quarter까지가 주어, is attached가 동사인 문장이다. 따라서 빈칸에는 명사 data를 목적어로 취하면서 앞에 나온 spreadsheet을 수식하는 준동사가 들어가야 하므로, 능동의 의미를 내포한 현재분사 (C) containing이 정답이다. (A) contains는 본동사, (B) contained는 본동사/과거분사로 빈칸에 들어갈 수 없다. (D) containable은 형용사로 두 명사 spreadsheet와 data를 연결해주지 못한다.

번역 4분기 소매 판매에 관한 데이터를 포함하는 스프레드시트가 첨부되어 있다.

어휘 retail 소매(의) quarter 분기 attach 첨부하다 contain 포함하다, ~이 들어 있다

123 명사 어휘

해설 빈칸에는 홍보 전단(promotional flyer)에 나올만한 것이 들어가야 한다. 따라서 '할인 품목(the discounted items)에 관한 설명'이라는 내용을 완성하는 (D) descriptions(설명, 기술)가 정답이다. description이 전치사 of와 자주 쓰인다는 것을 알아두면 좋다.

번역 할인 품목에 관한 모든 설명은 저희 주간 홍보 전단을 확인하세요.

어휘 promotional 홍보의 flyer 전단 complete 완전한, 전체의 exchange 교환 support 지원, 지지 receipt 영수증

124 형용사 어휘

해설 고객들(customers)의 특성을 적절히 묘사하는 형용사를 선택해야 한다. 처음 연락하기 전에(before contacting them for the first time) 조사를 해봐야 할 고객은 앞으로 거래할 가능성이 있는 잠재 고객이라고 볼 수 있다. 따라서 '잠재적인, 가능성이 있는'이라는 의미의 (B) potential이 정답이다. potential customer/buyer/client는

빈출 표현으로 암기해 두는 것이 좋다.

번역 신입 영업사원들은 잠재 고객에게 처음 연락하기 전에 그들의 업체에 대해 알아보라는 지시를 받는다.

어휘 be instructed to ~하도록 지시를 받다 total 전체의, 총 equal 동등한 factual 사실에 기반을 둔

125 접속사 자리

해설 두 개의 완전한 절을 이어주는 접속사 자리이다. 따라서 '~할 때마다, ~할 때는 언제든지'라는 의미의 부사절 접속사 (A) whenever가 정답이다. (B) simply, (C) accordingly, (D) quite는 모두 부사로 절을 이끌 수 없다.

번역 온라인 뱅킹을 이용하신다면 가장 편리한 때 요금을 납부하실 수 있습니다.

어휘 pay a bill 요금을 납부하다 convenient 편리한 simply 그저, 단지 accordingly 그에 맞춰 quite 꽤

126 상관접속사 자리

해설 정식 교육(formal instruction)과 직무 경험(professional experience)은 모두 인턴십을 통해 제공되어야 할(to provide) 사항이다. 따라서 빈칸에는 to provide의 목적어 역할을 하는 두 명사구를 이어줄 등위/상관접속사가 들어가야 하므로, '~뿐만 아니라 ~도'라는 의미의 (B) as well as가 정답이다. (A) above all은 부사로 품사상 빈칸에 들어갈 수 없고, 부사절 접속사 (C) now that 뒤에는 절이, to부정사 관용표현 (D) in order to 뒤에는 동사원형이 와야 한다.

번역 저희 인턴십에서는 정식 교육과 직무 경험을 모두 제공하기 위해 강의를 실제 프로젝트와 결합합니다.

어휘 combine 결합하다 lecture 강의 formal 정식의, 공식적인 instruction 교육, 설명 professional 직업의, 전문적인 above all 특히, 무엇보다도 now that ~이므로 in order to ~하기 위해

127 명사 자리 _ 동사의 주어 _ 복합명사

해설 문두에 온 명사 Employee가 동사 include와 수가 일치하지 않으므로, 빈칸에는 Employee와 함께 복합명사를 이루어 include의 주어 역할을 하는 복수명사가 들어가야 한다. 따라서 (C) benefits(혜택들)가 정답이다. (A) beneficial은 형용사, (B) beneficially는 부사, (D) benefited는 동사/과거분사로 품사상 빈칸에 들어갈 수 없다.

번역 메드마일 벤처의 직원 혜택에는 스톡옵션과 예정된 급여 인상이 포함된다.

어휘 include 포함하다 share option 스톡옵션 (주식매입권) scheduled 예정된 raise 급여 인상

128 명사 어휘

해설 필요한 허가서를 받고자(hope to get necessary permits) 하는 주체는 사람 또는 단체가 되어야 한다. 따라서 '개발업자, 개발업체'라는 의미의 (B) developers가 정답이다.

번역 도시 개발업자들은 미네르바 가에 20층짜리 사무실 건물을 짓기 위해 필요한 허가서를 받기를 바란다.

어휘 permit 허가증 agenda 의제 avenue 거리, 도로 boundary 경계

129 형용사 자리 _ 명사 수식

해설 '체계, 제도'라는 의미의 명사 framework을 수식하는 형용사 자리이다. 따라서 (D) regulatory(규제의, 규제력을 지닌)가 정답이다. (C) regulator는 '규제 기관[담당자]'이라는 뜻으로 framework과 복합명사를 이루기엔 어색하고, (A) regulate와 (B) regulates는 동사로 품사상 빈칸에 들어갈 수 없다.

번역 감사부 담당자들은 정기적으로 규제 제도의 변동사항을 감시한다.

어휘 compliance 준수 regularly 정기적으로

130 명사 어휘

해설 동사 achieves의 목적어 역할을 하는 명사 자리로, 성취의 대상을 나타내는 단어가 들어가야 한다. 따라서 desirable과 함께 '바람직한 결과[성과]'라는 의미를 완성하는 (C) outcomes가 정답이다. desirable outcome/result는 빈출 표현으로 암기해 두는 것이 좋다.

번역 X250 휴대용 히터는 특별히 고온에 도달하지 않고도 바람직한 결과를 낸다.

어휘 portable 휴대용의 achieve 성취하다, 달성하다 desirable 바람직한 reach 도달하다, ~에 이르다 practice 관행, 실천 factor 요인 dimension 크기, 규모

PART 6

131-134 정보

댄포스 패션즈 온라인 사이트에서 구입해 주셔서 감사합니다. 저희 품질관리팀은 고객 만족 보장을 위해 포장 131 **전** 모든 제품을 꼼꼼하게 검수하고 있습니다. 132 **구입하신 제품에 대해 전적으로 만족하시기를 바랍니다.** 그렇지 못한 경우 편리하게 교환 또는 환불해 드립니다. 다른 사이즈, 색상, 무늬 등이 필요하시거나 다른 어떤 이유로든 불만족스러우시다면 service@danforthfashions.com으로 연락해 주십시오. 교환이 즉시 133 **처리될 겁니다.** 제품을 환불하시려면 주문품에 포함된 선불 환불 배송 라벨을 이용하셔서, 사용 또는 손상되지 않은 원래 포장 상태 그대로 보내주십시오. 환불 배송비를 134 **제외하고** 원래 결제 수단으로 환불해 드립니다.

어휘 quality-control 품질관리 inspect 점검하다 packaging 포장 ensure 보장하다, 반드시 ~하게 하다 satisfaction 만족 exchange 교환 dissatisfied 불만스러운 refund 환불 prepaid 선불된 undamaged 손상되지 않은 issue a refund 환불해 주다 method of payment 결제 수단 shipping fee 배송비

131 전치사 자리 _ 어휘

해설 빈칸은 명사 packaging을 목적어로 취해 앞에 온 절(Our quality-control team carefully inspects all products)을 수식해 주는 전치사 자리이다. 제품 검수(inspects all products)는 포장(packaging) 전에 이루어지는 것이므로, '~전에, ~에 앞서'라는 의미의 (C) prior to가 정답이다. (A) in case는 뒤에 절이 와야 하고, (B) as much as는 '~만큼 많이', (D) in keeping with는 '~와 일치하여'라는 뜻으로 빈칸에 적절하지 않다.

132 문맥에 맞는 문장 고르기

번역 (A) 구입하신 제품에 대해 전적으로 만족하시기를 바랍니다.
(B) 올 여름 저희 웹사이트를 다시 디자인할 것으로 예상합니다.
(C) 단골 고객 여러분 모두를 소중하게 여깁니다.
(D) 귀하의 우편물 수신 주소가 변경되었음을 알았습니다.

해설 빈칸 앞 문장에서 고객 만족 보장을 위해 모든 제품을 꼼꼼하게 검수하고 있다(Our quality-control team carefully inspects all products ~ to ensure customer satisfaction)고 했고, 뒤 문장에서는 '그렇지 못한 경우 편리하게 교환 또는 환불이 가능하다(If not, we make exchanges or returns easy)'라고 했다. 따라서 빈칸에도 제품에 대한 고객 만족도와 관련된 내용이 들어가야 자연스러우므로, (A)가 정답이다. 참고로, 뒤 문장의 If not은 '만족하지 못했을 경우(=If you are not entirely pleased with your purchase)'를 나타낸다.

어휘 entirely 전적으로 purchase 구입 loyal customer 단골 고객 notice 알아차리다

133 동사 자리 _ 태 _ 시제

해설 주어 Your exchange의 동사 자리로, 보기에서 (A) will be processed, (B) was processed, (C) is processing 중 하나를 선택해야 한다. 교환(exchange)은 처리되는 대상이며, 회사에 연락할 시 이루어질 조치이므로, 수동태 미래동사인 (A) will be processed가 정답이 된다.

어휘 process 처리하다

134 전치사 어휘

해설 명사구 the return shipping fee를 목적어로 취하는 전치사 자리로, 환불 배송비(the return shipping fee)와 환불되는 금액(refunds)의 관계를 나타내는 단어가 들어가야 한다. 따라서 '~을 제외한, ~을 뺀'이라는 의미의 (D) minus가 정답이다.

어휘 aboard 탑승한

135-138 공지

> 알덴 아프너 인더스트리즈 직원 여러분께 알립니다.
>
> 새로운 이메일 소프트웨어로의 전환이 5월 2일 일요일 오후 11시에 시작된다는 점을 기억하시기 바랍니다. 연락처, 일정 이벤트 등을 포함해 계정에 있는 135기존 정보 일체는 5월 3일 월요일 오전 4시까지 새 시스템으로 이전될 것입니다. 모든 잠재적 문제들을 예측하고 이들에 대한 해결책을 제공해 드리기 위해 열심히 작업 중입니다만, 일부 직원들께서는 전환 이후 계정에 로그인을 시도할 136때 어려움을 겪으실 수도 있습니다. 아울러, 그럴 가능성은 희박하지만, 일부 정보가 손실될 수도 있습니다. 137그러니 중요한 이메일 파일은 가급적 빨리 백업해 두십시오. 138이와 관련해 도움이 필요하시면 IT 부서로 연락하십시오. 직원 여러분이 신규 소프트웨어의 주요 기능에 익숙해질 수 있도록 다음 주에 교육 일정이 잡힐 예정입니다.

어휘 attention 알립니다, 주목하세요 switch 전환 account 계정 diligently 열심히, 부지런히 anticipate 예측하다 potential 잠재적인, 가능성이 있는 attempt 시도하다 in addition 게다가 remote possibility 희박한 가능성 critical 대단히 중요한 familiarize 익숙하게 하다 function 기능

135 형용사 자리 _ 명사 수식 _ 현재분사

해설 빈칸이 한정사 All과 명사 information 사이에 있으므로, 빈칸에는 information을 수식하는 형용사 또는 information과 복합명사를 이루는 명사가 들어갈 수 있다. 문맥상 '현재 계정에 있는 정보'라는 내용이 되어야 자연스러우므로, '기존의, 현재의'라는 뜻의 현재분사형 형용사 (D) existing이 정답이다.

어휘 exist 존재하다 existence 존재

136 부사절 접속사 _ 부사절의 축약

해설 계정에 로그인 하려는 시도를 할(attempting to log in to their accounts) 때 어려움을 겪을지도 모른다는 내용이 되어야 자연스럽다. 따라서 절에서 축약된 분사구문과 쓰일 수 있는 (A) when(~할 때)이 정답이다. (B) plus는 전치사로 쓰여 빈칸에 들어갈 수 있지만, 어려움을 겪는 것과 로그인을 시도하는 것은 유사한 내용이 아니므로 문맥상 적절하지 않다. attempting이 명사 difficulty를 수식해주는 현재분사가 아니므로 부사인 (C) already는 빈칸에 들어갈 수 없다. 소유격 관계대명사 (D) whose 다음에는 「명사+동사」가 와야 한다.

137 접속부사

해설 앞 문장에서 새 소프트웨어로 전환 시 일부 정보가 손실될(some information may be lost) 가능성이 있다는 문제점을 언급했고, 빈칸 뒤에서는 중요한 이메일 파일은 가급적 빨리 백업하라(be sure to back up any critical e-mail files as soon as possible)며 당부했다. 즉 앞에서 설명한 문제점이 백업을 하라고 당부하는 이유가 되므로, '그러니(까)'라는 의미의 (D) For this reason이 정답이다.

어휘 previously 이전에 otherwise 그렇지 않으면 even so 그렇기는 하지만

138 문맥에 맞는 문장 고르기

번역 (A) 신규 소프트웨어는 이번 주에 주문할 예정입니다.
(B) 현재 시스템은 6월에 재가동될 예정입니다.
(C) 이와 관련해 도움이 필요하시면 IT 부서로 연락하십시오.
(D) 이러한 경우, 스스로 설치를 완료해야 합니다.

해설 빈칸 앞 문장에서 소프트웨어 전환 시 일부 정보가 손실될 가능성이 있으니 중요한 이메일 파일은 가급적 빨리 백업해 두라(be sure to back up any critical e-mail files as soon as possible)고 당부했고, 뒤 문장에서는 다음 주에 새로운 소프트웨어 관련 교육 일정이 잡힐 예정(A training session will be scheduled next week)이라며 다른 일정을 언급했다. 따라서 빈칸에는 이메일 백업이나 새 소프트웨어 관련 내용이 들어가야 하는데, 보기 중에서는 백업 관련 도움(assistance with this)을 받을 수 있는 부서를 안내한 (C)가 가장 적절하다. 새 소프트웨어가 곧 설치될 예정이므로 (A), (B)는 적절하지 않으며, 설치를 스스로 완료해야 할 경우가 앞에서 언급된 바 없으므로 (D)도 정답이 될 수 없다.

어휘 reactivate 재가동하다 assistance 도움 complete 완료하다 installation 설치

139-142 이메일

발신: 홍 트롱 〈htruong@jansenwebbfoundation.ca〉
발신일: 11월 16일 금요일
수신: 직원, 친구, 이해관계자 여러분
제목: JWF의 새로운 예산 담당자

JWF 팀원 여러분, 그리고 지역 협력단체 여러분께:

¹³⁹모두 잘 지내고 계시길 바랍니다. 소피아 바르가스 씨가 얀센 웹 재단의 새 예산 담당자로 ¹⁴⁰채용되었음을 알려드리고자 합니다. 바르가스 씨는 비영리 부문의 재정 ¹⁴¹관리 분야에서 훌륭한 경력을 갖추고 있습니다.

바르가스 씨는 최근 위니펙에 있는 로턴 어린이 센터에서의 경험을 비롯해, 기관 재무 분야에서 쌓은 풍부한 경험을 가져올 것입니다. 오늘 아침부터 근무하기 시작했으니 잠시 들러 그녀에게 ¹⁴²여러분 자신을 소개하는 시간을 가져 보세요.

홍 트롱

CEO, 얀센 웹 재단

어휘 stakeholder 이해당사자, 주주 budget 예산 foundation 재단 background 배경 fiscal 재정의, 회계의 nonprofit 비영리의 sector 부문 a wealth of 풍부한 organizational 조직의, 기관의 recently 최근 employment 근무, 고용

139 문맥에 맞는 문장 고르기

번역 (A) 이것은 신속한 요청입니다.
(B) 아낌없는 기부에 감사드립니다.
(C) 여기 오신 모두를 환영합니다.
(D) 모두 잘 지내고 계시길 바랍니다.

해설 빈칸이 이메일의 첫 문장이고, 뒤에서는 바르가스 씨의 채용 소식을 전하고 싶다고만(I just want to let you know that ~) 쓰여 있다. 따라서 빈칸에는 수신인들에게 전하는 인사말이 들어가야 자연스러우므로, 안부(I hope that all are well)를 전하는 (D)가 정답이다. 이 메일의 수신인 모두가 새로 채용된 사람들은 아니므로 (C)는 적절하지 않다.

어휘 request 요청 prompt 신속한, 지체 없는 generous 후한, 너그러운 contribution 기여, 기부금

140 동사 어형 _ 태 _ 시제

해설 that절의 주어 Sofia Vargas의 동사 자리이다. 바르가스 씨는 채용되는 대상이며, 두 번째 단락에서 그녀가 오늘 아침에 근무를 시작했다(Ms. Vargas started her employment with us this morning)고 했으므로, 채용이 이미 이루어졌음을 알 수 있다. 따라서 현재완료 수동태 동사인 (C) has been hired가 정답이다.

141 명사 어휘

해설 전치사 in의 목적어 역할을 하는 자리로, 형용사 fiscal과 어울려 쓰이는 명사를 선택해야 한다. 경력(background)은 특정 업계나 분야에서 쌓는 것이므로, fiscal과 함께 '재정 관리 (분야)'라는 의미를 완성하는 (D) management(관리, 운영)가 정답이다. (C) running도 '운영, 경영'이라는 뜻으로 쓰일 수 있지만, 분야가 아닌 운영되는 방식이나 행위를 가리키며 smooth(순조로운), day-to-day(그날그날의)와 같은 형용사와 어울려 쓰인다.

어휘 referral 소개, 위탁 administrator 관리자, 행정인

142 재귀대명사 _ 어휘

해설 명령문의 동사 introduce의 목적어 역할을 하는 자리이다. 바르가스 씨에게 소개할 대상은 명령문의 생략된 주어인 you와 동일한 사람이 되어야 자연스럽다. 따라서 2인칭 재귀대명사 (A) yourself가 정답이다.

143-146 전단

자메이카 국립 관광기구에서 무료 문화 입장권 제공

자메이카 국립 관광기구(JAMTO)에서 다양한 문화적 명소의 무료 입장을 제공하는 멋진 신규 프로그램을 발표했습니다. 이 프로그램은 본 전단의 뒷면에 실린 호텔 및 업체¹⁴³와 JAMTO가 후원합니다. 자메이카가 제공하는 최상의 문화 및 교육 체험 일부를 이용하실 수 있도록 여러분을 ¹⁴⁴초대합니다. ¹⁴⁵참여 명소에는 캐리비언 내셔널 가든스, 몬테고 베이 포터스 갤러리, 자메이카 뮤직 익스피리언스 및 기타 다수가 포함됩니다.

입장권을 받으시려면 저희 웹사이트 www.jamto.org/freepass를 방문하시거나 JAMTO 사무실을 찾아주세요. 입장권 1장당 최대 5인까지 유효합니다. ¹⁴⁶3일간 이용 가능합니다.

어휘 organization 기구, 단체, 조직 cultural 문화의 entry 입장 a variety of 다양한 attraction 명소 sponsor 후원하다 flyer 전단 take advantage of 이용하다 offer 제공하다 obtain 얻다, 구하다 valid 유효한

143 전치사 어휘

해설   후원의 주체로 나열된 the JAMTO와 the hotels and businesses를 적절히 연결해 주는 전치사를 선택해야 한다. 따라서 '~와 함께, ~에 덧붙여'라는 의미의 (D) along with가 정답이다.

어휘   despite ~에도 불구하고   instead of ~ 대신에   except for ~를 제외하고

144 동사 어형 _ 시제

해설   전단 전반에서 현재시제를 사용하여 신규 프로그램에 대해 설명한 후, 빈칸이 포함된 문장에서 이 프로그램의 이용을 권장하고 있다. 즉, 글을 쓰는 동시에 초대하는 행위를 하고 있으므로, 빈칸에도 현재시제가 쓰여야 자연스럽다. 따라서 (A) invite가 정답이다. (C) may invite는 가능성을 시사하므로, 실제로 초대하는 표현으로는 적절하지 않다.

145 형용사 어휘

해설   문장의 주어인 attractions를 적절히 묘사하는 형용사를 선택해야 한다. 동사 include 뒤에 나열된 다양한 명소가 무료 입장권 제공 프로그램을 통해 방문할 수 있는 곳이라고 볼 수 있다. 따라서 빈칸에 포함된 부분은 '참여하는 명소' 또는 '이용 가능한 명소'라는 의미가 되어야 자연스러우므로, (D) Participating이 정답이다.

어휘   affordable 감당할 수 있는, 가격이 알맞은

146 문맥에 맞는 문장 고르기

번역   (A) 주문해 주셔서 감사합니다.
      (B) 3일간 이용 가능합니다.
      (C) 버스는 주중에만 운행됩니다.
      (D) 모든 주요 신용카드를 받습니다.

해설   빈칸 앞에서 입장권을 받는 방법(To obtain your pass, visit our Web site ~ or stop by any JAMTO office) 및 유효인원(One pass is valid for up to five people)에 대해 안내했으므로, 빈칸에는 입장권과 관련된 추가 설명이나 전체 내용을 마무리하는 문장이 들어가야 자연스럽다. 따라서 보기 중 입장권의 유효기간을 언급한 (B)가 정답이다. 첫 번째 단락에서 무료 입장(free entry)임을 밝혔으므로, 지불 방법을 언급한 (D)는 정답이 될 수 없다.

어휘   accept 받아들이다, 수락하다

PART 7

147-148 문자메시지

> **준 캄바야시 [오전 10시 12분]** 레이첼, 다나카 씨가 탄 항공편이 오늘 오후에 30분 일찍 도착하는 것 같아요. 제가 모시러 가는 길입니다.
>
> **레이첼 뉴먼 [오전 10시 13분]** [147]그분이 마침내 저희와 함께 이곳에서 일하게 되어 직원들이 기뻐하고 있어요. 근무 시간이 끝나기 전에 두 분이 함께 사무실에 들를 시간이 있으세요?

> **준 캄바야시 [오전 10시 14분]** 아마도요. 그리고 저도 그래요. [147]다나카 씨가 우리 회사 치바 지점에서 훌륭하게 임무를 수행했잖아요.
>
> **레이첼 뉴먼 [오전 10시 15분]** 저도 항상 들어왔던 얘기예요. [148]다나카 씨가 환영 저녁 식사 전에 실험실을 빠르게 둘러보고 팀원들을 만날 수 있으면 좋을 것 같아요.
>
> **준 캄바야시 [오전 10시 16분]** 그게 좋겠네요. 항공편 일정을 예측할 수 없으니 공항에 도착하면 알려드릴게요.
>
> **레이첼 뉴먼 [오전 10시 17분]** 좋아요. 이따 봬요.

어휘   finally 마침내, 결국   probably 아마   lab 실험실   unpredictable 예측할 수 없는   keep ~ posted ~에게 정보를 알려주다

147 추론 / 암시

번역   다나카 씨는 누구이겠는가?
      (A) 새 실험실 주인
      (B) 중요 고객
      (C) 전근 오는 직원
      (D) 비행기 기장

해설   뉴먼 씨가 오전 10시 13분 메시지에서 다나카 씨가 마침내 우리와 함께 일하게 되었다(he finally is going to be working with us here)고 했고, 캄바야시 씨가 10시 14분 메시지에서 다나카 씨가 회사의 치바 지점에서 훌륭하게 임무를 수행했다(Mr. Tanaka has done great work at our Chiba branch)고 했다. 따라서 다나카 씨가 다른 지점에서 전근 오는 직원이라고 추론할 수 있으므로, (C)가 정답이다.

어휘   transfer 전근시키다, (장소를) 옮기다

148 의도 파악

번역   오전 10시 16분에 캄바야시 씨가 "그게 좋겠네요"라고 쓸 때, 그 의도는 무엇인가?
      (A) 저녁 식사 준비가 흡족하다.
      (B) 저녁 식사 전에 사무실에 들르라는 의견이 마음에 든다.
      (C) 다나카 씨의 직업적인 평판에 대해 인정한다.
      (D) 팀원들이 업무를 마쳐서 기쁘다.

해설   뉴먼 씨가 오전 10시 15분 메시지에서 다나카 씨가 환영 저녁 식사 전에 실험실을 둘러보면 좋을 것 같다(It would be nice for him to get a quick tour of the lab ~ before our welcome dinner)는 제안을 했는데, 이에 대해 캄바야시 씨가 긍정의 의사를 밝힌 것이다. 따라서 (B)가 정답이다.

어휘   arrangements 준비   appreciate 인정하다, (제대로) 인식하다   professional 직업에 관련된, 전문적인   reputation 평판   complete 완료하다

149-150 이메일

> 발신: jenkins@ourmarketfocus.au
> 수신: hardesty@gallusmail.au

날짜: 8월 11일
제목: 워크숍 공지

하디스티 씨께,

149 8월 18일 오후 4시에 있을 마케팅 기술 워크숍에 관해 중요한 변경 사항을 공유하고자 합니다. 많은 참석자들이 추가로 등록했기 때문에 행사 장소를 아래와 같이 변경했습니다.

더 릴 인; 퍼스

150 변경사항을 전달받았다고 알려주세요. 본 요청을 긴급으로 처리해 최대한 빨리 답신해 주시면 감사하겠습니다. 참가에 관한 질문이 있으시면 이메일을 보내주시면 됩니다.

감사합니다.

앤드류 젠킨스
워크숍 주최자

어휘   notice 공지   concerning ~에 관하여   attendee 참석자   sign up 등록하다   acknowledge 받음을 알리다   be aware of ~를 알다   appreciate 감사하다   treat ~라고 여기다, 처리하다   request 요청   urgent 긴급한   participation 참가

149 주제 / 목적

번역   이메일을 쓴 목적은?

(A) 행사를 취소하려고
(B) 새로운 장소를 알리려고
(C) 새로운 워크숍 발표자를 모집하려고
(D) 워크숍 자원봉사자를 요청하려고

해설   첫 번째 단락에서 중요한 변경사항을 공유하고자 한다(This is to share an important change)고 한 후, 변경된 행사 장소(we have changed the location of our event to The Rill Inn; PERTH)를 알려주었다. 따라서 (B)가 정답이다

어휘   cancel 취소하다   announce 알리다, 발표하다   recruit 모집하다

▶▶ Paraphrasing   지문의 location of our event → 정답의 venue

150 세부 사항

번역   하디스티 씨는 무엇을 하라고 요청받는가?

(A) 다른 참석자들에게 공지 공유하기
(B) 만나기 편한 시간을 선택하기
(C) 메시지 수신 확인해 주기
(D) 연락처 업데이트하기

해설   두 번째 단락에서 하디스티 씨에게 변경사항을 전달받았는지 알려달라(Please acknowledge you are aware of the update.)고 요청했으므로, (C)가 정답이다.

어휘   confirm 확인해 주다   receipt 수령, 받기

▶▶ Paraphrasing   지문의 acknowledge → 정답의 Confirm

151-152 광고

비렌스

151 최상의 텔레비전, 전화기, 태블릿 등을 찾는다면 비렌스로 오세요!

152 개점 기념 행사
라디오 방송국 KYX 93.8의 코미디언 겸 DJ 데클란 깁 특별 출연

152 10월 2일 토요일 오전 10시-오후 8시
모리스 가 234번지, 마이크 피자 옆

사라가 만든 맛있는 제과들이 모여있는 곳,
사라 베이커리에서 무료 간식 제공

본 광고를 지참하시고 10달러 이상 구입하시면 5달러를
할인해 드립니다.
10월 내내 유효.

어휘   grand opening 개장, 개점   celebration 기념 행사   feature 특별히 출연하다   complimentary 무료의   purchase 구입, 구매   valid 유효한

151 세부 사항

번역   비렌스는 어떤 유형의 업체인가?

(A) 제과점
(B) 라디오 방송국
(C) 전자제품 매장
(D) 피자 전문점

해설   첫 번째 단락에서 최상의 텔레비전, 전화기, 태블릿 등을 찾는다면 비렌스로 오라(Come to Virens for the best televisions, phones, tablets, and more!)고 했으므로, 전자제품 매장임을 알 수 있다. 따라서 (C)가 정답이다.

▶▶ Paraphrasing   지문의 televisions, phones, tablets, and more → 정답의 electronics

152 세부 사항

번역   광고에 따르면, 10월 2일에 어떤 일이 있을 것인가?

(A) 데클란 깁이 행사에서 공연을 할 예정이다.
(B) 두 개의 업체가 새로운 곳으로 이전할 것이다.
(C) 신상품이 출시될 예정이다.
(D) 쿠폰이 만료될 것이다.

해설   두 번째 단락에서 코미디언 겸 DJ인 데클란 깁이 특별 출연하는 개점 기념 행사(Grand Opening Celebration featuring comedian and DJ Declan Gibb from radio station)가 있다고 했다. 세 번째 단락에서 그 행사가 10월 2일임을 알 수 있으므로, (A)가 정답이다. 참고로, 쿠폰은 10월 내내 유효하다고 했으므로 (D)는 오답이다.

어휘   perform 공연하다   launch 출시하다   expire 만료되다

http://www.officenature.com

¹⁵³직원들의 건강과 사기를 증진하고 싶습니까? ¹⁵⁴오피스 네이처가 귀사의 휴게실까지 맛있는 음식이 가득 담긴 상자를 배달해 드립니다.

저희는 다음 사항에 중점을 두고 있습니다.
- 견과류, 그래놀라, 말린 과일 등 천연 간식 제공
- 지역 농부들과 협력해 가장 신선한 제품 제공
- 환경에 미치는 영향 감소
- 적정 가격으로 식품 제공

¹⁵⁴제품과 배송 요일만 선택하시면 건강에 좋은 음식이 담긴 신선한 상자가 매주 자동으로 배송됩니다. 첫 주문 고객은 주문 시 코드 YUM으로 10퍼센트 할인을 받으실 수 있습니다.

어휘 boost 북돋우다 morale 사기 deliver 배달하다 focus on ~에 중점을 두다 treat 간식 reduce 감소시키다, 줄이다 impact 영향 environment 환경 reasonable 합리적인, 타당한 automatically 자동으로

153 추론 / 암시

번역 웹페이지는 누구를 대상으로 하겠는가?

(A) 농부
(B) 회사 경영주
(C) 회사 직원
(D) 오피스 네이처 직원

해설 첫 번째 단락에서 직원들의 건강과 사기를 증진하고 싶은지(Want to boost the health and morale of your employees?)를 질문하면서 관심을 끌고 있다. 따라서 광고 대상이 회사 경영주라고 추론할 수 있으므로, (B)가 정답이다.

154 사실 관계 확인

번역 오피스 네이처에 대해 알 수 있는 것은?

(A) 건강한 간식을 배달한다.
(B) 주별 할인을 제공한다.
(C) 자체적으로 제과류를 만든다.
(D) 자체적으로 과일을 재배한다.

해설 첫 번째 단락에서 오피스 네이처가 맛있는 음식이 가득 담긴 상자를 배달한다(Office Nature delivers a box filled with delicious food)고 했으며, 세 번째 단락에서도 제품과 배송 요일만 선택하면 건강에 좋은 음식이 담긴 신선한 상자(a fresh box of healthy food items)가 매주 자동으로 배송된다고 했다. 따라서 (A)가 정답이다. 참고로, 지역 농부들과 협력해 가장 신선한 제품을 제공한다(working with local farmers to provide the freshest options)고 했으므로, (D)는 정답이 될 수 없다.

가이거 트래블에 세간의 관심이 집중되다

¹⁵⁵마커스 가이거는 여러 장소 및 문화를 탐험하고 싶은 자신의 열정과 기업 출장 상담가로서의 경력을 결합해 보고자 가이거 트래블 매니지먼트(GTM)를 창립했다. 10년이 지난 지금 회사는 미국, 캐나다와 남아메리카 여러 국가에 지사를 두고 있다. ¹⁵⁶비즈니스 전문가들을 위해 일정을 짜고 교통편과 숙소 마련을 돕는다.

¹⁵⁷GTM은 뭄바이에 있는 베일파이어 일렉트로닉스와의 협약을 통해 보안이 확실한 고속 컴퓨터, 전화 회의 시스템, 파일 관리 소프트웨어 등을 고객에게 제공하기도 한다. "저희의 성공은 베일파이어 덕분이죠." 가이거 씨가 설명한다. "이들의 서비스가 저희 고객으로 하여금 어디에 있든 효율적으로 일할 수 있게 해 주었기 때문입니다."

가이거 씨는 GTM이 본격적으로 더 성장할 것이라고 낙관하고 있다. ¹⁵⁷수리남 파라마리보에 있는 아푸라 항공과 바베이도스 브리지타운에 본사를 둔 음식점 체인 트리거피시, 이 두 업체도 추가로 8월에 GTM과 전략적 제휴를 맺기로 합의했다. 아울러 유럽에 사업체를 열 것을 고려해 현재 독일 전역에 지점을 둔 접객 서비스 업체 크로쿠스하우스 AG와 논의 중이다.

가이거 트래블 매니지먼트에 관해 더 자세한 정보를 알아보려면 www.gtm.com을 방문하면 된다.

어휘 combine 결합하다 passion 열정 corporate 기업의 found 설립하다 craft 공들여 만들다 itinerary 여행 일정 facilitate 용이하게 하다, 돕다 accommodation 숙소 arrangement 준비, 마련 secure 안전한, 확실한 conference call 전화 회의 management 관리 enable 가능하게 하다 efficiently 효율적으로 optimistic 낙관적인, 낙관하는 be on the horizon 본격화되다, 곧 일어날 듯하다 headquarter 본부를 두다 strategic 전략적인 operation 기업, 사업체 currently 현재 hospitality 접객(업), 환대

155 사실 관계 확인

번역 가이거 씨에 대해 알 수 있는 것은?

(A) 정기적으로 뭄바이에 출장을 간다.
(B) 회사의 확장을 감독해 왔다.
(C) 10년 전, 여행작가가 되기로 결심했다.
(D) 예전에 접객 서비스 업체에서 일했다.

해설 첫 번째 단락에서 가이거 씨가 가이거 트래블 매니지먼트(GTM)를 창립했다(Marcus Geiger founded Geiger Travel Management (GTM))고 한 후, 10년이 지난 지금 회사가 미국, 캐나다와 남아메리카 여러 국가에 지사를 두고 있다(Now ~ the company has offices in the United States, Canada, and several South American nations)고 했다. 따라서 가이거 씨가 사세를 확장했음을 알 수 있으므로, (B)가 정답이다. 참고로, 가이거 씨가 기업 출장 상담가로 일한 적은 있으나, 접객 서비스 업체에서의 근무 경험은 확인할 수 없으므로 (D)는 정답이 될 수 없다.

어휘 regularly 정기적으로 oversee 감독하다 expansion 확대, 확장

> ▸▸ Paraphrasing 지문의 the company has offices in the United States, Canada, and several South American nations
> → 정답의 the expansion of a business

156 세부 사항

번역 GTM은 어떤 서비스를 제공하는가?

(A) 임원들을 위한 호텔 예약
(B) 다양한 문화가 섞인 교육 워크숍 진행
(C) 회의 통역 서비스 제공
(D) 해외 지점 사무실에 가구 비치

해설 첫 번째 단락에서 GTM은 비즈니스 전문가들을 위해 일정을 짜고 교통편과 숙소 마련을 돕는다(It ~ facilitates travel and accommodation arrangements for business professionals)고 했으므로, (A)가 정답이다.

어휘 executive 경영진, 간부 cross-cultural 다양한 문화가 섞인 translation 번역 conference 회의 furnish (가구를) 비치하다 overseas 해외의

> ▸▸ Paraphrasing 지문의 accommodation arrangements for business professionals
> → 정답의 Booking hotels for executives

157 사실 관계 확인

번역 GTM은 어떤 회사와 협약을 맺지 않았는가?

(A) 베일파이어 일렉트로닉스
(B) 아푸라 항공
(C) 트리거피시
(D) 크로쿠스하우스 AG

해설 두 번째 단락에서 GTM과 베일파이어 일렉트로닉스의 협약이 언급되었고, 세 번째 단락에서 아푸라 항공 및 음식점 체인인 트리거피시와도 전략적 제휴를 맺기로 합의했다고 되어 있다. 하지만 세 번째 단락에서 현재 크로쿠스하우스 AG와는 논의 중(the company is currently in discussions with Krokushaus AG)이라고 했으므로, 아직 협약이 체결되지 않은 상태임을 알 수 있다. 따라서 (D)가 정답이다.

> ▸▸ Paraphrasing 지문의 is currently in discussions with
> → 질문의 does NOT have an agreement in place with

158-160 보도자료

> **즉시 배포용**
>
> **연락처: 셰릴린 스티븐스, sstevens@tearsoncorp.ca**
>
> 캘거리 (11월 2일) – 158티어슨 사의 최고 정보관리 책임자 이브 버니어는 지난 월요일, 티어슨 식료품 매장에 200대의 로봇이 곧 등장할 것이라고 발표했다. 159모두 베일리라는 이름이 붙은 이 로봇들

은 상자나 병이 떨어져 깨지면서 시리얼, 주스, 기타 물질 등이 바닥에 쏟아진 곳을 찾아내는 데 사용될 예정이다. 로봇은 유출물을 보고해 이들이 안전에 위협이 되기 전 매장 직원들이 해당 장소를 치우도록 할 것이다.

160로봇은 티어슨 본사가 위치한 캘거리에서 시범 사용되었다. 18개월의 시범 프로그램 동안, 매장 관리자들은 로봇들에게 일관되게 높은 점수를 주었다. 로봇이 회사 창고에서 몇 년간 사용돼 오기는 했지만, 매장에서 일하며 고객과 상호작용하는 것은 처음이다. 티어슨 전 매장은 12월 초까지 모두 로봇을 갖출 예정이다.

더 자세한 정보를 보려면 www.tearsoncorporation.ca로 티어슨 사를 방문하면 된다.

어휘 immediate 즉각적인 release 발표, 공개 announce 발표하다, 알리다 appear 나타나다, 생기다 locate ~의 정확한 위치를 찾아내다 spill 쏟다; 유출물(= 쏟아진 것) substance 물질 hazard 위험 pilot program(me) 시범 프로그램 consistently 지속적으로, 일관되게 warehouse 창고 interact 상호작용하다

158 주제 / 목적

번역 보도자료의 주제는?

(A) 회사 임원의 승진
(B) 매장에서의 기술 활용
(C) 신제품 출시
(D) 본사 이전

해설 첫 번째 단락에서 티어슨 식료품 매장에 200대의 로봇이 등장할 것이라는 소식(Yves Vernier ~ announced ~ that 200 robots will soon appear in Tearson's grocery stores)을 전한 후, 매장에서의 로봇 활용에 대한 정보를 제공하고 있다. 따라서 (B)가 정답이다.

어휘 promotion 승진 relocation 이전

159 세부 사항

번역 베일리는 무엇을 할 수 있는가?

(A) 어지럽혀진 바닥 청소하기
(B) 제품 라벨 만들기
(C) 유출물이 있는 구역 찾기
(D) 고객에게 제품 위치 찾아주기

해설 첫 번째 단락에서 베일리라는 이름이 붙은 로봇들이 상자나 병이 떨어져 깨지면서 시리얼, 주스, 기타 물질 등이 바닥에 쏟아진 곳을 찾아내는 데 사용될 예정(The robots, which are all named Bailey, will be used to locate areas ~ spilling cereal, juice, or other substances onto the floor)이라고 했다. 따라서 (C)가 정답이다. 참고로, 로봇은 위치를 알려주고 직원이 청소를 하게 되므로, (A)는 오답이다.

> ▸▸ Paraphrasing 지문의 locate areas ~ spilling cereal, juice, or other substances onto the floor
> → 정답의 Find areas that have spills

160 추론 / 암시

번역 보도자료에서 암시된 것은?

  (A) 캘거리에서 진행된 시범 프로그램이 성공을 거뒀다.
  (B) 티어슨 매장들은 12월에 개조 공사를 할 것이다.
  (C) 창고는 안전 장치에 대해 높은 점수를 받았다.
  (D) 매장 여러 곳에서 관리자들을 채용할 예정이다.

해설 두 번째 단락에서 로봇이 캘거리에서 시범 사용되었다(The robots were tested in Calgary)고 한 후, 시범 프로그램 동안 매장 관리자들이 로봇들에게 일관되게 높은 점수를 주었다(During the eighteen-month pilot programme, store managers consistently gave the robots high marks)고 했다. 따라서 결과가 성공적이었다고 볼 수 있으므로, (A)가 정답이다.

어휘 renovate 보수하다, 개조하다   safety feature 안전 장치

> ▸▸ Paraphrasing   지문의 high marks → 정답의 a success

161-163 이메일

발신: 헬렌 디트리히 〈hdietrich@morphospublishing.ca〉
수신: 알리아 세르반테스 〈alia.cervantes@gotomail.ca〉
날짜: 3월 3일
제목: 〈프랙티컬 가드닝〉

세르반테스 씨께,

¹⁶¹다음 달 〈프랙티컬 가드닝〉이 마지막 호라는 사실을 알려드리게 되어 유감스럽습니다. ¹⁶²62년 동안의 월간지 발행 후, 저희 모포스 출판사는 〈프랙티컬 가드닝〉을 폐간해야 할 정기 간행물에 포함시키는 것으로 결정했습니다. 비용 절감을 통해 얻은 자원을 현재 성장세인 도서 출판 및 교육용 동영상 제작 사업 쪽으로 보내려고 계획하고 있습니다.

〈프랙티컬 가드닝〉의 오랜 구독자로 성원해 주셔서 감사합니다. 귀하의 남은 구독 기간에, 야생 식물을 주제로 하는 저희의 인기 출판물인 〈플로라 디스커버리〉를 대신 보내드릴 수 있게 해 주셨으면 합니다. 하지만 구독 계정에 있는 ¹⁶³잔액을 환불 받고 싶으시다면 (822) 555-0127로 연락 주십시오.

헬렌 디트리히
구독 관리자, 모포스 출판사

어휘 issue (정기 간행물의) 호, 발행(물)   periodical 정기 간행물   discontinue 중단하다   redirect 다시 보내다   resource 자원   cost-cutting 비용 절감   publishing 출판   instructional 교육용의   grateful 감사하는   remainder 나머지   subscription 구독   term 기간   instead 대신   account 계정, 계좌   refund 환불해 주다

161 주제 / 목적

번역 이메일을 쓴 목적은?

  (A) 지연을 사과하려고
  (B) 신제품을 홍보하려고
  (C) 취소를 알리려고
  (D) 청구상의 오류를 해결하려고

해설 첫 번째 단락에서 다음 달 〈프랙티컬 가드닝〉이 마지막 호라는 사실을 알리게 되어 유감(I am sorry to report that next month's issue of *Practical Gardening* will be our last)이라고 했으므로, 월간지의 폐간으로 인한 구독 취소를 알리려는 이메일임을 알 수 있다. 따라서 (C)가 정답이다.

어휘 apologize 사과하다   promote 홍보하다   cancellation 취소   address 해결하다

162 추론 / 암시

번역 〈프랙티컬 가드닝〉은 무엇이겠는가?

  (A) 영화
  (B) 책
  (C) 웹사이트
  (D) 잡지

해설 첫 번째 단락을 보면 〈프랙티컬 가드닝〉이 월마다(monthly) 나오는 정기 간행물(periodical)임을 알 수 있다. 따라서 잡지라고 보는 것이 타당하므로, (D)가 정답이다.

163 동의어 찾기

번역 두 번째 단락, 네 번째 줄에 쓰인 "balance"와 의미가 가장 가까운 단어는?

  (A) 남아있는 금액
  (B) 안정성
  (C) 비용 인상
  (D) 생산량

해설 'balance'가 포함된 부분은 '구독 계정에 있는 잔액을 환불 받고 싶다면(if you would rather have the balance of your subscription account refunded to you)'이라는 의미로 해석되는데, 여기서 balance는 '잔액'이라는 뜻으로 쓰였다. 따라서 '남아있는 금액'이라는 의미의 (A) amount remaining이 정답이다.

164-167 온라인 채팅

린지 포코라 (오후 2시 15분) 안녕하세요, 코파린스키 씨. 사무용품 월별 주문을 넣어야 하는데요. 정기 주문 물품 이외에 별도로 필요한 게 있는지 알려주실 수 있을까요?

크레이그 코파린스키 (오후 2시 17분) 다른 관리자들에게 확인해 볼게요. ¹⁶⁴케이틀린, 제프리, 부서에 사무용품 요청이 있었나요?

케이틀린 데일리 (오후 2시 18분) 네, 화이트보드 마커가 더 필요해요.

크레이그 코파린스키 (오후 2시 19분) 회계부는요?

제프리 카튼 (오후 2시 20분) 없습니다.

린지 포코라 (오후 2시 22분) 마커요? 재고를 막 확인했는데 비품실에 아직 한 상자가 남아 있어요. 특별한 종류가 필요하신 건가요?

케이틀린 데일리 (오후 2시 23분) 아니요, 그냥 보통 검은색 마커요. 3상자면 충분할 거예요. ¹⁶⁵가지고 있는 상자의 마커를 써 봤는데 말라 버린 것 같아요. ¹⁶⁶신입사원들이 다음 주에 업무를 시작할 거라서 오리

엔테이션과 교육 시간에 마커가 필요할 겁니다.

크레이그 코파린스키 (오후 2시 24분) 알겠습니다. **167**린지, 마커 뿐만 아니라, 2층 회의실에 고장 난 의자를 교체할 새 의자를 주문해 주실 수 있나요? 모델번호를 찾아보셔야 할 겁니다. 고맙습니다.

어휘 place an order 주문을 넣다 office supply 사무용품 regular 정기적인 request 요청 department 부서 accounting 회계 inventory 물품 목록, 재고 in addition to ~에 더하여, ~이외에 conference 회의 replace 교체하다

164 의도 파악

번역 오후 2시 20분에 카든 씨가 "없습니다"라고 쓸 때, 그 의도는 무엇인가?

(A) 포코라 씨에게 아무 말도 듣지 못했다.
(B) 주문을 할 필요가 없다.
(C) 여분의 마커를 갖고 있지 않다.
(D) 비품실을 확인하지 않았다.

해설 코파린스키 씨가 오후 2시 17분 메시지에서 데일리 씨와 카든 씨에게 부서에 사무용품 주문 요청이 있는지(do you have any requests for office supplies in your departments?)를 물었는데, 이에 대해 카든 씨가 없다고 응답한 것이다. 따라서 (B)가 정답이다.

165 세부 사항

번역 데일리 씨가 알린 문제는 무엇인가?

(A) 일부 발표가 너무 길다.
(B) 사무실 지출 비용이 증가했다.
(C) 일부 사무용품을 사용할 수 없다.
(D) 회의실 크기가 충분하지 않다.

해설 데일리 씨가 오후 2시 23분 메시지에서 현재 상자에 있는 마커들을 써 봤는데 말라버린 것 같다(I tried some markers ~ but they seem to have dried up)고 했으므로, (C)가 정답이다.

어휘 presentation 발표 expense 비용

▶▶ Paraphrasing 지문의 markers
→ 정답의 office supplies

지문의 have dried up
→ 정답의 cannot be used

166 추론 / 암시

번역 데일리 씨는 어느 부서에서 일하겠는가?

(A) 회계
(B) 인사
(C) 구매
(D) 운송

해설 데일리 씨가 오후 2시 23분 메시지에서 신입사원들이 다음 주에 업무를 시작할 거라서 오리엔테이션과 교육 시간에 마커가 필요하다(A group of new employees will be starting next week, and we'll need markers for the orientation and training

sessions)고 했다. 따라서 그녀가 인사부에서 근무한다고 추론할 수 있으므로, (B)가 정답이다.

167 추론 / 암시

번역 포코라 씨는 다음으로 무엇을 하겠는가?

(A) 정보 찾기
(B) 교육 문서 검토하기
(C) 오리엔테이션 실시하기
(D) 부서 관리자에게 연락하기

해설 코파린스키 씨가 오후 2시 24분 메시지에서 포코라 씨에게 고장 난 의자를 교체할 새 의자를 주문해달라(Lindsay, ~ could you please order a new chair ~ to replace the one that is broken?)고 한 후, 모델번호를 찾아봐야 할 것(You'll need to look up the model number)이라고 덧붙였다. 따라서 포코라 씨가 요청에 따라 모델번호를 찾아볼 것이라고 추론할 수 있으므로, (A)가 정답이다.

어휘 locate ~의 정확한 위치를 찾다 conduct 하다

▶▶ Paraphrasing 지문의 look up the model number
→ 정답의 Locate some information

168-171 이메일

수신: 전 직원
발신: 잰 머천트
날짜: 10월 15일
제목: 레지날드 카르멘

동료 여러분께,

168에드먼튼 엔지니어링 컨설턴트 유한책임회사에 레지날드 카르멘 씨를 맞이하게 되어 기쁩니다.

카르멘 박사는 공학 및 교육에 전문성을 갖춰 저희 훌륭한 직원들에게 귀한 보탬이 될 것입니다. **169**대학을 졸업하고 아스트로파트 주식회사에서 통신 시스템을 설계하며 6년간 근무했습니다. 그리고 글래스 공과대학에서 지난 19년간 계신 뒤 바로 저희 회사로 오시는 것입니다. **170**그곳에서 10년간 전임교수로 근무하며 고급 수학 및 다양한 공학 특별 과정을 가르쳤습니다. 이후 학장으로 임명되어 나머지 임기 9년 동안 해당 직책을 맡았습니다. **171**이 기간 동안 학교의 전기공학 교육 과정을 다시 설계하는 팀을 이끌었습니다. 그러므로 저희 고객 교육 과정을 재설계할 적임자이십니다.

카르멘 박사님의 첫 근무일은 다음 주 화요일입니다.

잰 머천트, 인사부 이사

어휘 colleague 동료 LLC (Limited Liability Company) 유한책임회사 expertise 전문 지식, 전문성 valuable 귀중한 distinguished 유명한, 성공한, 뛰어난 graduate from ~를 졸업하다 directly 곧바로 advanced 고급의 appoint 임명하다 remaining 남아 있는 tenure 재임 기간 electrical 전기의

168 주제 / 목적

번역 머천트 씨가 이메일을 쓴 목적은?

(A) 자신이 퇴임하는 것을 알리려고
(B) 새 직원에 관한 세부 정보를 제공하려고
(C) 유명한 객원 발표자를 환영하려고
(D) 새로운 사업 부문 확장을 알리려고

해설 첫 번째 단락에서 회사에 레지널드 카르멘 씨를 맞이하게 되어 기쁘다(It is my pleasure to welcome Reginald Carmen to Edmonton Engineering Consultants, LLC)고 한 후, 그에 대한 추가 설명을 이어가고 있다. 따라서 새 직원에 대한 세부 정보를 제공하려는 목적이라고 볼 수 있으므로, (B)가 정답이다.

어휘 retire 은퇴하다 publicize 알리다 expansion 확대, 확장

169 사실 관계 확인

번역 카르멘 박사에 대해 명시된 것은?

(A) 통신 시스템 설계 경력이 있다.
(B) 과거에 에드먼튼 엔지니어링 컨설턴트에서 자문 위원으로 근무했다.
(C) 다른 회사에서 머천트 씨의 멘토였다.
(D) 글래스 공과대학을 졸업했다.

해설 두 번째 단락에서 카르멘 박사가 아스트로파트 주식회사에서 통신 시스템을 설계하며 6년간 근무했다(he spent six years designing telecommunications systems)고 했으므로, (A)가 정답이다. 참고로, 글래스 공과대학은 그가 근무만 했던 곳이므로 (D)는 오답이다.

어휘 consultant 자문 위원, 상담가

▸▸ Paraphrasing 지문의 spent six years
→ 정답의 has experience

170 세부 사항

번역 카르멘 박사는 글래스 공과대학에서 얼마나 오래 가르쳤는가?

(A) 6년
(B) 9년
(C) 10년
(D) 19년

해설 두 번째 단락에서 카르멘 박사가 글래스 공과대학에서 10년간 전임 교수로 근무하며 고급 수학 및 다양한 공학 특별 과정을 가르쳤다(he served as a full-time professor for ten years, teaching advanced mathematics and various special courses in engineering)고 했으므로, (C)가 정답이다. 학장으로 근무했던 9년은 가르친 기간에 포함될 수 없다.

171 문장 삽입

번역 [1], [2], [3], [4]로 표시된 곳 중에서 다음 문장이 가장 적합한 곳은?

"그러므로 저희 고객 교육 과정을 재설계할 적임자이십니다."

(A) [1]
(B) [2]
(C) [3]
(D) [4]

해설 주어진 문장에 인과관계를 연결하는 부사 thus가 있으므로, 앞에서 먼저 고객 교육 과정을 재설계할 적임자(the perfect choice for redesigning our client training modules)라고 판단한 근거가 언급되어야 한다. [4] 앞에서 카르멘 박사가 학교의 전기공학 교육 과정을 다시 설계하는 팀을 이끌었다(he led the team that redesigned the school's electrical engineering curriculum)며 관련 경력을 설명했다. 따라서 이 뒤에 주어진 문장이 들어가야 자연스러우므로, (D)가 정답이다.

172-175 후기

> ### 지역 미술관 방문자들, 대도시급 미술 작품을 감상하다
>
> **175**인상적인 미술 작품을 보기 위해 대도시를 찾아다닐 필요가 없어졌다. 미술 애호가들은 바로 이곳 잰포드에서 그것을 볼 수 있다.
>
> **172**지역 주민들은 잰포드를 등산객들이 좋아하는 숲 옆에 위치한 조용한 도시로만 알고 있다. 그러나 이곳은 또한 잰포드 대학교와 예상외로 훌륭한 미술관이 있는 장소이기도 하다. 전국에서 가장 훌륭한 대학 미술관 중 하나로 여겨지는 잰포드 대학교 미술관(JUAM)은 고대부터 현대에 이르기까지 94,000점 이상의 작품을 소장하고 있다. **173**소장품 규모 때문에 미술관은 작품들을 정기적으로 교대 전시한다. 또한 다른 기관에서 대여한 작품들을 전시하는 단기 전시회도 개최한다.
>
> **174**전문가들은 JUAM이 20세기의 광범위한 미술 수집품을 소장하고 있는 장소로서 주목할 만하다고 여긴다. 특히 조각가 로버트 대뷸리스가 만든 50점 이상의 작품과 스케치 모음을 포함하여, 그의 가장 많은 공개 소장품을 보유하고 있다.
>
> 미술관 입장은 무료이며 매일 오전 10시부터 오후 5시까지 문을 연다. 금요일 저녁에는 오후 10시까지 연장 운영한다.
>
> ---
>
> **어휘** patron 이용객, 후원자 venture into ~에 발을 들여놓다, 탐험하다 impressive 인상적인 situated 위치해 있는 likewise 마찬가지로, 또한 unexpectedly 예상외로, 뜻밖에 outstanding 뛰어난 house 소장하다 date from ~부터 시작되다 ancient 고대의 due to ~때문에 regularly 정기적으로 rotate 교대로 하다, 회전하다 host 주최하다 temporary 임시의, 일시적인 exhibition 전시회 institution 기관 comprehensive 광범위한 in particular 특히 sculptor 조각가 assortment 모음 admission 입장 extended hours 연장 근무 시간

172 사실 관계 확인

번역 후기에서 잰포드 시에 대해 명시된 것은?

(A) 조용한 환경에 위치해 있다.
(B) 역사가 100년 이상이다.
(C) 화가들이 활발하게 활동하는 공동체가 있다.
(D) 유명한 산림학 대학이 있다.

해설 두 번째 단락에서 지역 주민들은 잰포드를 숲 옆에 위치한 조용한 도시로만 알고 있다(Locals know Janford as a quiet town situated next to a forest)고 했으므로, (A)가 정답이다.

어휘 setting 환경, 배경 thriving 번성하는 forestry 산림학

▶▶ Paraphrasing 지문의 a quiet town situated next to a forest → 정답의 in a peaceful setting

173 사실 관계 확인

번역 미술관에 대해 언급된 것은?

(A) 고대 미술에 중점을 둔다.
(B) 전국적인 상을 여러 번 수상했다.
(C) 위치 때문에 관광객들이 찾기 어렵다.
(D) 한시적으로 소장품 중 일부를 전시한다.

해설 두 번째 단락에서 소장품 규모 때문에 미술관은 작품들을 정기적으로 교대 전시한다(Due to the size of its collection, the museum regularly rotates the works on display)고 했으므로, 소장품을 나눠서 한시적으로 전시 후 교체한다는 것을 알 수 있다. 따라서 (D)가 정답이다. 두 번째 단락에서 고대부터 현대에 이르는 작품(works dating from ancient times to the present)을 소장하고 있다고 했으므로, (A)는 정답이 될 수 없다.

어휘 award 상 location 위치 limited 제한된, 한정된

▶▶ Paraphrasing 지문의 regularly rotates
→ 정답의 for only a limited time

지문의 the works on display
→ 정답의 displays some items

174 추론 / 암시

번역 대뷸리스 씨에 대해 사실인 것은?

(A) 화가로 일을 시작했다.
(B) 특별히 JUAM을 위한 조각품을 만들었다.
(C) 20세기에 미술품을 창작했다.
(D) 잰포드 대학교에서 미술을 전공했다.

해설 세 번째 단락을 보면 JUAM이 20세기의 광범위한 미술 수집품을 소장하고 있는 장소(Experts consider JUAM noteworthy as a home to a comprehensive collection of twentieth-century art)이며 대뷸리스 씨의 작품이 다수 있다는 것(In particular, it holds the largest public collection of works by sculptor Robert Dabulis)을 알 수 있다. 따라서 대뷸리스 씨가 20세기에 미술품을 창작했다고 추론할 수 있으므로, (C)가 정답이다.

어휘 sculpture 조각 specifically 특별히

175 문장 삽입

번역 [1], [2], [3], [4]로 표시된 곳 중에서 다음 문장이 가장 적합한 곳은?

"미술 애호가들은 바로 이곳 잰포드에서 그것을 볼 수 있다."

(A) [1]
(B) [2]
(C) [3]
(D) [4]

해설 주어진 문장의 it이 가리키는 대상, 즉 미술 애호가들이 멀리 가지 않고 잰포드에서 감상할 만한 것이 앞에서 먼저 언급되어야 한다. [1] 앞에서 인상적인 미술 작품을 보기 위해 대도시를 찾아 다닐 필요

가 없어졌다(No need to venture into the big city to see an impressive art collection)고 했으므로, 이 뒤에 주어진 문장이 들어가야 자연스럽다. 따라서 (A)가 정답이다.

어휘 enthusiast 애호가, 열광적인 팬

176-180 주문서 + 이메일

레디 반

주문번호:	#13565
날짜:	6월 3일
배송:	24시간 특급 배송
[177]배송 주소:	헬렌 강
	스카이라이즈 로 45번지
	뉴텐, 뉴욕 12039
결제 수단:	신용카드 - 제이 심

제품번호	명세	가격
7563	[176]조리대 전기 그릴	49달러
[179]7564	[176/179]달걀 거품기	[179]14달러
7565	[176]찻주전자	27달러
7566	[176]토스터기	56달러
7567	[176]치즈 강판	16달러
	24시간 특급 배송	20달러
	합계	182달러

어휘 delivery 배송 shipping 배송, 운송 payment method 결제 수단 description 기술, 서술 countertop 조리대 grater 강판

수신: customerservice@readybarn.com
발신: jayshim@silyex.com
제목: 주문 #13565
날짜: 6월 6일

안녕하세요.

저는 최근 레디 반에서 주문(#13565)을 했습니다. [177]제가 구입한 제품은 최근 새 집을 구입한 제 조카 헬렌 강에게 줄 집들이 선물입니다. 그래서 조카의 주소를 배송 목적지로 제공했는데요. 내일 저녁에 있을 집들이 파티 전에 충분한 시간을 두고 물건이 도착하게 하고 싶어서 24시간 특급 배송으로 배송비를 더 많이 지불했어요. 며칠이 지났는데도 제 조카는 아직 해당 물품들을 받지 못했습니다. 무슨 일인지 알아봐 주시고 제 조카가 언제 배송을 받을 수 있을지 알려 주시면 감사하겠습니다. [178]아울러, 특급 배송으로 지불한 돈은 환불해 주시기 바랍니다.

[179]또한 영수증에 14달러가 청구된 7564번 제품은 주문한 기억이 없습니다. 돌려보낼 방법을 알려주십시오.

[180]레디 반을 오랫동안 이용해 왔고, 제품과 서비스에 대체적으로 아주 만족합니다. 최대한 빨리 답변 주세요.

제이 심

어휘 place an order 주문을 넣다 purchase 구입하다 housewarming 집들이 recently 최근 therefore 그러므로 destination 목적지 well ahead of ~보다 훨씬 더 전에 appreciate 감사하다 expedite 신속하게 처리하다 additionally 게다가 recognize 알아보다, 인지하다 charge 청구하다

176 추론 / 암시

번역 레디 반은 무엇을 전문으로 하겠는가?

(A) 주방 기구
(B) 파티 초대장
(C) 배송 용품
(D) 대형 기기

해설 주문서의 명세(Description) 목록을 보면 조리대 전기 그릴 (Countertop Electric Grill), 달걀 거품기(Egg Beater), 찻주전 자(Tea Kettle), 토스터기(Toaster), 치즈 강판(Cheese Grater)이 있다. 따라서 주방 기구 전문 업체라고 추론할 수 있으므로, (A)가 정답이다.

어휘 equipment 장비 appliance 기기

▶▶ Paraphrasing 지문의 Countertop Electric Grill, Egg Beater, Tea Kettle, Toaster, Cheese Grater → 정답의 Kitchen equipment

177 연계

번역 스카이라이즈 로 45번지에 대해 명시된 것은?

(A) 레디 반의 주소다.
(B) 심 씨의 청구서 발송지다.
(C) 강 씨의 새 주소지다.
(D) 심 씨의 이전 주소지다.

해설 주문서에 스카이라이즈 로 45번지는 헬렌 강이 물건을 받는 배송 주 소(Shipping Address)로 나와 있다. 이메일의 첫 번째 단락을 보 면, 심 씨가 최근 새 집을 구입한 조카 헬렌 강에게 집들이 선물(The items I purchased are housewarming gifts for my niece, Helen Kang, who recently purchased a new home)을 하려 고 그 주소로 물건을 주문했음을 확인할 수 있다. 따라서 (C)가 정답 이다.

어휘 billing address 청구서 발송지 former 이전의

178 세부 사항

번역 심 씨는 이메일에서 무엇을 요청하는가?

(A) 할인
(B) 환불
(C) 영수증
(D) 선물 목록

해설 이메일의 첫 번째 단락에서 특급 배송으로 지불했던 돈을 환불해달 라(I would like to ask you to return the money I paid for expedited shipping)고 요청했으므로, (B)가 정답이다.

어휘 refund 환불

▶▶ Paraphrasing 지문의 ask → 질문의 request
지문의 return the money I paid → 정답의 A refund

179 연계

번역 심 씨가 사려고 하지 않은 물품은?

(A) 치즈 강판
(B) 그릴
(C) 토스터기
(D) 달걀 거품기

해설 이메일의 두 번째 단락에서 심 씨는 14달러가 청구된 7564번 제품 을 주문한 기억이 없다(I do not recognize item number 7564 that I was charged $14)며 돌려보낼 방법을 알려달라(Please let me know how to send it back)고 했다. 주문서를 보면 제품번호 (Item Number)가 7564인 제품은 달걀 거품기(Egg Beater)이므 로, (D)가 정답이다.

180 사실 관계 확인

번역 이메일에 따르면, 심 씨에 대해 사실인 것은?

(A) 구입한 물품에 만족한다.
(B) 전에 레디 반에서 물건을 구입한 적이 있다.
(C) 예정대로 주문 물품을 받았다.
(D) 카탈로그를 보고 물건을 사는 것을 좋아한다.

해설 이메일의 세 번째 단락에서 심 씨가 레디 반을 오랫동안 이용해 왔다(I am a longtime customer of Ready Barn)고 했으므로, 전에 레 디 반에서 물건을 구입한 적이 있음을 알 수 있다. 따라서 (B)가 정답 이다. 참고로, 보통(=다른 때에는) 제품과 서비스에 만족하지만(I am usually very satisfied with your products and services) 이 번에 조카의 선물로 주문한 건에 대해서는 불만을 표시했으므로, (A) 는 정답이 될 수 없다.

어휘 on schedule 예정대로, 정시에 prefer 선호하다

▶▶ Paraphrasing 지문의 I am a longtime customer of Ready Barn → 정답의 He has shopped with Ready Barn before

181-185 이메일 + 탑승권

수신: 용선 체 〈ysche@buztech.com〉
발신: 지니 레드맨 〈gredman@silvervaleair.com〉
제목: 회신: 좌석 문제
날짜: 2월 12일
첨부: ◎ 상품권

체 씨께,

최근 이용하신 항공편에 대해 연락 주셔서 감사합니다. **181 귀하의 좌석 위 고장 난 에어컨 송풍구 때문에 비행 중 겪으신 불편에 대해 사과 드립 니다.**

181 저희는 귀하를 고객의 한 분으로서 소중히 생각하며, 귀하의 실버베일 항공 이용 경험이 긍정적인 기억으로 남았으면 합니다. **181/184** 그래서 200달러 상당의 상품권 789798을 첨부해 드립니다. 향후 저희 국내선 항공편 이용 시 **182** 적용 가능합니다. **183** 상품권은 12개월 후 만료됩니다.

실버베일 항공을 이용해 주셔서 감사합니다.

지니 레드맨
실버베일 항공 고객 서비스

어휘 attachment 첨부 voucher 상품권, 쿠폰 regarding ~에 관해 apologize 사과하다 discomfort 불편 vent 통풍구, 송풍구 positive 긍정적인 apply 적용하다 domestic 국내의 expire 만료되다

승객: 용선 체
항공권 번호: 0272125899649
확인 코드: CMOAAB

항공편	출발	도착	좌석
185 실버베일 항공 29	애틀랜타, GA (ATL)	로스앤젤레스, CA (LAX)	36D
	5월 6일 월요일	5월 6일 월요일	
	오전 11시 43분	**185** 오후 1시 35분	

항공료 요약

기본 요금	259.54달러
세금 및 수수료	33.76달러
184 상품권 789798	-200달러
합계	93.30달러

모든 승객은 무료로 기내용 가방 1개를 반입할 수 있으며, 위탁 수하물 가방 1개를 부칠 수 있습니다.

어휘 passenger 승객 confirmation 확인 depart 출발하다 arrive 도착하다 summary 요약 airfare 항공료 be entitled to ~할 자격이 있다 complimentary 무료의 carry-on (기내용) 휴대용 가방

---

181 주제 / 목적

번역 레드맨 씨가 체 씨에게 이메일을 보낸 목적은?

(A) 장비 수리에 관한 최근 정보를 알려주려고
(B) 항공료 책정에 관한 변동사항을 알리려고
(C) 새 좌석을 배정해 주려고
(D) 보상을 제공하려고

해설 이메일의 첫 번째 단락에서 체 씨가 비행 중 겪은 불편에 대해 사과 (We apologize for the discomfort you experienced during your flight)한 후, 실버베일 항공 이용 경험이 긍정적인 기억으로 남았으면 한다며 상품권을 첨부(we have attached Voucher)한다고 했다. 따라서 불편에 대해 보상을 제공하기 위한 이메일이라고 볼 수 있으므로, (D)가 정답이다.

어휘 pricing 가격 책정 assign 배치하다 compensation 보상

▸▸ Paraphrasing 지문의 Voucher → 정답의 compensation

---

182 동의어 찾기

번역 이메일의 두 번째 단락, 세 번째 줄에 쓰인 "applied to"와 의미가 가장 가까운 어구는?

(A) ~에 대해 요구되는
(B) ~에 사용되는
(C) 처리되는
(D) ~와 함께 보관되는

해설 'applied to'가 포함된 부분은 '향후 국내선 항공편 이용 시 적용 가능하다(This may be applied to a future domestic flight)'는 의미로 해석되는데, 여기서 applied to는 '~에 적용되는'이라는 뜻으로 쓰였다. 따라서 '~에 사용되는'이라는 의미의 (B) used for가 정답이다.

---

183 사실 관계 확인

번역 레드맨 씨가 상품권 789798에 대해 언급한 것은?

(A) 12개월간 유효하다.
(B) 아직 발송하지 않았다.
(C) 국제선 항공편 이용 시 사용할 수 있다.
(D) 다른 승객에게 양도할 수 없다.

해설 이메일의 두 번째 단락에서 상품권은 12개월 후 만료된다(The voucher expires after twelve months)고 했으므로, (A)가 정답이다. 상품권을 첨부했다(we have attached Voucher)고 했고, 향후 국내선 이용 시 적용된다(This may be applied to a future domestic flight)고 했으므로 (B)와 (C)는 오답이고, (D)는 언급되지 않았다.

어휘 valid 유효한 transfer 넘겨주다, 옮기다

▸▸ Paraphrasing 지문의 expires after twelve months → 정답의 is valid for twelve months

---

184 연계

번역 탑승권에서 체 씨에 대해 추론할 수 있는 것은?

(A) 상품권 전액을 사용했다.
(B) 업그레이드를 위해 추가요금을 지불했다.
(C) 왕복 항공편을 예약했다.
(D) 실버베일 항공의 상용 고객이다.

해설 탑승권을 보면 체 씨가 상품권 789798을 사용하여 항공료(airfare)의 200달러를 할인 받은 것으로 나오는데, 이메일의 두 번째 단락에서 해당 상품권이 200달러 상당(we have attached Voucher 789798 in the amount of $200)임을 알 수 있다. 즉, 그가 상품권 전액을 사용했다고 보는 것이 타당하므로, (A)가 정답이다.

어휘 redeem (현금, 상품 등으로) 교환하다 full value 전액 additional 추가의 round-trip 왕복 frequent 빈번한, 잦은

▸▸ Paraphrasing 지문의 **Voucher 789798 in the amount of $200** → 정답의 **the full value of a voucher**

185 사실 관계 확인

번역 실버베일 항공편 29에 대해 명시된 것은?

(A) 로스앤젤레스에서 출발한다.
(B) 오후에 도착한다.
(C) 승객들에게 좌석 배정이 되지 않는다.
(D) 승객들은 가방을 2개 위탁할 수 있다.

해설 탑승권에서 실버베일 항공편 29가 오후 1시 35분에 로스앤젤레스에 도착한다(Arrives)는 사실을 확인할 수 있으므로, (B)가 정답이다. 출발(Departs) 장소가 애틀랜타이고, 좌석(Seat)이 36D로 지정되어 있으며, 모든 승객은 1개의 가방을 위탁할 수 있다(All passengers are entitled to travel with ~ one checked bag)고 했으므로, (A), (C), (D)는 오답이다.

어휘 allow 허가하다

▸▸ Paraphrasing 지문의 **1:35 P.M.** → 정답의 **in the afternoon**

186-190 회의록 + 이메일 + 기사

카퍼 디지털 관리 운영위원회
회의록
11월 12일

1. 리피치 파일럿 테스트 준비가 완료되었다.

2. **186파일럿 테스트는 회계 연도 1분기인 1월 3일-3월 31일에 진행될 예정이다.**

3. 기존 고객사 다섯 곳에서 파일럿 테스트 기간 동안 리피치의 시험 버전을 이용해볼 것이다. **187향후 이들을 대상으로 소프트웨어의 유효성, 사용 편의성, 가격 적정성을 평가하는 설문 조사를 실시할 예정이다.**

4. **190리피치 파일럿 테스트가 성공을 거둘 경우, 대규모 마케팅 캠페인 설계 및 운영을 위한 거액의 자금 투자가 필요할 것이다.**

5. 회장님께서 본 캠페인의 가능한 재원을 알아보실 예정이다.

어휘 steering committee 운영위원회 minutes 회의록 pilot test 예비 시험하다; 시스템을 사용하기 전에 성능을 확인하는 점검 carry out 수행하다 fiscal year 회계 연도 existing 기존의 experimental 실험적인 rate 평가하다 effectiveness 유효성 affordability 가격 적정성 investment 투자 extensive 대규모의, 광범위한 potential 잠재적인, 가능성이 있는 funding source 재원

수신: sales@coffer.com
발신: tcao@ewest-taipei.com.tw
날짜: 4월 13일

제목: 파일럿 테스트

카퍼 디지털 귀하,

187귀사의 리피치 마케팅 소프트웨어에 관한 의견을 제출한 후 조금 덧붙이고 싶습니다. 188파일럿 테스트 관련 당사의 피드백은 매우 긍정적입니다. 그래서 본 제품이 출시되면 바로 알려주셨으면 합니다. 앞으로 계속될 당사의 디지털 마케팅 프로젝트에 리피치를 추가하고 싶은 생각이 간절합니다.

팅 카오, 글로벌 인터넷 마케팅 부장
이웨스트 클로딩 유한회사, 타이페이

어휘 follow up 덧붙이다 submit 제출하다 regarding ~에 관해 overwhelmingly 극도로, 압도적으로 immediately 즉시 rollout 첫 공개, 출시 be eager to ~하기를 간절히 바라다 permanent 영구적인, 앞으로 계속될 effort 활동, 프로젝트

업체 소식

카퍼 디지털은 어제 GPZ 캐피탈과의 협상을 매듭지었다. **190GPZ는 카퍼 디지털에 상당한 투자를 할 예정이며, 이는 리피치라는 이름의 새로운 온라인 마케팅 어플리케이션을 위한 자금을 조달해 줄 것이다. 189매출을 증대시키는 이 소프트웨어는 온라인 쇼핑객들이 제품 페이지에서 둘러보고 나간 후 이미 본 제품을 다시 한번 상기시키는 팝업창을 생성하는 방식으로 작동한다.**

GPZ는 데이터 및 마케팅 관련 지식으로 지난 5년간 다른 소프트웨어 개발업체 세 곳에 성공적으로 투자했다. 카퍼 디지털의 높은 명성과 최고의 직원들이 GPZ의 투자 결정을 뒷받침했다. "카퍼 디지털은 리피치 배포를 위해 확고한 계획을 갖고 있습니다. 그래서 투자를 결정하는 것이 쉬웠죠."라고 GPZ의 제시카 굴드 대변인은 말했다.

어휘 close a deal 협상을 매듭짓다 make an investment 투자하다 significant 중요한 funding 자금 제공 generate 만들어 내다 navigate (인터넷, 사이트 등을) 돌아다니다 knowledge 지식 reputation 평판 top-notch 최고의 solid 확고한, 탄탄한 distribute 배포하다, 유통하다 spokesperson 대변인

186 사실 관계 확인

번역 회의록에서 파일럿 테스트에 대해 명시된 것은?

(A) 테스트 기간은 약 3개월이 걸릴 것이다.
(B) 테스트 중 파악된 문제점은 즉시 보고되어야 한다.
(C) 테스트를 실시하는 데 비용이 많이 든다.
(D) 테스트 계획은 아직 회장의 승인을 받아야 한다.

해설 회의록의 2번 항목에서 파일럿 테스트가 1월 3일-3월 31일에 실시될 예정(The pilot test will be carried out during the first quarter of the fiscal year, January 3-March 31)이라고 했으므로, (A)가 정답이다.

어휘 identify 확인하다, 발견하다 immediately 즉시 costly 돈이 많이 드는 approval 승인

> ▸▸ **Paraphrasing** 지문의 **be carried out during the first quarter of the fiscal year, January 3-March 31**
> → 정답의 **last about three months**

187 연계

번역 카오 씨는 무엇을 했는가?
(A) 웹사이트 재디자인
(B) 연례 보고서 제출
(C) 설문 답변 작성
(D) 신사업 시작

해설 이메일의 초반부에서 카오 씨는 리피치 마케팅 소프트웨어에 관한 의견을 제출한 후 조금 덧붙이고 싶다(I wanted to follow up after having just submitted our thoughts regarding your Re-pitch marketing software)고 했는데, 회의록의 3번 항목을 보면 고객사들을 대상으로 소프트웨어를 평가하는 설문 조사를 실시할 예정(They will then take a survey to rate the software's ~ affordability)이라고 나와 있다. 따라서 카오 씨도 설문에 답변을 작성했음을 알 수 있으므로, (C)가 정답이다.

어휘 annual 연례의, 매년의 complete a survey 설문을 작성하다

> ▸▸ **Paraphrasing** 지문의 **take a survey**
> → 정답의 **completed a survey**

188 세부 사항

번역 카오 씨는 무엇을 요청하는가?
(A) 시험 결과 보기
(B) 향후 시험에 참여하기
(C) 소프트웨어를 구입할 수 있을 때 통지 받기
(D) 마케팅 협상 약속 잡기

해설 이메일의 중반부에서 리피치 마케팅 소프트웨어가 출시되면 바로 알려달라(we would like to be notified immediately upon the rollout of this product)고 요청했으므로, (C)가 정답이다.

어휘 participate in ~에 참가하다 available 이용 가능한 set up an appointment 약속을 정하다

> ▸▸ **Paraphrasing** 지문의 **immediately upon the rollout of this product** → 정답의 **when software is available for purchase**

189 세부 사항

번역 기사에 따르면, 리피치는 무엇을 하는가?
(A) 온라인 소매업체의 판매량 추적하기
(B) 인터넷 브라우저의 팝업창 방지하기
(C) 고객에게 제품 할인 제공하기
(D) 온라인 쇼핑객들이 구매를 고려할 수 있도록 제품 보여주기

해설 기사의 첫 번째 단락에서 리피치는 온라인 쇼핑객들이 구경했던 제품을 다시 한번 상기시키는 팝업창을 생성하는 방식으로 매출을 증대시

킨다(This sales-boosting software works by generating a pop-up window that reminds online shoppers of products they have already viewed)고 했다. 즉, 물건을 다시 한번 보여줌으로써 구매를 유도하는 소프트웨어이므로, (D)가 정답이다.

어휘 track 추적하다 retailer 소매업자 prevent 막다, 방지하다

> ▸▸ **Paraphrasing** 지문의 **generating a pop-up window** → 정답의 **displays products**

190 연계

번역 카퍼 디지털은 GPZ 캐피탈에서 받은 자금을 어떻게 이용하겠는가?
(A) 더 작은 회사 매입
(B) 제품 광고
(C) 신입사원 채용
(D) 새 장비에 투자

해설 기사의 첫 번째 단락에서 GPZ가 카퍼 디지털에 상당한 투자를 할 예정(GPZ will make a significant investment in Coffer Digital)이라고 한 후, 리피치를 위한 자금을 조달해 줄 것(enabling the funding of ~ Re-pitch)이라고 했다. 회의록의 4번 항목을 보면 리피치 파일럿 테스트가 성공을 거둘 경우, 대규모 마케팅 캠페인 설계 및 운영을 위한 거액의 자금 투자가 필요할 것(If the Re-pitch pilot is successful, a large dollar investment will be needed to ~ run an extensive marketing campaign)이라고 했으므로, 해당 자금이 광고에 쓰일 것으로 추론할 수 있다. 따라서 (B)가 정답이다.

어휘 advertise 광고하다 equipment 장비

> ▸▸ **Paraphrasing** 지문의 **enabling the funding** → 질문의 **use the funds**
> 지문의 **run an extensive marketing campaign** → 정답의 **advertise a product**

191-195 기사 + 이메일 + 안내판

C 터미널 다시 열려

(5월 23일) 해리슨 시 공항의 C 터미널이 2년간의 보수 공사 후, 6월 1일 다시 대중에게 개방된다.

해당 프로젝트는 11개의 새로운 탑승구를 추가해 터미널이 더 많은 항공편을 수용할 수 있도록 했다. **194보수 이전에 C 터미널을 이용했던 주요 항공사 세 곳은 다시 그곳에서 운영을 재개한다. 또한 노선을 확대하고 있는 지역 항공사 백 항공이 C 터미널에 새로 자리잡게 된다.**

터미널의 새 로비에는 효율적인 체크인 절차와 최신식 수하물 처리 시스템이 있다. 승객들은 대기 구역에서 무료 와이파이를 이용할 수 있으며, 이곳에는 상점과 음식점도 있다.

보수 공사가 진행 중이던 한 때, 공사팀이 기한을 맞추지 못할 것처럼 보이기도 했다. **191시에서 환경적 영향을 검토하는 과정에서 주차장 배치에 의문을 제기한 것이다. 설계자들은 주차장을 공항의 다른 쪽으로 옮기고 셔틀버스 서비스를 도입하여 이 문제를 해결했다.**

"**¹⁹²모든 이해당사자들의 협력 덕분에 프로젝트는 예산 초과 없이 기한까지 완료됐습니다.**" 공항 최고 운영 책임자인 아르투로 베네티가 말한다. "C 터미널 개선으로 해리슨 시에 안전하고 편안한 항공 교통편을 계속 제공할 수 있게 됐습니다."

어휘 renovation 개조, 보수 accommodate 수용하다 in operation 운영 중인, 가동 중인 carrier 항공사 expand 확장하다 efficient 효율적인 state-of-the-art 최신의 miss deadline 마감을 놓치다 environmental 환경의 impact 영향 placement 설치, 배치 institute 도입하다 cooperative 협력하는 stakeholder 이해당사자, 주주 budget overage 예산 초과 improvement 개선, 향상 enable 가능하게 하다

발신: 토마시나 이 〈thomasina.yee@cooverbrothers.com〉
수신: 스벤 폴슨 〈sven.paulsen@cooverbrothers.com〉
날짜: 7월 6일
제목: 슬로님 사 구매자들과의 회의

안녕하세요, 스벤.

¹⁹⁵집으로 돌아가는 3시 30분 비행기를 타려고 해리슨 시 공항에 있어요. 하지만 간략하게나마 소식을 알려드리려고 합니다. 슬로님에서의 회의는 잘 진행됐어요. **¹⁹³그들은 쿠버 브라더스의 제품에 매우 만족했고 내년에 주문량을 두 배로 늘리려고 하고 있어요. 사실 앞으로 있을 홈 앤 가든 박람회에 우리 침실 및 식당 세트를 포함시키자고 제안했습니다.** 내일 자세한 내용을 말씀드릴게요.

토마시나

어휘 feature 특별히 포함하다 upcoming 다가오는, 곧 있을 exposition 박람회, 전시회

---

¹⁹⁴해리슨 시 공항 - C 터미널
출발

항공사	항공편	탑승구	시간	목적지	상태
¹⁹⁴브라이트웨이	BR417	11	1:25	디트로이트	정시
플래닛 Z	PL700	3	2:06	오마하	취소
백	PA069	24	3:00	클리블랜드	정시
윈드로버	WI645	6	¹⁹⁵3:30	시카고	¹⁹⁵지연

어휘 departure 출발 status 상태 delayed 지연된

---

191 세부 사항

번역 주차장 위치를 변경해야 했던 이유는?

(A) 건축비를 줄이기 위해
(B) 환경을 보호하기 위해
(C) 승객들의 여행을 더 용이하게 만들기 위해
(D) 대형 차량을 위한 공간을 제공하기 위해

해설 기사의 네 번째 단락을 보면 시가 환경적 영향을 검토하는 과정에

서 주차장 배치에 의문을 제기했다(An environmental impact review conducted by the city questioned the placement of a parking lot)고 한 후, 설계자들이 주차장을 공항 다른 쪽으로 옮겨 문제를 해결했다(The planners solved the problem by moving the parking lot to the other side of the airport)고 했다. 따라서 환경을 보호하기 위해 주차장의 위치를 변경했음을 알 수 있으므로, (B)가 정답이다.

어휘 reduce 줄이다 construction 건축, 건설 passenger 승객

▸▸ Paraphrasing   지문의 **moving the parking lot to the other side of the airport**
→ 질문의 **to change the location of a parking lot**

---

192 세부 사항

번역 베네티 씨가 C 터미널에 대해 강조한 것은?

(A) 유일하게 무료 와이파이가 제공되는 터미널이다.
(B) 유명 건축가가 설계했다.
(C) 시에서 보수 자금을 댔다.
(D) 보수 공사가 제때 완료됐다.

해설 기사 마지막 단락에 나온 베네티 씨의 인터뷰를 보면, 프로젝트가 예산 초과 없이 기한까지 완료됐다(the project was completed by the deadline with no budget overage)고 했다. 따라서 (D)가 정답이다.

어휘 emphasize 강조하다 architect 건축가

▸▸ Paraphrasing   지문의 **by the deadline**
→ 정답의 **on time**

---

193 추론 / 암시

번역 쿠버 브라더스는 어떤 제품을 제조하겠는가?

(A) 가구
(B) 의류
(C) 주방기기
(D) 조경 도구

해설 이메일의 중반부를 보면 슬로님이 쿠버 브라더스의 제품에 매우 만족했다(They are very pleased with Coover Brothers products)고 한 후, 앞으로 있을 홈 앤 가든 박람회에 쿠버 브라더스의 침실 및 식당 세트를 포함시키자고 제안했다(they offered to feature our bedroom and dining room sets at the upcoming Home and Garden Exposition)고 덧붙였다. 따라서 가구를 제조하는 업체라고 추론할 수 있으므로, (A)가 정답이다.

---

194 연계

번역 브라이트웨이 항공에 대해 암시된 것은?

(A) 국제 항공사다.
(B) 오마하행 항공편을 제공한다.
(C) 보수 공사 전에 C 터미널을 이용했다.
(D) 승객을 위한 개인 전용 대기 구역이 있다.

해설 안내판을 보면 브라이트웨이 항공이 C 터미널을 이용하는 항공사 중 하나임을 확인할 수 있다. 기사의 두 번째 단락에서 보수 이전에 C 터미널을 이용했던 주요 항공사 세 곳이 다시 그곳에서 운영을 재개한다(The three major airlines that used Terminal C before the renovation will now be back in operation there)고 한 후, 백 항공이 C 터미널에 새로 자리잡게 된다(at Terminal C will be newcomer Paik Airways)고 했다. 즉, 백 항공을 제외한 나머지 항공사들은 보수 이전에도 C 터미널을 이용했다고 볼 수 있으므로, (C)가 정답이다.

어휘 private 개인 전용의

195 연계

번역 이 씨에 대해 암시된 것은?

(A) 오마하에서 일한다.
(B) 베네티 씨와 만났다.
(C) 이용하는 항공편이 늦게 출발했다.
(D) 수하물이 분실됐다.

해설 이메일의 초반부에서 이 씨가 3시 30분 비행기를 타려고 해리슨 시 공항에 있다(I'm at the Harrison City Airport to catch the 3:30 flight)고 했는데, 안내판을 보면 3시 30분 항공편이 지연(DELAYED)된 상태임을 알 수 있다. 따라서 (C)가 정답이다.

어휘 luggage 수하물

▸▸ Paraphrasing 지문의 **DELAYED** → 정답의 **departed late**

196-200 안내책자 + 양식 + 이메일

젤 익스테리어즈

젤 익스테리어즈의 금속 지붕 제품은 전통적인 지붕 자재에 비해 많은 장점을 제공합니다.

혜택 1 - 내후성:
우박, 바람, 비로부터 잘 보호해 주는 기술

197 혜택 2 - 다양한 선택사항:
패널 유형, 테두리 종류, 페인트 색상을 다양하게 선택 가능

혜택 3 - 만족 보장
마음을 더욱 편안하게 해 주는 30년 품질 보증

혜택 4 - 확실한 명성
신뢰받는 회사에서 제공하는 고품질 지붕

특정 제품에 관한 질문이 있으시거나 영업사원에게 견적을 요청하시려면, 저희 온라인 연락처 양식을 작성해 주십시오. **196 지붕 패널 일체는 당사의 지역 제조 시설 중 한 곳에서 제작되며, 귀하의 지붕에 필요한 크기로 미리 재단되어 가까운 지점으로 배송됩니다.** 그리고 나면 전문 설치업체가 그곳에서 물건을 가져갑니다.

어휘 advantage 장점 traditional 전통적인 material 재료, 자재 weather resistance 내후성 hail 우박 trim 테두리 satisfaction 만족 guarantee 보증, 보장 warranty 품질 보증

established 인정받는, 확실히 자리를 잡은 reputation 명성, 평판 specific 특정한 quote 견적 complete a form 양식을 작성하다 regional 지역의 dimension 크기, 규모

이름:	거스 키난
이메일:	g.keenan@autoewrite.net
전화번호:	555-0188
설명:	

197/198 여러 가지 지붕 자재를 살펴보았는데 다양한 페인트 옵션 때문에 귀사가 제 1순위가 됐습니다. 제 헛간 건물은 특이한 보라 색상인데요. 이를 보완할 색상을 찾고 싶어요. 그런데 질문이 있습니다. **199** 지금 있는 오래된 판자 지붕 위에 새로운 금속 지붕을 놓고 싶은데요. 이렇게 하면 시간, 인력, 폐기물 처리 측면에서 비용을 아낄 수 있을 것 같아요. 추천하시는 사항인가요? 오랜 시간을 들여 전문 도급 업자들을 위한 온라인 포럼을 살펴보았는데, 여기에 대한 견해가 엇갈려서 그렇습니다.

어휘 various 다양한, 여러 가지의 wide range of 다양한 shade 색조 complement 보완하다 shingle 지붕의 마감재, 판자 disposal 처리, 처분 contractor 도급업자, 계약자

수신: g.keenan@autoewrite.net
발신: nshertz@zellexteriors.com
날짜: 5월 20일
제목: 지붕 문의
첨부: ⬇ 젤 익스테리어즈 카탈로그

키난 씨께,

200 영업사원이 48시간 이내에 전화로 연락을 드리겠지만, 먼저 첨부된 제품 카탈로그를 확인해 주십시오. 저희는 여기에 있는 네 가지 기본 지붕 유형을 제공합니다.

SLP 스냅 록 - 빠른 설치를 가능하게 하는 잠금 기능이 있는 강철 패널
XM 패널 - 뛰어난 내식성을 지닌 알루미늄 패널. 비가 많이 오는 기후에 적합
199 QR 리지드 - 기존 지붕 위에 바로 설치 가능한 저비용 패널
WT 패널 - 가장 내구성이 뛰어난 상업용 등급 강철. 흰색과 회색만 가능

감사합니다.

니콜라 쉐르츠, 행정 보조, 젤 익스테리어즈

어휘 inquiry 문의 attachment 첨부 sales representative 영업사원 locking feature 잠금 기능 rapid 빠른 installation 설치 superior 우수한 corrosion 부식 resistance 저항 ideal 이상적인 existing 기존의 durable 내구성이 있는 commercial 상업의

196 사실 관계 확인

번역 안내책자에서 젤 익스테리어즈에 대해 언급한 것은?

(A) 사람들이 전시장을 방문하도록 독려한다.
(B) 몇 달 전에 미리 프로젝트 일정을 잡는다.
(C) 설치 전에 현장 조사를 요구한다.
(D) 배송 전에 주문 제작한 대로 제품을 자른다.

해설 안내책자의 마지막 단락을 보면 젤 익스테리어즈의 지붕 패널 일체는 고객의 지붕에 필요한 크기로 미리 재단되어 가까운 지점으로 배송된다(All our roofing panels are ~ precut to the necessary dimensions for your roof, and shipped to a branch near you)고 나와 있다. 따라서 (D)가 정답이다.

어휘 on-site 현장의 inspection 검사, 점검 prior to ~에 앞서

> ▸ Paraphrasing 지문의 precut to the necessary dimensions
> for your roof → 정답의 custom cuts
> 지문의 shipped → 정답의 delivery

197 연계

번역 키난 씨의 설명을 고려하면 목록 상의 어떤 혜택을 가장 마음에 들어 하겠는가?

(A) 혜택 1
(B) 혜택 2
(C) 혜택 3
(D) 혜택 4

해설 양식의 초반부에서 키난 씨는 다양한 페인트 옵션 때문에 젤 익스테리어즈가 자신의 1순위가 되었다(the wide range of paint options makes your company my top choice)고 했다. 안내책자를 보면 다양한 페인트 색상(Large selection of ~ paint colors to choose from)에 해당하는 혜택은 2번이므로, (B)가 정답이다.

어휘 attractive 매력적인

> ▸ Paraphrasing 지문의 top choice
> → 질문의 most attractive

198 사실 관계 확인

번역 양식에서 키난 씨에 대해 명시한 것은?

(A) 지붕 옵션에 대해 조사했다.
(B) 일부 자재를 설치할 때 실수했다.
(C) 자신의 프로젝트가 빨리 완료되기를 바란다.
(D) 이전 도급업체에 만족하지 못했다.

해설 키난 씨가 양식의 의견란에 본인이 여러 가지 지붕 자재를 살펴보았다(I have been looking at various roofing materials)고 적었으므로, (A)가 정답이다.

어휘 complete 완료하다 previous 이전의

> ▸ Paraphrasing 지문의 have been looking at various
> roofing materials → 정답의 has researched
> about roofing options

199 연계

번역 키난 씨는 어떤 유형의 지붕 제품을 선택하겠는가?

(A) SLP 스냅 록
(B) XM 패널
(C) QR 리지드
(D) WT 패널

해설 키난 씨는 양식의 의견란에 지금 있는 오래된 판자 지붕 위에 새로운 금속 지붕을 놓고 싶다(I would like the new metal roof to be placed on top of the old shingle roof I have)며 이렇게 하면 비용을 줄일 수 있을 것 같다(This would save money)고 덧붙였다. 이메일에 나열된 기본 지붕 유형(the four basic roofing types) 중 키난 씨의 조건에 가장 부합하는 제품은 기존 지붕 위에 바로 설치 가능한 저비용 패널(Low-cost panels that can be installed directly on top of an existing roof)이다. 따라서 (C)가 정답이다.

200 세부 사항

번역 쉐르츠 씨가 키난 씨에게 말하는 것은?

(A) 결정을 미루지 않음으로써 비용을 아낄 수 있다.
(B) 제안된 계약을 살펴봐야 한다.
(C) 젤 담당자가 전화를 걸 것이다.
(D) 예전에 자재를 잘못 주문했다.

해설 이메일의 첫 번째 단락에서 영업사원이 키난 씨에게 48시간 이내에 전화로 연락할 것(A sales representative will contact you by phone within 48 hours)이라고 했으므로, (C)가 정답이다.

어휘 delay 지연시키다 propose 제안하다

> ▸ Paraphrasing 지문의 contact you by phone
> → 정답의 He will be called

기출 TEST 4

101 (A)	102 (D)	103 (D)	104 (B)	105 (A)
106 (D)	107 (C)	108 (B)	109 (B)	110 (B)
111 (D)	112 (C)	113 (C)	114 (A)	115 (D)
116 (A)	117 (A)	118 (C)	119 (B)	120 (A)
121 (C)	122 (A)	123 (D)	124 (D)	125 (B)
126 (D)	127 (B)	128 (C)	129 (B)	130 (A)
131 (D)	132 (A)	133 (B)	134 (C)	135 (B)
136 (A)	137 (D)	138 (B)	139 (D)	140 (B)
141 (A)	142 (D)	143 (D)	144 (C)	145 (B)
146 (D)	147 (A)	148 (C)	149 (B)	150 (A)
151 (D)	152 (C)	153 (C)	154 (D)	155 (C)
156 (D)	157 (C)	158 (C)	159 (B)	160 (B)
161 (A)	162 (C)	163 (C)	164 (C)	165 (A)
166 (A)	167 (C)	168 (C)	169 (A)	170 (D)
171 (B)	172 (C)	173 (D)	174 (A)	175 (A)
176 (A)	177 (B)	178 (A)	179 (D)	180 (B)
181 (C)	182 (B)	183 (D)	184 (B)	185 (A)
186 (C)	187 (D)	188 (B)	189 (A)	190 (D)
191 (A)	192 (B)	193 (D)	194 (B)	195 (C)
196 (A)	197 (D)	198 (B)	199 (C)	200 (B)

PART 5

101 대명사 _ 수 일치

해설 빈칸에는 매진이 된(sold out) 대상을 가리키며 단수동사 was와 수가 일치하는 대명사가 들어가야 한다. 따라서 (A) it이 정답이다. 참고로, 여기서 it은 the concert를 가리키며, 표(tickets)가 매진되었다고 하려면 it was대신에 they were가 쓰여야 한다.

번역 콘서트가 매진되어 아카기 씨는 입장권을 구입할 수 없었다.

어휘 sold out (콘서트 등의) 표가 매진된, (상품 등이) 다 팔린

102 전치사 어휘

해설 빈칸은 동명사구 using the new employee scheduling software를 목적어로 취하는 전치사 자리이다. '신입 직원 일정 관리 소프트웨어 활용'은 강좌(Classes)의 주제를 나타내므로, '~에 관한'이라는 의미로 쓰일 수 있는 (D) on이 정답이다.

번역 신입 직원 일정 관리 소프트웨어 활용에 관한 강좌들은 12월에 시작될 것이다.

어휘 employee 직원 scheduling 일정 관리

103 형용사 자리 _ 명사 수식

해설 소유격 Hillsdale Fabrics'와 함께 명사 collection을 수식하는 형

용사 자리이므로, (D) diverse(다양한)가 정답이다. (A) diversity는 명사, (B) diversely는 부사, (C) diversify는 동사로 품사상 빈칸에 들어갈 수 없다.

번역 힐스데일 패브릭의 다양한 가죽 제품들은 이탈리아에서 수입되었다.

어휘 collection 컬렉션, 제품군 import 수입하다 diversity 다양성 diversely 다양하게 diversify 다양화하다

104 명사 어휘

해설 빈칸은 동사 spoke의 주어 역할을 하는 명사구를 이루는 부분으로, 전문가 그룹(four dental hygienists)을 나타내는 명사가 들어가야 자연스럽다. 따라서 '패널, 전문가 집단'이라는 의미의 (B) panel이 정답이다. A group/team/panel of는 빈출 표현이니 암기해 두는 것이 좋다.

번역 네 명의 치과위생사들은 자신들의 분야에서의 경력에 대해 이야기했다.

어휘 dental hygienist 치과위생사 a panel of ~로 구성된 집단, 합의체 support 지지, 성원

105 부사 자리 _ 동사 수식

해설 be동사 is와 현재분사 seeking 사이에서 동사를 수식하는 부사 자리이므로, (A) actively(적극적으로, 열심히)가 정답이다. (B) activate는 동사, (C) activity는 명사, (D) active는 형용사로 품사상 빈칸에 들어갈 수 없다.

번역 아덴틴 부동산은 보유 상품 목록에 넣을 새 임대 매물을 열심히 찾고 있다.

어휘 rental 임대 property 부동산, 건물 activate 작동시키다, 활성화하다

106 명사 어휘

해설 빈칸은 형용사 free의 수식을 받는 명사 자리로, 일반인들을 초청할 만한(invites the public to) 행사를 나타내는 명사가 들어가야 한다. 따라서 '워크숍, 연수회'라는 의미의 (D) workshop이 정답이다.

번역 이번 주 금요일, 존 플라이 카메라는 무료 항공사진 워크숍에 일반인들을 초청한다.

어휘 aerial photography 항공사진술

107 명사 자리 _ 전치사의 목적어

해설 빈칸은 뒤에 오는 명사 innovation과 함께 병렬 구조를 이루어 전치사 for의 목적어 역할을 하는 자리이다. 따라서 명사인 (C) creativity(창의성)가 정답이다. (A) creative는 형용사, (B) creatively는 부사, (D) creates는 동사로 품사상 빈칸에 들어갈 수 없다.

번역 앰버리 상은 창의성과 혁신성으로 주목할 만한 연구를 표창한다.

어휘 recognize (공로를) 인정하다, 표창하다 notable 주목할 만한, 유명한 innovation 혁신 creative 창의적인 create 만들다, 창조하다

108 동사 어휘

해설 빈칸은 주어 the harvest parade의 동사 자리로, 문맥상 행렬이 마을을 도는 행위를 나타내는 단어가 들어가야 한다. 따라서 '(원을 그리며 ~ 주위를) 순회하다'라는 의미의 (B) circle이 정답이다. 참고로, (A) spin은 제자리에서 회전시키는 행위를, (C) roll은 굴리는 행위를 나타내므로 빈칸에 적절하지 않다.

번역 올해 추수 행렬은 마을을 도는데, 마을 광장에서 시작하고 마무리될 것이다.

어휘 harvest 추수, 수확   square 광장   loosen 느슨하게 하다

109 동사 자리

해설 빈칸은 주어 Questwiz의 동사 자리로, a wide range of resource materials를 목적어로 취한다. 따라서 문장의 동사 역할을 할 수 있는 (B) contains(포함하다)가 정답이다. to부정사인 (A) to contain과 동명사/현재분사인 (D) containing은 본동사 역할을 할 수 없으며, (C) container는 명사이므로 빈칸에 들어갈 수 없다.

번역 도서관의 최신 데이터베이스인 퀘스트위즈에는 광범위한 자료가 들어 있다.

어휘 a wide range of 다양한   resource 자료   material 재료   container 용기

110 부사 어휘

해설 '3년도 더 걸린 후에야(After more than three years)'라는 시간 표현에 상응하는 부사가 들어가야 하므로, '마침내'라는 의미의 (B) finally가 정답이다.

번역 새 특허권 신청은 3년도 더 걸린 후에야 마침내 승인됐다.

어휘 application 신청, 지원   patent 특허권   approve 승인하다   already 이미   constantly 지속적으로   exactly 정확하게

111 동사 어형 _ 태

해설 빈칸의 주어인 it은 The First Street Hotel을 가리키는데, 빈칸 뒤에 목적어가 없으므로 문맥상 호텔이 개조되었다는 내용이 되어야 한다. 따라서 수동태인 (D) was renovated가 정답이다. (A) had renovated, (B) renovated, (C) was renovating은 모두 능동태 동사로 빈칸에 들어갈 수 없다.

번역 퍼스트 스트리트 호텔은 작년에 개조된 이래 거의 항상 만실이다.

어휘 book 예약하다   renovate 개조하다

112 형용사 어휘

해설 빈칸은 명사 amount를 수식하는 형용사 자리로, '지출해서는 안 된다(should not spend)'라는 동사구와 상응하는 단어가 들어가야 한다. 즉, 예산에서 너무 많은 금액을 지출하면 안 된다는 내용이 되어야 자연스러우므로, '과도한, 지나친'이라는 의미의 (C) excessive가 정답이다.

번역 부서들은 예산에서 과도한 금액을 사무용품에 지출해서는 안 된다.

어휘 department 부서   budget 예산   office supply 사무용품   equal 동일한   exciting 신나는   unknown 알려지지 않은

113 부사 자리 _ 동사 수식

해설 be동사 was와 과거분사 selected 사이에서 동사를 수식하는 부사 자리이므로, (C) carefully(신중하게)가 정답이다. (A) caring은 형용사/현재분사, (B) careful은 형용사, (D) cares는 동사/명사로 품사상 빈칸에 들어갈 수 없다.

번역 맥스웰 카피스는 품질과 내구성을 고려해 신중하게 선정한 두껍고 광택 나는 종이에 안내책자를 인쇄한다.

어휘 brochure 안내책자   glossy 광택[윤]이 나는   durability 내구성

114 부사절 접속사 자리

해설 빈칸은 뒤에 오는 절(Mr. Kamau has worked ~ two years)을 이끌어 주절(he has never taken time off)을 수식하는 자리이다. 따라서 '비록 ~이긴 하지만'이라는 의미의 부사절 접속사 (A) Although가 정답이다. 참고로, (B) But과 (D) Yet은 등위접속사로 해당 문장에서 콤마 뒤에 올 수는 있으나 빈칸에 들어갈 수는 없다.

번역 카마우 씨는 몸바사 커뮤니케이션즈에서 2년 동안 일했지만 한 번도 휴가를 쓴 적이 없다.

어휘 time off 휴가

115 형용사 자리 _ 명사 수식

해설 빈칸은 명사 importance를 수식하는 형용사 자리이므로, (D) critical(대단히 중요한, 중대한)이 정답이다. 참고로, 「of + 추상명사」는 의미상 형용사와 같은 역할을 하며, be of great/critical/vital importance 등은 '매우 중요하다'라는 뜻을 나타낸다. (A) critique는 명사/동사, (B) critic은 명사, (C) critically는 부사로 품사상 빈칸에 들어갈 수 없다.

번역 모리건 호텔에서는 고객 의견에 대처하는 일을 매우 중시한다.

어휘 address 다루다, 대처하다   critique 평론; 비평하다   critic 비평가   critically 비평적으로, 위태롭게

116 부사 어휘

해설 새로운 컴퓨터 프로그램(new computer program)이 데이터를 정리하고 검색하는(organize and retrieve data) 방식을 적절히 묘사하는 부사가 빈칸에 들어가야 한다. 따라서 '효율적으로'라는 의미의 (A) efficiently가 정답이다.

번역 액소페어의 새로운 컴퓨터 프로그램은 사용자가 데이터를 효율적으로 정리하고 검색할 수 있도록 해 준다.

어휘 enable 가능하게 하다   organize 정리하다   retrieve 검색하다   irreversibly 되돌릴 수 없게   vaguely 모호하게   especially 특히

117 명사 자리 _ 동사의 목적어

해설 빈칸은 동사 has just released의 목적어 역할을 하며 소유격 대명사 its의 수식을 받는 자리이다. 따라서 명사인 (A) analysis(분석)가 정답이다. (B) analytical은 형용사, (C) analyze는 동사, (D) analyzed는 동사/과거분사로 품사상 빈칸에 들어갈 수 없다.

번역 트렐모니 사는 세계 주식 시장 분석을 방금 발표했다.

어휘 release 공개하다, 발표하다   stock market 주식 시장
analytical 분석적인   analyze 분석하다

118 최상급 표현

해설 빈칸은 to reveal(알리다, 공개하다)의 목적어인 product를 수식하는 형용사 자리이다. '수프 제품군에서 가장 인기 있는 제품인 호박 수프'라는 내용이 되어야 자연스러우므로, the와 함께 최상급 표현을 완성하는 (C) most popular가 정답이다. (A) popularity of의 경우 구조상 빈칸에 들어갈 수 있으나, '인기'라는 뜻으로 앞뒤 문맥상 적절하지 않다.

번역 리우 푸즈는 자사의 유명한 수프 제품군에서 가장 인기 있는 제품인 호박 수프를 알리게 되어 기쁘게 생각한다.

119 전치사 자리

해설 빈칸은 명사구 renovations of the Fessler Road fire station을 목적어로 취해 앞에 온 절을 수식해 주는 전치사 자리이다. 따라서 분사형 전치사 (B) including(~을 포함하여)이 정답이다. (A) these는 형용사/지시대명사, (C) even though는 접속사, (D) always는 부사로 품사상 빈칸에 들어갈 수 없다.

번역 제안된 시 예산은 페슬러 로드 소방서 개조를 비롯해 다양한 프로젝트를 설명하고 있다.

어휘 budget 예산   outline 개요를 서술하다   various 다양한
renovation 개조

120 형용사 어휘

해설 명사 opening을 수식하는 자리로, 개업식이 연기된(opening ~ had to be postponed) 상황과 어울리는 일정 관련 형용사가 들어가야 자연스럽다. 따라서 '예정된'이라는 의미의 (A) scheduled가 정답이다.

번역 예정되었던 새 제과점 개업식은 주방에서 배관이 터지자 연기되어야 했다.

어휘 postpone 연기하다   burst 터지다, 파열하다   maintained 유지되는, 지원을 받는   motivated 자극 받은, 동기가 부여된
experienced 경험이 많은, 노련한

121 동사 어형 _ 태

해설 주어인 Two associates가 승진에(for promotions) 고려되는 대상이므로, 동사 consider가 수동태로 쓰여야 한다. 따라서 are being과 결합해 현재진행 수동태를 이루는 과거분사 (C) considered가 정

답이다. (A) consider는 능동태 동사원형, (B) considerable은 형용사, (D) consideration은 명사로 품사상 빈칸에 들어갈 수 없다.

번역 회계 부서에 있는 두 명의 직원들이 승진 대상으로 고려되고 있다.

어휘 associate 직원, 동료   accounting 회계   consider 고려하다
considerable 상당한   consideration 고려 (사항)

122 접속사 자리 _ 어휘

해설 빈칸은 완전한 절(the rock band Captain Zino decided to ~ concert)을 이끌어 주절을 수식하는 부사절 접속사 자리이다. 록밴드가 무료 입장권을 제공하기로 결정한 과거(decided) 시점 이후 기록적인 수치에 달했다(have reached)는 내용이므로, '~한 이래로, ~한 이후'라는 뜻의 (A) Since가 정답이다. (B) Besides는 전치사/부사로 완전한 절을 이끌 수 없다. (C) As much as는 접속사로 쓰일 수 있으나 '~한 만큼, ~일지라도'라는 뜻으로 문맥상 어색하다. (D) Not only는 문두에 올 경우 뒤따르는 주어와 동사가 도치되어야 하므로 구조상으로도 빈칸에 들어갈 수 없다.

번역 록밴드 캡틴 지노가 콘서트 무료 입장권을 제공하기로 결정한 이후, 앨범 판매량이 기록적인 수치에 달했다.

어휘 offer 제공하다   reach 도달하다   a record number 기록적인 수치

123 전치사 자리 _ 어휘

해설 명사구 her interview를 목적어로 취하는 전치사 자리로, 문맥상 '면접 후에 최고의 지원자로 평가되었다'라는 내용이 되어야 자연스럽다. 따라서 (D) After가 정답이다. (A) As in은 '~의 경우와 같이, ~와 마찬가지로', (B) Just as는 '딱 ~만큼'이라는 뜻으로 적절하지 않다. 부사 (C) Almost는 구조상 빈칸에 들어갈 수 없다.

번역 한 씨의 면접 후, 위원회는 그녀가 관리직에 가장 맞는 지원자라는 데 동의했다.

어휘 committee 위원회   candidate 후보자, 지원자   supervisor 관리자

124 전치사 어휘

해설 빈칸은 명사구 several days를 목적어로 취하는 자리이므로, 기간을 나타내는 전치사가 들어가야 자연스럽다. 따라서 '~ 동안'이라는 의미로 쓰일 수 있는 (D) for가 정답이다.

번역 자문 위원은 해셔 사의 재고 목록 관리 과정을 며칠 동안 지켜본 후 문제점을 찾아냈다.

어휘 inventory 재고 목록   process 절차, 과정   identify 찾다, 발견하다

125 부사 자리 _ 동사 수식

해설 빈칸은 앞에 온 동사 are fastened를 수식하는 부사 자리이므로, (B) securely(단단히)가 정답이다. (A) security는 명사, (C) secures는 동사, (D) securing은 현재분사/동명사로 품사상 빈칸에 들어갈 수 없다.

번역 크레인 기사는 기계 사용 전 모든 가동부가 단단히 고정되어 있는지 확인해야 한다.

어휘 moving part 가동부 fasten 매다, 고정하다 security 보안 secure 안전한; 확보하다

126 동사 어휘

해설 빈칸은 명사구 a free quote for cloud storage services를 목적어로 취하는 to부정사구의 동사 자리이다. 문맥상 무료 견적과 관계가 있는 행위가 들어가야 하므로, '받다, 획득하다'라는 의미의 (D) obtain이 정답이다.

번역 이 쿠폰을 이용해 클라우드 저장 서비스의 무료 견적을 받아보세요.

어휘 quote 견적 storage 저장 advertise 광고하다 discount 할인하다 develop 개발하다

127 명사 자리 _ 동명사의 목적어

해설 빈칸은 동명사 testing의 목적어 역할을 하며 전치사구 of the vehicle의 수식을 받는 자리이다. 따라서 명사인 (B) endurance(내구성)가 정답이다. (A) enduring은 형용사/현재분사, (C) endures와 (D) endure는 동사로 품사상 빈칸에 들어갈 수 없다. 참고로, the와 of 사이에 동명사가 들어갈 경우 of 뒤에 오는 명사가 동명사의 의미상 목적어 역할을 하게 되는데(eg. the supplying of equipment), 이 문장에서는 앞뒤 문맥상 어울리지 않으므로 enduring을 동명사로 본다 하더라도 (A)는 정답이 될 수 없다.

번역 설계자들은 사막 지역에서 차량의 내구성을 시험함으로써 혹독한 환경에서도 완벽하게 작동한다는 것을 입증했다.

어휘 terrain 지역, 지형 prove 입증하다 harsh 거친, 혹독한 endure 견디다

128 명사 어휘

해설 빈칸은 that절과 동격을 이루는 명사 자리로, 카메라 배터리를 충전해야 할 때 깜빡이는 노란 불빛(The flashing yellow light)의 역할(serves as)을 나타내는 단어가 들어가야 한다. 따라서 '경보, 알림'이라는 의미의 (C) alert가 정답이다.

번역 노란 불빛이 깜빡이는 것은 카메라 배터리를 충전해야 한다는 경보 역할을 한다.

어휘 serve as ~의 역할을 하다 charge 충전하다 example 예시 allowance 용돈, 허용량 administration 관리, 집행

129 대명사 어휘

해설 빈칸은 동사 did not say의 직접 목적어 역할을 하는 대명사 자리이다. 부정어 not과 어울려 쓰여 '계획에 대해 아무 말도 하지 않았다'라는 내용을 완성해야 하므로, (B) anything이 정답이다.

번역 로젠 씨는 새 직원휴게실 계획에 대해 아무 말도 하지 않았다.

어휘 break room 휴게실

130 전치사 어휘

해설 빈칸은 명사구 all business segments를 목적어로 취하는 전치사 자리로, 문맥상 '모든 사업부에 걸쳐서'라는 내용이 되어야 자연스럽다. 따라서 '전체에 걸쳐, 온 ~에'라는 의미의 (A) across가 정답이다. 참고로, across는 areas, regions, sectors, country, world와 같이 부문, 범위, 지역을 나타내는 명사와 자주 쓰인다.

번역 이번 분기에는 모든 사업부에서 2퍼센트가 넘는 수익 증가를 보였다.

어휘 revenue 수익 growth 증가, 성장 exceed 넘다, 초과하다 quarter 분기 prior to ~에 앞서

PART 6

131-134 이메일

수신: 수신인 다수
발신: 골드스타 은행 〈information@goldstarbank.co.in〉
제목: 골드스타 은행 앱
날짜: 7월 15일

고객 여러분께:

골드스타 은행에서는 고객과 고객의 요구사항을 중요하게 생각하고 있습니다. 여러분 중 아시는 분도 있겠지만, 저희가 모바일 앱 상에서 기술적 문제를 **131 겪고 있습니다.** **132 현재 저희 엔지니어들이 이 문제를 처리하고 있습니다.** 소프트웨어 버그 때문에 저희 시스템이 다운된 7월 14일에 이 문제가 시작됐습니다. 해당 앱은 앞으로 24시간 **133 이내에** 제대로 작동할 것으로 예상됩니다. **134 그동안** 저희 모든 지점에서 은행 업무를 보실 수 있으며, 자동 현금 인출기도 작동되고 있습니다.

불편을 끼쳐드려 죄송합니다.

라비 차다
고객관리부 부서장

어휘 recipient 받는 사람, 수신인 seriously 진지하게, 중요하게 technical 기술적인 up and running 제대로 작동되는 transaction 업무, 거래 branch 지점 automated 자동화된 cash machine 현금 인출기

131 동사 자리 _ 시제

해설 빈칸은 주어 we의 동사 자리로, technical difficulties를 목적어로 취한다. 뒷부분에서 모바일 앱의 기술적 문제가 시작된 시점이 7월 14일(The trouble started on 14 July)이며 편지를 쓴 시점(7월 15일)을 기준으로 24시간 이내에 해결이 될 것이라고 했으므로, 아직 문제를 겪고 있음을 알 수 있다. 따라서 현재진행형 동사 (D) are experiencing이 정답이다. (C) had experienced는 과거에 이미 완료된 일을 나타내므로 빈칸에 적절하지 않고, to부정사인 (A) to experience와 동명사/현재분사인 (B) experiencing은 본동사 자리에 들어갈 수 없다.

132 문맥에 맞는 문장 고르기

번역 (A) 현재 저희 엔지니어들이 이 문제를 처리하고 있습니다.
(B) 새 모바일 앱은 사용이 간편하며 무료로 이용 가능합니다.
(C) 고객 서비스 담당직에 공석이 다수 있습니다.
(D) 골드스타 은행의 신규 지점 개소를 알려드립니다.

해설 빈칸 앞 문장에서 모바일 앱 상에서 기술적 문제를 겪고 있다(we are experiencing technical difficulties with our mobile app)고 했고, 뒤 문장에서도 해당 문제에 대해 설명하고 있다. 따라서 빈칸에도 이와 관련된 내용이 들어가야 자연스러우므로, 문제를 처리 중이라고 한 (A)가 정답이다.

어휘 available 이용 가능한 opening 공석, 결원; 개업 representative 대표, 대리인 announce 알리다, 발표하다

133 전치사 자리

해설 빈칸은 기간을 나타내는 명사구 the next twenty-four hours를 목적어로 취하는 전치사 자리이다. 따라서 '24시간 이내에'라는 의미를 완성하는 (B) within이 정답이다. (C) as long as는 '~만큼 긴'이라는 뜻으로 문맥상 어색하며, (A) if는 부사절 접속사, (D) above all은 접속부사로 품사상 빈칸에 들어갈 수 없다.

어휘 above all 무엇보다도

134 접속부사

해설 빈칸 앞 문장에서는 모바일 앱이 제대로 작동할 시점(We expect the app to be up and running within the next twenty-four hours)을, 뒤 문장에서는 그때까지의 대안(banking transactions can be done at any of our branch locations, ~ also working)을 언급하고 있다. 따라서 '그동안에'라는 의미의 (C) In the meantime이 정답이다.

어휘 unusually 특이하게도, 대단히 eventually 결국 as an example 한 예로서

135-138 정보

비더니 인더스트리즈는 자사 제품이 구입일자로부터 최소 1년간 **135광고된** 대로 작동될 것을 보장합니다. **136특정 제품은 이 기간이 연장될 수 있습니다.** 본 **137품질보증서**는 비더니 인더스트리즈 매장 및 기타 공식 유통업체에서 판매된 제품에 한해 적용됩니다. 결함이 발견된 제품은 수리 또는 교환을 위해 저희 주소로 발송해 주시면 됩니다. 손상으로 인해 반품하는 제품은 가능한 한 **138원래** 포장 상태로 저희에게 반송되어야 합니다.

어휘 guarantee 보장하다 function 기능하다, 작용하다 at least 최소 purchase 구입 apply to ~에 적용되다 licensed 공식 인가를 받은 distributor 배급업체, 유통업체 defective 결함이 있는 exchange 교환 damage 손상 packaging 포장

135 분사구문

해설 as를 전치사로 볼 경우 명사가, 접속사로 볼 경우에는 부사절에서 축약된 과거분사가 빈칸에 들어갈 수 있다. 「function as 명사」는 '~로서 기능/역할을 하다', 「function as 과거분사」는 '~된 대로 작동하다'라는 뜻을 나타내는데, 문맥상 제품이 광고된 대로 작동될 것이라는 내용이 되어야 자연스러우므로 (B) advertised가 정답이다.

136 문맥에 맞는 문장 고르기

번역 (A) 특정 제품은 이 기간이 연장될 수 있습니다.
(B) 비더니 인더스트리즈 매장은 3개국에 있습니다.
(C) 그 당시 전자 영수증이 생성됐습니다.
(D) 제품 견본은 매장에서 보실 수 있습니다.

해설 빈칸 앞 문장에서 구입일자로부터 최소 1년간(for at least one year from date of purchase) 제품이 광고된 대로 작동될 것을 보장한다고 했고, 뒤 문장에서는 적용 대상에 대해 설명하고 있다. 따라서 빈칸에도 이와 관련된 내용이 들어가야 자연스러우므로, 특정 제품은 해당 보장 기간이 연장될 수 있다고 한 (A)가 정답이다.

어휘 certain 어떤 extend 연장하다 electronic receipt 전자 영수증 generate 생성하다, 만들어 내다

137 명사 어휘

해설 빈칸은 동사 applies의 주어 역할을 하는 명사 자리로, 제품에 적용될 만한 것들 중 앞서 언급된 보장 기간과 관련된 단어가 들어가야 한다. 따라서 '품질보증서'라는 의미의 (D) warranty가 정답이다.

어휘 agenda 안건 requirement 요구사항

138 형용사 자리 _ 명사 수식

해설 빈칸은 명사 packaging을 수식하는 자리이므로, 형용사 (B) original(원래의)이 정답이다. (A) originally는 부사로 품사상 빈칸에 들어갈 수 없고, (C) origin과 (D) originality는 둘 다 명사로 packaging과 복합명사를 이룰 수 없으므로 오답이다.

어휘 originally 원래, 본래 origin 기원, 출신 originality 독창성

139-142 공지

헬시 푸즈 마켓은 앞으로 몇 주 동안 진행될 멋진 개조 공사를 계획해 두었습니다. 이 기간 동안 매장은 계속 문을 열지만, 특정 코너는 일시적으로 이용 불가능합니다. 8월 3일부터 매장의 냉장 및 냉동 식품 코너 공사가 있을 **139예정입니다.** **140그러므로** 해당 구역의 식품은 공사가 완료되는 동안 구매하실 수 없습니다. 리모델링은 8월 9일에 종료됩니다. 매장 관리자들은 **141며칠간** 불편을 겪을 만한 가치가 충분히 있다고 확신합니다.

1428월 12일에는 특별 기념 행사가 열릴 예정입니다. 행사 때 새로운 식품들의 무료 시식이 있을 예정인데, 여기에는 즉석에서 먹을 수 있는 다양한 영양 만점 점심 및 저녁 식사 제품들이 포함됩니다.

어휘 renovation 개조, 보수 department 부문, 매장, 코너
temporarily 일시적으로, 임시로 unavailable 이용 불가능한,
구매할 수 없는 refrigerated 냉장의 section 구역, 코너
under construction 공사 중인 complete 완료하다
inconvenience 불편 well worth 충분히 가치 있는
complimentary 무료의 expanded 폭넓은, 다양한
nutritious 영양가 높은 ready-to-eat 즉석의, 바로 먹을 수 있는

139 동사 자리 _ 태

해설 빈칸은 주어 the refrigerated and frozen-food sections의 동
사 자리이다. schedule은 '일정을 잡다, 예정에 넣다'라는 의미이므
로, 여기서 수동태로 쓰여야 한다. 따라서 '~할 예정이다'라는 내용을
완성하는 (D) are scheduled가 정답이다. 참고로, schedule은 주
로 「be scheduled for 명사」, 「be scheduled to부정사」의 수동태
구조로 쓰인다. (A) schedules는 주어와 수가 일치하지 않으며 능동
태이므로 빈칸에 들어갈 수 없고, to부정사인 (B) to be scheduled
와 동명사/현재분사인 (C) scheduling은 본동사 역할을 할 수 없다.

140 접속부사

해설 빈칸 앞 문장에서는 식품 코너에 공사가 예정되어 있다(the
refrigerated and frozen-food sections ~ are scheduled to
be under construction)고 했고, 뒤 문장에서는 공사로 인해 해당
코너의 식품 이용이 불가능하다(food from these areas will be
unavailable)고 안내하고 있다. 따라서 '그러므로'라는 뜻으로 인과
관계를 나타내는 (B) Therefore가 정답이다.

어휘 however 그러나 besides 게다가 likewise 마찬가지로

141 형용사 어휘

해설 복수 가산명사 days와 결합하여 '며칠'이라는 의미를 완성하는 형용
사가 필요하므로, (A) few가 정답이다. 참고로, (C) less는 불가산명
사와 쓰인다.

142 문맥에 맞는 문장 고르기

번역 (A) 매장은 3일간 문을 닫아야 합니다.
(B) 고객은 최근에 추가된 주차 공간에 주차해야 합니다.
(C) 리모델링 기간 동안 아이스크림 제품을 구매할 수 있습니다.
(D) 8월 12일에는 특별 기념 행사가 열릴 예정입니다.

해설 빈칸 뒤 문장에서 '이 행사(At this event)'의 구체적인 내용이 언급
되고 있으므로, 빈칸에는 특정 행사가 열린다고 공지하는 내용이 들어
가야 자연스럽다. 따라서 특별 기념 행사가 열릴 예정이라고 한 (D)가
정답이다.

143-146 기사

밴쿠버 (2월 3일) - 오늘 포알레스코에서 연례 식물 공개 행사 제막식을
거행했다. 포알레스코 대변인 나치오 로자에 따르면, 이번 143**연례** 행

사에서는 식물 연구에 대한 회사의 최근 프로젝트를 선보인다고 한다.
이러한 프로젝트 중 상당수는 일반적인 문제들을 알아보고자 고안된 고
객 설문조사에 기인한다. 144**이후 연구개발팀은 이러한 문제점들을 해
결해 줄 품종을 개발하고자 노력한다.** 올해 포알레스코의 전문 묘목장
은 골드톤 사과나무처럼 가뭄에 강한 품종들을 생산해 냈다. 이 변종들
은 길어진 가뭄을 손상 없이 견딜 수 있다. "특히 사막 145**지역들**의 정
원사들이 골드톤의 진가를 알아볼 겁니다"라고 로자가 말했다. "그리고
146**그들은** 새로운 Q7 장미 나무에도 관심이 있을 겁니다. 이 나무도
유사한 기후에서 잘 자라거든요."

어휘 unveil 제막식을 거행하다, 발표하다 annual 연례의, 연간의
according to ~에 따르면 spokesman 대변인 offering
(사람들이 사용하거나 즐기도록) 제공된 것 highlight 강조하다,
돋보이게 하다 latest 최신의 effort 활동, 프로젝트, 노력
botanical 식물의 gain an understanding of ~를 알아내다,
이해하다 specialized 전문화된 nursery 묘목장 turn out
(제품을) 생산하다 drought-hardy 가뭄에 강한 breed 품종
varietal 변종, 품종 withstand 견디다 extended 길어진
sustain damage 손상을 입다 appreciate 진가를 알아보다 in
particular 특히 thrive 잘 자라다, 번창하다

143 형용사 어휘

해설 Showcase를 가리키는 this offering과 어울리는 형용사를 선택
해야 한다. 앞 문장에서 '연례(annual) 식물 공개 행사'라고 했으므
로, 빈칸에도 annual과 유사한 의미의 단어가 들어가야 한다. 따라서
(D) yearly가 정답이다.

144 문맥에 맞는 문장 고르기

번역 (A) 회사는 농업에서 가장 수익성이 높은 부문을 찾고 있다.
(B) 회사는 전 세계에서 오는 연구원들을 면접하고 있다.
(C) 이후 연구개발팀은 이러한 문제점들을 해결해 줄 품종을 개발하고
자 노력한다.
(D) 이들의 광범위한 연구는 가장 맛 좋은 식물들을 시장에 내놓고
있다.

해설 빈칸 앞 문장에서 이러한 프로젝트 중 상당수가 일반적인 문제들을
알아내고자 고안된 고객 설문조사에서 기인한다(Many of these
efforts result from customer surveys designed to gain an
understanding of common challenges)고 했고, 뒤 문장에서는
가뭄에 강한 품종(drought-hardy breeds)의 개발을 일례로 들고
있다. 따라서 빈칸에는 해당 프로젝트와 관련된 내용이 들어가야 자연
스러우므로, (C)가 정답이다.

어휘 seek out 찾아내다 profitable 수익성이 좋은 agriculture
농업 address 해결하다, 고심하다 flavorful 맛이 좋은

145 명사 자리 _ 전치사의 목적어 _ 가산 명사

해설 빈칸은 전치사 in의 목적어 역할을 하는 명사 자리로, 지역을 의미
하는 (A) region 혹은 (B) regions 중 하나를 선택해야 한다. 가
산명사는 앞에 한정사가 붙지 않을 경우 복수형으로 쓰여야 하므로,
(B) regions가 정답이 된다.

146 대명사 어휘

해설 빈칸은 동사 might also be interested의 주어 역할을 하는 자리이다. 새로운 장미 나무에 관심을 가질 사람은 앞부분에 나온 사막 지역들의 정원사들(Gardeners)이므로, 이들을 대신할 수 있는 (D) they가 정답이다.

PART 7

147-148 광고

스타 피트니스 클럽
4월 25일 개점 행사

147쉐도우 로 714번지에 있는 신축 건물 서머레이크 시티에 새 클럽을 여니, 오셔서 함께해 주십시오. 저희 최신 장비를 구경하시고, 건강에 좋은 간식을 맛보시며 노련한 트레이너와 강사들도 만나보세요.

특별 할인: 첫 3개월간 20퍼센트 할인을 받으세요! 148(D)이 할인 혜택은 신규 회원에게만 적용되며 기타 할인 혜택과 함께 이용하실 수 없습니다. 또한 148(B)스타 피트니스 클럽 전 지점에서 이용 가능하며, 148(A)6월 30일까지 유효합니다.

피트니스 강좌 시간표 및 클럽 운영시간을 비롯해 더 자세한 정보는 www.starfitness.ca에서 확인하세요.

어휘 grand opening 개점, 개장 brand-new 아주 새로운 state-of-the-art 최신의 equipment 장비 experienced 숙련된 refreshment 간식 special offer 특가 제공 be combined with ~와 결합되다, 함께 적용되다 good 유효한

147 사실 관계 확인

번역 스타 피트니스 클럽에 대해 알 수 있는 것은?
(A) 새로운 시설을 지었다.
(B) 유료 회원권에는 간식을 제공한다.
(C) 현재 중고 운동 장비를 판매하고 있다.
(D) 일주일 내내 문을 연다.

해설 첫 번째 단락에서 신축 건물에 새 클럽을 연다(we open our newest club in Summerlake City in our brand-new building ~)고 했으므로, 스타 피트니스 클럽이 새로운 시설을 지었음을 알 수 있다. 따라서 (A)가 정답이다. 참고로, 건강한 간식(healthy refreshments)을 언급하지만 유료 회원권에만 제공한다는 내용은 없으므로 (B)는 오답이다.

어휘 paid 유료의 currently 현재

▸▸ Paraphrasing 지문의 newest club ~ our brand-new building → 정답의 a new facility

148 사실 관계 확인

번역 특별 할인에 대해 언급되지 않은 것은?
(A) 6월 말에 만료된다.
(B) 모든 지점에서 이용할 수 있다.
(C) 개인 트레이너와 함께 하는 시간이 포함되어 있다.
(D) 신규 회원만을 대상으로 한다.

해설 두 번째 단락의 '특가 할인은 스타 피트니스 클럽 전 지점에서 이용 가능하며, 6월 30일까지 유효하다(The offer is available at all Star Fitness locations and is good until 30 June)'에서 (A)와 (B)를, '이 할인 혜택은 신규 회원에게만 적용된다(The offer is for new members only)'에서 (D)를 확인할 수 있다. 따라서 언급되지 않은 (C)가 정답이다.

어휘 be intended for ~를 대상으로 하다

▸▸ Paraphrasing 지문의 is good until 30 June
→ 보기 (A)의 expires at the end of June

지문의 available at all Star Fitness locations
→ 보기 (B)의 can be used at any location

지문의 for new members only
→ 보기 (D)의 for new customers only

149-150 쪽지

WH
웨스터리 호텔
프루던스 가 295번지
애틀랜타, GA 30317

손님 여러분,

애틀랜타에 오신 것을 환영합니다. 웨스터리 호텔을 선택해 주셔서 영광입니다.

매일 오전 6시부터 오전 10시 30분까지 로비에 있는 식사 공간에서 150무료 아침 식사가 제공됩니다. 달걀, 오트밀, 페이스트리, 신선한 과일, 시리얼, 주스, 커피, 차 등 여러 메뉴를 즐겨보세요. 149단, 5월 2일에는 해당 공간이 개인 행사에 사용될 예정이라 이날 아침 식사는 3층에 있는 핀 레스토랑에서 제공됨을 알려드립니다.

말콤 앤더슨, 관리자
웨스터리 호텔

어휘 complimentary 무료의 an array of 다수의 be aware 알다 accommodate 공간을 제공하다, 수용하다

149 주제 / 목적

번역 쪽지의 목적은 무엇인가?
(A) 최근 투숙 경험에 대한 의견을 요청하려고
(B) 투숙객에게 장소 변경 사항을 알리려고
(C) 투숙객을 개인 행사에 초청하려고
(D) 새로운 호텔 개소를 알리려고

해설 두 번째 단락에서 원래 아침 식사는 로비에 있는 식사 공간에서 제공되지만 5월 2일에는 3층에 있는 핀 레스토랑(Please be aware ~ on May 2 breakfast will be served in the Fin Restaurant, located on the third floor)에서 제공된다고 했으므로, 쪽지를 작성한 목적이 아침 식사 장소 변경을 알리기 위함임을 알 수 있다. 따라서 (B)가 정답이다.

어휘 request 요청하다 recent 최근의

150 사실 관계 확인

번역 아침 식사에 대해 명시된 것은?
(A) 무료이다.
(B) 주말에는 이용할 수 없다.
(C) 5월 2일에는 제공되지 않을 예정이다.
(D) 곧 더 많은 메뉴가 포함될 것이다.

해설 두 번째 단락에서 매일 무료 아침 식사가 제공된다(A complimentary breakfast is served daily)고 했으므로, (A)가 정답이다. 참고로, 5월 2일에 장소가 변경되었을 뿐 아침 식사는 여전히 제공될 것이므로 (C)는 오답이다.

어휘 free of charge 무료의 feature 특별히 포함하다

> ▶▶ Paraphrasing 지문의 complimentary
> → 정답의 free of charge

151-152 공지

사우스이스트 철도에 새로운 일들이 펼쳐집니다.- 참여해 보세요!

사우스이스트 철도 보수 계획이 진척되고 있습니다. 이러한 변화는 지역의 혼잡한 도로 교통에 더욱 빠르며 편리하며 믿을 만한 대안을 마련해 줄 것입니다. 151공사는 올해 9월에 시작됩니다. 152새로운 역 설계안에 관해 의견을 구하기 위한 공청회가 6, 7, 8월로 예정되어 있습니다. 공청회에 대한 더 자세한 내용은 www.southeastrailproject.com/communityaffairs를 방문해 확인해 보세요.

어휘 get involved 관여하다, 참여하다 move forward 전진하다, 진행되다 renovation 보수, 개조 reliable 믿을 만한, 의지할 수 있는 alternative 대안 congested 혼잡한 public meeting 공청회 solicit 간청하다, 구하려고 하다 regarding ~에 관해

151 세부 사항

번역 프로젝트 공사는 언제 시작될 것인가?
(A) 6월
(B) 7월
(C) 8월
(D) 9월

해설 중반부에서 공사는 올해 9월에 시작된다(Construction begins this September)고 했으므로, (D)가 정답이다.

152 세부 사항

번역 공청회에서는 무엇이 논의될 것인가?
(A) 도로 교통량 감소
(B) 공사 자재 공급원
(C) 기차역 설계
(D) 급행열차 시간표

해설 중반부에서 새로운 역 설계안에 관해 의견을 구하기 위한(to solicit comments regarding design options for the new stations) 공청회가 예정되어 있다고 했으므로, (C)가 정답이다.

어휘 reduction 감소 material 자재, 재료 express train 급행열차

153-154 문자 메시지

리사 도밍게스 (오후 3시 24분)
안녕하세요, 트래비스. 시장에서 토마토를 사고 있는데 익은 것이 하나도 없네요. 154지난주에 쓰던 냉동 토마토 소스가 남아 있는지 확인해 주실 수 있나요? 없으면 토마토 통조림을 사야 할 것 같아요.

트래비스 팔리 (오후 3시 27분)
다 쓴 것 같아요. 153주방장님께 얘기해 볼게요.

리사 도밍게스 (오후 3시 28분)
그게 좋겠어요.

트래비스 팔리 (오후 3시 32분)
대신 빨간 피망을 사 오면 된다고 하시네요. 메뉴 설명을 조금 변경해야 하겠지만, 다른 재료들은 그대로 쓰면 돼요.

리사 도밍게스 (오후 3시 34분)
좋아요. 알겠어요. 고마워요!

어휘 ripe 익은 on hand 구할 수 있는, 보유 중인 otherwise 그렇지 않으면 description 설명 ingredient 재료, 성분

153 추론 / 암시

번역 팔리 씨는 어떤 업체에서 일하겠는가?
(A) 농장
(B) 식료품점
(C) 음식점
(D) 배송 서비스 업체

해설 팔리 씨가 오후 3시 27분 메시지에서 주방장에게 얘기해본다(Let me speak to the chef)고 말하는 것으로 보아, 음식점에서 일한다고 추론할 수 있다. 따라서 (C)가 정답이다.

154 의도 파악

번역 팔리 씨가 오후 3시 27분에 "다 쓴 것 같아요"라고 말할 때, 그 의도는 무엇인가?
(A) 직원들은 더 이상 아이디어가 없다.
(B) 기한을 놓쳤다.
(C) 직원들이 퇴근했다.
(D) 제품이 없다.

해설 도밍게스 씨가 오후 3시 24분 메시지에서 지난주에 쓰던 냉동 토마토 소스가 남아 있는지 확인해달라(Can you check ~ if we have any frozen tomato sauce on hand from last week?)고 요청했는데, 이에 대해 팔리 씨가 '다 쓴 것 같아요(I'm afraid we are all out)'라고 응답한 것이다. 즉, 냉동 토마토 소스가 다 떨어졌음을 알리려는 의도라고 볼 수 있으므로, (D)가 정답이다.

어휘 deadline 마감 시간, 기한

▸▸ Paraphrasing   지문의 all out → 정답의 not available

155-157 공지

> 벨 커피 클럽 회원 여러분께 알립니다.
>
> ¹⁵⁵다음 주에 벨 커피가 커피 신제품인 '라테 슬로우 브루'를 선보입니다. 벨 커피 클럽 회원은 웰링턴 가 200번지에 있는 저희 본점에서 이 특별한 신제품을 처음 맛보실 수 있습니다. ^{155/157}1월 12일에 들르셔서 회원 카드를 제시하고 무료로 라테 슬로우 브루 한 잔과 지역 협력업체인 영 컨펙션즈에서 제공하는 시식용 빵을 받으세요. 특별히 벨 커피를 위해 제작된 맛인 초콜릿 에스프레소 머핀을 비롯해 갓 구워낸 다양한 머핀 중 선택하세요. <u>추가 커피 제품 및 제과류도 구입하실 수 있습니다.</u>
>
> ¹⁵⁶앞으로 4주에 걸쳐 벨 커피의 다른 지점에서도 출시가 이어질 예정입니다. 더 자세한 내용을 알아보려면 bellecoffee.ca를 방문하세요.
>
> 맛있게 드세요!

어휘 debut 신상품으로 소개하다, 데뷔시키다 creation 창작품, 제조품 treat 특별한 것, 대접 flagship store (체인점의) 본점 complimentary 무료의 pastry 밀가루 반죽으로 만든 빵이나 과자 confection 제과 제품 (회사) a variety of 다양한 rollout 출시, 첫 공개

155 세부 사항

번역 벨 커피는 1월 12일에 무엇을 할 것인가?

(A) 영 컨펙션즈와 합병
(B) 두 번째 지점 개점
(C) 신제품 소개
(D) 회원 프로그램 시작

해설 첫 번째 단락에서 다음 주에 커피 신제품 라테 슬로우 브루를 선보인다(Next week, Belle Coffee will debut our newest coffee creation, the Latte Slow Brew)고 한 후, 회원들에게 1월 12일에 이 신제품을 맛보라며 본점으로 초대(We invite you to stop by on January 12)했다. 따라서 이날 신제품을 소개할 것임을 알 수 있으므로, (C)가 정답이다.

어휘 merge 합병하다

▸▸ Paraphrasing   지문의 debut our newest coffee creation
→ 정답의 Introduce a new product

156 추론 / 암시

번역 공지에 따르면 웹사이트에서 무엇을 얻을 수 있는가?

(A) 쿠폰
(B) 조리법
(C) 신청서
(D) 일정표

해설 두 번째 단락에서 앞으로 4주에 걸쳐 벨 커피의 다른 지점에서도 신제품 출시가 이어질 예정(Rollout at our other Belle Coffee locations will follow over the next four weeks)이라며 더 자세한 내용을 알아보려면 웹사이트를 방문하라고 했다. 따라서 웹사이트에서 지점별 신상품 출시 일정을 볼 수 있을 거라 추론할 수 있으므로, (D)가 정답이다.

157 문장 삽입

번역 [1], [2], [3], [4]로 표시된 곳 중 다음 문장이 가장 적합한 곳은?

"추가 커피 제품 및 제과류도 구입하실 수 있습니다."

(A) [1]
(B) [2]
(C) [3]
(D) [4]

해설 주어진 문장에서 추가 커피 제품 및 제과류가 구입 가능하다(Additional coffee products and pastries will be available for purchase)고 했으므로, 앞서 먼저 동일한 종류의 제품이 언급되어야 한다. [3] 앞에서 라테 슬로우 브루(Latte Slow Brew), 시식용 빵(a pastry sample), 갓 구워낸 다양한 머핀(a variety of their fresh-baked muffins)이 언급되었으므로, 이 뒤에 주어진 문장이 들어가야 자연스럽다. 따라서 (C)가 정답이다.

어휘 additional 추가의 purchase 구매, 구입

158-160 공고

> ### 달스턴 오페라 뉴스
>
> #### 시즌 입장권 구매 가능
>
> 지금 www.dalstonopera.com/seasontickets에서 시즌 입장권을 구입하세요.
>
> 5월 4일-12일: 〈지그룬〉 (2시간, 중간 휴식 1회)
> ¹⁶⁰7월 6일-14일: 〈르 라팽〉 (3시간, 중간 휴식 2회)
> 9월 14일-22일: ¹⁵⁸〈더 쉽마스터스 가든〉 (90분, 중간 휴식 없음)
> 11월 30일-12월 8일: 〈오케스티아〉 (4시간, 중간 휴식 3회)
>
> *공연은 살로디 강당에서 진행되며, 오후 8시 정각에 시작합니다.*
>
> #### 입주 예술가 시리즈
>
> 저희 입주 예술가 순환 프로그램은 고정 출연진의 공연에 새로운 목소리를 불어넣기 위함입니다. 이러한 예술가들이 출연하는 정오 주간 공연 특별 시리즈에 함께 하셔서, ¹⁵⁹세계 곳곳에서 온 차세대 인재들이 오페라 무대에 오르는 것을 축하할 수 있도록 도와주십시오. 각 공연에

는 저희 입주 예술가들 중 한 명이 선정해 부르는 오페라 인기곡 메들리가 포함됩니다.

5월 4일: 다이앤 시모다

160 **7월 6일: 칼림 패턴**

9월 14일: 클라우디아 고딘

11월 30일: 니콜라이 수자

어휘   intermission (연극, 영화 등의) 중간 휴식 시간   take place 열리다   auditorium 강당   promptly 지체 없이, 시간을 엄수하여   rotating 순환하는   artist-in-residence 입주 예술가 (거주 지원을 받는 예술가)   aim ~을 목적으로 하다   regular cast 고정 출연진   matinee 마티네 (연극, 영화 등의 주간 공연, 상영)   generation 세대   feature 특별히 포함하다

158   세부 사항

번역   휴식 시간 없이 공연되는 오페라는?

(A) 〈지그룬〉
(B) 〈르 라팽〉
(C) 〈더 쉽마스터스 가든〉
(D) 〈오케스티아〉

해설   공고의 첫 번째 항목을 보면 중간 휴식 없이 90분간(90 minutes with no intermission) 진행되는 작품이 〈더 쉽마스터스 가든(The Shipmaster's Garden)〉임을 알 수 있다. 따라서 (C)가 정답이다.

▸▸ Paraphrasing   지문의 **with no intermission**
→ 질문의 **without a break**

159   추론 / 암시

번역   입주 예술가에 대해 사실에 가까운 것은?

(A) 모두 달스턴 지역 출신이다.
(B) 고정 출연 배우들보다 나이가 어리다.
(C) 무용가로 전문 훈련을 받았다.
(D) 세계적으로 잘 알려져 있다.

해설   입주 예술가 시리즈에 대한 공지에서 차세대 인재들이 오페라 무대에 오르는 것을 축하할 수 있도록 도와달라(help us celebrate the next generation of talent coming into the field of opera)고 했는데, 여기서 차세대(the next generation)라는 것은 입주 예술가들이 기존 공연자들보다 나이가 더 어리다는 것을 암시한다. 따라서 (B)가 정답이다. 참고로, 입주 예술가들이 세계 곳곳에서(from around the globe) 왔다고 했으나 유명한 지의 여부는 알 수 없으므로 (D)는 정답이 될 수 없다.

어휘   professionally 전문적으로

▸▸ Paraphrasing   지문의 **the next generation**
→ 정답의 **younger than the regular performers**

160   추론 / 암시

번역   누가 〈르 라팽〉에 출연하겠는가?

(A) 시모다 씨
(B) 패턴 씨
(C) 고딘 씨
(D) 수자 씨

해설   공고의 첫 번째 항목을 보면 〈르 라팽(Le Lapin)〉의 공연 기간이 7월 6일에서 7월 14일이라고 나와 있는데, 공고의 두 번째 항목에 나온 입주 예술가 중에서 7월 6일에 무대에 오르는 사람은 칼림 패턴(Kalim Patton) 씨임을 알 수 있다. 따라서 (B)가 정답이다.

161-163   기사

뮬커 조선소, 변화를 겪다

5월 2일 – 한때 바쁘게 돌아갔던 선박 제조 중심지 뮬커 조선소에 새 역할이 주어지고 있다. 한 팀의 기술자들이 뮬커 조선소를 **161 (D)** 음식점, **161 (C)** 10여 개의 소매업체, **161 (B)** 라이브 음악 공연이 열릴 야외 테라스 등을 갖춘 보행자 전용 야외 복합 공간으로 바꾸고 있다.

162 시에서는 작년 6월까지만 해도 조선소를 철거할 계획이었으나 이러한 결정은 지역 주민, 특히 조선소를 귀중한 역사적 산업 건물로 여기는 이전 조선소 직원들의 강한 반발을 일으켰다. 많은 조선소 직원들은 자신들의 노고가 후대에 기억되기를 바라며 입구 근처 벽에 자신들의 이름을 새겨 넣었었다.

"생산이 한창일 때는 조선소 직원들이 1년 만에 해군함정을 만들기도 했습니다." 수석 기술자인 바니 엔야트 씨의 말이다. "그 후 생산이 점차 줄어들고 결국 조선소는 문을 닫았어요. 이 프로젝트가 완료되면, 새로운 복합단지는 고용 기회와 오락을 위한 장소로서 **163** 역할을 하며 연중 내내 사랑 받는 한편, 조선소 과거의 유산 역시 지속될 것입니다."

어휘   shipyard 조선소   undergo 겪다   transformation 변화   bustling 부산한   manufacturing 제조   pedestrian mall 보행자 전용 쇼핑 단지   retail 소매   patio 테라스   demolish 철거하다   former 이전의   treasure 귀중히 여기다   industrial 산업의   etch 아로새기다   naval ship 해군함정   gradually 점차   eventually 결국   complete 완료된   employment 고용   opportunity 기회   legacy 유산   endure 지속되다, 오래 가다

161   사실 관계 확인

번역   조선소 관련 계획에서 언급되지 않은 것은?

(A) 사무 공간
(B) 오락
(C) 쇼핑 구역
(D) 식사 시설

해설   첫 번째 단락에서 기술자들이 조선소를 음식점, 10여 개의 소매업체, 라이브 음악 공연이 열릴 야외 테라스 등을 갖춘 공간(mall with restaurants, a dozen retail businesses and an outdoor patio that will feature live music performances)으로 바꾸고 있다고 했으므로, (B), (C), (D) 모두를 확인할 수 있다. 따라서 언급되지 않은 (A)가 정답이다.

어휘   establishment 시설, 기관

▸▸ Paraphrasing   지문의 live music performances
→ 보기 (B)의 Entertainment

지문의 retail businesses
→ 보기 (C)의 A shopping section

지문의 restaurants
→ 보기 (D)의 Eating establishments

162   추론 / 암시

번역   뮬커 조선소에 대해 암시된 것은?

(A) 동영상에 나올 것이다.
(B) 이전 직원들을 위한 기념물을 갖출 것이다.
(C) 지역 주민들이 조선소의 역사를 중요시한다.
(D) 현재 조선소에서 선박을 만들고 있다.

해설   두 번째 단락에서 조선소를 철거할 계획이었으나 지역 주민, 특히 조선소를 귀중한 역사적 산업 건물로 여기는 이전 조선소 직원들의 강한 반발(a strong reaction from community members, especially former shipbuilders who viewed the site as a treasured industrial landmark)을 일으켰다는 내용으로 보아, 지역 주민들이 조선소의 역사를 중요시함을 알 수 있다. 따라서 (C)가 정답이다. 참고로, 조선소 직원들이 입구 근처 벽에 자신들의 이름을 새겨 넣었다고는 했지만, 조선소 측에서 이들을 위한 기념물(monument)을 따로 세운다는 내용은 없으므로 (B)는 오답이다.

어휘   monument 기념물   currently 현재

▸▸ Paraphrasing   지문의 community members
→ 정답의 Local residents
지문의 viewed the site as a treasured industrial landmark
→ 정답의 appreciate its history

163   동의어 찾기

번역   세 번째 단락, 일곱 번째 줄에 쓰인 'serving'과 의미가 가장 가까운 단어는?

(A) 참석하며
(B) 기능을 하며
(C) 배부하며
(D) 제시하며

해설   'serving'이 포함된 부분은 '고용 기회와 오락을 위한 장소로서 역할을 하며'라는 의미로 해석되며, 여기서 serve as는 '~로서 역할을 하다'라는 뜻을 나타낸다. 따라서 '(특정) 기능을 하며'라는 의미의 (B) functioning이 정답이다.

164-167   회람

회람

수신: 고객 서비스팀
발신: 스콧 데이비스, 고객서비스 관리자
날짜: 7월 22일

---

¹⁶⁴오늘 하크니스 클로디어의 고객 서비스부 감사 주간이 시작됐습니다. 이 기회를 빌려 올해 여러분의 헌신과 전문성에 감사를 드리고 싶습니다. 여러분 각자가 탁월한 고객 서비스를 제공해 주셨습니다. 경영진은 여러분이 팀으로서 성취한 일들을 자랑스럽게 여깁니다. ¹⁶⁵작년에 진행된 스포팅 클로스 주식회사와의 합병이 때로는 혼란스럽고 힘들었다는 점을 알고 있습니다. 여러분의 서비스는 합병 과정 내내 한결같았고, 여러분들 덕분에 고객 관련 이행 작업이 매끄럽게 진행되었습니다. 이 얼마나 훌륭한 업적입니까!

저희 경영진은 감사를 표하기 위해 이번 주에 재미있는 시간을 보낼 수 있는 기회들을 제공할 것입니다. ^{164/166/167}화요일에는 오전 8시부터 모두에게 커피, 빵, 과일이 제공되는 아침 식사를 대접할 것입니다. 수요일 오후에는 각자 음식을 준비해 와서 나눠 먹는 점심 식사를 하겠습니다. 목요일에는 퇴근 후 모스 비스트로에서 팀 회식을 합니다. 금요일에는 점심 식사 후 상품을 받을 수 있는 대회들이 있을 예정입니다. 이번 주가 정말 기대됩니다. 여러분이 즐겁게 보내셨으면 합니다.

어휘   kick off 시작되다   appreciation 감사   opportunity 기회   dedication 헌신   professionalism 전문성   exceptional 특출한, 탁월한   management 경영진   merger 합병   at times 때로는   seamless 매끄러운, 순조로운   transition 이행   accomplishment 업적   potluck 각자 음식을 가져와서 조금씩 나눠 먹는 식사

164   주제 / 목적

번역   데이비스 씨가 회람을 쓴 목적은?

(A) 직원들에게 교육 시간 참석을 요청하려고
(B) 직원들에게 초과 근무를 요청하려고
(C) 기념 행사의 세부사항을 알려주려고
(D) 프로젝트 종료를 알리려고

해설   첫 번째 단락 도입부에서 고객 서비스부 감사 주간이 시작되었음을 알린 후, 두 번째 단락에서 고객 서비스팀을 대상으로 하는 요일별 행사 내용을 소개하고 있다. 따라서 기념 행사의 세부사항을 알리는 회람임을 알 수 있으므로, (C)가 정답이다.

어휘   attend 참석하다   request 요청하다   celebration 기념 행사, 기념

165   추론 / 암시

번역   하크니스 클로디어에 대해 암시된 것은?

(A) 다른 회사와 합쳤다.
(B) 매년 직원들에게 상을 준다.
(C) 방수 의류 제품을 제조한다.
(D) 규모가 매우 작은 고객 서비스팀이 있다.

해설   첫 번째 단락 중반부에서 작년에 진행된 스포팅 클로스 주식회사와의 합병이 때로는 혼란스럽고 힘들었다는 점을 알고 있다(We understand that last year's merger with Sporting Clothes, Inc., was confusing and difficult at times)고 했으므로, 다른 회사와 합쳤다는 사실을 알 수 있다. 따라서 (A)가 정답이다.

어휘   combine with ~와 결합되다   manufacture 제조하다   waterproof 방수의

166 세부 사항

번역 아침에 행사가 열리는 때는 언제인가?

(A) 화요일
(B) 수요일
(C) 목요일
(D) 금요일

해설 두 번째 단락에서 화요일에 커피, 빵, 과일이 제공되는 아침 식사를 대접할 것(On Tuesday ~ everyone will be treated to a breakfast)이라고 했으므로, (A)가 정답이다.

167 문장 삽입

번역 [1], [2], [3], [4]로 표시된 곳 중에서 다음 문장이 가장 적합한 곳은?

"저희 경영진은 감사를 표하기 위해 이번 주에 재미있는 시간을 보낼 수 있는 기회들을 제공할 것입니다."

(A) [1]
(B) [2]
(C) [3]
(D) [4]

해설 주어진 문장에서 경영진이 감사를 표하기 위해 이번 주에 재미있는 시간을 보낼 수 있는 기회들(some opportunities to have fun this week)을 제공할 것이라고 했으므로, 이러한 기회들을 소개한 문장을 찾아야 한다. [3] 뒤에서 요일별 행사 내용이 모두 언급되었으므로, (C)가 정답이다.

168-171 공고

프렌즈 오브 체스터턴 공립 도서관
도서 판매

체스터턴 공립 도서관은 이번 주말, 도서관 2층에서 연례 도서 판매 행사를 엽니다. 행사 시간은 11월 16일 토요일 오전 9시부터 오후 5시까지, 11월 17일 일요일 낮 12시부터 오후 5시까지입니다. **168 도서관의 자원봉사단인 프렌즈 오브 체스터턴 공립 도서관(FCPL)을 위한 특별 선판매 행사는 11월 15일 금요일 오후 4시부터 오후 8시까지 열릴 예정입니다.**

본 판매 행사에는 도서관에서 더 이상 대출하지 않는 도서뿐만 아니라 일반인이 기증한 도서도 포함됩니다. 수익금은 어린이 열람실 개설에 사용될 것입니다.

연령대와 장르를 불문하고 보급판과 양장본 도서의 기증을 모두 **169 환영합니다.** 단, 찢어지거나 다른 형태로 외관이 손상된 책은 받지 않음을 알려 드립니다. **170 죄송하지만 잡지나 학술지도 받지 않습니다.** 본 행사를 위한 기증품은 11월 8일 금요일까지 받을 예정이며, **171 다음 시간대에 안내 데스크로 갖다 주시면 됩니다.**

월-목요일: 오전 9시-오전 11시
171 수요일: 오후 1시-오후 8시
금요일: 오전 9시-오후 3시

여러분들의 성원에 감사 드립니다!

어휘 annual 연례의 preview sale 선판매 volunteer 자원봉사자 support group 협력 단체 donate 기부하다, 기증하다 proceeds 수익금 donation 기증(품) reading room 열람실 paperback 보급판 be torn 찢어지다 defaced 외관이 손상된 reject 거부하다, 거절하다 drop off 갖다 주다

168 세부 사항

번역 금요일 판매 행사에 누가 참석할 수 있는가?

(A) 유급 직원
(B) 자원봉사자
(C) 어린이
(D) 재정 기부자

해설 첫 번째 단락을 보면 특별 선판매 행사가 11월 15일 금요일에 열릴 예정(A special preview sale ~ will be held on Friday, November 15)이며 이 행사는 도서관의 자원봉사단(the library's volunteer support group)을 위한 것이라고 나와 있다. 따라서 (B)가 정답이다.

169 동의어 찾기

번역 세 번째 단락, 첫 번째 줄에 쓰인 'welcome'과 의미가 가장 가까운 단어는?

(A) 받아들이다
(B) 인사하다
(C) 존경하다
(D) 만족시키다

해설 'welcome'이 포함된 부분은 '연령대와 장르를 불문하고 보급판과 양장본 도서의 기증을 모두 환영한다'라는 의미로 해석되는데, 여기서 welcome은 '환영하다, 기꺼이 받아들이다'라는 뜻으로 쓰였다. 따라서 '받아들이다'라는 의미의 (A) accept가 정답이다.

170 사실 관계 확인

번역 학술지에 대해 명시된 것은?

(A) 2층에 비치되어 있다.
(B) 자원봉사자들에게만 판매될 예정이다.
(C) 대출할 수 없다.
(D) 기증할 수 없다.

해설 세 번째 단락 중반부에서 잡지나 학술지도 기증품으로 받지 않는다(Sorry, no magazines or journals, please)고 했으므로, 학술지는 기증할 수 없음을 알 수 있다. 따라서 (D)가 정답이다.

171 세부 사항

번역 저녁에 기증품을 갖다 줄 수 있는 때는 언제인가?

(A) 월요일
(B) 수요일
(C) 목요일
(D) 금요일

해설 공지 하단에 요일별로 기증품을 갖다 줄 수 있는 시간이 나와 있는데, 저녁 시간(1:00 P.M. to 8:00 P.M.)에 가능한 요일은 수요일이므로, (B)가 정답이다.

172-175 채팅

> **릴리 박 (오후 4시 3분)** 안녕하세요, 여러분. 주말 전에 여러분께 확인하고 싶어요. ¹⁷³카즈, 블룸필드 어소시에이츠와의 회의는 어땠나요?
>
> **카즈 페도로비츠 (오후 4시 10분)** 더할 나위 없이 좋았습니다. ¹⁷²그들은 서비스 계약과 함께 새 노트북 컴퓨터 40대를 구매할 예정이에요. 서명된 계약서를 받았고요.
>
> **릴리 박 (오후 4시 11분)** 훌륭해요! 한 주를 잘 마무리하는군요!
>
> **데이비드 에스포지토 (오후 4시 12분)** 축하합니다! 이번 건으로 선두에 올라서겠군요. 지금 3개월 연속 최다 판매사원이네요.
>
> **다니엘 베커 (오후 4시 13분)** 좋은 소식이네요, 카즈. 그건 그렇고, 사무실에 복귀하는 대로 저에게 모든 영수증을 갖다 주시면 ¹⁷⁵그 다음 주 초에 출장비 환급을 받으실 수 있어요.
>
> **카즈 페도로비츠 (오후 4시 14분)** 확실한가요? ¹⁷⁴마이클 림이 큰 판매 건을 따내지 않았나요?
>
> **릴리 박 (오후 4시 15분)** ^{173/174}안타깝게도 마이클의 고객들이 마지막 순간에 취소를 했어요. ¹⁷²새 장비를 구입하기보다 다른 업체에서 컴퓨터와 프린터를 대여하기로 결정했답니다.
>
> **카즈 페도로비츠 (오후 4시 17분)** 안타깝네요. 그리고 ¹⁷⁵챙겨 주셔서 감사합니다, 다니엘.
>
> **다니엘 베커 (오후 4시 18분)** 도움이 되어 기뻐요!
>
> **릴리 박 (오후 4시 19분)** 주말 잘 보내세요, 여러분.

어휘 Associates 합자 회사 purchase 구입하다 service agreement 서비스 계약 contract 계약(서) in a row 연속해서, 잇달아 receipt 영수증 reimbursement 환급, 상환 land (계약 등을) 따내다 back out 취소하다, 철회하다 lease 임대하다 equipment 장비

172 추론 / 암시

번역 글을 쓴 사람들은 어떤 유형의 업체에 관여하고 있는가?

(A) 부동산
(B) 여행 서비스
(C) 사무 기기
(D) 금융 자문

해설 페도로비츠 씨의 오후 4시 10분 메시지와 박 씨의 4시 15분 메시지에서 채팅 참여자들이 노트북, 컴퓨터, 프린터 등 사무 기기를 판매하는 업체에 근무하고 있음을 추론할 수 있다. 따라서 (C)가 정답이다.

▸▸ **Paraphrasing** 지문의 **laptops, computers, printers** → 정답의 **Office technology**

173 추론 / 암시

번역 박 씨의 직책은 무엇이겠는가?

(A) 광고 전문가
(B) 인사부장
(C) 경리사원
(D) 영업부 관리자

해설 박 씨는 오후 4시 3분 메시지에서 카즈에게 블룸필드 어소시에이츠와의 회의 결과(Kaz, how did your meeting with Blumfield Associates go?)를 묻고, 4시 15분 메시지에서 마이클의 고객들이 제품 주문을 취소한 사실(Michael's customers backed out at the last minute)을 알려주는 등 채팅의 흐름을 주도하고 있다. 따라서 영업부를 관리하는 직책으로 보는 것이 가장 타당하므로, (D)가 정답이다.

174 사실 관계 확인

번역 림 씨에 대해 알 수 있는 것은?

(A) 판매를 완수하지 못했다.
(B) 현재 출장 중이다.
(C) 채팅 참여자들이 속한 부서의 신입사원이다.
(D) 이제 막 계약서에 서명했다.

해설 페도로비츠 씨가 오후 4시 14분 메시지에서 마이클 림 씨가 큰 판매 건을 따내지 않았느냐(Didn't Michael Lim just land a big sale?)고 물었는데, 박 씨가 4시 15분 메시지에서 마이클의 고객들이 마지막 순간에 취소를 했다(Michael's customers backed out at the last minute)고 했다. 따라서 림 씨의 판매가 성공적으로 이루어지지 않았다고 볼 수 있으므로, (A)가 정답이다.

어휘 complete 완료하다 currently 현재

▸▸ **Paraphrasing** 지문의 **customers backed out** → 정답의 **was not able to complete a sale**

175 의도 파악

번역 베커 씨가 오후 4시 18분에 "도움이 되어 기뻐요!"라고 쓸 때, 그 의도는 무엇인가?

(A) 출장비 환급을 도울 수 있어 기쁘다.
(B) 신규 고객을 성공적으로 유치하게 되어 기쁘다.
(C) 한 주의 끝이라 마음이 편안하다.
(D) 장비 임대를 제안한 것이 기쁘다.

해설 베커 씨가 오후 4시 13분 메시지에서 페도로비츠 씨에게 출장비 환급에 대해 안내했고, 4시 17분 메시지에서 페도로비츠 씨가 베커 씨에게 챙겨 주어 고맙다(thanks for taking care of that, Danielle)고 인사하자 이에 대해 한 말이다. 따라서 (A)가 정답이다.

어휘 refund 환급하다 travel expense 출장비 relieved 안도하는,
다행으로 여기는

▶▶ Paraphrasing 지문의 **travel reimbursement check**
→ 정답의 **refunding some travel expenses**

176-180 광고 + 이메일

직접 주문 제작한 명함을 받아보세요

로레티 프린팅 사는 177**개인 맞춤형 명함 제작을 위한 새 온라인 플랫
폼** lorreticardprint.com을 알려 드리게 되어 기쁩니다. 176**고객 여
러분들은 약 10년간 해 오신 대로 직접 방문하여 주문하실 수도 있지만**,
이제 굉장히 빠르고 쉽게 명함을 주문할 수 있는 시스템도 갖췄습니다.
사용하기 편한 수백 개의 템플릿 중에서 선택하고 자신만의 글과 이미
지를 넣어, 몇 분 이내에 전문가급의 명함을 제작해 보세요.

4가지 종이 옵션을 제공합니다.

유형	설명	최소 주문 수량
178매트 - M1	표준 명함 인쇄용지, 번쩍임 감소	50장
글로시 - G4	광택, 색상 및 세부사양 강화	100장
텍스처드 - T3	독특한 격자 무늬, 흥미로운 촉감	100장
메탈릭 - M2	특별 광택, 독특함, 이목 집중	200장

저희에게 종이 유형별로 견본을 받아보고 싶으시다면 온라인 주문 전에
연락 주세요.

어휘 custom made 주문 제작의 announce 발표하다,
알리다 customized 맞춤형의, 개개인의 요구에 맞춘 place an
order 주문하다 in person 직접 방문하여 especially 특히,
유난히 easy-to-use 사용이 간편한 description 설명, 묘사
minimum 최소한의 standard 표준 card stock (명함의) 인쇄
용지 glare 환한 빛 enhance 높이다, 향상시키다 grid 격자
capture 붙잡다 attention 주목, 관심

수신: hello@loretticardprint.com
발신: felix@thibaultautoworks.com
날짜: 5월 22일 화요일
제목: 주문번호 28191 - 후속 조치
첨부: @ 로고_오토워크

제 주문을 즉시 중단시키고 필수 변경 사항을 반영하는 법을 설명해 주
셔서 감사합니다. 저의 명함이 출력에 들어가기 전에 연락이 닿아 정말
다행이었어요. 178**사용하지도 못하는 명함을 50장이나 받았으면 정말
안타까웠을 거예요.**

전화로 설명 드린 것처럼 179**이전 버전의 로고를 웹사이트에 잘못 올렸
습니다.** 파일 크기가 같은 현재 로고로 교체해 두었어요. 변경사항에 여
기 첨부한 이 로고가 180**반영됐는지** 확인해 주시기 바랍니다. 반영됐다
면 그대로 진행하시고 제 주문서를 제출해 주세요.

감사합니다.

펠릭스 티볼트

어휘 get in touch 연락하다 mention 언급하다 accidentally
잘못하여, 우연히 replace 교체하다 current 현재의 reflect
반영하다 submit 제출하다

176 추론 / 암시

번역 로레티 프린팅 사에 대해 암시된 것은?

(A) 오프라인 소매점이 있다.
(B) 카드 회사와 합병한다.
(C) 숙련된 디자이너들을 찾고 있다.
(D) 종이 옵션을 늘렸다.

해설 광고 초반에서 온라인 플랫폼을 열었지만 여전히 직접 방문하여 명
함을 주문할 수 있다(While our customers can still place
orders in person)고 했으므로, 오프라인 소매점이 있음을 추론할
수 있다. 따라서 (A)가 정답이다.

어휘 physical 실체가 있는 retail location 소매점 merge 합병하다
experienced 숙련된 expand 확대하다

▶▶ Paraphrasing 지문의 **our customers can still place orders
in person**
→ 정답의 **It has a physical retail location**

177 세부 사항

번역 광고에 따르면, 고객은 회사 웹사이트에서 무엇을 할 수 있는가?

(A) 회사에 대한 의견 제시하기
(B) 자신들만의 명함 디자인하기
(C) 회사의 우편물 수신자 명단에 들어가기
(D) 할인 코드 입력하기

해설 광고의 첫 번째 문장에서 회사 웹사이트를 소개하며 개인 맞춤형 명
함 제작을 위한 새 온라인 플랫폼(our new online platform for
creating customized business cards)이라고 했으므로, 여기서
고객들이 자신들만의 명함을 만들 수 있음을 알 수 있다. 따라서 (B)
가 정답이다.

어휘 mailing list 우편물 수신자 명단

▶▶ Paraphrasing 지문의 **creating customized business cards**
→ 정답의 **Design their own business cards**

178 연계

번역 티볼트 씨는 어떤 유형의 명함을 주문했겠는가?

(A) 매트
(B) 글로시
(C) 텍스처드
(D) 메탈릭

해설 이메일의 첫 번째 단락에서 사용하지도 못하는 명함을 50장이나 받았
으면 정말 안타까웠을 것(It would have been such a shame to
have printed 50 cards I can't use)이라고 했으므로, 티볼트 씨가
명함을 50장 주문했던 것을 알 수 있다. 광고에 나와 있는 표에 따르
면 50장 주문이 가능한 유형은 매트에 해당하므로, (A)가 정답이다.

179 세부 사항

번역 티볼트 씨가 주문상의 로고를 교체한 이유는?

(A) 제대로 정렬되지 않았다.
(B) 파일 크기가 잘못됐다.
(C) 다른 회사 로고였다.
(D) 예전 이미지였다.

해설 이메일의 두 번째 단락에서 명함 주문 시 자신의 로고를 이전 버전으로 잘못 올렸다(I had accidentally uploaded an older version of my logo)고 했으므로, (D)가 정답이다.

어휘 aligned 정렬된 properly 제대로 outdated 구식의, 예전의

▸▸ Paraphrasing 지문의 an older version of my logo
→ 정답의 an outdated image

180 동의어 찾기

번역 이메일의 두 번째 단락, 세 번째 줄에 쓰인 'reflects'와 의미가 가장 가까운 단어는?

(A) 돌려주다
(B) ~와 일치하다
(C) 고려하다
(D) 비추다

해설 'reflects'가 포함된 부분을 직역하면 '변경사항이 첨부한 이미지를 반영하는지 확인해 달라'라는 의미로 해석된다. 따라서 '~와 일치하다'라는 의미의 (B) matches가 정답이다.

181-185 웹페이지 + 이메일

http://www.greencityscreenwriters.org/workshopseries

그린 시티 시나리오 작가 워크숍

그린 시티 시나리오 작가 워크숍(GCSW)은 현직 시나리오 작가와 작가 지망생들에게 상호 교류 및 아이디어 교환의 장을 마련해 드립니다. **184GCSW는 지난 25년간 전국의 작가들이 창의적인 프로젝트를 개발할 수 있도록 지원했습니다.**

영화 대본 작업 중이십니까? 아니면 다음 블록버스터 영화에 관한 아이디어가 있나요? GCSW에서 다음에 열릴 강좌들을 신청해 보세요. 대본 쓰기 그룹, 무대독회, 객원 연사들과 함께 하는 세미나 등을 제공해 드립니다.

• 1월 10일에 6개 강좌가 시작되며 격주 목요일에 열립니다.
• 각 강좌는 그린 시티 예술 재단에서 오후 7시부터 9시까지 열립니다.
• 수업료는 총 500달러로, 납부 기한은 1월 1일입니다.
• 자격을 갖춘 분들은 소정의 학자금 지원을 받을 수 있습니다.
• **181강좌 수강생은 10명으로 제한됩니다.**

신청하기:
18220장 분량의 습작(모든 장르 가능)과 200단어 분량의 자기소개서를 apply@greencityscreenwriters.org로 보내주세요. 수락되면 강사가 문의사항에 응답해 드립니다.

어휘 screenwriter 시나리오 작가 aspiring 장차 ~이 되려 하는 practicing 활동하고 있는, 현직의 interaction 상호작용 exchange 교환 apply for ~에 신청하다 staged reading 무대독회 (배우들의 목소리만으로 연기하는 것) foundation 재단 tuition 수업료 financial aid 학자금 지원 qualify 자격이 있다 cap 제한을 두다 autobiographical 자서전의, 자전적인 statement 진술서, 소개서

발신: 조슈아 하트조그 〈jzog.2@greencityscreenwriters.org〉
수신: 테리 햄프턴 〈hampton100@webcentral.com〉
날짜: 12월 10일
제목: 곧 있을 시나리오 쓰기 강좌
첨부: 🔗 NSI 양식

햄프턴 씨께,

저는 조슈아 하트조그이며, 그린 시티 시나리오 작가 워크숍 강사입니다. **183저희 다음 강좌 시리즈에 승인되신 것을 알려드리게 되어 기쁩니다.** 저희 위원회는 귀하의 습작에 감명을 받았습니다.

184제 소개를 간략히 드리자면, GCSW가 시작되었을 때부터 강사로 있었습니다. 또한 여덟 편의 영화 각본을 썼는데, 이 중에는 〈언 인크레더블 서머〉, 〈토스트 오브 더 타운〉이 있으며 두 작품 모두 전국 작가 그룹상을 받았습니다.

185첨부한 신입생 정보 양식을 작성하셔서 1월 1일까지 이메일로 보내주시거나 그린 시티 예술 재단으로 직접 전달해 주세요. 1월 10일에 열릴 첫 강좌에서 귀하를 뵙게 되길 고대합니다. 첫 번째 과제는 이메일 수신함을 잘 보시기 바랍니다. 이 과제는 첫 번째 수업 때까지 해 오셔야 합니다.

감사합니다.

조슈아 하트조그

어휘 upcoming 앞으로 다가오는, 곧 있을 acceptance 수락, 승인 additionally 또한, 게다가 attached 첨부된 fill out a form 서식을 기입하다, 양식을 작성하다 in person 직접 look forward to ~를 고대하다 pay attention to ~에 주의를 기울이다 assignment 과제, 임무 due ~하기로 되어 있는

181 사실 관계 확인

번역 웹페이지에 따르면, 시나리오 쓰기 강좌 시리즈에 관해 사실인 것은?

(A) 오전 강좌를 들을 수 있다.
(B) 신청 마감 기한은 1월 10일이다.
(C) 강좌 규모는 10명으로 제한된다.
(D) 강좌는 매주 평일 밤에 열린다.

해설 웹페이지에서 '강좌 수강생은 10명으로 제한된다(Classes are capped at ten students)'고 했으므로, (C)가 정답이다. 강좌는 격주 목요일에 오후 7시부터 9시까지 열리며, 1월 10일은 수업 시작일이므로, (A), (B), (D)는 오답이다.

어휘 regarding ~에 관해 deadline 마감 기한 be limited to ~로 제한되다

> Paraphrasing   지문의 **Classes are capped at**
> → 정답의 **Class sizes are limited to**

182 세부 사항

번역 신청서에는 무엇이 포함되어야 하는가?

(A) 수업료 보증금
(B) 간단한 개인 이력
(C) 거주 증명서
(D) 출판된 영화 대본 두 편

해설 웹페이지 하단에서 신청 시 습작(writing sample)과 자기소개서 (autobiographical statement)를 제출하라고 했으므로, 보기 중에서는 (B)가 정답이다.

어휘 deposit 보증금   proof 증거, 증명   residency 거주   published 출판된

> Paraphrasing   지문의 **autobiographical statement**
> → 정답의 **A brief personal history**

183 주제 / 목적

번역 하트조그 씨가 이메일을 쓴 목적은?

(A) 수많은 상에 대해 설명하려고
(B) 첫 번째 수업 과제를 설명하려고
(C) 동료 작가에게 신청을 권장하려고
(D) 학생의 신청에 응답하려고

해설 이메일의 첫 번째 단락에서 다음 강좌 시리즈에 승인된 것을·알려주게 되어 기쁘다(I am pleased to inform you of your acceptance to our next series of classes)고 했으므로, 햄프턴 씨의 강좌 신청이 승인되었음을 알리는 이메일임을 알 수 있다. 따라서 (D)가 정답이다. 참고로, 첫 번째 수업 과제를 언급하긴 했지만 이는 별도의 이메일에 설명될 것이므로 (B)는 오답이다.

어휘 numerous 수많은   outline 개요를 서술하다   encourage 장려하다

184 연계

번역 하트조그 씨에 대해 명시된 것은?

(A) 신청서 심사 위원회의 책임자다.
(B) GCSW에서 25년간 가르쳤다.
(C) 그의 대본 여덟 편이 상을 받았다.
(D) 그의 대본 세 편이 그린 시티에서 상연된다.

해설 이메일의 두 번째 단락에서 하트조그 씨는 자신이 GCSW가 시작되었을 때부터 강사로 있었다(I have been a teacher at GCSW since it started)고 했는데, 웹페이지의 첫 번째 단락을 보면 GCSW는 지난 25년간 전국의 작가들을 지원했다(For the last 25 years, GCSW has helped writers from all over the country)고 되어 있다. 즉, 하트조그 씨가 25년간 강사로 있었음을 추론할 수 있으므로, (B)가 정답이다. 참고로, 하트조그 씨는 여덟 편의 대본을 썼으며 이 중 두 편이 상을 받았으므로(both of which won ~ awards) (C)는 오답이다.

어휘 head 이끌다, 책임지다   committee 위원회   take place 개최되다, 일어나다

> Paraphrasing   지문의 **have been a teacher**
> → 정답의 **has taught**

185 세부 사항

번역 햄프턴 씨는 무엇을 하라고 요청받았는가?

(A) 첨부된 양식 작성하기
(B) 연락처 보내기
(C) 학자금 지원 신청하기
(D) 습작 보내기

해설 이메일의 세 번째 단락에서 하트조그 씨는 햄프턴 씨에게 첨부된 신입생 정보 양식을 작성해서 보내달라(Please fill out the attached ~ form and return it to me)고 했다. 따라서 (A)가 정답이다.

> Paraphrasing   지문의 **fill out** → 정답의 **Complete**

186-190 이메일 + 리뷰 + 행사 일정표

수신: 제인 맥널리 〈jmcnally@aap.org.ie〉
발신: [188]요코 나라 〈ynara@insleyhotel.com.ie〉
날짜: 2월 3일
제목: 쿠폰

안녕하세요, 맥널리 씨.

[187]호텔 주방에 들어오는 온수 장치가 고장입니다. 냄비와 접시를 씻을 온수가 없어서 식사를 제공할 수가 없습니다. 기술자들이 열심히 이 문제를 해결하고 있습니다.

[188]모든 투숙객에게 바로 옆 사라스 카페에서 아침 또는 점심 식사를 할 수 있는 쿠폰을 제공하고 있습니다. [186/190]내일까지 해결되지 않으면 저녁 식사는 모리스 레스토랑으로 옮겨야 할 것 같아요. 모리 로블링 사장과 이미 논의해 두었으며, 그는 지금 [186]귀하의 전문직 단체를 맞을 준비를 하고 있습니다. 불편을 드려 죄송합니다.

감사합니다.

요코 나라

어휘 voucher 쿠폰, 상품권   technician 기술자   diligently 부지런히, 열심히   resolution 해결   apology 사과   inconvenience 불편

★★★★☆

"그곳은 훌륭했어요."

[188]저는 호텔로부터 쿠폰을 받아, 오늘 오후 사라스 카페에서 수프와 샌드위치 특선 요리를 먹었습니다. 딱 정오에 도착했는데 거의 25분 동안 자리가 나길 기다려야 했어요. 사라스 카페는 비교적 작기 때문에 조금 덜 바쁜 시간에 방문할 것을 추천합니다. 이 점만 제외하면, 제 식사가

무료가 아니었더라도 여전히 사라스 카페를 추천했을 거예요. 분위기는 따뜻하고 매력 있어요. 수제 수프가 맛있습니다.

—스테판 니콜스, 2월 3일

어휘 recommend 추천하다 relatively 비교적, 상대적으로 atmosphere 분위기 inviting 매력적인

https://www.app.org.ie/annualmeeting/schedule

전문 회계사 협회
연례 회의 - 행사 일정

2월 4일 금요일

객원 연사 오후 5시 30분, 인슬리 호텔 213호	콜포드 인터내셔널의 최고 재무 책임자 이안 배글리 씨가 '회계직에 관한 오랜 우려와 현재 동향'에 대해 이야기합니다.
¹⁹⁰친목 도모 저녁 식사 오후 7시, 모리스 레스토랑	유명 레스토랑에서 고급 저녁 식사를 즐기며 동료들과 편안한 시간을 보내세요.

2월 5일 토요일

취업박람회 오전 11시-오후 5시	새로운 기회를 찾으십니까? 그렇다면 당신을 위한 취업박람회가 될 것입니다. 지역 업체들의 대표들을 만나보세요. 이력서 사본을 지참하세요.
더블린 투어 오후 1시-오후 4시	개최 도시의 흥미로운 장소들을 방문하세요. ¹⁸⁹투어 참가자들은 2마일(3.2km) 가까이 이동해야 하니 편안한 신발을 착용하세요.

어휘 association 협회 accounting 회계 financial 재무의, 금융의 concern 우려, 걱정 profession 직업 gourmet 미식 colleague 동료 job fair 취업박람회 representative 대표 region 지역 approximately 대략, 가까이

186 추론 / 암시

번역 맥널리 씨는 누구이겠는가?

(A) 접수원
(B) 연회 주방장
(C) 행사 주최자
(D) 카페 사장

해설 이메일을 보면, 호텔 직원인 나라 씨가 맥널리 씨에게 호텔 주방의 온수 장치 고장에 대해 알린 후 내일까지 해결되지 않으면 맥널리 씨의 전문가 단체(your professional group)가 저녁 식사할 장소를 변경해야 할 것 같다(the evening's dinner will be moved to Maury's Restaurant)고 말했다. 이러한 사항을 맥널리 씨에게 공지하는 것으로 보아, 맥널리 씨가 단체 행사의 주최자라고 보는 것이 가장 타당하므로, (C)가 정답이다.

187 세부 사항

번역 이메일에서 어떤 문제를 이야기하는가?

(A) 행사가 취소됐다.
(B) 호텔이 문을 닫는다.
(C) 수리비가 제때 지불되지 않았다.
(D) 산업용 기기가 작동하지 않는다.

해설 이메일의 첫 번째 단락에서 호텔 주방에 들어오는 온수 장치가 고장이다(The water heater servicing the kitchen at the hotel is broken)라고 했으므로, (D)가 정답이다.

어휘 repair bill 수리비 on time 시간을 어기지 않고 industrial 산업의 appliance 기기

▸▸ Paraphrasing 　지문의 The water heater
　　　　　　　　　→ 정답의 An industrial appliance
　　　　　　　　　지문의 is broken
　　　　　　　　　→ 정답의 is not working

188 연계

번역 니콜스 씨에 대해 어떤 결론을 내릴 수 있는가?

(A) 맛있게 식사하지 않았다.
(B) 오찬에 25분 늦게 도착했다.
(C) 인슬리 호텔의 고객이다.
(D) 레스토랑 단골 고객이다.

해설 이메일의 두 번째 단락에서 인슬리 호텔 직원인 나라 씨(ynara@ insleyhotel.com.ie)가 모든 투숙객에게 사라스 카페에서 아침 또는 점심 식사를 할 수 있는 쿠폰을 제공하고 있다(I am offering vouchers to all guests that can be used ~ at Sarah's Café next door)고 했는데, 리뷰 초반부를 보면 니콜스 씨가 호텔에서 쿠폰을 받아서 사라스 카페에서 식사를 했다(I enjoyed a soup and sandwich special at Sarah's Café ~ because I received a voucher from my hotel)고 되어 있다. 따라서 니콜스 씨가 인슬리 호텔 고객임을 추론할 수 있으므로, (C)가 정답이다.

어휘 frequent customer 단골

189 사실 관계 확인

번역 행사 일정표에 명시된 것은?

(A) 투어 참가자들은 도보로 이동할 것이다.
(B) 로비에서 오락이 제공된다.
(C) 참가자들은 취업박람회에 등록해야 한다.
(D) 모든 활동은 오후에 이뤄진다.

해설 2월 5일 행사 일정을 보면, 투어 참가자들은 2마일(3.2km) 가까이 이동해야 하니 편안한 신발을 착용하라(Wear comfortable shoes, as tour participants will cover approximately two miles)고 되어 있으므로, 도보로 이동한다는 사실을 추론할 수 있다. 따라서 (A)가 정답이다. 참고로, 취업박람회가 열리기는 하지만 반드시 등록해야 하는 것은 아니므로 (C)는 오답이다.

어휘 on foot 도보로 attendee 참가자 register for ~에 등록하다 take place 일어나다, 발생하다

190 연계

번역 친목 도모 저녁 식사에 대해 암시된 것은?

(A) 배글리 씨의 연설이 포함될 것이다.
(B) 추후로 연기되어야 했다.
(C) 회계 수강생을 대상으로 한다.
(D) 원래 장소에서 옮겨졌다.

해설 행사 일정표를 보면 친목 도모 저녁 식사의 장소가 모리스 레스토랑으로 공지되어 있는데, 이메일의 두 번째 단락에서 호텔 직원인 나라 씨가 호텔 주방의 온수 장치 문제가 내일까지 해결되지 않으면 맥널리 씨의 전문가 단체(your professional group)가 저녁 식사할 장소를 모리스 레스토랑으로 변경해야 할 것 같다(the evening's dinner will be moved to Maury's Restaurant)고 말했다. 따라서 원래 다른 장소였다가 바뀐 것으로 추론할 수 있으므로, (D)가 정답이다.

어휘 feature 특별히 포함하다 postpone 연기하다 be intended for ~를 대상으로 하다

191-195 웹페이지 + 이메일 + 양식

http://www.antiziointernational.com

홈	소개	제품	연락처

안티지오 인터내셔널

191 안티지오 인터내셔널은 디자이너가 만든 도기, 자기, 석기 타일을 공급하는 선도 업체입니다. 저희 제품은 상업용 및 주거용 건물 공사 모두에 적합합니다. 당사는 지역 내 최고 품질의 공급업체가 되는 것을 사명으로 가지고 있습니다.

192 안티지오 인터내셔널과 협력하면 업계에서 가장 높이 평가 받는 브랜드 제품을 이용하실 수 있습니다. 저희의 전 세계 공급업체 목록은 제품 페이지에서 확인하세요.

이번 달 특별 행사: 벤타나 브랜드 타일
"브리타니" 시리즈 도기 타일
193 진빨강색, 보라색, 분홍색 (15퍼센트 할인)
회갈색, 황갈색, 연녹색 (20퍼센트 할인)

할인 가격은 3월 1일부터 15일까지 유효합니다.

어휘 ceramic 도자기 porcelain 자기 suitable for ~에 적합한 commercial 상업의 residential 주거의 have access to ~를 이용할 수 있다, ~에 접근할 수 있다 respected 높이 평가 받는, 훌륭한 supplier 공급자 valid 유효한

수신: 구매 담당자
발신: 안티지오 인터내셔널
날짜: 3월 24일
제목: 재고 목록 업데이트

193 4월 1일 자로 아래 제품들이 단종될 예정입니다.

제조업체	제품 라인
벤타나	"발렌티나" – 전 색상 (전 라인) 193 "브리타니" – 진빨강색, 보라색, 회갈색
메도로	"솔리드스톤" – 전 색상 195 "엘레멘타" – 검정색, 회색

해당 제품의 주문은 4월 1일 이후부터 불가합니다. 195 해당 제품의 반품은 5월 1일 이후부터 불가합니다.

어휘 purchasing 구매 agent 대리인 inventory 재고 목록 effective 시행되는, 발표되는 discontinue 생산을 중단하다 accept 수락하다, 받아들이다

안티지오 인터내셔널
- 상품 반품 -

본 양식 제출에 앞서 저희 반품 정책을 검토하십시오. 반품은 구매 후 60일 이내에 이루어져야 하며 사용하지 않은 원 상태여야 합니다.

195 반품일자:	5월 12일
고객명:	윌리엄 린, WKL 컨트랙터스 사
원송장 날짜:	3월 20일
195 제품명:	메도로 브랜드 – "엘레멘타" 타일
195 색상:	회색
수량:	20상자
상자당 가격:	70달러
194 반품 사유:	실제 색상이 카탈로그 사진과 맞지 않다.
환불 방식 요청:	☑ 환불 □ 매장 포인트 점수

어휘 merchandise 상품 return policy 환불 정책 submit 제출하다 invoice 송장 quantity 수량 request 요청하다

191 세부 사항

번역 안티지오 인터내셔널은 어떤 업계에서 영업하는가?

(A) 건축 자재
(B) 상업 광고
(C) 컴퓨터 제조
(D) 패션 디자인

해설 웹페이지의 첫 번째 단락에서 안티지오 인터내셔널은 디자이너가 만든 도기, 자기, 석기 타일을 공급하는 선도 업체(Antizio International is a leading provider of designer ceramic, porcelain, and stone tile)라고 했다. 타일은 건축 자재에 속하므로, (A)가 정답이다.

어휘 building material 건축 자재 commercial advertisement 상업 광고

▸▸ **Paraphrasing** 지문의 ceramic, porcelain, and stone tile → 정답의 Building materials

192 세부 사항

번역 안티지오 인터내셔널은 고객에게 어떤 이점을 제공하는가?

(A) 직원들이 이중 언어 사용자다.
(B) 제품의 평판이 좋다.
(C) 단골 고객은 배송비가 면제된다.
(D) 결제 방식에 융통성이 있다.

해설 웹페이지의 두 번째 단락에서 안티지오 인터내셔널과 협력하면 업계에서 가장 높이 평가받는 브랜드 제품을 이용할 수 있다(When you partner with Antizio International, you have access to the most respected brands in the industry)고 했으므로, (B)가 정답이다.

어휘 bilingual 이중 언어를 사용하는 have a good reputation 평판이 좋다 delivery fee 배송비 waive 면제하다 payment plan 결제 방식 flexible 유연한, 융통성이 있는

▸▸ **Paraphrasing** 지문의 **the most respected**
→ 정답의 **have a good reputation**

193 연계

번역 4월 1일 이후에는 브리타니 제품 라인의 어떤 색상을 주문할 수 있는가?

(A) 진빨강색
(B) 보라색
(C) 회갈색
(D) 연녹색

해설 이메일에서 4월 1일 자로 브리타니 제품 라인 중 진빨강색, 보라색, 회갈색 제품이 불가능하다(Orders for these products cannot be accepted after April 1)고 했는데, 웹페이지 하단을 보면 브리타니 제품 라인에는 진빨강색, 보라색, 분홍색, 회갈색, 황갈색, 연녹색이 있음을 확인할 수 있다. 따라서 이 중 단종되지 않는 색상은 분홍색, 황갈색, 연녹색이므로, 보기 중에서는 (D)가 정답이다.

194 세부 사항

번역 린 씨가 상품을 반품하는 이유는?

(A) 필요한 것보다 제품을 많이 구입했다.
(B) 상품의 색상이 마음에 들지 않는다.
(C) 발송된 제품의 크기가 잘못됐다.
(D) 제품이 배송 중 손상됐다.

해설 양식 하단에 나온 반품 사유(Reason for return) 항목에서 실제 색상이 카탈로그 사진과 맞지 않다(Actual color does not match catalog image)고 했으므로, (B)가 정답이다.

어휘 damage 손상하다

195 연계

번역 린 씨의 반품 요청은 왜 거절되겠는가?

(A) 주문 제작 디자인한 제품을 구입했다.
(B) 구매 증명서를 동봉하지 않았다.
(C) 기한이 만료된 후 제품을 반품했다.
(D) 반품 승인번호 요청을 잊어버렸다.

해설 양식에서 린 씨가 반품하려는 제품이 메도로 브랜드의 회색 엘레멘타 타일임을 알 수 있는데, 이메일을 보면 이 제품은 4월 1일 자로 단종되며, 5월 1일 이후부터는 단종된 제품의 반품은 불가하다(Return of these products cannot be accepted after May 1)고 나와 있다. 양식에 적힌 반품일자는 5월 12일이므로, 5월 1일이 지나서 반품을 하려는 린 씨의 요청이 거절될 것이라 추론할 수 있다. 따라서 (C)가 정답이다.

어휘 proof 증명, 증빙 expire 만료되다 authorization 허가, 인가

▸▸ **Paraphrasing** 지문의 **cannot be accepted after May 1**
→ 정답의 **after a deadline had expired**

196-200 이메일 + 일정표 + 이메일

수신: 전 직원
발신: 로널드 개리슨
날짜: 4월 20일
제목: 업데이트

동료 여러분,

지코모 솔루션즈에게는 즐거운 시기군요. 축하할 일이 많습니다! 우리 회사는 지난 일 년간 굉장한 성장을 이뤘습니다. 지난달에 목표치를 초과 달성하고 [197]그로튼 및 근교 지역 내 18개의 다양한 회사를 위해 25회의 고객 서비스 워크숍을 실시했습니다.

[196]성장에 대응하여, 각자의 업계에서 상당한 고객 서비스 경험을 갖춘 워크숍 진행자 세 분을 더 영입했습니다. 리사 오코로 씨는 텔레마케팅 업계에 중점을 둘 겁니다. [199]케일럽 파텔 씨는 의료 관련 분야에 있는 분들을 교육할 것입니다. 앨런 고로스페 씨는 주로 기술 업계 고객 서비스를 전문으로 할 예정입니다. 이들은 5월 첫째 주나 둘째 주에 워크숍 진행을 시작할 겁니다. [196]지코모 가족이 되신 전문가들을 함께 환영합시다.

로널드 개리슨
지코모 솔루션즈 CEO

어휘 tremendous 엄청난, 굉장한 growth 성장 exceed 넘다 conduct 실시하다 greater＋도시명 해당 지역과 근교를 포함하여 in response to ～에 대한 응답으로, 대응으로 respective 각자의 related to ～와 관련된 specialize in ～를 전문으로 하다

지코모 솔루션즈
임시 교육 일정표
5월 2일 주간

강좌명	강좌 길이	날짜	강사	장소
전화 응대 요령	[200]반일	[200]5월 2일	리사 오코로	[198]지코모, 그로튼
디지털 세계의 고객 서비스	전일	5월 3일	앨런 고로스페	[198]지코모, 그로튼

[199]병원 직원을 위한 환자와의 관계	전일	[199]5월 4일	추후 결정	피처 메디컬 그룹, 웨스트 그로튼
기술적 문제를 마케팅 기회로 변화시키기	반일	5월 5일	앨런 고로스페	캘리퍼 테크놀로지스, 페이엣빌

어휘 tentative 잠정적인 relation 관계 determine 결정하다

수신: 로널드 개리슨 〈rgarrison@zikomosolutions.net〉
발신: 재너 스나이더 〈jsnyder@snyder.com〉
날짜: 5월 8일
제목: 최근 워크숍

개리슨 씨께,

[200]저희 스나이더 굿즈 직원들 중 몇 명이 5월 2일과 3일 지코모 교육 세션에 참가했습니다. 피드백을 드리고 질문을 하고 싶은데요. [200]제 생각에 반일 교육 과정은 전일로 연장해도 될 것 같습니다. 흥미로운 주제와 훌륭한 진행자의 역량을 고려한다면 말이죠. 반대로 전일 과정은 흥미롭긴 해도 반일로 압축하는 게 나을 것 같습니다. 아울러 주차 공간을 좀 더 제공해 주실 수 있나요? 참가자를 위한 공간이 다 차서 스나이더 굿즈 직원 다수가 값비싼 유료 주차장에 주차해야 했습니다.

재너 스나이더
스나이더 굿즈

어휘 extend 연장하다 conversely 역으로 condense 압축하다 additionally 게다가 paid 유료의

196 주제 / 목적

번역 첫 번째 이메일을 쓴 목적은?
(A) 신입 직원 채용을 알리려고
(B) 직원들을 기념 행사에 초청하려고
(C) 회사 성장을 위한 계획을 설명하려고
(D) 실적이 좋은 직원의 공로를 인정하려고

해설 이메일의 두 번째 단락에서 회사가 성장함에 따라 워크숍 진행자 세 명을 더 영입했다(we have added three new workshop presenters)고 한 후 이들을 함께 환영해 주자(welcoming these professionals to the Zikomo family)고 했다. 따라서 신입 직원의 채용을 알리고자 한 이메일이라고 볼 수 있으므로, (A)가 정답이다.

어휘 celebration 기념 행사 outline 개요를 서술하다

▸▸ Paraphrasing 지문의 have added three new workshop presenters
→ 정답의 the hiring of new staff members

197 세부 사항

번역 지코모 솔루션즈는 어떤 분야에 특화되어 있는가?
(A) 컴퓨터 제조
(B) 회계
(C) 운송
(D) 고객 서비스

해설 첫 번째 이메일의 첫 단락에서 18개의 다양한 회사를 위해 25회의 고객 서비스 워크숍을 실시했다(we ~ conducted 25 customer service workshops for 18 different companies)고 했으므로, (D)가 정답이다.

198 사실 관계 확인

번역 일정표에서 워크숍에 대해 명시한 것은?
(A) 하루에 여러 개의 워크숍이 개최된다.
(B) 워크숍 일부는 지코모 사무실에서 개최된다.
(C) 보통 하루 종일 열린다.
(D) 보통 인원이 꽉 찬다.

해설 일정표를 보면 5월 2일과 5월 3일에 열리는 워크숍이 지코모에서 개최되므로, (B)가 정답이다. 4개의 워크숍이 각각 다른 날에 진행되며 5월 2일과 5월 5일에 열리는 워크숍은 반일이므로 (A)와 (C)는 오답이다.

어휘 typically 보통, 일반적으로 be filled to capacity 만원을 이루다, 꽉 차다

199 연계

번역 5월 4일에 워크숍을 진행할 적임자는?
(A) 개리슨 씨
(B) 오코로 씨
(C) 파텔 씨
(D) 고로스페 씨

해설 일정표에 따르면 5월 4일 워크숍은 병원 직원을 대상으로 하는 환자와의 관계(Patient Relations for Hospital Professionals) 강좌인데, 첫 번째 이메일의 두 번째 단락을 보면 케일럽 파텔 씨가 의료 관련 분야에 있는 사람들을 교육할 것(Caleb Patel will train those in fields related to medicine)이라고 나와 있다. 따라서 (C)가 정답이다.

어휘 qualified 자격을 갖춘

200 연계

번역 스나이더 씨가 직원들의 교육 경험에 대해 암시한 것은?
(A) 주차가 편리했다.
(B) 5월 2일 교육은 너무 짧았다.
(C) 주제가 흥미롭지 않았다.
(D) 진행자가 늦게 도착했다.

해설 두 번째 이메일의 초반부에서 스나이더 씨는 직원들이 5월 2일과 3일 지코모 교육에 참가했다(Several of my employees from Snyder Goods attended Zikomo training sessions on May

2 and 3)고 하면서, 반일 교육 과정은 전일로 연장해도 될 것 같다(I think the half-day session could be extended to a full day) 고 했다. 일정표에 따르면 반일로 진행된 워크숍이 2일이므로, (B)가 정답이다. 참고로, 주차 공간에 관해서는 자리가 부족해 유료 주차장 을 이용해야 했다고 했으므로 (A)는 오답이다.

기출 TEST 5

101 (C)	**102** (D)	**103** (D)	**104** (A)	**105** (C)
106 (C)	**107** (D)	**108** (A)	**109** (B)	**110** (B)
111 (C)	**112** (C)	**113** (D)	**114** (D)	**115** (B)
116 (C)	**117** (D)	**118** (A)	**119** (C)	**120** (A)
121 (D)	**122** (C)	**123** (B)	**124** (A)	**125** (B)
126 (A)	**127** (B)	**128** (B)	**129** (B)	**130** (C)
131 (B)	**132** (C)	**133** (B)	**134** (A)	**135** (C)
136 (A)	**137** (C)	**138** (B)	**139** (C)	**140** (C)
141 (B)	**142** (C)	**143** (B)	**144** (D)	**145** (A)
146 (D)	**147** (B)	**148** (C)	**149** (B)	**150** (B)
151 (A)	**152** (B)	**153** (A)	**154** (C)	**155** (B)
156 (C)	**157** (C)	**158** (B)	**159** (A)	**160** (D)
161 (C)	**162** (D)	**163** (B)	**164** (D)	**165** (D)
166 (B)	**167** (A)	**168** (C)	**169** (D)	**170** (D)
171 (B)	**172** (A)	**173** (A)	**174** (A)	**175** (C)
176 (D)	**177** (B)	**178** (A)	**179** (B)	**180** (A)
181 (B)	**182** (B)	**183** (C)	**184** (C)	**185** (A)
186 (C)	**187** (A)	**188** (D)	**189** (B)	**190** (B)
191 (D)	**192** (A)	**193** (B)	**194** (C)	**195** (D)
196 (C)	**197** (D)	**198** (D)	**199** (A)	**200** (D)

PART 5

101 접속사 자리 _ 등위접속사

해설 빈칸이 완전한 절과 주어 you가 생략된 명령문 사이에 있으므로, 빈칸에는 등위접속사가 들어가야 한다. 따라서 '그래서'라는 뜻의 (C) so가 정답이다. 상관접속사로 쓰이는 (A) than은 콤마 바로 뒤에 올 수 없고, (B) wait은 동사, (D) about은 전치사로 절과 절을 이어 줄 수 없다.

번역 아베 씨가 내일 물품을 주문할 예정이니, 필요한 것이 있으면 바로 그녀에게 얘기하세요.

어휘 supply 보급품, 물자

102 접속사 자리 _ 어휘

해설 두 개의 완전한 절을 이어주는 접속사 자리이다. 따라서 보기에서 등위접속사인 (B) but, 부사절 접속사인 (C) unless와 (D) before 중 하나를 선택해야 한다. 모든 전자기기를 무음으로 설정하는 것 (all electronic devices (should) be silenced)은 연극이 시작하기(the play begins) 전에 행해져야 하므로, '~ 전에'라는 의미의 (D) before가 정답이다. 참고로, 요청(requests)의 동사 뒤에 오는 that절에는 「(should)+동사원형」을 쓴다.

번역 크니샤 극장은 연극이 시작되기 전 모든 전자기기를 무음으로 해 달라고 요청한다.

어휘 request 요청하다 device 기기

103 명령문의 동사원형

해설 주어 You가 생략된 명령문에서 Human Resources를 목적어로 취하는 타동사 자리이다. 따라서 동사원형 (D) Contact가 정답이다.

번역 휴가 사용에 관한 문의사항이 있으면 인사부로 연락하십시오.

어휘 Human Resources 인사부 time off 휴가, 휴식 contact 연락하다

104 부사 어휘

해설 숫자 표현 eighty thousand를 적절히 수식하는 부사를 선택해야 한다. 따라서 '거의'라는 의미의 (A) Almost가 정답이다. 참고로, (B) More는 than과 함께 '~이상'이라는 뜻으로 쓰일 경우 빈칸에 들어갈 수 있다.

번역 거의 8만 명이 어제 축구 경기에 참석했다.

어휘 attend 참석하다

105 형용사 자리 _ 주격 보어 _ 분사

해설 부사 somewhat의 수식을 받으면서, 주어 our company's Web site를 보충 설명하는 주격 보어 자리이다. 따라서 빈칸에는 형용사가 들어가야 하므로, (C) confusing(혼란스럽게 하는, 헷갈리게 하는)이 정답이다. (A) confuse와 (B) confuses는 동사, (D) confusion은 명사로 품사상 빈칸에 들어갈 수 없다.

번역 온라인 방문자들은 우리 회사 웹사이트가 다소 혼동을 준다고 전합니다.

어휘 somewhat 다소 confuse 혼란스럽게 하다

106 명사 어휘

해설 traffic과 복합명사를 이루어 문장의 주어 역할을 하는 명사를 선택해야 한다. 도로에서 예상되는 교통 상황을 나타내는 단어가 들어가야 하므로, '정체, 지연'이라는 의미의 (C) delays가 정답이다. traffic/flight/travel delays 등의 빈출 표현은 암기해 두는 것이 좋다.

번역 다음 주 레이머스 로드를 따라 교통 정체가 예상된다.

어휘 expect 예상하다 driver 운전자 crowd 군중 need 요구, 필요

107 부사 어휘

해설 빈칸에는 형용사 qualified를 수식하는 부사가 필요하므로, '고도로(=높은/우수한 수준으로)'라는 의미의 (D) highly가 정답이다. high는 부사로 쓰일 경우 물리적 높이/비용/양을 나타내며, 분사를 수식해 하나의 형용사가 될 때는 하이픈을 동반한다. 예를 들어 highly paid 및 high-paid는 둘 다 가능하지만, qualified는 '자격을 갖춘'이라는 뜻이므로 high의 수식을 받을 수는 없다. qualified가 well/suitably/fully 등의 부사와도 어울려 쓰인다는 것을 알아두자.

번역 샬호브 병원은 우수한 자격을 갖춘 실험실 직원을 몇 명 더 채용하고 싶어 한다.

어휘 hire 채용하다 several more 몇 명[개] 더 qualified 자격을 갖춘 laboratory 실험실

108 형용사 / 명사 어휘

해설 빈칸에는 person을 수식하는 형용사 또는 person과 복합명사를 이루는 명사가 들어갈 수 있다. 소등해야(turn off the lights) 하는 사람을 명시하는 부분이므로, '방을 나가는 마지막 사람'이라는 표현을 완성하는 (A) last가 정답이다. (C) finish는 '종결, 끝손질'이라는 의미의 명사로 쓰일 수 있지만, person과 복합명사를 이루기엔 어색하다.

번역 본인이 방에서 마지막으로 나갈 때는 항상 불을 끄십시오.

어휘 exit 나가다

109 명사 자리 _ 전치사의 목적어

해설 분사형 전치사 Following의 목적어 역할을 하는 명사 자리로, 형용사 brief의 수식을 받는다. 따라서 (B) conversation(대화)이 정답이다. (A) converses는 동사, (C) conversational은 형용사, (D) conversationally는 부사로 품사상 빈칸에 들어갈 수 없다.

번역 무어 씨는 선임 기술자와 간단히 대화한 후 사용 설명서를 업데이트하는 데 동의했다.

어휘 following ~후에 operations manual 사용 설명서, 운영 매뉴얼 converse 대화를 나누다 conversational 대화의 conversationally 대화체로

110 전치사 어휘

해설 자동사 increased와 명사구 our expectations를 적절히 연결해 주는 전치사를 선택해야 한다. 문맥을 살펴보면, 기대치 (expectations)를 기준점으로 잡아 주가 상승 정도를 표현하고 있다. 따라서 '~ 이상으로, ~를 넘어서는'이라는 의미의 (B) beyond가 정답이다. beyond(기대 이상)/below(기대 이하) expectations는 필수 표현으로 암기해 두자.

번역 골든 삼록 쥬얼리는 기록적인 수익을 낸 후 주가가 기대 이상으로 상승했다.

어휘 record profit 기록적인 수익 stock price 주가

111 조동사 + 동사원형

해설 조동사 cannot 뒤에 오는 동사원형 자리로, the filming을 목적어로 취한다. 따라서 (C) complete가 정답이다. (A) completely는 부사, (B) completion은 명사, (D) completing은 동명사/현재분사로 빈칸에 들어갈 수 없다.

번역 충분한 자금 없이는 우리의 다큐멘터리 〈밤이 지나간 후의 아침〉 촬영을 완료하지 못한다.

어휘 sufficient 충분한 funding 자금 completion 완료

112 부사 어휘

해설 문맥상 도착 예정(will arrive) 시간(at 7:00 P.M.)을 강조하는 부사가 들어가야 자연스러우므로, '정확히, 시간을 엄수하여'라는 의미의 (C) promptly가 정답이다.

번역 수 씨가 탄 기차가 정확히 오후 7시에 도착할 테니 몇 분 일찍 역에 도착하십시오.

어휘 carefully 주의깊게 unexpectedly 뜻밖에, 예상외로 clearly 명백하게

113 대명사 어휘

해설 빈칸은 동사 can be done의 주어 역할을 하는 자리로, 주문 변경을 위해(to revise your order) 할 수 있는 것을 나타낸다. 물건이 이미 배송된 상태(the merchandise has already shipped)이므로 주문을 변경하기 위해 할 수 있는 일은 없다고 보는 것이 타당하다. 따라서 사물을 대신하며 부정의 의미를 지닌 (D) Nothing이 정답이다. (A) Ours는 '우리 것', (B) Nobody는 '아무도 ~않다, 무명인', (C) Others는 '다른 것들'을 의미하므로 빈칸에는 적절하지 않다.

번역 상품이 이미 배송됐기 때문에 귀하의 주문을 변경하기 위해 할 수 있는 것은 아무것도 없습니다.

어휘 revise 변경하다, 수정하다 merchandise 상품

114 동사 어휘

해설 명사 workplaces를 목적어로 취하는 타동사 자리로, 팀워크와 협력이 장려되는 직장에 대해 졸업생들이 어떤 경향을 보이는지 설명하는 단어가 들어가야 한다. 따라서 '선호하다'라는 의미의 (D) prefer가 정답이다. 참고로, 'A를 B라고 생각하는 경향이 있다'라고 말하려면 「think A (to be) B」 구조로 해야 하고, apply를 '~에 지원하다'라는 뜻으로 쓰려면 전치사 for나 to가 필요하다.

번역 최근 졸업자들은 팀워크와 협력이 장려되는 직장을 선호하는 경향이 있다.

어휘 graduate 졸업자 tend to ~하는 경향이 있다 collaboration 협력 encourage 권장하다, 장려하다 apply 적용하다, 바르다 extend 연장하다, 확대하다

115 명사 자리 _ 동사의 목적어 _ 복합명사

해설 cleaning과 함께 복합명사를 이루어 동사 follow의 목적어 역할을 하는 명사 자리이다. 의미상 따라야 하는 대상을 나타내야 하며, 형용사 specific 앞에 한정사가 없으므로 복수명사 또는 불가산명사가 되어야 한다. 따라서 '절차'라는 뜻의 복수명사 (B) procedures가 정답이다. (A) proceeds는 명사로 쓰일 경우 '수익금'이라는 의미로 문맥상 빈칸에 어색하다. (D) proceeding도 '소송 절차, 일련의 행위'라는 뜻의 가산명사로 쓰일 수 있지만, cleaning과 어울리지 않으며 단수 형태이므로 빈칸에 들어갈 수 없다.

번역 장 클리닝은 모든 직원들이 특정한 청소 절차를 따르도록 대단히 신경을 쓴다.

어휘 specific 특정한, 구체적인 proceed 진행되다 procedural 절차(상)의

116 전치사 자리 _ 어휘

해설 명사구 its delicious buffet dinners를 목적어로 취하는 전치사 자리로, 보기에서 전치사가 있는 (A) such as, (C) because of, (D) together with 중 하나를 선택해야 한다. 맛있는 뷔페 저녁 식사는 레스토랑이 호평 받는(acclaimed) 주된 이유이므로, '~ 때문에'라는 의미의 (C) because of가 정답이 된다. 참고로, (B) not only는 but (also)와 함께 '~뿐만 아니라 ~도'라는 뜻의 상관접속사로 쓰인다.

번역 뭄바이 쥬얼은 주로 맛있는 뷔페 저녁 식사 덕분에 널리 호평을 받고 있는 음식점이다.

어휘 be widely acclaimed 널리 호평을 받다

117 재귀대명사

해설 진주어 to prepare의 목적어 자리이다. prepare의 의미상 주어는 일반적인 사람(one)이며, 질문에 답하도록 준비시켜야 하는 대상은 면접을 보는 사람 자신이다. 따라서 one의 재귀대명사 (D) oneself가 정답이다. (A) whose와 (B) whichever는 접속사 역할을 하므로 바로 뒤에 전치사구가 올 수 없다.

번역 면접 전, 가장 많이 묻는 질문들에 답변하는 연습을 하는 것이 매우 중요하다.

어휘 critical 대단히 중요한 commonly 흔히

118 동사 어휘 _ 과거분사

해설 빈칸의 주어 it은 뒤에 나온 to read Joan Frantz's book *Balancing Work and Life*를 가리킨다. 주절에서 이 책을 읽는 것이 권장된다(are encouraged)고 했으므로, 양보의 접속사 While이 이끄는 절은 '그것이 필수는 아니지만'이라는 내용이 되어야 자연스럽다. 따라서 '요구되는, 필수의'라는 뜻의 (A) required가 정답이다.

번역 필수는 아니지만, 직원들은 조안 프란츠의 책 〈일과 삶의 균형 맞추기〉를 읽어보는 게 좋겠습니다.

어휘 encourage 격려하다, 권장하다 balance 균형을 유지하다 require 요구하다 publish 출판하다 guarantee 보장하다

119 형용사 자리 _ 주격 보어

해설 가주어 it(=to bring sturdy boots to wear on the hike)의 주격 보어 자리이다. 문맥상 부츠를 가져와 신는 행위에 대해 설명하는 형용사가 들어가야 자연스러우므로, (C) advisable(바람직한)이 정답이다. (B) advisor는 사람을 나타내는 가산명사로, 한정사가 없으며 주어와 동격 관계를 이루지 않으므로 빈칸에 들어갈 수 없다. (A) advise와 (D) advises는 동사로 품사상 오답이다.

번역 등반 시에는 튼튼한 부츠를 가져와 신는 것이 바람직하다.

어휘 sturdy 튼튼한, 견고한

120 부사 / 전치사 어휘

해설 빈칸 앞 reach는 '도달하다, 이르다'라는 뜻으로 15 degrees를 목적어로 취한다. 따라서 빈칸에는 수치와 어울리는 부사가 들어가야 하므로, '적어도, 최소'라는 의미의 (A) at least가 정답이다. 참고로, reach가 자동사로 쓰일 경우, '(손이) 닿다, (손을) 뻗다'라는 뜻을 나타내며 주로 전치사 for나 (in)to를 동반한다.

번역 노델 파크는 낮 평균 기온이 최소 15도에 이르면 시즌 개장을 할 것이다.

어휘 average 평균 temperature 기온 as of ~ 부로 along with ~와 함께 ahead of ~ 앞에, ~보다 빨리

121 명사 자리 _ 전치사의 목적어

해설 비교급 형용사 greater의 수식을 받으면서 전치사 for의 목적어 역할을 하는 명사 자리이므로, (D) assurance(확약, 확언)가 정답이다. (A) assure는 동사, (B) assured는 동사/과거분사, (C) assuredly는 부사로 품사상 빈칸에 들어갈 수 없다. 참고로, assurance와 that절은 동격 관계(~라는 확약)를 이루고 있다.

번역 황 씨는 투자하기 전, 브라이오머 테크가 프로젝트에 전념할 것이라는 더 강력한 확약을 기다릴 것이다.

어휘 invest 투자하다 be committed to ~에 전념하다, 헌신하다

122 부사 어휘

해설 빈칸을 포함한 to부정사구는 연간 수익(annual profits)이 5백만 유로를 넘을 거라는 예상(expected)을 나타내고 있다. 따라서 빈칸에는 이 결과를 강조하는 부사가 들어가야 자연스러우므로, '결국, 마침내'라는 의미의 (C) eventually가 정답이다. 참고로, (A) exactly(정확히)는 €5 million를 강조하는 자리에 더 어울리고, (B) extremely(극도로)는 주로 정도를 묘사하는 형용사/부사를 수식하므로 빈칸에 적절하지 않다.

번역 트라림 컨설팅의 연 수익은 결국 5백만 유로를 넘길 것으로 예상된다.

어휘 profit 수익, 수입 exceed 초과하다 evenly 고르게, 차분하게

123 형용사 자리 _ 주격 보어 _ 최상급

해설 정관사 the와 함께 최상급을 이루어 주어인 keeping customers satisfied를 보충 설명하는 주격 보어 자리이다. 따라서 최상급 형용사가 들어가야 하므로, (B) most essential(가장 필수적인)이 정답이다. (A) essential은 원급 형용사, (C) essentially와 (D) more essentially는 부사로 구조상 빈칸에 들어갈 수 없다.

번역 많은 요인들이 사업의 성공에 기여하고 있기는 하지만, 이 씨는 고객을 만족시키는 것이 가장 필수적이라고 생각한다.

어휘 factor 요인 contribute to ~에 기여하다 essential 필수적인, 중요한

124 동사 어휘

해설 명사구 each of the budget changes를 목적어로 취하는 타동사 자리이다. 예산 변동사항은 하나 하나 설명할 대상이라고 볼 수 있으므로, '상세히 알리다'라는 의미의 (A) detail이 정답이다. (B) attend는 참석하는 행사를 목적어로 취하므로 문맥상 적절하지

않다. (C) respond(응답하다)는 주로 자동사로 쓰이며, 타동사로 쓰일 경우 that절을 목적어로 취한다. (D) comply(따르다)는 자동사로서 단독으로 쓰이거나 전치사 with를 동반한다.

번역 알삼마리 씨는 직원 회의 중 예산 변동사항 각각을 상세히 알려주느라 한 시간을 꼬박 채웠다.

어휘 budget 예산

125 부사 어휘

해설 more than four months는 고객에게 권장하는 예약 시점을 정하는 기준이다. 즉, 이 기간 전에 예약하기를 권장한다는 내용이 되어야 하므로, '미리'라는 의미의 (B) in advance가 정답이다. 참고로, (D) far ahead가 '~보다 훨씬 앞서'라는 뜻을 나타낼 경우에는 주로 「far ahead of + 명사」의 구조로 쓰이며, far 앞에 기간을 나타내는 표현이 올 수 없다. far 없이 ahead만 있을 경우에는 가능하다 (eg. four months ahead).

번역 고객들은 행사를 위해 4개월 이상 전에 미리 데저트 로즈 볼룸을 예약하는 것이 권장된다.

어휘 book 예약하다 over time 오랜 시간에 걸쳐, 시간이 지나며 up to now 현재까지 far ahead 훨씬 앞에, 아득한 장래에

126 형용사 어휘

해설 as와 as possible 사이에서 주어인 data from oil-drilling sites를 보충 설명하는 형용사 자리이다. 생산 수준을 제대로 이해하는 데 (For a true understanding of our production levels) 필요한 데이터(data)의 특징을 나타내는 단어가 필요하므로, '정확한, 정밀한'이라는 의미의 (A) accurate가 정답이다.

번역 우리의 생산 수준을 제대로 이해하려면 유정 굴착 현장 데이터가 최대한 정확해야 한다.

어휘 oil-drilling 유정 굴착의 accurate 정확한 optimistic 낙천적인 exclusive 배타적인, 독점적인 competitive 경쟁력 있는, 경쟁을 하는

127 부사 자리 _ 동사 수식

해설 Adopting ~ software가 주어, would improve가 동사, Narrin Group's ~ process가 목적어인 완전한 절 뒤에서 개선될(would improve) 정도를 강조하는 부사 자리이다. 따라서 (B) substantially(상당히, 많이)가 정답이다. (A) substantial과 (C) more substantial은 형용사, (D) substances는 명사로 품사상 빈칸에 들어갈 수 없다.

번역 고급 계산서 청구 소프트웨어를 채택하면 나린 그룹의 회계 관리 절차가 상당히 개선될 것이다.

어휘 adopt 채택하다 advanced 고급의 fiscal 재정의, 회계의 substantial 상당한 substance 물질

128 명사 어휘

해설 형용사 effective의 수식을 받으면서 전치사 Thanks to의 목적

어 역할을 하는 명사 자리이다. 빈칸을 포함한 부분이 제품 출시 (product launch) 성공(a success)에 기여한 요인을 설명하고 있다. 따라서 effective와 함께 '효과적인 홍보'라는 의미를 완성하는 (B) promotion이 정답이다.

번역 드링크에버 첫 음료의 효과적인 홍보 덕분에 지난달 제품 출시가 성공을 거뒀다.

어휘 effective 효과적인 launch 출시, 개시 response 응답

129 동사 어형 _ 시제

해설 '내년 이맘때까지'라는 의미의 By this time next year가 빈칸이 포함된 절을 수식하고 있다. 따라서 미래의 특정 시점까지 완료될 일을 나타내는 미래완료시제 동사가 쓰여야 하므로, (B) will have opened가 정답이다.

번역 그라스웰 인더스트리즈는 내년 이맘때까지 동유럽에 새 공장 두 곳을 열 것이다.

어휘 plant 공장

130 형용사 어휘

해설 명사 supply를 수식하는 형용사 자리로, 카트에 비축해야 할 제품의 공급량을 나타내는 단어가 들어가야 한다. 따라서 '충분한, 적절한'이라는 의미의 (C) adequate이 정답이다.

번역 다음 항공편을 위해 카트에 충분한 양의 고급 간식 제품들을 구비해 두십시오.

어휘 supply 공급량 absolute 완전한, 완벽한 earned 얻은 energetic 활기에 찬

PART 6

131-134 기사

코펜하겐 (5월 25일) – 오덴세 미디어는 자사의 태블릿 제품인 버츄소닉의 최신 버전 초기 판매량이 회사의 기대치를 ¹³¹넘어섰다고 오늘 밝혔다. 회사 대변인 커스틴 베스테르가드 씨는 이 ¹³²인상적인 판매량이 많은 요인 덕분이라고 본다. 첫째로 태블릿의 고품질 케이스가 있다. ¹³³보호 케이스는 기기의 내구성을 보장해 준다. 게다가 버츄소닉은 화면 밝기 자동 조정 기능이 있다. 이 기능은 이상적이지 않은 ¹³⁴조명 환경에서도 기기가 자동으로 적응하게끔 해 준다. 베스테르가드 씨는 이러한 특징들로 버츄소닉이 소비자들에게 필수품이 됐다고 확신한다.

어휘 initial 초기의 expectation 기대, 예상 spokesperson 대변인 attribute A to B A를 B의 덕분으로 돌리다 factor 요인 in addition 게다가 adaptive 적응할 수 있는, (자동) 조정의 feature 기능, 특징 adjust to ~에 적응하다, 맞춰지다 automatically 자동으로 less-than-ideal 이상적이지 [바람직하지] 않은 condition 상태, 환경 characteristic 특징 must-have 필수품

131 동사 어휘

해설 주어인 초기 판매량(initial sales)과 목적어인 회사의 기대치(the company's expectations)의 관계를 나타내는 동사가 필요하다. 따라서 '뛰어넘다, 능가하다'라는 의미의 타동사 (B) surpassed가 정답이다. exceed one's expectations라고 표현할 수 있다는 것도 알아두자.

어휘 base ~에 근거지를 두다   invest 투자하다   progress 진전을 보이다, 진행시키다

132 형용사 자리 _ 명사 수식

해설 정관사 the와 명사 sales 사이에서 sales를 수식하는 형용사 자리이다. 예상을 뛰어넘는 판매량, 즉 판매 결과에 대해 평가하는 단어가 들어가야 자연스러우므로, '인상적인'이라는 의미의 (C) impressive가 정답이다. 현재분사 (B) impressing은 '감동시키는', 과거분사 (D) impressed는 '감동받은'이라는 뜻이므로 sales를 수식하기에 적절하지 않다. (A) impress는 동사로 품사상 빈칸에 들어갈 수 없다.

어휘 impress 감동시키다

133 문맥에 맞는 문장 고르기

번역 (A) 소비자는 태블릿을 어디에 쓸지 고려해야 한다.
(B) 버츄소닉은 다음 달 다른 색상으로도 구입할 수 있다.
(C) 새 기기 최저가는 매장에서 확인하면 된다.
(D) 보호 케이스는 기기의 내구성을 보장해 준다.

해설 인상적인 판매량의 요인(factors)으로 빈칸 앞 문장에서는 태블릿의 고품질 케이스(the tablet's high-quality case)를, 뒤 문장에서는 화면 밝기 자동 조정 기능(an adaptive screen brightness feature)을 언급했다. 따라서 빈칸에는 케이스에 대해 부연 설명을 하거나 또 다른 성공 요인을 제시하는 문장이 들어가야 자연스러우므로, (D)가 정답이다.

어휘 protective 보호하는   durability 내구성

134 명사 어휘

해설 해당 문장은 앞서 언급된 화면 자동 밝기 조정 기능(an adaptive screen brightness feature)에 대해 추가로 설명하고 있다. 화면 자동 밝기 조정 기능이란 환경에 따라 화면 밝기가 변하는 것을 말하는데, 안구 보호를 위해 어두운 곳에서는 어두워지고 밝은 곳에서는 밝아지는 기능이다. 빈칸이 포함된 부분(less-than-ideal ------- conditions)은 그 기능이 자동으로 실행되는 특정 환경을 나타내고 있으므로, 밝기(brightness)와 관련된 명사가 빈칸에 들어가야 한다. 따라서 '조명, 밝기'라는 의미의 (A) lighting이 정답이다.

어휘 temperature 온도

135-138 회람

수신: 전 직원
발신: 마커스 신두, IT 부서장
날짜: 6월 1일

제목: 웹사이트 관리

정기 서버 관리가 이번 주말에 실시되어 회사 웹사이트 콘텐츠에 영향을 미치게 될 거라는 점 유념해 주십시오. 서버는 6월 6일 토요일 오후 11시부터 6월 7일 일요일 오전 7시까지 대략 8시간 동안 다운될 **135예정입니다**. 이 시간 **136동안** 웹사이트 접속이 제한되고 이메일 전송이 중단될 겁니다. **137모든 웹사이트 기능은 일요일 아침에 재개됩니다**. 서버가 복구되면 시간을 내어 웹사이트의 **138업데이트된** 기능을 살펴보시기 바랍니다. 여기에는 새로운 스케줄러와 더욱 사용하기 쉬워진 검색 도구가 포함됩니다.

양해해 주시면 감사하겠습니다. 질문이 있으면 저에게 해 주십시오.

어휘 maintenance 관리, 유지보수   routine 정기의, 정례적인   perform 실시하다   approximately 대략   access 접속, 이용   restrict 제한하다   delivery 배송, 전달   pause 중단하다   explore 살펴보다, 탐험하다   user-friendly 사용하기 쉬운, 사용자 친화적인   patience 참을성, 인내심   appreciate 감사하다

135 동사 어형 _ 시제

해설 앞 문장에서 정기 서버 관리가 이번 주말에 실시될 예정(will be performed)이라고 했고, 서버가 다운되는 시기(from 11 P.M. on Saturday, June 6, to 7 A.M. on Sunday, June 7)가 이메일 날짜(Date: June 1)를 기준으로 미래임을 알 수 있다. 따라서 빈칸에도 미래 시제가 쓰여야 자연스러우므로, (C) will be가 정답이다.

136 전치사 어휘

해설 빈칸이 목적어로 취하는 this time은 앞 문장에서 언급된 서버 다운 시간(eight hours from 11 P.M. on Saturday ~ to 7 A.M. on Sunday, June 7)을 가리킨다. 빈칸 뒤에서 웹사이트 접속 및 이메일 전송이 중단될 거라고 안내했는데, 이는 서버가 다운되는 동안 발생할 일이라고 볼 수 있다. 따라서 '~ 동안'이라는 의미로 기간을 나타내는 (A) During이 정답이다.

어휘 despite ~에도 불구하고   following ~후에   prior to ~이전에

137 문맥에 맞는 문장 고르기

번역 (A) 작업은 업무시간 동안 이뤄집니다.
(B) 7명의 프로그래머로 구성된 팀이 열심히 작업할 것입니다.
(C) 모든 웹사이트 기능은 일요일 아침에 재개됩니다.
(D) 필요하시면 이메일을 자유롭게 확인하세요.

해설 빈칸 앞 문장에서는 서버 다운 시 제한 및 중단되는 것(access to the Web site will be restricted, and e-mail delivery will be paused)을 안내했는데, 뒤 문장에서는 서버가 복구되고 나면(Once the server is back up) 해야 할 일을 당부했다. 따라서 빈칸에는 추가로 제한되는 기능이나 웹사이트의 재개와 관련된 문장이 들어가야 자연스러우므로, 재개 시점을 안내한 (C)가 정답이다. 작업은 주말에 진행되며 이메일 전송이 중단된다고 했으므로 (A)와 (D)는 명백한 오답이다. 또한 웹사이트 이용이 불가능할 거라고 안내하다가 프로그래머들이 열심히 작업할 거라고 설명하는 것은 어색하므로, (B)는 정답이 될 수 없다. 앞뒤에 나온 단서(7 A.M. on Sunday→Sunday morning, is back up→resume)를 근거로 답을 선택하도록 한다.

어휘 be hard at work 열심히 일하다 resume 재개하다

138 명사 / 형용사 어휘

해설 뒤 문장에서 점검 후 새롭게 추가되거나 개선될 도구(These include a new scheduler and a more user-friendly search tool)를 나열했는데, 여기서 These는 the ------- features를 가리킨다. 따라서 빈칸에는 추가 및 개선될 기능과 어울리는 단어가 들어가야 하므로, '업데이트된, 최신의'라는 의미의 (B) updated가 정답이다.

어휘 safety 보안 portable 휴대용의 temporary 임시의

139-142 기사

소기업 비용: 초보자를 위한 개요

두 가지의 주요 비용이 있다. 하나는 변동 비용으로, 직원 임금이나 물품 비용이 포함된다. ¹³⁹**다른** 비용은 고정으로 간주된다. 여기에는 임대료 및 재산세 등이 포함된다.

세 번째 종류의 비용은 기회 비용이라고 한다. 다른 대안을 선택하는 ¹⁴⁰**대신** 어떤 특정한 일을 하기로 결정할 때마다 기회 비용을 발생시킨다. 이 비용은 다른 선택을 했더라면 이익을 얻었을 잃어버린 기회를 가리킨다. 잠재적인 기회 비용을 꼼꼼하게 고려하는 것이 중요하다. 이상적인 결과를 위해서는 이것이 의사 결정에 ¹⁴¹**영향을 주어야** 한다.

¹⁴²**다른 종류의 사업 비용도 있다.** 더 완전한 이해를 위해서는 공인회계사에게 자문을 구해야 한다.

어휘 overview 개요 variable 가변적인 wage 임금 supply 보급품, 물자 fixed 고정된 property tax 재산세 opportunity cost 기회 비용 incur 발생시키다 make a decision 결정을 내리다 specific 특정한 alternative 대안이 되는 refer to ~을 나타내다 benefit from ~로부터 이익을 얻다 potential 잠재적인 ideally 이상적으로는, 이상적인 결과를 위해서는 licensed 공인된, 면허를 소지한 accountant 회계사 complete 완전한

---

139 한정사 어휘

해설 앞 문장에서 두 가지의 주요 비용이 있다(There are two main kinds of costs)고 한 후, 주요 비용 중 하나(one kind)로 변동 비용(Variable costs)을 제시했다. 빈칸이 수식하는 비용은 고정된 것으로 간주된다(are considered fixed)고 했으므로, 앞서 언급된 변동 비용과는 반대되는 개념임을 알 수 있다. 따라서 '다른'이라는 의미의 (C) Other가 정답이다.

140 전치사 / 접속사 어휘

해설 다른 대안을 선택하는 것(choosing some alternative option)과 어떤 특정한 일을 하기로 결정하는 것(you make a decision to do one specific thing)은 양자택일의 대상이므로, '~ 대신'이라는 의미의 (C) rather than이 정답이다. 참고로, rather than은 상관접속사처럼 쓰여 뒤에 동사원형이 올 수도 있다.

어휘 except for ~를 제외하고 just as 꼭 ~처럼; ~한 대로 only if ~해야만

141 동사 어휘

해설 빈칸의 주어인 this는 앞 문장의 Careful consideration of potential opportunity costs를 가리킨다. 앞에서 잠재적 기회 비용을 고려하는 게 중요하다고 했으므로, 해당 문장은 이 과정을 거친 후 의사 결정을 하라고 권장하는 내용이 되어야 자연스럽다. 즉, 이 과정이 의사 결정에 영향을 주어야 한다는 취지이므로, (B) influence(영향을 미치다)가 정답이다.

어휘 eliminate 제거하다 replace 교체하다 automate 자동화하다

142 문맥에 맞는 문장 고르기

번역 (A) 직원 숫자가 계속 변동을 거듭하고 있다.
(B) 영업 관리자가 직원 위원회를 관리한다.
(C) 업체는 더 많은 재고 목록을 갖고 있었다.
(D) 다른 종류의 사업 비용도 있다.

해설 빈칸 앞에서 세 가지 소기업 비용(Small Business Costs)을 설명했고, 뒤 문장에서는 더 완전한 이해를 위해서는 면허를 소지한 회계사에게 자문을 구하라(You should consult a licensed accountant for a more complete understanding)고 조언했다. 따라서 빈칸에는 회계사에게 자문을 구해 배울만한 비용 관련 언급이 들어가야 자연스러우므로, (D)가 정답이다.

어휘 fluctuate 변동을 거듭하다 inventory 재고 목록

143-146 기사

몰런 홈 굿즈, 문을 열 예정

티스데일 (4월 2일) - 몰런 홈 굿즈가 이번 주 금요일, 예전에 빙클리 마켓이 ¹⁴³**있었던** 웨이벌리 로의 130제곱미터 크기의 공간에 문을 연다. 매장에는 전 세계에서 온 램프, 벽면 장식, 소형 가구 등 가정용 장식 제품이 있으며, 모두 적정한 가격에 판매된다. "몰런은 현대식 주거지를 위해 매우 다양한 멋진 상품을 갖추고 있습니다. 저희 물품 목록은 ¹⁴⁴**자주** 변경됩니다. 고객들이 신상품을 보러 종종 들르고 싶어 하거든요." 체인의 마케팅 담당자인 나오코 사사키의 설명이다. 이곳은 지역 내 첫 번째 몰런 매장이다. ¹⁴⁵**업체는 전국에 14개의 매장을 더 보유하고 있다.** 무료 음식과 경품, 할인 쿠폰 등이 주어질 개업 ¹⁴⁶**축하 행사**는 4월 13일 토요일 오전 10시부터 오후 6시까지 열릴 예정이다.

어휘 square meter 제곱미터 formerly 이전에 feature (특별히) 포함하다, 선보이다 affordable 가격이 적정한 a variety of 다양한 attractive 매력적인, 멋진 modern 현대(식)의 inventory 재고, 물품 목록 patron 이용자, 고객 local 지역의, 현지의 giveaway 증정품, 경품

---

143 동사 어형 _ 태

해설 주격 관계대명사 that이 이끄는 절에서 be동사 was와 함께 동사구를 이루는 자리이다. 뒤에 전치사 by가 있으므로 선행사인 a

130 square meter space (on Waverly Road)가 빙클리 마켓에 의해 점유되었던 곳임을 알 수 있다. 따라서 수동의 의미를 내포한 과거분사 (B) occupied가 정답이다. (A) occupation은 명사, (C) occupy는 동사, (D) occupying은 동명사/현재분사로 구조상 빈칸에 들어갈 수 없다.

어휘 occupation 직업 occupy 차지하다, 사용하다, 점령하다

144 부사 어휘

해설 앞 문장에서 매장에 다양한 물건이 있다고 했고, 뒤 문장에서는 고객들이 신상품을 보러 종종 들르고 싶어 한다(Patrons like to stop in often to see what is new)고 했다. 따라서 해당 문장은 고객의 주기적인 방문을 유도하기 위해 신상품을 계속 업데이트한다는 맥락이 되어야 한다. 즉, 물품 목록이 자주 바뀐다는 내용이 되어야 자연스러우므로, '자주, 빈번하게'라는 의미의 (D) frequently가 정답이다. 자동사 change는 변화 속도(rapidly, gradually 등), 빈도(frequently, often 등), 정도(dramatically, completely 등)를 나타내는 부사와 자주 쓰인다는 것도 알아두면 좋다.

어휘 elsewhere 다른 곳에서 afterward 후에 properly 적절히

145 문맥에 맞는 문장 고르기

번역 (A) 업체는 전국에 14개의 매장을 더 보유하고 있다.
(B) 저번 분기 이래로 수익이 25퍼센트 증가했다.
(C) 몰런의 최대 경쟁업체는 컨트리 홈이다.
(D) 빙클리 마켓은 올해 초에 폐업했다.

해설 빈칸 앞 문장에서는 지역 내 첫 번째 몰런 매장(This is the first Morlon in the local area)이라며 신규 매장의 의의를 설명했고, 뒤 문장에서는 개업(A grand opening)과 관련된 일정을 안내했다. 따라서 빈칸에도 몰런 매장과 관련된 내용이 들어가야 자연스러우므로, 전국에 있는 매장의 개수를 언급한 (A)가 정답이다. 수익(Profits), 경쟁사(competitor), 신규 매장 공간의 이전 임대 업체(Binkley's Market)에 대한 내용은 문맥상 어색하다.

어휘 profit 수익, 수입 quarter 분기 competitor 경쟁자 go out of business 폐업하다

146 명사 자리 _ 동사의 주어 _ 복합명사

해설 A grand opening ~ discount coupons까지가 주어, will be held가 동사인 문장이다. 구조상 빈칸에는 opening과 복합명사를 이루어 주어 역할을 하는 명사나 featuring을 수식하는 부사가 들어갈 수 있다. 따라서 보기 중 명사인 (D) celebration(축하 행사)이 정답이다. grand opening celebration은 '개업 축하 행사'라는 의미가 되며, 분사구 featuring 이하의 수식을 받는다. (A) celebrates와 (C) celebrate는 동사, (B) celebrating은 동명사/현재분사로 구조상 빈칸에 들어갈 수 없다.

PART 7
147-148 온라인 광고

```
http://www.yummygoodfoods.com
```

야미 굿 푸드
영양을 중요하게 여기십니까?
품질이 우수한 천연 제품을 좋아하시나요?
시간이 부족하세요?

147 그렇다면 건강에 좋고 영양가도 높으며 문 바로 앞까지 배송해 드리는 저희의 식사 제품을 고려해 보세요. *야미* 굿 푸드는 한 번의 기회인 특별 판매를 진행하고 있습니다. 147/148 첫 주 동안 '헬시 밀' 메뉴의 맛있는 식사를 무료 배송으로 보내드리겠습니다!

www.yummygoodfoods.com으로 가셔서
BetterHealth4Me 코드를 입력하세요.
148 특별 판매는 6월 중 한 달 단위로 첫 구매 시 유효합니다.

어휘 nutrition 영양 natural 천연[자연]의 short on ~이 부족하여 nutritional 영양가 높은 offer 특별 판매, 특가 할인 complimentary 무료의 valid 유효한 purchase 구입

147 주제 / 목적

번역 광고의 목적은?
(A) 매장 개업을 홍보하려고
(B) 새 고객을 유치하려고
(C) 새 메뉴를 알리려고
(D) 웹사이트 업그레이드를 보고하려고

해설 중반부에서 문 바로 앞까지 배송되는 야미 굿 푸드의 식사 제품을 고려해보라(consider our ~ meals shipped right to your door)며 주문 시 첫 주 동안 맛있는 식사를 무료 배송으로 보내주겠다(We will send your first week of delicious meals ~ with complimentary shipping!)고 했다. 이는 신규 고객을 위한 특별 혜택이므로, (B)가 정답이다.

어휘 promote 홍보하다 attract 끌어들이다, 유치하다

148 세부 사항

번역 6월 중 이용 가능한 것은?
(A) 식단 분석
(B) 견본 조리법
(C) 무료 배송
(D) 잡지 구독

해설 광고의 마지막 문장에서 특별 판매는 6월 중 한 달 단위로 첫 구매 시 유효하다(Offer valid through June with your first monthly purchase)고 했는데, 중반부를 보면 해당 혜택이 첫 번째 주의 식사를 무료 배송해 주는 것(We will send your first week of delicious meals ~ with complimentary shipping!)임을 알 수 있다. 따라서 (C)가 정답이다.

▶▶ Paraphrasing   지문의 complimentary shipping
　　　　　　　　　 → 정답의 free delivery

149-150 이메일

수신: 전 입주민
발신: 댄 매드슨
날짜: 9월 20일
제목: 조지타운 마라톤

톰슨 타워의 모든 입주민 여러분께,

¹⁴⁹다음 주 토요일에 제25회 연례 조지타운 마라톤 대회가 열립니다. 올해는 최초로 경주가 리버 가에서 갈라져 엘몬트 가로 이어집니다. ¹⁵⁰따라서 토요일에는 등록 참가자 거의 5천 명이 우리 톰슨 타워 주차 건물 입구로 통하는 유일한 도로를 따라 달릴 예정입니다. ¹⁴⁹당연히 엘몬트 가는 오전 7시부터 오전 10시 45분 사이에 모든 차량이 통제됩니다. 따라서 해당 행사 중에는 입주민 차량이 우리 주차 건물에 출입할 수 없습니다. 이 시간 동안 차량을 쓰셔야 한다면 일찍 출발하시거나 다른 곳에 주차할 수 있도록 사전에 준비하시기를 권장합니다.

지도, 등록 안내, 대체 주차 장소 등 경주에 관한 더 자세한 사항을 알고 싶으시다면 www.gergetownmarathon.co.uk를 방문하십시오.

댄 매드슨
건물 관리인, 톰슨 타워

어휘   resident 거주자, 주민   turn off (가고 있던 길에서) 빠져나가다   proceed 계속해서 ~하다, 나아가다   register 등록하다   contestant (대회) 참가자   stretch 길게 뻗은 구간, 직선 코스   provide 제공하다   access 접근(권), 이용   parking garage 주차장   entrance 입구   unsurprisingly 당연하게도, 아니나다를까   mean 결국 ~하게 되다, (어떤 결과를) 뜻하다   recommend 권고하다   make arrangements 준비하다, 마련하다   ahead of time 시간보다 빨리, 사전에   elsewhere 다른 곳에서   registration 등록   alternative 대안이 되는

149 주제 / 목적

번역   이메일을 쓴 목적은?
(A) 경주 참가를 독려하려고
(B) 앞으로 있을 도로 봉쇄에 대해 통지하려고
(C) 세입자 회의 일정을 다시 잡으려고
(D) 공사 계획을 알리려고

해설   첫 번째 단락에서 제25회 연례 조지타운 마라톤 대회가 열린다(The 25th annual Georgetown Marathon will be held)고 한 후, 엘몬트 가에 모든 차량의 통행이 통제된다(Elmont Avenue will be closed to all vehicle traffic)는 점을 안내했다. 따라서 마라톤 대회로 인한 도로 봉쇄를 알리는 이메일임을 알 수 있으므로, (B)가 정답이다.

어휘   encourage 독려하다   participation 참가   warn 예고하다, 경고하다   upcoming 곧 있을, 다가오는   reschedule 일정을 다시 잡다   tenant 세입자   construction 건설, 공사

150 사실 관계 확인

번역   조지타운 마라톤에 대해 알 수 있는 것은?
(A) 참가자가 대략 5천 명이다.
(B) 최초로 개최된다.
(C) 엘몬트 가에서 출발한다.
(D) 톰슨 타워에서 온 참가자들도 있다.

해설   첫 번째 단락에서 거의 5천 명의 등록된 참가자들이 있을 것(there will be nearly 5,000 registered contestants)이라고 했으므로, (A)가 정답이다. 제25회 연례 조지타운 마라톤 대회(The 25th annual Georgetown Marathon)라고 했고, 경주가 리버 가에서 갈라져 엘몬트 가로 이어진다(the race will turn off of River Street and proceed onto Elmont Avenue)고 했으므로, (B)와 (C)는 명백한 오답이다. (D)는 확인되지 않으므로 정답이 될 수 없다.

어휘   close to 대략   participant 참가자

▶▶ Paraphrasing   지문의 nearly 5,000 registered contestants
　　　　　　　　　 → 정답의 close to 5,000 participants

151-152 안내서 페이지

¹⁵¹골판지가 신선 채소 및 과일 배송용으로 굉장히 인기 있는 자재가 된 한 가지 이유는 용기 라벨 작업이 쉽기 때문이다. 농산물의 상표, 크기, 등급 등의 정보가 상자를 만들고 난 후 그 위에 바로 인쇄될 수 있다. '후인쇄'로 알려진 이 방식이 골판지 용기에 라벨 작업을 하는 가장 경제적인 방법이긴 하지만, 한두 가지 색으로만 제한된다. 컬러 그래픽은 상자를 만들기 전 그 위에 정보를 인쇄해서 얻을 수 있다. ¹⁵²'선인쇄'라고 알려진 이 방식은 약 15퍼센트 비용이 더 들지만, 많은 슈퍼마켓 관리자들이 이를 선호한다. 고객들이 다채로운 진열에 매료되면 이것이 곧 매출 증가로 이어지기 때문이다.

어휘   corrugated fiberboard 골판지   material 재료, 자재   label 라벨 작업을 하다, 라벨을 붙이다   container 용기   produce 농산물   method 방식, 방법   economical 경제적인   obtain 얻다, 구하다   prefer 선호하다   be attracted to ~에 끌리다   display 진열, 전시   lead to ~로 이어지다

151 사실 관계 확인

번역   골판지 상자에 대해 알 수 있는 것은?
(A) 라벨 작업이 쉽다.
(B) 다른 용기보다 더 많이 들어간다.
(C) 채소를 신선하게 보관한다.
(D) 다른 유형보다 덜 자주 사용된다.

해설   초반부에서 골판지가 인기 있는 자재가 된 한 가지 이유가 용기 라벨 작업이 쉽기 때문(One reason that corrugated fiberboard has become such a popular material ~ is the ease of labeling the containers)이라고 했으므로, (A)가 정답이다.

▶▶ Paraphrasing   지문의 the ease of labeling the containers
　　　　　　　　　 → 정답의 easy to label

TEST 5

152 세부 사항

번역 매장 관리자들이 일반적으로 컬러 그래픽이 들어간 상자를 선호하는 이유는?

(A) 씻어서 재활용할 수 있다.
(B) 매우 다양한 크기로 나온다.
(C) 고객들이 자주 요청한다.
(D) 고객의 구매를 늘린다.

해설 후반부에서 슈퍼마켓 관리자들은 컬러 인쇄를 할 수 있는 '선인쇄' 방식을 선호한다며 고객들이 다채로운 진열에 매료되고 이것이 매출 증가로 이어지기 때문(because customers are attracted to the colorful displays, which leads to increased sales)이라고 했다. 따라서 (D)가 정답이다.

어휘 a variety of 다양한 request 요청하다 increase 늘리다, 증가시키다

> ▸▸ Paraphrasing 지문의 leads to increased sales
> → 정답의 increase customers' purchases

153-155 구인광고

행정 사무원

직책 개요:
통신업계에서 세계적인 선도 제조업체로 꼽히는 나이두 라이 일렉트로닉스가 자이푸르 사무실에서 일할 상근직 행정 사무원을 찾습니다.

책무:
1. 153제품 디자인 팀원들에게 출장 및 경비 보고서를 포함해 행정적인 지원 제공
2. 153잠재 고객 및 디자이너와의 약속 일정 수립
3. 파일 관리, 문서 처리, 보고서 편집

필요 자격/학력:
고등학교 졸업증명서 필수, 경영학과 수료증 우대

역량:
1. 뛰어난 대인관계 역량
2. 뛰어난 조직 및 기획력
3. 소프트웨어 능숙

154후보로 고려되려면 s.mohta@naiduraielec.in으로 이력서와 자기소개서를 보내주십시오. 155면접에 선발된 지원자는 기본적인 소프트웨어 숙련도 시험을 치러야 합니다.

어휘 administrative 관리의, 행정의 assistant 사무원, 보조자 summary 요약, 개요 leading 가장 중요한, 선두의 telecommunications 통신 industry 업계 full-time 상근직의 support 지원 including ~를 포함하여 expense 지출, 경비 appointment 약속 prospective 장래의, 미래의 maintain 유지하다, 관리하다 process 처리하다 compile 편집[편찬]하다 qualification 자격 certificate (과정 이수 후 받는) 증명서 mandatory 의무적인, 필수의 certification 증명, (주로 시험 합격 후 받는) 증명서 preferred 우대되는 interpersonal 대인관계의 organizational 조직의

---

proficiency 능숙함, 숙련도 consider (선발 대상이나 후보로) 고려하다 candidate 지원자, 후보자

---

153 사실 관계 확인

번역 해당 직책에 대해 알 수 있는 것은?

(A) 제품 디자이너들과의 업무를 수반한다.
(B) 출장을 자주 가야 한다.
(C) 임시직이다.
(D) 몇 개월간 비어 있었다.

해설 나열된 책무(Responsibilities) 중 '제품 디자인 팀원들에게 행정적인 지원 제공(Provide administrative support for members of the product design team)'과 '잠재 고객 및 디자이너와의 약속 일정 수립(Schedule appointments with prospective clients and designers)'에서 제품 디자이너들과 함께 일한다는 것을 알 수 있다. 따라서 (A)가 정답이다.

어휘 involve 수반하다 frequent 잦은, 빈번한 temporary 임시의, 일시적인

---

154 세부 사항

번역 광고에 따르면, 지원하기 위해 무엇을 해야 하는가?

(A) 고객 목록 제공하기
(B) 학교 성적증명서 보내기
(C) 이력서 제출하기
(D) 추천서 보내기

해설 마지막 단락에서 후보로 고려되려면 이력서와 자기소개서를 이메일로 보내달라(To be considered, e-mail your résumé and cover letter)고 했으므로, (C)가 정답이다.

어휘 forward 보내다 transcript 성적증명서 submit 제출하다 reference letter 추천서

> ▸▸ Paraphrasing 지문의 To be considered →
> 질문의 to apply
> 지문의 e-mail → 정답의 submit

---

155 세부 사항

번역 지원자는 면접에서 무엇을 하게 될 것인가?

(A) 전화 응대하기
(B) 컴퓨터 시험 치르기
(C) 작문 견본 제출하기
(D) 보고서 편집하기

해설 마지막 단락에서 면접에 선발된 지원자는 기본적인 소프트웨어 숙련도 시험을 치러야 한다(candidates selected for an interview will be required to take a basic software proficiency test)고 했으므로, (B)가 정답이다.

> ▸▸ Paraphrasing 지문의 candidates → 질문의 applicant
> 지문의 take a basic software proficiency test → 정답의 Take a computer test

156-158 웹페이지

http://www.moorecountylibrary.gov/seminars

| 홈 | 소개 | **세미나** | 연락처 |

마케팅 기초
¹⁵⁶4월 15일 오후 6시
무어 카운티 도서관 시스템, 뉴버그 분관
발표자: 살 쿼트로치

¹⁵⁸사업체를 효과적으로 마케팅하는 방법을 배우고 싶습니까?

이 유익한 강좌를 함께 하십시오. 여기서 다음의 방법을 배우게 됩니다.

- ^{157(A)}타깃 고객 및 그들에게 구매 동기를 부여하는 요소 알아보기
- 고객에게 도달하는 최상의 방법 선택하기
- ^{157(B)}경쟁업체를 파악하고 이들과 차별화하기
- ^{157(D)}한정된 마케팅 예산을 최대한 활용하기

강좌는 무료이지만 등록이 필요하며, 등록은 3월 1일에 시작됩니다.

¹⁵⁸'마케팅 기초'는 무어 카운티 도서관에서 새롭게 진행 중인
〈소기업을 위한 마케팅〉 시리즈의 일환입니다. 5월 6일 랭커스터
분관에서 열릴 다음 강좌인 '디지털 전략'에도 참석하세요.
등록은 4월 5일에 시작됩니다.

어휘 presenter 발표자, 진행자   effectively 효과적으로
informative 유익한, 유익한 정보를 주는   determine 알아내다,
밝히다, 결정하다   target customer 타깃 고객, 영업 대상으로 삼는
고객   motivate 동기를 부여하다   reach 도달하다, 닿다   identify
확인하다, 파악하다   competitor 경쟁자   stand out from ~와
구별되다, ~중에 두드러지다   get the most out of ~를 최대한
활용하다   limited 한정된   budget 예산   registration 등록
ongoing 진행 중인   strategy 전략

156 세부 사항

번역 마케팅 기초 강좌는 언제 열릴 것인가?

(A) 3월 1일
(B) 4월 5일
(C) 4월 15일
(D) 5월 6일

해설 '마케팅 기초(MARKETING BASICS)'라는 제목 아래에서 강좌가
4월 15일 오후 6시(April 15, 6 P.M.)에 진행될 예정임을 확인할 수
있다. 따라서 (C)가 정답이다. (A)는 강좌 등록일(registration is
required and begins on March 1)이며, (B)와 (D)는 다음 강좌인
디지털 전략(Digital Strategy)과 연관된 일정이므로 오답이다.

어휘 take place 열리다

157 사실 관계 확인

번역 마케팅 기초 강좌에서 다루지 않을 주제는?

(A) 잠재 고객 파악하기
(B) 사업체가 경쟁자들과 차별화되는 방법 보여주기
(C) 광고를 만들 그래픽 디자이너 선발하기
(D) 마케팅 비용을 효율적으로 사용하기

해설 중반부를 보면 마케팅 기초 강좌에서 배우는 내용(you will learn
how to)이 나열되어 있다. '타깃 고객 알아보기(Determine your
target customers)'에서 (A)가, '경쟁업체를 파악하고 이들과 차별
화하기(Identify your competitors and stand out from them)'
에서 (B)가, '한정된 마케팅 예산을 최대한 활용하기(Get the most
out of your limited marketing budget)'에서 (D)가 다뤄진다는
것을 확인할 수 있다. 따라서 언급되지 않은 (C)가 정답이다.

어휘 potential 잠재적인, 가능성 있는   advertisement 광고
efficiently 효율적으로

▸▸ Paraphrasing   지문의 Determine your target customers
→ 보기 (A)의 Identifying potential customers
지문의 stand out from
→ 보기 (B)의 Showing how a business is
different from
지문의 Get the most out of your limited
marketing budget
→ 보기 (D)의 Spending marketing money
efficiently

158 사실 관계 확인

번역 마케팅 기초 강좌에 대해 알 수 있는 것은?

(A) 마케팅 교수가 가르친다.
(B) 사업체 소유주들에게 제공되는 여러 강좌 중 하나다.
(C) 회사 임원들을 위해 고안됐다.
(D) 가까운 시일 내에 다시 제공될 예정이다.

해설 초반부에서 사업체를 효과적으로 마케팅하는 방법을 배우고 싶은
지(Do you want to learn how to effectively market your
business?)를 물으며 주의를 끌었고, 마지막 단락에서는 마케
팅 기초가 무어 카운티 도서관에서 새롭게 진행 중인 〈소기업을 위
한 마케팅〉 시리즈의 일환(Marketing Basics is part of Moore
County Library's new ongoing series, Marketing for Small
Businesses)이라고 했다. 따라서 마케팅 기초가 사업체 소유주들
을 대상으로 하는 여러 강좌 중 하나임을 알 수 있으므로, (B)가 정
답이다. 참고로, 가까운 시일 내에 제공되는 것은 다른 강좌(Digital
Strategy)이므로, (D)는 정답이 될 수 없다.

어휘 corporate 회사의   executive 임원, 경영진

159-161 웹페이지

http://www.coltonhotels.com.au/accommodations

멜버른 콜튼 호텔은 야라 리버 신관 공사가 완료되었음을 기쁜 마음으
로 알려드립니다. ¹⁵⁹이 새로운 공간은 장기 투숙용 아파트를 제공하는
데, 근무지 이동 중인 경영진이나 1주일 이상 출장 중인 사람들에게 이
상적입니다. ¹⁶¹가구가 비치되어 있고 거실, 업무 공간, 조리 가능한 주
방을 갖춘 침실 한 개짜리 또는 두 개짜리 아파트를 제공합니다. 아울러
장기 투숙객을 위한 선택 서비스도 이용 가능합니다.

저희는 다음을 제공합니다.

- 다양한 가격대의 객실 관리비
- 다양한 저가 인터넷 및 전화 요금제

- 최소 요금으로 예약 가능한 회의 시설
- 인근 피트니스 센터 여러 곳의 단기 회원권
- ¹⁶⁰매일 아침 로비에서 무료 커피 제공

멜버른 콜튼 호텔은 교통편, 관광 명소, 쇼핑 지역과 가깝습니다. 더 자세한 내용은 reservations@coltonhotels.com.au 또는 61 3 7010 9921로 연락하세요.

> 어휘 construction 공사 complete 완료하다 extended-stay 장기 체류 ideal 이상적인 relocate 이전하다 furnished 가구가 비치된 pricing 가격 책정 a variety of 다양한 facility 시설 book 예약하다 minimal 최소의, 아주 적은 complimentary 무료의

159 세부사항

번역 정보는 주로 누구를 대상으로 하는가?

(A) 출장자
(B) 관광객
(C) 호텔 직원
(D) 공사 인부

해설 첫 번째 단락에서 호텔이 제공하는 장기 투숙용 아파트가 근무지 이동 중인 경영진이나 1주일 이상 출장 중인 사람들에게 이상적(extended-stay apartments, which are ideal for executives who are relocating or for people on company travel for more than a week)이라고 한 후, 이에 대해 광고하고 있다. 따라서 (A)가 정답이다.

> ▸▸ Paraphrasing 지문의 executives who are relocating, people on company travel
> → 정답의 Business travelers

160 세부 사항

번역 호텔은 무엇을 무료로 제공하는가?

(A) 객실 관리
(B) 인터넷
(C) 회의실
(D) 커피

해설 두 번째 단락에 호텔이 제공하는 서비스(We offer:)가 나열되어 있는데, 마지막 항목에서 매일 아침 로비에서 무료 커피를 제공한다(Complimentary coffee served each morning in the lobby)고 했다. 따라서 (D)가 정답이다.

> ▸▸ Paraphrasing 지문의 offer → 질문의 provide
> 지문의 Complimentary
> → 질문의 at no charge

161 문장 삽입

번역 [1], [2], [3], [4]로 표시된 곳 중에서 다음 문장이 가장 적합한 곳은?

"아울러 장기 투숙객을 위한 선택 서비스도 이용 가능합니다."

(A) [1]
(B) [2]
(C) [3]
(D) [4]

해설 주어진 문장에서 추가적으로(In addition) 제공되는 선택 서비스(optional services)를 언급하고 있으므로, 이 앞에서 먼저 기본 서비스에 대한 설명이 나와야 한다. [3] 앞에서 아파트에 기본적으로 제공하는 시설을 소개(We offer furnished one- and two-bedroom apartments with a living room, work space, and full kitchen)하고 있으며, 뒤에서는 부가 서비스를 나열하고 있으므로, 이 사이에 주어진 문장이 들어가야 자연스럽다. 따라서 (C)가 정답이다.

어휘 optional 선택적인

162-163 문자 메시지

> [오후 2시 11분] 프랭크 스턴:
> 안녕하세요, 페트라. ¹⁶²손님이 양면 광택 컬러 포스터 1,000매를 원해요. ^{162/163}오늘 할 수 있을까요? 안 되면 다른 곳에 일을 맡길 것 같다라고요.
>
> [오후 2시 12분] 페트라 키트조스:
> 아마 안 될 겁니다. 노블 아키텍트의 큰 건으로 일이 밀려 있어요. 내일 아침 첫 작업으로 하면 어때요?
>
> [오후 2시 12분] 프랭크 스턴:
> 물어볼게요.
>
> [오후 2시 13분] 프랭크 스턴:
> ¹⁶³오전 10시까지 완료될 수 있는지 알고 싶어 해요.
>
> [오후 2시 13분] 페트라 키트조스:
> ¹⁶³그럼요.
>
> [오후 2시 14분] 프랭크 스턴:
> 그럼 안심이네요. 고맙습니다.

> 어휘 glossy 광택의, 윤이 나는 elsewhere 다른 곳으로 probably 아마도 be backed up with ~로 밀려 있다, 꽉 막혔다 relief 안도, 안심

162 추론 / 암시

번역 스턴 씨와 키트조스 씨는 어디에서 일하겠는가?

(A) 배송 매장
(B) 건축 사무소
(C) 회계 사무소
(D) 인쇄소

해설 스턴 씨가 오후 2시 11분 메시지에서 손님이 양면 광택 컬러 포스

터 1,000매를 원한다(A customer wants 1,000 glossy color posters)고 한 후, 오늘 할 수 있는지(Any chance we can do this today?)를 물었다. 따라서 그들이 인쇄소에서 일한다고 추론할 수 있으므로, (D)가 정답이다.

163 의도 파악

번역 오후 2시 14분에 스턴 씨가 "그럼 안심이네요"라고 쓸 때, 그 의도는 무엇인가?

(A) 키트조스 씨가 시간 외 근무를 해주어 감사하다.
(B) 회사가 고객을 잃지 않을까 더 이상 걱정하지 않는다.
(C) 키트조스 씨가 빠르게 응답해서 고마워한다.
(D) 아침 일찍 올 필요가 없어서 기쁘다.

해설 오후 2시 11분 메시지에서 스턴 씨는 주문이 들어왔는데 오늘 하지 못하면 다른 곳으로 넘어갈 것 같다(they might take the job elsewhere)고 했다. 내일 아침에 하면 어떠냐는 키트조스 씨의 제안에 따라 고객에게 확인 후, 고객이 원하는 시간(if it can be done by 10 A.M.)까지 작업이 가능할지 물었는데, 키트조스 씨가 그렇다(Sure)고 하자 안심을 표한 것이다. 스턴 씨가 고객을 잃게 될 염려가 없어진 것에 안도하고 있다고 볼 수 있으므로, (B)가 정답이다.

어휘 grateful 감사하는 no longer 더 이상 ~아닌 respond 응답하다

164-167 기사

호컴, 로즈빌 도심을 주목하다

(4월 22일) - [165]주에서 가장 선도적인 통신업체인 호컴이 로즈빌에 사무실을 설립할 듯하다. [164]전해진 바에 따르면 호컴은 디지털 미디어 업계로 확장하는 신규 사업의 일환으로 로즈빌 사무실을 여는 것을 고려하고 있다. [166]호컴 대변인들은 계획의 세부적인 내용을 전혀 알려주지 않았지만, 해당 프로젝트와 관계된 두 명의 건축가들이 제안된 사무용 건물 설계가 직원 100명 이상을 수용할 수 있을 거라는 내용을 확인해 주었다. [167]이 정보통에 따르면, 곧 공사에 들어갈 건물의 예상 위치는 로즈빌 중심부의 베어 광장에 인접한 부지다.

어휘 eye 쳐다보다, 주목하다 establish 설립하다, 수립하다 reportedly 전해진[보고된] 바에 따르면 venture 신규 개발 사업, (사업상의) 모험 expansion 확대, 확장 spokespeople 대변인들 architect 건축가 involved with ~와 관계된 proposed 제안된 accommodate 수용하다 likely 예상되는, 그럴 듯한 soon-to-be 곧 ~할 according to ~에 따르면 property 부동산, 재산 adjacent to ~에 인접한

164 세부 사항

번역 호컴은 로즈빌에서 무엇을 하려고 계획하는가?

(A) 새로운 전화 서비스 제공
(B) 하도급업체에게 공간 임대
(C) 본사 이전
(D) 새로운 사업 부문 개시

해설 두 번째 문장에서 호컴이 디지털 미디어 업계로 확장하는 신규 사업의 일환으로 로즈빌 사무실을 여는 것을 고려하고 있다(Houkcomm is ~ looking to open a Roseville office as part of a new venture for the company: an expansion into the digital media industry)고 했으므로, (D)가 정답이다.

어휘 lease 임대하다 subcontractor 하도급업자 relocate 이전하다 headquarters 본사

▸▸**Paraphrasing** 지문의 **looking to**
　　　　　　　→ 질문의 **planning to**
　　　　　　　지문의 **a new venture for the company: an expansion into the digital media industry** → 정답의 **a new business division**

165 사실 관계 확인

번역 호컴에 대해 맞는 것은?

(A) 주에서 유일한 통신업체이다.
(B) 현재 로즈빌 중심가에서 공간을 임대하고 있다.
(C) 최근 100명 이상의 신규 직원을 채용했다.
(D) 주에서는 이미 일류로 입지를 구축하고 있다.

해설 첫 번째 문장에서 호컴을 주에서 가장 선도적인 통신업체 중 하나(one of the state's leading telecommunications companies)로 소개하고 있으므로, (D)가 정답이다.

어휘 currently 현재 recently 최근 major 주요한, 일류의 presence 입지, 존재

▸▸**Paraphrasing** 지문의 **leading**
　　　　　　　→ 정답의 **has a major presence**

166 추론 / 암시

번역 기자는 기사에 쓸 정보를 어떻게 얻었겠는가?

(A) 호컴 대표들이 쓴 보도자료에서
(B) 호컴을 위해 일하고 있는 업체 직원을 인터뷰해서
(C) 공문서와 건축 허가서를 통해
(D) 로즈빌에서 열린 기자회견에 참석해서

해설 세 번째 문장에서 호컴의 로즈빌 프로젝트와 관계된 두 명의 건축가들이 제안된 사무용 건물 설계에 관한 내용을 확인해 주었다(two architects involved with the project confirmed that one proposed office building design would accommodate over 100 workers)고 했으므로, 관련 업체 직원으로부터 정보를 얻었다고 추론할 수 있다. 따라서 (B)가 정답이다.

어휘 press release 보도자료 representative 대표, 대리인 permit 허가증 press conference 기자회견

▸▸**Paraphrasing** 지문의 **two architects involved with the project** → 정답의 **employees of a firm that is doing work for Houkcomm**

167 추론 / 암시

번역 기사에 따르면, 곧 어떤 일이 있겠는가?

(A) 새 건물에서 공사가 시작될 것이다.
(B) 베어 광장의 모든 거주지가 매입될 것이다.
(C) 호컴은 새로운 공급 계약 협상을 할 것이다.
(D) 로즈빌의 제조업 일자리가 늘어날 것이다.

해설 마지막 문장에서 곧 공사에 들어갈 건물의 예상 위치(The likely location for this soon-to-be constructed building)를 언급했으므로, 건물 공사가 시작될 거라고 추론할 수 있다. 따라서 (A)가 정답이다.

어휘 residence 거주지 negotiate 협상하다 contract 계약 manufacturing 제조

> ▸▸ **Paraphrasing** 지문의 **soon-to-be** → 질문의 **happen soon**

168-171 이메일

발신: 다케시 이시구로
수신: 세바스티야 전 직원
제목: 최신 소식
날짜: 12월 13일

세바스티야 직원 여러분께,

올해 지금까지의 판매량에 관한 최신 소식을 전해드리려고 합니다. 현재 우리 판매량이 작년보다 20퍼센트 상승했음을 알리게 되어 기쁩니다. 이는 부분적으로 우리의 해외 진출 확장이 매우 성공적이었다는 사실에 기인합니다.

여기 전 세계의 수치가 나와 있습니다. **168/169/171 브라질에서는 매출이 57퍼센트 상승했으며, 이는 우리 야회복을 선보인 리우데자네이루 패션쇼 덕분일 겁니다.** 비슷한 동향이 러시아에서도 나타났는데, 여기서는 판매량이 32퍼센트 증가했습니다. **168 러시아에서는 특히 겨울 옷 제품으로 올해 나머지 기간에도 성장이 지속될 것이라 예상합니다.** 아랍에미리트에서도 매출 성장이 있었는데 극심한 경쟁으로 인해 성장률은 불과 10퍼센트 정도였습니다. 그렇기는 하지만, 이 시장에서 우리 신용카드 가입 실적이 좋았습니다. 마지막으로, 지금까지의 해외 시장 출시 중 가장 큰 성공을 거둔 한국에서는 우리 제품에 대한 우호적인 기사가 강력한 판매량을 이끌어 냈습니다.

그러므로 지금까지 대체로 훌륭한 한 해였습니다. **170 우리 매장에서 쇼핑하도록 다른 사람을 초대한 고객에게 할인을 제공하는 새 프로그램이 모든 지역에서 매출 성장을 북돋울 것이라고 확신합니다.**

다케시 이시구로
영업 부서장

어휘 currently 현재 expand 확대하다 be attributed to ~덕분이다 emerge 나오다, 부상하다 anticipate 기대하다, 예상하다 sustained 지속된 apparel 의복 modest 그다지 대단하지는 않은, 불과 ~인 fierce 극심한 competition 경쟁 that said 그렇기는 하지만 credit card (특정 브랜드 매장용) 신용카드 launch 론칭, 출시 favorable 호의적인 boost 북돋우다, 신장시키다

168 세부 사항

번역 세바스티야는 어떤 종류의 업체인가?

(A) 여행사
(B) 잡지 출판사
(C) 의류 소매업체
(D) 호텔 체인

해설 두 번째 단락에서 세바스티야의 야회복이 선보인 리우데자네이루 패션쇼(the Rio de Janeiro Fashion Show where our evening wear was featured) 덕분에 브라질에서 매출이 상승했다고 했고, 겨울 옷 제품(our winter apparel line)으로 올해 나머지 기간에도 러시아에서 성장이 지속될 것으로 예상한다고 했다. 이를 통해 세바스티야가 의류를 판매하는 업체임을 알 수 있으므로, (C)가 정답이다.

어휘 publisher 출판사 retailer 소매업자

169 세부 사항

번역 이메일에 따르면, 관객에게 회사 제품을 선보인 곳은?

(A) 브라질
(B) 러시아
(C) 아랍에미리트
(D) 한국

해설 두 번째 단락에서 브라질에서 매출이 상승했다며 이는 야회복이 선보인 리우데자네이루 패션쇼 덕분(In Brazil, sales increased ~ attributed to the Rio de Janeiro Fashion Show where our evening wear was featured)이라고 했다. 따라서 (A)가 정답이다.

> ▸▸ **Paraphrasing** 지문의 **featured** → 질문의 **seen**

170 추론 / 암시

번역 이시구로 씨에 따르면, 앞으로 무엇이 사업을 증대시키겠는가?

(A) TV 광고
(B) 신용카드 프로그램 확대
(C) 회사에서 후원하는 대회
(D) 고객의 소개

해설 세 번째 단락을 보면 세바스티야 매장에서 쇼핑하도록 다른 사람을 초대한 고객에게 할인을 제공하는 새 프로그램이 매출 성장을 북돋울 것(our new program, which offers discounts to customers who invite others to shop with us, will begin to boost sales growth)이라고 확신하고 있다. 따라서 (D)가 정답이다.

어휘 commercial 광고 sponsor 후원하다 referral 소개, 위탁

> ▸▸ **Paraphrasing** 지문의 **boost sales growth**
> → 질문의 **bring increased business**
> 지문의 **customers who invite others to shop with us**
> → 정답의 **Referrals from customers**

171 문장 삽입

번역 [1], [2], [3], [4]로 표시된 곳 중에서 다음 문장이 가장 적합한 곳은?

"여기 전 세계의 수치가 나와 있습니다."

(A) [1]
(B) [2]
(C) [3]
(D) [4]

해설 주어진 문장이 '여기 전 세계의 수치가 나와 있다(Here are some figures from around the world)'이므로, 이 뒤에 각 나라별 수치가 제시되어야 한다. [2] 뒤에서 브라질(Brazil), 러시아(Russia), 아랍에미리트(United Arab Emirates), 한국(Korea)의 사례를 나열하고 있으므로, (B)가 정답이다.

어휘 figures 수치

172-175 문자 메시지

> 린다 맥캔 (오후 1시 8분) 안녕하세요, 베르나데트, 해리슨. 172우리 프로젝트 관련 업무를 시작할 수 있도록 급히 팀 회의 일정을 잡아야 해요.
>
> 베르나데트 에코 (오후 1시 10분) 네. 172마케팅 전 직원 회의를 원하시는 건가요? 제가 도와드릴 수 있는지 알려주세요.
>
> 린다 맥캔 (오후 1시 12분) 아뇨, 173전 오닐 프로젝트를 말한 거예요. 그 팀에 있는 우리 세 명만 회의를 해야 하죠.
>
> 베르나데트 에코 (오후 1시 14분) 알겠습니다. 저는 수요일이나 금요일 이른 오후에 시간이 돼요.
>
> 해리슨 밀러 (오후 1시 15분) 174저는 그거 대신 맥밀란 프로젝트로 다시 배정된 줄 알고 있었는데요.
>
> 베르나데트 에코 (오후 1시 17분) 174아니요. 그 팀 마지막 자리는 제이콥 에이켄스로 채워졌어요. 이전에 그렐러 프로젝트, 올포드 프로젝트 등 비슷한 프로젝트를 맡은 적이 있거든요.
>
> 해리슨 밀러 (오후 1시 18분) 네, 알겠습니다.
>
> 린다 맥캔 (오후 1시 19분) 저도 수요일과 금요일에 시간이 되긴 하는데 오후 3시 이전에만 가능해요. 수요일에는 오후 3시에 영업팀과 회의가 있고 금요일 오후 3시 30분엔 연구팀과 회의가 있거든요.
>
> 해리슨 밀러 (오후 1시 21분) 175저는 수요일은 안 되고 금요일 오후 1시에 됩니다.
>
> 린다 맥캔 (오후 1시 23분) 좋아요! 베르나데트?
>
> 베르나데트 에코 (오후 1시 23분) 좋습니다! 소회의실을 예약할게요.

어휘 urgently 급히 assist 돕다 reassign 다시 맡기다, 새로 발령내다 instead (앞서 언급한 것) 대신 slot 자리 similar 비슷한, 유사한 available 시간이 되는 reserve 예약하다 conference room 회의실

172 추론 / 암시

번역 문자 메시지 작성자들은 어떤 부서에서 일하겠는가?

(A) 영업
(B) 마케팅
(C) 청구서 발송
(D) 연구

해설 맥캔 씨가 오후 1시 8분 메시지에서 팀 회의 일정을 잡자고 제안하자 에코 씨가 1시 10분 메시지에서 마케팅 전 직원 회의를 원하는지(Are you wanting an all-marketing-staff meeting?) 물었다. 따라서 문자 메시지 작성자들이 마케팅 부서에서 일한다고 추론할 수 있으므로, (B)가 정답이다.

173 세부 사항

번역 세 명의 문자 메시지 작성자들은 어떤 프로젝트에 배정되었는가?

(A) 오닐 프로젝트
(B) 맥밀란 프로젝트
(C) 그렐러 프로젝트
(D) 올포드 프로젝트

해설 맥캔 씨가 오후 1시 12분 메시지에서 오닐 프로젝트(I was thinking of the O'Neil project)를 언급한 후, 그 팀에 있는 자신들 세 명만 회의해야 한다(only the three of us who are on that team need to meet)고 했다. 따라서 (A)가 정답이다.

174 의도 파악

번역 오후 1시 18분에 밀러 씨가 "네, 알겠습니다"라고 쓸 때, 그 의도는 무엇인가?

(A) 다른 팀으로 이동되지 않은 이유를 이해했다.
(B) 제시간에 회의에 오지 않았다는 것을 알았다.
(C) 고객을 만나지 않을 것이라는 사실을 받아들였다.
(D) 임무를 완수하지 않았다는 것을 인정했다.

해설 밀러 씨가 오후 1시 15분 메시지에서 오닐 프로젝트 대신 맥밀란 프로젝트로 다시 배정된 줄 알고 있었다(I had been reassigned to the McMillan project)고 했는데, 이에 대해 에코 씨가 오후 1시 17분 메시지에서 아니라고 한 후, 밀러 씨가 배정되지 않은 이유(the final slot on that team was filled by Jacob Aikens, since he's worked on similar projects in the past)를 설명했다. 이 설명에 대해 밀러 씨가 '네, 알겠습니다(Okay, I see)'라고 응답한 것이므로, 자신이 다른 팀으로 배정되지 않은 이유를 이해한 거라고 추론할 수 있다. 따라서 (A)가 정답이다.

어휘 recognize 알다 acknowledge 인정하다

175 세부 사항

번역 수요일이 아닌 금요일로 회의 일정을 잡은 이유는?

(A) 맥캔 씨가 그 날 다른 팀과 약속이 있다.
(B) 이번 달에 에코 씨의 일정이 무척 바쁘다.
(C) 밀러 씨가 수요일에 시간이 안 된다.
(D) 영업팀이 수요일에 회의실을 사용할 예정이다.

해설 회의 일정을 잡는 중에 밀러 씨가 오후 1시 21분 메시지에서 수요일은 안 되고 금요일 오후 1시에 된다(Wednesday won't work for me, but I could do Friday at 1 P.M.)고 했으므로, (C)가 정답이다.

어휘 commitment 약속

> ▸▸ Paraphrasing 지문의 **Wednesday won't work**
> → 정답의 **unavailable on Wednesday**

176-180 이메일 + 웹페이지

수신: 브로디 디믹 ⟨bdimmick@greerscoffee.com.au⟩
발신: 파우지아 구르마니 ⟨fgurmani@greerscoffee.com.au⟩
제목: 최근 전화에 대한 후속 조치
날짜: 9월 17일
첨부: ⬭ 제안서

디믹 씨께,

¹⁷⁷최근 전화 주셔서 감사합니다. 지역 매장 관리자들께서 연락을 주시면 항상 반갑습니다. ¹⁷⁸그리어 커피 클럽을 다시 되돌리자는 의견이 굉장히 좋다고 생각합니다. ¹⁷⁹또한 클럽 펀치카드에 대해 고객들께서 문의해 주시고 계시다는 사실을 알게 되어 기쁩니다. 지금이 프로그램을 다시 되돌리기에 적기라는 데 저도 동의합니다. 회사 브랜드 이미지를 쇄신하는 작업을 하고 있기 때문입니다. ¹⁷⁶디믹 씨의 제안을 문서로 작성했고, 내일 소라 오 마케팅 부서장님께 보낼 예정인데요. 그 전에 한 번 보시고 제가 혹시 세부사항을 빠뜨린 게 있는지 알려 주시겠습니까? 오늘 업무 종료 시까지 의견을 보내 주십시오.

감사합니다.

파우지아 구르마니
지부장

어휘 follow up 후속 조치를 하다, 덧붙이다 proposal 제안, 제안서 reinstate 복귀시키다, 회복시키다 bring back 되돌리다 rebrand ~의 브랜드 이미지를 쇄신하다 draw up 작성하다 forward 보내다 vice president 부서장, 부사장

http://www.greerscoffee.com.au/rewards

커피와 대화, 간식을 위한 장소 그리어가 이제 더욱 좋아졌습니다!

저희가 그리어 커피 클럽을 부활시켰습니다. ¹⁷⁹다만 새로운 점은 이제 이용이 훨씬 간편해졌다는 것입니다! 그저 새 모바일 앱을 다운로드하고 등록만 하면 됩니다. 그리어 커피의 어느 매장이든 방문 시마다 앱을 이용해 영수증을 스캔하세요. 그러면 포인트를 적립할 수 있습니다. 100 포인트를 모을 때마다 커피, 음식 및 기타 제품을 할인받는 데 포인트를 ¹⁸⁰사용하실 수 있습니다.

어휘 register 등록하다 receipt 영수증 accrue 누적하다, 쌓다 redeem (현금, 상품 등으로) 교환하다, 상환하다

176 주제 / 목적

번역 구르마니 씨가 이메일을 보낸 목적은?
(A) 신입사원을 환영하려고
(B) 클럽 가입 방법을 설명하려고
(C) 디믹 씨를 회의에 초대하려고
(D) 제안서 세부 사항을 확인하려고

해설 이메일의 후반부에서 구르마니 씨는 디믹 씨의 제안을 문서로 작성했다(I have drawn up your proposal)고 한 후, 한 번 보고 세부 사항을 빠뜨린 게 있으면 알려달라(can you please look it over and let me know if I have missed any details?)고 요청했다. 따라서 (D)가 정답이다.

어휘 describe 설명하다 confirm 확인하다

177 세부 사항

번역 디믹 씨는 누구인가?
(A) 새 공급업자
(B) 매장 관리자
(C) 부서장
(D) 지부장

해설 이메일의 초반부에서 디믹 씨의 최근 전화에 대해 감사(Thank you for your recent call)를 전한 후, 지역 매장 관리자들이 연락을 주면 항상 반갑다(We are always pleased to hear from one of our many local store managers)고 했다. 따라서 디믹 씨가 지역 매장 관리자 중 한 명임을 알 수 있으므로, (B)가 정답이다.

178 추론 / 암시

번역 구르마니 씨는 그리어 커피에 대해 무엇을 암시하는가?
(A) 전에 커피 클럽을 운영한 적이 있다.
(B) 신생 회사다.
(C) 마케팅 자문 위원을 채용했다.
(D) 새로운 맛의 커피를 출시한다.

해설 이메일의 초반부에서 그리어 커피 클럽을 다시 되돌리자는 디믹 씨의 의견이 좋다고 생각한다(I think your idea to reinstate the Greer's Coffee Club is excellent)고 했으므로, 그리어 커피가 전에 커피 클럽을 운영한 적이 있었다고 추론할 수 있다. 따라서 (A)가 정답이다.

어휘 consultant 자문 위원 launch 출시하다 flavor 맛, 향

179 연계

번역 웹페이지에서 그리어 커피 클럽에 대해 암시된 것은?
(A) 고객이 온라인으로 주문할 수 있다.
(B) 더 이상 펀치 카드 사용이 필요하지 않다.
(C) 더 이상 모든 지점에서 제공되지 않는다.
(D) 고객이 한 달 단위로 구매를 해야 한다.

해설 웹페이지의 초반부에서 그리어 커피 클럽의 이용이 훨씬 간편해졌다(it is now even easier to use)는 점을 강조한 후, 새 모바일 앱을 다운로드하고 등록만 하면 된다(Simply download our new mobile app and register)고 했다. 하지만 이메일 중반부를 보면 고객들이 커피 클럽 펀치카드에 대해 문의하고 있다(your customers have been asking about the club punch cards)는 소식을 언급한 것으로 보아 예전에는 앱이 아닌 펀치카드로 운영되었음을 알 수 있다. 따라서 펀치카드가 앱으로 대체되었다고 추론할 수 있으므로, (B)가 정답이다.

어휘   no longer 더 이상 ~아닌   require 요구하다   purchase 구입

180   동의어 찾기

번역   웹페이지의 첫 번째 단락, 네 번째 줄에 쓰인 'redeem'과 의미가 가장 가까운 단어는?

(A) 교환하다
(B) 변제하다
(C) 풀어주다
(D) 포섭하다

해설   'redeem'을 포함한 부분은 '할인을 받는 데 포인트를 사용할 수 있다(you can redeem the points for discounts)'라는 의미로 해석되는데, 여기서 redeem은 '(현금, 상품 등으로) 교환하다'라는 뜻을 나타낸다. 즉, 포인트를 할인금액으로 교환하여 사용할 수 있다는 것이므로, '교환하다, 거래하다'라는 의미의 (A) trade in이 정답이다.

181-185   구인광고 + 이메일

공시일자: 4월 10일
모집: 매우 숙련된 재무 부장
고용업체: 비맥소 재무 서비스(VFS)

업무 포함사항:
- [181]연간 재무 목표 설정
- 회계 담당 직원 업무 관리
- [181]투자 및 현금 유동성 관리 감독
- [181]건전한 재무 전략 개발

필수 요건:
- [185]재무 부장 경력 5년
- 경제학 또는 유사 분야 학사 학위
- 훌륭한 의사소통 능력
- 뛰어난 분석력

지원 방법: [182/183]지원서 및 증빙 서류를 5월 15일까지 인사부장 셀레스트 조모로디 씨에게 zomorodi.c@vfs.com으로 보내주세요. 6월 21일까지 가장 적합한 지원자를 채용하고 7월 1일자로 근무를 시작하도록 하려고 합니다.

어휘   experienced 능숙한, 경험이 풍부한   finance 금융, 재무   include 포함하다   annual 연간의   accounting 회계   oversee 관리하다, 감독하다   investment 투자   cash flow 현금 유동성   strategy 전략   prerequisite 전제 조건, 필수 조건   economics 경제학   outstanding 뛰어난, 두드러진   analytical 분석적인   application 지원   supporting document 증빙 서류, 뒷받침하는 서류   ideal 이상적인, 가장 알맞은

발신: 노리타카 호소카와
수신: 셀레스트 조모로디
날짜: 4월 11일
제목: 재무 부장

셀레스트 씨께,

[183]어제 우리 부서에서 낸 재무 부장 구인광고에 대해 여쭤보고 싶습니다. 제게 미카엘라 샤비비라고 하는 친구가 있는데, 이 직책에 [184]딱 맞는 사람인 것 같아요. 한 번 지원하라고 해볼까요?

[185]미카엘라는 3년 전 그레나다 대학교에서 재무 석사 학위를 받고 졸업했으며 그때부터 사우스사이드 투자은행에서 재무 부장으로 근무해오고 있어요. 숙련된 직무 훈련가이며 그녀의 분석력은 견줄 데가 없습니다. 알려주세요.

감사합니다.

노리타카 호소카와

어휘   job posting 구인광고, 일자리 공시   release 공개하다, 발표하다   fit 딱 맞는 사람[것]   encourage 권하다, 장려하다   Master's degree 석사 학위   investment 투자   analytical 분석적인   unparalleled 견줄 데 없는, 비할 바 없는

181   세부 사항

번역   구인광고에 따르면, 선발된 지원자의 책무 중 하나는 무엇인가?

(A) 세금 정책 검토하기
(B) 재무 계획 감독하기
(C) 홍보 캠페인 평가하기
(D) 모금 담당자 만나기

해설   구인광고의 업무 포함사항(Duties include:)을 보면 '연간 재무 목표 설정(Setting annual financial targets)', '투자 및 현금 유동성 관리 감독(Overseeing investments and cash flow)', '건전한 재무 전략 개발(Developing sound financial strategies)' 등이 나열되어 있다. 따라서 재무 계획 감독이 책무 중 하나임을 알 수 있으므로, (B)가 정답이다.

어휘   policy 정책   evaluate 평가하다   promotional 홍보의   fund-raising 모금

182   세부 사항

번역   지원 마감 기한은 언제인가?

(A) 4월 10일
(B) 5월 15일
(C) 6월 21일
(D) 7월 1일

해설   구인광고의 지원 방법(To apply:)에서 지원서 및 증빙 서류를 5월 15일까지 인사부장에게 보내라(Send application and supporting documents to our director of Human Resources ~ by May 15)고 했으므로, (B)가 정답이다.

183 연계

번역 호소카와 씨와 조모로디 씨에 대해 어떤 것이 사실이겠는가?

　　(A) 대학교에서 만났다.
　　(B) 샤비비 씨의 친구이다.
　　(C) 인사부서에서 일한다.
　　(D) 어린 시절부터 서로 알고 지냈다.

해설 이메일의 첫 번째 단락에서 호소카와 씨가 조모로디 씨에게 '우리 부서에서 낸 재무 부장 구인광고에 대해 물어보고 싶다(I wanted to ask you about the finance director job posting released by our department)'고 했으므로, 둘이 같은 부서에서 일한다는 것을 알 수 있다. 구인광고의 지원 방법(To apply:)을 보면 조모로디 씨가 인사부장(our director of Human Resources, Celeste Zomorodi)이라고 나와있으므로, (C)가 정답이다.

184 동의어 찾기

번역 이메일의 첫 번째 단락, 두 번째 줄에 쓰인 'fit'과 의미가 가장 가까운 단어는?

　　(A) 동의
　　(B) 성공
　　(C) 어울리는 사람
　　(D) 준비

해설 'fit'을 포함한 부분은 '이 직책에 딱 맞는 사람(a good fit for this position)'이라는 의미로 해석되는데, 여기서 fit은 '적합한 사람[것]'이라는 뜻으로 쓰였다. 따라서 '어울리는 사람[것]'이라는 의미의 (C) match가 정답이다.

어휘 agreement 동의 preparation 준비

185 연계

번역 조모로디 씨의 설명으로 볼 때, 샤비비 씨가 충족하지 못할 것 같은 직책 요건은?

　　(A) 직무 관련 경험
　　(B) 학사 학위
　　(C) 훌륭한 의사소통 능력
　　(D) 뛰어난 분석력

해설 이메일의 두 번째 단락에서 샤비비 씨가 3년 전 재무 석사 학위를 받고 졸업했으며 그때부터 사우스사이드 투자은행에서 재무 부장으로 근무해오고 있다(Michaela graduated with a Master's degree in Finance ~ three years ago and has worked since then as finance director at Southside Investment Bank)고 했다. 하지만 구인광고의 필수 요건(Prerequisites:)을 보면 재무 담당자 경력이 5년(5 years of experience as a finance director)이어야 하므로, 샤비비 씨의 직무 관련 경험이 부족하다고 볼 수 있다. 따라서 (A)가 정답이다.

어휘 related 관련된

▸▸ Paraphrasing　　지문의 experience as a finance director
　　　　　　　　　　→ 정답의 Job-related experience

186-190 웹페이지 + 설문 응답 + 회람

http://www.nozawamotors.ca/newsroom

| 노자와 소개 | **뉴스룸** | 포럼 | 운전자 이야기 |

186새로운 노자와 10이 드디어 나왔습니다! 저희 계기판 내비게이션 시스템을 완전히 음성 지원이 되게끔 만들었습니다. **190**저희 노자와 네비게이션 인터페이스(NNI)를 이용하면 운전자들은 도로 상황에만 계속 집중할 수 있습니다. **187/189**또한 앞 좌석 사이의 컵홀더, 향상된 뒷좌석 스피커, 29리터 더 커진 짐칸 등을 추가했습니다. 노자와 모터스 대리점에서 신모델을 확인하시고 의견을 알려주십시오!

어휘 dashboard 계기판 voice enabled 음성 지원이 되는 enhanced 향상된 expanded 확장된 cargo 짐, 수하물

의견이나 질문, 우려사항이 있으십니까?

188저는 10년 이상 노자와 고객이었고 최근 새로운 노자와 10을 구입했어요. **189**대체적으로 구매에 대해 만족하는데 컵홀더의 새 위치가 마음에 들지 않습니다. 거기 통기구가 대신 놓였어야 합니다. 그러면 난방과 냉방 시스템이 더욱 효율적이었을 겁니다.

다른 운전자들처럼, 저도 NNI 시스템에서 문제들을 몇 가지 겪었어요. 하지만 트렁크를 더 채울 수 있다는 점이 정말 좋아요. 그리고 이 모델은 이전 모델에 비해 가속력이 향상된 것 같습니다.

설문 응답에 개인적으로 답신을 원하시면, 연락처를 입력하십시오.

| **이름:** | 미셸 헤레라 | **이메일 주소:** | mherrera@notezip.com |

어휘 decade 10년 purchase 구입(품) position 위치 air vent 통기구, 공기 구멍 place 놓다 efficient 효율적인 acceleration 가속 compared with ~와 비교하여 previous 이전의 response 응답

회람

발신: 타비타 마크스
수신: 노자와 서비스 센터 관리자
제목: 새로운 출시

190새로운 노자와 10 모델의 NNI 시스템에 대해 부정적인 고객 의견을 접수했습니다. 이에 대응하여 오류를 수정한 새로운 NNI 소프트웨어 업데이트를 출시했습니다. 정비를 위해 매장에 들어온 올해 노자와 10 모델 전체에 즉시 업데이트 설치를 시작하십시오. 본 업데이트가 이용 가능하다는 것을 모든 소유주들에게 알릴 예정이므로 정비를 위해 들어오는 노자와 10의 수량이 증가할 수 있습니다.

어휘 release 출시; 출시하다 receive 접수하다, 받다 negative 부정적인 in response (~에) 대응하여 fix 고치다, 수정하다 bug (컴퓨터나 시스템 상의) 오류 install 설치하다 immediately 즉시, 지체없이 current 현재의 servicing 정비 notify 알리다 available 이용 가능한

186 주제 / 목적

번역 웹페이지의 목적은?

(A) 최근 고객 설문조사에 대해 설명하려고
(B) 제품 출시 지연에 대해 설명하려고
(C) 차량 업데이트를 알리려고
(D) 차량 유용성 시험에 대해 보고하려고

해설 노자와 모터스의 웹페이지 첫 번째 문장에서 새로운 노자와 10이 드디어 나왔다(The new Nozawa 10 is finally here!)고 한 후, 개선된 점에 대한 상세 설명을 이어가고 있다. 따라서 차량 업데이트를 알리는 웹페이지라고 볼 수 있으므로, (C)가 정답이다.

어휘 delay 지연 usability 유용성

187 세부 사항

번역 웹페이지에 따르면, 새 노자와 10 모델에서 더 커진 것은?

(A) 보관 공간
(B) 핸들
(C) 엔진
(D) 미러

해설 웹페이지의 중반부에서 짐칸을 29리터 확장했다(We have ~ expanded the cargo area by 29 liters)고 했으므로, 보관 공간이 더 커졌음을 알 수 있다. 따라서 (A)가 정답이다.

어휘 storage 저장, 보관

> **▸▸ Paraphrasing** 지문의 expanded → 질문의 bigger
> 지문의 cargo area → 정답의 storage space

188 사실 관계 확인

번역 헤레라 씨가 설문 응답에서 명시한 것은?

(A) 지부장에게 연락했다.
(B) 대리점에 차량 수리를 맡길 계획이다.
(C) 최근 새 직책으로 승진했다.
(D) 노자와 차량을 한 대 이상 운전해본 적이 있다.

해설 설문 응답의 첫 번째 단락에서 헤레라 씨가 10년 이상 노자와 고객이었고 최근 새로운 노자와 10을 구입했다(I've been a Nozawa customer for more than a decade, and I recently got a new Nozawa 10)고 했으므로, 노자와 차량을 한 대 이상 운전해본 적이 있다는 사실을 확인할 수 있다. 따라서 (D)가 정답이다.

어휘 district 구역 dealership 자동차 대리점 promote 승진시키다

189 연계

번역 헤레라 씨는 차량의 어느 부분에 통기구가 있는 것을 선호하는가?

(A) 뒷좌석 근처
(B) 앞 좌석 사이
(C) 디스플레이 화면 옆
(D) 계기판

해설 설문 응답의 첫 번째 단락에서 컵홀더의 새 위치가 마음에 들지 않는다(I am not pleased with the new position of the cupholders)고 한 후, 그 자리에 통기구가 대신 놓였어야 한다(Some air vents could have been placed there instead)고 했다. 웹페이지의 중반부를 보면 앞 좌석 사이에 컵홀더를 추가했다(We have ~ added cupholders between the front seats)고 되어 있으므로, 헤레라 씨는 통기구가 앞 좌석 사이에 있는 것을 더 선호한다고 볼 수 있다. 따라서 (B)가 정답이다.

어휘 rear 뒤쪽

190 연계

번역 무엇을 고쳐야 하는가?

(A) 차량 정비 기록
(B) 내비게이션 장치
(C) 고객 연락처
(D) 스테레오 시스템

해설 회람의 초반부에서 새로운 노자와 10 모델의 NNI 시스템에 대해 부정적인 고객 의견을 접수했다(We received negative customer feedback about the new Nozawa 10 model's NNI system)고 했으므로, NNI 시스템이 고쳐야 할 대상임을 알 수 있다. 웹페이지의 중반부를 보면 노자와 내비게이션 인터페이스(NNI)를 이용하면 운전자들은 도로 상황에만 계속 집중할 수 있다(With our Nozawa Navigation Interface (NNI), drivers can stay focused on the road)고 했으므로, NNI 시스템이 내비게이션 장치임을 알 수 있다. 따라서 (B)가 정답이다.

191-195 웹페이지 + 공지 + 후기

---

http://www.pinkbegoniafarms.com

핑크 베고니아 농장

핑크 베고니아 농장은 식물에 관한 모든 요구사항을 위한 원스톱 매장입니다. 여러분이 조경 전문가이든, 뒤뜰 정원사이든, 실내용 화초 애호가이든 상관없이, 저희는 여러분이 필요로 하는 모든 것을 갖추고 있습니다! **191 일부 씨앗, 비료, 장비는 온라인으로 주문할 수 있지만 더 많은 제품을 보시려면 직접 저희 묘목장을 방문해 주세요.**

규모가 꽤 큰 저희 시설은 아래의 네 가지 개별 구역으로 나뉩니다.

- 북문
  - 실내용 화초, 열대 식물, 외래종
- **193 남문**
  - 식물과 조경 제품을 대량으로 도매가에 판매
- **195 동문**
  - 우리 지역에서 잘 자라고 관리가 거의 필요하지 않은 지역 조경 식물
- 서문
  - 약초, 채소, 과일 및 견과가 열리는 나무, 기타 식용 식물

어휘 one-stop shop 한 곳에서 다 살 수 있는 매장 related 관련된 landscape 조경 professional 전문가 gardener 정원사 houseplant 실내용 화초 enthusiast 애호가 seed 씨앗 fertilizer 비료 equipment 장비 nursery 묘목장 in person 직접, 몸소 selection (선택 가능한) 제품 sizable 상당한 크기의, 꽤 큰 facility 시설 be divided into ~로 나뉘다 distinct 별개의, 구분되는 tropical 열대의 exotic 외래종 in bulk 대량으로 wholesale 도매 require 필요로 하다 maintenance 관리 edible 식용, 먹을 수 있는 것

핑크 베고니아 농장 고객 여러분께 알립니다!

4월 1일자로 소유주가 바뀝니다. ¹⁹³여러 가지 다른 변화가 있을 예정이며, 무엇보다도 특히 보수 공사가 진행되어 대량 주문 고객들을 위해 서비스를 제공하는 공간이 4월 1일부터 5월 5일까지 문을 닫습니다.

¹⁹²아울러, 구입하신 물품을 차로 옮기기 위해 바구니나 수레를 사용하실 경우 주차장 한가운데 놓고 가지 마시길 당부 드립니다. 감사합니다!

어휘 attention 주목하세요, 알립니다 most notably 무엇보다도 특히 renovation 보수, 개조 cause 야기하다 service 서비스를 제공하다 bulk-order 대량 주문 request 요청하다 wagon 수레, 마차 leave 남겨 두다

---

http://www.retaileropinion.com/reviews/pinkbegoniafarms

핑크 베고니아 농장에서 기분 좋게 쇼핑을 했습니다. ¹⁹⁴최근 고객의 부동산 매각을 준비하고 있었는데 대규모 조경 작업이 필요했어요. 잠재 구매자들에게 집을 보여 드리기 전에 앞쪽 입구에 꽃과 녹색 식물이 더 필요했거든요. ¹⁹⁵식물에 대해 전혀 알지 못해서 손수 물을 주거나 돌봐야 하는 수고가 거의 없는 지역 인기 식물 모음을 골라 달라고 매장 직원에게 도움을 청했어요. 끝마쳤을 때 집은 훨씬 그럴듯해 보였습니다. 핑크 베고니아 농장의 뛰어난 서비스에 감사드려요!

-다프네 웨이건드
4월 15일

어휘 recently 최근 property 부동산, 건물 extensive 대규모의, 광범위한 entryway 입구 color and greenery (다양한 색의) 꽃과 녹색 식물 potential 잠재적인 assortment 모음 manual 손으로 하는, 육체노동의 care 관리, 돌봄 inviting 마음을 끄는, 매력적인

191 사실 관계 확인

번역 웹사이트에서 온라인 매장에 대해 언급한 것은?

(A) 계절에 따라 특별 상품을 제공한다.

(B) 4월에 개시될 예정이다.

(C) 홈페이지에서 가장 인기 있는 식물을 선보이고 있다.

(D) 실제 매장보다 판매 상품이 적다.

해설 웹페이지의 첫 번째 단락에서 일부 씨앗, 비료, 장비 등은 온라인으로 주문할 수 있지만 더 많은 제품을 보려면 직접 묘목장을 방문하

라(Some seeds, fertilizer, and equipment can be ordered online, but please come visit our nursery in person for a much larger selection)고 권고했다. 따라서 온라인 매장이 실제 매장보다 판매 상품이 적다는 것을 알 수 있으므로, (D)가 정답이다.

어휘 be scheduled to ~할 예정이다 feature 특별히 포함하다 physical 물리적인

▸▸ Paraphrasing 지문의 nursery → 정답의 physical store

192 추론 / 암시

번역 공지에서 핑크 베고니아 농장에 대해 암시된 것은?

(A) 식물을 옮길 용기를 제공한다.

(B) 이름이 곧 바뀔 것이다.

(C) 주차장이 공사 중이다.

(D) 더 이상 할인 상품의 반품을 받지 않는다.

해설 공지의 두 번째 단락에서 구입한 물품을 차로 옮기기 위해 바구니나 수레를 사용할 경우(if you use our baskets or wagons to move your purchased items to your car) 주차장 한가운데 놓고 가지 말라고 당부했다. 따라서 농장이 식물을 옮길 용기를 제공한다고 추론할 수 있으므로, (A)가 정답이다.

어휘 transport 운송하다 under construction 공사 중인

▸▸ Paraphrasing 지문의 our baskets or wagons → 정답의 containers

지문의 to move your purchased items → 정답의 transporting plants

193 연계

번역 핑크 베고니아의 어떤 구역이 5월에 다시 문을 여는가?

(A) 북문

(B) 남문

(C) 동문

(D) 서문

해설 공지의 첫 번째 단락에서 보수 공사가 진행되어 대량 주문 고객들을 위해 서비스를 제공하는 공간이 4월 1일부터 5월 5일까지 문을 닫는다(renovation work that will cause the area where we service our bulk-order customers to be closed from April 1 through May 5)고 했다. 웹페이지에 나열된 묘목장의 네 개 구역 중, 식물과 조경 제품을 대량으로 판매(plants and landscaping products sold in bulk quantities)하는 구역은 남문(South Gate)이므로, (B)가 정답이다.

194 추론 / 암시

번역 웨이건드 씨의 직업은 무엇이겠는가?

(A) 조경업자

(B) 행사 기획자

(C) 부동산 중개인

(D) 묘목장 인부

해설 후기의 초반부에서 웨이건드 씨가 고객의 부동산 매각을 준비하고 있었다(I was preparing a client's property for sale)며 잠재 구매자들에게 집을 보여주기 전에(before I could show the house to the potential buyers) 조경 작업이 필요했다고 말했다. 따라서 그녀가 부동산 중개인이라고 추론할 수 있으므로, (C)가 정답이다.

195 연계

번역 웨이건드 씨에 대해 암시된 것은?

(A) 정기적으로 꽃을 배송받는다.
(B) 고객을 통해서 이 매장을 알게 됐다.
(C) 가까운 장래에 집을 살 계획이다.
(D) 묘목장의 동문 구역에서 물건을 샀다.

해설 후기의 중반부에서 웨이건드 씨는 손수 물을 주거나 돌봐야 하는 수고가 거의 없는 지역 인기 식물 모음을 골라 달라(pick out an assortment of local favorites that would require very little manual watering or care)고 매장 직원에게 도움을 청했다고 했다. 웹페이지에 나열된 묘목장 구역을 보면, 지역에서 잘 자라고 관리가 거의 필요하지 않은 지역 조경 식물(local landscape plants that grow well in our area and require little maintenance)이 동문(East Gate)에서 판매됨을 확인할 수 있다. 따라서 웨이건드 씨가 이곳에서 해당 식물을 구매했다고 추론할 수 있으므로, (D)가 정답이다.

어휘 on a regular basis 정기적으로

196-200 이메일 + 이메일 + 영수증

수신: 산다 피터슨 〈thandapeterson@thandapeterson.com〉
발신: 밀로스 아다멕 〈milosa@wistartravel.org〉
제목: 여행 준비
날짜: 4월 17일

안녕하세요, 산다.

잘 지내고 계시길 바랍니다. 작가 회의를 위해 이용하실 수 있는 콩코드발 섬니펠트행 항공편을 살펴보았는데요. 저가 항공사인 알터 항공이 해당 노선 직항 서비스를 매일 제공한다는 사실을 알았습니다. 잠정적인 일정은 다음과 같습니다.

콩코드 출발: 5월 8일 금요일 오전 8시 50분
섬니펠트 도착: 5월 8일 금요일 오전 11시 05분

섬니펠트 출발: 5월 11일 월요일 오후 1시 20분
콩코드 도착: 5월 11일 월요일 오후 3시 35분

확정해 주시는 대로 예약하겠습니다. ¹⁹⁶돌아오시는 여정에, 섬니펠트 공항이 현재 진행되는 대규모 보수 공사로 인해 탑승객들이 출발 2시간 전에 도착하도록 권고하고 있음을 기억해 두시기 바랍니다.

¹⁹⁹그건 그렇고, 섬니펠트 공항 근처의 훌륭한 페루식 점심식사 장소에 관심이 있으실 지도 모르겠습니다. 말씀해 주시면 이름을 알려드리겠습니다.

밀로스

어휘 arrangement 준비 conference 회의 discount carrier 저가 항공사 direct service 직항 서비스 tentative 잠정적인 itinerary 일정 depart 출발하다 arrive 도착하다 book 예약하다 keep in mind 명심하다, 기억해 두다 advise 권고하다 passenger 승객 extensive 대규모의 renovation 보수, 개조

수신: 밀로스 아다멕 〈milosa@wistartravel.org〉
발신: 산다 피터슨 〈thandapeterson@thandapeterson.com〉
제목: 회신: 여행 준비
날짜: 4월 18일

밀로스,

예약하시기 전에 얼른 새로운 상황을 알려드립니다. ²⁰⁰섬니펠트로 5월 8일에 출발할지 아니면 하루 더 일찍 출발해야 하는지 며칠 더 생각해 봐야 합니다. 5월 7일 저녁에 제가 참석할지도 모르는 조기 회의 워크숍이 있어요. ¹⁹⁸제 최근 원고와 관련해 이야기 나누고 싶은 출판사 직원이 참석할지도 모르거든요! 곧 알려드리겠습니다.

¹⁹⁷늘 도와주셔서 감사합니다.

산다

어휘 consider 고려하다 attend 참석하다 actually 사실 publisher 출판사 representative 직원, 대표 regarding ~에 관하여 manuscript (책의) 원고, 필사본 be in attendance 참석하다 shortly 곧

섬니펠트 퀵 택시
555-0194

날짜: ²⁰⁰5월 7일	
출발: 섬니펠트 공항	
도착: ¹⁹⁹페루 드리밍 카페, 트리탑 가 98번지	
픽업: 오전 11시 55분	
하차: 오후 12시 4분	
거리: 1.2마일	
총액: 8달러	
결제 종류: ☒ 신용카드 ☐ 현금	
신용카드 상의 이름: 산다 피터슨	
신용카드 번호: xxxx xxxx xxxx 5523	

196 사실 관계 확인

번역 섬니펠트 공항에 대해 알 수 있는 것은?

(A) 피터슨 씨의 호텔과 매우 가깝다.
(B) 새로운 체크인 직원이 있다.
(C) 공사 중이다.
(D) 종종 항공편 출발이 연착된다.

해설 첫 번째 이메일의 세 번째 단락을 보면, 섬니펠트 공항에서 현재 대규모 보수 공사가 진행되고 있음(the Sumneyfeld Airport ~

because of extensive renovations being done there)을 언급했다. 따라서 (C)가 정답이다.

어휘   undergo 겪다   departure 출발

> ▸▸ **Paraphrasing**   지문의 **extensive renovations being done** → 정답의 **undergoing construction work**

197 추론 / 암시

번역   피터슨 씨에 대해 암시된 것은?

(A) 종종 알터 항공사를 이용한다.
(B) 예전에 섬니펠트를 방문했다.
(C) 종종 회사 출장을 간다.
(D) 전에 아다멕 씨의 서비스를 이용했다.

해설   두 번째 이메일의 마지막 단락에서 피터슨 씨가 '늘(as always)'이라는 표현과 함께 아다멕 씨에게 감사를 전했으므로, 전에 아다멕 씨의 서비스를 이용한 적이 있다고 추론할 수 있다. 따라서 (D)가 정답이다.

어휘   frequently 자주, 빈번하게

198 추론 / 암시

번역   피터슨 씨는 누구이겠는가?

(A) 뉴스 기자
(B) 여행잡지 작가
(C) 음식 평론가
(D) 책 저자

해설   두 번째 이메일의 첫 번째 단락에서 피터슨 씨가 자신의 최근 원고와 관련해 이야기 나누고 싶은 출판사 직원이 워크숍에 참석할 지도 모른다(a publisher representative with whom I would like to talk regarding my latest manuscript may be in attendance)고 했다. 따라서 그녀가 책 저자라고 추론할 수 있으므로, (D)가 정답이다.

199 연계

번역   피터슨 씨는 조언에 대한 응답으로 무엇을 했겠는가?

(A) 음식점을 방문했다.
(B) 무료 셔틀 서비스를 이용했다.
(C) 대표와 만났다.
(D) 항공사를 바꿨다.

해설   첫 번째 이메일의 마지막 단락에서 아다멕 씨는 피터슨 씨에게 섬니펠트 공항 근처의 훌륭한 페루식 점심식사 장소(an excellent Peruvian lunch place near the Sumneyfeld Airport)를 언급하며 원하면 어딘지 말해주겠다고 했다. 택시 영수증을 보면, 5월 7일 점심 때쯤 피터슨 씨의 도착지(To:)가 페루 드리밍 카페(Peru Dreaming Café)이므로, 아다멕 씨의 추천대로 음식점에 방문했다고 추론할 수 있다. 따라서 (A)가 정답이다.

어휘   in response to ～에 응하여

> ▸▸ **Paraphrasing**   지문의 **lunch place** → 정답의 **restaurant**

200 연계

번역   영수증을 보고 피터슨 씨에 대해 어떤 결론을 내릴 수 있는가?

(A) 교통비를 현금으로 지불했다.
(B) 권장된 것보다 공항에 늦게 도착했다.
(C) 회의 장소까지 버스를 타고 갔다.
(D) 추가 회의 행사에 참석하기로 결정했다.

해설   두 번째 이메일의 첫 번째 단락에서 섬니펠트로 5월 8일에 출발할지 아니면 하루 더 일찍 출발해야 하는지 생각해 봐야 한다(I will need ～ to consider whether I should depart for Sumneyfeld on May 8 or leave one day earlier)고 한 후, 5월 7일 저녁에 참석할 지도 모르는 조기 회의 워크숍이 있다(There is an early conference workshop the evening of May 7 that I might attend)며 고심의 이유를 덧붙였다. 택시 영수증을 보면, 택시를 이용한 날짜(Date:)가 5월 7일(May 7)이므로, 피터슨 씨가 이날 열리는 추가 회의 행사에 참석하기로 결정했다고 추론할 수 있다. 따라서 (D)가 정답이다.

어휘   pay in cash 현금으로 지불하다   venue 장소

> ▸▸ **Paraphrasing**   지문의 **an early conference workshop** → 정답의 **an extra conference event**

기출 TEST 6

101 (A)	**102** (D)	**103** (D)	**104** (B)	**105** (A)
106 (C)	**107** (D)	**108** (A)	**109** (A)	**110** (B)
111 (B)	**112** (A)	**113** (D)	**114** (C)	**115** (C)
116 (D)	**117** (A)	**118** (B)	**119** (B)	**120** (C)
121 (C)	**122** (B)	**123** (A)	**124** (C)	**125** (D)
126 (C)	**127** (A)	**128** (C)	**129** (D)	**130** (B)
131 (C)	**132** (A)	**133** (D)	**134** (B)	**135** (D)
136 (B)	**137** (A)	**138** (C)	**139** (C)	**140** (B)
141 (C)	**142** (A)	**143** (B)	**144** (A)	**145** (C)
146 (D)	**147** (C)	**148** (B)	**149** (C)	**150** (B)
151 (B)	**152** (D)	**153** (D)	**154** (A)	**155** (C)
156 (A)	**157** (C)	**158** (B)	**159** (D)	**160** (A)
161 (C)	**162** (D)	**163** (A)	**164** (C)	**165** (D)
166 (C)	**167** (D)	**168** (B)	**169** (D)	**170** (A)
171 (B)	**172** (D)	**173** (A)	**174** (B)	**175** (D)
176 (C)	**177** (D)	**178** (D)	**179** (D)	**180** (A)
181 (B)	**182** (A)	**183** (A)	**184** (D)	**185** (C)
186 (A)	**187** (B)	**188** (B)	**189** (D)	**190** (B)
191 (A)	**192** (D)	**193** (B)	**194** (B)	**195** (C)
196 (D)	**197** (B)	**198** (C)	**199** (A)	**200** (C)

PART 5

101 인칭대명사의 격 _ 소유격

해설 전치사 with의 목적어 역할을 하는 sophisticated entrées를 한정 수식하는 자리이므로, 소유격 인칭대명사 (A) his가 정답이다.

번역 다니엘스 주방장은 그의 세련된 메인 요리로 고객들에게 깊은 인상을 준다.

어휘 impress 깊은 인상을 주다, 감명을 주다 sophisticated 세련된, 정교한 entrée 메인[주] 요리

102 동사 자리 _ 수 일치

해설 주어 Oil production의 동사 자리이므로, 빈칸에는 불가산명사 production과 수가 일치하는 동사가 들어가야 한다. 따라서 수의 영향을 받지 않는 과거 동사 (D) dropped가 정답이다. (A) drop은 production과 수가 일치하지 않고, (B) to drop과 (C) dropping은 준동사이므로 빈칸에 들어갈 수 없다.

번역 석유 생산은 1월부터 2월까지 5퍼센트 감소했다.

어휘 production 생산 drop 떨어지다, 감소하다

103 형용사 자리 _ 명사 수식

해설 문제를 해결할 제안을 가지고 있다는 내용이므로, 제안의 성격을 나타

내는 형용사가 빈칸에 들어가야 자연스럽다. 따라서 (D) helpful(유용한, 도움이 되는)이 정답이다. (C) helped는 has와 함께 현재완료를 이룰 수 있지만, 이 경우 helped 뒤에 도움을 받는 대상이 와야 하므로 빈칸에는 적절하지 않다.

번역 이토 씨는 컴퓨터 문제를 해결할 유용한 제안을 가지고 있다.

어휘 suggestion 제안, 의견 resolve 해결하다

104 동사 어휘

해설 보기에서 to부정사구 to construct a fountain in the front entryway를 목적어로 취할 수 있는 타동사를 선택해야 한다. 따라서 '(~하려고) 계획하다'라는 의미의 (B) plans가 정답이다.

번역 바이돈 호텔은 전면 출입로에 분수를 건설할 계획이다.

어휘 construct 건설하다 fountain 분수 match 어울리다, 일치하다 praise 칭찬하다

105 명사 어휘

해설 music과 함께 복합명사를 이루어 전치사 for의 목적어 역할을 하는 자리로, 빈칸을 포함한 전치사구가 명사 events를 수식한다. 따라서 빈칸에는 세부 행사(events)를 포괄하는 단어가 들어가야 하므로, '축제'라는 의미의 (A) festival이 정답이다.

번역 음악 축제 행사 일정은 금요일에 게시될 것이다.

어휘 post 게시하다 situation 상황 instrument 기구, 악기 issue 문제

106 부사 자리 _ 동사 수식

해설 주어가 the attending physician, 동사가 must fill out, 목적어가 a form인 완전한 절 뒤에서 동사를 수식하는 부사 자리이므로, (C) completely(완전하게, 전적으로)가 정답이다. 과거분사 (B) completed가 form 뒤에 올 수도 있지만(eg. get a form completed), 이 문장에서는 '완성된 양식을 작성해야 한다'는 뜻이 되므로 문맥상 적절하지 않다. (A) completes는 동사, (D) completeness는 명사로 품사상 빈칸에 들어갈 수 없다.

번역 병가 신청을 처리할 때 주치의가 전적으로 양식을 작성해야 한다.

어휘 medical leave 병가 request 요청 attending 주치의로 근무하는 physician 의사, 내과의사 fill out a form 서식에 기입하다, 양식을 작성하다 complete 완성하다 completeness 완성도

107 동사 어휘

해설 명사구 their online portfolios를 목적어로 취하는 동사 자리로, 패션 스타일리스트(fashion stylists)가 온라인 포트폴리오와 관련해 정기적으로(on a regular basis) 하는 일을 나타낸다. 따라서 '업데이트하다, 갱신하다'라는 의미의 (D) update가 정답이다.

번역 많은 패션 스타일리스트들이 온라인 포트폴리오를 정기적으로 업데이트한다.

어휘 on a regular basis 정기적으로 dress 옷을 입히다 invite 초청하다 range 범위가 ~에 이르다, 배치하다

108 명사 자리 _ 전치사의 목적어 _ 어휘

해설 전치사 of의 목적어 역할을 하는 명사 자리로, a ~ blanket of(짙게 드리운)와 어울리는 불가산명사가 들어가야 한다. 따라서 '안개'라는 의미의 명사로 쓰일 수 있는 (A) fog가 정답이다. (B) fogger는 '분무기'라는 뜻의 가산명사, (C) foggy는 형용사, (D) fogged는 동사/과거분사로 구조상 빈칸에 들어갈 수 없다.

번역 짙게 드리운 안개 때문에 모든 항공편이 3시간 연착됐다.

어휘 delay 지연시키다 fog 안개; 수증기가 서리게 하다, 혼란스럽게 만들다 foggy 안개가 낀

109 전치사 어휘

해설 동사 will perform과 장소 명사 Reverbury Hall을 자연스럽게 연결해주는 전치사를 선택해야 한다. Reverbury Hall은 오케스트라가 공연하는 장소이므로, '~에서'라는 의미의 (A) at이 정답이다.

번역 노스윅 오케스트라는 이번 달 중에 리버버리홀에서 공연할 예정이다.

어휘 perform 공연하다

110 부사 어휘

해설 과거분사 based를 수식하는 부사 자리로, 빈칸을 포함한 수식어구 (------- based in the Toronto office)는 회의실을 예약할 수 있는 직원들의 자격을 나타낸다. 현재 토론토 사무실에 근거지를 둔 직원만 가능하다는 내용이 되어야 자연스러우므로, '현재'라는 의미의 (B) currently가 정답이다.

번역 현재 토론토 사무실에 근거지를 둔 직원들만 회의실을 예약할 수 있다.

어휘 reserve 예약하다 conference room 회의실 possibly 아마 immediately 즉시 exactly 정확히, 틀림없이

111 (대)명사 어휘 _ 수 일치

해설 복수동사 have placed의 주어 역할을 하는 명사 자리로, 보기에서 (A) Any와 (B) Several 중 하나를 선택해야 한다. 문맥상 직원들 몇 명이 주문했다는 내용이 되어야 자연스러우므로, '몇몇, 여러 명'이라는 의미의 (B) Several이 정답이다. (A) Any는 부정문, 조건문, 의문문에서 '아무도, 누군가'라는 뜻으로 쓰이거나, 긍정문에서 '누구라도'라는 의미를 나타내므로 빈칸에 적절하지 않다. (C) Another(또 다른 것)과 (D) Either(둘 중 하나)는 단수로 have placed 및 their와 수가 일치하지 않는다.

번역 직원들 중 몇몇이 새 스탠딩 책상을 주문했다.

어휘 place an order 주문을 넣다

112 형용사 어휘

해설 명사 volunteers를 수식하는 형용사 자리로, 박물관 견학에 지원(support)을 해줄 만한 자원봉사자들의 특성을 나타내는 단어가 들어가야 한다. 따라서 예전에 유사한 업무를 해 본 경험이 있다는 것을 암시하는 (A) former(이전의)가 정답이다. 참고로, (C) entire는 '하나로서의 전체'를 강조하는 형용사이므로, the entire group of volunteers와 같은 형태로 쓰일 수는 있으나 volunteers만을 수식할 수는 없다.

번역 벳시 라일리는 변경된 박물관 견학에 이전 자원봉사자들의 지원을 구할 것이다.

어휘 seek 구하다, 청하다 revise 변경하다, 수정하다 following 다음의 entire 전체의 gradual 점진적인

113 명사 어휘

해설 store와 함께 복합명사를 이루어 동사 receive의 목적어 역할을 하는 자리로, 반품 시 현금 환불 대신(instead of a cash refund) 받을 수 있는 것이 들어가야 한다. 따라서 '상점 포인트'라는 의미를 완성하는 (D) credit이 정답이다.

번역 카소라마 고객은 제품 반품 시 현금 환불 대신 상점 포인트를 받는다.

어휘 refund 환불 acceptance 수락, 동의 training 교육, 훈련 preference 선호 store credit 상점 포인트, 물건 값을 상점의 채무(credit)로 처리하는 것

114 부사 어휘

해설 동사 needs를 수식하는 부사 자리이므로, 보기에서 동사를 수식할 수 있는 (C) still과 (D) even 중 하나를 선택해야 한다. 접속사 but이 두 절을 연결하고 있으므로, 작년에 공장이 개선된(was upgraded) 것과는 대조적으로 현재 하역장에 작업이 필요한(needs work) 상황을 강조하는 부사가 필요하다. 따라서 '아직도, 여전히'라는 의미의 (C) still이 정답이다. (D) even은 '심지어'라는 의미로 문맥상 빈칸에 적절하지 않다. (A) such는 한정사/대명사인데, 비격식체에서 부사처럼 쓰일 경우 형용사를 수식하고, (B) very는 형용사/부사를 수식하므로 빈칸에 들어갈 수 없다.

번역 만하임에 있는 우리 공장은 작년에 개선됐지만 하역장은 여전히 작업이 필요하다.

어휘 loading dock 짐 싣는 곳, 하역장

115 형용사 자리 _ 명사 수식 _ 분사

해설 빈칸은 부사 recently의 수식을 받으며 명사 mayor를 꾸며주는 형용사 자리이다. 따라서 보기에서 형용사 역할을 하는 분사 (A) electing과 (C) elected 중 하나를 선택해야 한다. 시장은 선출되는 대상이므로, 수동의 의미를 내포한 과거분사 (C) elected가 정답이 된다. (B) election은 명사, (D) elects는 동사로 품사상 빈칸에 들어갈 수 없다.

번역 최근 선출된 시장은 시의 교통 문제를 곧 해결할 계획이라고 말했다.

어휘 recently 최근 mayor 시장 address a problem 문제를 해결하다, 해결하려 하다 elect 선출하다; 당선자(명사 뒤에 붙여서) election 선거

116 부사 자리 _ 동사 수식

해설 전치사구 in their nutritional content와 함께 자동사 differ를 수식하는 부사 자리이므로, (D) significantly(상당히)가 정답이다. (A) significant는 형용사, (B) signify는 동사, (C) significance는 명사로 품사상 빈칸에 들어갈 수 없다.

번역 김 씨의 연구는 건초의 유형이 영양 성분에 따라 상당히 다르다는 사실을 밝혔다.

어휘 reveal 드러내다, 밝히다 differ 다르다 nutritional content 영양 성분 significant 중요한 signify 의미하다, 중요하다 significance 중요성, 의의

117 전치사 어휘

해설 보기에서 extend our warmest welcome과 Mr. Lam Keong Wu, our new vice president of marketing을 적절히 연결해 주는 전치사를 선택해야 한다. 신임 마케팅 부사장에게 따뜻한 환영을 베풀자(extend)라는 내용이므로, '~에게'라는 의미의 (A) to가 정답이다.

번역 신임 마케팅 부사장이신 람 케옹 우 씨를 따뜻하게 맞이합시다.

어휘 extend a warm welcome 따뜻하게 맞이하다

118 명사 자리 _ 동사의 목적어

해설 「과거분사(increased)+형용사(public)」의 수식을 받으면서 동사 shows의 목적어 역할을 하는 명사 자리이므로, (B) approval(승인, 인정)이 정답이다. (A) approve는 동사, (C) approving은 형용사/동명사/현재분사, (D) approvingly는 부사로 품사상 빈칸에 들어갈 수 없다.

번역 최근 여론 조사는 경기장 보수 프로젝트에 대한 대중의 지지가 높아졌음을 보여준다.

어휘 polling 여론 조사, 투표 renovation 보수, 개조 approve 승인하다 approving 찬성하는 approvingly 찬성하여

119 형용사 어휘

해설 주어인 Oshka Landscape Supply revenue를 보충 설명하는 자리로, 빈칸 뒤 전치사 on과 어울려 쓰이는 형용사를 선택해야 한다. 계절별 매출(seasonal sales)에 대한 수익(revenue) 의존도가 높다는 내용이므로, on과 함께 '~에 의존하는'이라는 의미를 완성하는 (B) dependent가 정답이다. be dependent on은 빈출 표현이니 반드시 암기해 두도록 하자. 참고로, (C) accessible은 전치사 to(~에 접근하기 쉬운)나 from(~로부터 접근하기 쉬운)과 자주 쓰인다.

번역 오쉬카 조경용품점의 수익은 계절별 매출에 크게 의존한다.

어휘 extensive 광범위한, 대규모의 insightful 통찰력 있는

120 전치사 어휘

해설 빈칸이 목적어로 취하는 the unseasonably cold weather(때아닌 추운 날씨)는 관광업이 둔화된(Tourism ~ has slowed) 원인이라

고 볼 수 있다. 따라서 '~ 때문에'라는 의미의 (C) because of가 정답이다.

번역 때아닌 추운 날씨 때문에 코크의 관광업은 최근 몇 주간 둔화됐다.

어휘 recent 최근의 unseasonably 계절에 맞지 않게, 때아니게 as long as ~하는 한; ~만큼 긴 in case of ~의 경우에 except for ~를 제외하고

121 형용사 자리 _ 명사 수식 _ 최상급

해설 최상급 표현 the most와 함께 복합명사 business ideas를 수식하는 형용사 자리로, '창의적인 사업 아이디어'라는 내용이 되어야 자연스럽다. 따라서 '창의적인, 상상력이 풍부한'이라는 의미의 (C) imaginative가 정답이다. (B) imagining은 동명사/현재분사로 '상상하는 것', 혹은 '상상하는'을 뜻하므로 적절치 않고, (A) imagine은 동사, (D) imagination은 명사로 품사상 빈칸에 들어갈 수 없다.

번역 아즈넷 재단은 가장 창의적인 사업 아이디어가 있는 기업가 세 명에게 각 5천 달러의 보조금을 제공한다.

어휘 foundation 재단 grant 보조금 entrepreneur 기업가 imagine 상상하다 imagination 상상

122 형용사 자리 _ 명사 수식

해설 소유격 인칭대명사 her와 함께 명사 performance를 수식하는 형용사 자리이므로, '지난'이라는 의미의 (B) past가 정답이다. 참고로, past는 명사, 전치사, 부사로도 쓰일 수 있다. (C) apart는 형용사로 쓰일 수 있지만 명사 앞에 올 수 없고, (A) neither는 한정사/대명사/부사, (D) twice는 부사로 구조상으로도 빈칸에 들어갈 수 없다.

번역 소아레스 씨의 지난 성과로 볼 때, 50미터 경주에서 잘 해 낼 것 같다.

어휘 based on ~에 기반하여, ~로 볼 때 performance 실적, 성과

123 명사 어휘

해설 동사 provides의 목적어 자리로, 설명서(manual)가 카메라의 주요 기능(primary features)에 관해 제공하는 것을 나타낸다. 따라서 '개요, 개관'이라는 의미의 (A) overview가 정답이다.

번역 설명서는 R25100 카메라의 주요 기능에 대한 기본 개요를 제공한다.

어휘 primary 주된, 주요한 feature 기능, 특징 adviser 조언자 challenge 도전, 어려움 instance 예

124 동사 어휘

해설 빈칸은 명사구 the wireless Internet option을 목적어로 취하는 자리로, 추가 데이터 요금을 피하기 위해(to avoid additional data fees) 휴대전화에 해야 하는 일을 나타낸다. 따라서 '(기능 등을) 활성화시키다, ~할 수 있게 하다'라는 의미의 (C) enable이 정답이다.

번역 추가 데이터 요금을 피하려면 회사 휴대전화의 무선 인터넷 옵션을 켜십시오.

어휘 avoid 막다, 피하다 additional 추가의 return 반환하다 pull 당기다 inflate 부풀리다, 올리다

125 부사 어휘

해설 현재시제 동사 hires(채용하다)를 수식하는 자리이므로, 중개인 채용이라는 반복적인 행위와 어울리는 부사가 들어가야 문맥상 자연스럽다. 따라서 '항상, 늘'이라는 의미의 (D) always가 정답이다. (A) soon은 '곧, 이내'라는 뜻으로 문맥상 어울리지 않고, (B) most와 (C) enough는 동사를 뒤에서 수식하므로 구조상으로도 빈칸에 들어갈 수 없다.

번역 트루홈 에스테이트의 최고경영자는 항상 자신의 삶에서 장애물을 극복한 중개인을 채용한다.

어휘 overcome 극복하다 obstacle 장애물

126 전치사 자리

해설 명사구 twenty business days (of finishing a project)를 목적어로 취하는 전치사 자리이므로, (C) within(~ 이내에)이 정답이다. (A) whether, (B) whose, (D) while은 모두 명사를 목적어로 취할 수 없으며 주로 절을 이끈다.

번역 대금을 받으려면, 판매업체들은 프로젝트 완료부터 영업일 기준 20일 이내에 온라인으로 청구서를 제출해야 한다.

어휘 vendor 판매업자[업체] submit 제출하다 invoice 청구서, 송장

127 전치사 / 부사절 접속사 _ 어휘

해설 opening을 명사로 볼 경우 전치사가, 분사로 볼 경우 부사절에서 축약된 분사구문을 이끄는 일부 접속사(eg. When)가 들어갈 수 있다. 콤마 뒤 절에서 과거완료 시제(had worked)를 사용해 락살트 씨의 이전 경력을 설명하고 있으므로, '~ 전에'라는 의미의 전치사 (A) Prior to가 정답이 된다. 접속사인 (B) Although와 (D) If는 현재분사 구문과는 쓰이지 않고, 부사인 (C) Then은 구조상 빈칸에 들어갈 수 없다.

번역 락살트 씨는 제과점을 열기 전 식품업계에서 15년간 일해왔었다.

어휘 industry 산업, 업

128 형용사 어휘

해설 빈칸은 복합명사 sales report를 수식하는 형용사 자리로, 투자자들의 초기 두려움(Investors' initial fears)을 가라앉힌 판매 실적 보고서의 성격을 나타낸다. 따라서 '안심시키는, 고무적인'이라는 의미의 (C) reassuring이 정답이다.

번역 투자자들이 초기에 느꼈던 두려움은 이번 주 발행된 고무적인 판매 실적 보고서에 의해 잠잠해졌다.

어휘 initial 처음의, 초기의 issue 발행하다 remote 먼, 외진 attentive 주의를 기울이는, 신경쓰는 restful 평화로운, 편안한

129 명사 자리 _ 주격 보어

해설 her almost comic의 수식을 받는 명사 자리로, 주어인 One distinctive aspect의 보어이다. 따라서 (D) exaggeration(과장)이 정답이다. (A) exaggerate는 동사, (B) exaggerated는 동사/과거분사, (C) exaggeratedly는 부사로 품사상 빈칸에 들어갈 수 없다.

번역 화가 채핀 쿠렉의 초상화 방식에서 독특한 점 하나는 얼굴의 특징을 우스꽝스러울 정도로 과장하는 것이다.

어휘 distinctive 독특한, 구별되는 aspect 양상, 측면 facial feature 얼굴의 특징 exaggerate 과장하다 exaggeratedly 과장되게

130 동사 어형 _ 태 _ 시제

해설 주어인 Ramirez Instruments의 동사 자리로, 명사구 high-quality acoustic guitars를 목적어로 취한다. 따라서 능동태 동사 중 하나를 선택해야 하는데, 뒤에 과거부터 현재까지의 기간을 나타내는 표현(for over a century)이 있으므로, 능동태 현재완료진행 동사인 (B) has been designing이 정답이 된다.

번역 라미레즈 악기는 100년 이상 품질이 우수한 어쿠스틱 기타를 디자인해오고 있다.

어휘 instrument 악기 high-quality 고품질의, 품질이 우수한

PART 6

131-134 편지

10월 9일

에바 아처, 소유주
아처 카페
소프 가 40번지
포트 페러리, 빅토리아 3284

아처 씨께,

귀하의 식당 점검이 9월 16일 보건안전부 **131직원들**에 의해 시행되었습니다. **132이러한 방문은 1년에 한 번 이뤄집니다.** 본 점검의 목적은 귀하의 사업체가 모든 지역 규정을 따르며 모든 **133필수** 허가증이 최근 것인지 확인하기 위한 것입니다. 보건안전부는 모든 규정이 **134만족스럽게** 지켜지고 있다는 결론을 내렸습니다. 따라서 귀하 측에서 취해야 할 추가 조치는 없습니다.

올리버 우
보건안전부

어휘 inspection 점검, 시찰 conduct 실시[시행]하다 purpose 의도, 목적 in compliance with ~에 따라 regulation 규정, 규제 permit 허가증 up-to-date 최신의 determine 판단하다, 결정하다 therefore 그러므로 further 추가의 action 조치

131 명사 자리 _ 전치사의 목적어 _ 어휘

해설 전치사 by의 목적어 역할을 하는 명사 자리인데, 빈칸 앞에 한정사가 없으므로 빈칸에는 복수명사 또는 불가산명사가 들어가야 한다. 문맥상 점검 시행(An inspection ~ was conducted)의 주

체를 나타내는 사람 명사가 필요하므로, '직원들'이라는 뜻의 복수명사인 (C) representatives가 정답이다. (A) represents는 동사, (B) representative는 형용사/단수명사로 구조상 빈칸에 들어갈 수 없고, (D) representations는 '묘사, 대의권, 항의'라는 의미로 적절하지 않다.

어휘 represent 대표하다, 대변하다 representative 직원, 대표; (특징 단체를) 대표하는

132 문맥에 맞는 문장 고르기

번역 (A) 이러한 방문은 1년에 한 번 이뤄집니다.
(B) 식당은 점검을 위해 문을 닫을 예정입니다.
(C) 규정은 저희 웹사이트에 게시되어 있습니다.
(D) 부서는 오전 9시에 엽니다.

해설 빈칸 앞 문장에서는 식당 점검이 시행된(An inspection of your restaurant was conducted) 일정(16 September) 및 주체(representatives of the Department of Health and Safety)를, 뒤 문장에서는 점검의 목적(The purpose of the inspection)을 설명했다. 따라서 빈칸에도 점검과 관련된 보건안전부의 설명이 들어가야 자연스러우므로, 시행 빈도를 언급한 (A)가 정답이다.

어휘 post 게시하다

133 형용사 어휘

해설 명사 permits를 수식하는 자리로, 최신 상태(up-to-date)로 유지해야 하는 허가증의 유형을 나타내는 형용사가 들어가야 한다. 따라서 '필수의, 필연적인'이라는 의미의 (D) necessary가 정답이다.

어휘 meaningful 의미 있는 fortunate 운 좋은 persistent 끈질긴, 끊임없이 지속되는

134 부사 어휘

해설 동사구 are being followed를 수식하는 부사 자리이다. 뒤 문장에서 식당 측에서 취해야 할 추가 조치는 없다(no further action is required on your part)고 했으므로, 해당 부분은 모든 규정이 적절히 지켜지고 있다는 내용이 되어야 자연스럽다. 따라서 '흡족스럽게, 만족스럽게'라는 의미의 (B) satisfactorily가 정답이다.

어휘 potentially 잠재적으로 inconsistently 모순되게, 대중없이 temporarily 일시적으로, 임시로

135-138 이메일

수신: 서튼 부티크〈info@certainboutique.co.uk〉
발신: 프리미엄 타이 캔들즈〈orders@prethaican.com〉
날짜: 10월 28일
제목: 주문 상황

고객님께,

귀하를 프리미엄 타이 캔들즈의 고객으로 135**맞이하게 되어** 기쁩니다. 귀하의 양초 40상자 대량 주문이 현재 처리되고 있습니다. 136**구매해 주셔서 감사합니다.**

주문하신 물건 대부분은 현재 재고가 있으며 10일 이내에 영국에 도착할 예정입니다. 137**그러나** 장미향 양초는 재고 부족으로 주문이 밀려 있음을 알려드립니다. 지금부터 3주 후 이용 가능하며 최대한 빨리 배송해 드리겠습니다.

프리미엄 타이 캔들즈의 새로운 고객으로서 귀하의 138**첫** 주문에 만족하시기를 간절히 바랍니다.

사마라야 샤르마

어휘 status 상황 delighted 기쁜 customer 고객 wholesale 도매의, 대량의 process 처리하다 currently 현재 be in stock 재고가 있다 please be advised that ~를 알려드립니다 back order 재고가 없어 처리되지 않은 주문, 이월 주문 available 이용 가능한 sincerely 진심으로, 간절히

135 to부정사

해설 빈칸이 완전한 절(We are delighted)과 대명사 you 사이에 있으므로, you를 목적어로 취하면서 형용사 delighted를 수식하는 준동사가 들어가야 한다. 따라서 부사적 용법으로 감정(delighted)의 원인을 나타내는 to부정사 (D) to welcome이 정답이다. (A) welcome은 동사/형용사/명사, (B) welcomed는 과거동사/과거분사, (C) will welcome은 미래시제 동사로 구조상 빈칸에 들어갈 수 없다.

136 문맥에 맞는 문장 고르기

번역 (A) 이번 한시적 할인으로 비용을 아끼세요.
(B) 구매해 주셔서 감사합니다.
(C) 다른 상자도 갖고 있습니다.
(D) 현재 저희 웹사이트를 이용하실 수 있습니다.

해설 빈칸 앞 문장에서는 고객의 대량 주문이 처리 중(Your wholesale order ~ is being processed)이라고 했고, 뒤에서는 주문한 물건의 재고 여부(in stock) 및 도착 예정 시기(within ten days) 등을 안내했다. 따라서 빈칸에도 고객의 주문과 관련된 내용이 들어가야 자연스러우므로, 주문에 대해 감사를 전한 (B)가 정답이다.

어휘 limited 한정된

137 접속부사

해설 앞 문장에서는 주문한 물건 대부분이 현재 재고가 있으며 10일 이내에 도착할 예정(Most of your order is currently in stock and will arrive ~ within ten days)이라고 했는데, 빈칸 뒤에서는 장미향 양초는 재고 부족으로 주문이 밀려 있다(the rose-scented candles are on back order)고 했다. 따라서 빈칸에는 상반되는 상황을 연결하는 접속부사가 들어가야 자연스러우므로, '하지만, 그러나'라는 의미의 (A) However가 정답이다.

어휘 given that ~을 고려하면 as you can imagine 상상이 되시겠지만 at that point 그 지점에서

138 형용사 어휘

해설 order를 수식하는 형용사 자리로, 신규 고객(as a new customer)이 한 주문의 특징을 나타내는 단어가 필요하다. 따라서 '처음의, 초기의'라는 의미의 (C) initial이 정답이다.

어휘 proper 적절한 usual 보통의, 평상시의 rapid 빠른

139-142 기사

그린웨이 (12월 15일) - 막 발표된 정부 통계에 ¹³⁹**따르면**, 10월과 11월 중 국가 고용 일자리가 4만 개 이상 증가했다. 가장 큰 증가를 보인 곳은 새롭게 9천 개의 일자리가 창출된 소매 부문이었다. 서비스 부문은 8천 4백 개의 추가 일자리로 전체 활동에서 ¹⁴⁰**두 번째**를 차지했다. 전문 서비스 및 사업 서비스 분야에서도 일자리가 늘었다. 보건 서비스와 교육은 각각 4천 2백 개의 일자리가 늘어 강한 증가세를 보였다. ¹⁴¹**성장이 제자리인 유일한 부문은 농업이었다.** 회사 규모로 보면, 직원 수가 50명에서 499명 사이인 중견기업들이 가장 많은 직원을 채용했다. 직원 500명 이상의 대기업들은 1만 2천 명을 채용했다. "취업 시장은 활기를 유지하고 있으며 계속 그럴 것으로 ¹⁴²**예상합니다**,"라고 경제학자 케이샤 후가 말했다.

어휘 employment 고용 statistics 통계 release 발표하다 increase 증가; 증가하다 retail 소매 sector 부문, 분야 overall 전체적인, 전반적인 professional service 전문 서비스 (전문직) business service 사업 서비스 gain 얻다; 증가 hire 채용하다 remain ~한 상태를 유지하다 robust 활기를 띠는, 탄탄한 economist 경제학자

139 전치사 자리 _ 어휘

해설 명사구 government statistics를 목적어로 취하는 전치사 자리로, (C) according to와 (D) instead of 중 하나를 선택해야 한다. 정부 통계는 고용 증가(employment rose) 소식의 출처이므로, '~에 따르면'이라는 의미의 (C) according to가 정답이 된다. 참고로, release는 타동사로서 목적어가 필요하며, 통계는 발표되는 대상이므로 released는 동사가 아닌 government statistics를 수식하는 과거분사로 봐야 한다. (A) because와 (B) whereas는 부사절 접속사로 뒤에 절이 와야 한다.

어휘 whereas 반면에 instead of ~대신

140 형용사 / 부사 어휘

해설 앞 문장에서 가장 큰 증가를 보인 곳은 새롭게 9천 개의 일자리가 창출된 소매 부문(The biggest increase was in the retail sector)이라고 했고, 해당 문장에서는 8천 4백 개가 늘어난 서비스 부문, 그 뒤에서는 4천 2백 개가 증가한 부문들을 언급했다. 즉, 서비스 부문은 전체에서 2위를 차지한 것이므로, came in과 함께 '두 번째를 차지했다, 2위로 들어왔다'라는 의미를 완성하는 (B) second가 정답이다. 참고로, 여기서 came in은 구동사, second는 부사로 볼 수 있으며, in 없이 came second라고 해도 무방하다. 또한 come in handy(유용하다) 등 비격식체에서는 형용사와도 쓰일 수 있으니 고정된 표현으로 알아두도록 하자.

어휘 primary 주된, 주요한

141 문맥에 맞는 문장 고르기

번역 (A) 공익사업 주가가 평균 약 5퍼센트 상승했다.
(B) 그러나 새 자동차 제조 공장이 다음 달에 문을 연다.
(C) 성장이 제자리인 유일한 부문은 농업이었다.
(D) 대학 등록자 수는 4퍼센트만 증가했다.

해설 빈칸 앞에서는 부문(sector)별 일자리 수 변화를, 뒤 문장에서는 화제를 전환하여 회사 규모(company size)별 채용 인원수를 설명했다. 따라서 빈칸에는 앞에서 언급된 부문별 일자리 수와 관련된 내용이 이어져야 자연스러우므로, 성장이 제자리인 분야(agriculture)를 밝힌 (C)가 정답이다.

어휘 utility 공익사업 stock 주식 on average 평균적으로 zero growth 제로 성장, 성장하지 않은 상태 agriculture 농업 enrollment 등록, 등록자 수

142 동사 어형 _ 시제

해설 주어 we와 목적어 it 사이의 동사 자리로, 보기에서 현재동사인 (A) expect와 과거동사인 (C) expected 중 하나를 선택해야 한다. 대명사 it이 현재시제 remains를 포함한 절(The job market remains robust)을 대신하고, 빈칸을 포함한 절이 이러한 상태가 지속될 거라고 예측하고 있으므로, 현재시제인 (A) expect가 정답이 된다.

어휘 expect 예상[기대]하다 expectant 기대하는

143-146 공지

로플러 모바일 뱅킹

앞으로 몇 주 간, 로플러 은행은 더욱 안전하고 사용자 친화적인 경험을 제공하고자 모바일 앱을 업그레이드할 예정입니다. 고객님께서는 이제 로플러 계좌 전체를 동시에 볼 수 있고 지문 인식 스캔을 통해 ¹⁴³**향상된** 보안을 누릴 수 있을 것입니다. ¹⁴⁴**아울러**, 사용자는 온라인 대시보드를 원하는 대로 바꿔서 지출 및 예산을 추적하게 될 수도 있습니다.

특히 빠른 기술 발전을 고려하면, 개인에게는 이러한 변화들이 버거울지도 모릅니다. ¹⁴⁵**저희 팀원들은 이러한 사실을 잘 알고 있습니다.** 따라서 저희 앱의 어떤 기능에 ¹⁴⁶**대해서**든 도움이 필요하시면 555-0133으로 전화하시거나 온라인 www.lofflerbank.com/faq를 방문해 주십시오.

어휘 secure 안전한 user-friendly 사용하기 쉬운 account 계좌 simultaneously 동시에 fingerprint 지문 identification 식별, 인식 customize 원하는 대로 만들다 [바꾸다] dashboard 대시보드, 사용자 인터페이스 track 추적하다 budget 예산 challenging 버거운, 도전적인 individual 개인 particularly 특히 in light of ~를 고려하여 advancement 진보, 발전 assistance 도움 feature 기능

143 형용사 자리 _ 명사 수식 _ 분사

해설   동사 enjoy와 명사 security 사이에 있으므로, 빈칸에는 enjoy의 목적어 역할을 하는 동명사, security를 수식하는 형용사/분사, 또는 security와 복합명사를 이루는 명사가 들어갈 수 있다. 지문 인식 스캔(a fingerprint identification scan)을 통해 고객이 누릴 수 있는 것은 '향상된 보안'이므로, 과거분사 (B) enhanced가 정답이 된다.

어휘   enhance 향상시키다   enhancement 향상, 상승

144 접속부사

해설   빈칸 앞뒤 문장에서 고객(Customers), 즉 사용자(users)를 위한 모바일 앱(mobile application)의 기능을 설명하고 있으므로, 빈칸에는 추가 설명을 덧붙일 때 쓰이는 접속부사가 들어가야 자연스럽다. 따라서 '게다가, 아울러'라는 의미의 (A) Additionally가 정답이다.

어휘   consequently 그 결과, 따라서   ultimately 궁극적으로   conversely 정반대로, 역으로

145 문맥에 맞는 문장 고르기

번역   (A) 새 보안조치는 이 문제를 해결할 목적입니다.
(B) 이번 개발을 면밀히 감시할 것입니다.
(C) 저희 팀원들은 이러한 사실을 잘 알고 있습니다.
(D) 이번 실수에 대해 진심으로 사과드립니다.

해설   빈칸 앞 문장에서는 개인에게 모바일 앱 업데이트와 같은 변화들이 버거울 지도 모른다(Changes can prove to be challenging for individuals)고 했는데, 뒤 문장에서는 도움이 필요한 경우(should you ever need assistance) 연락을 달라며 대안을 제시했다. 따라서 이러한 사실(=고객의 어려움)을 잘 알고 있다며 이해를 표현한 (C)가 빈칸에 들어가야 가장 자연스럽다. 참고로, 여기서 this fact는 앞 문장 전체를 가리킨다.

어휘   measure 조치, 방법   aim 목표하다   development 발전, 개발   be aware of ~을 알다   apologize for ~에 대해 사과하다

146 전치사 어휘

해설   명사 assistance와 any of the features of our app을 적절히 연결해 주는 전치사를 선택해야 한다. '앱의 기능'은 도움이 필요한 부분이므로, '~에 대해서, ~에 있어서'라는 뜻으로 쓰일 수 있는 (D) with가 정답이다. 참고로, assistance는 전치사 with(도움이 필요한 부분)나 in(도움이 필요한 행위)과 함께 자주 쓰인다.

PART 7

147-148 광고

147 **켄드릭스 어플라이언스 세일**
3월 5일, 6일

147/148 본 행사는 1년 전 사우스 워터프론트 구역에 새로 문을 연 저희 매장을 환영해 주신 친구 및 이웃 여러분께 감사를 표하기 위한 것입니

다. 147 브로드 가 동쪽과 리버사이드 가 서쪽에 거주하는 지역 주민 여러분은 이번 주말에 들르셔서 지정된 상품에 추가 할인을 받으세요. 거주 증빙서를 잊지 말고 가져오십시오.

어휘   appliance 기기, 가전제품   neighborhood 인근, 동네   community 지역, 지역 사회   be invited to ~하러 오세요   claim 받다, 청구하다   additional 추가의   selected 지정된, 엄선된   merchandise 상품, 물품   proof 증명, 증거   residency 거주

147 주제 / 목적

번역   무엇을 광고하는가?
(A) 최근 업체 이전
(B) 지점 개소
(C) 지역 주민을 위한 특별 판촉 행사
(D) 신제품 브랜드 소개

해설   첫 번째 문장에서 1년 전 사우스 워터프론트 구역에 새로 문을 연 매장을 환영해 준 친구 및 이웃에게 감사를 표하기 위해 할인 행사를 진행한다고(This event is our way of saying thank you to our friends and neighbors for welcoming our new business to the South Waterfront neighborhood)한 후, 지역 주민들(Members of the community)을 초대했다. 따라서 (C)가 정답이다.

어휘   relocation 이전   promotion 홍보   local 지역의   resident 거주자

▸▸ Paraphrasing   지문의 sale → 정답의 promotion
지문의 Members of the community → 정답의 local residents

148 사실 관계 확인

번역   켄드릭스 어플라이언스에 대해 알 수 있는 것은?
(A) 1년 동안 영업을 해 왔다.
(B) 브로드 가에 있는 매장이다.
(C) 배송 서비스는 사우스 워터프론트로 한정되어 있다.
(D) 주말에는 영업시간이 연장된다.

해설   첫 번째 문장에서 1년 전 사우스 워터프론트 구역에 문을 열었다는 것(welcoming our new business to the South Waterfront neighborhood one year ago)을 언급했으므로, (A)가 정답이다.

어휘   be limited to ~로 제한되다, 한정되다   extend 연장하다, 확대하다

▸▸ Paraphrasing   지문의 one year ago → 정답의 for one year

149-150 회람

회람

수신: 이스트랜드 지역 병원 전 직원

발신: 패트릭 멘잘레스

날짜: 2월 1일

제목: 소개

이스트랜드 지역 병원은 공인 간호사, 엑스레이 기사, 카페테리아 및 시설 관리 직원을 추가로 채용할 계획입니다. ¹⁴⁹**2월 27일 수요일 오후 2시부터 5시까지 윙클러 강당에서 채용 및 정보 행사를 개최하려고 합니다.** 이곳에서 일하는 데 관심이 있는 친구나 가족이 있다면 해당 공석에 대해 알아볼 좋은 기회입니다. 입장료는 없으며 예약이 필요치 않습니다.

¹⁵⁰**여러분이 소개한 지원자가 채용되고 고용 상태가 최소 3개월 지속될 경우, 여러분은 소중한 직원으로서 보너스를 받게 됩니다.** 해당 지원자에게 지원서 상에서 '소개한 사람'이라고 되어 있는 칸에 당신의 이름을 넣어 달라고 요청하십시오. 보너스는 급여에 추가됩니다.

문의사항이 있으시면 저에게 연락 주십시오.

어휘 referral 소개, 추천 registered 등록된, 공인된 technician 기술자 housekeeping 시설 관리 hold 열다, 개최하다 hiring 채용 auditorium 강당 opportunity 기회 open position 공석 entry 입장 make an appointment 예약하다 valued 소중한, 귀중한 candidate 지원자, 후보자 employment 고용, 근무 last 지속되다 include 포함시키다 application 지원, 지원서 labeled ~라고 표시된, ~라고 적힌 paycheck 급료 contact 연락하다

149 사실 관계 확인

번역 채용 및 정보 행사에 대해 알 수 있는 것은?

(A) 카페테리아에서 열릴 예정이다.
(B) 입장료가 부과된다.
(C) 오후에 열릴 것이다.
(D) 참석자는 미리 등록하라는 요청을 받을 것이다.

해설 첫 번째 단락에서 2월 27일 수요일 오후 2시부터 5시까지 채용 및 정보 행사를 개최하려고 한다(We will be holding a hiring and information event on Wednesday, February 27, from 2 P.M. to 5 P.M.)고 했으므로, (C)가 정답이다. 행사는 윙클러 강당(in the Winkler Auditorium)에서 열릴 예정으로 입장료가 없고(no fee for entry) 예약도 필요치 않다(It is not necessary to make an appointment)고 했으므로, (A), (B), (D)는 정답이 될 수 없다.

어휘 admission fee 입장료 charge 청구하다 attendee 참석자 register 등록하다 in advance 미리

▸▸ Paraphrasing 지문의 **from 2 P.M. to 5 P.M.**
→ 정답의 **in the afternoon**

150 세부 사항

번역 멘잘레스 씨는 직원들에게 무엇을 하라고 권하는가?

(A) 프로젝트 진행 지원
(B) 직원 채용을 위해 지원자 소개
(C) 초과 근무로 보너스 획득
(D) 급여가 더 높은 직책에 지원

해설 두 번째 단락에서 공석에 소개한 지원자가 채용되고 고용 상태가 최소 3개월 지속될 경우 직원들은 보너스를 받게 된다(As a valued employee, you will receive a bonus if you refer a candidate ~ whose employment lasts at least three months)며 우회적으로 직원들에게 지원자를 소개하라고 권하고 있다. 따라서 (B)가 정답이다.

어휘 applicant 지원자 work overtime 초과 근무하다 apply for ~에 지원하다

▸▸ Paraphrasing 지문의 **candidate**
→ 정답의 **applicant(s)**

151-152 공지

쳄스베리 시민협회 회의

장소: 알바 매드슨 커뮤니티 센터, 후버 로 4141번지

일시: 6월 14일 화요일 오후 7:00-오후 8:30

안건

- 새로운 이웃 소개
- 도로 공사 관련 새 소식
- ¹⁵¹**부회장 선거**
- 다과

참고 바랍니다:

현재 올해 회비를 걷고 있습니다. 회비는 25달러입니다. 아직 회비를 내지 않으셨다면 납부해 주시기 바랍니다. ¹⁵²**회의 석상에서 납부하시거나, 셸턴 길 595번지의 밥 롭슨에게 회비를 보내주시면 됩니다.**

회의에서 뵙게 되기를 바랍니다!

수잔 울프, 쳄스베리 시민협회 회장
하모니 길 784번지

어휘 civic 시의, 시민의 association 협회 agenda 안건, 의제 목록 neighbor 이웃 construction 건설, 공사 election 선거 vice president 부회장, 부사장 refreshments 다과 currently 현재 collect 모으다, 걷다 dues 회비

151 사실 관계 확인

번역 앞으로 있을 회의에 대해 명시된 것은?

(A) 하모니 길에서 열릴 예정이다.
(B) 임원을 뽑는 선거가 포함될 것이다.
(C) 롭슨 씨가 진행할 것이다.
(D) 지역 커뮤니티 센터에서 연사가 나올 것이다.

해설 회의 안건(Agenda)에 협회 부회장 선거(Election of Vice president)가 포함되어 있으므로, (B)가 정답이다.

어휘 voting 투표 local 지역의

▸▸ Paraphrasing 지문의 **Election of vice president**
→ 정답의 **voting for an office**

152 사실 관계 확인

번역 롭슨 씨에 대해 사실인 것은?

  (A) 협회 부회장이다.
  (B) 회비 납부를 잊어버렸다.
  (C) 회의에서 다과를 제공한다.
  (D) 협회 회원들의 회비를 걷는다.

해설 참고 사항을 보면, 회비를 회의 석상에서 납부하거나 밥 롭슨에게 보내면 된다(You may pay at the meeting, or you may send your payment to Bob Robsen)고 쓰여 있다. 이를 통해 롭슨 씨가 회비 걷는 일을 맡고 있음을 알 수 있으므로, (D)가 정답이다.

어휘 provide 제공하다

153-154 문자 메시지

> **에릭 오자와 (오후 12시 6분)**
> 안녕하세요, 카라. ¹⁵³제가 탄 기차가 늦을 예정이라는 걸 알려드리고 싶어서요.
>
> **카라 무라토 (오후 12시 10분)**
> 아, 안타깝네요. 3시 회의에 시간 맞춰 오실 수 있나요?
>
> **에릭 오자와 (오후 12시 11분)**
> 잘 모르겠어요. 기차 차장은 출발까지 최소 1시간이 더 걸릴 거라고 생각하네요.
>
> **카라 무라토 (오후 12시 12분)**
> 회의를 연기해야 할까요?
>
> **에릭 오자와 (오후 12시 14분)**
> 시작하셔야 할 것 같아요. 병원의 새로운 별관 계획이 제 책상에 있습니다. 원래 설계에서 변경된 사항을 전부 알고 계시잖아요. ¹⁵⁴대답할 수 없는 질문을 고객이 할 경우, 저에게 전화하면 돼요.
>
> **카라 무라토 (오후 12시 15분)**
> 좋아요. 도착 시간에 관해 새 소식이 있으면 알려주세요.
>
> **에릭 오자와 (오후 12시 16분)**
> 네. 고맙습니다.

어휘 make it 참석하다, 시간 맞춰 가다 conductor (버스나 기차의) 차장, 승무원 at least 최소한 postpone 연기하다 wing 부속 건물, 별관 original 원래의 be unable to ~할 수 없다 arrival 도착

153 주제 / 목적

번역 오자와 씨가 무라토 씨에게 연락한 이유는?

  (A) 새 고객을 소개하려고
  (B) 지연을 알리려고
  (C) 기차표 예약을 부탁하려고
  (D) 프로젝트 마감 기한 변경에 대해 감사하려고

해설 오자와 씨가 오후 12시 6분 메시지에서 자신이 탄 기차가 늦을 예정이라는 걸 알려주고 싶다(I wanted to let you know that my train is going to be late)고 했으므로, (B)가 정답이다.

어휘 inform 알리다 delay 지연 book 예약하다

> ▸▸ **Paraphrasing** 지문의 let you know that my train is going to be late → 정답의 inform her of a delay

154 의도 파악

번역 오후 12시 15분에 무라토 씨가 "좋아요"라고 쓸 때, 그 의도는 무엇인가?

  (A) 질문이 있으면 오자와 씨에게 연락할 것이다.
  (B) 전화로 회의에 참석할 것이다.
  (C) 오자와 씨를 역까지 태워 줄 것이다.
  (D) 회담 일정을 변경할 것이다.

해설 오자와 씨는 오후 12시 14분 메시지에서 무라토 씨가 대답할 수 없는 질문을 고객이 할 경우, 자신에게 전화하라(You can call me if the client has any questions that you are unable to answer)고 했다. 이에 대해 무라토 씨가 '좋아요(Sounds good)'라고 한 것이므로, 질문이 있을 경우 오자와 씨에게 연락할 거라고 추론할 수 있다. 따라서 (A)가 정답이다.

어휘 reschedule 일정을 변경하다 consultation 회담, 상담

> ▸▸ **Paraphrasing** 지문의 call → 정답의 contact

155-157 이메일

> 발신: noreply@vacationsiteseer.com
> 수신: vneuman@gzetmail.com
> 날짜: 7월 16일 오후 2시 52분
> 제목: 다가오는 여행
>
> 뉴먼 씨께,
>
> 귀하의 밀라노 여행이 1주일밖에 남지 않았습니다. 클라시코 호텔 객실이 확정되었습니다. ¹⁵⁵체크인은 7월 23일 오후 2시이며 체크아웃은 7월 28일 오전 11시입니다. 체크아웃이 완료될 때까지는 결제가 요구되지 않으므로, 지금 결제하실 필요가 없습니다.
>
> 렌터카 관련해서 미리 계획을 세우실 것을 권장합니다. ¹⁵⁶베이케이션 사이트시어의 고객으로서, 지금 차량을 예약하시면 20퍼센트 할인을 받으실 수 있습니다. ¹⁵⁷저희 렌터카 협력업체들이 7월 20일까지만 이 특별 할인을 제공하니 기다리지 마세요. 저희 웹사이트에 있는 옵션을 살펴보시고 오늘 예약하십시오.
>
> 밀라노에서의 숙박을 예약하기 위해 저희 베이케이션 사이트시어를 선택해 주셔서 감사합니다.
>
> 즐거운 여행 되십시오!
>
> 베이케이션 사이트시어 팀

어휘 upcoming 다가오는, 곧 있을 confirm 확정하다 payment 결제, 지불 require 요구하다, 필요로 하다 urge 강력히 권고하다 regarding ~에 관해 car rental 자동차 대여, 렌터카 be entitled to ~할 자격이 주어지다 deal 특가 거래,

할인   journey 여행, 여정

155 세부 사항

번역   뉴먼 씨는 언제부터 밀라노에서 머무르기 시작하는가?

(A) 7월 16일
(B) 7월 20일
(C) 7월 23일
(D) 7월 28일

해설   첫 번째 단락에서 뉴먼 씨의 체크인이 7월 23일 오후 2시(Check-in is on July 23 at 2 P.M.)라고 했으므로, (C)가 정답이다.

▸▸ Paraphrasing   지문의 **Check-in** → 질문의 **begin his stay**

156 세부 사항

번역   이메일에 포함된 제안은?

(A) 렌터카 할인
(B) 늦은 체크아웃 시간
(C) 호텔 객실 업그레이드
(D) 무료 관광 투어

해설   두 번째 단락에서 베이케이션 사이트시어의 고객은 지금 렌터카를 예약하면 20퍼센트 할인을 받을 수 있다(you are entitled to a discount of 20% if you book your car now)고 했으므로, (A)가 정답이다.

어휘   sightseeing 관광

157 문장 삽입

번역   [1], [2], [3], [4]로 표시된 곳 중에서 다음 문장이 가장 적합한 곳은?

"저희 웹사이트에 있는 옵션을 살펴보시고 오늘 예약하십시오."

(A) [1]
(B) [2]
(C) [3]
(D) [4]

해설   주어진 문장에서 웹사이트에 있는 옵션을 살펴보고 오늘 예약할 것(Explore your options on our Web site and make a reservation today)을 촉구했으므로, 앞에서 먼저 예약을 서둘러야 하는 이유가 제시되어야 한다. [3] 앞에서 렌터카 협력업체들이 7월 20일까지만 특별 할인을 제공하니 기다리지 말라(Our car rental partners are offering this special deal only until July 20, so do not wait)고 했으므로, 이 뒤에 주어진 문장이 들어가야 자연스럽다. 따라서 (C)가 정답이다.

어휘   explore 검토하다   make a reservation 예약하다

158-161 기사

크레이버튼, 평상시처럼 업무로 복귀하다

- 브리애나 와이블 기자

¹⁵⁸어제 발생한 정전으로 크레이버튼 도심의 많은 업체들과 지역 명소

가 문을 닫았다. 정전의 원인은 아직 알려지지 않았지만 아마 새벽의 궂은 날씨가 일조한 것으로 보인다.

¹⁵⁹도심의 몇몇 유적지 투어를 진행하던 남성민 씨는 여행 일정표를 변경했다. "다행히 제가 이 지역을 잘 알고 있어서요." 남 씨가 이야기했다. "단체를 다시 버스로 인솔해서 그랜트우드 파크, 홀트롭 타워 등 다른 대체 장소를 찾기 위해 시의 다른 지역으로 갔습니다."

¹⁶⁰/¹⁶¹크레이버튼 미술관에는 정전이 수익에 변동을 주지 않았는데, 갤러리가 화요일마다 일반 대중에게 비공개 되기 때문이다. 그러나 직원들은 휴무를 하긴 했다. 크레이버튼 대학교는 강의를 취소했지만 발전기로 기숙사 및 카페테리아에 전력을 공급했다. 어제 오후 늦게까지 대부분의 지역 업체에 전력이 복구됐다. 그리고 오늘 크레이버튼은 평상시처럼 업무로 복귀했다.

어휘   return to business 업무에 복귀하다   as usual 평상시처럼   power outage 정전   cause A to부정사 A가 ~하도록 야기하다   attraction 명소   stormy 폭풍우가 몰아치는, 험악한   play a part 한몫 하다, 일조하다   historic site 유적지   itinerary 여행 일정표   discover 발견하다, 찾다   alternative 대안이 되는   make a difference 변화를 가져오다, 차이를 낳다   earnings 수익, 수입   generator 발전기   power 전력을 공급하다   residence hall 기숙사, 생활관   restore 회복하다, 복구하다

158 주제 / 목적

번역   기사의 주제는?

(A) 크레이버튼으로 이주하는 이유
(B) 크레이버튼의 예기치 못한 상황
(C) 믿을 만한 일기예보 소식통
(D) 관광 명소로 가능한 장소

해설   첫 번째 단락에서 어제 발생한 정전으로 크레이버튼 도심의 업체들과 지역 명소가 문을 닫았다(A power outage yesterday caused ~ businesses and area attractions in downtown Craverton to close)고 한 후, 상황에 대한 추가 설명을 이어가고 있다. 따라서 (B)가 정답이다.

어휘   unexpected 예기치 않은, 뜻밖의   reliable 믿을 만한   forecast 예보, 예측

▸▸ Paraphrasing   지문의 **A power outage** → 정답의 **An unexpected situation**

159 추론 / 암시

번역   남 씨는 누구이겠는가?

(A) 기자
(B) 교수
(C) 미술사학자
(D) 투어 가이드

해설   두 번째 단락에서 유적지 투어를 진행하던 남성민 씨가 여행 일정표를 변경했다(Sun Min Nam, who was leading a tour of some of the historic sites ~ changed his itinerary)고 했으므로, 남 씨가 투어 가이드라고 추론할 수 있다. 따라서 (D)가 정답이다.

160 사실 관계 확인

번역 기사에서 크레이버튼 미술관에 대해 언급한 것은?

(A) 어제 손해를 보지 않았다.
(B) 크레이버튼 도심 근처에 위치해 있다.
(C) 화요일마다 방문객에게 개방된다.
(D) 미술 강좌 시리즈를 시작할 예정이다.

해설 세 번째 단락에서 크레이버튼 미술관에는 정전이 수익에 변동을 주지 않았다(For the Craverton Art Museum, the outage did not make a difference in earnings)고 했으므로, (A)가 정답이다.

▸▸ **Paraphrasing** 지문의 did not make a difference in earnings → 정답의 did not lose money

161 문장 삽입

번역 [1], [2], [3], [4]로 표시된 곳 중에서 다음 문장이 가장 적합한 곳은?

"그러나 직원들은 휴무를 하긴 했다."

(A) [1]
(B) [2]
(C) [3]
(D) [4]

해설 주어진 문장에서 조동사 did를 사용해 직원들이 휴무했던 사실을 강조한 것으로 보아, 정전 때문에 발생한 상황임을 짐작할 수 있다. 문장이 However로 시작하고 있으므로 이 앞에는 상반되는 내용, 즉 평소와 같았던 상황이 제시되어야 하며, 직원들의 소속도 언급되어야 한다. [3] 앞에서 정전이 있던 날은 원래 크레이버튼 미술관(the Craverton Art Museum) 갤러리가 일반 대중에게 비공개 되는 화요일이라 수익에는 변동이 없었다(the outage did not make a difference in earnings)며 평소와 같았던 점을 설명하고 있다. 따라서 이 뒤에 주어진 문장이 들어가야 자연스러우므로, (C)가 정답이다.

162-165 문자 메시지

이사벨 포터 (오전 8시 15분): 안녕하세요. ¹⁶²우리 새 인턴 밀라 에르벤이 내일 도착해요. 밀라가 착수할 업무가 있나요?

오마르 시라니 (오전 8시 16분): 정말 죄송해요. ¹⁶³지난주에 JNTD 회의 때문에 사무실을 비웠어요. 이따가 다시 연락 드려도 될까요?

리코 알바레즈 (오전 8시 16분): 지금 밀라에게 줄 업무는 없습니다.

이사벨 포터 (오전 8시 17분): 헷갈리네요. 여러분의 부서장님께서 인턴이 있으면 팀에 크게 도움이 될 거라고 하셨거든요. 다같이 밀라가 할 일을 찾아봐 줄 수 있을까요?

오마르 시라니 (오전 8시 17분): ¹⁶²대학교에서 뭘 전공하는지 다시 얘기해 주시겠어요?

이사벨 포터 (오전 8시 18분): 회계요. 그녀의 이력서에는 회계 감사관이 되고 싶다고 쓰여 있어요.

리코 알바레즈 (오전 8시 19분): ¹⁶⁴음, 좀 따분하긴 하지만 몇 가지 업무가 있을 것 같아요.

이사벨 포터 (오전 8시 20분): 그거면 될 거예요. 저도 복사를 부탁할 서류가 있을 거예요. 밀라의 첫 주는 그걸로 충분할 겁니다. ¹⁶⁵하지만 목요일까지 팀과 회의해서 밀라가 다음 주에 할 추가 업무를 정리해 주시면 고맙겠습니다.

어휘 convention 회의, 대회 confused 혼란스러운 department 부서 mention 언급하다, 말하다 benefit from ~로부터 이익을 얻다 remind 상기시키다 accounting 회계 auditor 회계 감사관 task 업무 dull 따분한, 재미없는 document 서류, 문서 appreciate 감사하다 organize 정리하다, 준비하다 additional 추가의

162 추론 / 암시

번역 에르벤 씨에 대해 암시된 것은?

(A) 회계사다.
(B) 부서 관리자다.
(C) 대회 기획자다.
(D) 학생이다.

해설 밀라 에르벤 씨는 새로 올 인턴(Our new intern, Mila Erben)이며, 문자 메시지 작성자들은 그녀가 할 만한 일에 대해 논의하고 있는 중이다. 시라니 씨가 오전 8시 17분 메시지에서 에르벤 씨가 대학교에서 뭘 전공하는지(what she's studying at the university?) 물었으므로, 그녀가 학생임을 추론할 수 있다. 따라서 (D)가 정답이다.

163 세부 사항

번역 시라니 씨는 지난주에 무엇을 했는가?

(A) 회의 참석
(B) 지점에서 근무
(C) 휴가
(D) 새로운 일 시작

해설 시라니 씨가 오전 8시 16분 메시지에서 지난주에 JNTD 회의에 있었다(I was ~ last week at the JNTD Convention)고 했으므로, (A)가 정답이다.

어휘 attend 참석하다 take a vacation 휴가를 쓰다

▸▸ **Paraphrasing** 지문의 was ~ at the JNTD Convention → 정답의 Attend a convention

164 의도 파악

번역 오전 8시 20분에 포터 씨가 "그거면 될 거예요"라고 쓸 때, 그 의도는 무엇인가?

(A) 혼자서 프로젝트를 완료할 것이다.
(B) 그 업무를 하는 데 2주가 걸릴 것이라고 생각한다.
(C) 알바레즈 씨의 제안에 동의한다.
(D) 나중에 시라니 씨에게 정보를 더 줄 것이다.

해설 새로 올 인턴인 에르벤 씨에게 배정할 업무에 대해서 논의하던 중, 알바레즈 씨가 오전 8시 19분 메시지에서 좀 따분하긴 하지만 에르벤 씨가 할 만한 몇 가지 업무가 있을 것 같다(I might have a few tasks, although they may be a bit dull)고 했는데, 이에 대해 포터 씨가 '그거면 될 거예요(That will do)'라고 한 것이다. 따라서 포터 씨가 알바레즈 씨의 의견에 동의한다고 추론할 수 있으므로, (C)가 정답이다.

어휘 complete 완료하다 propose 제안하다

165 세부 사항

번역 포터 씨는 메시지 작성자들에게 목요일 전에 무엇을 하라고 요청하는가?

(A) 인턴 채용하기
(B) 문서 복사하기
(C) 자신에게 이메일 보내기
(D) 업무 계획하기

해설 포터 씨가 오전 8시 20분 메시지에서 목요일까지 각자 팀과 회의해서 에르벤 씨가 다음 주에 할 추가 업무를 정리해 주면 고맙겠다(I'd appreciate it if you could meet with your team by Thursday and organize additional tasks for Mila for next week)고 했으므로, (D)가 정답이다.

> ▸▸ Paraphrasing 지문의 organize additional tasks
> → 정답의 Plan a set of tasks

166-168 이메일

발신: 베라 페르난데즈
수신: 칼라 로사
발송일자: 6월 7일 오후 12시 47분
제목: 원격 교육 계획

로사 씨께,

168돌리나 재단을 대표해 연락 드립니다. 166저희 임무는 전원 지역 및 지리적으로 고립된 지역사회에서의 원격 교육 플랫폼 이용을 촉진하는 것입니다. 저희는 기술업계 협력망을 통해 이를 실현하고 있습니다. 167귀사를 저희 협력망에 모실 수 있다면 영광이겠습니다.

6월 25일 오후 2시에 돌리나는 "지방 도서관 원격 교육"이라는 제목의 발표를 후원합니다. 발표는 저희 협력업체들이 개발한 기술을 이용해 온라인에서 웨비나로 이뤄집니다. 재단의 시스템 통합 담당자인 제이 랄스턴이 학문 및 직업 교육 프로그램을 지원하는 데 사용되는 기술에 대해 설명할 것입니다. 아울러 사서 5인이 저희 협력업체가 개발하고 공급하는 기술을 이용해 자신들의 지역에서 다양한 교육 프로그램을 어떻게 제공하고 있는지 논의할 것입니다. 167웨비나에 등록하고 저희 재단 프로그램에 대해 더 알고 싶으시면 웹사이트 www.dolinafoundation.org를 방문하십시오.

문의사항이 있으시면 저에게 언제든지 연락 주십시오. 초청을 고려해 주시기를 바랍니다.

168베라 페르난데즈, 대외 지원 담당자

어휘 initiative 계획 distance learning 원격 교육 on behalf of ~를 대표하여 foundation 재단 mission 임무, 사명 promote 촉진하다, 홍보하다 isolated 고립된 geographically 지리적으로 sponsor 후원하다 presentation 발표 entitled ~라는 제목의 webinar 웨비나, 온라인 세미나 (web + seminar) integration 통합 vocational 직업과 관련된 in addition 게다가 librarian 사서 a variety of 다양한 region 지역 develop 개발하다 deliver 전달하다, 공급하다 register for ~에 등록하다 consider 고려하다 invitation 초청, 초대 outreach 원조, 지원

166 세부 사항

번역 돌리나 재단은 어떤 일을 하는가?

(A) 학교에 소프트웨어 판매
(B) 학교에서 쓰는 교과서 인쇄
(C) 기술을 이용한 교육 지원
(D) 대도시에 도서관 건립

해설 첫 번째 단락에서 돌리나 재단의 임무가 전원 지역 및 지리적으로 고립된 지역사회에서의 원격 교육 플랫폼 이용을 촉진하는 일(Our mission is to promote the use of distance-learning platforms)이라고 했으므로, (C)가 정답이다.

> ▸▸ Paraphrasing 지문의 promote the use of distance-learning platforms → 정답의 Use technology to support learning

167 세부 사항

번역 로사 씨는 무엇을 하라고 요청받았는가?

(A) 보조금 승인
(B) 웨비나 참가
(C) 공석에 지원
(D) 도서관 방문

해설 첫 번째 단락에서 로사 씨의 회사가 재단의 협력업체가 되었으면 좋겠다고 한 후, 두 번째 단락에서 로사 씨에게 웨비나에 등록하고 재단의 프로젝트에 대해 알아보려면 웹사이트를 방문하라(To register for the webinar, ~ visit our Web site)고 권했다. 따라서 (B)가 정답이다.

어휘 approve 승인하다 grant 보조금 job opening (회사의) 빈자리, 채용공고

> ▸▸ Paraphrasing 지문의 register for the webinar → 정답의 Participate in a webinar

168 추론 / 암시

번역 페르난데즈 씨는 누구이겠는가?

(A) 재단 프로그램 학생
(B) 기술업체 임원
(C) 지방 도서관 연구원
(D) 재단 직원

해설 이메일 서명에서 페르난데즈 씨가 대외 지원 담당자임을 알 수 있는
데, 첫 번째 단락을 보면 자신이 돌리나 재단을 대표해 연락한다(I am
contacting you on behalf of the Dolina Foundation)고 했으므
로, 페르난데즈 씨가 재단 직원이라고 추론할 수 있다. 따라서 (D)가
정답이다.

169-171 편지

7월 29일

샤리 맥컬리

이스턴 길 103번지

토민톨, 발린다로크 AB37 9EX

맥컬리 씨께,

169 **스코티시 커넥션 집 바꿔 살기 프로그램의 일환으로 7월 22일부터
한 주 동안 귀하의 집에 머무르게 되어 영광이었습니다.**

저희 가족 모임을 위한 완벽한 장소였어요. 제 딸과 사위는 마을의 평온
과 고요함을 즐기는 한편, 손주들은 집 뒤편 널찍한 야외 공간에서 즐겁
게 놀았습니다. 제 남편은 거실에 있는 대화면 TV를 아주 좋아했어요.

여분의 이불을 그렇게 많이 제공해 주시다니 정말 사려 깊으십니다. 7
월 밤이 그렇게 추울 거라고는 예상하지 못했거든요.

170 **7월 25일, 제 결혼기념일 파티 때 제가 거실 탁자에 남긴 메모에 쓴
것처럼, 저희가 식사를 준비하면서 믹서기 뚜껑에 금이 갔어요.** 당일에
교체품을 주문했는데, 아직 도착하지 않은 것 같아 말씀 드리자면, 곧
댁으로 배송될 겁니다. 작은 사고를 일으킨 점 진심으로 죄송합니다.

171 **저희가 귀하의 산장 주택에서 즐거운 시간을 보냈던 것처럼, 귀하와
친구분들이 여기 애버딘에 있는 저희 아파트에서 좋은 시간 보내셨기를
바랍니다.** 그러셨다면 향후 다시 저희와 집 바꿔 살기를 해 주셨으면 합
니다.

클라라 브린월

어휘 privilege 특권, 특전 home exchange 집 바꿔 살기
location 위치 setting 배경, 장소 gathering 모임 relish
즐기다 thoughtful 배려심 있는, 사려 깊은 lid 뚜껑 food
processor 다용도 조리기, 믹서기 crack 금이 가다, 갈라지다
replacement 교체(품) assuming (that) ~라고 가정하면, ~라고
생각하고 sincerely 진심으로 apologize 사과하다 mishap
작은 사고 be willing to 흔쾌히 ~하다

169 주제 / 목적

번역 편지를 쓴 목적은?

(A) 가풍을 설명하려고

(B) 소포 수신을 확인하려고

(C) 집에 대한 감사를 표시하려고

(D) 휴가로 얻을 수 있는 혜택을 서술하려고

해설 첫 번째 단락에서 스코티시 커넥션 집 바꿔 살기 프로그램의 일환으로
맥컬리 씨의 집에 머무르게 되어 영광이었다(It was a privilege to
stay in your home ~ as part of the Scottish Connections

home exchange program)고 했으므로, 집에 대한 감사를 전하는
편지임을 알 수 있다. 따라서 (C)가 정답이다.

어휘 tradition 전통 appreciation 감사 outline 개요를 서술하다

170 세부 사항

번역 7월 25일에 어떤 일이 있었는가?

(A) 물건이 손상됐다.

(B) 주문품이 배송됐다.

(C) 행사에 음식이 공급됐다.

(D) 결혼식이 진행됐다.

해설 네 번째 단락에서 브린월 씨는 자신의 결혼기념일 파티 날인 7월 25
일에 믹서기 뚜껑에 금이 갔다(As I said in the note I left ~ on
25 July, the day of my wedding anniversary party, the lid
of your food processor cracked)고 했으므로, (A)가 정답이다.

어휘 damage 손상을 주다 cater 음식을 공급하다

▶▶ Paraphrasing 지문의 **the lid of your food processor
cracked**
→ 정답의 **An item was damaged**

171 추론 / 암시

번역 맥컬리 씨에 대해 암시된 것은?

(A) 집 바꿔 살기 프로그램을 이끌고 있다.

(B) 산간 지역에 산다.

(C) 브린월 씨의 친척이다.

(D) 애버딘으로 이사할 계획이다.

해설 마지막 단락에서 브린월 씨는 자신과 가족들이 맥컬리 씨의 산장 주택
에서 즐거운 시간을 보냈다(we enjoyed your mountain home)
고 했다. 따라서 맥컬리 씨가 산간 지역에 산다고 추론할 수 있으므로
(B)가 정답이다.

어휘 relative 친척

▶▶ Paraphrasing 지문의 **mountain home** → 정답의 **lives in a
mountainous area**

172-175 이메일

수신: 히엔 팸 〈hpham@ngoc.com〉

발신: 테레사 그리핀 〈tgriffin@throngsoftware.com〉

제목: 정보

날짜: 9월 20일

팸 씨께,

스롱 소프트웨어에 오신 것을 환영합니다. 172 **저희는 팸 씨께서 입사
하시게 되어 기쁩니다. 10월 3일 월요일 업무 첫날은 오전 8시 45분에
14동으로 출근하십시오.** 프런트 데스크에서 체크인하시면 임시 신분증
이 지급될 것입니다. 거기서 뵙고 사무실로 안내해 드린 다음, 건물을
둘러보면서 동료들에게 소개해 드리겠습니다. 이후 정보기술 (IT) 부서

로 가시면 노트북, 비밀번호, 보안 정보를 받으실 겁니다. ¹⁷³다 마치고 나면 누군가가 12동 인사부서로 안내해 드릴 것이니, 급여 및 복지 서류를 작성하시면 됩니다.

오전 11시 30분에는 저를 비롯한 동료 여러 명과 함께해 주십시오. 사무실 근처에 저희가 가장 좋아하는 식당 중 한 곳으로 모시고 가겠습니다. 오후 시간 ¹⁷⁴나머지는 자유 시간이 될 테니 사무실에 자리를 잡으신 후 그날 받은 정보를 검토하실 수 있을 것입니다. ¹⁷⁵제가 이 날 오후 중에 사무실에 들러 모든 사무기기의 위치를 알려드리겠습니다.

그 때 뵙겠습니다.

테레사 그리핀
인사부서, 스롱 소프트웨어

어휘　**report to** ~로 가서 도착했다고 알리다, 출근하다　**temporary** 임시의　**colleague** 동료　**Information Technology** 정보기술부서　**security** 보안　**Human Resources** 인사부서　**fill out** 기입하다, 작성하다　**payroll** 급여　**benefit** 혜택, 복리후생　**settle into** 자리잡다　**review** 검토하다　**equipment** 장비

172　세부 사항

번역　10월 3일에 어떤 일이 있을 것인가?

(A) 직원들에게 새 노트북이 지급될 것이다.
(B) 카페테리아에서 오찬이 열릴 것이다.
(C) 개조된 건물 견학이 이뤄질 것이다.
(D) 신입 직원이 업무를 시작할 것이다.

해설　첫 번째 단락에서 팸 씨가 입사하게 되어 기쁘다(We are pleased that you are joining the company)고 한 후, 10월 3일 월요일이 업무 첫날(On your first day of work, Monday, October 3)이라고 했다. 따라서 10월 3일이 신입 직원인 팸 씨가 업무를 시작하는 날임을 알 수 있으므로, (D)가 정답이다.

어휘　**issue** 지급하다, 교부하다　**renovate** 개조하다, 보수하다

173　세부 사항

번역　팸 씨는 어디서 문서를 작성할 것인가?

(A) 12동
(B) 14동
(C) 자신의 사무실
(D) IT 사무실

해설　첫 번째 단락에서 누군가 팸 씨를 12동 인사부서로 안내하면 그곳에서 급여 및 복지 서류를 작성하면 된다(someone will guide you to Human Resources in building 12 so you can fill out payroll and benefits forms)고 했으므로, (A)가 정답이다.

> ▸▸ **Paraphrasing**　지문의 **fill out payroll and benefits forms** → 질문의 **complete some documents**

174　동의어 찾기

번역　두 번째 단락, 두 번째 줄에 쓰인 "rest"와 의미가 가장 가까운 단어는?

(A) 다수
(B) 나머지
(C) 휴식 시간
(D) 의도

해설　'rest'를 포함한 부분은 '오후 시간 나머지(The rest of the afternoon)'라는 의미로 해석된다. 따라서 동일한 뜻의 (B) remainder(나머지)가 정답이다.

175　세부 사항

번역　팸 씨는 오후에 무엇을 하겠는가?

(A) 장비 시험하기
(B) 그리핀 씨 사무실 방문하기
(C) 프로젝트 제안서 검토하기
(D) 장비 위치 알기

해설　두 번째 단락에서 그리핀 씨가 이 날 오후 중에 팸 씨의 사무실에 들러 모든 사무기기의 위치를 알려주겠다(I will stop by your office later in the day to make sure you know where all the office equipment is)고 했으므로, (D)가 정답이다.

어휘　**be located** 위치해 있다

> ▸▸ **Paraphrasing**　지문의 **later in the day** → 질문의 **in the afternoon**
> 지문의 **know where all the office equipment is** → 정답의 **Learn where equipment is located**

176-180　후기 + 편지

칼보 컷
★★★☆☆

^{176/177}저의 칼보 컷 첫 방문은 실망스러웠습니다. 도착했을 때 문에 있는 표지판에는 "예약하지 않은 고객도 환영"이라고 붙어 있었습니다. ¹⁷⁷하지만 접수원은 이발하려면 약 한 시간 기다려야 한다고 통명스럽게 말했습니다. 매장엔 다른 고객이 한 명 밖에 없고 스타일리스트는 세 명이었는데도 말이죠. 작업 품질은 좋았습니다. 이발 가격은 15달러로 적당했고 제가 했던 남성 일반 컷은 만족스러웠습니다. 하지만 스타일리스트는 말 한 마디 없이 이발을 했습니다. ^{177/179}모든 사람이 잡담을 좋아하는 것은 아니지만 저를 맡은 스타일리스트가 말 한 마디 하지 않는 것은 무례해 보였습니다. ¹⁷⁷이발을 마치자 머리를 말려주겠다는 제안도 없이 이발 가운을 벗겼습니다.

- 마틴 실버, 비숍빌

어휘　**first-time customer** 처음 이용하는 고객　**disappointing** 실망스러운　**walk-in** 예약 없이 오는 고객　**receptionist** 접수원　**bluntly** 직설적으로, 통명스럽게　**quality** 품질　**fairly priced** 가격이 적정하게 책정된　**cape** 어깨 망토

offer to 부정사 ~해 주겠다고 제안하다 blow-dry 드라이어로
머리를 말리다

칼보 컷 · 7번 가 678번지 · 라마, 사우스 캐롤라이나 · 29069

마틴 실버
오크 가 51번지
비숍빌, 사우스 캐롤라이나 29010

실버 씨께,

시간을 내어 저희에게 후기를 남겨 주셔서 감사합니다. 저희는 항상 가능한 최상의 서비스를 제공하고자 노력하고 있습니다. ¹⁷⁸저희 직원 중 누구라도 불친절하거나 전문가답지 못하다고 느끼셨다면 귀하의 불만사항에 대해 더 자세히 듣고 싶습니다. 803-555-0110으로 저에게 직통으로 전화해 주세요.

칼보 컷은 진심으로 귀하를 계속 모시고 싶습니다. ¹⁷⁹마리사 로페즈에게 이발 및 드라이 예약을 잡아드릴 수 있으면 좋겠습니다. 귀하께서 기대하시는 이발 경험을 그녀가 제공해 드릴 수 있으리라 확신합니다. ¹⁸⁰아울러 다음 번 칼보 컷 방문 시에는 저희 최다 판매 제품 중 하나인 천연 샴푸 한 병을 무료로 제공해 드리고자 합니다. 머리 손질이 필요하시면 언제든 칼보 컷을 다시 찾아 주시길 바랍니다.

제나 마코브스키
칼보 컷 사장

어휘 available 이용 가능한 unaccommodating 불친절한
unprofessional 전문가답지 못한 regarding ~에 관해
complaint 불만, 불평 directly 직접 serious ~에 진지한,
진심인 earn one's business 거래를 따내다, 손님으로 받다
appointment 예약 provide A with B A에게 B를 제공하다
in addition 게다가 complimentary 무료의 best-selling
product 최다 판매 제품 trim 다듬기, 손질

176 추론 / 암시

번역 후기에 따르면, 실버 씨에 대해 암시된 것은?
(A) 예약 시간에 늦었다.
(B) 일반 이발을 요청하지 않았다.
(C) 칼보 컷을 딱 한 번 방문했다.
(D) 문에 있는 표지판을 보지 못했다.

해설 후기의 첫 문장에서 실버 씨가 칼보 컷 첫 방문이 실망스러웠다 (My visit to Calbo Cuts as a first-time customer was disappointing)고 평가했으므로, 실버 씨가 칼보 컷에 딱 한 번 방문했다고 추론할 수 있다. 따라서 (C)가 정답이다.

▸▸ Paraphrasing 지문의 as a first-time customer
→ 정답의 only once

---

177 세부 사항

번역 칼보 컷의 어떤 점이 실버 씨를 실망하게 했는가?
(A) 가격
(B) 위치
(C) 영업시간
(D) 고객 서비스

해설 후기의 첫 문장에서 칼보 컷 첫 방문이 실망스러웠다(My visit to Calbo Cuts as a first-time customer was disappointing)고 평가한 후, 접수원(the receptionist bluntly told me)과 스타일리스트(I found my stylist's total silence to be rude ~ she removed the haircutting cape without even offering to blow-dry my hair)의 응대 태도에 대해 불만을 표했다. 따라서 (D)가 정답이다.

---

178 세부 사항

번역 마코브스키 씨는 왜 실버 씨가 자신에게 연락해야 한다고 제안했는가?
(A) 예약 변경을 위해
(B) 세부 사항을 추가로 제공하기 위해
(C) 개인적인 만남을 주선하기 위해
(D) 연락처를 업데이트하기 위해

해설 편지의 첫 번째 단락에서 마코브스키 씨는 실버 씨의 불만사항에 대해 더 자세히 듣고 싶다(I would like to hear more details regarding your complaint)며 직통으로 전화해달라(Feel free to call me directly)고 했다. 즉, 불만에 대한 세부 사항을 추가로 제공해 달라는 요청으로 볼 수 있으므로, (B)가 정답이다.

어휘 additional 추가의 arrange 마련하다, 주선하다

▸▸ Paraphrasing 지문의 more details
→ 정답의 additional details

---

179 연계

번역 로페즈 씨에 대해 암시된 것은?
(A) 한 시간을 꼬박 들여 이발을 한다.
(B) 예약하지 않은 고객을 받지 않는다.
(C) 현재 가장 인기 있는 스타일리스트다.
(D) 고객에게 이야기하는 것을 좋아한다.

해설 마코브스키 씨는 편지의 두 번째 단락에서 로페즈 씨와의 이발 및 드라이 예약을 잡아주고 싶다(I would be happy to schedule an appointment for you for a haircut and blow-dry with Marissa Lopez)고 제안한 후, 실버 씨가 기대하는 이발 경험을 그녀가 제공해 줄 수 있을 것(she can provide you with the haircut experience you are looking for)이라고 덧붙였다. 실버 씨가 쓴 후기의 후반부를 보면, 모든 사람이 잡담을 좋아하는 것은 아니지만 자신을 맡은 스타일리스트가 말 한 마디 하지 않는 것이 무례해 보였다(not everyone likes to make small talk, but I found my stylist's total silence to be rude)고 쓰여 있다. 따라서 실버 씨에게 추천된 로페즈 씨가 고객과 이야기하는 것을 좋아한다고 추론할 수 있으므로, (D)가 정답이다.

> ▸▸ **Paraphrasing** 　지문의 likes to make small talk
> 　　　　　　　　　　　→ 정답의 enjoys talking

180 세부 사항

번역　실버 씨는 다음 번 칼보 컷 방문 시 무엇을 무료로 얻겠는가?

(A) 샴푸 한 병
(B) 이발
(C) 드라이
(D) 신제품

해설　편지의 두 번째 단락에서 실버 씨가 다음 번에 칼보 컷을 방문할 때 천연 샴푸 한 병을 무료로 제공하겠다(on your next visit to Calbo Cuts, we would like to offer you a complimentary bottle of our all-natural shampoo)고 했으므로, (A)가 정답이다.

> ▸▸ **Paraphrasing** 　지문의 complimentary → 질문의 for free

181-185 기사 + 이메일

업계 소식

글 해리엇 멜러스

런던 (4월 1일) – 관리자나 팀장이 직원과 동료에게 피드백을 주는 최선의 방법을 배우는 건 종종 181**어려운** 일이다. 182**사미아 비샤라의 새 저서 〈피드백에 관한 진실〉 (폭스 밀 출판사)은 이 문제에 대한 조언을 제공한다.** 185**비샤라 씨는 회사 경영 문제 및 해결책 관련 전문 상담가다.** 그녀는 관리자들에게 조언과 비판보다는 사실을 말하고 반응을 해 주라고 조언한다.

182/184**비샤라 씨는 4월 6일 월요일 오후 2시, 스톤클리프 서점에서 강연할 예정이다.** 더 자세한 내용을 보려면 www.stonecliff.co.uk를 방문하면 된다.

어휘　employee 직원　colleague 동료　expert 전문가의, 전문적인　consultant 상담가, 자문 위원　advise 조언하다 reaction 반응　advice 충고　criticism 비판, 비평

수신: 오스카 버튼 〈oburton@harstonindustries.com.hk〉
발신: 판미숙 〈mpan@harstonindustries.kr〉
제목: 제안
날짜: 4월 10일

안녕하세요, 오스카.

오닉스 호텔에서 있을 전문성 개발 프로그램을 맡을 워크숍 진행자들을 아직 다 예약하지는 않은 걸로 알고 있어요. 183**며칠 전 필립스 사 업무를 보며 런던에 있었는데요.** 184**4월 6일에 거기서 사미아 비샤라 씨를 만나 그녀의 새 저서 〈피드백에 관한 진실〉을 주제로 한 강연을 들을 수 있었어요.** 저희 워크숍 진행자 중 한 분으로 훌륭한 선택이 될 거라고 생각합니다. 185**비샤라 씨의 경력과 시간이 되는지 여부에 대해 세부 정보를 더 모아서 곧 보내드릴게요.** 목요일 원격 기획 회의에 당신과 함께

하기를 고대할게요.

판미숙

어휘　suggestion 제안　book 예약하다　upcoming 다가오는, 곧 있을　professional 직업의, 전문가의　development 개발 account 고객(사), 거래(관계), 계정　gather 모으다　further 추가의　availability (이용) 가능성, 시간 가능 여부　shortly 곧 teleconference 원격 회의

181 동의어 찾기

번역　기사의 첫 번째 단락, 첫 번째 줄에 쓰인 "hard"와 의미가 가장 가까운 단어는?

(A) 내구성이 있는
(B) 어려운
(C) 견고한
(D) 사실인

해설　'hard'를 포함한 부분은 '피드백을 주는 최선의 방법을 배우는 건 종종 어려운 일이다(It is often hard ～ to learn the best way to give feedback)'라는 의미로 해석되는데, 여기서 hard는 '어려운'이라는 뜻으로 쓰였다. 따라서 (B) difficult가 정답이다.

182 주제 / 목적

번역　기사를 쓴 목적 중 하나는?

(A) 곧 있을 행사를 알리기 위해
(B) 새로운 출판사에 관해 보고하기 위해
(C) 상담가의 서비스를 광고하기 위해
(D) 새 서점을 홍보하기 위해

해설　기사의 첫 번째 단락에서는 비샤라 씨의 새 저서(Samia Bishara's new book, *Facts on Feedback*)를 소개했고, 두 번째 단락에서는 비샤라 씨가 4월 6일에 스톤클리프 서점에서 강연을 할 예정(Ms. Bishara will be speaking at Stonecliff Bookstore on ～ 6 April)이라고 했다. 따라서 기사의 목적 중 하나가 곧 있을 행사를 알리기 위함이라고 볼 수 있으므로, (A)가 정답이다.

어휘　announce 알리다, 발표하다　advertise 광고하다　promote 홍보하다

183 추론 / 암시

번역　이메일에서 판 씨에 대해 암시된 것은?

(A) 출장에서 돌아왔다.
(B) 책 집필에 관심이 있다.
(C) 행사에 참석할 수 없다.
(D) 런던으로 이사할 계획이다.

해설　이메일의 초반부에서 판 씨가 며칠 전 필립스 사 업무를 보며 런던에 있었다(I was in London a few days ago working on the Phillips account)고 했으므로, 판 씨가 출장에서 돌아왔다고 추론할 수 있다. 따라서 (A)가 정답이다.

184 연계

번역 판 씨는 비샤라 씨를 어디서 만났겠는가?

(A) 호텔
(B) 기획 회의
(C) 회계사무소
(D) 서점

해설 이메일의 초반부에서 판 씨는 4월 6일에 비샤라 씨를 만나 새 저서를 주제로 한 강연을 들을 수 있었다(on 6 April, I had a chance to meet Samia Bishara and hear her speak on the topic of her new book)고 했다. 기사의 두 번째 단락을 보면, 비샤라 씨가 4월 6일에 스톤클리프 서점에서 강연을 할 예정(Ms. Bishara will be speaking at Stonecliff Bookstore on Monday, 6 April)이라고 되어 있으므로, 판 씨가 비샤라 씨를 서점에서 만났다고 추론할 수 있다. 따라서 (D)가 정답이다.

185 연계

번역 판 씨는 버튼 씨에게 무엇을 줄 계획인가?

(A) 예산 제안서
(B) 회의 프로그램
(C) 사업 상담가에 대한 정보
(D) 필립스 고객에 관한 문서

해설 이메일의 후반부에서 비샤라 씨의 경력과 시간이 되는지 여부에 대해 정보를 더 모아서 보내겠다(I will gather further details about Ms. Bishara's background and availability and send that to you)고 했다. 기사의 첫 번째 단락을 보면 비샤라 씨가 회사 경영 문제 및 해결책 관련 전문 상담가라고 되어 있으므로, (C)가 정답이다.

어휘 budget 예산 proposal 제안, 제안서 related to ~에 관한

▸▸ Paraphrasing 지문의 send → 질문의 give

지문의 further details
→ 정답의 Some information

186-190 이메일 + 웹페이지 + 이메일

발신: 미칼 제줄라 〈m.zezula@gerlach-kozey.com.au〉
수신: 당 티 리엔 〈dtlien@hermiston.com.au〉
날짜: 9월 21일 목요일 오후 1시 44분
제목: 회의 저녁 식사

리엔 씨께,

다음 달에 시드니에서 열릴 비즈니스 리더십 회의에서 뵙기를 고대하고 있습니다. 187저희 토론단의 일원이 되어 주셔서 기쁩니다. 지방 자치 정부 계획 관련 논문에 대해 이야기하시는 것을 듣기를 고대하고 있습니다.

189저는 토론단 의장으로서, 토론회 직후에 모든 연사들을 위한 저녁 식사를 준비하고 있습니다. 186그 지역에 근거지를 두고 계시니 회의 웹사이트에 열거된 장소에 대해 잘 알고 계실 것 같아요? 186/188항구가 내려다보여서 빅토리아 그릴로 마음이 기울고 있긴 하지만, 그래도 의견을 듣고 싶습니다. 규모가 큰 단체를 수용할 수 있는 장소라면 특히 좋겠습니다. 이곳들을 제가 직접 방문하고 싶은데 토론회 참석일까지 시드니

에 도착하지 못하거든요. 10월 1일까지 모든 준비를 마치고 싶습니다.

미칼 제줄라

어휘 delighted 아주 기뻐하는 panel 토론단, 토론회 paper 논문 local government 지방 자치 정부 initiative 계획 chair 의장 organize 준비하나, 조직하다 immediately 바로, 즉시 locally 해당 지역에, 현지에 insight 통찰력, 이해 lean towards ~로 기울다 overlook 내려다보다 harbor 항구 accommodate 수용하다 especially 특히 desirable 바람직한 arrangement 준비(사항), 마련

---

http://www.blcsydney.com.au/thingstodo

일정	숙소	지도	연락처	**할 일**

음식점 추천

190이 음식점들은 모두 회의장에서 걸어서 갈 수 있는 거리에 있습니다. 예상되는 활동을 고려할 때, 특히 대규모 단체의 경우에는 예약을 권장합니다.

◎ **봄베이 팰리스**: 현대 인도 요리. 여러 가지 채식주의 식단이 포함된 광범위한 메뉴. 가격: 적당

◎ **빅토리아 그릴**: 창의적인 호주 요리. 풍광이 멋진 시드니 항구가 내려다보이는 헤시오드 빌딩 꼭대기층에 위치. 가격: 고가

◎ **아미르 키친**: 현대적인 스타일의 레바논 요리. 개별실 이용 가능. 파티나 단체 행사에 이상적. 가격: 저렴

어휘 recommendation 추천 within walking distance 걸어서 갈 수 있는 거리에 있는 given ~를 고려해 볼 때 anticipated 예상[기대]되는, 예정된 reservation 예약 contemporary 동시대의 cuisine 요리 moderate 보통의, 적당한 innovative 획기적인, 창의적인 spectacular 장관을 이루는 flair (특이하고 매력적인) 스타일, 솜씨 ideal 이상적인 inexpensive 저렴한

발신: 당 티 리엔 〈dtlien@hermiston.com.au〉
수신: 미칼 제줄라 〈m.zezula@gerlach-kozey.com.au〉
날짜: 9월 22일 금요일 오전 10시 2분
제목: 회신: 회의 저녁 식사

제줄라 씨께,

저도 뵙기를 고대하고 있습니다. 추천해 주신 음식점에 대해 말씀 드리면, 웹사이트에 있는 세 곳을 제가 가 봤어요. 모두 음식이 맛있고 분위기가 좋아요. 190빅토리아 그릴은 가격이 다소 높고, 사실 회의장에서 택시를 타고 가야 할 겁니다. 제 의견으로는 봄베이 팰리스가 저희 단체 규모에 가장 좋을 것 같습니다. 제 사무실 건물 바로 옆에 있어요. 189원하시면 퇴근하고 들러서 10월 6일 봄베이 팰리스 저녁 식사 예약에 대해 문의해 볼 수 있습니다.

당 티 리엔

어휘   ambience 분위기   somewhat 다소, 어느 정도   pricey
값비싼   require 필요로 하다, 요구하다   stop by 들르다   inquire
문의하다

186   주제 / 목적

번역   첫 번째 이메일을 쓴 목적은?

(A) 행사에 대한 조언을 요청하려고
(B) 관광 명소에 대한 정보를 주려고
(C) 논문 주제를 제안하려고
(D) 업체 대표들을 회의에 초청하려고

해설   첫 번째 이메일의 두 번째 단락에서 리엔 씨가 회의 장소 인근에 근거지를 두고 있으니 회의 웹사이트에 열거된 식당에 대해 잘 알고 있을 것 같다(Since you are locally based, perhaps you have insights about the places listed on the conference Web site)며 장소를 결정하기 전에 의견을 듣고 싶다(I would like to hear your opinion)고 했다. 따라서 리엔 씨에게 행사에 대한 조언을 구하고자 이메일을 썼다고 볼 수 있으므로, (A)가 정답이다.

어휘   propose 제안하다

▶▶ Paraphrasing   지문의 would like to hear your opinion
→ 정답의 request advice

187   세부 사항

번역   회의에서 리엔 씨의 역할은?

(A) 토론단 의장직 맡기
(B) 발표하기
(C) 케이터링 업체에 연락하기
(D) 안내 데스크에서 일하기

해설   첫 번째 이메일의 첫 단락을 보면, 리엔 씨가 비즈니스 리더십 회의에서 토론단의 일원(you will be part of our panel)으로서 지방 자치 정부 계획 관련 논문에 대한 이야기를 할 것(discuss your paper on local government initiatives)임을 알 수 있다. 따라서 (B)가 정답이다.

어휘   presentation 발표   staff 직원으로 일하다

▶▶ Paraphrasing   지문의 discuss your paper
→ 정답의 Giving a presentation

188   세부 사항

번역   제줄라 씨가 빅토리아 그릴에서 식사하고 싶어 하는 이유는?

(A) 채식 식단을 제공한다.
(B) 개별실을 제공한다.
(C) 비교적 늦게 문을 연다.
(D) 멋진 전망을 갖추고 있다.

해설   첫 번째 이메일의 두 번째 단락을 보면, 제줄라 씨는 빅토리아 그릴로 마음이 기울고 있다(I am leaning towards Victoria Grill)고 한 후, 항구가 내려다보인다(it overlooks the harbor)는 이유를 덧붙였다. 따라서 멋진 전망 때문에 그곳에서 식사하길 원한다고 볼 수 있

으므로, (D)가 정답이다.

어휘   relatively 비교적, 상대적으로   attractive 매력적인, 멋진

▶▶ Paraphrasing   지문의 leaning towards
→ 질문의 interested in
지문의 overlooks the harbor
→ 정답의 has an attractive view

189   연계

번역   토론은 언제 이뤄질 예정인가?

(A) 9월 21일
(B) 9월 22일
(C) 10월 1일
(D) 10월 6일

해설   첫 번째 이메일의 두 번째 단락에서 제줄라 씨가 토론회 직후에 모든 연사들을 위한 저녁 식사를 준비하고 있다(I am organizing a dinner for all the speakers immediately following the panel)고 했으므로, 토론회와 저녁 식사가 같은 날 진행될 예정임을 알 수 있다. 두 번째 이메일의 후반부를 보면, 리엔 씨는 제줄라 씨가 원하면 10월 6일 봄베이 팰리스 저녁 식사 예약에 대해 자신이 문의해 볼 수 있다(If you like, I could ~ inquire about a dinner reservation at Bombay Palace on 6 October)고 회신했다. 즉, 10월 6일에 토론회 및 저녁 식사 일정이 잡혀 있는 것이므로, (D)가 정답이다.

190   연계

번역   리엔 씨는 회의 웹사이트의 어떤 정보가 잘못됐다고 생각하는가?

(A) 봄베이 팰리스의 대규모 단체 접객 가능 여부
(B) 회의장에서 빅토리아 그릴까지의 거리
(C) 음식점의 요리 가격
(D) 저녁 식사 예약 필요성

해설   웹페이지의 초반부를 보면 음식점 세 곳 모두 회의장에서 걸어서 갈 수 있는 거리에 있다(All of these restaurants are located within walking distance of the conference site)고 되어 있다. 하지만 두 번째 이메일의 중반부에서 리엔 씨가 세 곳 중 빅토리아 그릴은 회의장에서 택시를 타고 가야 한다(Victoria Grill ~ would require a taxi ride from the conference site)고 했으므로, (B)가 정답이다.

어휘   distance 거리   make a reservation 예약하다

191-195   이메일 + 제품 정보 + 청구서

발신: amartin@netforceevents.com
수신: mpresser@gerenukofficedesign.com
날짜: 9월 3일
제목: 의자 (제품 번호 10405)

프레서 씨께,

191 지난봄에 이뤄진 회사 확장의 결과로, 당사는 더 큰 시설로 이전하게

되어 새 가구가 필요했습니다. ¹⁹⁴그 당시에 게레누크 오피스 디자인에서 사무용 의자 22개(제품 번호 10405-파란색)를 주문했습니다. 두 달새, 의자 중 다수가 고장 나거나 사용할 수 없게 되었습니다. 처음에는 무료로 배송해 주신 교체품 의자가 마음에 들었지만. 그 중 몇 개는 또 고장 났습니다.

^{192/194}그래서 신제품인 이그제큐티브 라인(제품 번호 10612)의 품질이 더 낫다는 가정 하에, 의자 22개를 그 제품으로 추가 비용 없이 교체해 주실 것을 요청하는 바입니다. 저희가 원래 구입했던 모델과 가격 면에서 비슷하더군요. ¹⁹⁴그렇게 하실 수 없다면 가구가 필요할 때 다른 업체를 찾을 수밖에 없습니다.

알렉산드라 마틴, 사무실 관리자
넷포스 이벤츠

어휘 expansion 확장, 확대 facility 시설 unusable 사용할 수 없는 initially 처음에 replacement 교체, 교체품 deliver 배송하다 free of charge 무료로 hereby 이로써, 그래서 at no extra charge 추가 비용 없이 assuming (that) ~라고 가정하면 comparable 비교할 만한, 비슷한 original 원래의 purchase 구입하다 be forced to 하는 수 없이 ~하다 furnishing 가구, 비품

---

http://www.hansons-office.com/ergonomic-task-chair

핸슨즈: 사무용품 원스톱 매장

홈	**제품**	고객 지원	소개

인체공학 업무용 의자

¹⁹³**인체공학 업무용 의자는 당사의 최다 판매 회전 의자입니다.** 특별히 좋은 자세를 촉진하고 불편함을 방지하도록 설계되어, 사무실에서의 장시간 근무에 완벽한 제품입니다. 무엇보다도 오래 가도록 견고하게 만들어졌으며 평생 품질 보증서를 함께 드립니다. 해당 모델은 4가지 멋진 색상이 있습니다.
개당 159달러

· 검은색, 제품 코드 429BL
· 파란색, 제품 코드 469BB
· ¹⁹⁵**녹색, 제품 코드 490GN**
· 빨간색, 제품 코드 459RD

어휘 office supply 사무용품 ergonomic 인체공학의 swivel 회전 promote 촉진하다 posture 자세 avoid 피하다, 막다 discomfort 불편함 built to last (오래 사용할 수 있도록) 견고하게 만들어진 lifetime 평생 warranty 품질 보증서 attractive 멋진, 매력적인

---

¹⁹⁴**핸슨즈: 사무용품 원스톱 매장**
청구서

¹⁹⁴**고객: 넷포스 이벤츠**

주소: 콜라드 대로 342번지, 햄프턴, 메인
날짜: 9월 10일

제품	수량	단가	합계
인체공학 업무용 의자, ¹⁹⁵**제품 490GN**	22	159달러	3,498달러
		소계	3,498달러
		첫 주문 고객 할인:	-159달러
		합계	3,339달러

문의사항이 있으시면 customerhelp@hansons-office.com으로 연락 주십시오.

---

191 사실 관계 확인

번역 넷포스 이벤츠에 대해 사실인 것은?

(A) 최근 다른 건물로 이전했다.
(B) 가구를 제조한다.
(C) 새 매장을 막 열었다.
(D) 지난봄에 창립됐다.

해설 이메일의 첫 번째 단락에서 지난봄에 이뤄진 회사 확장의 결과로 넷포스 이벤츠가 더 큰 시설로 이전했다(As a result of our company's expansion last spring, we moved into a larger facility)고 했으므로, (A)가 정답이다.

어휘 recently 최근 manufacture 제조하다 found 설립하다

▸▸ Paraphrasing 지문의 a larger facility
→ 정답의 another building

192 주제 / 목적

번역 이메일을 쓴 목적은?

(A) 이용 가능한 의자 색상에 대해 불만을 제기하려고
(B) 일부 의자들의 수리를 요청하려고
(C) 사무용 문구류 주문을 넣으려고
(D) 가구의 교체를 요청하려고

해설 이메일의 두 번째 단락에서 원래 구매 했던 의자 22개를 신제품인 이그제큐티브 라인 의자로 추가 비용 없이 교체해 줄 것을 요청한다(I am hereby requesting that you replace all 22 with chairs from your new Executive line)고 했으므로, (D)가 정답이다.

어휘 repair 수리하다 place an order 주문을 넣다 stationery 문구류

▸▸ Paraphrasing 지문의 requesting that you replace all 22 with chairs
→ 정답의 To ask that some furniture be replaced

193 사실 관계 확인

번역 인체공학 업무용 의자에 대해 명시된 것은?

(A) 가격이 적당하다.
(B) 인기 있는 모델이다.
(C) 한정 품질 보증서가 주어진다.
(D) 물빨래가 가능한 직물로 만들어졌다.

해설 제품 정보의 첫 번째 문장에서 인체공학 업무용 의자가 핸슨즈의 최다 판매 회전 의자(The Ergonomic Task Chair is our best-selling swivel model)라고 했으므로, (B)가 정답이다. 평생 품질 보증서가 포함되어 있다(it ～ comes with a lifetime warranty)고 했으므로 (C)는 틀린 내용이고, (A)와 (D)는 명시되지 않았다.

어휘 reasonably 합리적으로, 타당하게 limited 한정된 fabric 직물, 천

> ▸▸ **Paraphrasing** 지문의 **our best-selling swivel model**
> → 정답의 **a popular model**

194 연계

번역 게레누크 오피스 디자인에 대해 암시된 것은?

(A) 최초 고객에게 할인을 제공한다.
(B) 마틴 씨의 요청에 동의하지 않았다.
(C) 이그제큐티브 의자가 빠르게 품절됐다.
(D) 새 경영진 체제 하에 있다.

해설 이메일의 두 번째 단락에서 마틴 씨는 게레누크 오피스에서 주문했던 의자 22개 모두를 추가 비용 없이 신제품으로 교체해달라(you replace all 22 with chairs ～ at no extra charge)고 요청한 후, 그렇게 할 수 없다면 가구가 필요할 때 다른 업체를 찾을 수밖에 없다(If you are unable to do this, we will be forced to look elsewhere for our furnishing needs)고 했다. 청구서를 보면, 마틴 씨의 회사인 넷포스 이벤츠(Client: Netforce Events)가 핸슨즈(HANSON'S)에서 제품을 주문했다는 사실을 확인할 수 있으므로, 게레누크 오피스 디자인이 마틴 씨의 교체 요청을 수락하지 않았다고 추론할 수 있다. 따라서 (B)가 정답이다. 참고로, 첫 주문 고객 할인(Discount for first-time customers)은 핸슨즈가 제공한 것이므로, (A)는 오답이다.

어휘 sell out 매진되다, 다 팔리다 management 경영, 경영진

195 연계

번역 넷포스 이벤츠가 핸슨즈에서 주문한 의자 색상은?

(A) 검은색
(B) 파란색
(C) 녹색
(D) 빨간색

해설 청구서에 나온 표에서 넷포스 이벤츠가 인체공학 업무용 의자(Ergonomic Task Chair) 중 490GN을 주문했다는 사실을 확인할 수 있다. 제품 정보를 보면, 제품 코드가 490GN(Item Code 490GN)인 의자는 녹색(Green)이므로, (C)가 정답이다.

196-200 공지 + 도표 + 이메일

클루프 포토그래피 행사

[196]11월 21일, 영업 5주년을 기념하기 위한 축하 행사에 클루프 전 직원 여러분을 초대합니다. 전통 바비큐 파티뿐만 아니라 라이브 음악, 게임 경기 등이 있는 회사 야유회에 참석해 주십시오. 전통 바비큐 스타일로 준비된 그릴에서 갓 구운 고기를 제공하며, [198]음료도 드립니다. [199]그 대신, 참석자들은 함께 나눠 먹을 곁들임 음식을 가져오시거나 장소 준비팀에 자원해 주시기 바랍니다. 행사를 원활히 진행하기 위해, 준비를 도와줄 사람이 최소 두 분 필요합니다.

[197]모임은 본사 건물 테라스에서 오후 1시부터 8시까지 열립니다. 참석하고자 하시면 회사 드라이브에 저장된 참가 신청서를 열고, 어떻게 기여할 것인지 그곳에 명시해 주세요. 직원들은 손님 동반 의사를 표해주시기만 한다면 마음껏 데려오실 수 있습니다. 문의사항은 저희 행사 담당자인 녹솔로 누수에게 nwwosu@kloofphoto.sa로 보내주시면 됩니다.

어휘 celebration 축하 행사, 기념 행사 commemorate 기념하다 feature (특별히) 포함하다 traditional 전통적인 braai 바비큐 파티 competitive 경쟁하는 fresh off the grill 그릴에서 갓 구운 beverage 음료 in exchange 그 대가로, 대신 attendee 참석자 smoothly 순조롭게, 원활히 at least 최소한 gathering 모임 convene 회합하다, 개최되다 patio (정원식) 테라스 headquarters 본사, 본부 sign-up sheet 참가 신청서 indicate 명시하다, 나타내다 contribute 기여하다, 이바지하다 intention 의도 direct 전달하다, 보내다 coordinator 진행 담당자

클루프 포토그래피 참가 신청서

이름	곁들임 음식	손님 동반 여부
메이슨 키분두	옥수수	아니요
클라라 싱	감자 샐러드	예
칼 윌리엄스	마늘빵	예
세이드 디알로	잡탕밥	예
세쿠 롬바드		예
[198]패트리샤 윌리엄슨	[198]음료	예

발신: 데이비드 존슨
수신: 녹솔로 누수
제목: 클루프 하계 행사
날짜: 11월 3일

누수 씨께,

곧 있을 행사를 준비해 주셔서 감사합니다. 저희 클루프 동료 몇 명이 가져올 요리에 대해 이야기 나눴습니다. [200]그런데 제가 남아프리카공화국에 이제 막 도착해서 바비큐 야유회 관련 문화가 상당히 생소해요. [199]또한 요리를 그다지 잘하지 못합니다만, 성공적인 야유회를 위해 힘

을 보태고 싶습니다. 가장 도움이 되는 일을 알려주세요.

데위드 존슨

어휘 organize 준비하다, 조직하다 upcoming 다가오는, 곧 있을 colleague 동료 discuss 논의하다 surrounding ~를 둘러싼, ~와 관련된 not much of 잘 못하는, 별로인

196 세부 사항

번역 행사의 목적은?

(A) 제품을 홍보하려고
(B) 매장 개점을 축하하려고
(C) 회사 신임 회장을 환영하려고
(D) 회사 기념일을 축하하려고

해설 공지의 첫 번째 단락에서 영업 5주년을 기념하기 위한 축하 행사에 클루프 전 직원을 초대한다(all Kloof employees are invited to a celebration to commemorate our first five years in business)고 했으므로, (D)가 정답이다.

어휘 promote 홍보하다 mark an anniversary 기념일을 축하하다, 주기를 기념하다

▸▸ Paraphrasing 지문의 a celebration → 질문의 the event
지문의 to commemorate our first five years in business
→ 정답의 To mark a company anniversary

197 세부 사항

번역 공지에 따르면, 행사는 어디서 열릴 것인가?

(A) 공원
(B) 사무실 건물 근처
(C) 소매점
(D) 경기장

해설 공지의 두 번째 단락에서 모임은 본사 건물 테라스에서 있을 것(Our gathering will convene ~ on the patio of our headquarters building)이라고 했으므로, (B)가 정답이다.

어휘 retail 소매

▸▸ Paraphrasing 지문의 convene → 질문의 be held
지문의 on the patio of our headquarters building → 정답의 Near an office building

198 연계

번역 도표의 정보에 따르면 윌리엄슨 씨는 어떤 실수를 했는가?

(A) 가져올 음식을 아무 것도 신청하지 않았다.
(B) 참가 의사를 확정하지 않았다.
(C) 회사에서 제공하는 것을 본인도 가져올 계획이다.
(D) 허가된 것보다 더 많은 손님을 데려오려고 한다.

해설 도표에서 윌리엄슨 씨가 곁들임 음식(Side dish)으로 음료(drinks)를 적었다는 사실을 확인할 수 있다. 하지만 공지의 첫 번째 단락에서

음료는 제공된다(Beverages will also be provided)고 했으므로, 회사에서 제공하는 음식을 본인도 가져가려고 계획한 것이 실수라고 볼 수 있다. 따라서 (C)가 정답이다.

어휘 confirm 확정하다, 확인하다 permit 허가하다

199 연계

번역 누수 씨는 존슨 씨에게 무엇을 하라고 권하겠는가?

(A) 장소 준비 돕기
(B) 고기 가져오기
(C) 굽는 것 돕기
(D) 경기 진행하기

해설 이메일의 후반부에서 존슨 씨가 자신이 요리를 그다지 잘하진 못하지만 성공적인 야유회를 위해 힘을 보태고 싶다(I am not much of a cook, but I do want to contribute to the success of the picnic)고 한 후, 가장 도움이 되는 일을 알려달라(Please let me know what would be most helpful)고 누수 씨에게 요청했다. 공지의 첫 번째 단락을 보면, 참가자들이 함께 나눠 먹을 곁들임 음식을 가져오거나 장소 준비팀에 자원해주길(attendees either plan to bring a side dish to share or volunteer to join the setup crew) 바란다고 되어 있다. 따라서 누수 씨가 존슨 씨에게 장소 준비 돕는 일을 제안할 거라고 추론할 수 있으므로, (A)가 정답이다.

어휘 assist with ~를 돕다

▸▸ Paraphrasing 지문의 volunteer to join the setup crew → 정답의 Help with setting up

200 추론 / 암시

번역 이메일에서 존슨 씨에 대해 암시된 것은?

(A) 신참 사진작가가 아니다.
(B) 요리를 즐겨 한다.
(C) 남아프리카공화국 출신이 아니다.
(D) 실내 행사를 선호한다.

해설 이메일의 중반부에서 존슨 씨는 자신이 남아프리카공화국에 이제 막 도착해서 바비큐 야유회 관련 문화가 상당히 생소하다(since I have just arrived in South Africa, the culture surrounding a braai picnic is quite new to me)고 했다. 따라서 남아프리카공화국 출신이 아니라고 추론할 수 있으므로, (C)가 정답이다.

어휘 prefer 선호하다

기출 TEST 7

101 (B)	**102** (D)	**103** (D)	**104** (B)	**105** (A)
106 (A)	**107** (B)	**108** (C)	**109** (A)	**110** (D)
111 (C)	**112** (D)	**113** (D)	**114** (A)	**115** (D)
116 (B)	**117** (B)	**118** (D)	**119** (D)	**120** (D)
121 (A)	**122** (B)	**123** (D)	**124** (A)	**125** (A)
126 (C)	**127** (C)	**128** (C)	**129** (B)	**130** (D)
131 (A)	**132** (B)	**133** (B)	**134** (D)	**135** (B)
136 (D)	**137** (C)	**138** (A)	**139** (C)	**140** (B)
141 (A)	**142** (B)	**143** (C)	**144** (A)	**145** (D)
146 (B)	**147** (D)	**148** (B)	**149** (C)	**150** (D)
151 (D)	**152** (C)	**153** (C)	**154** (B)	**155** (C)
156 (A)	**157** (D)	**158** (C)	**159** (B)	**160** (A)
161 (B)	**162** (B)	**163** (C)	**164** (C)	**165** (A)
166 (C)	**167** (B)	**168** (B)	**169** (C)	**170** (D)
171 (D)	**172** (D)	**173** (C)	**174** (A)	**175** (D)
176 (C)	**177** (A)	**178** (D)	**179** (D)	**180** (C)
181 (A)	**182** (B)	**183** (B)	**184** (B)	**185** (C)
186 (C)	**187** (B)	**188** (C)	**189** (B)	**190** (D)
191 (A)	**192** (C)	**193** (D)	**194** (C)	**195** (D)
196 (A)	**197** (D)	**198** (D)	**199** (B)	**200** (C)

PART 5

101 인칭대명사의 격 _ 소유격

해설 전치사 about의 목적어인 명사구 recent order를 한정 수식해 주는 자리이다. 따라서 소유격 인칭대명사 (B) your가 정답이다.

번역 귀하의 최근 주문에 대한 모든 질문은 고객관리센터로 보내주십시오.

어휘 direct ~로 보내다 recent 최근의

102 명사 어휘

해설 Ms. Wu에 대해 설명하는 주격 보어 자리로, of the contest의 수식을 받는다. 뒤에서 우 씨가 상을 받는다(collect her prize)고 했으므로 '대회의 우승자'라는 내용이 되어야 자연스럽다. 따라서 (D) winner가 정답이다.

번역 우 씨는 대회 우승자였고 다음 주에 상을 받을 것이다.

어휘 collect one's prize 상을 받다 partner 협력자 member 회원 player 선수

103 형용사 자리 _ 명사 수식 _ 과거분사

해설 명사 time을 수식하는 자리로, 보기에서 형용사로도 쓰이는 현재분사 (B) limiting(제한하는, 극단적인)과 과거분사 (D) limited(제한된, 한정된) 중 하나를 선택해야 한다. 보너스를 지급하는 기간은 한시적

으로 제한되는 것이므로, 수동의 의미를 내포한 (D) limited가 정답이다. 참고로, limit은 동사/명사로 time 뒤에 붙어서 '시간 제한'이라는 뜻의 복합명사가 될 수는 있지만 빈칸의 위치에 들어갈 수는 없다.

번역 마르코 은행은 한시적으로 처음 거래하는 고객이 계좌를 개설할 때 100달러의 보너스를 지급한다.

어휘 open an account 계좌를 개설하다 limit 제한; 제한시키다

104 형용사 어휘

해설 '온실 화원'이라는 뜻의 greenhouse를 적절히 수식하는 형용사를 선택해야 한다. 시청의 로비에 화분을 기증할 만한 곳은 해당 지역에 있는 온실 화원이므로, '지역의, 현지의'라는 의미의 (B) local이 정답이다.

번역 한 지역 온실 화원에서 시청 로비를 아름답게 꾸미기 위해 화분에 심은 식물 여러 개를 기증했다.

어휘 donate 기부[기증]하다 potted 화분에 심은 beautify 아름답게 꾸미다 potential 잠재적인 main 주요한

105 명사 자리 _ to부정사의 목적어

해설 to report의 목적어 역할을 하는 명사 자리로, 한정사 any 및 과거분사구 incurred during business travel의 수식을 받는다. 따라서 (A) expenses(비용, 지출)가 정답이다. (B) expensed는 과거동사/과거분사, (C) expensively는 부사, (D) expensive는 형용사로 품사상 빈칸에 들어갈 수 없다.

번역 첨부된 문서는 출장 중 발생된 일체의 비용을 보고하는 방법을 알려 준다.

어휘 attach 붙이다, 첨부하다 incur (비용을) 발생시키다 expense 비용; ~을 필요 경비로 청구하다

106 명사 어휘

해설 admission과 복합명사를 이루어 동사 pay의 목적어 역할을 하는 자리이다. 비회원이 체육관을 이용하기 위해 지불해야 하는 것은 '입장료'이므로, '요금, 수수료'라는 뜻의 (A) fee가 정답이다. admission fee는 고정된 표현으로 암기해 두는 것이 좋다.

번역 비회원은 일일 입장료를 지불하고 배상책임 면책서약서에 서명했다면 체육관을 이용해도 된다.

어휘 guest waiver 배상책임 면책서약서 income 수입 salary 월급

107 인칭대명사의 격 _ 소유격

해설 전치사 for의 목적어인 명사 employees를 한정 수식하는 자리이다. 따라서 소유격 인칭대명사 (B) its가 정답이다.

번역 샤리크 제약회사는 헤인 파크에서 자사의 직원들을 위한 야유회를 개최할 예정이다.

어휘 pharmaceuticals 제약회사 host 열다, 개최하다 employee 직원

108 접속사 어휘

해설 굴뚝(Chimney) 점검 및 청소(inspection and cleaning)는 겨울이 시작되기 전에 의뢰해야 할 작업이라고 볼 수 있으므로, '~ 전에'라는 의미의 (C) before가 정답이다.

번역 겨울이 시작되기 전, 완벽한 점검과 청소를 위해 바우튼 침니에 전화하세요.

어휘 complete 완벽한 inspection 점검, 검사 now that ~이므로 even though ~일지라도 since ~이래로, ~이므로

109 동사 자리

해설 빈칸은 주어 Ikeda Real Estate Group의 동사 자리로, text messages를 목적어로 취한다. 따라서 (A) uses(이용하다)가 정답이다. (B) users는 복수명사, (C) useful은 형용사, (D) using은 동명사/현재분사로 구조상 빈칸에 들어갈 수 없다.

번역 이케다 부동산 그룹은 이제 고객들에게 관심 부동산에 대한 새로운 정보를 주기 위해 문자 메시지를 이용한다.

어휘 property 부동산, 건물 of interest 흥미 있는, 관심 있는

110 형용사 어휘

해설 병원 기록을 바탕으로(According to our records) 상대방이 어떤 상태인지 알려주는 주격 보어 자리로, '검진 시기를 놓친'이라는 의미를 완성하는 (D) overdue(기한이 지난, 시기를 놓친)가 정답이다. 참고로, (A) willing은 to부정사와 어울려 쓰인다. (B) helpful과 (C) concerned는 뒤에 각각 도움을 받는 대상, 걱정하는 대상이 와야 한다.

번역 저희 기록에 따르면, 귀하는 배럴 박사 병원에서의 연례 건강 검진 시기를 놓쳤습니다.

어휘 according to ~에 따르면 checkup 검사, 건강 진단 willing 기꺼이 ~하는 helpful 도움이 되는 concerned 걱정하는, 관심이 있는

111 부사절 접속사 자리

해설 빈칸은 완전한 절(the Human Resources offices are being renovated)을 이끄는 접속사 자리로, 빈칸이 이끄는 절이 앞에 있는 주절을 수식하고 있다. 직원 업무 지원 데스크가 530호로 옮겨지는 일은 인사부서 사무실이 개조되는 동안 일어날 일이므로, '~ 하는 동안에'라는 의미의 부사절 접속사 (C) while이 정답이다. (A) opposite은 형용사/부사/명사/전치사, (B) that은 대명사/한정사/명사절 접속사/형용사절 접속사(관계대명사), (D) anywhere는 대명사/부사로 구조상으로도 빈칸에 들어갈 수 없다.

번역 인사부서 사무실이 개조되는 동안 직원 업무 지원 데스크는 530호로 옮겨질 예정이다.

어휘 employee help desk 직원 업무 지원 데스크 renovate 개조하다, 보수하다

112 전치사 어휘

해설 동사 is located와 Elm Road를 연결하는 자리로, 도로와 어울리는 전치사를 선택해야 한다. 따라서 '~를 따라가는 길 어디에, (기다란 길, 강 등의) 옆에'라는 의미로 쓰일 수 있는 (D) along이 정답이다.

번역 브레이 팜 마트는 엘름 로를 따라가다 보면 와이 길과의 교차로 근처에 있다.

어휘 intersection 교차로, 교차점

113 형용사 자리 _ 명사 수식 _ 어휘

해설 동사 offers의 목적어인 명사 hours를 수식하는 형용사 자리이다. 보기에서 형용사 역할을 할 수 있는 현재분사 (A) extending(연장하는)과 과거분사 (D) extended(연장된) 중 하나를 선택해야 한다. 영업 시간은 연장되는 것이므로, 수동의 의미를 내포한 과거분사 (D) extended가 정답이 된다. (B) extends와 (C) extend는 동사로 품사상 빈칸에 들어갈 수 없다.

번역 우리 사무실은 고객에게 더 많은 유연성을 부여하기 위해 연장 영업 시간을 제공한다.

어휘 offer 제공하다 provide 제공하다 additional 추가의 flexibility 유연성 extend 연장하다

114 명사 어휘

해설 동사 has created의 목적어 자리로, 판매를 촉진하기 위해(to encourage sales) 만든 것을 나타내는 명사가 들어가야 한다. 따라서 '판촉 (광고)'라는 의미의 (A) promotion이 정답이다.

번역 어레네오 그룹은 특히 젊은 층에서의 판매를 촉진하기 위해 온라인 판촉 광고를 만들었다.

어휘 specifically 특별히, 구체적으로 encourage 권장하다, 촉진하다

115 부사 자리 _ 동사 수식

해설 be동사 is와 현재분사 looking 사이에서 동사를 수식하는 부사 자리이므로, (D) continually(계속해서)가 정답이다. (A) continued는 과거동사/형용사/과거분사, (B) continuation은 명사, (C) continual은 형용사로 품사상 빈칸에 들어갈 수 없다.

번역 코라카 주식회사는 운송망을 확장할 새로운 방법들을 계속해서 찾고 있다.

어휘 expand 확장하다 transportation 운송, 수송 continuation 계속, 연속

116 전치사 자리 _ 어휘

해설 명사 the presentation을 목적어로 취하는 전치사 자리이다. 발표가 진행되는 중에 식사를 해도 된다는 내용이므로, '~도중에, ~동안에'라는 의미의 (B) during이 정답이다. (C) into는 '~안으로'라는 뜻으로 문맥상 어색하고, (A) in case와 (D) although는 부사절 접속사로 품사상 빈칸에 들어갈 수 없다.

번역 직원들은 회의 때 각자 점심 식사를 가져와서 발표 도중 먹어도 된다.

117 명사 자리 _ 동사의 목적어

해설 빈칸은 타동사 requires의 목적어 역할을 하는 명사 자리이므로, (B) reorganization(재편성)이 정답이다. (A) reorganize와 (C) reorganizes는 동사, (D) reorganized는 과거동사/과거분사로 품사상 빈칸에 들어갈 수 없다.

번역 로건 클로딩의 상품은 매 시즌 초반에 재편성을 해야 한다.

어휘 merchandise 상품 require 요구하다, 필요로 하다 reorganize 재편성하다, 개편하다

118 명사 어휘

해설 빈칸은 new hire(신규 채용자)와 복합명사를 이루어 동사 complete and return의 목적어 역할을 하는 자리이다. 따라서 작성해서 다시 보낼 수 있는 대상이 들어가야 하므로, '서류'라는 의미의 (D) paperwork이 정답이다.

번역 인턴들은 근무 첫날까지 신규 채용자 서류 작성을 완료해 반송해야 한다.

어휘 complete 완료하다 background 배경 management 관리 publication 출판, 출간물

119 전치사 어휘

해설 빈칸 앞에 온 완전한 절과 명사구 the high volume of customers를 적절히 이어주는 전치사를 선택해야 한다. '많은 수의 고객'은 식사 예약이 필수가 된 원인이므로, '~때문에'라는 의미의 (D) due to가 정답이다.

번역 제이크 다운타운 비스트로에서의 평일 식사는 많은 수의 고객 때문에 예약을 통해서만 가능하다.

어휘 high volume of 다량의, 다수의 regarding ~에 관해

120 동사 어휘

해설 전치사 with와 어울려 쓰이는 자동사 자리로, 데 솔라 씨와 함께하는 행위를 나타내야 한다. 따라서 '상의하다, 의논하다'라는 의미의 (D) consult가 정답이다. 참고로, consult는 '(의사, 변호사 등에게) 상담하다, 조언을 구하다'라는 뜻의 타동사로도 쓰인다.

번역 누구든 데 솔라 씨와 상의할 필요가 있다면, 반드시 오늘 회의 이전에 하세요.

어휘 reflect 반영하다, 숙고하다 arrange 준비하다 regard ~를 …로 여기다

121 형용사 자리 _ 명사 수식

해설 빈칸에는 명사 students를 수식하는 형용사나 students와 복합명사를 이루는 명사가 들어갈 수 있다. 문맥상 직업의 날(Career Day) 행사에 오는 학생들(students)의 특성을 묘사하는 형용사가 필요

하므로, (A) ambitious(포부 넘치는, 야심찬)가 정답이다. 명사인 ambition은 '야심, 야망'이라는 뜻으로 students와 복합명사를 이룰 수 없으며, (C) ambitiously는 부사로 품사상 빈칸에 들어갈 수 없다.

번역 라우 씨는 직업의 날 행사에서 포부 넘치는 학생들을 만나기를 고대한다.

어휘 career 직업, 진로

122 명령문의 동사원형

해설 Please로 시작하는 명령문의 동사 자리로, 명사구 daily spending records를 목적어로 취한다. 따라서 동사원형인 (B) keep이 정답이다. (A) kept는 과거동사/과거분사, (C) keeps는 현재동사, (D) keeping은 동명사/현재분사로 구조상 빈칸에 들어갈 수 없다.

번역 온라인 잔액 명세서가 최근 계좌 활동을 반영하지 않을 수 있으니, 일일 지출 기록을 해두세요.

어휘 spending 지출 keep a record 기록해 두다 balance 잔고, 잔액 statement 명세서, 거래내역서 account 계좌, 회계

123 부사 어휘

해설 접속사 but이 두 절을 연결하고 있으므로, 빈칸이 포함된 절은 바트 씨가 '최근에(recently)' 시설 책임자를 교체하기 위해 '조직 외부로(outside of the organization)' 나가서 사람을 영입해 온 것과는 상반되는 내용이 되어야 한다. 따라서 '보통은 회사 내부 사람들(people within the company)'을 책임자로 승진시킨다는 의미를 완성하는 (D) normally(보통, 일반적으로)가 정답이다.

번역 바트 씨는 보통 회사 내부 사람들을 승진시키지만, 최근에는 시설 책임자를 교체하기 위해 조직 외부로 나가서 구했다.

어휘 promote 승진시키다 organization 조직, 단체 replace 교체하다, 바꾸다 facilities 시설 director 책임자, 이사 forgetfully 깜빡 잊어서

124 동사 자리

해설 주어 The National Health Agency's latest report의 동사 자리로, that절을 목적어로 취한다. 따라서 (A) concludes(결론을 내리다)가 정답이다. 동명사/현재분사인 (B) concluding과 to부정사인 (D) to conclude는 본동사 역할을 할 수 없으며, (C) conclusion은 명사로 품사상 빈칸에 들어갈 수 없다.

번역 국립보건청의 최근 보고서는 근래에 채택된 보건 규정이 성공적이었다는 결론을 내렸다.

어휘 latest 최근의 adopt 채택하다 regulation 규정, 규제 conclusion 결론

125 대명사 어휘 _ 수 일치

해설 관계대명사 who의 선행사 자리로, 관계사절의 단수동사 wants와 수가 일치하는 대명사가 들어가야 한다. 따라서 (A) Anyone이 정답이다. (C) Those는 복수형 대명사이므로 빈칸에 들어가려면 관계사

절에 want가 쓰여야 한다. (B) Some(몇몇의 사람)은 수가 일치하지 않으며 문맥상으로도 어색하고, (D) Other는 the 없이 단독으로 대명사 역할을 할 수 없다.

번역 다음 주 오찬에 참석하고 싶은 사람은 내일 정오까지 하세가와 씨에게 이야기해야 한다.

어휘 attend 참석하다 luncheon 오찬

126 동사(과거분사) 어휘

해설 주어 they가 앞에 나온 orders를 가리키므로, 빈칸에는 주문이 처리되고 나서(Once orders are processed) 48시간 내에 이루어지는 일을 나타내는 동사가 들어가야 한다. 따라서 '이행된다'라는 의미를 완성하는 (C) filled가 정답이다. 여기서 fill은 '(요청 받은 것을) 제공하다'라는 뜻을 나타내며, fill an order는 고정된 표현으로 알아두는 것이 좋다.

번역 영업소에서 주문을 처리하면 48시간 이내에 이행된다.

어휘 process 처리하다 commit 저지르다, 약속하다 position ~에 두다 occur 일어나다

127 과거분사

해설 빈칸은 명사구 new figures를 뒤에서 수식하는 자리이다. 수치는 회사에 의해(by the company) 발표되는 것이므로, 수동의 의미를 내포한 과거분사 (C) released가 정답이다. to부정사 (A) to release와 현재분사로 쓰일 수 있는 (B) releasing은 능동의 의미를 나타내며 타동사로서 목적어가 필요하므로 오답이다. 또한 according to가 전치사이기 때문에 본동사 형태인 (D) have released도 구조상 빈칸에 들어갈 수 없다.

번역 사측에서 발표한 새 수치에 따르면, 탈히 베버리지 사의 수익은 작년에 약 4퍼센트 올랐다.

어휘 profit 수익, 수입 rise 오르다 figures 수치 release 발표하다, 공개하다

128 상관접속사

해설 빈칸은 and와 함께 상관접속사를 이루어 최고 경영자(the CEO)와 최고 재무 책임자(the CFO)를 연결해주고 있다. 따라서 'A와 B 둘 다'라는 뜻을 완성하는 (C) Both가 정답이다. 참고로, (A) Each는 한정사로 쓰일 경우 뒤에 관사 없이 단수명사가 와야 하고, (B) Either는 and가 아닌 or와 함께 상관접속사를 이룬다. (D) Whoever는 명사절/부사절 접속사 역할을 하므로 구조상 빈칸에 들어갈 수 없다.

번역 최고 경영자와 최고 재무 책임자 둘다 10,000달러 이상의 수표에 서명할 권한이 있다.

어휘 be authorized to ~할 권한이 있다

129 전치사 자리

해설 빈칸 앞에 '여러 가지 이유가 있다'라는 완전한 절이 왔으므로, 빈칸 뒤 cost는 명사, to negotiate a new agreement는 reasons를 수식하는 to부정사구로 보아야 한다. 따라서 빈칸에는 cost를 목적어

로 취해 수식어구를 이루는 전치사가 들어가야 하므로, '~이외에도'라는 의미의 (B) besides가 정답이다. (A) also, (C) indeed는 부사, (D) yet은 부사/접속사로 품사상 빈칸에 들어갈 수 없다.

번역 비용 이외에도 신규 계약을 협상할 이유는 많다.

어휘 multiple 많은, 다수의 negotiate 협상하다 agreement 협정, 계약 indeed 사실

130 부사 어휘

해설 동명사구 reading texts를 적절히 수식하는 부사를 선택해야 한다. 편집자들이 오류를 고치고 글을 다듬기 위해 지문을 읽는 방식을 묘사하는 단어가 들어가야 하므로, '면밀하게, 주의 깊게'라는 의미의 (D) closely가 정답이다.

번역 벤칠리 프레스의 편집자들은 오류를 고치고 글을 다듬기 위해 지문을 면밀히 읽는 것에 능숙하다.

어휘 be skilled at ~를 잘하다 polish 다듬다 prose 산문 sensibly 현저히, 합리적으로 perfectly 완벽하게 tightly 단단히, 꽉

PART 6

131-134 이메일

수신: 전 직원 〈staff@TFF.com〉
발신: 월터 C. 핸디 〈wchandy@TFF.com〉
제목: 영업 인센티브 프로그램
날짜: 11월 15일

TFF 영업팀 여러분께,

올해 4분기를 위한 새로운 더블 인센티브 제도를 소개하고자 이메일을 드립니다! 기본 현금 보너스 방침에 더해, 영업사원 여러분은 이제 음악회, 스포츠 행사, 극장 공연 입장권을 ¹³¹**얻을** 기회를 갖게 됩니다. 이 추가 인센티브는 올해를 사상 최대 판매를 기록한 해로 만들기 위해 고안된 것입니다. ¹³²**저는 우리가 이 목표를 달성할 수 있으리라 확신합니다.**

며칠 후 더 ¹³³**자세한 내용을** 알려드릴 예정입니다. ¹³⁴**그동안** 이 제도에 대한 질문이 있으시면 인사부서에 연락하십시오.

계속되는 성공을 기원하며,

최고 경영자 월터 C. 핸디

어휘 incentive 장려금, 장려책 quarter 분기 in addition to ~에 더하여 standard 표준의, 기본의 sales associate 영업사원 opportunity 기회 performance 공연 continued 지속적인

131 to부정사 _ 형용사적 용법

해설 빈칸은 명사구 tickets to concerts, sporting events, and

theater performances를 목적어로 취하면서 앞에 있는 명사 opportunity(동사 have의 목적어)를 수식하는 역할을 한다. opportunity는 to부정사와 함께 쓰여 '~할 기회'라는 뜻을 나타내므로, (A) to earn이 정답이다. (B) earning도 앞에 오는 명사를 수식할 수는 있지만(eg. people earning more than $150,000), 여기서 opportunity는 티켓을 얻는 주체가 아니므로 정답이 될 수 없다. 참고로, to부정사의 수식을 받는 명사에는 chance(기회), ability(능력), plan(계획) 등이 있다.

132 문맥에 맞는 문장 고르기

번역 (A) 회계연도는 10월에 종료됩니다.
(B) 저는 우리가 이 목표를 달성할 수 있으리라 확신합니다.
(C) 행사 참석은 의무입니다.
(D) TFF는 내년에 사무실 개조를 고려하고 있습니다.

해설 빈칸 앞 문장에서 추가 인센티브 제도는 올해를 사상 최대 판매를 기록한 해로 만들기 위해(to help make this our greatest sales year ever) 고안된 것이라고 했으므로, 빈칸에도 이러한 취지와 관련된 내용이 이어져야 문맥상 자연스럽다. 따라서 해당 목표를 달성할 수 있으리라 확신한다고 말한 (B)가 정답이다.

어휘 fiscal year 회계연도 confident 확신하는, 자신감 있는 attendance 참석 mandatory 의무적인 renovate 개조하다, 보수하다

133 명사 어휘

해설 빈칸은 동사 will be provided의 주어 역할을 하는 명사 자리이다. 앞서 언급된 인센티브 제도에 대해 더 자세한 내용을 알려주겠다고 하는 것이 가장 자연스러우므로, '세부 내용'이라는 의미의 (B) details가 정답이다.

어휘 supply 보급품 product 제품 receipt 영수증

134 접속부사

해설 앞 문장에서는 며칠 후 더 자세한 내용을 알려주겠다(More details will be provided in the next few days)고 했고, 빈칸 뒤에서는 그때까지 질문이 있을 경우 문의할 곳(if you have any questions about this program, contact the Human Resources Department)을 제시하고 있다. 따라서 '그동안에'라는 의미의 (D) In the meantime이 빈칸에 들어가야 자연스럽다.

어휘 similarly 마찬가지로 therefore 그러므로 above all 특히, 그 중에서도

135-138 정보

어카운터리움: 회계사들을 위한 계간지

기고 요청

올해 마지막 4분기 호에는 이직한 회계사들에 대한 특집 기사가 포함될 예정입니다. 회계사들이 획득한 재무 서비스 ¹³⁵역량은, 재무가 아닌 다른 분야의 직책을 채용하고자 하는 이들에게도 수요가 높습니다.

¹³⁶따라서 많은 전문 회계사들이 다른 역할을 맡으라는 권유를 받고 있습니다.

이와 같은 직업상의 변화가 있으셨다면 그에 관해 듣고 싶습니다. 회계 분야의 경력을 기술하고 그것이 새 직업에 ¹³⁷어떻게 유용한지 800자 이내로 적어 주세요. features@accountarium.com으로 문서를 첨부해서 보내주십시오. ¹³⁸제출 마감 기한은 10월 15일입니다. 유감스럽지만 해당 날짜 이후 수신된 제출물은 고려 대상이 될 수 없습니다.

어휘 -arium ~에 관련된 물건[장소] quarterly 분기별의 accountant 회계사 call for ~를 요청하다 submission 제출(물), (의견) 개진, 기고 feature 특집 기사 career shift 이직 financial 금융의, 재무의 in demand 수요가 많은 professional 전문적인, 직업의 persuade 설득하다, ~하라고 권유하다 take on a role 역할을 맡다 background 배경, 경력 profession 직업 attachment 첨부(물) regret 후회하다, 유감으로 여기다 consider 고려하다

135 명사 어휘

해설 빈칸은 that accountants gain의 수식을 받는 자리로, 회계사들이 획득한 것을 나타낸다. 따라서 (B) skills(역량, 기술)가 정답이다.

어휘 industry 산업 need 요구, 필요 field 분야

136 접속부사

해설 앞 문장에서는 회계사들의 역량이 재무 이외의 분야에서 채용하고자 하는 이들에게도 수요가 높다(The financial service skills that accountants gain are in demand even by those seeking to hire for positions outside of finance)고 했고, 빈칸 뒤에서는 많은 전문 회계사들이 다른 역할을 맡으라는 권유를 받고 있다(many professional accountants have been persuaded to take on other roles)고 했다. 뒤 문장이 필연적인 결과를 나타내므로, (D) Consequently(따라서)가 정답이다.

어휘 nevertheless 그럼에도 불구하고 once again 다시 한 번 in addition 게다가

137 명사절 접속사

해설 빈칸은 완전한 절(it is useful in your new profession)을 이끌어 동사 explain의 목적어 역할을 한다. 문맥상 그것이(it=your background in accounting) 새 직업에 어떻게 유용한지에 대해 글을 써달라는 내용이 되어야 자연스러우며, 완전한 절을 이끄는 명사절 접속사가 필요하다. 따라서 (C) how가 정답이다. 참고로, (A) what, (B) whose, (D) which가 의문형용사로서 명사절 접속사 역할을 할 경우, 바로 뒤에는 대명사가 아닌 일반 명사가 와야 한다.

138 문맥에 맞는 문장 고르기

번역 (A) 제출 마감 기한은 10월 15일입니다.
(B) 모든 경력 단계의 회계사를 채용합니다.
(C) 이 자격증은 널리 인정되고 있습니다.
(D) 오늘 수신된 귀하의 답장에 감사드립니다.

해설 빈칸 앞 문장에서는 글을 이메일로 보내달라고 했고, 뒤 문장에서는 '이 날짜' 이후 수신된 제출물은 고려 대상이 될 수 없다 (any submissions received after this date cannot be considered)고 했다. 따라서 빈칸에 제출 마감 기한이 언제인지 언급되어야 하므로, (A)가 정답이다.

어휘 deadline 마감 일자, 기한 at all stages of 모든 단계의 credential 자격증, 신임장 recognize 인정하다 response 응답

139-142 추천 글

수 개월 동안, 장 사무용품의 소유주인 이 장 씨는 **139매출**을 증대할 방법을 모색해 왔습니다. 그리고 정말 우연히 고객의 소리(VOC)라고 하는 접근법에 대해 듣게 됐습니다. "싱 마켓 리서치에 전화해 그 방법에 대한 설명을 들었을 때, 전 무척 흥미를 느꼈어요. 저와 얘기 나눈 상담원은 **140그걸** 한번 시도해보라고 설득하더군요." 장 씨는 VOC가 특정 대상을 목표로 하는 광고를 고안하는 수단으로 시장 조사를 이용한다는 사실을 알게 됐습니다. 그는 이 방법을 이용해 잠재 고객이 사무용품을 구입할 때 **141정확히** 어떤 점을 우려하고 어떤 것을 원하는지를 먼저 파악했습니다. 이후 자신의 웹사이트 광고를 만들기 위해 시장 조사에 참여한 사람들의 솔직한 말들을 그대로 인용했습니다. **142그는 다이렉트 이메일 광고에서도 그것들을 활용했습니다.** "VOC 덕분에 저의 고객층은 전에 없이 늘어났습니다." 그가 미소 지으며 말합니다.

어휘 office supply 사무용품 search for ~를 찾다 increase 증대시키다 by chance 우연히 sheer 순전한 approach 접근법, 처리 방법 intrigued 아주 흥미로워 하는 method 방법 present 제시하다, 설명하다 representative 직원, 대리인 convince 확신시키다, 설득하다 give it a try 시도하다, 한번 해보다 market research 시장 조사 aid 도움, 지원 targeted advertisement 특정 대상을 목표로 하는 광고 determine 알아내다, 밝히다 potential 잠재적인 be concerned about ~에 대해 우려하다, 걱정하다 candid 솔직한 quote 인용구 participate in ~에 참여하다 expand 확대되다

139 명사 어휘

해설 빈칸은 to increase의 목적어 자리로, 장 씨가 증대시키고자 한 것을 나타낸다. 뒤에서 효과적인 광고 방법에 대한 조언을 받아 고객층이 늘었다고 했으므로, 장 씨가 매출을 증대시킬 방법을 모색한 것임을 알 수 있다. 따라서 (C) sales가 정답이다.

어휘 production 제작 capacity 용량, 능력 wage 임금

140 대명사 어휘

해설 give의 목적어 자리로, 한번 시도(a try)를 해볼 만한 대상이 들어가야 한다. 문맥상 상담원이 '고객의 소리'라는 접근법(approach, method)을 시도해보라고 했다는 내용이 되어야 자연스러우므로, (B) it이 정답이다.

141 부사 자리

해설 he가 주어, determined가 동사, 명사절인 what potential customers are concerned about ~ when shopping for office supplies가 목적어인 완전한 문장이므로, 빈칸에는 문장 구성에 영향을 미치지 않는 부사가 들어가야 한다. 따라서 (A) exactly(정확히)가 정답이다. exactly는 종종 의문사와 결합해 이를 강조하는 역할을 한다(eg. exactly what/when/where). (B) exact는 형용사/동사, (C) exacting은 형용사/현재분사, (D) exactness는 명사로 구조상 빈칸에 들어갈 수 없다.

어휘 exact 정확한; 요구하다, 강요하다 exacting 힘든, 까다로운 exactness 정확함, 정밀성

142 문맥에 맞는 문장 고르기

번역 (A) 그는 11년간 사업을 해 왔습니다.
(B) 그는 다이렉트 이메일 광고에서도 그것들을 활용했습니다.
(C) 그는 지역 슈퍼마켓도 소유하고 있습니다.
(D) 그는 더 작은 건물로 이사할 계획입니다.

해설 빈칸 앞 문장에서 웹사이트 광고에 사람들의 솔직한 말을 인용했다(he used candid quotes from the people ~ to create advertisements for his Web site)고 했고, 뒤에서는 '고객의 소리(VOC)'라는 이 방식 덕분에 고객층이 늘었다고 했다. 따라서 빈칸에도 해당 방식과 관련된 내용이 들어가야 자연스러우므로, 다이렉트 이메일 광고에서도 그것들(=candid quotes from the people)을 활용했다고 한 (B)가 정답이다.

어휘 in business 사업을 하는, 영업을 하는 direct e-mail (소비자나 잠재 고객에게) 직접적으로 발송되는 이메일 local 지역의

143-146 공지

교통 혼잡을 줄이고 주차가 더 쉬워지도록, 뉴그레인지 타운십에서는 올해의 뉴그레인지 카운티 박람회를 오가는 무료 버스를 제공할 예정입니다. **143차량**은 6월 5일 금요일부터 6월 7일 일요일까지 이용 가능합니다. 계획된 픽업 장소에는 38번 도로의 라인스베르그 초등학교와 메인 가의 뉴그레인지 지자체 건물이 포함됩니다.

박람회장으로 가는 버스는 오전 8시부터 오후 5시까지 매시 정각에 해당 장소에서 출발합니다. 또한 오전 8시 30분부터 오후 7시 30분까지 30분마다 박람회장에서 버스가 **144출발합니다.** 16세 미만 어린이는 반드시 성인과 동행해야 합니다. **145버스 내 음식이나 음료 섭취는 불가합니다.**

뉴그레인지 카운티 박람회 위원회는 올해 버스 및 **146기사**를 제공해 주신 점에 대해 관대한 후원사들께 감사를 드립니다. 뉴그레인지 카운티 박람회를 함께해 주시기 바랍니다!

어휘 reduce 감소시키다 congestion 혼잡 township 지방 자치 단체, 구군(행정 단위) available 이용 가능한 elementary school 초등학교 municipal 지방 자치의 depart 출발하다, 떠나다 fairground 박람회장 accompany 동반하다, 동행하다 generous 관대한, 후한 sponsor 후원사, 후원자

143 명사 어휘

해설 빈칸 앞 문장에서 언급된 무료 버스(free bus rides)의 이용 가능 기간을 설명한 문장이다. 따라서 '교통편, 차량'이라는 의미의 (C) Transportation이 빈칸에 들어가야 자연스럽다.

어휘 refreshments 간식 information 정보 entertainment 유흥

144 동사 자리 _ 시제

해설 빈칸은 주어 Buses의 동사 자리로, the fairgrounds를 목적어로 취한다. 앞으로 열릴 지역 박람회에서 새롭게 제공되는 무료 버스의 출발 시간을 설명하는 문장인데, 바로 앞 문장에서 미래시제(will depart)가 쓰였으므로, 빈칸에도 미래시제가 들어가야 자연스럽다. 따라서 (A) will leave가 정답이다. (B) have left와 (D) left는 시제가 맞지 않으며, 동명사/현재분사인 (C) leaving은 본동사 자리에 들어갈 수 없으므로 오답이다.

145 문맥에 맞는 문장 고르기

번역 (A) 올해 자동차 전시회에 와 주셔서 감사합니다.
(B) 서비스 비용이 상승될 예정입니다.
(C) 호텔에 투숙하시는 동안 즐거우셨기를 바랍니다.
(D) 버스 내 음식이나 음료 섭취는 불가합니다.

해설 빈칸 앞 문장에서 16세 미만 어린이는 반드시 성인과 동행해야 한다(children under the age of 16 must be accompanied by an adult)며 버스 이용 시 주의할 사항을 고지했으므로, 빈칸에도 이와 비슷한 내용이 들어가야 문맥상 자연스럽다. 따라서 버스 내 음식이나 음료 섭취가 불가하다고 한 (D)가 정답이다.

어휘 permit 허가하다

146 명사 자리 _ 어휘

해설 앞에 나온 buses와 함께 동명사 providing의 목적어 역할을 하는 명사 자리이다. 후원사들이 박람회를 위해 버스와 함께 제공할 만한 것은 '기사들'이므로, (B) drivers가 정답이다. (D) drive도 명사로 쓰일 수 있지만, '자동차 여행, 충동, 추진력' 등을 뜻하므로 문맥상 어색하다.

어휘 drivable 주행 가능한

PART 7

147-148 이메일

수신: 와얀 카효

발신: 아디 스포츠 클럽

날짜: 3월 10일

제목: 통지서

카효 씨께,

본 이메일은 3월 5일 자 귀하의 편지가 수신되었음을 통지하기 위함입니다.

147귀하의 요청이 처리되었습니다. 귀하의 스포츠 클럽 회원권은 하단에 명시된 날짜에 종료될 예정입니다. 그때까지 저희 시설을 이용하고 단체 강좌에 참석하셔도 좋습니다. 148이 기한까지 사물함에서 개인 소지품을 비워 주십시오.

148종료 발효일: 3월 31일

감사합니다.

조디 소머즈, 고객 서비스 담당자

어휘 acknowledgement 답신, 접수 통지 acknowledge 받았음을 알리다 receipt 수신, 접수 be scheduled to ~할 예정이다 indicated 명시된 facilities 시설 attend 참석하다 personal belongings 개인 소지품 termination 종료 effective 실행되는, 발효되는

147 주제 / 목적

번역 이메일을 쓴 목적은?
(A) 정보 일부를 정정하려고
(B) 회원 할인을 제공하려고
(C) 새 단체 강좌를 홍보하려고
(D) 취소를 확정하려고

해설 두 번째 단락에서 카효 씨의 요청이 처리되었다고 한 후, 스포츠 클럽 회원권이 하단에 명시된 날짜에 종료될 예정(Your athletic club membership is scheduled to end on the date indicated below)이라고 했다. 따라서 회원권의 만료, 즉 회원 자격이 취소될 예정임을 알리는 이메일이라고 볼 수 있으므로, (D)가 정답이다.

어휘 correct 정정하다, 바로잡다 discount 할인 promote 홍보하다 cancellation 취소

148 세부 사항

번역 카효 씨는 3월 31일까지 무엇을 해야 하는가?
(A) 수표를 우편 발송하기
(B) 사물함 비우기
(C) 강사에게 편지 쓰기
(D) 소머즈 씨에게 전화하기

해설 3월 31일은 회원권이 만료되는 날(Termination effective: March 31)인데, 두 번째 단락을 보면 이 기한까지 사물함에서 개인 소지품을 비워야 한다(Please be sure to clear out your locker of any personal belongings by this deadline)고 되어 있다. 따라서 (B)가 정답이다.

어휘 instructor 강사

▸▸ Paraphrasing 지문의 clear out → 정답의 Empty

공지

9월 23일 월요일에, 컨스터레이션 인터넷 서비스가 이곳 블루스톤 타워에 새로운 최신 시스템을 설치할 예정입니다. 이날은 거의 인터넷 서비스가 되지 않을 것입니다. ¹⁴⁹이는 입주민들이 건물의 무선 네트워크에 접속할 수 없으며 저희 관리팀이나 유지보수 직원에게 이메일로 연락하실 수 없다는 의미입니다. ¹⁵⁰9월 23일 오전 9시에서 오후 5시 사이에 인터넷 접속이 필요하신 분은 다른 방법을 마련해야 할 것입니다. 불편을 드려 죄송합니다.

클레어 조
블루스톤 타워 건물 관리자

어휘 install 설치하다 state-of-the-art 최신의 resident 거주자, 입주민 access 접속하다 wireless 무선의 management 관리 maintenance 유지보수 require 요구하다, 필요로 하다 arrangement 방식, 준비, 마련 apologize for ~에 대해 사과하다 inconvenience 불편 property 건물, 부동산

149 추론 / 암시

번역 공지는 누구를 대상으로 하는가?

(A) 공사 인력
(B) 인터넷 제공업체
(C) 건물 입주민
(D) 유지보수 인부

해설 중반부에서 입주민들은 9월 23일에 건물의 무선 네트워크에 접속할 수 없으며 관리팀이나 유지보수 직원에게 이메일로 연락할 수 없다(residents will not be able to access the building's wireless network, ~ to contact our management or maintenance staff by e-mail)고 한 후, 필요 시 다른 방안을 찾으라고 공지했다. 따라서 건물 입주민을 대상으로 하는 공지라고 추론할 수 있으므로, (C)가 정답이다.

150 추론 / 암시

번역 공지는 9월 23일 오후 5시에 어떤 일이 있을 것을 암시하는가?

(A) 새 웹사이트가 개시될 것이다.
(B) 새 서비스 요금이 적용될 것이다.
(C) 건물 출입이 제한될 것이다.
(D) 인터넷 서비스가 복구될 것이다.

해설 후반부에서 9월 23일 오전 9시에서 오후 5시 사이에 인터넷에 접속해야 하는 사람은 다른 방법을 마련해야 한다(Those who require access to the Internet between 9:00 A.M. and 5:00 P.M. on 23 September will need to make other arrangements)고 공지한 것으로 보아, 오후 5시 이후에는 인터넷 사용이 가능해질 것임을 추론할 수 있다. 따라서 (D)가 정답이다.

어휘 charge 요금 take effect 시행되다, 발효되다, 적용되다 restrict 제한하다 restore 복구하다, 복원하다

수신: a.thompson@pepperfam.com
발신: customerservice@dixons_clothing.com
날짜: 11월 4일 오전 11시 31분
제목: 귀하의 최근 주문 건

톰슨 씨께,

저희 기록에 의하면 귀하의 딕슨 클로딩 주문번호 5409281이 배송되었습니다.

제품: 캔버스 우비 재킷 (남성용):	85달러
운송비:	4.50달러
합계:	89.50달러

귀하가 제품에 만족하셨는지 확인하는 일이 저희에게는 중요합니다. ^{151/152}그러니 질문, 의견, 우려사항 등이 있으시다면 월-금요일 오전 8시-오후 7시, 토-일요일 오전 10시-오후 5시 사이에 555-0142로 전화 주십시오. ¹⁵¹customerservice@dixons_clothing.com으로 이메일을 주셔도 됩니다. 다시 모실 수 있기를 고대합니다.

고객 서비스 부서
딕슨 클로딩

어휘 recent 최근의 deliver 배달하다 shipping fee 운송료 therefore 그러므로 concern 우려, 걱정 look forward to -ing ~하기를 고대하다

151 주제 / 목적

번역 이메일을 쓴 목적은?

(A) 고객에게 배송 지연을 알리려고
(B) 교환 요청을 확인하려고
(C) 주문 건에 대한 지불을 요청하려고
(D) 고객에게 피드백 제시 방법을 알리려고

해설 두 번째 단락에서 질문, 의견, 우려사항 등이 있다면 전화를 달라(if you have any questions, comments, or concerns about it, call us)고 했고, 이메일로도 가능하다(You can also e-mail us)고 덧붙였다. 피드백 제시 방법을 고객에게 알려주는 것이 이메일을 쓴 목적 중 하나라고 볼 수 있으므로, (D)가 정답이다.

어휘 delivery 배송 confirm 확인해 주다, 확정하다 request 요청; 요청하다 exchange 교환 payment 지불

▸▸ Paraphrasing 지문의 questions, comments, or concerns → 정답의 feedback

152 사실 관계 확인

번역 딕슨 클로딩에 대해 알 수 있는 것은?

(A) 여러 개의 지점이 있다.
(B) 무료 배송을 제공한다.
(C) 고객 서비스 직원과 매일 상담 가능하다.
(D) 웹사이트에 고객이 쓴 제품 리뷰가 있다.

TEST 7

해설 두 번째 단락을 보면 월-금요일 오전 8시-오후 7시, 토-일요일 오전 10시-오후 5시 사이에 고객 서비스 부에 연락할 수 있음(call us at 555-0142, Monday through Friday between 8:00 A.M. and 7:00 P.M., and Saturday and Sunday between 10:00 A.M. and 5:00 P.M.)을 알 수 있다. 즉 평일과 주말 모두 상담이 가능한 것이므로, (C)가 정답이다.

어휘 free shipping 무료 배송 available 이용 가능한, 시간이 있는 feature 보여주다, 특집으로 다루다

> **▶▶ Paraphrasing** 지문의 Monday through Friday ~ and Saturday and Sunday
> → 정답의 daily

153-154 문자 메시지

리앤 올리버 (오전 9시 20분)
안녕하세요, 라파엘. ¹⁵³오늘 오후 채용위원회 회의에 오실 예정인가요?

라파엘 소세다 (오전 9시 21분)
계획에 없었어요. 제가 거기 있어야 할까요?

리앤 올리버 (오전 9시 22분)
¹⁵³그 직책에 예상했던 것보다 많은 지원자가 지원했어요. 누구를 면접할지 결정해야 하는데 당신의 전문 지식이 굉장히 유용할 것 같아요.

라파엘 소세다 (오전 9시 23분)
¹⁵⁴기꺼이 도와드려야죠. 4시 맞죠?

리앤 올리버 (오전 9시 24분)
정확해요. B 회의실입니다. 거기서 봬요. 감사합니다.

어휘 committee 위원회 candidate 지원자, 후보자 apply for ~에 지원하다 anticipate 예상하다 expertise 전문 지식 exactly 정확히, 꼭 conference 회의

153 세부 사항

번역 올리버 씨가 언급한 회의의 목적은?
(A) 공석 지원자를 면접하려고
(B) 채용공고를 승인하려고
(C) 직책에 맞는 지원자를 고려하려고
(D) 채용위원회 위원을 선발하려고

해설 올리버 씨가 오전 9시 20분 메시지에서 오늘 오후에 채용위원회 회의(the hiring committee meeting this afternoon)가 예정되어 있다고 말한 후, 9시 22분 메시지에서 누구를 면접할지 결정해야 한다(We need to decide who to interview)고 했다. 따라서 면접에 적합한 지원자를 선별하는 것이 회의의 목적이라고 볼 수 있으므로, (C)가 정답이다.

어휘 approve 승인하다 job announcement 채용공고 applicant 지원자

> **▶▶ Paraphrasing** 지문의 candidates
> → 정답의 applicants

154 의도 파악

번역 오전 9시 24분에 올리버 씨가 "정확해요"라고 쓸 때, 그 의도는 무엇인가?
(A) 회의실은 4층에 있다.
(B) 회의는 오후 4시로 예정되어 있다.
(C) 4명이 회의에 참석할 예정이다.
(D) 위원회는 네 차례 회의할 것이다.

해설 소세다 씨가 오전 9시 23분에 회의 참석 요청을 승낙하며 4시가 맞는지(It's at 4, right?) 물어봤는데, 이에 대해 올리버 씨가 '정확해요(Exactly)'라고 응답했다. 즉, 회의가 4시임을 확인해 준 것이므로, (B)가 정답이다.

어휘 be scheduled for ~로 예정되어 있다 attend 참석하다

155-157 기사

제조업체, 중요한 시점을 경축하다

미니애폴리스 (8월 13일)—정밀기계 부품 제조업체인 린드그렌 머시너리는 최근 창립 100주년을 경축했다. ¹⁵⁵이 회사는 조나 린드그렌이 창업했는데, 그는 스웨덴의 금속 부품 업체에서 견습공으로 일을 시작했다. 결국 미국으로 이주해 미니애폴리스 시 외곽에 정착했다. 린드그렌 씨는 수익의 대부분을 주문 제작 기계 부품 생산에서 창출하며 성장하는 소규모 회사를 설립했다.

¹⁵⁵30년 전, 린드그렌 머시너리는 제임스 월린에게 매각됐다. ¹⁵⁵/¹⁵⁷오늘날 이 회사는 가족 소유 및 경영 사업체로 유지되고 있다. 현재 회장이자 최고 경영자인 메리 월린은 최근 몇 년간 부친으로부터 대표의 역할을 점차 ¹⁵⁶가져왔다.

린드그렌 머시너리는 항공기, 운동장비, 의료기기 부품을 제조한다. 월린 씨에 따르면, 제품 목록이 늘어나고 다각화함에 따라 회사의 시설을 확충하고 생산력을 증대할 계획이라고 한다.

어휘 manufacturer 제조업체 milestone 이정표, 획기적인 사건 precision 정밀 anniversary 기념일 founding 창립 apprentice 견습공 eventually 결국 immigrate 이주하다 settle 정착하다 outskirt 교외, 변두리 establish 설립하다 modest 소규모의, 그리 대단하지 않은 generate 발생시키다 revenue 수익, 수입 custom 주문 제작의 purchase 구입하다, 매입하다 operation 사업체 current 현재의 gradually 점차 assume (역할 등을) 맡다 equipment 장비 expand 확대하다 facility 시설 capacity (공장 등의) 생산 능력 diversify 다각화하다

155 주제 / 목적

번역 기사를 쓴 주된 목적은?
(A) 회사의 공석을 알리려고
(B) 회사의 이전에 대해 이야기하려고
(C) 회사의 역사를 요약하려고
(D) 성공적인 제조 전략에 대해 설명하려고

해설 첫 번째 단락에서 회사의 창업(The company was started by

Jona Lindgren) 과정을 설명한 뒤, 두 번째 단락에서 매각된 시기(Thirty years ago, Lindgren Machinery was purchased by James Wallin)와 현 소유주에 대해 서술하고 있다. 즉, 100주년을 맞이한 린드그렌 머시너리의 역사를 개괄한 기사이므로, (C)가 정답이다.

어휘 announce 발표하다, 알리다 relocation 이전, 재배치 summarize 요약하다 strategy 전략

156 동의어 찾기

번역 두 번째 단락, 여섯 번째 줄에 쓰인 "assumed"와 의미가 가장 가까운 단어는?

(A) 책임을 맡았다
(B) ~인 척 행동했다
(C) 생각했다
(D) 시도했다

해설 'assumed'가 포함된 부분은 '부친으로부터 대표의 역할을 가져왔다'라는 의미로 해석되는데, 여기서 assumed는 '(역할 등을) 맡았다'라는 뜻이다. 따라서 '(일, 책임 등을) 맡았다'라는 의미의 (A) undertaken이 정답이다.

157 사실 관계 확인

번역 린드그렌 머시너리에 대해 현재 사실인 것은?

(A) 새로운 경영진을 교육하고 있다.
(B) 최근 본사를 이전했다.
(C) 시에서 직원을 가장 많이 고용한 회사다.
(D) 가족이 경영하는 업체다.

해설 두 번째 단락에서 '오늘날 이 회사는 가족 소유 및 경영 사업체로 유지되고 있다(Today, the firm continues as a family-owned and family-directed operation)'고 했으므로, (D)가 정답이다.

어휘 management 경영진 headquarters 본사

▸▸ Paraphrasing 지문의 family-directed operation
→ 정답의 family-operated business

158-160 이메일

발신: 예약 ⟨reservations@panticohotels.com⟩
수신: 로저 언더힐 ⟨runderhill@monthpress.com⟩
날짜: 2월 10일
제목: 판티코 리스본

언더힐 씨께,

판티코 호텔 그룹에 예약해 주셔서 감사합니다. 3월 8일부터 3월 12일까지 리스본에 있는 저희 호텔에 투숙하실 것을 고대하고 있습니다.

158저희는 24시간 커피숍, 피트니스 센터, 비즈니스 라운지 등을 비롯해 다양한 서비스를 제공해 드리고 있습니다. 차로 여행하길 원하시는 159투숙객을 위한 주차 공간도 마련되어 있습니다. 하지만, 판티코 리스본은 위치가 좋으며, 수많은 고급 쇼핑, 오락, 식사 장소까지 도보로 갈

수 있는 거리에 있습니다. 또한 대중교통을 편리하게 이용하실 수 있으며, 요금을 지불하시면 공항 교통편도 예약 가능합니다.

160저희에 대해 더 많은 내용을 알고 싶으시면, 웹사이트 www. panticohotels.com/lisbon을 방문하세요. 호텔 및 주변 지역에서 앞으로 열릴 행사 관련 세부사항이 담긴 일정표도 찾아보실 수 있습니다.

질문이나 우려 사항이 있으시면 본 이메일에 바로 회신 주시기 바랍니다.

브랜카 로페스
판티코 리스본 호텔

어휘 reservation 예약 book 예약하다 upcoming 다가오는, 곧 있을 a range of 다양한 well situated 위치가 좋은 be within walking distance 걸어서 갈 수 있는 거리에 있다 public transportation 대중교통 transfer 이동, 환승 surrounding 인근의, 주위의 concern 우려, 걱정

158 주제 / 목적

번역 이메일을 쓴 주된 목적은?

(A) 객실 예약 건에 변경을 요청하려고
(B) 호텔 신입 직원을 소개하려고
(C) 호텔 편의시설에 대해 설명하려고
(D) 최근 고객에게 의견을 구하려고

해설 첫 번째 단락에서 호텔에 예약해 준 것에 대해 감사를 표한 뒤, 두 번째 단락에서 24시간 커피숍, 피트니스 센터, 비즈니스 라운지 등을 비롯해 다양한 서비스를 제공한다(We are proud to offer a range of services)며 호텔 시설에 대해 중점적으로 설명하고 있다. 따라서 (C)가 정답이다.

어휘 description 서술 amenities 편의시설 obtain 얻다, 구하다

▸▸ Paraphrasing 지문의 24-hour coffee shop, a fitness center, a business lounge, a parking area
→ 정답의 hotel amenities

159 세부 사항

번역 호텔은 투숙객에게 무엇을 제공하는가?

(A) 무료 공항 셔틀 서비스
(B) 주차 시설
(C) 지역 내 식당 식사권
(D) 가이드가 동행하는 시티 투어

해설 두 번째 단락에서 투숙객을 위한 주차 공간도 마련되어 있다(There is also a parking are for guests)고 했으므로, 보기 중에서는 (B)가 정답이다. 참고로, 공항 교통편은 유료(for a fee)로 예약이 가능하다고 했으므로 (A)는 명백한 오답이다.

어휘 complimentary 무료의 voucher 쿠폰, 상품권

▸▸ Paraphrasing 지문의 a parking area
→ 정답의 A parking facility

160 세부 사항

번역 이메일에 따르면, 언더힐 씨는 웹사이트에서 무엇을 볼 수 있는가?

    (A) 행사 관련 정보
    (B) 지역 지도
    (C) 직원 목록
    (D) 상세 영수증

해설 세 번째 단락을 보면, 웹사이트에서 앞으로 열릴 행사 관련 세부사항이 담긴 일정표를 찾아볼 수 있다(A calendar with details about upcoming events ~ can be found there)고 되어 있다. 따라서 (A)가 정답이다.

> **Paraphrasing** 지문의 details about upcoming events
> → 정답의 Information about some events

161-163 편지

11월 23일

마테오 페르난데즈
레볼 가 5196번지
레이크턴, 캘리포니아 97999

페르난데즈 씨께,

¹⁶¹하단에 명시된 귀하의 면허증이 올해 말 만료될 예정임을 알려드리고자 글을 씁니다.

¹⁶²면허 유형: 오토바이

면허 번호: 297461

만료일: 12월 31일

주 법률에 따라 모터가 달린 모든 운송수단의 면허는 정기적으로 갱신되어야 합니다. 비용은 선박 및 스노모빌 20달러, ¹⁶²오토바이 30달러, 자동차 40달러, 트럭 50달러입니다. 트럭 면허에 해당하는 추가 요건 및 기타 유형의 운송수단 면허 비용과 관련된 내용은 웹사이트 www.motorvehiclelicense.net을 확인하십시오.

¹⁶³온라인으로 갱신하는 것이 빠르고 쉽습니다. 그렇게 하시려면 저희 웹사이트를 방문하세요. 우편으로도 갱신 가능합니다. 이 옵션을 선택하실 경우, 본 고지서 사본을 비용과 함께 귀하의 지역에 있는 모터 운송수단 면허청 사무실로 보내주십시오.

베티 차이
행정담당자, 모터 운송수단 면허청

어휘 notify 알리다 license 면허 described 명시된, 설명된 expire 만료되다 require 요구하다, 필요로 하다 motor vehicle 모터가 달린 운송수단 renew 갱신하다 periodically 정기적으로 regarding ~에 관해 requirement 요구사항, 요건 administrator 행정인, 관리자

161 주제 / 목적

번역 편지를 쓴 목적은?

    (A) 요금 인상 이유를 설명하려고
    (B) 면허 현황을 제공하려고
    (C) 레이크턴에서의 회의 일정을 잡으려고
    (D) 사용자의 신분증 번호를 업데이트하려고

해설 첫 번째 단락에서 페르난데즈 씨의 면허증이 올해 말 만료될 예정임을 알리고자 글을 쓴다(We are writing to notify you that your license ~ will expire at the end of the year)고 했으므로, (B)가 정답이다.

어휘 status 상태, 상황 identification 신원, 신분

162 세부 사항

번역 편지에 따르면, 페르난데즈 씨는 얼마를 지불해야 하는가?

    (A) 20달러
    (B) 30달러
    (C) 40달러
    (D) 50달러

해설 페르난데즈 씨의 면허 유형은 오토바이(License Type: Motorcycle)인데, 두 번째 단락을 보면 오토바이 면허 갱신 수수료가 30달러($30 for motorcycle licenses)임을 알 수 있다. 따라서 (B)가 정답이다.

163 문장 삽입

번역 [1], [2], [3], [4]로 표시된 곳 중에서 다음 문장이 가장 적합한 곳은?

"그렇게 하시려면 저희 웹사이트를 방문하세요."

    (A) [1]
    (B) [2]
    (C) [3]
    (D) [4]

해설 주어진 문장에서 그렇게 하려면 웹사이트를 방문하라(To do so, please visit our Web site)고 했으므로, 웹사이트를 통해 할 수 있는 것이 앞에서 먼저 언급되어야 한다. [3] 앞에서 온라인으로 갱신하는 것이 빠르고 쉽다(It is quick and easy to renew online)고 했으므로, 이 뒤에 주어진 문장이 들어가야 자연스럽다. 따라서 (C)가 정답이다.

164-167 온라인 채팅

데이비드 탐 [오전 8시 4분] 안녕하세요, 켈리, 조나단. 다음 주에 홍콩에서 누가 도착할지 확정됐나요?

켈리 크롬웰 [오전 8시 5분] ¹⁶⁴/¹⁶⁵홍콩 사무실에서 사라 왕과 네하 아가월을 보낼 예정입니다. 다른 사람들은 필요 시 전화로 참여할 수 있어요.

데이비드 탐 [오전 8시 7분] 사라와 네하는 도착하면 어디서 일하죠?

켈리 크롬웰 [오전 8시 9분] B 회의실에 자리잡을 겁니다. 그렇지 않으면 인사부서 마이클 클라인 근처에 있는 빈 책상을 사용할 수 있고요.

조나단 리 [오전 8시 11분] 잠시만요. 사실 세 명이 되겠네요. ¹⁶⁵릴리안 장도 오거든요.

데이비드 탐 [오전 8시 12분] 그럼 다른 업무공간이 필요하겠군요. 그들이 함께 있었으면 합니다. 회계부서에 여분의 사무실이 있을 것 같은데요.

켈리 크롬웰 [오전 8시 13분] ¹⁶⁶장 씨는 왜 오는 거죠? 마케팅 팀만인 줄 알았는데요.

조나단 리 [오전 8시 14분] ¹⁶⁶이번 프로젝트에서는 포장재 디자이너들이 마케팅 부서와 긴밀히 협력해오고 있거든요.

켈리 크롬웰 [오전 8시 17분] 알겠습니다. 제가 처리할게요. 점심시간 전에 최종 일정표를 보내드리겠습니다. ¹⁶⁷조나단, 전화 참석자 명단과 번호를 업데이트해서 우리 모두에게 보내주세요.

어휘 confirm 확인해 주다, 확정하다 conference 회의 otherwise 그렇지 않으면 Human Resources 인사부 actually 사실 accounting 회계 packaging 포장재 participant 참석자

164 세부 사항

번역 홍콩 사무실에서 누가 방문할 예정인가?
(A) 탐 씨
(B) 크롬웰 씨
(C) 아가왈 씨
(D) 클라인 씨

해설 크롬웰 씨의 오전 8시 5분 메시지를 보면, 홍콩 사무실에서 사라 왕과 네하 아가왈을 보낼 예정(The Hong Kong office is sending Sara Wang and Neha Agarwal)이라고 했으므로, 보기 중에서는 (C)가 정답이다.

165 의도 파악

번역 리 씨가 오전 8시 11분에 "세 명이 되겠네요"라고 쓸 때, 그 의도는 무엇인가?
(A) 또 다른 방문자가 도착할 것이다.
(B) 다른 회의실을 이용할 수 있다.
(C) 회계부서에 여러 개의 개방형 업무공간이 있다.
(D) 일정표에 회의들이 진행될 하루가 더 포함될 것이다.

해설 크롬웰 씨와 탐 씨가 홍콩 지사에서 오는 직원 두 명이 사용할 업무공간에 대한 대화를 나누던 도중, 리 씨가 '세 명이 되겠네요(there are going to be three)'라고 한 후 릴리안 장도 온다(Lillian Zhang is coming, too)고 덧붙였다. 따라서 세 번째 방문자가 있다는 사실을 알리려는 의도라고 볼 수 있으므로, (A)가 정답이다.

어휘 additional 추가의 available 이용 가능한

166 추론 / 암시

번역 장 씨는 누구이겠는가?
(A) 회계사
(B) 인사부서 직원
(C) 마케팅 전문가
(D) 포장재 디자이너

해설 크롬웰 씨가 오전 8시 13분 메시지에서 장 씨가 오는 이유를 물으며 본인은 마케팅 팀만 오는 줄 알았다(Why is Ms. Zhang coming? I thought it was just the marketing team)고 하자, 리 씨가 8시 14분 메시지에서 이번 프로젝트에서는 포장재 디자이너들이 마케팅 부서와 긴밀히 협력하고 있다(The packaging designers have been working closely with Marketing on this project)며 장 씨가 오는 이유를 우회적으로 드러냈다. 이를 통해 장 씨가 마케팅 팀 소속이 아닌 포장재 디자이너로서 함께 오는 것임을 추론할 수 있으므로, (D)가 정답이다.

167 세부 사항

번역 크롬웰 씨는 리 씨에게 무엇을 하라고 요청하는가?
(A) 회의 일정표 출력
(B) 연락처 목록 준비
(C) 점심 메뉴 배포
(D) 방문자를 사무실로 배정

해설 크롬웰 씨가 오전 8시 17분 메시지에서 리 씨에게 전화 참석자 명단과 번호를 업데이트해서 모두에게 보내달라(Jonathan, please update the list of call-in participants' names and numbers and send it to all of us)고 했으므로, (B)가 정답이다.

어휘 distribute 분배하다, 배포하다 assign 배정하다, 배치하다

▸▸ Paraphrasing 지문의 update the list of call-in participants' names and numbers
→ 정답의 Prepare a list of contacts

168-171 정보

제안서 요청

목적
¹⁶⁸뉴랭스턴 시에서는 시 전역의 버스 정류장 전광판 제작 및 설치를 위한 제안을 구하고 있습니다. ¹⁶⁹뉴랭스턴은 버스 탑승자들에게 실시간 도착 정보를 보여줄 새로운 전광판을 배치할 계획입니다.

배경
현재 뉴랭스턴의 버스 정류장은 정류장 위치 및 해당 위치에 정차하는 노선들만 보여주는 단순한 금속 알림판으로 표시되어 있습니다. 전 세계의 도시들은 버스 정류장 표지판에 실시간 도착 정보를 포함하기 시작했습니다. 전광판은 탑승자들에게 매우 호응이 높은 것으로 입증되고 있으며, ¹⁷⁰연구들은 이러한 전광판의 도입이 수많은 도시에서 승객 수가 증가한 데 일조했음을 보여줍니다.

프로젝트 설명
선발된 입찰사는 뉴랭스턴 시에 최대 350개의 전광판을 제공하게 됩니

다. ^{171 (A)}전광판은 태양 에너지로 작동되어야 하며 ^{171 (B)}야간, 흐린 날 및 모든 기상 상황에서 작동할 수 있도록 하는 예비 배터리 장치가 있어야 합니다. ^{171 (C)}전광판은 최소 99퍼센트의 신뢰도를 가져야 합니다. 전광판에는 최소 3줄에서 최대 5줄의 글이 표시되어야 하며, 버스 탑승자들에게 실시간 정보를 제공하기 위해 인터넷에 연결되어야 합니다.

비용을 정리한 자세한 입찰 내용을 5월 31일 밤 11시 59분까지 뉴랭스턴 시 지역위원회 regionalcouncil@cityofnewlangston.gov로 제출해 주십시오.

어휘 request 요청 proposal 제안, 제안서 manufacture 제조 installation 설치 electronic signage 전광판 deploy 배치하다 display 보여주다, 드러내다 real-time 실시간의 arrival 도착 incorporate 포함시키다 contribute 기여하다, 공헌하다 ridership 이용자 수, 승객 수 numerous 수많은 bidder 응찰자, 입찰사 solar energy 태양 에너지 reliability factor 신뢰도, 신뢰지수 be connected to ~에 연결되다 submit 제출하다 outline 정리하다, 개요를 설명하다 regional 지역의

168 주제 / 목적

번역 정보의 목적은?

(A) 시의 대중교통 문제를 상세히 알려주려고
(B) 시의 프로젝트에 입찰을 요청하려고
(C) 버스 이용 수요의 역사를 설명하려고
(D) 환경적 책임을 고취하려고

해설 첫 번째 단락에서 뉴랭스턴 시 전역의 버스 정류장 전광판 제작 및 설치를 위한 제안을 구하고 있다(The City of New Langston is seeking proposals for the manufacture and installation of electronic signage at bus stops throughout the city)고 한 후, 아래에서 입찰 방법을 안내했다. 따라서 (B)가 정답이다.

어휘 public transportation 대중교통 solicit 간청하다, 얻으려고 하다 encourage 장려하다, 고취하다 environmental 환경의 responsibility 책임

169 사실 관계 확인

번역 제안되는 표지판에 대해 명시된 것은?

(A) 뉴랭스턴의 현재 버스 정류장 표지판과 정확히 똑같이 보일 것이다.
(B) 뉴랭스턴에 소재한 회사에서 제조될 것이다.
(C) 탑승자들에게 다음 버스 도착에 대해 알릴 것이다.
(D) 한 달에 한 번만 프로그램이 설정될 것이다.

해설 첫 번째 단락에서 버스 탑승자들에게 실시간 도착 정보를 보여줄 새로운 전광판을 배치할 계획(New Langston plans to deploy new electronic signs that display real-time arrival information to bus riders)이라고 했으므로, 제안되는 표지판에 다음 버스의 도착 시간이 나와야 함을 알 수 있다. 따라서 (C)가 정답이다.

어휘 current 현재의

170 세부 사항

번역 정보에 따르면, 다른 도시들의 전광판 설치 결과는 어떠했는가?

(A) 대중교통 이용 증가
(B) 버스 요금 상승
(C) 버스 정류장 조명 개선
(D) 정시 도착 버스 증가

해설 두 번째 단락의 후반부를 보면, 실시간 버스 정보를 알려주는 전광판의 도입이 승객 수 증가에 일조했다(the introduction of such signage has contributed to increased ridership in numerous cities)는 것을 연구에서 보여준다고 했다. 따라서 (A)가 정답이다.

어휘 fare 요금 lighting 조명

▸▸ Paraphrasing 지문의 ridership
→ 정답의 use of public transportation

171 사실 관계 확인

번역 새 표지판에 대한 요구사항이 아닌 것은?

(A) 태양 에너지로 작동해야 한다.
(B) 우천시에 작동해야 한다.
(C) 신뢰할 수 있어야 한다.
(D) 정보를 컬러로 보여줘야 한다.

해설 세 번째 단락의 '전광판은 태양 에너지(solar energy)로 작동해야 하며 야간, 흐린 날 및 모든 기상 상황에서(at night, on cloudy days, and in all weather conditions) 작동할 수 있도록 하는 예비 배터리 장치가 있어야 한다'에서 (A)와 (B)를, '전광판은 최소 99퍼센트의 신뢰도(a reliability factor of at least 99 percent)를 가져야 한다'에서 (C)를 확인할 수 있다. 따라서 언급되지 않은 (D)가 정답이다.

어휘 reliable 믿을 만한

▸▸ Paraphrasing 지문의 operate ~ in all weather conditions
→ 보기 (B)의 operate in the rain
지문의 have a reliability factor of at least 99 percent → 보기 (C)의 be reliable

172-175 채용공고

하급 프로젝트 관리자

트래스킨 홍보 회사
시애틀, 워싱턴

트래스킨 홍보 회사는 접객업에 주력하는 마케팅 홍보 업체입니다. 시애틀에 본사를 두고 있으며, 20년 이상 영업해 왔습니다. ¹⁷²**근래의 빠른 사세 확장에 발맞추기 위해, 트래스킨에서 새로운 하급 프로젝트 관리자를 찾습니다.** 귀중한 전략적, 창의적 과정 속에서 훈련을 받을 수 있는 기회입니다. ¹⁷³**본 교육 프로그램은 현재 상급 프로젝트 관리자로 있는 여러 사람의 출발점이 되기도 했습니다.** 트래스킨은 전 직원에게 타사에 뒤지지 않는 대우와 혜택을 제공합니다.

책무에는 관리자 및 고객과의 조정, 회의 및 발표 일정 잡기, 예산 관리 등이 포함됩니다. 아울러, ¹⁷⁴합격자는 내부 팀원 및 고객을 위한 주간 최신 소식 이메일을 작성하게 됩니다.

¹⁷⁵자격 요건은 유사한 대행사에서 최소 2년 이상의 관리 경력, 프로젝트 관리 소프트웨어 관련 지식, 뛰어난 조직력입니다. 예산 준비 경력은 가산점이 됩니다.

careers@traskinpr.com에 이력서와 자기소개서를 올려주세요.

어휘 public relations 홍보 focus on ~에 중점을 두다 hospitality 환대, (접객) 서비스업 be based 본사를 두다 keep up with ~를 따라잡다, ~에 뒤지지 않다 expansion 확장, 확대 valuable 귀중한 strategic 전략적인 creative 창의적인 serve as ~의 역할을 하다 competitive 경쟁력 있는, 뒤지지 않는 compensation 보상 benefit 혜택 responsibility 책임 coordinate 조정하다 budget 예산 additionally 게다가 successful applicant 합격자 qualification 자격 similar 유사한 knowledge 지식 organizational 조직의

172 사실 관계 확인

번역 트래스킨 홍보 회사에 대해 명시된 것은?

(A) 신생업체이다.
(B) 해외 지사들이 있다.
(C) 웹사이트 개발에 중점을 둔다.
(D) 규모가 커지고 있다.

해설 첫 번째 단락에서 근래의 빠른 사세 확장에 발맞추기 위해(To keep up with our recent rapid expansion, Traskin is now seeking a new junior project manager) 새로운 하급 프로젝트 관리자를 찾고 있다고 했으므로, 회사가 성장 중임을 알 수 있다. 따라서 (D)가 정답이다.

어휘 development 개발

▸ Paraphrasing 지문의 expansion
→ 정답의 growing in size

173 추론 / 암시

번역 광고된 직책에 대해 암시된 것은?

(A) 출장 기회를 제공한다.
(B) 신입사원 교육 경력을 필요로 한다.
(C) 승진으로 이어질 수 있다.
(D) 임시직이다.

해설 첫 번째 단락에서 하급 프로젝트 관리자가 받는 교육 프로그램은 현재 상급 프로젝트 관리자로 있는 여러 사람의 출발점이 되기도 했다(This training program served as the starting point for several of our current senior project managers)고 했다. 따라서 이들이 junior project manager로 시작해 senior project manager로 승진했음을 추론할 수 있으므로, (C)가 정답이다.

어휘 lead to ~로 이어지다 promotion 승진 temporary 임시의

174 세부 사항

번역 해당 직책의 책무는?

(A) 정기적으로 최신 소식 발송
(B) 주간 팀 회의 주재
(C) 시장 조사 실시
(D) 팀원들에게 업무 배정

해설 두 번째 단락에서 합격자는 내부 팀원 및 고객을 위한 주간 최신 소식 이메일 작성을 하게 된다(the successful applicant will create weekly e-mail updates for internal teammates and clients)고 했으므로, (A)가 정답이다.

어휘 regularly 정기적으로 conduct 실시하다 market research 시장 조사 assign 배당하다, 배정하다

▸ Paraphrasing 지문의 weekly → 정답의 regularly

175 문장 삽입

번역 [1], [2], [3], [4]로 표시된 곳 중에서 다음 문장이 가장 적합한 곳은?

"예산 준비 경력은 가산점이 됩니다."

(A) [1]
(B) [2]
(C) [3]
(D) [4]

해설 주어진 문장에서 예산 준비 경력은 가산점이 된다(Experience preparing budgets is a plus)며 우대 조건을 제시했으므로, 이 앞에 필수 요건이 먼저 언급되어야 한다. [4] 앞에서 자격 요건(Qualifications)이 나열되었으므로, 이 뒤에 주어진 문장이 들어가야 자연스럽다. 따라서 (D)가 정답이다.

176-180 웹페이지 + 이메일

https://www.zoliorentals.ca

졸리오 렌탈 주식회사는 시간별 또는 일별 대여가 가능한 중장비 및 공사 도구를 다수 보유하고 있습니다. 귀하의 작업이 어떤 것이든, 그 일을 처리하시는 데 필요한 것을 저희가 갖추고 있을 것입니다. 캐나다 전역에 50개가 넘는 지점이 있으며, ¹⁷⁶일부 매장에서는 제한적으로 배송도 가능합니다. 도움이 필요하시면 604-555-0129로 전화하시거나 info@zoliorentals.ca로 이메일을 보내주세요.

검색:

도랑 파는 기계

결과:

	45cm 트렌처	60cm 트렌처
4시간 대여	166달러	194달러
24시간 대여	¹⁸⁰237달러	275달러

어휘   inventory 물품 (목록)   heavy machine 중장비
construction 공사, 건설   available 이용 가능한   tackle
처리하다, (힘든 문제 상황과) 씨름하다   location 매장, 지점
limited 한정된, 제한된   delivery 배송   assistance 도움, 지원
trench 도랑   trencher 트렌처, 도랑 파는 기계

수신: 샬라 스탠턴 〈sharla@stantonacres.ca〉
발신: 랄프 피츠패트릭 〈rfitzpatrick@fitzgreenways.ca〉
날짜: 4월 6일
제목: 트렌처 기계

안녕하세요, 샬라.

당신의 토지에 관개 도랑을 파야 할 것 같다고 지난번에 말씀하신 적 있
었잖아요. 저도 마찬가지였고요. 그래서 제가 졸리오 렌탈 웹사이트에
서 검색했고, 180이용 가능한 가장 작은 트렌처를 내일 대여하기로 결정
했다는 걸 알려드리고 싶었어요. 저는 기계가 한두 시간만 필요해요. 그
런데 가장 가까운 대여점이 여기서 45분 거리인 더럼에 있고 제 트럭에
실어 집과 더럼을 오고 가는 데 시간이 걸릴 것 같아서, 177/180전일 대
여하기로 결정했어요.

177/179저에게 기계가 있는 동안 사용하시겠어요? 만약 그렇다면 일정
을 조정해서 제가 마치고 난 후 가져다 드릴 수 있어요. 179그러면 그 다
음날 아침 제가 졸리오 렌탈에 트렌처를 반납할 수 있고요. 대여료 전액
은 기꺼이 제가 178부담할게요. 지난 가을 잔디 깎는 기계를 쓸 때 도와
주신 것에 대한 제 답례입니다. 알려주세요.

랄프

어휘   mention 언급하다   anticipate 예상하다   irrigation 관개
property 부동산, 토지   coordinate 조정하다   entire 전체의
lawn mower 잔디 깎는 기계

176   세부 사항

번역   웹페이지에서 졸리오 렌탈에 대해 무엇이라고 설명하는가?

(A) 물품 목록을 확장하고 있다.
(B) 새로운 고객 서비스 담당자들을 교육시키고 있다.
(C) 특정 지역에 장비를 배송해 줄 수 있다.
(D) 최근 지점들을 열었다.

해설   웹페이지의 세 번째 문장에서 일부 매장에서는 제한적으로 배송도 가
능하다(with limited delivery available in some locations)고
했으므로, (C)가 정답이다.

어휘   equipment 장비   branch 지점

▶▶ Paraphrasing   지문의 with limited delivery available in
some locations
→ 정답의 deliver equipment to certain areas

177   주제 / 목적

번역   피츠패트릭 씨가 이메일을 쓴 이유는?

(A) 도움을 제공하려고
(B) 실수에 대해 사과하려고
(C) 제품에 관한 피드백을 요청하려고
(D) 프로젝트를 연기하려고

해설   이메일의 첫 번째 단락에서 피츠패트릭 씨는 도랑 파는 기계를 대여했
다고 한 후, 두 번째 단락에서 샬라 씨가 원한다면 사용 후 가져다 줄
수 있다(Would you want to use the machine while I have it?
If so, we can coordinate our schedules, and I can bring it
to you after I finish)고 했다. 따라서 도움을 제공하고자 쓴 이메일
임을 알 수 있으므로, (A)가 정답이다.

어휘   apologize 사과하다   oversight 실수, 간과   postpone 연기하다

178   동의어 찾기

번역   이메일의 두 번째 단락, 세 번째 줄에 쓰인 "cover"와 의미가 가장 가
까운 단어는?

(A) ~에 대해 보고하다
(B) 보호하다
(C) 숨기다
(D) ~의 값을 지불하다

해설   'cover'가 포함된 부분은 '대여료 전액을 부담하겠다'라는 의미로 해석
되는데, 여기서 cover는 '요금 등을 부담하다'라는 뜻으로 쓰였다. 따
라서 '~의 값을 지불하다'라는 의미의 (D) pay for가 정답이다.

179   추론 / 암시

번역   이메일에서 피츠패트릭 씨에 대해 암시된 것은?

(A) 그의 가족은 더럼으로 이주할 계획이다.
(B) 수년간 관개 자문위원으로 일했다.
(C) 졸리오 렌탈에서 정기적으로 장비를 대여한다.
(D) 그의 소유지는 스탠턴 씨의 소유지와 가깝다.

해설   이메일의 두 번째 단락에서 피츠패트릭 씨는 샬라 씨에게 기계를 빌려
주겠다고 한 후, 그 다음날 아침에 본인이 졸리오 렌탈에 반납할 수 있
다(Then I can return the trencher to Zolio Rentals the next
morning)고 했다. 하루 안에 두 명 모두 기계를 사용한 후 다음날 아
침에 반납이 가능할 정도로 두 사람의 토지가 가깝다고 추론할 수 있
으므로, (D)가 정답이다.

어휘   relocate 이주하다, 이전하다   regularly 정기적으로

180   연계

번역   피츠패트릭 씨는 졸리오 렌탈에 얼마를 지불하겠는가?

(A) 166달러
(B) 194달러
(C) 237달러
(D) 275달러

해설   이메일의 첫 번째 단락에서 피츠패트릭 씨는 가장 작은 트렌처(the
smallest trencher that is available)를 대여하겠다고 했고, 같은

단락 마지막 문장에서 전일 대여하기로 결정했다(I have decided to rent the machine for a full day)고 언급했다. 웹페이지를 보면, 가장 작은 45cm 트렌처의 24시간 대여 요금이 237달러라고 되어 있으므로, (C)가 정답이다.

181-185 기사 + 채용공고

웰리나라스 기업, 연구개발 부문 이전

푸네 (3월 12일) - ¹⁸³푸네에 본사를 둔 보건의료 기술 회사인 웰리나라스 기업은 5월 1일부로 연구개발(R&D) 부서가 뭄바이에 근거지를 두게 될 예정이라고 오늘 발표했다. "뭄바이는 우리가 생산을 추진하는 데 필요한 기업 풍토, 시설, 창의적 인재 등을 갖추고 있습니다"라고 지난달 회사의 3대 회장이 된 라짓 자다브 씨가 말했다. 현재 이 회사는 뉴델리, 하이데라바드 등 인도의 다른 도시 두 곳에 지사를 두고 있다.

웰리나라스 기업은 고품질 기술 장비를 생산하는 업체이다. ¹⁸¹수요가 가장 높아서 수익성 있는 제품은 '비질런트'이다. 자다브 씨가 발명해 인도 전역에서 구할 수 있는 이 장비는 건강 문제가 있는 사람들을 위해 고안되었다. ¹⁸²주요 기능은 응급 상황 시 중요할 수 있는 정보인 환자의 상태 관련 데이터를 정기적으로 수집하고 업데이트하는 것이다.

어휘 corporation 회사 division 부문 headquarter in ~에 본사를 두다 research and development (R&D) 연구개발 effective (~부로) 시행되는 climate 풍토 facility 시설 production 생산 currently 현재 manufacturer 제조업체 equipment 장비 in demand 수요가 많은 thus 그러므로 profitable 수익성이 있는 intended for ~를 대상으로 하는, ~를 위해 고안된 feature 기능 gather 모으다 condition 상태 crucial 결정적인, 중요한 emergency 응급, 비상

웰리나라스 기업

¹⁸³**직책: 연구개발 수석 엔지니어**
작성일: 3월 23일
¹⁸⁴**지원 마감일: 4월 25일**

착용 가능한 건강 상태 모니터링 기기 설계 및 시험 책임자

학력 및 역량:

- 생명의학 공학 석사 학위
- 최소 5년 이상 의료용 기기 개발 및 임상시험 실시 경력
- ¹⁸⁵**최소 3년 이상 연구팀 관리 경력**
- 뛰어난 서면 및 구두 의사소통 능력
- 전 세계 다문화 환경에서의 협업 능력

¹⁸³**지원자는 6월 8일 근무 시작에 앞서, 5월 25일 예비 교육 과정에 참석해야 합니다.**

어휘 job title 직위, 직책 apply 지원하다 responsible for ~에 책임이 있는 wearable 착용 가능한 health-monitoring 건강 상태를 관찰하는 education 교육 graduate degree 석사 학위 biomedical 생명의학의 conduct 실시하다 clinical trial 임상시험 oral 구두의 collaboratively 협력적으로

---

multicultural 다문화의 environment 환경 candidate 지원자, 후보자 attend 참석하다 preliminary 예비의 prior to ~에 앞서

181 사실 관계 확인

번역 자다브 씨에 대해 알 수 있는 것은?

(A) 회사 제품 중 하나를 만들었다.
(B) 웰리나라스 기업의 창립자다.
(C) 연구개발 부문의 책임자였다.
(D) 3년간 회사의 회장이었다.

해설 기사의 두 번째 단락에서 수요가 가장 높아 수익성 있는 제품이 '비질런트'(Its product that is most in demand and, thus, profitable, is called *Vigilant*)라고 했는데, 바로 다음 문장에서 이것은 자다브 씨가 발명한(Invented by Mr. Jadhav) 장비라고 했다. 따라서 자다브 씨가 회사 제품인 비질런트를 발명했음을 알 수 있으므로, (A)가 정답이다. 참고로, 자다브 씨는 지난달에 3대 회장(the company's third president)이 된 것이므로, (B)와 (D)는 명백한 오답이다.

어휘 founder 창립자 be in charge of ~를 책임지다

> ▸▸ Paraphrasing 지문의 Its product ~ Invented by Mr. Jadhav → 정답의 He created one of the company's products

182 사실 관계 확인

번역 비질런트에 대해 알 수 있는 것은?

(A) 해외에 판매된다.
(B) 정보를 수집한다.
(C) 값이 저렴하다.
(D) 신제품이다.

해설 기사의 두 번째 단락 후반부에서 비질런트의 주요 기능은 응급 상황 시 중요할 수 있는 정보인 환자의 상태 관련 데이터를 정기적으로 수집하고 업데이트하는 것(A key feature is its ability to regularly gather and update data about the patient's condition, information that might be crucial in emergencies)이라고 했다. 따라서 (B)가 정답이다.

어휘 collect information 정보를 수집하다 inexpensive 비싸지 않은

> ▸▸ Paraphrasing 지문의 gather ~ data → 정답의 collects information

183 연계

번역 선발된 지원자는 어디에서 일하겠는가?

(A) 푸네
(B) 뭄바이
(C) 뉴델리
(D) 하이데라바드

해설 채용공고에서 모집하는 직책은 연구개발 수석 엔지니어(Senior

Research and Development Engineer)이며 5월 25일에 교육을 받고 6월 8일부터 근무를 시작하게 된다. 기사의 첫 번째 단락을 보면, 웰리나라스 기업이 연구개발(R&D) 부서를 5월 1일로 뭄바이로 옮길 예정이라고 되어 있다. 따라서 새로 선발된 연구개발 수석 엔지니어는 뭄바이에서 근무하게 될 것이라 추론할 수 있으므로, (B)가 정답이다.

184 세부 사항

번역 지원 마감 기한은 언제인가?

(A) 3월
(B) 4월
(C) 5월
(D) 6월

해설 채용공고의 소제목 부분을 보면 4월 25일까지 지원하라(Apply by: 25 April)고 되어 있으므로, (B)가 정답이다.

185 세부 사항

번역 해당 직책의 요건은?

(A) 학술 기사 발표 경력
(B) 의술 제공 경력
(C) 관리 경력
(D) 해외 근무 경력

해설 채용공고에서 최소 3년의 연구팀 관리 경력(Minimum of three years' experience in managing research teams)이 필요하다고 명시되어 있으므로, 보기 중에서는 (C)가 정답이다.

어휘 publish 출판하다, 발표하다 scholarly 학술적인 managerial 관리의, 경영의

▸▸ Paraphrasing 지문의 experience in managing research teams → 정답의 managerial experience

186-190 이메일 + 일정표 + 이메일

수신: 도서관 회원 전체
발신: 에이다 카운티 도서관
날짜: 3월 20일
제목: 앞으로 있을 강좌
첨부: 📎봄_일정표

에이다 카운티 도서관 회원 여러분께,

오래 기다리시던 봄 강좌 일정표가 마무리되었습니다. 이 강좌들의 참여도가 훌륭하리라고 기대하고 있습니다. [187]가장 흥미로운 부분은 아랍어 시 번역에 관한 발표로, 에이다 카운티 도서관을 처음 방문하시는 강사께서 발표해 주시겠습니다.

도서관 행사 입장은 항상 무료이며 선착순입니다. 그러니 그에 맞춰 계획을 세우시고, 특히 가장 협소한 장소 두 곳, 좌석 35석이 있는 헬름스 룸과 [186]20대의 컴퓨터 스테이션만 있는 에이버리 룸에서의 행사에 유의하십시오.

어휘 upcoming 앞으로 있을, 곧 다가올 lecture 강좌, 강의 long-awaited 오래 기다리던 finalize 마무리하다, 완결 짓다 turnout 참가자 수, 참여도 presentation 발표 translation 번역 present 발표하다 access 이용(권), 접근(권) first-come, first-served 선착순의 accordingly 그에 맞춰 especially 특히 venue 장소 seat (특정 수의) 좌석이 있다 computer station 컴퓨터가 있는 자리

에이다 카운티 도서관
봄 강좌 일정표

주요 주제	초청 강사	날짜 및 시간	장소
아이다호 문학	이본 브릭스	4월 10일, 오후 4-6시	헬름스 룸
[187]아랍어 시 번역	[187]캐롤 엘긴	4월 17일, 오후 3-5시	스톡스 룸
효과적인 이력서 디자인	마크 댄젤로	4월 24일, 오후 3-5시	에이버리 룸
[189]사전의 역사	잭스 모리슨	[189]5월 8일, 오후 4-6시	스톡스 룸
철학 관련 논픽션	달라 와이스	5월 15일, 오후 3-5시	프레드릭스 룸
프로그래밍 역량	앨리사 레이놀즈	5월 22일, 오후 4-6시	에이버리 룸

어휘 literature 문학 effective 효과적인 philosophical 철학에 관련된

수신: 메리 칼튼 〈mcarlton@adacountylibrary.org〉
발신: 잭스 모리슨 〈jmorrison@bookpress.com〉
날짜: 4월 3일
제목: 예정된 도서관 행사

칼튼 씨께,

[188/189]5월 8일 도서관에서 계획된 제 행사의 일정이 변경되어야 함을 알려드리려 메일을 씁니다. 제가 그 주에 출장을 떠날 예정이라서요. 도서관 회원들이 정말 재미있어 할 것 같은 흥미로운 자료들을 이미 준비했습니다. 그래서 여전히 강의를 하고 싶어요. [190]현재 스톡스 룸에서 진행될 예정인데, 제가 원하는 청중 규모와 딱 맞는 크기입니다. 제 강의에 필요한 장비도 모두 갖추고 있어서, 계속 그 방을 사용하기를 바랍니다.

[188]일정을 변경해야 하는 불편을 드려서 죄송합니다만, 본 행사를 다시 예약하도록 도와주시면 감사하겠습니다. 저의 주제를 무척 발표하고 싶어서요.

잭스 모리슨

어휘 scheduled 예정된 reschedule 일정을 변경하다 material 자료 patron 이용자, 회원 take place 개최되다,

열리다 draw (관객 등을) 끌다, 끌어모으다 apologize 사과하다 inconvenience 불편 appreciate 감사하다 rebook 다시 예약하다

186 세부 사항

번역 20명만 앉을 수 있는 장소는?

(A) 헬름스 룸
(B) 스톡스 룸
(C) 에이버리 룸
(D) 프레드릭스 룸

해설 첫 번째 이메일의 두 번째 단락 후반부에서 에이버리 룸에는 컴퓨터 스테이션이 20개밖에 없다(the Avery Room, which has only 20 computer stations)고 명시했으므로, (C)가 정답이다.

187 연계

번역 에이다 카운티 도서관에서의 새로운 연사로 강조된 사람은?

(A) 브릭스 씨
(B) 엘긴 씨
(C) 와이스 씨
(D) 레이놀즈 씨

해설 첫 번째 이메일의 첫 단락 후반부에서 가장 흥미로운 부분은 아랍어 시 번역에 관한 발표로, 에이다 카운티 도서관을 처음 방문하는 강사가 발표한다(A highlight is a presentation on Arabic poetry translation, presented by a lecturer who will make her first visit to Ada County Library)고 했다. 일정표에 따르면 아랍어 시 번역을 발표하는 강사는 캐롤 엘긴 씨이므로, (B)가 정답이다.

▸▸ Paraphrasing 지문의 a lecturer who will make her first visit → 문제의 a new speaker

188 추론 / 암시

번역 칼튼 씨의 직업은 무엇이겠는가?

(A) 대학 강사
(B) 컴퓨터 프로그래머
(C) 행사 담당자
(D) 여행사 직원

해설 두 번째 이메일의 첫 단락에서 모리슨 씨는 칼튼 씨에게 사정을 설명하며 도서관 행사 중 자신의 강의 시간을 변경되어야 한다(my planned event at the library ~ will need to be rescheduled)고 했다. 이후 두 번째 단락에서 발표를 꼭 하고 싶다며 다시 예약해달라고 부탁(I appreciate your help in getting this event rebooked, as I am excited to present my topic)하고 있으므로, 칼튼 씨가 도서관 행사 담당자라고 추론할 수 있다. 따라서 (C)가 정답이다.

189 연계

번역 어떤 행사의 일정을 변경해야 하는가?

(A) 아이다호 문학
(B) 사전의 역사
(C) 철학 관련 논픽션
(D) 프로그래밍 역량

해설 두 번째 이메일의 첫 단락에서 모리슨 씨는 5월 8일 도서관에서 계획된 행사(자신의 강의) 일정이 변경되어야 함을 알리려 메일을 쓴다(I am writing to let you know that my planned event at the library on May 8 will need to be rescheduled)고 했다. 일정표에 따르면 5월 8일에 예정된 강의의 주제는 '사전의 역사'이므로, (B)가 정답이다.

190 사실 관계 확인

번역 모리슨 씨에 대해 알 수 있는 것은?

(A) 강의 준비를 아직 시작하지 않았다.
(B) 5월 8일에 도서관을 방문할 예정이다.
(C) 출장을 갈 필요가 없다.
(D) 발표 시 장비를 사용할 계획이다.

해설 두 번째 이메일의 첫 단락 후반부에서 모리슨 씨는 기존에 강의하기로 예정되었던 스톡스 룸에 자신이 필요한 장비가 모두 갖춰져 있어서(It also has all the necessary technology for my lecture) 일정을 변경하더라도 이 방을 사용하고 싶다고 했다. 따라서 모리슨 씨가 장비를 사용할 예정임을 알 수 있으므로, (D)가 정답이다.

어휘 be required to ~하도록 요구되다 utilize 사용하다

▸▸ Paraphrasing 지문의 It ~ has all the necessary technology for my lecture
→ 정답의 He plans to utilize technology in his presentation

191-195 웹페이지 + 이메일 + 이메일

http://www.crfoundation.org/volunteer

강 보호 운동가

센트럴강 재단은 센트럴강 및 지류를 따라 여러 장소에서 이뤄질 수질 감시 작업을 조직하고 있습니다. 재단에서는 지역 공동체 사람들이 정기적인 수질 검사를 실시하도록 교육하고자 합니다.

강 보호 운동가가 되는 데 관심이 있으시다면 www.crfoundation.org로 연락 주십시오.

요건:

▸ 확실한 교통 수단은 필수입니다. 비교적 외딴 지역에서 작업하기 때문입니다.
▸ 세부적인 것에 주의를 기울이는 세심함 및 정확한 측정을 할 수 있는 역량
▸ 191/192 수질 변화 감지를 위해 최소 4주에 1회 검사를 할 수 있는 여건

어휘 **advocate** 옹호자, (환경 등의) 보호 운동가 **foundation** 재단 **coordinate** 조직하다 **tributary** (강 등의) 지류 **individual** 개인, 사람 **conduct** 실시[수행]하다 **periodic** 주기적인, 정기적인 **requirement** 요건, 필수 조건 **reliable** 믿을 만한 **transportation** 교통편 **essential** 필수적인 **relatively** 비교적, 상대적으로 **remote** 거리가 떨어진, 먼 **attention to detail** 세부적인 것에 주의를 기울이는 것, 세심함 **take a measurement** 측정하다 **precise** 정밀한, 정확한 **availability** 이용 가능성, ~할 시간이 되는 것 **detect** 감지하다

수신: 재니스 구티에레즈, 미치 그레고리, 메리 코너스, 로스 하워드
발신: 클레어 슈뢰더 〈cschroeder@crfoundation.org〉
제목: 교육
날짜: 5월 5일

192센트럴강 재단의 강 보호 운동가로 참여하는 데 관심을 보여주셔서 감사합니다.

193교육 시간은 클리포드 공원에서 5월 8일 토요일 오전 9시부터 정오까지로 예정되어 있습니다. 교육 중에 여러분은 표본 키트 사용을 연습하고 각자의 멘토에게 소개될 겁니다. 가실 때는 첫 과제와 수료증을 받게 됩니다. 그러고 나면 한 시간 분량의 첫 번째 과제를 하시는 데 멘토가 동행해 드립니다. 이는 여러분이 추후 독자적으로 활동하실 수 있게끔 준비를 시켜줄 것입니다.

저희가 교육을 클리포드 공원에서 진행하지만, 여러분은 보통 다른 장소에서 활동하게 됩니다. 각 개별 검사 장소를 아래에서 확인하세요.

수질 검사 장소	자원봉사자
서튼 브리지	재니스 구티에레즈
브래드포드 벤드	미치 그레고리
194앨더윅 코브	194메리 코너스
태너 파크	로스 하워드

토요일에 여러분 모두를 뵙게 되길 고대합니다!

클레어 슈뢰더

어휘 **participate** 참여하다 **training session** 교육 시간 **practice** 연습하다 **introduce** 소개하다 **assignment** 임무, 과제 **certificate of completion** 수료증 **accompany** 동행하다, 동반하다 **prepare** 준비시키다 **independently** 독립하여, 자주적으로

수신: 수잔 림
발신: 메리 코너스
날짜: 5월 13일
제목: 현장 방문

안녕하세요, 수잔.

194저는 5월 20일에 첫 수질 검사를 완료하도록 되어 있는데요. 거기에서 만나 제가 제대로 할 수 있게 도와주실 시간이 있으세요? 저는 오후 3시부터 오후 6시까지 언제든 시간이 됩니다. 온라인으로 장소를 찾아

봤는데, 강에서 0.5킬로미터 떨어진 곳에 주차를 하고 현장까지 걸어가야 할 것 같아요. 슈뢰더 씨가 말씀하시길, 여정에 약 30분이 더해질 거래요.

195그리고 수질 검사 키트를 여분으로 갖고 계시나요? 제 것은 일부 부품이 빠진 것 같아요. 제 용품을 교체 받을 수 있을 때까지 당신 것 중 하나를 써도 될까요?

감사해요.

메리

어휘 **be supposed to** ~하기로 되어 있다 **complete** 완료하다 **available** 시간이 되는 **correctly** 바르게, 정확하게 **mention** 말하다, 언급하다 **supply** 용품 **replace** 교체하다

191 세부 사항

번역 강 보호 운동 자원봉사자들에게 어떤 책임이 있는가?

(A) 수질 변화 감시
(B) 물 보호 관행 홍보
(C) 강둑을 청결하게 유지
(D) 강과 시내 견학 주관

해설 웹페이지 하단을 보면 강 보호 운동가의 요건이 나와 있는데, 세 번째 항목에서 그들이 수질 변화를 감지하는 일(to detect any changes in water quality)을 한다는 것을 알 수 있다. 따라서 (A)가 정답이다.

어휘 **promote** 홍보하다 **conservation** 보호, 보존 **practice** 관례, 관행 **riverbank** 강둑

192 연계

번역 첫 번째 이메일 수신자들에 대해 암시된 것은?

(A) 차량을 공유할 예정이다.
(B) 자원봉사자들을 모집하는 데 도움을 주었다.
(C) 한 달에 1회 시간을 낼 것을 약속했다.
(D) 컴퓨터 시스템에 기록을 입력할 것이다.

해설 첫 번째 이메일의 첫 단락을 보면 이메일의 수신자들이 센트럴강 재단의 강 보호 운동가(a river advocate for the Central River Foundation)로 활동할 예정임을 알 수 있다. 웹페이지 하단에 나온 요건 중 세 번째 항목에 따르면, 강 보호 운동가는 수질 변화 감지를 위해 최소 4주에 1회 검사할 수 있어야 한다(Availability to conduct testing at least once every four weeks to detect any changes in water quality)고 되어 있다. 따라서 이메일의 수신자들이 여기에 동의했다고 추론할 수 있으므로, (C)가 정답이다.

어휘 **recruit** 모집하다 **commit to** ~을 확실히 약속하다

> ▸▸ Paraphrasing 지문의 **once every four weeks**
> → 정답의 **once a month**

193 사실 관계 확인

번역 첫 번째 이메일에서 교육에 대해 명시된 것은?

(A) 센트럴강 재단 건물에서 개최될 것이다.
(B) 오전에 개최될 것이다.
(C) 한 시간 동안 계속될 것이다.
(D) 여러 장소에서 열릴 것이다.

해설 첫 번째 이메일의 두 번째 단락에서 교육 시간은 5월 8일 토요일 오전 9시부터 정오까지로 예정되어 있다(A training session has been scheduled at Clifford Park on Saturday, May 8, from 9:00 A.M. to 12 noon)고 했으므로, 교육이 오전 중에 이루어짐을 알 수 있다. 따라서 (B)가 정답이다.

어휘 be held 개최되다 take place 개최되다, 열리다 multiple 많은, 다수의

194 연계

번역 림 씨는 어디에서 코너스 씨를 만나겠는가?

(A) 서튼 브리지
(B) 브래드포드 벤드
(C) 앨더윅 코브
(D) 태너 파크

해설 두 번째 이메일의 첫 번째 단락에서 코너스 씨는 림 씨에게 자신이 5월 20일에 첫 수질 검사를 완료하도록 되어 있는데(I'm supposed to complete my first water testing on May 20), 거기에서 만나 도와줄 수 있는지(Are you available to meet me there to help me do it correctly?) 물었다. 첫 번째 이메일의 표에 따르면, 코너스 씨가 수질 검사를 해야 하는 장소는 앨더윅 코브이므로, (C)가 정답이다.

195 세부 사항

번역 두 번째 이메일에서 코너스 씨는 림 씨에게 무엇을 해 달라고 요청하는가?

(A) 차에 태워 주기
(B) 슈뢰더 씨에게 연락하기
(C) 30분 일찍 출발하기
(D) 수질 검사 키트 가져오기

해설 두 번째 이메일의 두 번째 단락에서 코너스 씨는 림 씨에게 수질 시험 키트 여분이 있는지 물은 후, 림 씨 것 중 하나를 써도 되는지(do you have an extra water-testing kit? ~ Can we use one of yours ~?) 물었다. 즉, 림 씨의 수질 시험 키트를 가져와 달라고 요청한 것이므로, (D)가 정답이다.

어휘 give a ride 태워 주다

196-200 이메일 + 이메일 + 웹페이지

수신: 크리스토프 자즈 〈kszasz@budaceramics.com〉
발신: 아누크 아얄라 〈aayala@ayala.net〉
제목: 태양열 발전 옵션
날짜: 1월 25일

자즈 씨께,

196 귀하의 도자기 회사용 태양열 발전 옵션 추천을 요청하는 최근 이메일에 감사 드립니다. 어느 업체가 귀하의 요구사항에 가장 잘 부합하는지 추천을 드리기에 앞서, 이 질문들에 대한 답을 주시겠습니까?

1. **198 (A)** 태양 전지판 구입 및 설치 예산은 어느 정도로 유동성이 있습니까?

2. 작업 기간은 언제입니까? **197** 정부는 태양열 발전 설치 비용에 재정적인 혜택을 제공할 계획이며, 이는 약 2년 후 시행 예정입니다.

3. **198 (B)** 건물 배치는 어떻게 됩니까? **200** 공간이 있다면, 주차장과 지면 중 한 곳에 태양 전지판을 설치하도록 선택하실 수 있습니다. 첫 번째 선택사항은 주차장 덮개로 이루어지며, 두 번째 선택사항은 사용하지 않는 대규모 구역에 아주 좋습니다.

4. **198 (C)** 지붕은 어떤 종류입니까? **200** 평평한 지붕은 이상적이지 않습니다. 위에 장비가 많이 있는 지붕도 안 됩니다. 대형 태양 전지판을 둘 공간이 충분치 않기 때문입니다.

5. 향후 사업체 확장 계획이 있습니까?

곧 연락 주시기를 고대합니다.

아누크 아얄라

어휘 solar power 태양열 발전 request 요청하다 recommendation 추천 ceramics 도자기류 serve one's needs 요구를 충족시키다, 요구사항에 부합하다 flexible 유연한, 융통성이 있는 installation 설치 financial 재정적인, 재무의 incentive 장려책, 혜택 take effect 시행되다, 발효되다 configuration 배치, 배열 property 건물, 부동산 consist of ~로 이루어지다 ideal 이상적인 expand 확대하다, 확장하다

수신: 아누크 아얄라 〈aayala@ayala.net〉
발신: 크리스토프 자즈 〈kszasz@budaceramics.com〉
제목: 회신: 태양열 발전 옵션
날짜: 1월 27일

아얄라 씨께,

저희 본사는 수도 외곽에 있습니다. **198 (B)/200** 도자기 공장이 저희 구내의 절반 정도를 차지합니다. **198 (C)/199/200** 충분한 냉각을 보장하기 위해, 지붕 공간의 대부분은 산업용 크기의 에어컨 및 오븐을 위한 통기 구조물이 차지하고 있습니다. **198 (B)/200** 구내의 나머지 부분에는 꽤 큰 주차장이 있는데, 이 지역에 대중교통이 없어서 150명의 직원들이 자가용으로 출근하기 때문입니다.

저희가 선택할 태양열 발전 업체는 안정적이어야 합니다. 현재 프로젝트는 기한을 융통성 있게 조절할 수 없습니다. 따라서 **198 (A)/200** 비용을 희생해서라도 최대한 빨리 패널을 설치했으면 합니다. 이 답변들이 추천하시는 데 도움이 됐으면 합니다.

크리스토프 자즈

어휘 headquarters 본사, 본부 occupy 점유하다, 차지하다 approximately 거의, 대략 ensure 보장하다, ~하게 하다

sufficient 충분한   industrial 산업의, 공업의   venting 통기
silo 원통형의 구조물, 저장고   contain 포함하다   sizeable 꽤
큰   public transportation 대중교통   well-established
자리를 잘 잡은, 안정된   inflexible 융통성이 없는, 변경이 불가능한
sacrifice 희생시키다

---

http://www.solarinsider.com

최근 고객 설문조사를 바탕으로, 아래에 있는 수도권 지역 내의 태양열
발전 업체 네 곳이 가장 성공적이라는 평가를 받았다.

회사	전문 분야	의견
AKX 솔라	지붕	비용이 매우 저렴함, 매우 안정적인 업체
선365	모든 유형	우수한 품질, 매우 철두철미하나 다소 느림
200 베라넥 시스템즈	200 주차장	200 빠른 작업 완료 시간, 꽤 비쌈
플루토솔라	지면 설치	3월까지 시작 불가

어휘 based on ~를 기반으로, ~를 바탕으로 survey 설문 be
rated 평가되다 specialty 전문 분야 stable 안정된 superior
우수한 thorough 철두철미한, 빈틈없는 turnaround 처리 시간,
소요 시간

---

196 추론 / 암시

번역 아얄라 씨의 직업은 무엇이겠는가?

(A) 기술 자문위원
(B) 공장 감독관
(C) 잡지 기자
(D) 유지보수 인부

해설 첫 번째 이메일의 첫 단락을 보면, 자즈 씨가 자신의 도자기 회사를 위
한 태양열 발전 옵션을 추천해달라고 아얄라 씨에게 요청했음(your
recent e-mail requesting recommendations for solar
power options for your ceramics company)을 알 수 있다. 아
얄라 씨는 어느 업체가 자즈 씨의 요구에 부합할 지 추천하기에 앞
서(Before I make a recommendation for which company
would best serve your needs) 몇 가지 질문을 하며 이에 답해 달
라고 요청하고 있으므로, 그녀가 기술 관련 자문위원이라고 추론할 수
있다. 따라서 (A)가 정답이다.

---

197 사실 관계 확인

번역 아얄라 씨가 태양열 발전에 대해 명시한 것은?

(A) 많은 정부 건물들이 태양 전지판을 갖추고 있다.
(B) 해외 태양열 업체들은 매우 빠르게 성장하고 있다.
(C) 지붕 전지판은 가장 높은 에너지 효율성을 제공한다.
(D) 태양 전지판 설치를 2년간 미루면 비용을 낮출 수 있다.

해설 첫 번째 이메일의 2번 질문에서 아얄라 씨는 정부에서 2년 후에 태
양열 발전 설치 시 재정적인 혜택을 제공할 계획(The government
plans to provide financial incentives toward the cost of

installing solar power that will take effect in about two
years)이라고 설명했다. 따라서 2년 후에 태양열 전지판을 설치하면
정부의 보조금을 받아 비용을 절감할 수 있으므로, (D)가 정답이다.

어휘 be equipped with ~를 갖추고 있다   extremely 극도로, 극히
efficiency 효율성

---

198 연계

번역 자즈 씨는 아얄라 씨의 어떤 질문에 답변하지 못했는가?

(A) 1번
(B) 3번
(C) 4번
(D) 5번

해설 두 번째 이메일은 자즈 씨가 아얄라 씨의 질문에 답장한 내용이다.
첫 번째 단락에서 도자기 공장이 구내의 절반 정도를 차지하고(The
ceramics factory occupies approximately one-half of our
property) 나머지 부분에는 큰 주차장이 있다(The rest of our
property contains a sizable parking lot)고 한 것은 3번 질문
에 대한 답변이고, 지붕 공간의 대부분은 산업용 크기의 에어컨과 오
븐을 위한 통기 구조물이 차지하고 있다(much of the roof space
is taken up by industrial-sized air-conditioning units and
venting silos for our ovens)고 설명한 것은 4번 질문에 대한 답
변이다. 그리고 두 번째 단락에서 기한을 융통성 있게 조절할 수 없
으니(inflexible deadline) 비용을 희생해서라도 최대한 빨리 패널
을 설치했으면 한다(I am willing to sacrifice money to get the
panels installed as soon as possible)고 했는데, 이는 1번 및 2
번 질문에 대한 답변으로 볼 수 있다. 사업 확장 가능성을 묻는 5번 질
문에는 답하지 않았으므로, (D)가 정답이다.

---

199 추론 / 암시

번역 두 번째 이메일에 따르면, 도자기 공장에 대해 암시된 것은?

(A) 도로에서 먼 곳에 있다.
(B) 광범위한 냉각이 필요하다.
(C) 대중교통 노선상에 위치해 있다.
(D) 최근 수도권 지역으로 이전했다.

해설 두 번째 이메일의 첫 단락에서 충분한 냉각을 보장하기 위해 공장 지
붕 공간의 대부분에 산업용 크기의 에어컨 및 오븐을 위한 통기 구
조물이 있다(To ensure sufficient cooling, much of the roof
space is taken up by industrial-sized air-conditioning
units and venting silos for our ovens)고 했다. 따라서 공장에
광범위한 냉각이 필요하다고 추론할 수 있으므로, (B)가 정답이다.

어휘 situated 위치해 있는   extensive 대규모의, 광범위한

---

200 연계

번역 아얄라 씨는 어떤 업체를 추천하겠는가?

(A) AKX 솔라
(B) 선365
(C) 베라넥 시스템즈
(D) 플루토솔라

해설 두 번째 이메일의 첫 단락을 보면, 자즈 씨의 회사는 절반이 공장이고, 나머지 부분에는 큰 주차장이 있으며, 공장 지붕에 장비가 많음을 알 수 있다. 첫 번째 이메일의 3번 질문에서 주차장이나 지면에 태양 전지판 설치가 가능하다고 했고, 4번 질문에서 지붕도 가능하지만 위에 장비가 많으면 불가능하다고 했으므로, 결론적으로 자즈 씨의 회사에서 설치가 가능한 곳은 주차장이 된다. 두 번째 이메일의 두 번째 단락에서 자즈 씨는 비용을 희생하더라도 최대한 빨리 패널을 설치하길 원한다고 했으므로, 이 요건을 충족하는 업체를 웹페이지에서 찾아야 한다. 웹페이지에 따르면, 주차장에 전지판 설치가 가능하며 다소 비싸지(quite expensive)만 작업 속도가 빠른(fast turnaround) 업체는 베라넥 시스템즈로, 아얄라 씨가 이 업체를 추천할 것으로 볼 수 있다. 따라서 (C)가 정답이다. (A) AKX 솔라는 지붕을 전문으로 하고, (B) 선365과 (D) 플루토솔라는 일정이 맞지 않으므로 추천 대상이 될 수 없다.

ETS TEST 8

101 (B)	102 (C)	103 (C)	104 (D)	105 (B)
106 (B)	107 (A)	108 (A)	109 (B)	110 (A)
111 (D)	112 (C)	113 (B)	114 (D)	115 (B)
116 (C)	117 (A)	118 (B)	119 (B)	120 (C)
121 (B)	122 (D)	123 (A)	124 (D)	125 (D)
126 (C)	127 (A)	128 (A)	129 (D)	130 (C)
131 (A)	132 (B)	133 (D)	134 (D)	135 (D)
136 (C)	137 (A)	138 (B)	139 (C)	140 (C)
141 (A)	142 (B)	143 (B)	144 (A)	145 (C)
146 (B)	147 (C)	148 (A)	149 (A)	150 (C)
151 (D)	152 (B)	153 (C)	154 (A)	155 (D)
156 (C)	157 (A)	158 (D)	159 (C)	160 (B)
161 (B)	162 (A)	163 (A)	164 (D)	165 (C)
166 (D)	167 (A)	168 (B)	169 (B)	170 (A)
171 (D)	172 (C)	173 (D)	174 (A)	175 (B)
176 (B)	177 (A)	178 (C)	179 (D)	180 (B)
181 (D)	182 (B)	183 (D)	184 (A)	185 (D)
186 (A)	187 (B)	188 (D)	189 (B)	190 (C)
191 (D)	192 (D)	193 (C)	194 (A)	195 (D)
196 (C)	197 (D)	198 (B)	199 (A)	200 (C)

PART 5

101 인칭대명사의 격 _ 소유격

해설 전치사 in의 목적어 역할을 하는 명사 office를 한정 수식하는 자리이므로, 소유격 인칭대명사 (B) his가 정답이다.

번역 피어스 씨는 정오에 전 직원이 그의 사무실에서 만날 것을 요청했다.

어휘 request 요청하다

102 명사 자리 _ 동사의 목적어

해설 소유격 your의 수식을 받으면서 동사 appreciate의 목적어 역할을 하는 명사 자리이므로, (C) cooperation(협조, 협력)이 정답이다. (A) cooperates, (B) cooperated, (D) cooperate는 모두 동사로 품사상 빈칸에 들어갈 수 없다.

번역 곧 있을 이전을 위한 사무실 준비 작업에 협조해 주셔서 매우 감사합니다.

어휘 appreciate 감사하다 upcoming 다가오는, 곧 있을

103 동사 어휘

해설 who가 이끄는 관계사절의 동사 자리로, to부정사구 to contribute to the company picnic을 목적어로 취할 수 있는 타동사가 들어가야 한다. 따라서 (C) wish(~하기를 바라다)가 정답이다. 참고로,

(A) require는 5형식 동사로 쓰일 경우 「require＋목적어＋목적격 보어(to부정사)」 구조가 되어야 하며, (B) supply와 (D) express는 to부정사를 목적어로 취하지 않는다.

번역 회사 야유회를 돕고 싶은 직원은 리우 씨에게 연락해야 한다.

어휘 contribute to ~에 기여하다, ~를 돕다 require 요구하다 supply 제공하다 express 표현하다

104 전치사 어휘

해설 명사 the luncheon을 목적어로 취하는 전치사 자리이다. 여기서 오찬(luncheon)은 수상 발표(the awards announcement)가 있을 행사이므로, '~에서'라는 의미의 (D) at이 정답이다.

번역 응고 씨는 다음 주 오찬에서 시상 발표를 할 것이다.

어휘 make an announcement 공표하다 award 상

105 명사 자리 _ 동사의 목적어 _ 어휘

해설 travel과 함께 복합명사를 이루어 동사 will be planning의 목적어 역할을 하는 자리로, 보기에서 명사인 (B) budget(예산)과 (D) budgeter(예산 담당자) 중 하나를 선택해야 한다. 기획할만한 대상은 예산이므로, (B) budget이 정답이다. (A) budgeted가 과거분사로서 travel을 수식한다고 가정하더라도, '짜여진 여행을 기획하다'라는 의미가 되므로 어색하다. (C) budgetary는 명사 앞에 오는 형용사로 품사상 빈칸에 들어갈 수 없다.

번역 기븐스 씨는 10월 1일자로 우리 부서의 출장 예산을 기획할 것이다.

어휘 as of ~일자로, ~현재 budget 예산; 예산을 세우다 budgetary 예산상의

106 부사 어휘

해설 be동사 are와 과거분사 encouraged 사이에서 동사를 수식하는 부사 자리로, 빈칸에는 권장되는(encouraged) 정도를 나타내는 단어가 들어가야 자연스럽다. 따라서 '강하게, 적극'이라는 의미의 (B) strongly가 정답이다. strongly encouraged/recommended/ advised 등은 빈출 표현이니 암기해 두는 것이 좋다.

번역 지원자는 업무 포트폴리오 및 이력서 제출이 적극 권장된다.

어휘 applicant 지원자 encourage 권장하다, 장려하다 submit 제출하다 rapidly 빨리, 신속히 nearly 거의, 대략 tightly 단단히, 꽉

107 to부정사

해설 앞에는 명령문 형태의 절(Join us for dinner on Friday)이 왔고, 뒤에는 명사구(Mr. Yi's promotion to Vice President of Marketing)가 있으므로, 빈칸에는 Mr. Yi's promotion 이하를 목적어로 취하며 앞에 온 절을 수식하는 준동사가 들어가야 한다. 따라서 '승진을 축하하기 위해'라는 목적을 나타내면서 부사적인 역할을 하는 to부정사 (A) to celebrate가 정답이다. (B) celebrates, (C) will celebrate, (D) celebrated는 본동사 형태로 구조상 빈칸에 들어갈 수 없다.

번역   이 씨의 마케팅 부서장 승진을 축하하기 위한 금요일 저녁 식사 자리에 저희와 함께해 주십시오.

어휘   promotion 승진   vice president 부서장, 부사장   celebrate 축하하다

108   명사 어휘

해설   빈칸에는 배달(will be delivered)의 대상인 21개의 도구(21 tools)와 어울리는 명사가 들어가야 하므로, '세트, 한 조'라는 의미의 (A) set가 정답이다.

번역   주문된 21개 도구 세트는 오늘 오후 애비 스트리트 창고로 배송될 예정이다.

어휘   warehouse 창고

109   전치사 자리

해설   명사 November를 목적어로 취해 앞에 온 절을 수식하는 전치사 자리이므로, '~동안'이라는 의미의 전치사 (B) during이 정답이다. (A) entire는 형용사, (D) ever는 부사, (C) while은 접속사/명사로 품사상 빈칸에 들어갈 수 없다.

번역   갤럭시 헬스 클럽은 11월 동안 모든 강좌에 20퍼센트 할인을 제공한다.

어휘   offer 제공하다   entire 전체의

110   부사절 접속사 자리 _ 어휘

해설   완전한 절(the printer cartridge was installed correctly)을 이끄는 접속사 자리로, 빈칸이 이끄는 절이 콤마 뒤 주절을 수식하고 있다. 카트리지가 바르게 설치된 것(the printer cartridge was installed correctly)과 잉크가 약간 새는 것(it leaked some ink)은 상충되는 상황이므로, 대조/양보의 접속사인 (A) Although(비록 ~ 이지만)가 정답이다. 참고로, (B) So는 등위접속사로 절이나 문장 사이에 들어갈 수 있다. (D) However는 접속사로 쓰일 경우 '아무리 ~해도'라는 의미로 바로 뒤에 형용사나 부사가 온다.

번역   프린터 카트리지는 바르게 설치되었지만 잉크가 좀 샜다.

어휘   install 설치하다   correctly 바르게, 정확하게   leak 새게 하다, 새다

111   인칭대명사의 격 _ 소유격

해설   동사 can protect의 목적어 역할을 하는 명사 equipment를 한정 수식하는 자리이므로, 소유격 인칭대명사인 (D) their가 정답이다.

번역   추 씨는 공장 인부들이 손상으로부터 그들의 장비를 보호할 수 있는 방법을 설명할 것이다.

어휘   equipment 장비   damage 훼손, 손상

112   동사 어휘 _ 과거분사

해설   주어인 Promotional ideas 및 행위의 주체(by)인 the publicity

---

team과 어울리는 동사를 선택해야 한다. 홍보를 위한 아이디어는 홍보팀에 의해 논의되는 대상이므로, '논의되는, 검토되는'이라는 의미의 (C) discussed가 정답이다.

번역   다음 달 홍보팀에 의해 바이올리니스트 젤리나 오티즈의 홍보를 위한 아이디어가 논의될 것이다.

어휘   promotional 홍보의   publicity 홍보   escort 호위하다   tutor 가르치다   subscribe 구독하다, 가입하다

113   형용사 자리 _ 명사 수식

해설   빈칸이 전치사 in과 명사 sales 사이에 있으므로, sales를 수식하는 형용사 또는 sales와 복합명사를 이루는 명사가 들어갈 수 있다. 해당 부분이 최고의 수치를 기록한 부문을 나타내고 있으므로, '디지털의'라는 의미의 형용사인 (B) digital이 정답이다. 참고로, digit은 '숫자'라는 뜻으로 sales와 복합명사를 이루기엔 어색하다. (D) digitize는 동사로 품사상 빈칸에 들어갈 수 없다.

번역   〈기퍼즈 글로벌 인베스터 잡지〉는 지난 분기에 디지털 매출 부문에서 최고치를 경험했다.

어휘   quarter 분기   digit (0부터 9까지의 아라비아) 숫자   digitize 디지털화하다

114   부사절 접속사 자리

해설   빈칸은 완전한 두 절을 연결해 주는 접속사 자리이다. 따라서 '~일지라도'라는 의미의 부사절 접속사인 (D) even though가 정답이다. 해당 문장에서 opening이 that절을 목적어로 취하는 타동사나 that절의 수식을 받는 명사로 쓰인 것이 아니므로, (B) that은 빈칸에 들어갈 수 없다. (A) among과 (C) prior to는 전치사로 절을 이끌 수 없다.

번역   인근에 이미 3개의 다른 이발소가 있는데도 새 이발소가 문을 연다.

어휘   neighborhood 인근   prior to ~이전에

115   형용사 어휘

해설   빈칸을 포함한 절은 록커 기타 스쿨이 추가 강사를 채용할 여력(it can afford to hire additional teachers)이 되는 이유(Now that)를 나타낸다. 따라서 '수익성이 있는, 벌이가 많은'이라는 의미의 (B) profitable이 빈칸에 들어가야 자연스럽다.

번역   록커 기타 스쿨은 수익성이 있는 업체라서 추가로 강사들을 채용할 여력이 있다.

어휘   enterprise 기업, 사업   afford to ~할 여유가 있다, ~할 형편이 되다   additional 추가의   compact 소형의, 간편한

116   동사 자리 _ 시제 / 수 일치

해설   명사 the way를 수식하는 절(Ms. Garcia ~ it would)의 동사 자리이다. (A) imagine은 3인칭 단수 주어(Ms. Garcia)와 쓰일 수 없으므로, 주어의 수에 영향을 받지 않으며 시제상 앞뒤에 나온 과거동사(did not look, would)와도 어울리는 (C) imagined가 정답이다. (B) imagining은 동명사/현재분사, (D) imagination은 명사로 구

조상 빈칸에 들어갈 수 없다.

번역 개조된 사무실 건물은 가르시아 씨가 상상했던 것처럼 보이지 않았다.

어휘 renovate 개조하다, 보수하다 imagination 상상

117 명사 어휘

해설 전치사 until(~까지)의 목적어 역할을 하는 명사 자리로, 특정 시점을 나타내는 명사가 들어가야 한다. 따라서 '여름'이라는 의미의 (A) summer가 정답이다. 참고로, (B) year가 until the와 쓰이려면 year 다음에 숫자(eg. until the year 2031)가 와야 한다. (C) hours는 기간을 나타내므로 until과 어울리지 않는다.

번역 아소브 컨설팅은 우리에게 신상품 스웨터 수송을 하려면 여름까지 기다리라고 조언했다.

어휘 advise 조언하다 ship 운송하다, 수송하다

118 한정사 _ 수 일치

해설 단수가산명사 department를 수식하는 한정사 자리로, 보기에서 단수명사와 쓰일 수 있는 (A) its 또는 (B) each 중 하나를 선택해야 한다. 빈칸을 포함한 전치사구가 복수명사 heads를 수식하므로, 부서장과 부서가 여럿임을 알 수 있다. 따라서 빈칸에는 각기 다른 부서를 나타내는 단어가 들어가야 하므로, '각각의'라는 의미의 (B) each가 정답이다. (C) most는 복수명사와 불가산명사를, (D) several은 복수명사를 수식한다.

번역 회사의 각 부서장은 콜카타에서 열리는 교육에 참석해야 한다.

어휘 attend 참석하다 several 몇의, 수개의

119 동사 어휘

해설 be동사 is와 함께 수동태를 이루는 과거분사 자리로, to부정사구와 어울려 쓰이는 동사가 들어가야 한다. 또한 문맥상 soon과 어울려 곧 일어날 일을 묘사하는 단어가 필요하므로, '(~할 것으로) 예상되는'이라는 뜻의 (B) expected가 정답이다. 참고로, expect는 타동사로서 「expect+목적어+목적격 보어(to부정사)」의 5형식 구조로 쓰일 수 있으며, 수동태로 쓰일 경우 해당 문장 구조가 된다. be expected to는 빈출 표현이니 암기해 두는 것이 좋다.

번역 산업용 재봉틀 제조업체인 버크 주식회사는 곧 가정용 제품을 내놓을 것으로 예상된다.

어휘 manufacturer 제조업체 industrial 산업의 sewing machine 재봉틀 apply 적용하다, 응용하다 inquire 문의하다 object 반대하다

120 명사 자리 _ 동사의 목적어 _ 어휘

해설 빈칸은 to부정사 to answer의 목적어 역할을 하는 명사 자리로, 관계사절 that hotel guests may have의 수식을 받는다. 프런트 데스크 직원이 답해야 하는 것은 호텔 투숙객들이 할 질문이므로, (C) questions가 정답이다. (A) questioner는 '질문자'라는 뜻으로 문맥상 어색하며, (B) questioned는 과거 동사/과거분사, (D) questionable은 형용사로 품사상 빈칸에 들어갈 수 없다.

번역 프런트 데스크 직원은 호텔 투숙객이 할 수 있는 모든 질문에 대답할 수 있도록 철저히 교육을 받는다.

어휘 reception 환영, 접수처[프런트] personnel 직원들 thoroughly 철저히, 완전히

121 부사 어휘

해설 빈칸에는 월 50파운드로 가격이 책정된(is priced) 상황을 평가하는 부사가 들어가야 하므로, '합리적으로, 타당하게'라는 의미의 (B) reasonably가 정답이다. 참고로, highly(높게)/realistically(현실적으로)/sensibly(합리적으로) 등의 부사도 priced와 어울려 쓰인다.

번역 위크셔 모바일의 통화, 문자, 데이터 무제한 요금제는 월별 50파운드로 가격이 합리적으로 책정됐다.

어휘 unlimited 무제한의 promptly 지체없이 partially 부분적으로 loyally 충성스럽게

122 숫자 수식 표현

해설 빈칸 없이도 완전한 문장으로, 바로 뒤에 오는 5,000과 어울려 쓰이는 단어가 빈칸에 들어가야 한다. 따라서 '~ 이상'이라는 뜻으로 숫자를 수식할 수 있는 (D) over가 정답이다. 참고로, (A) many는 의미상 5,000과 같은 특정 숫자를 수식할 수 없다.

번역 캅 스태퍼는 지역 또는 업계별로 분류한 5천 개 이상 회사들의 국제 데이터베이스 인수를 발표했다.

어휘 acquisition 인수, 매입 sort 분류하다

123 형용사 어휘

해설 독수리 둥지를 보기 위해 특정 장소를 방문하는 새 관찰자(bird watchers)의 성향을 묘사하는 형용사 자리이다. 따라서 '열렬한, 열광적인'이라는 의미의 (A) enthusiastic이 정답이다.

번역 힐탑 그로브는 여러 개의 독수리 둥지가 있어서 열광적인 새 관찰자들이 가장 좋아하는 장소다.

어휘 presence 있음, 존재 watcher 연구가, 관찰자 affordable 가격이 알맞은, 입수 가능한 elaborate 정교한 comparable 비슷한, 비교할 만한

124 부사 자리 _ to부정사 수식 _ 비교급

해설 비교급 more와 함께 to부정사 to fill을 수식하는 부사 자리이므로, (D) quickly(빠르게)가 정답이다. 참고로, quick은 비격식체에서 부사로서 동사를 뒤에서 수식할 수 있는데, 그렇다 하더라도 (A) quick은 원급, (B) quickest는 최상급, (C) quicker는 비교급으로 more와 함께 쓰일 수 없으므로 오답이다.

번역 총괄 관리자는 모조 보석류 온라인 주문에 더 빠르게 응대할 시스템을 시행했다.

어휘 implement 시행하다 fill an order 주문에 응하다 costume jewelry 모조 보석류

125 전치사 어휘

해설 공장 배기가스를 줄이려는 목표(the goal of reducing its factory emissions)는 퀄렛 모터스가 지향하는 바이므로, '~를 향해'라는 의미의 (D) toward가 정답이다. work toward(s)는 고정된 표현으로 암기해 두면 시간을 단축할 수 있다.

번역 퀄렛 모터스는 작년부터 공장 배기가스를 25퍼센트 줄인다는 목표로 나아가고 있다.

어휘 work toward(s) ~를 목표로 나아가다   emission 배출, 배기가스   opposite 반대의

126 형용사 자리 _ 명사 수식 _ 어휘

해설 소유격 Gribson & Kim's와 함께 주어인 brand identity를 수식하는 형용사 자리로, 브랜드 정체성의 특징을 나타내는 단어가 들어가야 한다. 따라서 '강력한'이라는 의미의 (C) powerful이 정답이다. 과거분사형 형용사인 (B) powered는 '전동의, 동력을 이용하는'이라는 뜻으로 문맥상 어색하며, (A) powers는 명사/동사, (D) powerfully는 부사로 품사상 빈칸에 들어갈 수 없다.

번역 그립슨 앤 킴의 강력한 브랜드 정체성은 회사의 이미지와 가치를 정확하게 전달한다.

어휘 brand identity 브랜드 정체성   accurately 정확히   convey 전달하다

127 전치사 자리

해설 명사 opposition을 목적어로 취하는 전치사 자리이므로, (A) in spite of(~에도 불구하고)가 정답이다. (B) in order that은 부사절 접속사로 뒤에 완전한 절이 와야 하고, (C) even so와 (D) on the contrary는 부사로 품사상 빈칸에 들어갈 수 없다.

번역 시 의회는 지역 주민들의 반대에도 불구하고 쇼핑센터 건립을 위한 렘코의 신청을 승인했다.

어휘 approve 승인하다   application 신청, 지원   opposition 반대   resident 거주자   in order that ~하기 위해, ~할 수 있도록   even so 그렇기는 하지만   on the contrary 그와는 반대로

128 목적격 보어 _ (to) + 동사원형

해설 「help + 목적어(any business) + 목적격 보어」 구조에서 목적격 보어에 해당하는 자리로, 뒤에 오는 명사구 its products를 목적어로 취한다. help의 목적격 보어로는 to부정사나 동사원형이 쓰이므로, (A) promote가 정답이다. (B) promoted는 동사/과거분사, (C) promotable은 형용사, (D) promoter는 명사로 품사상 빈칸에 들어갈 수 없다.

번역 말리엣 마케팅은 어떤 업체든 멀티미디어 광고 패키지를 통해 제품을 홍보하도록 도울 수 있다.

어휘 advertising 광고   promote 홍보하다   promotable 증진시킬 수 있는   promoter 촉진물, (홍보 업무를 하는) 기획사

129 명사 어휘

해설 빈칸은 sought의 목적어 자리로, 전치사구 with the department manager의 수식을 받는다. 따라서 지역 기자(Local reporters)가 부서장(the department manager)을 대상으로 요청할 수 있는 일을 나타내는 명사가 들어가야 하므로, '인터뷰'라는 의미의 (D) interviews가 정답이다.

번역 지역 기자들은 시청 지하실에서 오래된 부동산 기록을 찾아낸 부서장과의 인터뷰를 요청했다.

어휘 seek 청하다, 구하다   property 부동산   permit 허가증   material 자료   condition 조건, 환경

130 부사 자리 _ 동사 수식

해설 the sportswear company가 주어, is shifting이 동사, its marketing tactics가 목적어인 완전한 절 뒤에서 변화(shift)의 정도를 강조하는 부사 자리이다. 따라서 (C) dramatically(극적으로, 크게)가 정답이다. (A) drama는 명사, (B) dramatic과 (D) more dramatic은 형용사로 품사상 빈칸에 들어갈 수 없다.

번역 그 스포츠웨어 업체는 아시아 전역의 젊은 소비자들을 매료시키기 위해 마케팅 전략을 크게 바꾸고 있다.

어휘 appeal 관심을 끌다   tactic 전략, 전술   dramatic 극적인

PART 6

131-134 정보

> 당신의 **131집 앞**까지 맛있는 고품질 식사를 배달하는 온라인 서비스, 다이닝 티켓에 오신 것을 환영합니다. 다이닝 티켓 **132이용**을 시작하시려면 그저 장소를 입력하고 귀하의 지역 배송 선택사항을 살펴보시면 됩니다. 다음으로 원하는 가격대, 요리 유형, 식당 이름 등으로 정보를 필터링하십시오. 그러고 나서 다이닝 티켓 배달원에 의해 배송될 때 주문을 추적해 보세요. **133이처럼 아주 쉽습니다.** 집에서 **134편안**하게 좋아하는 식당의 음식을 즐기시려면 오늘 바로 다이닝 티켓을 이용해 보세요!

> **어휘** deliver 배달하다   desired 원하는, 바라는   price range 가격대   cuisine 요리   track 추적하다   transport 운송하다, 수송하다   fare 음식

131 명사 어휘

해설 빈칸은 전치사 to의 목적어 역할을 하는 자리로, 고품질 식사가 배달되는(delivers ~ to) 장소를 나타낸다. 따라서 '문간, 집 앞'이라는 의미의 (A) doorstep이 정답이다.

어휘 station 역   market 시장

132 동명사

해설 고유명사 Dining-Ticket을 목적어로 취하면서 To start의 목적어 역할을 하는 자리이므로, 보기 중에서 동명사 (B) using이 정답이다. 참고로, start는 동명사와 to부정사 모두를 목적어로 취할 수 있다. (A) usage와 (D) users는 명사, (C) usable은 형용사로 품사상 빈칸에 들어갈 수 없다.

어휘 usage 사용(법) usable 사용 가능한 user 이용자

133 문맥에 맞는 문장 고르기

번역 (A) 현재 배달 직원을 추가로 모집하고 있습니다.
(B) 귀하의 주문은 매장 내 픽업으로 1시간 이내에 준비될 것입니다.
(C) 저희 교육은 철저하고 빠릅니다.
(D) 이처럼 아주 쉽습니다.

해설 빈칸 앞에서는 온라인 식사 주문 배달 서비스인 다이닝 티켓의 이용 방법을 안내했고, 뒤 문장에서는 오늘 바로 다이닝 티켓을 이용해 보라(try Dining-Ticket today)고 권했다. 따라서 빈칸에도 서비스 이용과 관련된 내용이 들어가야 자연스러우므로, 이용 방법이 쉽다고 강조한 (D)가 정답이다.

어휘 additional 추가의 recruit 모집하다 thorough 철저한, 빈틈없는

134 명사 자리 _ 전치사의 목적어

해설 전치사 from의 목적어 자리로, 정관사 the 및 전치사구 of your own home의 수식을 받는다. 따라서 명사인 (D) comfort(편안함, 안락)가 정답이다. from/in the comfort of your (own) home은 '집에서 편안하게'라는 뜻의 고정 표현으로 암기해 두면 좋다. 참고로, 「the+동명사+of+명사」 구조가 가능하려면 명사가 동명사의 "의미상" 목적어 역할을 해야 하는데(eg. the widening of the road), 해당 문장에서는 이 관계가 성립되지 않으므로 (B) comforting은 오답이다. (A) comforted는 동사/과거분사, (C) comfortable은 형용사로 품사상 빈칸에 들어갈 수 없다.

135-138 이메일

수신: 라쉬다 윌리스 〈rwillis@pintaur.net〉
발신: 고객 계정 관리부 〈accounts@stauntonnaturalgas.com〉
날짜: 8월 4일
제목: 종이를 쓰지 않는 전자 청구서 발부

윌리스 씨께,

귀하의 스턴튼 천연 가스 계정에서 종이를 쓰지 않는 전자 청구서 **135옵션**을 선택해 주셔서 감사합니다. 8월 20일을 **136시작으로** 월 내역서를 전자로 받으시게 됩니다. 청구서를 꼭 받으실 수 있도록 저희 이메일 계정을 연락처 목록에 추가해 주십시오. 언제라도 계정 설정에서 선택만 하시면 종래의 종이 청구서로 **137복귀할** 수 있습니다.

138청구서 발부 절차의 다른 사항은 변경되지 않았습니다. 귀하의 청구서는 계속 매월 1일까지 납부되어야 합니다.

스턴튼 천연 가스

어휘 Customer Accounts 고객 계정 (관리부) paperless 종이를 쓰지 않는, 전자화된 billing 청구서 발부 account 계정 statement 내역서 electronically 전자로, 컴퓨터로 ensure 보장하다, ~하게 하다 receipt 수령, 수신 traditional 전통적인, 종래의 due (돈을) 지불해야 하는

135 명사 어휘

해설 동명사 selecting의 목적어 자리로, 선택되는 대상이 들어가야 한다. 따라서 '(종이를 쓰지 않는) 전자 청구서 옵션'이라는 의미를 완성하는 (D) option이 정답이다.

어휘 value 가치 degree 정도

136 분사구문

해설 전치사구 on August 20와 함께 콤마 뒤 절을 수식하는 자리이다. 앞에서 윌리스 씨가 종이 청구서 대신 전자 청구서를 선택했다고 명시했으므로, 8월 20일은 월 내역서를 전자로 받기(you will receive your monthly statement electronically) 시작하는 시점이라고 볼 수 있다. 따라서 (C) Beginning이 정답이다. (A) Until은 '~까지'라는 뜻을 나타내며 전치사 on과 연달아 쓰일 수 없으므로 빈칸에 들어갈 수 없고, (B) Only와 (D) Even은 의미상 적절하지 않다.

137 조동사(may) + 동사원형

해설 빈칸이 조동사 may와 전치사구 to traditional paper billing 사이에 있으므로, 빈칸에는 동사원형이 들어가야 한다. 따라서 (A) return(되돌아가다, 복귀하다)이 정답이다. (B) returnable은 형용사, (C) to return과 (D) returning은 준동사로 조동사 뒤에 올 수 없다.

어휘 returnable 반환할 수 있는

138 문맥에 맞는 문장 고르기

번역 (A) 계정 잔금이 현재 미불 상태입니다.
(B) 청구서 발부 절차의 다른 사항은 변경되지 않았습니다.
(C) 회사 직원이 곧 연락 드릴 것입니다.
(D) 계정은 매월 말일 폐쇄될 것입니다.

해설 빈칸 앞 단락에서는 변경된 청구서 발급 방식(paperless billing)을 설명했는데, 뒤 문장에서는 청구서 납기일이 계속 그대로(Your bill will still be due on the first of each month)라고 했다. 따라서 청구서 발급 방식 외에 다른 사항은 변경되지 않았다고 한 (B)가 빈칸에 들어가야 자연스럽다.

어휘 account balance 지불 잔액, 잔금, 잔고 overdue (지불, 반납 등의) 기한이 지난, 미불 상태인 representative 직원, 대리인

139-142 회람

수신: 레드 디비전 영업팀 팀원

발신: 마티아스 가마, 이사

제목: 정보

날짜: 11월 22일

첨부: 3분기 결과

지난 분기 뛰어난 실적을 낸 것에 대해 여러분 모두를 칭찬합니다! 첨부된 보고서를 직접 확인해 보시면, 모든 세부사항이 나와있을 겁니다. **139그럼에도 불구하고** 성장의 여지는 항상 존재합니다. 그것이 바로 우리가 새 **140교육** 프로그램을 시작하는 이유입니다. 우리의 요구사항을 꼼꼼하게 **141분석한** 외부 대행사가 이를 제공할 것입니다. 조직 전체에 학습 모듈이 제공되겠지만, 시작은 우리 부서에서 할 예정입니다. **142날짜는 곧 알려드리겠습니다.** 그동안, 계속해서 훌륭하게 업무를 수행해 주십시오.

어휘 attachment 첨부 quarter 분기 commend (공개적으로) 칭찬하다 outstanding 뛰어난 room for ~의 여지 organization 조직, 단체 be scheduled to ~할 예정이다 division (조직의) 분과, 부 in the meantime 당분간, 그동안에 carry on with ~를 계속하다 good work 업무 등을 잘 하는 것

139 접속부사 자리 _ 어휘

해설 빈칸 앞에서는 뛰어난 실적(outstanding work)에 대해 칭찬했는데(commend), 뒤에서는 성장의 여지는 항상 존재한다(there's always room for growth)는 반전의 내용이 왔다. 따라서 '그럼에도 불구하고'라는 의미의 (C) Nevertheless가 정답이다. 참고로, (D) Even if는 완전한 절과 절을 연결하는 부사절 접속사로 빈칸에 들어갈 수 없다.

어휘 similarly 마찬가지로 in that case 그 경우에

140 명사 어휘

해설 program과 함께 복합명사를 이루는 명사 자리로, 새로 시작하는 (are launching) 프로그램의 취지를 나타내는 단어가 들어가야 자연스럽다. 뒤에서 회사 전체에 학습 모듈이 제공된다(the learning modules will be offered across the organization)고 했으므로, 프로그램이 교육용임을 알 수 있다. 따라서 '교육, 훈련'이라는 의미의 (C) training이 정답이다.

어휘 exercise 운동, (기량을 닦기 위한) 연습 benefit 혜택

141 현재완료 _ 태

해설 빈칸이 has carefully 다음에 왔으므로, 빈칸에는 has와 현재완료시제를 이루는 과거분사가 들어가야 한다. 따라서 보기에서 (A) analyzed와 (D) been analyzed 중 하나를 선택해야 하는데, 뒤에 목적어 our needs가 있으므로 능동태인 (A) analyzed가 정답이 된다. (B) analyzing은 현재분사/동명사, (C) to analyze는 to부정사로 빈칸에 들어갈 수 없다. 참고로, '~해야 한다'라는 뜻의 have to 사이에는 부사가 들어갈 수 없다.

어휘 analyze 분석하다

142 문맥에 맞는 문장 고르기

번역 (A) 이번이 최고의 분기입니다!
　　 (B) 날짜는 곧 알려드리겠습니다.
　　 (C) 고객들도 매우 흡족해하고 있습니다.
　　 (D) 현재 등록이 다 찼습니다.

해설 빈칸 앞 문장에서는 학습 모듈이 우리 부서에서 시작할 예정(they are scheduled to begin in our division)이라고 했는데, 뒤 문장에서는 그동안(In the meantime) 계속해서 훌륭하게 업무를 수행해 달라고 요청하고 있다. '그동안'이라는 것은 프로그램이 시작할 때까지 시간의 공백이 있다는 뜻이므로, 일정을 곧 알려주겠다고 한 (B)가 빈칸에 들어가야 자연스럽다.

어휘 registration 등록

143-146 이메일

발신: 조안나 마키앤

수신: 관리자 전체

제목: 애더코프 임원진과의 회의

날짜: 1월 11일

크레듈럭스 동료 여러분께,

수요일 이사회 회의에서는 **143곧 있을** 애더코프 주식회사와의 합병에 초점을 맞출 예정임을 알려드립니다. 애더코프 최고 경영자 및 여러 관리자뿐만 아니라 양사 법무팀원들도 참석할 예정입니다. **144회의에 직접 참석하도록 계획하시기 바랍니다.**

이 회의의 목적은 합병 절차의 추진 일정을 명확히 하기 위함입니다. 이사회에 질문이 있으신 **145분은 누구나** 질의할 시간이 충분히 주어질 예정입니다. **146이러한 이유로,** 급하지 않은 모든 안건은 2월 초 우리의 경영진 회의 의제로 남겨 두시라는 요청을 드리고자 합니다.

조안나 마키앤

어휘 management 관리진, 경영진 colleague 동료 Please be advised that ~를 알려드립니다(알아두십시오) Board of Directors 이사회 merger 합병 legal 법률과 관련된 purpose 목적, 의도 clarify 명확히 하다 ample 충분한 nonurgent 급하지 않은 agenda 안건

143 형용사 어휘

해설 company merger를 수식하는 자리이다. 애더코프 주식회사와 회의를 통해 합병에 대해 논의할 예정인 것으로 보아, 합병이 이루어지기 전임을 알 수 있다. 따라서 '다가오는, 곧 있을'이라는 의미의 (B) upcoming이 정답이다.

어휘 selected 선정된, 엄선된 occasional 가끔의 assorted 여러 가지의, 갖은

TEST 8

144 문맥에 맞는 문장 고르기

번역 (A) 회의에 직접 참석하도록 계획하시기 바랍니다.
(B) 인턴들이 애더코프에서의 경력에 대해 보고할 예정입니다.
(C) 대신 회의를 1시간 연장할 것입니다.
(D) 곧 새 법률을 알려드리겠습니다.

해설 빈칸 앞 문장에서 예정된 합병 관련 회의의 참석자들(We will be joined by Adacorp's CEO and several managers as well as members of both companies' legal teams)을 구체적으로 밝히고 있으므로, 빈칸에도 해당 회의와 관련된 내용이 들어가야 자연스럽다. 따라서 경영진들 대상으로 회의에 직접 참석하도록 권한 (A)가 정답이다. 회의 시간을 변경하는 내용은 아니므로 (C)는 빈칸에 적절하지 않다.

어휘 in person 직접 instead 대신 extend 늘리다, 연장하다 be notified of ~를 통보받다

145 대명사 어휘

해설 동사 will be given의 주어 역할을 하는 자리로, 전치사구 with questions for our Board of Directors의 수식을 받는다. 따라서 질문이 있는 사람을 나타내는 대명사가 들어가야 하므로, (C) Anyone이 정답이다. (A) Each other는 '서로'라는 뜻으로 주어 자리에 들어갈 수 없고, 소유대명사인 (B) Yours는 '너의 사람/것'을 의미하므로 문맥상 빈칸에 적절하지 않다. (D) Whoever는 주어 자리에 올 경우 명사절 접속사 역할을 하며, will be given 앞에 동사가 하나 더 와야 한다(eg. Whoever has questions for our Board of Directors ~).

146 접속부사

해설 앞 문장에서 질문이 있는 사람에게는 누구나 질의할 시간이 충분히 주어지게 된다(Anyone with questions ~ will be given ample time to ask them)고 했고, 빈칸 뒤에서는 급하지 않은 모든 안건은 경영진 회의 의제로 남겨두라(all nonurgent agenda items (should) be saved for our management team meeting)고 요청하고 있다. 충분한 질의 시간을 제공하기 위해 급하지 않은 안건을 다음 회의로 미루라고 한 것이므로, '이러한 이유로'라는 의미의 (B) For this reason이 정답이다.

어휘 on the contrary 그와는 반대로, 이에 반해 soon after 곧 for example 예를 들면

PART 7

147-148 정보

스미스 카운티 교통부
현재 게시물

교량 조사관 (BI9253) — [147]멋지고 다채로운 풍경으로 잘 알려진 아름다운 스미스 카운티에서 교량 조사관으로서의 경력을 새로운 단계로 높여 보세요! [147]우리 자치구의 지형은 넓고 언덕이 많아 주민과 관광객 모두가 많은 교량과 터널을 이용해야 합니다. [148]본 직책은 기존

의 교량, 터널, 지하 배수로, 관련 도로 표지판 평가와 수리 제안 및 감독 등의 업무를 수반합니다. 경쟁력 있는 급여와 훌륭한 복지 혜택을 제공합니다. 요건에 관한 세부사항 및 지원 방법을 알아보려면 www.smithcounty.gov/jobs를 방문하세요. 마감 기한은 1월 15일입니다.

어휘 current 현재의 inspector 조사관, 감독관 spectacular 멋진, 황홀한 varied 다양한, 다채로운 landscape 풍경 geography 지리, 지형 necessitate ~를 필요하게 만들다 resident 거주자, 주민 alike 둘 다, 모두 involve 수반하다 assess 평가하다 existing 기존의 culvert 지하 배수로 related 관련된 oversee 감독하다 competitive 경쟁력 있는, 업계 평균 이상의 requirement 요구사항, 요건 apply 지원하다

---

147 추론 / 암시

번역 정보에서 스미스 카운티에 대해 암시된 것은?
(A) 인구가 빠르게 증가하고 있다.
(B) 터널 시스템의 현대화가 필요하다.
(C) 거주하고 방문하기에 매력적인 장소다.
(D) 현재 새 고속도로를 많이 건설하고 있다.

해설 첫 번째 문장에서 스미스 카운티를 멋지고 다채로운 풍경으로 잘 알려진 곳(known for its spectacular and varied landscape)이라고 소개하였으며, 그 다음 문장에서 주민과 관광객 모두(residents and tourists alike)가 많은 교량과 터널을 이용한다고 했다. 따라서 스미스 카운티가 거주하고 방문하기에 매력적인 장소라고 추론할 수 있으므로, (C)가 정답이다.

어휘 population 인구 rapidly 빠르게 modernization 현대화, 근대화 currently 현재

148 세부 사항

번역 정보에 따르면, 교량 조사관의 책무인 것은?
(A) 유지보수 공사 감독
(B) 새 교량 기획
(C) 교량 및 터널 통행료 징수
(D) 신호등 설계

해설 중반부에서 교량 조사관 직책은 기존의 교량, 터널, 지하 배수로, 관련 도로 표지판 평가와 수리 제안 및 감독 등의 업무를 수반한다(The position involves assessing the condition of existing bridges ~ as well as proposing and overseeing repairs)고 했으므로, (A)가 정답이다.

어휘 supervise 감독하다 collect tolls 통행료를 징수하다

▸▸ Paraphrasing 지문의 overseeing repairs
→ 정답의 Supervising maintenance work

149-150 공지

---

[149]역사적인 월튼 증기선의 투어 입장권을 구입해 주셔서 감사합니다. 예약을 취소 또는 변경해야 할 경우, 취소 정책을 숙지해 주시기 바랍니다.

예정된 투어 하루 전까지 취소하시면 입장권당 50%를 환불받으실 수 있습니다. 당일에 취소하거나 예정된 투어 시간에 나타나지 않는 경우에는 환불되지 않습니다. 모든 환불 금액은 입장권 구매 시 사용된 카드로 입금됩니다.

150투어는 증기선 내부와 외부 갑판에서 모두 이뤄집니다. 날씨로 인한 취소는 매우 드문 일입니다. 150춥거나 비가 오는 날씨를 겪을 때를 대비해 적절한 복장을 갖춰주십시오.

어휘 purchase 구입하다 steamship 증기선 appointment 예약, 약속 be aware of ~를 알다 cancellation 취소 policy 정책 refund 환불 appear 나타나다 credit 입금하다 conduct 하다 rarely 드물게, 좀처럼 ~하지 않는 due to ~ 때문에 appropriate 적절한 experience 경험하다, 겪다

149 추론 / 암시

번역 공지는 누구를 대상으로 하겠는가?

(A) 현재 티켓 소지자
(B) 증기선 선원들
(C) 고객 서비스 상담직원
(D) 교육을 받고 있는 투어 가이드

해설 첫 번째 단락에서 공지의 대상에게 투어 입장권을 구입해 주어 감사하다(Thank you for purchasing tickets for a tour)고 했으므로, (A)가 정답이다.

150 세부 사항

번역 공지에서 사람들에게 무엇을 권장하는가?

(A) 연락처 업데이트하기
(B) 역사 관련 참고 자료 출력하기
(C) 야외에서 시간을 보내기 위한 복장 갖추기
(D) 투어 당일 일찍 도착하기

해설 두 번째 단락에서 투어는 증기선 내부와 외부 갑판에서 모두 이뤄진다(tours are conducted both inside the ship and outside on deck)고 한 후, 춥거나 비가 오는 날씨를 대비해 적절한 복장을 갖추라(Please wear appropriate clothing in case we experience cold or wet weather)고 했다. 따라서 (C)가 정답이다.

어휘 reference material 참고 자료

▸▸ Paraphrasing 지문의 wear appropriate clothing
→ 정답의 Dress
지문의 outside on deck → 정답의 outdoors

151-152 이메일

발신: support@volunix.com
수신: 암리타 다스 〈adas@myfastmail.com〉
발신일자: 9월 6일
제목: 사건 030924

소중한 고객님께,

의약품 온라인 매장 볼류닉스 주식회사에 연락 주셔서 감사합니다. 151온라인 구매와 관련해 겪고 계신 기술적 문제에 대해 사과를 드립니다. 152귀하의 서비스 지원 요청서는 9월 6일 수요일 오후 10시 12분에 제출되었습니다. "사건 상황" 기능을 이용해 귀하의 사건 상황을 추적하실 수 있습니다. 또한 해당 기능을 이용해 언제든 지원 요청서에 정보를 추가하실 수도 있습니다.

볼류닉스팀은 지원이 필요한 문제에 최대한 빨리 대응하고 있습니다. 152정규 업무시간 (월-금요일 오전 8시-오후 6시) 중에는 1시간 이내에 답변을 들으실 수 있습니다. 업무시간 이후 및 주말에 제출된 요청서는 다음 영업일 정오 이전까지 답변 드리겠습니다.

감사합니다.

볼류닉스 웹 팀

어휘 incident 사건, 사고 valued 귀중한 supplies 필수품, 물자 apologize for ~에 대해 사과하다 technical 기술적인 difficulty 어려움, 문제 purchase 구입 support ticket 서비스 지원 요청서 submit 제출하다 track 추적하다 status 상태, 상황 feature 특색, 기능 respond to ~에 대응하다 support issue 서비스 지원이 필요한 문제, 지원 문의 regular 정기적인

151 추론 / 암시

번역 다스 씨는 어떤 문제를 겪고 있겠는가?

(A) 자신의 회사 웹사이트에 접속이 안 된다.
(B) 자신의 컴퓨터에 시스템 업데이트를 해야 한다.
(C) 환불을 받지 못했다.
(D) 제품을 구입할 수 없다.

해설 첫 번째 단락에서 온라인 구매와 관련해 다스 씨가 겪고 있는 기술적 문제에 대해 사과(We apologize for the technical difficulty you are experiencing with your online purchase)했으므로, 다스 씨가 온라인으로 제품을 구매할 수 없다고 추론할 수 있다. 따라서 (D)가 정답이다.

어휘 accessible 접속 가능한, 접근할 수 있는 refund 환불

152 사실 관계 확인

번역 서비스 지원 요청서에 대해 알 수 있는 것은?

(A) 잘못 제출됐다.
(B) 업무시간 이후 제출됐다.
(C) 1시간 이내에 해결됐다.
(D) 볼류닉스 관리자에 의해 처리됐다.

해설 첫 번째 단락에서 다스 씨의 서비스 지원 요청서가 수요일 오후 10시 12분에 제출되었다(Your support ticket was submitted on Wednesday, ~ at 10:12 p.m.)고 했는데, 두 번째 단락을 보면 정규 업무시간(regular business hours)이 오후 6시까지라고 나와 있다. 따라서 업무시간 이후 제출되었음을 알 수 있으므로, (B)가 정답이다.

어휘 incorrectly 부정확하게 resolve 해결하다

TEST 8

153-155 이메일

수신: 메리 림 〈mlim412@mailhouz.com〉

발신: 조지 시스코스 〈gsiskos@crehcorp.com〉

날짜: 9월 24일

제목: 조 아젠토의 소개

154 첨부: 🔗 정보

림 씨께,

크레코프 주식회사의 채용 담당자 조지 시스코스라고 합니다. **153현재 경리 직원을 채용하려는 중인데 조 아젠토가 귀하를 추천했습니다.** **154조의 말에 따르면 귀하의 경력이 본 직책(첨부된 공고)에 안성 맞춤이라고 합니다.** 크레코프와 본 직책에 대해 더 알고 싶으시다면, 기꺼이 추가 정보를 제공해 드리겠습니다. **155언제 이야기할 시간이 되시는지 알려 주십시오.** 전화 드리겠습니다.

155곧 답변을 들을 수 있기를 고대합니다!

조지 시스코스

어휘 referral 소개 currently 현재 accounting clerk 경리 직원 recommend 추천하다 background 경력, 배경 a good fit for ~의 적임자, 딱 맞는 것 available 시간이 되는, 이용 가능한 look forward to ~를 고대하다

153 주제 / 목적

번역 이메일을 쓴 목적은?

(A) 크레코프를 광고하려고

(B) 추천서를 요청하려고

(C) 직원을 채용하려고

(D) 승진을 알리려고

해설 첫 번째 단락 초반부에서 현재 경리 직원을 채용하려는 중(We are currently looking to hire an accounting clerk)이라고 한 후, 조 아젠토가 림 씨를 추천했다(Joe Argento recommended you)고 했다. 따라서 림 씨를 고용하고자 이메일을 썼다고 볼 수 있으므로, (C)가 정답이다.

어휘 advertise 광고하다 reference 추천서, 추천인 recruit 모집하다 promotion 승진

154 세부 사항

번역 시스코스 씨는 무엇을 첨부했는가?

(A) 직무기술서

(B) 재무 보고서

(C) 회의 초청장

(D) 운전 경로 정보 링크

해설 첫 번째 단락 중반부에서 림 씨의 경력이 모집하고 있는 직책에 잘 맞다(your background makes you a good fit for the role)며 해당 공고를 첨부했다(posting attached)고 했다. 따라서 직책에 대해 설명한 파일임을 알 수 있으므로, (A)가 정답이다.

155 세부 사항

번역 림 씨는 무엇을 하라고 요청받았는가?

(A) 크레코프 웹사이트 방문

(B) 아젠토 씨에게 연락

(C) 이력서 우편 발송

(D) 이메일에 답신

해설 첫 번째 단락 후반부에서 림 씨에게 언제 이야기할 시간이 되는지 알려달라(Let me know when you are available to talk)고 요청한 후, 두 번째 단락에서 답변을 들을 수 있기를 고대한다(I look forward to hearing back from you!)고 했다. 따라서 (D)가 정답이다.

156-157 문자 메시지

프랜시스 창 [오후 4시 32분]

안녕하세요, 코니. 하계 일정을 취합하고 있는데요. **156계속 한 달에 두 번 금요일 오후 워크숍을 맡아 지도해 주실 수 있나요?** 서로 교대해서 하면 제가 나머지 두 번의 금요일을 맡을 수 있어요.

코니 케호 [오후 4시 39분]

연락 주셔서 감사합니다, 프랜시스. **156여전히 함께 하고 싶긴 하지만, 이번 여름엔 더 바빠질 것 같아요.** 배구 리그를 조직하고 있거든요.

프랜시스 창 [오후 4시 40분]

아, 알겠습니다. **156제가 한 달에 세 번 금요일에 워크숍을 맡을 수 있을 것 같기도 해요.**

코니 케호 [오후 4시 42분]

그럼 딱이겠네요. 그러면 제가 다른 임무를 수행할 시간이 충분할 것 같아요.

프랜시스 창 [오후 4시 43분]

157또 한 가지, 이번 여름에는 기본 데생보다 수채화 그리기에 중점을 두고 싶어요.

코니 케호 [오후 4시 44분]

제가 예전 수업 계획들을 훑어볼 거긴 한데, 그건 문제 없을 거예요. 그리고 곧 만나서 수업 재료 예산을 짜기로 해요.

어휘 take turns 교대하다 involve 수반하다, 관여시키다 coordinate 조직하다, 조정하다 obligation 의무 rather than ~보다는 budget 예산 material 재료

156 의도 파악

번역 오후 4시 42분에 케호 씨가 "그럼 딱이겠네요"라고 쓸 때, 그 의도는 무엇인가?

(A) 여름을 고대하고 있다.

(B) 워크숍 인기가 높을 것으로 본다.

(C) 제안된 일정에 만족한다.

(D) 창 씨가 채용될 예정이라 기쁘다.

해설 창 씨가 오후 4시 32분 메시지에서 한 달에 두 번 수업을 해 줄 수 있는지 물었는데, 케호 씨가 39분 메시지에서 바빠서 힘들 것 같다고 했

다. 이에 창 씨가 그럼 자신이 세 번을 맡을 수도 있다(I could cover the workshops three Fridays a month)고 했고, 케호 씨가 이를 받아들이며 '그럼 딱이겠네요'라고 한 것이다. 즉 제안된 일정에 만족한다는 의미이므로, (C)가 정답이다.

어휘 proposed 제안된

---

157 세부 사항

번역 어떤 종류의 워크숍을 계획하고 있는가?

(A) 미술
(B) 개인 금융
(C) 여행
(D) 고객 서비스

해설 창 씨가 오후 4시 43분 메시지에서 이번 여름에는 기본 데생보다 수채화 그리기에 중점을 두고 싶다(this summer we want to focus on painting with watercolors, rather than basic drawing)고 했으므로, (A)가 정답이다.

어휘 finance 금융, 재무

▸▸ Paraphrasing 지문의 painting with watercolors
→ 정답의 Art

158-160 편지

> 5월 15일
>
> 로저 랭 씨, 전무 이사
> 파커 솔루션즈 재단
> 노스사이드 길 40번지, 500호
> 포틀랜드, 오레곤 97215
>
> 랭 씨께,
>
> ¹⁵⁸본 편지의 목적은 이사회를 대표해 귀하를 국제 그린 솔루션 연구소(IGSRI) 회의의 기조연설자로 초청하고자 하는 것입니다. ¹⁵⁹회의는 12월 3일부터 5일까지 미주리 주 세인트 루이스의 페어뷰 컨퍼런스 센터에서 개최될 예정입니다. ¹⁶⁰저의 많은 동료들이 귀하를 추천했습니다. 그들은 귀하의 전문성에 대해 극찬했습니다.
>
> 수잔 베네데토 교수가 12월 3일 오전에 개회사를 할 예정입니다. 회의에서 중점적으로 다뤄질 주제에 대한 감을 잡으실 수 있도록 2주 후에 프로그램 초안을 보내드리겠습니다.
>
> 올해는 2천 5백여 명의 대표단과 40명의 연사 등, 참석률이 역대 최고일 것으로 예상합니다. 여기에는 최근 문을 연 제네바 지부의 대규모 대표단도 포함됩니다.
>
> 1주 후 연락 드려서 추가 정보를 드리고 질문이 있으시면 답해 드리고자 합니다.
>
> 브라이언 모건

어휘 foundation 재단 on behalf of ~를 대표하여 board of directors 이사회 keynote speaker 기조연설자 conference 회의 colleague 동료 deliver a speech 연설하다

---

highlight 강조하다 attendance 참석률, 참석자 수 delegate 대표 contingent 대표단 chapter 지부 follow up 후속 조치를 취하다, 추가 정보를 주다

---

158 주제 / 목적

번역 랭 씨에게 편지를 쓴 이유는?

(A) 추천서를 요청하려고
(B) 회의 주제를 평가해 달라고 요청하려고
(C) 수상을 축하하려고
(D) 회의 참석을 요청하려고

해설 첫 번째 단락에서 편지의 목적이 랭 씨를 국제 그린 솔루션 연구소 회의의 기조연설자로 초청하고자 하는 것(The purpose of this letter is to invite you ~ to be the keynote speaker at the International Green Solutions Research Institute (IGSRI) Conference)이라고 했으므로, (D)가 정답이다.

어휘 recommendation 추천 evaluate 평가하다 congratulate 축하하다 participate in ~에 참가하다

▸▸ Paraphrasing 지문의 to invite you ~ to be the keynote speaker at
→ 정답의 To ask him to participate in

---

159 세부 사항

번역 IGSRI 회의는 어떤 도시에서 개최되는가?

(A) 포틀랜드
(B) 페어뷰
(C) 세인트 루이스
(D) 제네바

해설 첫 번째 단락에서 회의가 미주리 주 세인트 루이스의 페어뷰 컨퍼런스 센터에서 개최될 예정(It will be held at the Fairview Conference Center in Saint Louis, Missouri)이라고 했으므로, (C)가 정답이다.

---

160 문장 삽입

번역 [1], [2], [3], [4]로 표시된 곳 중에서 다음 문장이 가장 적합한 곳은?

"그들은 귀하의 전문성에 대해 극찬했습니다."

(A) [1]
(B) [2]
(C) [3]
(D) [4]

해설 주어진 문장이 They로 시작하므로, 앞에서 먼저 랭 씨의 전문성을 극찬했던 사람들이 누구인지 언급되어야 한다. [2] 앞에서 많은 동료들이 랭 씨를 추천했다(You were recommended by a number of my colleagues)며 They가 가리킬 만한 대상을 명시했으므로, (B)가 정답이다.

어휘 speak highly of ~를 극찬하다 expertise 전문성

www.sergeyparksandrec.gov/survey

환영합니다!

¹⁶¹귀하는 세르게이 공원 여가과 웹사이트 페이지, 에콜로지 얼라이브의 최신 온라인 소식지, 또는 친구의 소셜미디어 페이지를 통해 본 설문에 오셨습니다. 오시게 된 경로에 상관없이, 설문 작성을 위해 시간을 내 주신 점 감사드립니다.

¹⁶²본 설문은 지역 야생물 단체가 헌신적이고 믿을 만한 자원봉사자들을 모집하는 데 있어서 실질적인 접근법을 찾을 수 있도록 돕고자 합니다. 설문은 작성하는 데 약 15분이 소요되며, 참여는 전적으로 귀하의 선택에 달려 있습니다. ¹⁶³특정 질문에 답하고 싶지 않으신 경우 다음 질문으로 넘어갈 수 있습니다.

본 설문이 어떻게 이용될 지에 관해 문의사항이 있으시면, stefan_mchann@sergeyparksandrec.gov로 스테판 맥한에게 연락 주시기 바랍니다.

설문 번호 4123

이름: 켄숀 오데예미

어휘 survey (설문) 조사 recent 최근의 regardless of ~에 상관없이 appreciate 감사하다 complete 기입하다, 작성하다 aim 목표로 하다 organization 조직, 단체 practical 실질적인, 현실적인 approach 접근법, 처리 방법 dedicated 헌신적인 reliable 믿을 수 있는 participation 참여 optional 선택적인 particular 특정한 regarding ~에 관해

161 사실 관계 확인

번역 설문 조사에 대해 알 수 있는 것은?

(A) 최근 수정됐다.
(B) 여러 온라인 정보원으로부터 접속할 수 있다.
(C) 작성하는 데 한 시간이 필요하다.
(D) 대학생들에게만 전송되고 있다.

해설 첫 번째 단락에서 설문 조사 페이지로 올 수 있는 세 가지 방법(through a page on the Sergey Parks and Recreation Department's Web site, from one of Ecology Alive's most recent online newsletters, or from a friend's social media page)을 나열했으므로, 다양한 온라인 접속 경로가 있다는 것을 알 수 있다. 따라서 (B)가 정답이다.

어휘 modify 수정하다, 바꾸다 access 접속하다 multiple 다수의

▸▸ Paraphrasing 지문의 **You have been directed to this survey**
→ 정답의 **It can be accessed**

지문의 **a page on ~ Web site, ~ online newsletters, ~ social media page**
→ 정답의 **multiple online sources**

162 세부 사항

번역 설문 조사의 목적은?

(A) 자원봉사자 모집 방법을 찾으려고
(B) 단체의 강점을 평가하려고
(C) 지역 야생생물 개체 수를 산정하려고
(D) 중요한 리더십 특성을 알아보려고

해설 두 번째 단락에서 설문 조사를 통해 지역 야생생물 단체가 헌신적이고 믿을 만한 자원봉사자들을 모집하는 데 있어서 실질적인 접근법을 찾을 수 있도록 돕고자 한다(This survey aims to help local wildlife organizations find practical approaches to attracting a dedicated and reliable volunteer base)고 했으므로, (A)가 정답이다.

어휘 evaluate 평가하다 assess 평가하다, 산정하다 determine 알아보다, 결정하다 trait 특질, 특성

▸▸ Paraphrasing 지문의 **This survey aims to**
→ 질문의 **the purpose of the survey**

지문의 **find practical approaches to attracting a ~ volunteer base**
→ 정답의 **To find ways to recruit volunteers**

163 추론 / 암시

번역 설문 응답자들에 대해 암시된 것은?

(A) 질문 일부를 건너뛸 수 있다.
(B) 에콜로지 얼라이브를 구독해야 한다.
(C) 참여하고 돈을 받을 것이다.
(D) 맥한 씨로부터 추가 설문 조사를 받을 것이다.

해설 두 번째 단락에서 설문 응답 시 특정 질문에 답하고 싶지 않으면 다음 질문으로 넘어갈 수 있다(If you do not wish to answer a particular question, you can move on to the next one)고 했으므로, (A)가 정답이다.

어휘 subscribe 구독하다, 가입하다 additional 추가의

▸▸ Paraphrasing 지문의 **move on to the next one**
→ 정답의 **skip some of the questions**

12월 1일

<u>전 직원께 알립니다.</u>

¹⁶⁴1월 1일부터 바클리 스티븐스 코퍼레이션(BSC)은 통합 신분증을 사용하는 보안 시스템으로 이행할 예정입니다. 지금까지 BSC 직원들은 보안 직원이 건물 입구에서 확인했던 전통적인 신분증을 사용해 왔습니다. 그들은 그저 신분증의 사진을 직원의 얼굴과 비교하기만 했습니다. 새로운 시스템은 기술적으로 더욱 진보되어 신분증 정보를 우리 시설 내 다양한 출입 ¹⁶⁵지점과 통합하게 됩니다.

통합된 신분증은 직원들이 허용된 건물 구역으로만 출입할 수 있게 해줍니다. ¹⁶⁶아울러 누가 건물의 어떤 구역에, 언제 들어갔는지 전자 기

록을 생성합니다. 비정규직 직원의 경우 재직 기간이 종료되면 신분증이 비활성화됩니다.

¹⁶⁷12월 중순에 전 직원의 사진을 새로 촬영할 예정이며, 이때 신분증 처리 절차 완료를 위해 모두에게 간단한 서식 작성을 요청할 것입니다.

어휘   attention 알립니다, 주목하세요   transition 이행하다
integrated 통합된   traditional 전통적인   identification
신원 확인, 신분 증명   personnel 직원(들)   entrance 입구
appearance 외모, 겉모습   technologically 기술적으로
advanced 선진의, 고급의   access 이용, 접근, 출입   facility
시설   permit 허가하다   moreover 게다가   temporary 임시의
tenure 재임 기간   fill out a form 서식에 기입하다   complete
완료하다

164   주제 / 목적

번역   공지의 목적은?

(A) 직원들에게 정보 제출을 요청하려고
(B) 시설을 더 잘 활용하도록 권장하려고
(C) 건물 보수에 대해 논의하려고
(D) 보안 시스템 변경사항을 알리려고

해설   첫 번째 단락에서 1월 1일부터 통합 신분증을 사용하는 보안 시스템으로 이행할 예정(Beginning on January 1, Barkley-Stephens Corporation (BSC) will transition to a security system that uses integrated ID badges)이라고 한 후, 보안 시스템 변경 관련 설명을 이어가고 있다. 따라서 (D)가 정답이다.

어휘   submit 제출하다   encourage 권장하다, 장려하다   renovation
개조, 보수

165   동의어 찾기

번역   첫 번째 단락, 여섯 번째 줄에 쓰인 "points"와 의미가 가장 가까운 단어는?

(A) 의도
(B) 세부사항
(C) 장소
(D) 순간

해설   'points'를 포함한 부분은 '신분증 정보를 우리 시설 내 다양한 출입 지점과 통합하게 된다(integrating ID badge information with various access points around our facility)'라는 의미로 해석되는데, 여기서 points는 '지점, 장소'라는 뜻으로 쓰였다. 따라서 '장소'라는 의미의 (C) places가 정답이다.

166   사실 관계 확인

번역   새 신분증에 대해 명시된 장점은?

(A) 편리하게 주머니에 꼭 맞다.
(B) 추가적인 건물 구역에 출입할 수 있게 한다.
(C) 이전 신분증보다 내구성이 더 좋다.
(D) 현장에서 직원 위치를 추적할 수 있다.

해설   두 번째 단락에서 통합된 신분증은 직원들이 허용된 건물 구역으로만 출입할 수 있게 해준다고 한 후, 누가 건물의 어떤 구역에, 언제 들어 갔는지 전자 기록을 생성한다(the badges create an electronic record of who has entered which areas of the building and when)고 덧붙였다. 따라서 직원의 위치 추적이 가능하다는 것을 알 수 있으므로, (D)가 정답이다.

어휘   conveniently 편리하게, 알맞게   durable 내구성이 있는
location 위치   on-site 현장의

▸▸ Paraphrasing   지문의 who has entered which areas of the
building
→ 정답의 an employee's location on-site

167   세부 사항

번역   공지에 따르면, 현재 신분증의 어떤 특징이 업데이트되는가?

(A) 사진
(B) 회사 로고
(C) 형태
(D) 직원 직책

해설   마지막 단락에서 12월 중순에 전 직원의 사진을 새로 촬영할 예정(New photographs of all staff will be taken in mid-December)이라고 했으므로, 신분증의 사진이 업데이트된다는 것을 알 수 있다. 따라서 (A)가 정답이다.

▸▸ Paraphrasing   지문의 New → 질문의 updated
지문의 photographs → 정답의 photo

168-171   온라인 채팅

프랭클린 스미스 (오전 7시 51분)
안녕하세요, 조세핀, 칼. 둘 중 한 분이라도 사무실에 계신가요? ¹⁶⁸제가 탄 기차가 늦어져서 오전 8시 30분 워크숍 준비가 다 됐는지 확인하고 싶습니다.

조세핀 말리언 (오전 7시 56분)
지금 들어가고 있어요. ¹⁶⁸뭘 도와드릴까요, 프랭클린?

칼 도밍고 (오전 7시 57분)
저는 한 10분 뒤에 도착합니다. ¹⁶⁹애스터 룸에서 있을 워크숍을 말씀하시는 건가요? 오벨 홀에서 열리는 다른 워크숍도 있어서요.

프랭클린 스미스 (오전 7시 59분)
¹⁶⁹네, 애스터 룸에서 있을 새비 스틸 영업 워크숍이에요. ¹⁷⁰좌석을 원형으로 재배열하고 프로젝터를 켜서 오디오를 비롯한 모든 것이 잘 되는지 확인할 수 있도록 어젯밤 보낸 발표 슬라이드를 예행연습해 주시면 감사하겠습니다.

칼 도밍고 (오전 8시 2분)
알겠습니다. 사실 의자는 어젯밤에 정리해 두었어요.

조세핀 말리언 (오전 8시 4분)
감사합니다, 칼. ¹⁷¹제가 나머지를 처리하는 동안 의제 15부를 출력해 주실 수 있나요?

칼 도밍고 (오전 8시 5분)

알겠습니다. 최대한 빨리 해 둘게요.

프랭클린 스미스 (오전 8시 7분)

두 분 모두 감사합니다. 기차가 지금 도착해요. 제시간에 갈 수 있을 것 같아요.

조세핀 말리언 (오전 8시 8분)

괜찮습니다, 프랭클린. 드실 커피도 충분히 준비할게요!

> 어휘 take place 개최되다, 열리다 appreciate 감사하다 rearrange 재배열하다 run through 예행연습하다 presentation 발표 actually 사실 plenty of 많은

168 주제 / 목적

번역 스미스 씨가 첫 번째 메시지를 보낸 이유는?

(A) 초대하려고
(B) 도움을 요청하려고
(C) 실수에 대해 사과하려고
(D) 출장 예약을 확정하려고

해설 스미스 씨가 첫 번째 메시지에서 자신이 탄 기차가 늦어져서(My train is running late) 오전 8시 30분 워크숍 준비가 다 됐는지 확인하고 싶다(I want to make sure everything is set up for our 8:30 A.M. workshop)고 하자 말리언 씨가 어떻게 도와줄 지 물었다. 따라서 워크숍 진행과 관련해 도움을 요청하기 위해 메시지를 보냈음을 알 수 있으므로, (B)가 정답이다.

어휘 extend an invitation 초대하다, 초대장을 보내다 apologize 사과하다 reservation 예약

169 추론 / 암시

번역 새비 스틸 회의에 대해 암시된 것은?

(A) 다른 장소로 옮겨졌다.
(B) 당일에 열리는 두 개 회의 중 하나이다.
(C) 말리언 씨의 발표가 포함될 것이다.
(D) 계획보다 늦게 시작할 것이다.

해설 도밍고 씨가 오전 7시 57분 메시지에서 애스터 룸에서 있을 워크숍에 대해 말하는 것인지(Are you talking about the workshop in the Aster Room?)를 확인하며 오벨 홀에서 열리는 다른 워크숍도 있다(there is another workshop taking place in Obell Hall)고 했다. 이에 대해 스미스 씨가 오전 7시 59분 메시지에서 애스터 룸에서 있을 새비 스틸 영업 워크숍(the one in the Aster Room— the Savvy Steel sales workshop)이라고 응답했으므로, 새비 스틸 회의를 포함해 당일 두 개의 워크숍이 있다고 추론할 수 있다. 따라서 (B)가 정답이다.

170 의도 파악

번역 오전 8시 2분에 도밍고 씨가 "알겠습니다"라고 쓸 때, 그 의도는 무엇인가?

(A) 장비를 확인할 것이다.
(B) 애스터 룸을 열 것이다.
(C) 의자를 더 가져올 것이다.
(D) 회의 의제를 변경할 것이다.

해설 스미스 씨가 오전 7시 59분 메시지에서 좌석을 원형으로 재배열하고 프로젝터를 켜서 오디오를 비롯한 모든 것이 잘 되는지 확인할 수 있도록 발표 슬라이드를 예행연습해달라(rearrange the seats into a circle, turn on the projector, and run through the presentation slides ~ just to make sure that everything, including the audio, is working)고 요청했다. 이를 도밍고 씨가 수락한 것이므로, 그가 워크숍에 필요한 장비를 확인할 것이라고 추론할 수 있다. 따라서 (A)가 정답이다.

어휘 revise 변경하다

> ▸▸ Paraphrasing 지문의 make sure → 정답의 check
> 지문의 projector → 정답의 equipment

171 세부 사항

번역 도밍고 씨는 무엇을 하라고 요청받는가?

(A) 동료들에게 커피 갖다 주기
(B) 슬라이드 변경하기
(C) 역에서 스미스 씨 만나기
(D) 사본 만들기

해설 말리언 씨가 오전 8시 4분 메시지에서 도밍고 씨에게 의제 15부를 출력해달라(Would you mind printing out fifteen copies of the agenda)고 요청했으므로, (D)가 정답이다.

어휘 coworker 동료

> ▸▸ Paraphrasing 지문의 printing out fifteen copies of the agenda → 정답의 Make some copies

172-175 편지

폭스테일 항공

7월 30일

지나 카라시아 씨
총괄 담당자
옵시디언 빌라
마린 대로 1121번지
시애틀, 워싱턴 98101

카라시아 씨께,

저는 폭스테일 항공 마케팅 이사 아이작 볼튼이라고 합니다. **172양사에 도움이 될 수 있는 마케팅 아이디어를 공유하고자 편지를 드립니다.** 과

거에 시애틀로 비행하는 당사 승무원들은 수차례 옵시디언 빌라에 투숙했습니다. ^{173/175}승무원들은 객실이 한결같이 편안하고 청결하며 직원들이 친절하고 유능하다고 이야기했습니다. 같은 내용의 긍정적인 후기도 많이 읽었고요. 그러나 귀사의 훌륭한 시설에 종종 빈방이 없어서 당사 승무원들이 다른 곳에 묵어야 하는 상황이 발생합니다. 당사는 전 세계 여러 도시에 있는 호텔들과 협약을 맺어 해당 호텔들에 승무원용 객실을 미리 예약할 수 있게 하고 있습니다. 폭스테일 항공은 이러한 호텔들을 기내 잡지에 대폭 할인된 가격으로 광고합니다. ¹⁷²옵시디언 빌라와도 유사한 협력관계를 발전시키고 싶습니다.

¹⁷⁴당사가 제공하는 광고 가능안이 어떤지 보여 드리기 위해, 그래픽 디자인팀에서 예상 광고 네 편을 제작했으며, 본 편지에 동봉해 드렸습니다. 매년 저희 항공사를 이용하는 300만 이상의 승객들에게 옵시디언 빌라를 홍보하는 일에 저희가 얼마나 열의를 갖고 있는지 이 견본들을 통해 보여드릴 수 있었으면 합니다. 이 아이디어에 대해 더 알아보시고 싶다면, 저에게 546-555-0182로 전화하시거나 i.r.bolton@foxtailairlines.com으로 이메일을 보내주십시오. 귀사와 협력할 기회를 얻게 되길 바랍니다.

아이작 볼튼, 마케팅 이사
폭스테일 항공

동봉

어휘 beneficial 유익한 consistently 일관되게, 한결같이 efficient 유능한, 효율적인 vacancy 빈방[자리] establishment 시설 have an arrangement with ~와 협약을 맺고 있다 reserve 예약하다 in advance 미리 advertise 광고하다 in-flight 기내의 significant 커다란, 중요한 similar 유사한 possibility 가능성, 가능안 potential 잠재적인, 가능성 있는, 예상의 enclose 동봉하다 demonstrate 보여주다, 입증하다 enthusiastic 열광적인, 열렬한 promote 홍보하다 opportunity 기회

172 주제 / 목적

번역 편지를 쓴 목적은?

(A) 제품을 소개하려고
(B) 예약하려고
(C) 새로운 협력관계를 제안하려고
(D) 승진을 알리려고

해설 첫 번째 단락 초반부에서 양사에 도움이 될 수 있는 마케팅 아이디어를 공유하기 위해 편지를 쓴다(I am writing to share a marketing idea with you that would be beneficial for both our companies)고 한 후, 후반부에서 옵시디언 빌라와도 협력관계를 발전시키고 싶다(We would like to develop a similar partnership with Obsidian Villa)고 덧붙였다. 따라서 새로운 협력관계를 제안하기 위해 쓴 편지라는 것을 알 수 있으므로, (C)가 정답이다.

어휘 make a reservation 예약하다 propose 제안하다 promotion 승진

번역 옵시디언 빌라에 대해 알 수 있는 것은?

(A) 대개 이용 가능한 방이 있다.
(B) 최근 관리자들을 추가로 채용했다.
(C) 1년에 300만 명의 고객이 온다.
(D) 훌륭한 고객 서비스를 제공한다.

해설 첫 번째 단락에서 옵시디언 빌라에 투숙했던 승무원들에 따르면 객실이 한결같이 편안하고 청결하며 직원들이 친절하고 유능하다(They report that the rooms are consistently comfortable and clean and that the staff is friendly and efficient)고 했다. 따라서 옵시디언 빌라가 훌륭한 고객 서비스를 제공한다는 것을 알 수 있으므로, (D)가 정답이다.

어휘 available 이용 가능한 additional 추가의 provide 제공하다

▸▸ **Paraphrasing** 지문의 **that the rooms are consistently comfortable and clean and that the staff is friendly and efficient**
→ 정답의 **good customer service**

174 세부 사항

번역 볼튼 씨는 편지와 함께 무엇을 보냈는가?

(A) 광고 견본
(B) 기내 잡지
(C) 항공권
(D) 고객 여행 일정표

해설 두 번째 단락에서 그래픽 디자인팀이 기내 잡지에 실을 만한 광고 네 편을 제작했다(our graphic design team has created four potential advertisements)고 한 후, 본 편지에 동봉했다(They are enclosed with this letter)고 했다. 따라서 (A)가 정답이다.

▸▸ **Paraphrasing** 지문의 **are enclosed with this letter**
→ 질문의 **send with the letter**

지문의 **four potential advertisements**
→ 정답의 **Sample advertisements**

175 문장 삽입

번역 [1], [2], [3], [4]로 표시된 곳 중에서 다음 문장이 가장 적합한 곳은?

"같은 내용의 긍정적인 후기도 많이 읽었고요."

(A) [1]
(B) [2]
(C) [3]
(D) [4]

해설 주어진 문장에서 같은 내용의 긍정적인 후기도 많이 읽었다(I have read numerous positive reviews that say the same)고 했으므로, 이 앞에 먼저 긍정적인 평가가 언급되어야 한다. [2] 앞에서 객실이 한결같이 편안하고 청결하며 직원들이 친절하고 유능하다(They report that the rooms are consistently comfortable and clean and that the staff is friendly and efficient)는 승무원들

의 평가를 인용했으므로, 이 뒤에 주어진 문장이 들어가야 자연스럽다. 따라서 (B)가 정답이다.

어휘 numerous 많은 positive 긍정적인

176-180 일정표 + 이메일

스폿티드 캣 서점 월간 낭독회 시리즈
6월 일정표

6월 2일 토요일　　　브라이언 스테닉, 〈바다 속으로: 시 모음집〉 저자
6월 3일 일요일　　　**180데이비드 칼랜더, 〈위로의 기술〉 저자**
6월 11일 월요일　　　니나 브라운, 〈가족이라는 연대〉 저자
179 6월 13일 수요일　버니스 샌딘, 〈복고풍: 운동복의 역사〉 저자

낭독회는 오후 7시에 시작하며, 끝나고 가벼운 다과를 곁들인 연회가 있습니다.

7월에 있을 시리즈에서 낭독하고 싶은 출판 작가는 readings@ spottedcatbooks.com으로 작품 5페이지를 첨부해 제출해 주십시오. **177작품 견본과 함께 한 단락의 자기소개를 보내주세요.** 자기소개에서는 학력 및 전속 기간, 그리고 해당될 경우에 한해 출판물, 낭독 경험, 강의에 대해 언급해야 합니다. **176본 시리즈에서는 확실히 자리를 잡은 작가와 신진 작가 모두를 환영합니다.**

어휘 author 저자 mastery 숙달, 전문적 기술 thread 연결된 실, 연대 retroactive (패션) 복고풍의, (법률) 소급하는 athletic wear 운동복 refreshments 다과 afterward 그 후에 publish 출판하다 submit 제출하다 attachment 첨부 biography 자기소개, 전기 residency (화가, 작가 등의) 전속, 전속 기간 publication 출판물 lecture 강의 if applicable 해당된다면 well-established (성공하여) 확실히 자리를 잡은 emerging 새롭게 등장하는, 신흥의

발신: 조 앤 로드클리프 〈jrodcliff@weeklycourier.com〉
수신: 데이비드 칼랜더 〈dcallander@elwyn.edu〉
날짜: 5월 16일
제목: 낭독회

칼랜더 교수님께,

179교수님과 샌딘 교수님께서 몇 주 후 스폿티드 캣에서 낭독하실 거라는 이야기를 들었습니다. 정말 기대됩니다! 179두 분의 낭독회 모두 참석하고 싶고 두 분 모두 다시 뵙기를 고대하고 있습니다.

저는 작년에 엘윈 대학교를 졸업한 후, 〈위클리 쿠리어〉에서 문화예술 칼럼니스트로 일하고 있습니다. 시에서 열리는 미술전시회, 음악회, 기타 문화 행사에 대한 논평을 주로 씁니다. 악력과 서평도 쓰고요. **180제 다음 칼럼에서 교수님과 교수님의 저서를 다룰 수 있을지 여쭤보고 싶습니다.** 해당 칼럼은 낭독회 전날 게재될 예정입니다.

178교수님의 저서에 무척 감명을 받아서, 〈위클리 쿠리어〉에서 논평할 수 있다면 무척 기쁠 것 같습니다. 내일 통화할 시간이 되십니까? 물론 직접 뵙고 인터뷰하는 편이 더 좋지만 다음 주까지 업무 때문에 외지에 나와 있습니다. 관심 있으면 알려 주십시오.

조 앤 로드클리프

어휘 attend 참석하다 look forward to ~를 고대하다 review 논평, 비평 cultural 문화와 관련된 feature (신문, 잡지 등에서) 다루다, 특별히 포함하다 fascinate 매료시키다, 사로잡다 available 시간이 되는 in person 직접 assignment (주어진) 업무, 과제

176 사실 관계 확인

번역 낭독회 시리즈에 대해 명시된 것은?

(A) 한 달에 한 번 열린다.
(B) 신진 작가와 유명 작가가 모두 출연한다.
(C) 참석하려면 입장권이 필요하다.
(D) 최근 출판된 책들을 강조한다.

해설 일정표의 마지막 단락에서 낭독회 시리즈에서는 확실히 자리를 잡은 작가와 신진 작가 모두를 환영한다(The series welcomes both well-established and emerging writers)고 했으므로, (B)가 정답이다. 6월 일정표(June Schedule)에 4번의 낭독회가 예정되어 있으므로 (A)는 명백한 오답이다.

어휘 require 요구하다, 필요로 하다 highlight 강조하다

▸▸Paraphrasing　지문의 well-established and emerging
→ 정답의 new and well-known

177 세부 사항

번역 작가들은 서점에 무엇을 보내야 하는가?

(A) 자신의 배경에 대한 정보
(B) 고객들에게 읽어주고 싶은 책
(C) 강의하기에 선호하는 장소
(D) 서명한 계약서

해설 일정표의 마지막 단락에서 낭독회에 참여하고 싶다면 작품 견본과 함께 한 단락의 자기소개를 보내달라(send a one-paragraph biography)고 했으므로, (A)가 정답이다.

어휘 contract 계약서

▸▸Paraphrasing　지문의 biography → 정답의 background

178 주제 / 목적

번역 로드클리프 씨가 이메일을 쓴 이유는?

(A) 자신을 새 고객에게 소개하려고
(B) 자신의 경험을 잠재 고용주에게 설명하려고
(C) 업무의 일부로 인터뷰를 잡으려고
(D) 대학교 방문 일정을 잡으려고

해설 이메일의 세 번째 단락에서 로드클리프 씨는 칼랜더 교수의 저서를 〈위클리 쿠리어〉에서 논평하고 싶다(it would be my pleasure to review it in the *Weekly Courier*)고 한 후, 내일 통화할 시간이 되는지(Are you available for a phone call tomorrow?) 물었다. 따라서 칼랜더 교수에게 전화 인터뷰를 요청하기 위해 쓴 이메일임을 알 수 있으므로, (C)가 정답이다.

어휘 potential 잠재적인 arrange 마련하다, 주선하다

179 연계

번역 로드클리프 씨는 샌딘 교수의 낭독을 며칠에 듣고 싶어하는가?

(A) 6월 2일
(B) 6월 3일
(C) 6월 11일
(D) 6월 13일

해설 이메일의 첫 번째 단락에서 로드클리프 씨는 칼랜더 교수와 샌딘 교수가 스폿티드 캣에서 낭독할 예정(you and Professor Sandene are reading at the Spotted Cat)이라고 들었다며 두 낭독회 모두 참석하고 싶다(I am hoping to attend both readings)고 했다. 일정표를 보면, 샌딘 교수의 낭독회는 6월 13일에 있을 예정이므로, (D)가 정답이다.

▸▸ Paraphrasing   지문의 attend both readings
→ 질문의 hear Professor Sandene read

180 연계

번역 로드클리프 씨는 자신의 칼럼에서 어떤 책을 논평하고 싶어하는가?

(A) 〈바다 속으로: 시 모음집〉
(B) 〈위로의 기술〉
(C) 〈가족이라는 연대〉
(D) 〈복고풍: 운동복의 역사〉

해설 이메일의 두 번째 단락에서 로드클리프 씨는 다음 칼럼에서 칼랜더 교수와 그의 저서를 다루고(whether I may feature you and your book in my next column) 싶다는 의사를 표현했다. 일정표를 보면, 칼랜더 교수가 〈위로의 기술〉의 저자(author of The Mastery of Comfort)라고 나와 있으므로, (B)가 정답이다.

▸▸ Paraphrasing   지문의 would like to ask whether I may feature → 질문의 want to review

181-185 웹페이지 + 이메일

케릴린 패션 - 귀사의 브랜드를 위한 특별한 의류

자사의 브랜드로 만들 제품을 찾고 있는 의류 소매업체이신가요? 저희는 기업 대상 도매업체로서 셔츠, 바지, 신발, 패션 액세서리를 제공합니다. 폭넓은 저희의 컬렉션을 둘러보시고 귀사의 고객층을 위한 제품을 선택하세요. 182(C)귀사의 브랜드 로고가 있는 라벨을 주문하신 제품에 박음질해 드립니다. 주문 건은 3-4주 후 도착합니다. 케릴린 패션은 귀사의 제품 생산 시간을 아껴 제품을 시장에 빠르게 내놓을 수 있도록 해드립니다. 181시즌마다 산뜻한 새 디자인을 제공하며 182(A)요청 시 견본 제품을 발송해 드릴 수 있습니다.

대량 주문 건에는 할인을 제공합니다. 전 세계 어디든 주문 물품의 무게에 기반한 요금으로 배송해 드립니다.

상품은 환불이 불가하며 훼손된 상태로 도착한 일체의 상품에 대해서는 신용 전표를 발행합니다. 첫 주문을 시작하려면, 온라인 계정을 만드

셔야 합니다. 그러면 182(D)/183귀사에 계정 관리자가 배정되며, 이 관리자가 24시간 이내에 연락을 드려 첫 주문 및 향후 주문을 용이하게 도와드릴 것입니다.

어휘 exceptional 이례적일 정도로 우수한, 특출한 apparel 의류, 의복 retailer 소매업체 business-to-business 기업간의 wholesaler 도매업체 extensive 광범위한, 폭넓은 catalog (제품 등의) 모음, 컬렉션, 또는 이를 소개한 책 customer base 고객층 badge (라벨, 표 등을) 달다, 견장[기장]을 달다 sewn 박음질된 save A time A가 시간을 절약하게 해주다 merchandise 상품 upon request 요청 시 extend 베풀다, 주다 charge 요금 nonrefundable 환불되지 않는 credit (다음 거래 시 해당 금액을 공제 받을 수 있는) 신용 전표 issue 발행하다 damaged 훼손된, 손상된 account 계정, 고객사 assign 배정하다 account manager 계정 관리자, 영업 관리자 facilitate 가능하게 하다, 용이하게 하다

수신: 테렌스 앤더슨 〈tanderson@kerilynfashions.com〉
발신: 산딥 발리가 〈sbaliga@baligadesigns.in〉
날짜: 8월 15일
제목: 신규 주문을 위한 문의

앤더슨 씨께,

183지난달 케릴린 패션에서 면 혼방 티셔츠로 첫 주문을 할 수 있도록 효과적으로 도와주셔서 진심으로 감사합니다. 185잘 만들어진 제품이라 저희 고객들이 아주 좋아했고 덕분에 2주만에 품절됐어요. 같은 제품을 요청하고 싶은데 더 많은 수량이 필요할 것으로 184예상합니다. 저희가 가격 할인을 받으려면 주문 수량이 얼마나 되어야 할까요? 빠른 응답 주실 것으로 알고, 미리 감사드립니다.

산딥 발리가

어휘 enquiry 문의 thank you very kindly 진심으로 감사하다 effectively 효과적으로 blend 혼방 anticipate 예상하다, 기대하다 quantity 양 in advance 미리 response 응답, 답변

181 사실 관계 확인

번역 케릴린 패션에 대해 알 수 있는 것은?

(A) 가족이 경영하는 업체이다.
(B) 익일 배송을 제공한다.
(C) 가격이 경쟁력 있다.
(D) 제품군이 정기적으로 업데이트된다.

해설 웹페이지의 첫 번째 단락 후반부에서 시즌마다 산뜻한 새 디자인을 제공한다(we offer fresh, new designs every season)고 했으므로, 정기적으로 제품군을 업데이트한다는 것을 알 수 있다. 따라서 (D)가 정답이다.

어휘 competitive 경쟁력 있는 regularly 정기적으로

▸▸ Paraphrasing   지문의 offer fresh, new designs every season
→ 정답의 Its products selection is updated regularly.

182 사실 관계 확인

번역 케릴린 패션의 서비스에 대한 장점으로 명시되지 않은 것은?

(A) 주문 전 검토할 수 있도록 견본 제품을 제공할 수 있다.

(B) 대량 주문의 경우 배송비가 면제된다.

(C) 상품은 고객의 업체명으로 미리 라벨이 붙여져 도착한다.

(D) 특별 관리자를 배정해 신규 고객을 도울 수 있도록 한다.

해설 케릴린 패션의 서비스에 대한 장점은 웹페이지에서 확인 가능하다. 첫 번째 단락의 '요청 시 견본 제품을 발송한다(sample items can be sent to you upon request)'에서 (A)를, '브랜드 로고가 있는 라벨을 주문한 제품에 박음질해 준다(We will badge the products in your order with sewn-in labels carrying your company's branded logo)'에서 (C)를, 마지막 단락의 '계정 관리자가 배정되어 첫 주문 및 향후 주문을 용이하게 도와준다(You will be assigned an account manager who will ~ facilitate your first and future orders)'에서 (D)를 서비스의 장점으로 확인할 수 있다. 하지만 대량 주문에 제공되는 것은 할인(We extend discounts on large orders)이며, 전 세계 어디든 주문 물품의 무게에 기반한 요금으로 배송한다(We ship ~ with charges that are based on the weight of the order)고 했으므로, 사실이 아닌 (B)가 정답이다.

어휘 charge 요금 waive 면제하다

> **▸ Paraphrasing** 지문의 sample items can be sent to you upon request
> → 보기 (A)의 can provide sample products ~ in advance of ordering
> 지문의 sewn-in labels carrying your company's branded logo
> → 보기 (C)의 a client's business prelabeled
> 지문의 an account manager who ~ facilitate your first and future orders
> → 보기 (D)의 special managers to assist new clients

183 연계

번역 앤더슨 씨는 누구이겠는가?

(A) 패션모델

(B) 패션 디자이너

(C) 계정 관리자

(D) 사무실 관리자

해설 이메일의 초반부에서 발리가 씨는 지난달 케릴린 패션에서 첫 주문을 할 수 있도록 효과적으로 도와준 것(so effectively facilitating our very first order last month from Kerilyn Fashions)에 대해 앤더슨 씨에게 감사를 전했다. 웹페이지의 마지막 단락을 보면, 계정 관리자가 첫 주문 및 향후 주문을 가능하게 도와준다(You will be assigned an account manager who ~ facilitate your first and future orders)고 했으므로, 앤더슨 씨가 발리가 씨에게 배정된 계정 관리자라고 추론할 수 있다. 따라서 (C)가 정답이다.

184 동의어 찾기

번역 이메일의 첫 번째 단락, 네 번째 줄에 쓰인 "anticipate"와 의미가 가장 가까운 단어는?

(A) 예상하다

(B) 막다

(C) 고대하다

(D) 의존하다

해설 'anticipate'를 포함한 부분은 '더 많은 수량이 필요할 것으로 예상한다(we anticipate needing a larger quantity)'라는 의미로 해석되는데, 여기서 anticipate는 '예상하다, 예측하다'라는 뜻으로 쓰였다. 따라서 '예상하다, 기대하다'라는 의미의 (A) expect가 정답이다.

185 사실 관계 확인

번역 발리가 씨가 언급한 것은?

(A) 그의 업체는 지점들을 열 계획이다.

(B) 그의 티셔츠 재고가 너무 많다.

(C) 티셔츠를 여러 색으로 주문했다.

(D) 케릴린 패션 제품의 품질이 좋다고 확신한다.

해설 이메일의 초반부에서 발리가 씨는 처음 주문한 티셔츠가 잘 만들어진 제품이라 고객들이 아주 좋아했고 덕분에 2주만에 품절됐다(They were well made, and our customers liked them so much that we sold out in two weeks)고 했다. 따라서 그가 케릴린 패션 제품의 품질에 대한 확신을 갖고 있음을 알 수 있으므로, (D)가 정답이다.

어휘 branch 지점 stock 재고품

> **▸ Paraphrasing** 지문의 well made
> → 정답의 of high quality

186-190 표지판 + 영수증 + 이메일

베스 중고 가구
보관 규정

1. 구입한 상품은 7일간 보관할 수 있습니다.

2. **186**7일 이후까지 찾아가지 않은 상품은 재고로 반환되어 재판매됩니다.

3. 당사는 수거 대기 중인 물품의 훼손에 책임지지 않습니다.

4. 대형 가구는 요청 시 배송 서비스를 제공해 드립니다. **188**무게 25kg 이상이 대형 가구로 간주됩니다.

5. **187**판매 후 교환 및 반품은 불가합니다.

어휘 secondhand 중고의 purchase 구입하다 merchandise 상품 unclaimed 찾아가지 않은, 주인이 나서지 않는 inventory 재고, 물품 목록 await 기다리다 collection 수집, 수거 on request 요청 시 consider 간주하다 final 변경할 수 없는

```
영수증
베스 중고 가구
```

189물품 번호: 39235

영수증 번호: 47712

188무게: 18kg

189구입일자: 8월 8일

고객명: 에드워드 하세가와

총 금액: 135달러

결제 방식: 신용카드

메모: 찾아갈 수 있도록 보관 바랍니다.

수신: 고객 서비스 〈customerservice@bethssecondhand.ca〉

발신: 에드워드 하세가와 〈e.hasegawa@abodemail.com〉

제목: 가구 픽업

날짜: 8월 10일

제 이름은 에드워드 하세가와입니다. **1898월 8일 화요일에 매장에서 책상을 구입했어요.** 책상을 찾으러 가려고 동료의 트럭을 빌릴 계획이었는데 그 트럭이 앞으로 2주간 수리점에 들어갈 예정이라는 사실을 오늘 알게 됐습니다. **190예기치 못한 사정 때문에 보관 기간을 연장할 수 있는지 여쭤보고 싶습니다.** 저는 가게의 오랜 고객으로 소파, 선반, 식탁, 기타 물품 등을 구입한 바 있습니다.

에드워드

어휘   coworker 동료   extend 연장하다, 늘리다   unforeseen 예측하지 못한, 뜻밖의   circumstances 상황, 사정   shelving 선반

186   세부 사항

번역   표지판에 따르면, 찾아가지 않은 가구는 어떻게 되는가?

(A) 다시 판매용으로 내놓아진다.

(B) 지역 자선단체에 기부된다.

(C) 즉시 폐기된다.

(D) 장기 보관소로 옮겨진다.

해설   보관 규정(Hold Rules) 2번 항목에서 7일 이후까지 찾아가지 않는 상품은 재고로 반환되어 재판매된다(Merchandise unclaimed after 7 days will be returned to inventory and resold)고 했으므로, (A)가 정답이다.

어휘   be made available 사용 가능하다   donate 기부하다   charity 자선단체   promptly 즉시, 지체없이   be disposed of 처리되다, 폐기되다   storage 보관

> ▶▶ **Paraphrasing**   지문의 returned to inventory and resold
> → 정답의 made available for sale again

187   추론 / 암시

번역   베스 중고 가구에 대해 암시된 것은?

(A) 새 경영진 하에 있다.

(B) 반품을 받지 않는다.

(C) 비영리 업체이다.

(D) 다른 매장을 연다.

해설   표지판의 보관 규정(Hold Rules) 5번 항목에서 판매 후 교환 및 반품은 불가하다(All sales are final)고 했으므로, (B)가 정답이다. 참고로, 'All sales are final'은 '교환 및 반품 불가'라는 고정 표현으로, 여기서 final은 변경되거나 다시 할 수 없음을 의미한다.

어휘   management 관리, 경영, 경영진   nonprofit 비영리적인

> ▶▶ **Paraphrasing**   지문의 All sales are final.
> → 정답의 It does not accept returns.

188   연계

번역   하세가와 씨의 구입품에 대해 알 수 있는 것은?

(A) 100달러 이하이다.

(B) 이틀 안에 찾으러 가야 한다.

(C) 훼손으로 인해 가격이 낮아졌다.

(D) 대형 가구로 분류되지 않는다.

해설   영수증에서 하세가와 씨가 구입한 제품의 무게(Weight)가 18kg임을 확인할 수 있다. 표지판의 보관 규정(Hold Rules) 4번 항목을 보면 무게 25kg 이상이 대형 가구로 간주된다(Large furniture is considered 25kg or heavier)고 나와 있으므로, 하세가와 씨의 구입품은 대형 가구로 분류되지 않는다는 것을 알 수 있다. 따라서 (D)가 정답이다.

어휘   reduce 낮추다, 줄이다

189   연계

번역   물품 번호 39235는 무엇이겠는가?

(A) 소파

(B) 책상

(C) 선반

(D) 탁자

해설   영수증을 보면, 물품 번호 39235(Item Number: 39235)는 하세가와 씨가 베스 중고 가구에서 8월 8일에 구입한 제품(Date of Purchase: 8 August)임을 확인할 수 있다. 이메일의 초반부에서 하세가와 씨가 8월 8일 화요일에 매장에서 책상을 구입했다(On Tuesday, 8 August, I bought a desk from your store)고 했으므로, 물품 번호 39235가 책상이라고 추론할 수 있다. 따라서 (B)가 정답이다.

190   주제 / 목적

번역   이메일을 쓴 목적은?

(A) 배송 시간을 잡으려고

(B) 구입 금액을 확인하려고

(C) 보관 기간 연장을 요청하려고

(D) 물품 교환에 대해 문의하려고

해설 이메일의 중반부에서 예기치 못한 사정 때문에 제품을 찾아갈 수 없게 되어 보관 기간을 연장할 수 있는지 문의하고 싶다(I'd like to ask whether the hold time can be extended because of these unforeseen circumstances)고 했으므로, (C)가 정답이다.

어휘 delivery 배송 extension 연장 exchange 교환

> ▶ Paraphrasing 지문의 **to ask whether the hold time can be extended** → 정답의 **To request an extension for a hold**

191-195 웹페이지 + 광고 + 이메일

---

http://www.lelandskilledstaffing.com

귀사의 다음 작업을 위해 숙련된 주거시설 배관공이나 상업시설 배관공이 필요하십니까? 많은 업체들이 그들이 필요로 하는 자격을 갖춘 배관공을 구하는 데 어려움을 겪고 있습니다. **191최근 설문 조사에 따르면, 자격증을 소지한 배관공에 대한 수요가 향후 10년간 20퍼센트 증가할 것이라고 합니다.**

릴런드 스킬드 스태핑은 공인 배관공을 찾을 수 있도록 도와, 귀사가 채용에 들이는 시간과 비용을 절약해 드립니다. 장기 프로젝트이든 긴급 배관 작업이 필요한 상황을 처리할 인부가 필요하든, 저희는 다양한 전문성을 갖춘 숙련된 인부를 요구에 맞춰 보내드립니다. **193저희가 작업자의 배경 및 경력을 확인하니 여러분은 업무에만 집중하실 수 있습니다.**

오늘 연락 주시면 귀하의 채용 요구사항을 충족하게끔 도와드리겠습니다.

어휘 skilled 숙련된, 노련한 residential 주거의, 주거시설의 commercial 상업의, 상업시설의 plumber 배관공 licensed 자격증을 소지한, 허가를 받은, 공인된 according to ~에 따라 demand 수요 staffing 직원 채용, 채용 대행사 certified 공인된 recruitment 모집, 채용 on-demand 필요시 이용 가능한, 주문[요구]형의 a range of 광범위한, 다양한 confirm 확인해 주다

자격증을 소지한 배관공
황 서비스
직책: 주거시설 배관공

직책 요약: **192스프링필드 최신 지점에서 일할 상근직 직원.** 신규 건축물과 기존 주택에서 모두 작업. 배관과 붙박이 세간, 가스 파이프 등의 정비, 수리, 교체 포함.

직책 요건: 배관 자격증, **195경력 3년 이상,** 운전면허증, 현대적 기술 활용 능력.

급여 범위: 경력에 따라 50,000-90,000달러, 유급 휴가.

근무시간: 특정 시기의 필요에 따라 달라짐. 일부 저녁 시간 작업 필요.

s.huang@huangservices.com으로 이력서를 보내주세요. **193철저한 신원 조사를 통과한 분들은 연락을 드려 인터뷰 일정을 잡게 됩니다.**

어휘 job title 직책, 직위 summary 요약 construction 건축물 existing 이미 존재하는 service 정비하다 replace 교체하다 fixture 붙박이 세간 requirement 요구사항, 요건 depending on ~에 따라 vary 달라지다 thorough 철저한 background check 신원 조사[조회], 배경 조사

수신: info@lelandskilledstaffing.com
발신: s.huang@huangservices.com
날짜: 4월 15일
제목: 직원 구합니다

담당자께,

제 업체에서 일할 주거시설 배관공을 찾고 있어서 이메일을 드립니다. **194얼마간 구인 공고를 게시했지만 적합한 지원자를 찾는데 성공하지 못했습니다. 195요구사항은 지원자가 배관 자격증을 소지해야 하는 것이며, 2년 이상의 경력이면 수용하겠습니다.** 지원자는 운전면허증도 필요하며 가끔 저녁 시간에 일할 수 있어야 합니다. 5월 5일 월요일에 근무를 시작할 수 있는 분들의 명단을 보내주시겠어요? 저희 회사가 그날 지역 내 신규 주택 단지에서 배관 설치를 시작할 예정입니다.

스테파니 황

어휘 to whom it may concern 담당자께 job advertisement 구인 공고 for a while 잠시 동안 require 필요로 하다 candidate 지원자, 후보자 accept 받아들이다, 수용하다 occasionally 가끔 install 설치하다 housing development 주택 단지

---

191 세부 사항

번역 웹페이지에 따르면, 무엇이 증가할 것으로 예상되는가?

(A) 교육 기간
(B) 장비 가격
(C) 인건비
(D) 숙련된 배관공 수요

해설 웹페이지의 첫 번째 단락에서 자격증을 소지한 배관공에 대한 수요가 향후 10년간 20퍼센트 증가할 것(the demand for licensed plumbers will increase by 20 percent in the next ten years)이라고 했다. 따라서 (D)가 정답이다.

어휘 equipment 장비 labor 노동, 근로

> ▶ Paraphrasing 지문의 **the demand for licensed plumbers** → 정답의 **The need for skilled plumbers**

---

192 추론 / 암시

번역 광고에서 황 서비스에 대해 암시된 것은?

(A) 3년간 영업해 왔다.
(B) 특정 계절에 문을 닫는다.
(C) 시간제 근로만 이용 가능하다.
(D) 지점이 한 곳 이상 있다.

해설 구인 광고의 직책 요약(Position Summary) 부분에서 스프링필드 최신 지점에서 일할 정규직 직원(Full-time position available at newest location in Springfield)을 찾고 있다고 했는데, '최신 지점'이라는 것은 해당 지점 이외에 다른 지점도 있음을 의미한다. 따라서 (D)가 정답이다.

어휘 certain 특정한

193 연계

번역 릴런드 스킬드 스태핑과 황 서비스의 공통점은?

(A) 모두 황 씨가 설립했다.
(B) 스프링필드에 있다.
(C) 작업자의 자격을 확인한다.
(D) 상업시설 배관 전문이다.

해설 웹페이지의 두 번째 단락 후반부를 보면, 릴런드 스킬드 스태핑에서 채용 대행 시 작업자의 배경 및 경력을 확인한다(We confirm the background and experience of the workers)고 되어 있다. 황 서비스에서 게시한 채용 공고 하단에서도 철저한 신원 조사를 통과한 지원자(those who pass a thorough background check)만 면접을 볼 수 있다고 했으므로, 두 회사 모두 작업자의 자격을 확인한다는 것을 알 수 있다. 따라서 (C)가 정답이다.

어휘 have in common 공통점이 있다 found 설립하다 verify 확인하다, 입증하다 qualification 자격 specialize in ~를 전문으로 하다

194 사실 관계 확인

번역 황 씨가 구인 공고에 대해 언급한 것은?

(A) 성공적이지 못했다.
(B) 곧 삭제될 것이다.
(C) 올바른 정보가 들어 있지 않았다.
(D) 인기 있는 웹사이트에 게시되었다.

해설 이메일의 초반부에서 황 씨가 구인 공고를 게시했지만 적합한 지원자를 찾는 데 성공하지 못했다(I have had a job advertisement posted ~ but have not had success in finding the right candidate)고 했으므로, (A)가 정답이다.

어휘 delete 삭제하다 contain 들어 있다 correct 올바른, 맞는

▸▸ Paraphrasing 지문의 a job advertisement posted
→ 질문의 a job posting

지문의 have not had success
→ 정답의 was not successful

195 연계

번역 황 서비스에서 해당 직책에 대해 변경한 것은?

(A) 초봉
(B) 필요한 자격증의 수
(C) 근무시간
(D) 요구하는 경력 연수

해설 구인 광고의 직책 요건(Position Requirements)을 보면, 황 서비

스는 지원자에게 3년 이상의 경력(3 years' experience)을 요구했다. 하지만 이메일의 중반부에서 황 씨가 2년 이상의 경력도 수용하겠다(We ~ will accept two years of experience)고 했으므로, 요구하는 경력 연수가 변경되었음을 알 수 있다. 따라서 (D)가 정답이다.

196-200 기사 + 일정표 + 이메일

웬포드 테크놀로지스의 신규 회의 장학금

(1월 2일)—인터넷 서비스 업계의 대표주자 웬포드 테크놀로지스가 [200]4월 21일부터 23일까지 뉴저지 주 뉴어크에서 열릴 '컴퓨터 과학 분야의 돌파구' 회의에 참석하고 싶은 후보자 중 자격을 갖춘 6인에게 장학금을 지급할 계획이라고 발표했다. [196]회의 참가자들에게 더 넓은 세계적 관점을 독려하기 위해 남아메리카, 아프리카, 아시아에서 각각 2인이 장학금 수혜자로 선발될 예정이다.

"다양한 관점이 우리 업계가 성장하고 번영하게끔 도와준다고 확신합니다." 웬포드 테크놀로지의 최고경영자인 데일 켈빈 씨가 설명했다. "이를 위해 지리적으로 특정 지역 출신의 전문가들에게 기회를 주고자 합니다."

[197/199]지원자는 자격을 갖추려면 1-5년의 기간 동안 컴퓨터 과학 분야에서 상근직으로 고용된 상태여야 한다. 장학금에 관한 더 자세한 정보를 알아보려면 wenfordtech.com/scholarships를 방문하면 된다.

어휘 scholarship 장학금 offer 제공하다 qualified 자격을 갖춘 candidate 후보자, 지원자 breakthrough 돌파구, 약진 encourage 권하다, 장려하다 perspective 관점, 안목 individual 개인 recipient 받는 사람, 수혜자 a variety of 다양한 thrive 번창하다 to this end 이것을 위해 extend 주다, 베풀다 geographic 지리학상의, 지리적인 applicant 지원자 eligible 자격이 있는

'컴퓨터 과학 분야의 돌파구' 회의
예비 일정표, 4월 21-23일

회의에서 있을 활동 개요는 아래와 같습니다. 매일 동일한 구성 방식을 따릅니다. [198]연사 이름 및 소속이 표시된 최종 일정표는 행사 2개월 전에 보실 수 있습니다.

오전 8시 30분 - 오전 9시	유럽식 아침 식사 - 음식은 리셉션 홀에 마련됩니다.
오전 9시 - 오전 9시 30분	공표
[200]오전 9시 40분 - 정오	발표
정오 - 오후 1시	점심시간—회의 참석자들은 각자 점심을 먹습니다. 회의장에서 도보로 갈 수 있는 거리에 가격이 적당한 음식점이 많이 있습니다.
오후 1시 - 오후 4시	워크숍
오후 4시 - 오후 5시 15분	패널 토론 및 세션 평가

어휘 preliminary 예비의 outline 개요 affiliation 소속 prior to ~전에 announcement 공표, 발표 presentation 발표 attendee 참석자 reasonably priced 적정하게 가격이 매겨진 establishment 시설 within walking distance of ~에서 도보로 갈 수 있는 거리의 venue 장소 evaluation 평가

수신: 신디 코넬리 〈cconnelly@wenfordtech.com〉
발신: 아다무 아데바요 〈aadebayo@spmail.co.za〉
날짜: 2월 3일
제목: 장학금 감사합니다

코넬리 씨께,

199웬포드 테크놀로지스에서 저의 '돌파구' 회의 참석을 지원해 주셔서 점 진심으로 감사드립니다. 저에겐 흥미로운 경험입니다. 세계 여러 곳에서 같은 분야에 종사하는 사람들로부터 많이 배우기를 고대하고 있습니다.

200제가 오후 2시 30분(요하네스버그 시간)에 고객과 일일 전화 회의를 진행하는데, 이는 취소가 불가능하다는 점을 말씀드리고 싶습니다. 이 업무는 뉴어크 시간으로 오전 9시 30분에 시작하며, 제가 30분 정도 주의를 기울여야 합니다. 그 외에는 모든 회의 행사에 전부 참석하고 싶습니다. 저에게 더 필요하신 정보가 있으면 알려주세요.

아다무 아데바요

어휘 sincere 진심 어린 attendance 참석, 출석 opportunity 기회 mention 말하다, 언급하다 conference call 전화 회의 require an attention 주의를 요하다 otherwise 그 외에는 proceeding 행사, 일련의 행위

196 세부 사항

번역 웬포드 테크놀로지스는 장학금으로 무엇을 촉진하고자 하는가?

(A) 빠른 성장
(B) 공동 작업
(C) 다양한 관점
(D) 혁신적 문제 해결

해설 기사의 첫 번째 단락에서 회의 참가자들에게 더 넓은 세계적 관점을 독려하기 위해(To encourage a greater global perspective among conference participants) 남아메리카, 아프리카, 아시아에서 각각 2인이 장학금 수혜자로 선발될 예정이라고 했다. 따라서 장학금이 다양한 관점을 촉진하고자 지급됨을 알 수 있으므로, (C)가 정답이다.

어휘 rapid 빠른 collaborative 공동의 diverse 다양한 innovative 혁신적인

▸▸Paraphrasing 지문의 encourage → 질문의 promote
지문의 a greater global perspective
→ 정답의 Diverse perspectives

197 세부 사항

번역 기사에 따르면, 장학금 지원자에게 무엇이 요구되는가?

(A) 온라인 설문 조사에 응해야 한다.
(B) 워크숍 주제를 제안해야 한다.
(C) 회의 시간을 미리 선택해야 한다.
(D) 경력 초기 단계에 있어야 한다.

해설 기사의 마지막 단락에서 장학금 지원자는 1-5년의 기간 동안 상근직으로 고용된 상태여야 한다(Applicants must be employed full-time ~ for a period of between one and five years in order to be eligible)고 했다. 따라서 경력의 초기 단계에 있는 사람들에게 장학금 지원 자격이 주어진다는 것을 알 수 있으므로, (D)가 정답이다.

어휘 respond to ~에 응하다 in advance 미리 early stage 초기 단계

▸▸Paraphrasing 지문의 for a period of between one and five years → 정답의 at an early stage

198 추론 / 암시

번역 일정표에서 회의에 대해 암시한 것은?

(A) 매일 출장 요리로 점심 식사를 제공한다.
(B) 일부 세부사항을 마무리하고 있다.
(C) 토론 진행은 자원봉사자에게 의존한다.
(D) 매일 구성 방식이 달라진다.

해설 일정표의 상단을 보면, 연사 이름 및 소속이 표시된 최종 일정표는 행사 2개월 전에 볼 수 있다(A final schedule with speakers' names and their affiliations will be available two months prior to the event)고 되어 있다. 따라서 일부 세부 사항이 조율 중임을 추론할 수 있으므로, (B)가 정답이다.

어휘 finalize 마무리 짓다, 완결하다 rely on ~에 기대다, 의존하다 vary 달라지다

199 연계

번역 아데바요 씨에 대해 어떤 결론을 내릴 수 있겠는가?

(A) 컴퓨터 과학 분야에 종사한다.
(B) 웬포드 테크놀로지스로부터 일자리 제의를 받았다.
(C) 해외 고객을 얻고 싶어 한다.
(D) 뉴어크에서 직업 교육을 완수했다.

해설 이메일의 첫 번째 단락에서 아데바요 씨는 자신의 회의 참석을 지원해 준 것(supporting my attendance at the Breakthroughs conference)에 대해 웬포드 테크놀로지스에 감사를 전했다. 기사의 마지막 단락을 보면, 지원자는 컴퓨터 과학 분야에서 상근직으로 고용된 상태여야 한다(Applicants must be employed full-time in computer science ~ in order to be eligible)고 했으므로, 아데바요 씨도 컴퓨터 과학 분야에 종사한다고 볼 수 있다. 따라서 (A)가 정답이다.

어휘 acquire 획득하다, 얻다 complete 완료하다

▸▸Paraphrasing 지문의 must be employed → 정답의 works

200 연계

번역 아데바요 씨는 회의의 어떤 행사 도중에 매번 자리를 비울 것인가?

    (A) 아침 식사

    (B) 공표

    (C) 발표

    (D) 패널 토론

해설 이메일의 두 번째 단락에서 아데바요 씨는 자신이 매일 오후 2시 30분(요하네스버그 시간)에 고객과 전화 회의를 진행하며 이는 취소가 불가능하다고 한 후, 뉴어크 시간으로 오전 9시 30분에 시작해서 30분 정도 주의를 기울여야 한다(This task would start at 9:30 A.M. in Newark, and it will require my attention for 30 minutes or so)고 덧붙였다. 기사의 첫 번째 단락에서 회의가 뉴어크에서 개최된다고 했고, 일정표를 보면 해당 시간과 겹치는 일정은 오전 9시 40분에 시작하는 발표(Presentations)이므로, (C)가 정답이다.

어휘 absent 결석한, 부재한

> ▸▸ **Paraphrasing**   지문의 **daily** → 질문의 **each day**

101 (B)	**102** (B)	**103** (D)	**104** (C)	**105** (A)
106 (A)	**107** (B)	**108** (C)	**109** (B)	**110** (C)
111 (A)	**112** (B)	**113** (C)	**114** (A)	**115** (C)
116 (A)	**117** (D)	**118** (D)	**119** (D)	**120** (A)
121 (B)	**122** (B)	**123** (D)	**124** (D)	**125** (C)
126 (D)	**127** (B)	**128** (C)	**129** (B)	**130** (D)
131 (B)	**132** (C)	**133** (A)	**134** (D)	**135** (A)
136 (D)	**137** (D)	**138** (B)	**139** (B)	**140** (D)
141 (A)	**142** (D)	**143** (A)	**144** (B)	**145** (C)
146 (B)	**147** (C)	**148** (A)	**149** (A)	**150** (B)
151 (D)	**152** (C)	**153** (B)	**154** (C)	**155** (C)
156 (A)	**157** (D)	**158** (B)	**159** (A)	**160** (D)
161 (B)	**162** (B)	**163** (C)	**164** (D)	**165** (A)
166 (C)	**167** (B)	**168** (B)	**169** (A)	**170** (C)
171 (A)	**172** (C)	**173** (D)	**174** (A)	**175** (C)
176 (A)	**177** (B)	**178** (D)	**179** (C)	**180** (B)
181 (C)	**182** (C)	**183** (D)	**184** (A)	**185** (C)
186 (D)	**187** (C)	**188** (D)	**189** (B)	**190** (B)
191 (D)	**192** (A)	**193** (B)	**194** (A)	**195** (C)
196 (D)	**197** (C)	**198** (D)	**199** (A)	**200** (B)

PART 5

101 동사 자리 _ 수 일치

해설 주격 관계대명사 who가 이끄는 절의 동사 자리로, 보기에서 (A) want와 (B) wants 중 하나를 선택해야 한다. 관계사절의 동사는 선행사와 수가 일치해야 하는데, anyone은 단수로 취급되므로 (B) wants가 정답이 된다. (C) wanting과 (D) to want는 준동사로 빈칸에 들어갈 수 없다.

번역 회의 전 커피 한 잔을 원하는 모든 사람을 위해 휴게실에 커피가 있습니다.

어휘 break room 휴게실

102 전치사 자리 _ 어휘

해설 명사구 a ten-year warranty를 목적어로 취하는 전치사 자리로, 자동사 comes와 어울려 쓰이는 단어가 필요하다. 10년간의 품질보증서(warranty)는 여행용 가방(suitcase)과 함께 제공되는 것이므로, comes와 함께 '~이 딸려 있다, ~와 함께 나오다'라는 의미를 완성하는 (B) with가 정답이다. (A) if와 (C) so는 접속사로 빈칸에 들어갈 수 없다.

번역 모든 레디 웨어 여행용 가방은 10년짜리 품질보증서와 함께 나온다.

어휘 warranty 품질보증서

103 전치사 어휘

해설 장소를 나타내는 두 명사구 the new apartment building과 the river를 연결해주는 전치사 자리이다. 따라서 위치 관계를 나타내는 단어가 들어가야 자연스러우므로, '~ 옆에[가에]'라는 의미의 (D) by가 정답이다.

번역 오설리반 씨는 강가에 있는 새 아파트 건물의 전기 작업을 감독했다.

어휘 oversee 감독하다   electrical 전기의

104 인칭대명사의 격 _ 소유격

해설 동사 telephone의 목적어 역할을 하는 명사구 booking department를 한정 수식하는 자리이므로, 소유격 인칭대명사 (C) our가 정답이다.

번역 호텔 예약에 관한 문의사항은 저희 예약 부서 555-0109로 전화하십시오.

어휘 reservation 예약   department 부서

105 부사 자리 _ 동명사 수식

해설 빈칸 뒤에 오는 defending the company's reputation(회사의 명성을 지킨 것)은 자넷 로즈가 칭찬을 받은 이유(was commended for)를 나타낸다. 따라서 이 동명사구를 수식할 수 있는 부사가 빈칸에 들어가야 하므로, (A) assertively(적극적으로)가 정답이다. defending을 현재분사로 보고 빈칸에 명사를 넣을 수 있다고 가정하더라도, (D) assertion은 '주장, 행사'라는 뜻으로 칭찬을 받는 이유가 되기엔 어색하며 회사의 명성을 지키는 주체가 될 수 없으므로 적절치 않다. (B) assert는 동사, (C) assertive는 형용사로 품사상 빈칸에 들어갈 수 없다.

번역 자넷 로즈는 회사의 명성을 적극적으로 지켜내 칭찬을 받았다.

어휘 commend 칭찬하다, 추천하다   defend 지키다, 옹호하다   reputation 명성, 평판   assert 강하게 주장하다   assertive 적극적인, 확신에 찬

106 동사 어형 _ 태

해설 주어 A second order for 500 recycled paper cups의 동사 자리로, 보기에서 (A) was placed, (B) was placing, (D) placed 중 하나를 선택해야 한다. 주문(order)은 누군가에 의해 행해지는 대상이므로, 수동태 동사인 (A) was placed가 정답이 된다. (C) to place는 준동사로 빈칸에 들어갈 수 없다.

번역 재활용 종이컵 500개의 두 번째 주문이 지난주에 이뤄졌다.

어휘 place an order 주문을 넣다   recycle 재활용하다

107 명사 어휘

해설 One of the ------- for the position이 주어, is가 동사, three years of customer service experience가 주격 보어인 문장이다. 3년간의 고객 서비스 경력은 특정 직책에 요구되는 조건 중 하나라고 볼 수 있으므로, '(자격) 요건, 필요조건'이라는 의미의

(B) requirements가 정답이다. requirement가 전치사 for와 자주 쓰인다는 것은 반드시 알아 두자.

번역 해당 직책의 요건 중 하나는 3년간의 고객 서비스 경력이다.

어휘 associate (직장) 동료   assistant 보조, 조수

108 명사 자리 _ 동사의 주어

해설 동사 will receive의 주어 역할을 하는 명사 자리로, 이메일을 받는(receive a weekly e-mail) 주체가 들어가야 한다. 따라서 (C) Supervisors(관리자)가 정답이다. 동명사인 (D) Supervising도 주어 자리에 들어갈 수 있지만 문맥상 빈칸에는 적절치 않고, (A) Supervises는 동사, (B) Supervisory는 형용사로 품사상 빈칸에 들어갈 수 없다.

번역 관리자들은 근무 시간 기록표를 승인하라고 상기시키는 주간 이메일을 받을 것이다.

어휘 remind 상기시키다   approve 승인하다

109 전치사 어휘

해설 the hotel chain Contempo Inns와 new management의 관계를 적절히 나타내는 전치사가 들어가야 한다. 호텔은 특정 경영진이나 체제 하에 있는 것이므로, (B) under가 정답이다. 참고로, management, supervision, direction, leadership과 같이 관리나 감독을 의미하는 명사 앞에는 전치사 under가 자주 쓰인다.

번역 다음 주부터 콘템포 인 호텔 체인이 새 경영 체제 하에 들어갈 것이다.

어휘 management 경영(진)

110 한정사 자리 _ 수 일치

해설 전치사 about의 목적어 역할을 하는 복수가산명사 staff members를 한정 수식하는 자리이므로, 소유격 인칭대명사 (C) their가 정답이다. (A) whose도 명사를 수식할 수 있지만 문장 중간에 들어갈 경우 접속사 역할을 하므로 뒤에 절이 와야 한다. (B) while은 부사절 접속사로 구조상 빈칸에 들어갈 수 없으며, (D) much는 불가산명사와 쓰여야 하므로 오답이다.

번역 관리자는 인사부서에 연락을 취해 직원들에 대한 정보를 얻을 수 있다.

어휘 access information 정보를 얻다

111 명사 어휘

해설 customer와 복합명사를 이루는 명사 자리로, 회사가 전념할 만한(committed to) 분야를 나타내는 단어가 들어가야 한다. 따라서 customer와 함께 '고객 만족'이라는 의미를 완성하는 (A) satisfaction이 정답이다. customer satisfaction은 빈출 표현이니 암기해 두는 것이 좋다.

번역 추 홈 헬스 서비스는 18년간 영업한 후에도 고객 만족에 계속 전념하고 있다.

어휘 remain 계속[여전히] ~이다   committed to ~에 전념하는   production 생산   opportunity 기회

112 관계대명사 _ 주격

해설 문장에 동사가 2개(are working, will now be working) 있으므로, The obstetrics nurses부터 Dorothy Caramella까지를 주어, will (now) be working을 본동사로 보는 것이 타당하다. 빈칸이 이끄는 절의 의미를 따져보면, 주어가 빠진 불완전한 절(are working under Dorothy Caramella)임을 알 수 있다. 따라서 빈칸에는 해당 절을 이끌어 The obstetrics nurses를 수식하는 주격 관계대명사가 들어가야 하므로, (B) who가 정답이다. (A) they 및 (D) these는 절을 이끌 수 없으며, (C) when은 관계부사로 쓰일 경우 완전한 절을 이끌게 되므로 빈칸에 들어갈 수 없다.

번역 도로시 카라멜라 밑에서 일하는 산과 간호사들은 이제 피에르 콕토를 위해 일할 것이다.

어휘 obstetrics 산과

113 형용사 어휘

해설 주어인 Visitor parking 및 위치를 묘사하는 전치사구 behind the office complex와 가장 잘 어울리는 형용사를 선택해야 한다. 사무실 단지 뒤는 방문객 주차장이 있는 장소라고 볼 수 있으므로, '이용 가능한'이라는 의미의 (C) available이 정답이다.

번역 방문객 주차장은 메이필드 가에 있는 사무실 단지 뒤에서 이용할 수 있다.

어휘 complex 복합 건물, 단지   adjusted 조절된, 보정된   visual 시각의   urgent 긴급한

114 명사 자리 _ 전치사의 목적어 _ 수 일치

해설 빈칸은 전치사 Among의 목적어 역할을 하는 명사 자리로, other의 수식을 받는다. Among이 '(셋 이상) 중에서, 사이에'라는 뜻이므로, 가산명사 task의 복수형태인 (A) tasks가 정답이다. 「Among other+복수명사」는 여러 대상 중 하나를 언급할 때 쓰이는 표현이다.

번역 여러 업무 중에서도 구매 부서는 최상의 가격으로 물품을 조달하기 위해 계약을 협상하는 일을 한다.

어휘 purchasing 구매   negotiate 협상하다   contract 계약   procure 구하다, 조달하다

115 전치사 자리 _ 어휘

해설 동사 will be constructed와 명사구 three separate stages를 적절히 연결해 줄 전치사가 필요하다. 수영장 공사가 각기 다른 세 단계에 걸쳐 진행된다는 내용이므로, stages와 함께 '단계별로, 단계적으로'라는 표현을 완성하는 (C) in이 정답이다. (D) at은 stage와 쓰일 경우 '(특정) 단계에서'라는 시점을 나타내므로 빈칸에는 적절하지 않다.

번역 지역사회 수영장은 각기 다른 세 단계에 걸쳐 지어질 것이다.

어휘 construct 건설하다   separate 별개의, 서로 다른

TEST 9

116 동사 어휘

해설 명사구 its debut를 목적어로 취하는 타동사 자리이다. debut는 '첫선, 데뷔'라는 뜻으로 make와 어울려 쓰이므로, (A) made가 정답이다. make one's debut(데뷔를 하다, 첫선을 보이다)는 고정된 표현으로 암기해 두는 것이 좋다.

번역 라나야 7 노트북 컴퓨터는 연례 델바 기술 회담에서 첫선을 보였다.

어휘 summit (정상)회담

117 등위접속사 자리 _ 어휘

해설 루스터에서 제공하는 서비스(service)인 e-mail과 Web hosting을 연결하는 자리이므로, 등위접속사 (D) and가 정답이다. (B) yet과 (C) but은 대조적인 내용을 연결하는 등위접속사로 문맥상 빈칸에 적절하지 않고, (A) then은 부사로 품사상 빈칸에 들어갈 수 없다.

번역 루스터 이메일 및 웹 호스팅 서비스에서 개업 시 한 달간 무료로 이용하세요.

어휘 Web hosting 웹사이트 저장 공간을 제공하는 서비스[사업]

118 부사 자리 _ 형용사 수식

해설 빈칸 없이도 의미상 완전한 구조를 이루는 문장으로, 비교급 형용사 higher (than expected)가 turned out to be(~인 것으로 드러났다)의 보어 역할을 한다. 따라서 빈칸에는 higher를 강조하는 부사가 들어가야 하므로, (D) considerably(상당히)가 정답이다. (A) considering은 동명사/현재분사, (B) consider는 동사, (C) consideration은 명사로 품사상 빈칸에 들어갈 수 없다.

번역 교량 프로젝트 입찰가는 기대했던 것보다 상당히 높은 것으로 드러났다.

어휘 bid 경매 입찰(가) consider 고려하다, 숙고하다 consideration 사려, 숙고

119 부사 어휘

해설 빈칸은 형용사 close와 전치사구 to completion 사이에서 close를 강조하는 역할을 하므로, 형용사를 뒤에서 수식할 수 있는 부사가 들어가야 한다. 따라서 (D) enough(~할 만큼 충분히)가 정답이다. (A) already는 '이미, 벌써'라는 의미로 문맥상 빈칸에 적절하지 않고, (B) quite와 (C) such는 부사처럼 쓰일 경우 형용사 앞에 와야 한다.

번역 계약 협상은 목요일까지 체결될 수 있을 만큼 완료 상태에 가까워졌다.

어휘 negotiation 협상 completion 완료 sign the deal 계약에 서명하다, 협상을 체결하다

120 현재분사 _ 명사 수식

해설 동사 will cause의 목적어인 명사 damage를 수식하는 형용사 자리이므로, 보기에서 (A) lasting(영구적인, 지속적인)과 (C) last(지난, 마지막의) 중 하나를 선택해야 한다. 문맥상 직사광선(direct sunlight)이 가구에 미칠 손상의 정도를 묘사하는 단어가 들어가야 자연스러우므로, (A) lasting이 정답이 된다. (B) lasts는 동사,

(D) lastly는 부사로 품사상 빈칸에 들어갈 수 없다.

번역 필버 목공소는 고객들에게 직사광선이 가구에 영구적인 손상을 입힐 수 있다고 상기시킨다.

어휘 damage 손상, 훼손 lastly 마지막으로, 끝으로

121 한정사 어휘 _ 수 일치

해설 복수명사 employees를 수식하는 자리이므로, (B) All이 정답이다. (A) Each와 (C) Every는 단수명사와 쓰여야 하므로 오답이며, (D) Total은 '총계'를 강조하는 형용사이므로 빈칸에 적절치 않다.

번역 휴가를 쓰고 싶어 하는 모든 직원은 2주 전 미리 요청서를 제출해야 한다.

어휘 submit 제출하다 request 요청

122 형용사 자리 _ 명사 수식

해설 동사 make의 목적어인 명사 decisions를 수식하는 형용사 자리이므로, (B) strategic(전략적인, 전략상 중요한)이 정답이다. (A) strategized와 (C) strategize는 자동사, (D) strategically는 부사로 빈칸에 들어갈 수 없다.

번역 브론코 건축 설비는 데이터를 이용해 전략적 결정을 내리고 향후 운영을 계획한다.

어휘 make a decision 결정하다 plot 계획하다 strategize 전략을 짜다 operation 영업[운영] (활동)

123 부사 자리 _ 어휘

해설 미래진행 동사를 이루는 will과 be hosting 사이에서 동사를 수식하는 부사 자리이다. 문맥을 살펴보면, 저녁 음악회 시리즈 외에(In addition to the evening concert series) 어린이를 위한 행사(several events for children)도 개최할 예정이라는 내용이 되어야 자연스럽다. 따라서 '또한'이라는 의미의 (D) also가 정답이다. 참고로, (B) although는 접속사로 품사상 빈칸에 들어갈 수 없다.

번역 센테니얼 파크는 올 여름 저녁 음악회 시리즈 외에 어린이를 위한 여러 행사도 개최할 예정이다.

어휘 in addition to ~외에도, ~에 더하여 nevertheless 그럼에도 불구하고 consequently 그 결과, 따라서

124 한정사 자리 _ 수 일치

해설 Because가 이끄는 부사절의 주어인 복수명사 spaces를 수식하는 자리이므로, 복수가산명사와 쓰일 수 있는 (D) so many가 정답이다. (A) that much는 불가산명사와 쓰이고, (B) after which와 (C) in case는 접속사 역할을 하므로 구조상 빈칸에 들어갈 수 없다.

번역 몰의 아주 많은 공간에 임차인이 있어서 유동 인구수가 크게 증가했다.

어휘 tenant 임차인, 세입자 foot traffic 유동 인구수[규모] increase 증가하다

125 형용사 자리 _ 명사 수식

해설 빈칸은 ensure(보장하다, ~하게 하다)의 목적어 역할을 하는 명사 processing(처리)을 수식하는 자리로, 정관사 the와 함께 최상급을 이루는 형용사가 들어가야 한다. 따라서 (C) most rapid가 정답이다. (D) rapidity는 '민첩, 속도'라는 뜻으로 processing과 복합명사를 이룰 수 없고, (A) rapidly 및 (B) more rapidly는 부사이므로 품사상 빈칸에 들어갈 수 없다.

번역 신청이 가장 빠르게 처리될 수 있도록 서식을 꼼꼼히 작성해 주십시오.

어휘 complete a form 서식을 작성하다, 용지에 써넣다 application 신청 rapid 빠른

126 동사 어휘

해설 음료의 조제법을 변경한 것(Changes to the ~ formulation)이 고객의 마음에 끄는 데 실패했다는 내용이 되어야 자연스러우며, 구조상으로는 전치사 to와 어울려 쓰이는 동사가 들어가야 한다. 따라서 (D) appeal(~에게 매력적이다, ~의 마음을 끌다)이 정답이다. 참고로, (A) remain(남아 있다, 계속 ~이다)은 단독으로 쓰이거나 형용사 혹은 to부정사와 자주 쓰이고, (B) result는 보통 in(~를 초래하다)이나 from(~로부터 유래하다)과 짝을 이룬다. (C) appreciate는 자동사로 쓰일 경우 '가치가 오르다'라는 뜻을 나타낸다.

번역 톱 피즈 청량음료의 조제법 변경은 고객의 마음을 끄는 데 실패했다.

어휘 formulation 조제법 appreciate 감사하다, 진가를 알아보다

127 명사 자리 _ 동사의 주어 _ 어휘

해설 문장에 접속사 한 개(that)와 동사 두 개(will take, came)가 있으므로, The부터 next month까지를 주어, came as a surprise를 본동사구로 보는 것이 타당하다. 그렇다면 빈칸에는 놀라움으로 다가온 대상을 나타내며 that절(that Jennifer Chan will take over as CEO next month)과 동격을 이루는 명사가 들어가야 한다. 즉, 놀라움을 준 것은 제니퍼 찬이 다음 달에 CEO가 된다는 소식이므로, (B) announcement(발표, 소식)가 정답이 된다. 참고로, 문두에 정관사 The가 있기 때문에 Liu Supermarket이 고유명사임에도 불구하고 명사인 announcement를 의미상 수식할 수 있다(cf. the government('s) announcement 정부의 발표). 만일 앞에 The가 없다면 Liu Supermarket 뒤에 소유격을 나타내는 접미사('s)가 반드시 붙어야 한다. (D) announcer(발표자)는 사람 명사로 that절과 동격 관계를 이루지 않으므로 오답이다. 빈칸 뒤에 또 다른 접속사 that이 생략되었다고 가정하여 (A) announced를 빈칸에 넣게 되면 '리우 슈퍼마켓은 제니퍼 찬이 다음 달 최고경영자 직을 맡을 예정이라는 것이 놀라움으로 다가왔다고 발표했다'라는 의미가 되므로 어색하다. (C) announcing을 현재분사로 보더라도 문맥상 Liu Supermarket을 수식하기에는 적절치 않다.

번역 제니퍼 찬이 다음 달 최고경영자 직을 맡는다는 리우 슈퍼마켓의 발표는 놀라움으로 다가왔다.

어휘 take over as ~ 직을 맡다 announce 알리다, 발표하다 come as a surprise 놀라움으로 다가오다

128 전치사 자리 _ 어휘

해설 명사구 extensive renovations를 목적어로 취하는 전치사 자리로, 보기에서 (B) Since(~ 이래로)와 (C) Due to(~ 때문에) 중 하나를 선택해야 한다. 광범위한 보수 작업은 임시 이전(temporarily relocate)을 유발한 원인이므로, (C) Due to가 정답이 된다. 참고로, (B) Since는 접속사와 전치사 둘 다 될 수 있는데, '~(하기) 때문에'라는 의미를 나타내려면 접속사로 쓰여야 한다. (A) If only와 (D) Though는 접속사이므로 빈칸에 들어갈 수 없다.

번역 메인 볼트 은행은 광범위한 보수 작업 때문에 바리스터 가 1450번지로 임시 이전할 예정이다.

어휘 extensive 폭넓은, 광범위한 renovation 개조, 보수 temporarily 임시로, 일시적으로 relocate 이전하다

129 명사 자리 _ 동사의 목적어 _ 불가산명사

해설 빈칸은 loyalty(충실함, 충성심)와 함께 동사 promises의 목적어 역할을 하는 명사 자리이다. 따라서 (B) transparency와 (C) transparencies 중 하나를 선택해야 하는데, 고객에게 약속할 만한 것은 충실함과 투명함이므로, (B) transparency가 정답이 된다. 참고로, transparency는 불가산명사로서 '투명(도), 투명함', 가산명사로서 '유리판, 슬라이드'라는 뜻을 나타낸다. (A) transparent는 형용사, (D) transparently는 부사로 품사상 빈칸에 들어갈 수 없다.

번역 도넬 앤 프랭클린 인베스트먼츠는 고객을 향한 비할 데 없는 충실함과 투명성을 약속한다.

어휘 incomparable 비할 데 없는 loyalty 충실함, 충성심

130 명사 어휘

해설 빈칸은 음악가 발굴 작업(seek out ~ musicians)을 하는 회사의 직원(who work for ARF Recordings)을 가리킨다. 따라서 '에이전트, 중개인'이라는 의미의 (D) agents가 정답이다.

번역 ARF 레코딩즈에서 일하는 에이전트들은 첫 앨범을 녹음하고 싶어 하며 재능은 있지만 잘 알려지지 않은 음악가들을 찾아낸다.

어휘 seek out ~을 찾아내다, 발굴하다 talented 재능이 있는 unknown 유명하지 않은, 알려지지 않은

TEST 9

PART 6

131-134 공지

> **공청회 공지**
>
> 폴버그 시립 도서관은 8월 19일 오후 6시에 월례 이사회를 개최합니다. 지역사회 일원은 **131 참석하시기를** 권합니다. 의사 일정은 도서관 웹사이트에서 볼 수 **132 있으며** 시의 동부에 제안된 도서관 건물에 대한 설명회가 포함됩니다. 프로젝트 매니저인 안드레 카잘이 해당 건물의 디자인 컨셉을 공유해 드릴 것입니다. **133 아울러**, 건설 자금을 어떻게 조달할 것인지에 관해 토론도 진행할 예정입니다. 정기 안건들에 이어 대중의 의견을 듣는 시간이 마련될 것입니다. **134 이때 참석자들은 의견**

을 공유할 기회를 얻게 됩니다.

어휘 **public meeting** 공청회 **board meeting** 이사회 **be encouraged to** ~하도록 장려되다, ~해 주십시오 **agenda** 안건, 의사 일정 **proposed** 제안된 **construction** 건설 **fund** 자금을 대다 **comment** 의견 **regular** 정기적인, 정규의

131 동사 어휘

해설 앞 문장에서 폴버그 시립 도서관이 월례 이사회를 개최한다(The Fallberg City Library will hold its monthly board meeting)고 했으므로, 이 회의와 관련해 지역사회 일원에게 권장될 만한 행위가 빈칸에 들어가야 한다. 따라서 '(회의 등에) 참석하다'라는 의미의 (B) attend가 정답이다.

어휘 **donate** 기부하다 **volunteer** 자원봉사를 하다

132 관계대명사 _ 계속적 용법

해설 빈칸이 포함된 부분은 문장 중간에 삽입되어 앞에 나온 사물명사 agenda를 보충 설명하는 역할을 한다. 따라서 「주격 관계대명사 +be동사」로 구성된 (C) which is가 정답이다. 참고로, (B) being을 현재분사로 본다고 하더라도, '의사 일정을 웹사이트에서 볼 수 있다는 것'은 부가적인 정보일 뿐, '일정에 설명회가 포함된 것'과는 관계가 없기 때문에 분사구문이 성립될 수 없다. (D) what can be는 앞에 선행사가 올 수 없으므로 오답이다.

133 접속부사

해설 빈칸 앞뒤로 프로젝트 매니저인 안드레 카잘이 회의에서 할 일(share design concepts for the building, lead a discussion about how construction should be funded)을 열거하고 있다. 따라서 내용을 덧붙일 때 쓰이는 접속부사가 필요하므로, '게다가, 아울러'라는 의미의 (A) In addition이 정답이다.

어휘 **as a result** 결과적으로 **as mentioned** 언급된 대로 **in the meantime** 당분간, 그동안

134 문맥에 맞는 문장 고르기

번역 (A) 새 이사회 임원이 9월에 임명될 예정입니다.
(B) 본점은 추가 공지가 있을 때까지 문을 닫을 것입니다.
(C) 프로젝트는 공적 자금의 부족으로 취소됐습니다.
(D) 이때 참석자들은 의견을 공유할 기회를 얻게 됩니다.

해설 빈칸 앞 문장에서 대중의 의견을 듣는 시간이 마련될 것(There will be a period for public comment)이라고 했으므로, 이에 대해 부연 설명을 하거나 공지를 마무리하는 문장이 이어져야 자연스럽다. 따라서 그때 참석자들이 의견을 제시할 수 있다고 한 (D)가 정답이다. 참고로, 여기서 at that time은 앞 문장의 a period for public comment를 가리킨다.

어휘 **appoint** 임명하다 **further** 추가의 **due to** ~때문에 **lack** 부족, 결핍 **opportunity** 기회

135-138 이메일

수신: 전 영업사원
발신: 딘 버든
날짜: 6월 27일
제목: 매장 개선

브이 앤 제이 캠핑용품에 근무하는 우리에게, 하나의 조직으로서 서로 협력하는 것은 매우 중요합니다. 팀워크는 생산성을 향상시킬 뿐 아니라 고객과 직원의 만족도를 높여주는 결과를 가져옵니다. **135이러한 이유로**, 직원, 경영진, 고객을 행복하게 만들 수 있는 매장 내 개선 계획과 팀워크 조성 훈련을 결합하려고 합니다.

매장 벽을 제품이 진열될 수 **136있는** 푹 들어간 **136공간**을 갖춘 나무처럼 보이게 다시 설계할 것입니다. 야외를 테마로 한 이 선반은 사실 간편하게 조립할 수 있는 모듈식 벽면 장치입니다. 영업사원들에게는 팀별로 서로 협력하여 그것들을 조립하는 임무가 **137주어질 것입니다**. **138본 프로젝트는 하루가 소요될 겁니다**. 완료되면 선반에 상품을 채우고 고객을 위한 재개업식 행사를 치르며 즐겁게 보낼 것입니다.

더 자세한 내용은 곧 알려드리겠습니다.

딘 버든
건물 책임자

어휘 **sales associate** 영업사원 **improvement** 개선, 향상 **productivity** 생산성 **satisfaction** 만족 **combine** 결합하다 **in-store** 매장 내의 **redesign** 재설계하다 **hollow** 빈, 푹 파인 **actually** 사실 **assemble** 조립하다 **modular** 모듈식의(규격화된 부품을 조립하여 만들 수 있는) **cooperatively** 협력하여 **complete** 완료하다 **forthcoming** 곧 있을, 다가오는

135 접속부사

해설 빈칸 앞 문장에서는 팀워크의 이점(Teamwork not only improves productivity but also leads to increased satisfaction for customers and employees)을 설명했고, 빈칸 뒤에서는 매장 내 개선 계획과 팀워크 조성 훈련을 결합하려 한다(we will be combining a team-building exercise with an in-store improvement plan)며 팀워크를 강화할 계획을 발표했다. 즉, 계획을 실행하기 위해 팀워크의 이점을 명분으로 내세운 것이므로, '그러한 이유로'라는 의미의 (A) For that reason이 빈칸에 들어가야 자연스럽다.

어휘 **for instance** 예를 들어 **on the other hand** 반면에

136 관계부사

해설 빈칸은 완전한 절(products can be displayed)을 이끌어 장소 명사인 spaces를 수식하는 역할을 한다. 따라서 관계부사 (D) where이 정답이다. 참고로, (A) for는 접속사로 쓰일 경우 이유를 나타내며 앞에 콤마가 와야 한다. (B) that이 빈칸에 들어가려면 that이 이끄는 완전한 절과 앞에 나오는 명사가 동격 관계가 되어야 하는데, 해당 문장에서는 성립되지 않는다. 복합관계대명사인 (C) whatever(~하는 것은 무엇이든지, 어떤 ~일지라도)는 명사절을 이끌어 문장의 주어/목적어 역할을 하거나 부사절을 이끌어 콤마 앞에 오는 주절을 수식하

는데, 빈칸 바로 앞에 명사(spaces)가 있으므로 구조상으로도 빈칸에 들어갈 수 없다.

137 동사 어형 _ 태 _ 시제

해설 빈칸은 주어 Associates의 동사 자리이다. 만일 the task가 동사의 직접목적어라고 한다면 이 뒤에 수령 대상(「전치사 to + 사람」)이 와야 하는데, 여기서는 task를 수식하는 to부정사가 왔다. 따라서 주어인 영업 사원들이 특정 임무를 받는 대상이라고 보는 것이 타당하므로, 보기에서 수동태인 (B) were given과 (D) will be given 중 하나를 선택해야 한다. 해당 임무는 앞으로 있을 활동에서 주어지는 것이므로, 미래시제인 (D) will be given이 정답이 된다. give는 4형식 동사로 쓰일 경우 뒤에 간접목적어 및 직접목적어가 순서대로 오는데, 수동태로 바뀌면서 간접목적어가 주어 자리에 가면 직접목적어는 동사 뒤에 그대로 남겨져 해당 문장과 같은 구조가 된다.

138 문맥에 맞는 문장 고르기

번역 (A) 고객들은 안내를 받았습니다.
(B) 본 프로젝트는 하루가 소요될 겁니다.
(C) 곧 발표가 이루어질 예정입니다.
(D) 이 유닛들은 여러 색으로 나옵니다.

해설 빈칸 앞 문장에서 영업사원들에게 팀별로 서로 협력하여 선반을 조립하는 임무가 주어질 것(Associates will be given the task to work cooperatively in teams to assemble them)이라고 했고, 뒤 문장에서는 해당 작업이 완료된 후(When it is completed) 하게 될 일을 나열했다. 따라서 빈칸에도 조립을 위한 협력 작업과 관련된 내용이 들어가야 자연스러우므로, 작업 소요 시간을 예상한 (B)가 정답이다.

어휘 inform 알리다 announcement 발표, 공지 available 이용 가능한

139-142 이메일

수신: 도널드 해로웨이 〈dharoway@indomail.co.nz〉
발신: 픽스잇 배관
날짜: 8월 4일
제목: 정비 요청

해로웨이 씨께,

본 이메일은 픽스잇 배관이 헤론 가 458번지에 있는 귀하의 자택에서 가스관을 139설치할 수 있다는 확인증 역할을 합니다. 8월 10일 월요일 오전 10시에서 11시 사이에 작업을 수행할 수 있도록 공인된 자격증을 갖춘 전문 배관공 브래들리 번즈를 140보낼 예정입니다. 가스관을 넣는 데 1시간 정도 소요될 것입니다. 141그리고 나면 가스레인지를 사용하실 수 있을 겁니다.

142예약을 취소해야 할 경우 저희에게 바로 연락 주십시오. 지금이 연중 특히 바쁜 시기라 저희 일정이 꽉 차 있습니다.

엘나 들라미니
픽스잇 배관

어휘 plumbing 배관 serve as ~의 역할을 하다 confirmation 확인(증), 확정 residence 거주지, 주택 certified 공인된 licensed 자격증을 갖춘 particularly 특히 quite 완전히, 꽤

139 동사 어휘

해설 뒤 문장에서 배관을 넣는 데 1시간 정도 소요된다(It should take about an hour to put in the line)고 했으므로, 가스관(a gas line)이 설치될 예정이라고 보는 것이 타당하다. 따라서 (B) install이 정답이다.

어휘 fill 채우다 inspect 점검하다 examine 점검하다

140 동사 어형 _ 시제

해설 주격 인칭대명사 We의 동사 자리로, 전치사구 on Monday, 10 August의 수식을 받는다. 이메일을 보낸 날짜(Date: 4 August)를 기준으로 8월 10일은 미래이며, 앞 문장에서도 미래시제(will be able to)가 쓰였으므로, (D) will send가 정답이다.

141 문맥에 맞는 문장 고르기

번역 (A) 그리고 나면 가스레인지를 사용하실 수 있을 겁니다.
(B) 에반스 씨는 지난주 귀하의 구역에서 작업을 했습니다.
(C) 전날 오전 9시 30분까지 저희에게 전화해 주십시오.
(D) 저희는 이 작업을 경쟁업체들보다 잘 합니다.

해설 앞 문장에서 작업 예정일에 배관을 넣는 데 1시간 정도 소요될 것(It should take about an hour to put in the line)이라고 했으므로, 빈칸에는 해당 작업에 대한 추가 내용이 들어가야 자연스럽다. 따라서 순서상 설치 이후 가능한 일을 설명한 (A)가 정답이다.

어휘 competitor 경쟁자

142 명사 어휘

해설 첫 번째 단락에서 8월 10일 월요일 오전 10시에서 11시 사이에 작업을 수행할 수 있도록 번즈 씨를 보낼 예정(We will send Bradley Burns ~ to do this on Monday, 10 August, between 10:00 A.M. and 11:00 A.M.)이라고 했으므로, 취소(cancel)할 만한 대상은 예정된 작업이라고 볼 수 있다. 따라서 '약속, 예약'이라는 의미의 (D) appointment가 정답이다.

어휘 subscription 구독, 가입 membership 회원(권) celebration 기념

143-146 이메일

수신: 매장 관리자
발신: 알랭 마호
날짜: 10월 4일
제목: 재활용 계획

여러분 안녕하세요.

오스트레일리아 제일의 전자제품 소매업체로서, 우리는 항상 업계 선두라는 지위를 유지 [143]**하려고 합니다.** 올해, 고객들이 중고 전자 기기를 매장으로 가져와 재활용할 수 있도록 하는 신규 프로그램을 시험하기 시작했습니다. 그 대가로, 고객들은 구매 시 할인을 받았습니다. 이 계획은 우리의 기대를 넘어섰습니다. [144]**그러므로 금년 중에 하반기에 본 프로그램을 전 지점으로 확대할 것입니다.**

11월 말, 모든 매장 관리자들은 물품을 수거하고 재활용 협력업체에 보내는 방법에 관해 [145]**상세한** 지시사항을 받을 겁니다. [146]**아울러,** 11월 중순부터 시작해 소셜미디어와 인쇄 광고를 통해 본 프로그램을 대중에게 알릴 것입니다.

흥미진진한 이 계획에 대한 추가 업데이트 및 안내 사항을 기대해 주십시오.

알랭 마호
제품개발 부서장

> 어휘 initiative 계획 retailer 소매업자 maintain 유지하다 standing 지위 allow 허락하다 in exchange 그 대가로, 그 대신 purchase 구입 exceed 넘다 expectation 예상, 기대 instruction 설명, 지시 announce 알리다, 발표하다 anticipate 기대하다, 예상하다

143 동사 어휘

해설 빈칸의 목적어 역할을 하는 to maintain our standing as an industry leader와 어울리는 동사를 선택해야 한다. 업계 선두라는 지위를 유지하는 것은 업체가 추구하는 목표라고 볼 수 있으므로, '추구하다, ~하려고 하다'라는 의미의 (A) seek가 정답이다. (D) remember는 to부정사와 쓰일 경우 '~할 것을 기억하다'라는 뜻을 나타내므로 빈칸에 적절치 않다. (B) imply(암시하다)와 (C) predict(예측하다)는 to부정사를 목적어로 취하지 않으므로, 구조상으로도 불가능하다.

144 문맥에 맞는 문장 고르기

번역 (A) 전자제품 재활용은 환경에 도움이 됩니다.
(B) 그러므로 금년 중에 본 프로그램을 전 지점으로 확대할 것입니다.
(C) 안타깝게도 고객들 영수증을 갖고 있지 못했습니다.
(D) 전국의 업체들은 이미 많은 재료를 재활용하고 있습니다.

해설 빈칸 앞에서는 올해 시험하기 시작한 신규 프로그램이 기대를 넘어섰다(The initiative exceeded our expectations)고 했고, 뒤에서는 모든 매장 관리자들에게 관련 내용을 안내하고 대중에게 해당 프로그램을 발표하겠다고 했다. 따라서 빈칸에도 해당 프로그램과 관련된 내용이 들어가야 자연스러우므로, 시험 성공에 따른(Thus) 결정을 밝힌 (B)가 정답이다.

어휘 environment 환경 thus 그러므로 expand 확대하다 unfortunately 불행히도, 안타깝게도 retain 보유하다, 간직하다

145 형용사 자리 _ 명사 수식

해설 빈칸은 명사 instructions를 수식하는 형용사 자리로, 문맥상 '상세한(=상세히 설명된) 지시사항'이라는 내용이 되어야 자연스럽다. 따라서 (C) detailed가 정답이다. 현재분사로 쓰일 수 있는 (D) detailing은 명사를 뒤에서 수식해야 하며, 목적어를 취해야 한다. 참고로, send는 4형식 동사로 쓰일 경우 뒤에 간접목적어 및 직접목적어가 순서대로 오는데, 수동태로 바뀌면서 간접목적어가 주어 자리에 가면 직접목적어는 동사 뒤에 그대로 남겨져 해당 문장과 같은 구조가 된다.

어휘 detail 세부사항; 상세히 알리다 detailing 세부장식; ~를 상세히 설명하는

146 접속부사

해설 빈칸 앞뒤로 신규 프로그램의 확장과 관련된 11월 일정(all store managers will be sent detailed instructions ~ we will be announcing the program to the public)을 안내하고 있다. 따라서 연관 있는 내용을 덧붙일 때 쓰이는 접속부사가 빈칸에 들어가야 자연스러우므로, '게다가, 또한'이라는 의미의 (B) Additionally가 정답이다.

어휘 instead 대신 however 그러나 for example 예를 들면

PART 7

147-148 광고

> **웨인 임대물 있음**
>
> 볼링 그린의 중심지에서 15마일 떨어진 웨인 마을에 방 두 개, 욕실 한 개짜리의 훌륭한 아파트가 나와 있습니다. [147]**10년 된 중층 건물에 위치한 이 아파트는 상점과 카페가 가까우며 기차역까지 도보로 갈 수 있는 거리입니다.** [148](C)**오븐과** [148](D)**식기세척기가 얼마 전에 교체되었으며 새로운 타일 조리대가 주방에 설치됐습니다. 새 세탁기 및** [148](B)**건조기 세트는 식료품 저장실 옆에 있습니다.** 월 임대료는 공과금을 포함해 950달러입니다. 1년 짜리 임대 계약하시고 빠르면 8월 1일에 입주하실 수 있습니다. 둘러볼 약속을 잡으시려면 (419) 555-0145로 전화하세요.

> 어휘 available 이용 가능한 sparkling 반짝이는, 아주 좋은 situated in ~에 있는, 위치한 convenient (~에) 접근하기 편리한, 가까운 within walking distance of ~에 도보로 갈 수 있는 거리에 있는 replace 교체하다 countertop 조리대 install 설치하다 utility (수도, 전기, 가스 등의) 공익사업, 공과금 sign a lease 임대 계약하다 arrange 주선하다, 마련하다

147 추론 / 암시

번역   아파트 건물에 대해 암시된 것은?

    (A) 새 관리 체제 하에 있다.

    (B) 큰 주차 공간이 있다.

    (C) 대중교통과 가깝다.

    (D) 1년 전에 지어졌다.

해설   초반부에서 아파트가 기차역까지 도보로 갈 수 있는 거리에 있다 (the apartment is ~ within walking distance of the train station)고 했으므로, 대중교통과 가깝다고 추론할 수 있다. 따라서 (C)가 정답이다.

어휘   management 관리   public transportation 대중교통

> ▸▸ Paraphrasing   지문의 within walking distance of the train station → 정답의 close to public transportation

148 사실 관계 확인

번역   새로운 기기로 언급되지 않은 것은?

    (A) 냉장고

    (B) 의류 건조기

    (C) 오븐

    (D) 식기세척기

해설   중반부에서 오븐과 식기세척기가 얼마 전에 교체되었으며(The oven and dishwasher have just been replaced), 세탁기 및 건조기 세트도 새 것(A new washer and dryer set)이라고 했으므로, 언급되지 않은 (A)가 정답이다.

어휘   appliance (가정용) 기기

> ▸▸ Paraphrasing   지문의 been replaced → 질문의 new

149-150 공지

드레이프 어 랏에서 구입해 주셔서 감사합니다!

결제, 교환, 반품에 관한 문제는 가까운 드레이프 어 랏 소매점에 연락하십시오. 149훼손되거나 없어진 부품, 셀프 설치 관련 설명, 제품 관련 문의 등에 관한 도움을 받으시려면 드레이프 어 랏 고객 지원 (713) 555-0101로 전화하세요. 상담원들이 월-금요일 오전 9시부터 오후 5시까지 문의사항에 답변해 드립니다. 150전화하시기 전 다음의 정보를 미리 준비하세요: 이름, 전화번호, 구입 주문번호, 구입 장소

어휘   appreciate 감사하다   purchase 구입   regarding ~에 관해   exchange 교환   retailer 소매점, 소매업자   damaged 손상된   missing 없어진, 빠진   instructions 설명(서), 안내(문) do-it-yourself installation 셀프 설치   representative 직원, 대리인

149 추론 / 암시

번역   공지에서 드레이프 어 랏에 대해 암시한 것은?

    (A) 설치 서비스를 제공하지 않는다.

    (B) 반품을 받지 않는다.

    (C) 온라인 고객 지원을 제공한다.

    (D) 최근 소매점을 열었다.

해설   중반부에서 셀프 설치 설명 등에 관한 도움을 받으려면 드레이프 어 랏 고객 지원에 전화하라(For help with damaged or missing parts, instructions for do-it-yourself installation, ~, call Drapes-A-Lot customer support)고 했으므로, 드레이프 어 랏이 아닌 고객이 직접 설치해야 한다는 것을 추론할 수 있다. 따라서 (A)가 정답이다. 반품에 관한 문제는 가까운 드레이프 어 랏 소매점에 연락하라(For issues regarding ~ returns, please contact your nearest Drapes-A-Lot retailer)고 했으므로 (B)는 명백한 오답이다.

어휘   accept 받아주다   recently 최근

150 세부 사항

번역   공지에 따르면, 고객 지원처에 연락할 때 어떤 정보가 필요한가?

    (A) 제품 일련번호

    (B) 제품을 구입한 매장 위치

    (C) 구입에 사용한 신용카드 번호

    (D) 고객 이메일 주소

해설   후반부에서 전화하기 전에 이름, 전화번호, 구입 주문번호, 구입 장소와 같은 정보를 미리 준비하라(Before calling, please have the following information ready: your name and phone number, the purchase order number, and where you made your purchase)고 했으므로, 보기 중에서는 (B)가 정답이다.

어휘   location 매장, 장소

> ▸▸ Paraphrasing   지문의 where you made your purchase → 정답의 The store location where the product was bought

151-152 문자 메시지

키스 오돔 (오전 10시 15분) 151로비 입구 근처 관목과 나무 손질을 거의 마쳤어요. 점심 식사 후엔 뒤뜰 전체를 손질할 겁니다. 하지만 앞쪽에 있는 동안엔 화단의 잡초를 뽑을 거예요.

레베카 트루스델 (오전 10시 18분) 152이번 주에 다 뽑혔던 걸로 알고 있었는데요.

키스 오돔 (오전 10시 20분) 152비가 왔다는 사실을 기억하세요. 수요일에 잡초 뽑기를 하지 못했잖아요.

레베카 트루스델 (오전 10시 25분) 맞네요. 네, 앞쪽 구역부터 끝마치죠. 내일로 예정된 큰 파티 두 건이 있으니 호텔 입구와 구내가 깔끔해 보였으면 합니다.

키스 오돔 (오전 10시 27분) 알겠습니다. 한 시간 넘게 걸리진 않을 겁니다.

레베카 트루스델 (오전 10시 28분) 뒤뜰을 끝마치면 알려주세요. 이따가 오후에 새 테라스 가구가 배송될 걸로 예상합니다. 도착하는 대로 설치될 거예요.

어휘 trim 다듬다, 손질하다 entrance 입구 weed 잡초를 뽑다 out front 앞쪽 구역 scheduled for ~로 예정된 grounds 구내 delivery 배송 patio (주로 뒤뜰에 있는) 테라스 furniture 가구

151 추론 / 암시

번역 오돔 씨는 누구이겠는가?

   (A) 호텔 관리자
   (B) 행사 기획자
   (C) 준공 검사자
   (D) 구내 관리인

해설 오돔 씨가 오전 10시 15분 메시지에서 로비 입구 근처의 관목과 나무를 손질하는 일(trimming the bushes and trees around the lobby entrance)을 거의 마쳤다고 한 후, 앞으로 뒤뜰 전체를 손질하는 일(trim everything in the back garden)과 화단의 잡초를 뽑는 일(weed the flower beds)을 할 것이라고 했다. 오돔 씨가 열거한 작업들로 미루어 보아 그가 구내 관리인이라고 추론할 수 있으므로, (D)가 정답이다.

152 의도 파악

번역 오전 10시 25분에 트루스델 씨가 "맞네요"라고 쓸 때, 그 의도는 무엇인가?

   (A) 나무를 손질해야 한다고 요청했다.
   (B) 손님 예약을 확인했다.
   (C) 일이 처리되지 못한 이유가 기억났다.
   (D) 가구가 배송되지 않은 이유를 알았다.

해설 오전 10시 18분 메시지에서 트루스델 씨가 이번 주에 잡초가 다 뽑힌 걸로 알고 있었다(I thought they were cleaned up earlier this week)고 하자, 10시 20분 메시지에서 오돔 씨는 비가 왔다는 사실을 기억하라(Remember it rained)며 수요일에 잡초 뽑기를 하지 못했다(We couldn't get to the weeding on Wednesday)고 덧붙였다. 이에 대해 트루스델 씨가 '맞네요(That's right)'라고 한 것이므로, 잡초 뽑기가 처리되지 못했던 이유를 기억해 냈다고 추론할 수 있다. 따라서 (C)가 정답이다.

어휘 request 요청하다 reservation 예약

153-154 광고

새프트 서점
이전 세일

9월 23일부터 9월 30일까지, 하이 가 312번지에 있는 새프트 서점은 매장의 설비 및 가구, 장비 일체를 판매할 예정입니다. **¹⁵³여기에는 매장 전면 유리창에서 보이는 멋진 골동품 책장도 포함됩니다.** 조심해서

사용한 가구를 구입해서 여러분의 매장에 비치할 좋은 기회를 놓치지 마세요. 놀라운 가격에 물품을 판매하며, 기꺼이 가격을 협상할 의향도 있습니다.

¹⁵⁴새프트 서점은 2월, 분다 가 4900번지에서 새로 개점합니다. 공간이 상당히 넓어지고 전혀 다른 실내 디자인을 선보일 예정입니다. 새 매장도 꼭 방문해 주세요.

어휘 fixture 고정 세간, 설비 equipment 장비 antique 골동품 opportunity 기회 purchase 구입하다 furnish (가구를) 비치하다 negotiate 협상하다 significantly 상당히, 크게 spacious 널찍한 feature 특징으로 삼다, 선보이다 distinct 전혀 다른, (구분이) 확실한

153 사실 관계 확인

번역 골동품 책장에 대해 알 수 있는 것은?

   (A) 분다 가에 있는 매장으로 옮길 것이다.
   (B) 진열창에 전시해 왔다.
   (C) 상태가 좋지 않다.
   (D) 유명 디자이너가 만들었다.

해설 첫 번째 단락에서 판매 품목에는 매장 전면 유리창에서 보이는 골동품 책장도 포함된다(This includes the beautiful antique bookshelves from our main storefront window)고 했으므로, 책장이 진열창에 전시되어 있다는 것을 알 수 있다. 따라서 (B)가 정답이다.

어휘 be on display 전시되어 있다

▸▸ Paraphrasing   지문의 **from our main storefront window**
                    → 정답의 **on display in a shop window**

154 추론 / 암시

번역 새로운 새프트 서점에 대해 암시된 것은?

   (A) 현재 위치와 같은 거리에 있다.
   (B) 일주일 내내 문을 열 예정이다.
   (C) 이전 매장보다 더 커질 것이다.
   (D) 대다수의 직원을 그대로 유지할 것이다.

해설 두 번째 단락에서 새프트 서점이 다른 곳에서 새로 개점한다(Saft's Bookshop will reopen its doors)고 한 후, 공간이 상당히 넓어진다(It will be significantly more spacious)고 덧붙였다. 따라서 (C)가 정답이다.

어휘 retain 유지하다

▸▸ Paraphrasing   지문의 **reopen its doors** → 질문의 **new**
                    지문의 **more spacious** → 정답의 **larger**

155-157 소식지

버치힐 예술 센터 위원회
후원자 소식지

저희 위원회는 올 한 해 열심히 노력했습니다! 아름다운 버치힐 주민 모두에게 도움이 될 지역 예술 센터를 건립하고자 하는 목표 달성에 가까워지고 있습니다. 다음은 저희가 지금까지 성취한 내용입니다.

- ¹⁵⁶1월에 새로운 버치힐 예술 센터에서 제공할 활동에 대해 지역 사회 설문 조사를 완료했습니다.
- 2월에 실천 가능성 보고서를 완료했으며 잠재적 건축 부지들을 가능성이 있는 세 곳으로 압축했습니다.
- ¹⁵⁵4월에 승인을 위해 프로젝트 예산 제안서를 시 의회에 제출했습니다.
- 5월에 운영 이사 직책 지원자 몇 명을 면접했습니다.

앞으로 두 달 간은 다음 업무를 하겠습니다.
- 신임 운영 이사 선정
- 센터 위치 선정
- 공사 청사진 완료
- 공사 예산 및 일정 확정
- 행사 일정표 초안 작성

올 가을에는 버치힐 예술 센터의 공사를 시작해야 합니다!

항상 그렇듯, 저희는 진행 과정에서 여러분의 의견을 환영합니다. 문의사항이나 의견은 project@bhca.org로 위원회에 보내주십시오. ¹⁵⁷위원회에서 일하는 데 관심이 있으시면 952-555-0128로 전화 주세요.

어휘 committee 위원회 reach a goal 목표를 달성하다 serve 도움이 되다, 기여하다 accomplish 성취하다 complete 완료하다 feasibility 타당성, 실현 가능성 potential 잠재적인 possibility 가능안, 가능한 선택지 submit 제출하다 budget 예산 approval 승인 candidate 후보자, 지원자 blueprint 계획, 청사진 finalize 마무리짓다, 완결하다 draft 초안을 작성하다

155 세부 사항

번역 위원회는 시에 예산 제안서를 언제 보냈는가?
(A) 1월
(B) 2월
(C) 4월
(D) 5월

해설 첫 번째 단락 아래에 나열된 지금까지의 업적(what we have accomplished so far)을 보면, 4월에 프로젝트 예산 제안서를 시 의회에 제출했다(In April, we submitted our project budget proposal to the city council)고 되어 있다. 따라서 (C)가 정답이다.

▸▸ Paraphrasing   지문의 submitted our project budget proposal → 질문의 send a proposed budget

156 세부 사항

번역 위원회는 제공할 활동 관련 정보를 어디서 모았는가?
(A) 설문조사를 통해
(B) 보고서를 통해
(C) 제안서를 통해
(D) 개인 인터뷰를 통해

해설 첫 번째 단락 아래에 나열된 지금까지의 업적(what we have accomplished so far)을 보면, 1월에 새롭게 지어질 센터에서 제공할 활동에 대해 지역사회 설문 조사를 완료했다(we completed a community survey about what activities to offer)고 되어 있다. 따라서 설문조사를 통해 관련 정보를 모았음을 알 수 있으므로, (A)가 정답이다.

어휘 gather 모으다

157 세부 사항

번역 위원회에 참여하고 싶은 사람은 무엇을 하라고 지시받는가?
(A) 설문조사 작성하기
(B) 이메일 보내기
(C) 웹사이트 방문하기
(D) 전화하기

해설 마지막 단락에서 위원회에서 일하는 데 관심이 있으면 952-555-0128로 전화하라(If you are interested in serving on the committee, please call 952-555-0128)고 했으므로, (D)가 정답이다.

어휘 questionnaire 설문지

▸▸ Paraphrasing   지문의 are interested in serving on the committee → 질문의 wants to join the committee
지문의 call → 정답의 Make a phone call

158-160 구인광고

패튼 광고에서 채용 중입니다!

당사의 디자인, 재무, IT 부서에서 일할 의욕적이고 열정적인 분들을 찾습니다. 광고 ¹⁵⁸부문에서의 이전 경력은 도움이 되지만 필수는 아닙니다.

업무
패튼에서는 다양한 고객을 위한 광고를 만들고 마케팅 전략을 세워 왔습니다. 해당 업무에는 로고 및 웹사이트 디자인과 지역 라디오 및 전국광고판을 위한 광고 제작이 포함됩니다. 최고경영자 아미 아데시나의 지휘 하에 새로운 방향으로의 확장을 모색하고 훨씬 더 흥미로운 프로젝트를 다루고자 합니다.

직원들의 한 마디
- "^{159/160}패튼에서 디자이너로 보낸 첫 6개월만에, 이미 여러 고객과 협업하고 팀을 이끌기까지 할 기회를 얻었습니다. 일이 항상 쉬운 건 아니지만 빠르게 진행되는 도전적인 환경을 좋아한다면 여기서 정말 잘 해 나갈 수 있어요." ^{159/160}토마스 커티

- "¹⁶⁰패튼에서 법률 자문으로 일한 지 일 년이 채 안 됐는데 매 순간이 즐겁습니다. 체육관 회원권 및 자원봉사활동을 위한 유급 휴가를 비롯해 후한 직원 혜택을 갖춘 훌륭한 직장 문화가 있어요. 지금껏 일한 회사 중 최고입니다." ¹⁶⁰사비나 후세인

공석을 확인하고 지원하시려면 저희 웹사이트 www.pattonads.com/careers를 방문하세요.

어휘 advertising 광고 motivated 동기가 부여된, 의욕이 있는 enthusiastic 열정적인, 열렬한 individual 개인, 사람 finance 재무, 금융 strategy 전략 a wide range of 광범위한, 다양한 include 포함하다 billboard (옥외) 광고판 look to ~하려고 하다 expand 확장하다 tackle 다루다 fast-paced 속도가 빠른, 빠르게 진행되는 challenging 도전적인 environment 환경 thrive 잘 해내다, 번창하다 legal 법률과 관련된 generous 후한, 관대한, 넉넉한 paid time off 유급 휴가 vacancy 공석, 결원 apply for ~에 지원하다

158 동의어 찾기

번역 첫 번째 단락, 두 번째 줄에 쓰인 "sector"와 의미가 가장 가까운 단어는?

(A) 부분
(B) 업계
(C) 지역
(D) 운영

해설 'sector'를 포함한 부분은 '광고 부문에서의 경력(Previous experience in the advertising sector)'이라는 의미로 해석되는데, 여기서 sector는 '부문, 분야'라는 뜻으로 쓰였다. 따라서 '업계'라는 의미의 (B) industry가 정답이다.

159 세부 사항

번역 커티 씨의 직업은?

(A) 디자이너
(B) 변호사
(C) IT 기술자
(D) 최고경영자

해설 직원들의 한 마디(Some Employee Comments) 부분에서 커티 씨는 패튼에서 디자이너로 보낸 첫 6개월(In my first six months as a designer at Patton)에 대한 소회를 밝혔다. 따라서 (A)가 정답이다.

160 사실 관계 확인

번역 커티 씨와 후세인 씨 모두에 대해 맞는 것은?

(A) 여가시간에 자원봉사를 즐긴다.
(B) 모두가 패튼에서의 근무를 즐길 것이라고 생각한다.
(C) 부서 내 팀장이다.
(D) 패튼에서 1년 미만으로 근무했다.

해설 직원들의 한 마디(Some Employee Comments) 부분에서 커티 씨는 패튼에서 디자이너로 보낸 첫 6개월만에 이미 여러 고객과 협업하고 팀을 이끌기까지 할 기회를 얻었다(In my first six months as a designer at Patton, I've already had the chance to ~ lead my own team)고 했고, 후세인 씨도 패튼에서 법률 자문으로 일한 지 일 년이 채 안 됐지만(I've been working as a legal consultant at Patton for just under a year now) 매 순간이 즐겁다고 적었다. 따라서 두 사람 모두 패튼에서 근무한 기간이 1년 미만임을 알 수 있으므로, (D)가 정답이다. 참고로, 커티 씨가 빠르게 진행되는 도전적인 환경을 좋아한다면(if you enjoy a fast-paced,

challenging environment) 패튼에서 잘 해 나갈 수 있다며 특정 조건을 걸었으므로, (B)는 정답이 될 수 없다.

어휘 spare time 여가시간

161-163 편지

7월 31일

샤말리 모와트 박사
콘월 대학병원
빅토리아 가 22-28번지
킹스턴 6

모와트 박사님께,

161 간호 프로그램에 레날도 실바 씨를 추천하게 되어 기쁩니다. 실바 씨는 서머 캠프 웨스트에서 지난 2년의 여름 동안, 주 4일 현장의 공인 간호사 두 명의 보조 역할을 한 바 있습니다. 이곳의 어린 캠핑 참여자들은 실바 씨를 꽤 좋아하게 됐습니다. 그들은 친절하면서도 헌신적이기도 한 실바 씨의 돌봄을 고마워한답니다. 그는 참을성 있고 보살피는 성격입니다. 박사님의 간호 프로그램 같은 곳에서 성공할 거라고 확신합니다.

162/163제 자신이 30년 이상 간호사로서, 대형 병원, 소형 의원, 학교 등의 다양한 환경에서 젊은 전문인들과 함께 일해 보았고, 그 중 지난 몇 년간은 서머 캠프 웨스트에서만 그렇게 해왔습니다. 그래서 저는 실바 씨의 전문성과 돌봄이 필요한 사람들에 대한 그의 온정을 증언할 수 있습니다. 따라서 실바 씨가 적극적이고 성공적인 프로그램 참여자가 될 수 있으리라 확신합니다.

실바 씨에 대한 질문이 있으시면 언제든 (876) 555-0140으로 전화해 주십시오.

베니타 올리베이라

어휘 recommend 추천하다 on-site 현장의 registered nurse 공인[등록된] 간호사 appreciate 고마워하다, 진가를 인정하다 dedicated 헌신적인, 전념하는 approach to wellness 건강에 대한 접근 방법, 돌보는 방법 nurturing 보살피는, 배려하는 decade 10년 various 다양한 setting 환경, 배경 exclusively 독점적으로, 오로지 therefore 그러므로 participant 참여자

161 추론 / 암시

번역 모와트 박사는 누구이겠는가?

(A) 여름 캠프 주인
(B) 교육 프로그램 담당자
(C) 의료직 지원자
(D) 인간 생물학 교수

해설 첫 번째 단락에서 올리베이라 씨가 모와트 박사의 간호 프로그램에 레날도 실바 씨를 추천하게 되어(to recommend Mr. Renaldo Silva for your nursing programme) 기쁘다고 했으므로, 모와트 박사가 간호 프로그램의 담당자라고 추론할 수 있다. 따라서 (B)가 정답이다.

어휘 candidate 후보자, 지원자 biology 생물학

▸▸ Paraphrasing 지문의 nursing programme
→ 정답의 training program

162 사실 관계 확인

번역 올리베이라 씨에 대해 알 수 있는 것은?

(A) 자녀가 서머 캠프 웨스트에 참가한다.
(B) 30년 이상 의료 부문에 고용되어 있었다.
(C) 서머 캠프 웨스트에서 주 4일 일한다.
(D) 병원에서 간호 인력을 감독한다.

해설 두 번째 단락에서 올리베이라 씨 자신이 30년 이상 간호사로서 다양한 환경에서 젊은 전문인들과 함께 일했다(As a nurse myself for more than three decades, I have worked with young professionals in various settings)고 했으므로, (B)가 정답이다.

어휘 attend 참석하다 supervise 감독하다

▸▸ Paraphrasing 지문의 As a nurse ~ for more than three decades
→ 정답의 in health care for over 30 years

163 문장 삽입

번역 [1], [2], [3], [4]로 표시된 곳 중에서 다음 문장이 가장 적합한 곳은?

"그래서 저는 실바 씨의 전문성과 돌봄이 필요한 사람들에 대한 그의 온정을 증언할 수 있습니다."

(A) [1]
(B) [2]
(C) [3]
(D) [4]

해설 주어진 문장의 As such가 '그래서'라는 뜻을 나타내므로, 실바 씨의 전문성과 온정을 증언할 수 있는(I can attest to) 근거가 앞에서 먼저 언급되어야 한다. [3] 앞에서 올리베이라 씨는 자신이 30년 이상 간호사로 다양한 환경에서 젊은 전문인들과 함께 일해왔다(As a nurse myself for more than three decades, I have worked with young professionals in various settings)고 했는데, 이 경험을 토대로 실바 씨의 자질을 높이 평가하여 증언하는 것으로 볼 수 있다. 따라서 이 뒤에 주어진 문장이 들어가고 그 다음에 실바 씨가 성공적인 프로그램 참여자가 될 거라고 이어지는 것이 자연스러우므로, (C)가 정답이다.

어휘 attest 입증하다, 증언하다 compassion 동정, 온정

164-167 문서

스카이 하이 지붕 공사

¹⁶⁴지붕에서 공사 또는 수리 작업을 하는 인부들은 많은 잠재적 위험에 직면합니다. 사다리, 채광창, 자연적 요소에의 신체적 노출 등은 위험을 수반합니다. ¹⁶⁴상식적인 ¹⁶⁵관행을 행하여 안전한 상태를 유지하십시오. 이와 같은 지침을 따라 주십시오.

안전을 위한 복장을 착용하세요.

- ¹⁶⁶더운 날씨에도 긴 소매 셔츠를 입고 소맷단의 단추를 채우십시오.
- ¹⁶⁶단이 없는 긴 바지를 입으십시오. 지붕 공사 자재에 걸려 찢어지거나 파편이 붙을 수 있기 때문입니다.
- ¹⁶⁷⁽ᶜ⁾발목을 덮는 작업화를 착용하고 밑창이 지나치게 마모된 게 보이면 신발을 교체하십시오.

개인 보호 장비를 이용하세요.

- 손목을 감싸는 장갑을 착용하고 장갑 목과 소맷단 끝 사이에 틈이 없도록 하십시오.
- ¹⁶⁷⁽ᴬ⁾보호 안경을 착용하십시오.

일과를 올바르게 시작하세요.

- 모든 팀원들과 함께 작업 계획을 검토하십시오.
- ¹⁶⁷⁽ᴰ⁾사다리 및 모든 안전 장비의 상태를 확인하십시오.

지침을 검토하고 숙지했습니다.

서명: _____ 날짜: _____

어휘 roofing 지붕 공사 repair 수리 multiple 많은, 다양한 potential 잠재적인 hazard 위험 skylight (채광을 위한) 천창 physical 신체적인 exposure 노출 element 요소 involve 수반하다 guideline 지침 cuff 단 snag on ~에 걸려 찢어지다 material 자재 debris 쓰레기, 잔해, 파편 replace 교체하다 excessive 지나친 wear 마모 protective 보호용의, 보호하는

164 추론 / 암시

번역 문서는 누구를 대상으로 하겠는가?

(A) 사다리 제조업자
(B) 의상 디자이너
(C) 주택 검사관
(D) 지붕 설치업자

해설 첫 번째 단락에서 지붕에서 공사 또는 수리 작업을 하는 인부들은 많은 잠재적 위험에 직면한다(Workers doing construction or repair work on roofs face multiple potential hazards)고 한 후, 상식적인 관행을 행하여 안전을 유지하고(Stay safe by using commonsense practices), 아래 열거된 지침을 따르라(Follow these guidelines)고 조언했다. 따라서 지붕 설치업자를 대상으로 한 문서라고 추론할 수 있으므로, (D)가 정답이다.

165 동의어 찾기

번역 첫 번째 단락, 세 번째 줄에 쓰인 "practices"와 의미가 가장 가까운 것은?

(A) 관례에 맞는 행동
(B) 신체 운동
(C) 전문적인 업체
(D) 공연 리허설

해설 'practices'를 포함한 문장은 '상식적인 관행을 행하여 안전을 유지하다(Stay safe by using commonsense practices)'라는 의미로 해석되는데, 여기서 practices는 '관행, 관례'라는 뜻으로 쓰였다. 따

TEST 9

라서 '관례에 맞는[적절한] 행동'이라는 의미의 (A) regular actions 가 정답이다.

166 사실 관계 확인

번역 문서에서 알 수 있는 것은?

(A) 스카이 하이 지붕 공사는 태양 전지판 설치 전문이다.
(B) 주택 소유주들은 위험 지역을 표시할 책임이 있다.
(C) 팔과 다리를 감싸는 옷이 필수적이다.
(D) 지붕 인부들은 회사 워크숍에 참가해야 한다.

해설 복장(Dress for safety)에 대한 지침의 첫 번째 및 두 번째 항목을 보면, 더운 날씨에도 긴 소매 셔츠를 입고(Wear long-sleeved shirts, even in warm weather) 단이 없는 긴 바지를 입으라(Wear long pants without cuffs)고 되어 있다. 따라서 팔과 다리를 감싸는 옷이 필수임을 알 수 있으므로, (C)가 정답이다.

어휘 specialize in ~를 전문으로 하다 solar panel 태양 전지판 installation 설치 hazardous 위험한 essential 필수적인

167 사실 관계 확인

번역 문서에서 안전 조치로 언급되지 않은 것은?

(A) 보호 안경 사용
(B) 귀마개 사용
(C) 견고한 신발 착용
(D) 장비 확인

해설 보호 장비 이용(Use personal protective equipment)에 대한 지침 중 '보호 안경을 착용할 것(Use protective eyewear)'에서 (A)를, 복장 착용(Dress for safety)에 대한 지침 중 '밑창이 지나치게 마모된 게 보이면 신발을 교체할 것(replace boots when the soles show excessive wear)'에서 (C)를, 일과 시작법(Begin the day right)에 대한 지침 중 '사다리 및 모든 안전 장비의 상태를 확인할 것(Check the condition of ladders and all safety equipment)'에서 (D)를 확인할 수 있다. 따라서 언급되지 않은 (B)가 정답이다.

어휘 earmuff 귀마개 sturdy 견고한

▶▶ **Paraphrasing** 지문의 **protective eyewear** → 보기 **(A)**의 **safety glasses**

지문의 **replace boots when the soles show excessive wear** → 보기의 **(C)**의 **Wearing sturdy footwear**

지문의 **Check the condition of** → 보기 **(D)**의 **Performing ~ checks**

168-171 기사

공공사업부 어려움에 직면하다

카베리 (4월 15일)—카베리 공공사업부 건물이 시초부터 대중의 환영을 거의 받지 못하고 있다. [168]**건축가들이 구조물 청사진을 공개하자, 오래 거주한 주민들은 건물의 밝은 색상과 각진 모양이 카베리의 독특한**

붉은 벽돌 건물들과 어울리지 않는다고 주장했다. [171]지역 주민들의 우려는 소셜미디어 그룹의 생성까지 촉발했는데, 이 회원들은 주민들에게 읍 의회 회의와 기타 공개 포럼에서 의견을 밝히라고 촉구했다. 수십 명의 사람들이 정말 그렇게 했다.

[169]결국 건물의 원래 디자인보다 더 보수적인 버전의 초안이 만들어졌고, 개소는 4월 28일로 계획됐었다. 그러나 인근 건물 소유주들이 상당한 양의 빗물로 야기된 배수 문제를 신고하기 시작했다.

"대지가 풀과 나무가 있는 노지였을 때는 과도한 양의 빗물도 땅으로 빠르게 흡수됐습니다." 악시오스 사무실 건물 소유주인 트루디 몰리나가 설명한다. "[170]지금은 비가 많이 오면 물이 고여서 인접한 주차장으로 흘러 넘칩니다."

읍장인 버트 몬티엘에 따르면, 건물 프로젝트의 유감스러운 결과는 예측하지 못한 것이었으며 건축공학자들이 공공사업부 건물 개소 전 문제를 해결하기 위해 신속히 노력하고 있다고 한다. [170]팀에서는 물을 인근 지하 하수관으로 우회시키기 위해 배수로 및 연결 배수관을 추가로 설치하기 시작했다. [169]작업은 5월 하순에 건물 개소를 기념할 수 있도록 때맞춰 완료되어야 한다.

어휘 public work 공공사업(부) inception 시초, 시작 appreciation 환영, 공감 architect 건축가 unveil 발표하다 blueprint 계획, 청사진 resident 거주자 angular 각진 distinctive 독특한 concern 우려 spark 촉발하다 urge 강력히 권고하다, 촉구하다 voice one's opinion 견해를 말하다 conservative 보수적인 draft 초안을 만들다 drainage 배수 significant 중대한 water runoff 땅 위를 흐르는 빗물 excess 과도한 absorb 흡수하다 adjacent 인접한 unforeseen 예측하지 못한, 뜻밖의 swiftly 신속히 installation 설치 gutter 배수로 drain 배수관 divert 우회시키다 sewer 하수관

168 세부 사항

번역 카베리 공공사업부 건물에 대한 초기 불만의 주제는 무엇이었는가?

(A) 규모
(B) 디자인
(C) 위치
(D) 목적

해설 첫 번째 단락을 보면, 건축가들이 구조물 청사진을 공개하자 오래 거주한 주민들은 건물의 밝은 색상과 각진 모양이 카베리의 독특한 붉은 벽돌 건물들과 어울리지 않는다(its bright colors and angular shapes did not blend well with Carberry's distinctive redbrick buildings)고 주장했다고 되어 있다. 따라서 초기의 불만 사항이 디자인과 관련된 것임을 알 수 있으므로, (B)가 정답이다.

▶▶ **Paraphrasing** 지문의 **bright colors and angular shapes** → 정답의 **design**

169 추론 / 암시

번역 카베리읍에 대해 암시된 것은?

(A) 행사를 연기할 것이다.

(B) 새로운 읍장을 찾고 있다.

(C) 내년을 위한 많은 프로젝트가 있다.

(D) 인근 읍보다 주민이 적다.

해설 두 번째 단락 초반부에서 카베리 공공사업부 건물 개소가 4월 28일로 계획됐다(the grand opening was planned for April 28)고 했지만 반전(However)이 있음을 시사한 후, 마지막 단락에서 5월 하순에 건물 개소를 기념할 것(The work should be completed in time to celebrate the building's opening in late May)이라고 되어 있다. 따라서 계획된 행사가 연기될 것이라고 추론할 수 있으므로, (A)가 정답이다.

어휘 postpone 연기하다, 미루다

▸▸ **Paraphrasing** 지문의 grand opening → 정답의 event

170 세부 사항

번역 읍에서는 몰리나 씨의 우려를 어떻게 해결할 것인가?

(A) 악시오스 사무실 건물의 신호 체계를 개선해서

(B) 공과금을 변제해서

(C) 물을 지역으로부터 먼 곳으로 끌어내서

(D) 건물 주차장을 확장해서

해설 세 번째 단락을 보면, 몰리나 씨가 비가 많이 오면 물이 고여서 인접한 주차장으로 흘러 넘친다(water pools up and floods adjacent parking areas during heavy rains)는 문제를 보고했음을 알 수 있다. 이에 대한 해결책은 네 번째 단락에 나와 있는데, 팀에서 물을 인근 지하 하수관으로 우회시키기 위해 배수로 및 연결 배수관을 추가로 설치하기 시작했다(A team has begun the installation of ~ to divert the water to the neighborhood's underground sewer system)고 했으므로, (C)가 정답이다.

어휘 signage 신호 체계　reimburse 변제하다, 배상하다　expand 확장하다

▸▸ **Paraphrasing** 지문의 to divert the water to the neighborhood's underground sewer system → 정답의 By directing water away from an area

171 문장 삽입

번역 [1], [2], [3], [4]로 표시된 곳 중에서 다음 문장이 가장 적합한 곳은?

"수십 명의 사람들이 정말 그렇게 했다."

(A) [1]

(B) [2]

(C) [3]

(D) [4]

해설 주어진 문장은 수십 명의 사람들이 누군가가 말한 대로 '정말 그대로(just that)' 했다'는 의미이므로, 이 앞에 '누가 어떤 행위를 하라고 말했는지'를 설명하는 문장이 나와야 한다. [1] 앞 문장을 보면, 소셜미

디어 그룹의 회원들이 주민들에게 읍 의회 회의와 기타 공개 포럼에서 의견을 밝히라고 촉구했다(whose members urged residents to voice their opinions at town council meetings and in other public forums)고 쓰여 있으므로, 이 뒤에 주어진 문장이 들어가야 자연스럽다. 따라서 (A)가 정답이다.

172-175 온라인 채팅

리즈, 타마라 [오후 1시 30분] 그린 시티 투어에 연락 주셔서 감사합니다. 어떻게 도와드릴까요?

체임버스, 커티스 [오후 1시 32분] 안녕하세요. [172]요크 코퍼레이션의 다가오는 밴쿠버 여행에 대해 씁니다. [173]참가자들을 위해 모든 식사가 포함되게끔 그린 시티 투어에서 주선하신다고 알고 있습니다. 맞나요?

리즈, 타마라 [오후 1시 33분] 아니요. [173]계약 조건에서 "참가자들을 위해 환영 연회와 환송 정찬이 모두 열릴 것이다. 프로그램 동안 다른 모든 식사는 참가자 자비로 처리되어야 한다."라고 명확히 명시하고 있습니다. 이 여행에 대해 문의사항이 더 있으시면 알려주세요.

체임버스, 커티스 [오후 1시 35분] 실망스럽네요! 이전 직원 여행에는 모든 식사가 포함됐거든요. [174]관리자와 연결해 주실 수 있나요? 이 선택사항이 계약에 포함되었어야 한다고 확신해요.

디아즈, 마타 [오후 1시 37분] [174]안녕하세요, 체임버스 씨. 요크 코퍼레이션과 그린 시티 투어의 계약 조건에 관해 오해가 있으셨다면 죄송합니다. 계약서는 귀사의 최고 재무책임자인 프랭클린 왕 씨의 요청에 맞춰 작성되었습니다. 중간 식사는 포함되지 않는 것이 그의 조건이었습니다. 다른 식사 선택사항을 추천해 드릴 수 있습니다.

체임버스, 커티스 [오후 1시 40분] 됐습니다. 두 분 모두 도와주셔서 감사합니다. [175]이 상황에 대해 왕 씨와 협의해 보겠습니다. 곧 다시 연락드리죠.

어휘 arrange 마련하다, 주선하다　participant 참가자　terms 조건　specifically 분명히, 명확하게　expense 돈, 비용　apologize 사과하다　concerning ~에 관한　in accordance with ~에 맞춰서　stipulation 조건, 조항　intervening ~사이에 있는, 중간의　make a recommendation 추천하다　consult with ~와 협의하다

172 주제 / 목적

번역 체임버스 씨가 그린 시티 투어에 연락한 이유는?

(A) 신입사원을 위한 여행을 계획하려고

(B) 신용카드 대금에 관해 문의하려고

(C) 여행 세부사항에 관해 문의하려고

(D) 비상연락처를 제공하려고

해설 체임버스 씨가 오후 1시 32분 메시지에서 요크 코퍼레이션의 다가오는 밴쿠버 여행에 대해(about ~ upcoming trip to Vancouver) 메시지를 쓴다고 한 후, 참가자들을 위한 식사 관련 문의를 하고 있다. 따라서 (C)가 정답이다.

어휘 inquire 문의하다　emergency 비상

173 의도 파악

번역 체임버스 씨가 오후 1시 35분에 "실망스럽네요"라고 쓸 때, 그 의도는 무엇인가?

(A) 음식점 추천에 동의하지 않는다.
(B) 여행에 참가할 수 없어서 좌절감을 느낀다.
(C) 리즈 씨가 자신의 질문에 답변할 수 있다고 생각하지 않는다.
(D) 계약 조건 일부가 마음에 들지 않는다.

해설 오후 1시 32분 메시지에서 체임버스 씨는 여행 참가자들을 위해 모든 식사가 포함되게끔 그린 시티 투어에서 주선하는 것으로 알고 있다며 리즈 씨에게 이를 확인했는데, 리즈 씨가 1시 33분 메시지에서 계약 조건상(the terms of the contract specifically state) 환영 연회와 환송 정찬을 제외한 다른 모든 식사는 참가자 자비로 처리해야 한다(All other meals are to be covered at the participants' own expense during the program)고 설명했다. 이에 대해 체임버스 씨가 실망스럽다고 한 것이므로, (D)가 정답이다.

어휘 frustrated 좌절감을 느끼는

174 추론 / 암시

번역 디아즈 씨의 직업은 무엇이겠는가?

(A) 고객 서비스 관리자
(B) 밴쿠버시 행정 담당자
(C) 여행 블로그 작가
(D) 호텔 안내원

해설 체임버스 씨가 오후 1시 35분 메시지에서 리즈 씨에게 관리자와 연결해달라(Could I be connected with a supervisor?)고 요청했는데, 이에 오후 1시 37분에 디아즈 씨가 등장해 체임버스 씨를 응대했다. 따라서 디아즈 씨가 고객 서비스 관리자라고 추론할 수 있으므로, (A)가 정답이다.

> ▸▸ **Paraphrasing** 지문의 supervisor
> → 정답의 Customer service manager

175 세부 사항

번역 체임버스 씨는 다음으로 무엇을 할 것인가?

(A) 환영사 준비
(B) 유적지 조사
(C) 동료와 대화
(D) 음식 시식

해설 체임버스 씨가 오후 1시 40분 메시지에서 앞서 자신이 문의했던 식사 관련 계약 조건에 대해 왕 씨와 협의해 보겠다(I'm going to consult with Mr. Wang)고 했으므로, (C)가 정답이다.

어휘 speech 연설 historical 역사의 colleague 동료

> ▸▸ **Paraphrasing** 지문의 consult with Mr. Wang
> → 정답의 Speak with a colleague

176-180 이메일 + 기사

수신: 나디아 버튼 〈manager_publicaffairs@
jaspertonintlairport.com〉
발신: 론 힐튼 〈rhylton@cityofjasperton.gov〉
날짜: 10월 3일
제목: 개통식 기념행사

안녕하세요, 버튼 씨.

176예기치 못하게 일정이 겹친 관계로, 브라운 시장님이 다음 주 행사 출연을 취소해야 한다는 소식을 전해드리게 되어 유감입니다. 177시장님은 재스퍼턴 국제공항과 인근 주택 소유주들 간 소음 감소 협정을 협상하는 데 일조한 것을 자랑스럽게 생각하며, 축하하러 갈 수 없어서 유감스러워하십니다. 176/180시 의회 의장이 시장님을 대신할 예정입니다.

179그건 그렇고, 아로비온 항공에 대한 희소식을 들었습니다. 축하드립니다! 179동아시아로 출장을 가는 많은 사람들이 이를 즐겁게 이용할 것입니다.

론 힐튼, 커뮤니케이션 담당자
시장실

어휘 ribbon-cutting 개관식, 개통식 unexpected 예기치 못한 scheduling conflict 일정이 겹치는 것 appearance 나타남, 출연 play a part 일조하다, 역할을 하다 negotiate 협상하다 reduction 감소 agreement 협정, 합의 chairperson 의장 take advantage of ~를 이용하다

공항 및 시 지도층, 프로젝트 완성을 기념하다

재스퍼턴 (10월 5일)—17810월 12일 재스퍼턴 국제공항에서 개통 기념식이 개최될 예정이다. 이 행사는 공항 15번 활주로 확장 완료를 기념한다. 180시 의회 의장인 로잘리 콜맨과 공항 담당자 노리스 유안이 오전 9시 30분에 다른 초청객들과 함께 모여 커팅식을 진행할 것이다.

활주로 확장 프로젝트는 5개월 전 시작됐는데, 다소 논란이 있었다. 소음공해를 우려하는 주택 소유주 단체가 제기한 불만사항은 결국 프로젝트 초기 계획에는 없었던 콘크리트 방음벽의 건설로 이어졌다.

17915번 활주로 확장으로 지역 내 여행의 새로운 시대가 열리게 되었다. 현재 활주로는 장거리 해외 노선을 갈 수 있는 광폭 동체 항공기를 수용할 만큼 충분히 길다. 장거리 항공사 중 적어도 한 곳이 이미 재스퍼턴에서 동아시아로 가는 직항편을 준비하고 있다.

어휘 completion 완료 extension 확장 gather 모이다 not without 다소 있는, 없진 않은 controversy 논란 complaint 불만 concerned about ~를 염려하는 pollution 공해 eventually 결국 noise barrier 방음벽 initial 초기의, 원래의 usher in ~이 시작되게 하다 era 시대 accommodate 수용하다 long-haul 장거리의 carrier 항공사

176 주제 / 목적

번역 이메일을 쓴 목적은 무엇이겠는가?

(A) 계획 변경을 알리기 위해

(B) 초청장을 보내기 위해

(C) 항공편 예약을 바꾸기 위해

(D) 최근 회의를 요약하기 위해

해설 이메일의 첫 번째 단락에서 블라우 시장이 다음 주 행사 출연을 취소해야 한다는 소식을 전하게 되어 유감(I am sorry to tell you that ~ Mayor Blau must cancel her appearance at next week's event)이라고 한 후, 시 의회 의장이 시장을 대신할 예정(The city council chairperson will take her place)이라고 했다. 따라서 계획의 변경을 알리기 위해 쓴 이메일이라고 추론할 수 있으므로, (A)가 정답이다.

어휘 notification 알림, 통지   modify 수정하다   reservation 예약
summarize 요약하다

> ▸▸Paraphrasing   지문의 **cancel her appearance at next week's event / take her place**
> → 정답의 **a change**

177 세부 사항

번역 블라우 시장은 어떻게 프로젝트를 지원했는가?

(A) 건설 허가를 받을 수 있도록 도왔다.

(B) 두 단체가 합의에 이르도록 도왔다.

(C) 해외 항공사와 관계를 정립했다.

(D) 시 의회와 자금 인상을 협상했다.

해설 이메일의 첫 번째 단락에서 블라우 시장이 재스퍼턴 국제공항과 인근 주택 소유주들 간 소음 감소 협정을 협상하는 데 일조했다(The mayor is ~ to have played a part in negotiating a noise-reduction agreement between Jasperton International Airport and nearby homeowners)고 했으므로, (B)가 정답이다.

어휘 permit 허가증   reach an agreement 합의에 이르다
establish a relationship 관계를 맺다, 관계를 정립하다
funding 자금

> ▸▸Paraphrasing   지문의 **have played a part in negotiating a noise-reduction agreement between Jasperton International Airport and nearby homeowners** → 정답의 **helped two groups reach an agreement**

178 세부 사항

번역 기사에서 알리고 있는 것은?

(A) 신공항 개관식

(B) 공항 담당자 임명

(C) 새 광폭 동체 항공기 디자인

(D) 확장 활주로 개통식

해설 기사의 첫 번째 단락을 보면, 10월 12일 재스퍼턴 국제공항에서 개통 기념식이 개최될 예정이며, 이 행사에서 공항 15번 활주로 확장

완료를 기념한다(The event will mark the completion of the extension of airport runway 15)고 나와 있다. 따라서 (D)가 정답이다.

어휘 dedication 개관식, 헌정식   appointment 임명

> ▸▸Paraphrasing   지문의 **A ribbon-cutting ceremony**
> → 정답의 **The opening**

179 연계

번역 아로비온 항공사에 대해 암시된 것은?

(A) 새 경영 체제 하에 있다.

(B) 저가 항공권으로 인기가 높다.

(C) 장거리 항공편을 제공할 것이다.

(D) 최근 본사를 이전했다.

해설 이메일의 두 번째 단락에서 힐튼 씨는 아로비온 항공에 대한 희소식을 들었다(we heard the good news about Arovion Air)고 한 후, 동아시아로 출장을 가는 많은 사람들이 이를 즐겁게 이용할 것 같다(A lot of people traveling to East Asia on business will be happy to take advantage of this)고 덧붙였다. 기사의 마지막 단락을 보면 활주로 확장으로 인해 새로운 여행길이 열려 한 장거리 항공사가 재스퍼턴에서 동아시아로 가는 직항편(nonstop from Jasperton to East Asia)을 준비하고 있다고 나와 있으므로, 아로비온 항공사가 해당 항공편을 제공한다고 추론할 수 있다. 따라서 (C)가 정답이다.

어휘 long-distance 장거리의   relocate 이전하다   headquarters
본부, 본사

> ▸▸Paraphrasing   지문의 **long-haul carrier**
> → 정답의 **long-distance flights**

180 연계

번역 기념식에서 누가 재스퍼턴 시장을 대신하겠는가?

(A) 버튼 씨

(B) 콜맨 씨

(C) 힐튼 씨

(D) 유안 씨

해설 이메일의 첫 번째 단락에서 시 의회 의장이 시장을 대신하여(The city council chairperson will take her place) 기념식에 참여할 예정이라고 했다. 기사의 첫 번째 단락을 보면, 시 의회 의장인 로잘리 콜맨이 다른 초청객들과 함께 모여 커팅식을 진행할 것(City council chairperson Rosalie Colman ~ will gather with other invited guests to cut the ribbon)이라고 되어 있으므로, (B)가 정답이다.

어휘 represent 대표하다, 대신하다

> ▸▸Paraphrasing   지문의 **take her place** → 질문의 **represent Jasperton's mayor**

12월 2일

182/184폴 레거, 점장

182펠더 안경점

메인 가 930번지

태미스빌, 버몬트 05003

레거 씨께,

182최근 귀하의 매장을 방문했는데 저에게 맞는 사이즈의 안경테를 찾을 수가 없었습니다. 모건 씨가 응대해 주셨고 매우 도움이 됐지만 사실상 저의 작고 좁은 얼굴형에 맞는 성인용 스타일은 없었어요. 앞으로는 더 작은 여성용 안경테를 갖춰 주셨으면 합니다.

자그마한 크기의 예쁜 안경을 온라인 몰인 유어 베스트 프레임에서 발견했는데요. 이번 주에 구입하려고 합니다. **181/183제가 테를 구입하고 매장으로 바로 가게끔 배송시키면 렌즈를 제작하고 끼워 주실 수 있나요? 바로 답변 주시기를 기다리겠습니다.**

스테파니 포츠

어휘 optician 안경사, 안경점 recently 최근 wait on ~을 응대하다, 시중을 들다 virtually 사실상 petite 자그마한 purchase 구입하다 insert 끼우다, 삽입하다 promptly 즉시

유어 베스트 프레임

www.yourbestframes.com

날짜:	12월 5일
고객:	스테파니 포츠
	브로드 가 201번지, 태미스빌, 버몬트 05003
184배송지:	**점장, 펠더 안경점**
	주제: S. 포츠 주문 건
	메인 가 930번지, 태미스빌 버몬트 05003
주문번호:	28734T2
	주문 세부사항: 수 레인 제작 여성용 안경테 1개
	색상/스타일: 검정/작은 안경테 9374-87
가격:	127달러
	신용카드: 라나 은행 **** **** **** 7872
처리자:	사이먼 줄러
183비고:	**포트 씨의 요청 대로 펠더 안경점으로 직배송.**
	12월 12일까지 배송 예상. **185완불.**

어휘 per ~의 요청대로 expected 예상되는 paid in full 전액 지불된

181 주제 / 목적

번역 편지를 쓴 목적은?

(A) 제품의 반품 방법을 문의하려고

(B) 수리에 대해 문의하려고

(C) 특별 요청을 하려고

(D) 배송일자에 관해 문의하려고

해설 편지의 두 번째 단락에서 포트 씨는 자신이 테를 구입하고 레거 씨의 매장(=펠더 안경점)으로 바로 가게끔 배송시키면 렌즈를 제작하고 끼워 줄 수 있는지(If I buy the frames, could I have them shipped directly to your store for you to make and insert the lenses?) 물어보며 답을 요청했다. 따라서 (C)가 정답이다.

어휘 repair 수리 make a request 요청하다

182 세부 사항

번역 모건 씨는 어디서 일하는가?

(A) 배송업체

(B) 의류 소매점

(C) 안경점

(D) 신용카드 회사

해설 편지의 첫 번째 단락에서 포트 씨는 최근 레거 씨의 매장(=펠더 안경점)을 방문했는데 안경테를 찾을 수가 없었다(I recently visited your store and was unable to find eyeglass frames)고 한 후, 방문 당시 모건 씨가 자신을 응대했다(Ms. Morgan waited on me)고 했다. 따라서 모건 씨가 펠더 안경점에서 일한다는 것을 알 수 있으므로, (C)가 정답이다.

183 연계

번역 펠더 안경점에 대해 암시된 것은?

(A) 브로드 가에 있다.

(B) 작은 안경 제품이 많이 있다.

(C) 안경테를 판매하는 온라인 매장이 있다.

(D) 다른 곳에서 구입한 테에 렌즈를 끼워줄 것이다.

해설 편지의 두 번째 단락에서 포트 씨는 자신이 테를 구입하고 레거 씨의 매장(=펠더 안경점)으로 바로 가게끔 배송시키면 렌즈를 제작하고 끼워줄 수 있는지(If I buy the frames, could I have them shipped directly to your store for you to make and insert the lenses?) 문의했는데, 유어 베스트 프레임에서 발급한 영수증의 비고란을 보면 포트 씨의 요청에 따라 안경테를 펠더 안경점으로 바로 배송하라(Ship directly to Pelder Opticians, per Ms. Potts)고 되어 있다. 이를 통해 펠더 안경점에서 포트 씨의 요청, 즉 다른 곳에서 주문한 안경테에 렌즈를 끼워주는 작업을 해주기로 수락했다고 추론할 수 있으므로, (D)가 정답이다.

어휘 elsewhere 다른 곳에서

184 연계

번역 유어 베스트 프레임은 누구에게 소포를 보낼 것인가?

(A) 레거 씨

(B) 포츠 씨

(C) 레인 씨

(D) 줄러 씨

해설 영수증의 배송지(Ship to) 정보에서 소포가 펠더 안경점의 점장(Manager, Pelder Opticians) 앞으로 보내진다는 것을 알 수 있다. 펠더 안경점의 점장은 편지의 수신인인 레거 씨(Paul Reggar, Manager)이므로, (A)가 정답이다.

185 사실 관계 확인

번역 주문 건에 대해 알 수 있는 것은?

(A) 12월 2일에 제출됐다.
(B) 12월 5일까지 도착할 것으로 예상된다.
(C) 이미 결제됐다.
(D) 안경테 한 쌍이 여분으로 들어 있다.

해설 영수증의 비고란(Notes)에 완불(Paid in full)되었다고 쓰여 있으므로, (C)가 정답이다. 영수증이 12월 5일(Date: December 5)에 작성되었고, 배송 예정일은 12월 12일(Expected delivery by December 12)이라고 나와 있으며, 안경테는 한 쌍(1 pair women's frame)만 들어 있으므로, 나머지는 오답이다.

어휘 submit 제출하다 contain ~이 들어 있다

186-190 웹페이지 + 일정표 + 편지

http://www.milfordjanitorialservice.com

밀포드 청소 용역 서비스
메도우베일 로 956번지, 밀포드, 코네티컷 06460

밀포드 청소 용역 서비스(MJS)가 여러분의 일터를 가장 보기 좋게 만들 수 있도록 도와드리겠습니다. 가장 좋은 평가를 받은 청소용품을 사용하여, MJS는 크고 작은 회사들의 특정 요구사항 및 일정에 따라 서비스를 제공합니다. ¹⁸⁶전문적으로 공인된 직원들이 주 7일 고품질의 스트레스 없는 청소 서비스를 제공해 드립니다. 관심이 있으십니까? 절차는 다음과 같습니다.

1. ¹⁸⁹MJS에 연락해 요청사항을 주시고, 저희가 어떻게 해야 최적의 서비스를 제공해 드릴 수 있을지 말씀해 주십시오.

2. ¹⁸⁹무료 상담을 위해 귀사를 방문합니다.

3. 72시간 이내에 연락 드려 추천사항 및 가격 견적을 알려드립니다.

4. 저희 견적서를 검토하시고 만족하신다면 계약에 서명하십시오.

어휘 janitorial 용역의, 잡역부의 top-rated 가장 인기 있는, 가장 좋은 평가를 받은 specific 특정한, 구체적인 needs 요구사항 professionally 전문적으로 certified 입증된, 공인된 process 과정, 절차 request 요청 consultation 상담 recommendation 추천 estimate 견적서, 추산 contract 계약(서)

밀포드 청소 용역 서비스 (MJS)
¹⁸⁷6월 10일 월요일 저녁 업무 일정표

장소	세부사항	팀
핼렌더 사무용품	먼지 털기 및 진공청소	실버팀
쇼어사이드 은행	창문 청소	¹⁹⁰블루팀 *
라리마 카페	화장실 청소	그린팀
파우더 빨래방	¹⁹⁰바닥 청소 및 광내기	¹⁹⁰골드팀 *
¹⁸⁸J. 맬러리 회계	먼지 털기 및 진공청소	¹⁸⁸실버팀

* ^{187/190}다음 달부터 블루팀과 골드팀이 청소 업무를 바꿀 예정입니다.

어휘 assignment 임무, 과제 office supply 사무용품 dusting 먼지 털기 vacuuming 진공청소 laundromat 빨래방 polishing 광내기 accounting 회계 switch 바꾸다, 전환하다

아이린 예복 · 캐노피 로 1800번지 · 밀포드, 코네티컷 06461

6월 17일

밀포드 청소 용역 서비스
메도우베일 로 956번지
밀포드, 코네티컷 06460

안녕하세요.

제 고객 중 한 분이 귀사를 추천해 주셨습니다. ^{189/190}특정 요구사항이 있는데요. 제 사업체의 대규모 로비에서 바닥 청소 및 광내기 작업을 전문적으로 해 주십사 요청 드립니다. 로비가 항상 반짝거리는 건 중요한 일이니까요. ^{189/190}7월 1일부터 매주 서비스를 받고 싶습니다. 답변 기다리겠습니다.

아이린 노게이라
아이린 예복

어휘 formal wear 예복, 정장 refer 추천하다, 보내다 require 요청하다 sparkling 반짝거리는 provide 제공하다

186 사실 관계 확인

번역 MJS에 대해 명시된 것은?

(A) 새 경영 체제 하에 있다.
(B) 연간 계약을 갱신하고 있다.
(C) 주택 청소를 전문으로 한다.
(D) 매일 서비스를 제공한다.

해설 웹페이지의 첫 번째 단락에서 전문적으로 공인된 직원들이 주 7일 청소 서비스를 제공한다(Our professionally certified staff delivers ~ cleaning services seven days a week)고 했으므로, (D)가 정답이다. MJS가 '일터'를 보기 좋게 만들 수 있도록 도와준다(Let ~ MJS help you showcase your workplace in its best light)고 했으므로 (C)는 정답이 될 수 없고, (A)와 (B)는 언급되지 않았다.

어휘 renew a contract 계약을 갱신하다 specialize in ~를 전문으로 하다 residential 주택지의

▸▸ **Paraphrasing** 지문의 delivers ~ cleaning services seven days a week → 정답의 provides services every day of the week

187 세부 사항

번역 일정표는 누구를 대상으로 하는가?

(A) MJS 고객
(B) 청소용품 공급업체
(C) MJS 직원
(D) 구직자

해설 일정표의 상단에 6월 10일 월요일 저녁 업무 일정표(Assignment schedule for the evening of Monday, June 10)라고 명시되어 있고, 하단에는 다음 달부터 블루팀과 골드팀이 청소 업무를 바꿀 예정(beginning next month, the Blue Team and the Gold Team will switch cleaning roles)이라며 주의 사항을 전달하고 있다. 따라서 MJS의 직원들을 대상으로 한 일정표라고 보는 것이 타당하므로, (C)가 정답이다.

188 세부 사항

번역 실버팀은 6월 10일에 어디에 있을 것인가?

(A) 쇼어사이드 은행
(B) 라리마 카페
(C) 파우더 빨래방
(D) J. 맬러리 회계

해설 일정표에서 실버팀이 6월 10일에 핼렌더 사무용품(Hallender Office Supply)과 J. 맬러리 회계(J. Mallery Accounting)에서 업무를 수행할 예정임을 알 수 있다. 따라서 보기 중에서는 (D)가 정답이다.

189 연계

번역 MJS 직원은 편지에 대한 응답으로 다음에 무엇을 하겠는가?

(A) 아이린 예복에 전화하여 증빙 서류 제공하기
(B) 아이린 예복 방문하기
(C) 노게이라 씨에게 이메일로 견적서 보내기
(D) 노게이라 씨에게 계약서 보내기

해설 편지에서 노게이라 씨는 회사 로비의 바닥 청소 및 광내기 작업(professional floor cleaning and polishing in the large lobby of my business)을 요청하며 7월 1일부터 매주 서비스를 받고 싶다(I would like this service provided weekly, beginning on July 1)고 했다. 웹페이지의 서비스 신청 절차(process)를 보면, MJS에 연락해 요청 사항을 전달하는 것(Contact MJS with your request, describing how we can best serve you)은 첫 번째 단계에 해당한다. 따라서 MJS 직원이 그 다음 단계인 무료 상담(We will visit your place of business for a free consultation)을 위해 노게이라 씨의 회사, 즉, 아이린 예복을 방문할 거라고 추론할 수 있으므로, (B)가 정답이다.

어휘 reference 증빙 서류, 추천서

▸▸ Paraphrasing 지문의 **visit your place of business** → 정답의 **Make a visit to Irene's Formal Wear**

190 연계

번역 7월에는 아이린 예복에 어떤 팀이 배정되겠는가?

(A) 실버팀
(B) 블루팀
(C) 그린팀
(D) 골드팀

해설 편지에서 노게이라 씨는 회사(=아이린 예복) 로비의 바닥 청소 및 광내기 작업(professional floor cleaning and polishing in the large lobby of my business)을 요청하며 7월 1일부터 서비스를 받고 싶다고 했다. 일정표에 따르면 6월 10일 바닥 청소 및 광내기(Floor cleaning and polishing) 작업은 골드팀(Gold Team) 담당이지만, 하단을 보면 다음 달부터 블루팀과 골드팀이 청소 업무를 바꿀 예정(beginning next month, the Blue Team and the Gold Team will switch cleaning roles)이라고 되어 있다. 따라서 7월부터 서비스를 요청한 아이린 예복에는 블루팀이 배정될 것이라고 추론할 수 있으므로, (B)가 정답이다.

191-195 메뉴 + 청구서 + 이메일

딜리쉬 바비큐 케이터링 메뉴

바비큐 및 곁들임 요리 뷔페: 1인당 17.95달러
육류 두 가지와 곁들임 요리 두 가지를 선택하세요.
    육류: 소고기, 닭고기, 돼지고기, 소시지
    곁들임 요리: 껍질콩과 양파, 감자 샐러드, 마카로니와 치즈,
    구운 콩
191샐러드, 음료(탄산음료, 커피, 차), 빵(옥수수빵, 디너롤빵)과 함께 제공.

추가 곁들임 요리는 파운드 단위로 이용 가능
6.50달러: 껍질콩과 양파
1936달러: 감자 샐러드
5달러: 마카로니와 치즈
4달러: 구운 콩

아침 식사 뷔페 (1인당 가격)
옵션 A (8.95달러): 페이스트리와 신선 과일 모둠, 음료(커피, 차, 우유, 생과일 주스)
옵션 B (10.95달러): 팬케이크와 시럽, 옵션 A의 모든 메뉴
옵션 C (13.95달러): 오믈렛 모둠, 옵션 A의 모든 메뉴

194문의사항이나 주문 관련사항은 저희 행사 관리자에게 연락해 주십시오.

어휘 catering 음식 조달[공급] fixing 요리에 곁들인 음식
available 이용 가능한

<table>
<tr><td colspan="4" align="center">청구서
딜리쉬 바비큐 케이터링</td></tr>
<tr><td>**물품**</td><td>**단가**</td><td>**수량**</td><td>**총액**</td></tr>
<tr><td>바비큐 및 곁들임 요리 뷔페</td><td>17.95달러</td><td>30</td><td>538.50달러</td></tr>
<tr><td>**193** 추가 곁들임 요리</td><td>6달러</td><td>3</td><td>18달러</td></tr>
<tr><td>**192** 배달료</td><td></td><td></td><td>20달러</td></tr>
<tr><td>**192** (6월 23일에 배달되도록 주문)</td><td></td><td></td><td></td></tr>
<tr><td>아침 식사 옵션 C</td><td>13.95달러</td><td>30</td><td>418.50달러</td></tr>
<tr><td>**192** 배달료</td><td></td><td></td><td>20달러</td></tr>
<tr><td>**192** (6월 24일에 배달되도록 주문)</td><td></td><td></td><td></td></tr>
<tr><td>소계</td><td></td><td></td><td>1,015달러</td></tr>
<tr><td>시식료</td><td></td><td></td><td>14달러</td></tr>
<tr><td>판매세 (6%)</td><td></td><td></td><td>61.74달러</td></tr>
<tr><td>**총 금액**</td><td></td><td></td><td>**1,090.74달러**</td></tr>
</table>

수신: 데릭 아너드 〈darnaud@deelishbbq.com〉
발신: 마리사 금 〈mkeum@keumaccountancy.com〉
날짜: 6월 3일
제목: 청구서

아너드 씨께,

청구서 보내주셔서 감사합니다. **194** 청구서에 대해 몇 가지 문의사항이 있는데 도와주셨으면 합니다.

지난주 전화로 이야기했을 때, 시식료(2인 14달러)는 전체 구매금액에서 공제해주실 거라고 말씀하셨는데요. 청구서에는 이게 반영되어 있지 않네요.

잔금 중 절반은 지금 지불하고 나머지 절반은 음식이 배달됐을 때 지불할 수 있는지도 여쭤봤는데요. 이 방식이 아직 유효한가요? **195** 만약 그렇다면, 새 청구서를 받을 때 보증금을 지불하겠습니다.

마리사 금

어휘 deduct 공제하다 balance 잔금 arrangement (주선된) 방식 deposit 착수금, 보증금 make a payment 지불하다, 결제하다

191 사실 관계 확인

번역 메뉴에 따르면, 바비큐 및 곁들임 요리 뷔페에 포함되지 않은 것은?

(A) 샐러드
(B) 음료
(C) 빵
(D) 과일

해설 바비큐 및 곁들임 요리 뷔페(BBQ and Fixings Buffet)에 대한 설명을 보면, 샐러드, 음료, 빵이 함께 제공(Comes with salads, drink ~, and bread)된다고 나와 있다. 따라서 언급되지 않은 (D)가 정답이다.

192 세부 사항

번역 청구서에 따르면, 고객에게 배달료가 두 번 청구되는 이유는?

(A) 배달이 각각 다른 날 이뤄질 예정이다.
(B) 일반 배달 지역 범위를 넘어서 배달이 이뤄질 예정이다.
(C) 딜리쉬 바비큐에서 잘못 청구했다.
(D) 고객이 결제 시 실수했다.

해설 청구서의 배달료(Delivery charge) 내역을 보면, 6월 23일(Order to be delivered June 23)과 6월 24일(Order to be delivered June 24)에 각각 다른 메뉴가 배달되어야 함을 알 수 있다. 즉, 배송이 두 번 이루어지는 것이므로, (A)가 정답이다.

어휘 occur 발생하다, 일어나다 separate 별개의, 서로 다른

193 연계

번역 금 씨는 어떤 곁들임 음식을 추가로 구입했는가?

(A) 껍질콩과 양파
(B) 감자 샐러드
(C) 마카로니와 치즈
(D) 구운 콩

해설 청구서 내역에서 금 씨가 단가(Unit Cost) 6달러의 곁들임 음식(Extra side)을 구입한 사실을 확인할 수 있다. 메뉴를 보면, 파운드 단위로 이용 가능한 추가 곁들임 요리(Extra sides available by the pound) 중 6달러인 것은 감자 샐러드($6.00: Potato salad)이므로, (B)가 정답이다.

194 연계

번역 아너드 씨는 누구이겠는가?

(A) 케이터링 관리자
(B) 고객
(C) 음식점 주인
(D) 음식 평론가

해설 이메일의 첫 번째 단락에서 금 씨는 아너드 씨에게 청구서에 대해 몇 가지 문의사항이 있다(I just have a few questions about the invoice)며 도와달라(you could help)고 요청했다. 메뉴의 마지막 단락을 보면, 문의사항이나 주문 관련 사항은 행사 관리자에게 연락하라(Contact our events manager with any questions or issues with your order)고 되어 있으므로, 문의사항을 받은 아너드 씨가 행사 관리자라고 추론할 수 있다. 따라서 (A)가 정답이다.

▸▸ Paraphrasing 지문의 events manager
→ 정답의 catering supervisor

195 세부 사항

번역 이메일에 따르면, 금 씨는 아너드 씨가 다음으로 무엇을 하기를 기대하는가?

(A) 자신에게 전화해서 주문 검토
(B) 배달 일정 변경
(C) 새 청구서 발송
(D) 시식 견본 제공

해설 이메일의 세 번째 단락에서 새 청구서를 받으면 보증금을 지불하겠다(I will make the deposit payment once I receive the new invoice)고 했으므로, 아너드 씨가 새로 청구서를 발송하기를 기대한다는 것을 알 수 있다. 따라서 (C)가 정답이다.

어휘 reschedule 일정을 변경하다

196-200 기사 + 보도자료 + 이메일

클레어톤 비즈니스 다이제스트

(2월 8일)—196많은 업체들, 특히 중간 가격대의 의류 브랜드를 판매하는 업체들이 흥미로운 전략을 수용했다. 제품을 위해 현지 및 지역 시장에 중점을 두는 대신, 의도적으로 소매점을 다각화한다. 일례로, 동아시아 전역에 10개의 매장을 여는 대신, 동아시아에서는 몇 개의 매장만으로 제한하고 남아메리카나 중동에 새 매장을 추가하는 방법을 선택하는 것이다.

마케팅 자문위원 체스터 마우는 "196이러한 접근법은 어느 한 지역의 경기 침체나 성장 둔화 시기에 완충 역할을 합니다."라고 설명했다.

이미 해당 전략을 따르는 업체 중에는 카리스마 패션과 베이비 클로짓 등이 포함되어 있다. 198롤로 스포츠웨어는 4월로 계획된 남아메리카 시장의 진출로 이 전례를 따를 것이다.

어휘 especially 특히 apparel 의류 embrace 수용하다, 받아들이다 strategy 전략 regional 지역의 purposely 일부러 diversify 다각화하다 opt to ~하기로 선택하다 approach 접근법 serve as ~의 역할을 하다 buffer 완충 economic downturn 경기 침체 geographical area 지리적 영역, 지역 pursue 추구하다 follow suit 전례를 따르다

즉시 배포용
6월 13일

연락처: 모라 킬, mkeele@lolosportswear.com

(클레어톤) - 197롤로 스포츠웨어는 조셉 차카타가 신임 최고경영자 자리에 오를 것이라고 오늘 발표했다. 차카타 씨는 7월에 직책을 맡게 될 예정이다. 그는 이전에 선도적인 패션 디자인 업체인 컬러스프라이트 주식회사에서 8년간 최고경영자로 일했다.

199/200차카타 씨는 롤로 스포츠웨어를 창립하고 18년간 최고경영자직을 맡은 셜리 알덴을 대신하게 된다. 알덴 씨는 "롤로 스포츠웨어를 이토록 유능한 손에 맡기고 떠나게 되어 기쁩니다. 이제 회사는 중요한 다음 시기를 맞을 준비가 됐습니다."라고 발언했다. 1984월에 회사의 첫 해외 매장을 성공적으로 연 뒤 대표직 이행이 이뤄진다. 연말에는 추가 확장이 계획되어 있다.

어휘 immediate 즉각적인 assume responsibility 직책을 맡다 previously 이전에 replace 대신하다 found 설립하다 capable 유능한 transition 이행 additional 추가의 expansion 확장

수신: 셜리 알덴 〈salden@mailenvy.com〉
발신: 조셉 차카타 〈jchakata@lolosportswear.com〉
날짜: 9월 10일
제목: 소식

알덴 씨께,

200함께 아는 지인 체스터 마우 씨로부터 당신이 또 다른 상업 회사를 시작할 준비가 되셨다는 얘기를 최근에 들었습니다. 이번에는 가구 업계라고요. 큰 성공을 거두시리라 확신합니다. 제 축하 인사를 받아주십시오.

조셉 차카타

어휘 recently 최근 commercial 상업적인 venture 벤처 기업, 신규 회사 accept 받아주다

---

196 세부 사항

번역 기사에서 설명한 사업 전략을 회사에서 이용하는 이유는?

(A) 대표직을 더 빠르게 구하려고
(B) 브랜드 가시성을 높이려고
(C) 더 다양한 구성원이 있는 일터를 만들려고
(D) 어느 한 지역에 의존하는 것을 피하려고

해설 기사의 첫 번째 단락에서 언급된 사업 전략은 현지 및 지역 시장에 중점을 두는 대신 의도적으로 소매점을 다각화하는 것(Instead of focusing on local and regional markets for their products, they purposely diversify their retail locations)이다. 두 번째 단락에 인용된 전문가의 말에 따르면, 이러한 접근법은 어느 한 지역의 경기 침체나 성장 둔화 시기에 대하여 완충 역할을 하므로(This approach serves as a buffer against economic downturns or periods of slower growth in any one geographical area), 한 군데에 의존하지 않기 위해 이 전략을 사용한다는 것을 알 수 있다. 따라서 (D)가 정답이다.

어휘 visibility 가시성 diverse 다양한 workforce 직원, 노동력 dependence 의존, 의지

---

197 세부 사항

번역 롤로 스포츠웨어는 몇 월에 대표직이 바뀌었는가?

(A) 4월
(B) 6월
(C) 7월
(D) 12월

해설 보도자료의 첫 번째 단락에서 차카타 씨가 롤로 스포츠웨어의 신임 최고경영자 자리에 오를 것(Joseph Chakata will become its new chief executive officer)이라고 한 후, 7월에 직책을 맡게 될 예정(Mr. Chakata will assume responsibilities in July)이라고 덧붙였다. 따라서 (C)가 정답이다.

▸▸ Paraphrasing 지문의 **its new chief executive officer**
→ 질문의 **leadership change**

198 연계

번역 차카타 씨에 대해 암시된 것은?

(A) 패션 디자이너이다.
(B) 중동에 거주한다.
(C) 최근 경영대학원을 졸업했다.
(D) 남아메리카 매장들을 관리할 것이다.

해설 보도자료의 두 번째 단락에서 롤로 스포츠웨어가 4월에 첫 해외 매
장을 연 뒤 대표직 이행이 이뤄진다(The leadership transition
comes after the successful launch in April of the
company's first overseas stores)고 했는데, 기사의 마지막 단
락을 보면 롤로 스포츠웨어가 4월에 남아메리카 시장으로 진출할 계
획(With its planned April move into the Latin American
market, Lolo Sportswear will follow suit)이라고 나와 있다.
따라서 4월 이후에(=7월) 롤로 스포츠웨어의 최고경영자가 되는 차카
타 씨가 남아메리카 매장들을 관리하게 될 거라고 추론할 수 있으므
로, (D)가 정답이다.

어휘 graduate from ~를 졸업하다 oversee 감독하다, 관리하다

199 세부 사항

번역 보도자료에 따르면, 알덴 씨는 누구인가?

(A) 성공적인 회사의 창업주
(B) 마케팅 자문위원
(C) 인사 전문가
(D) 비즈니스 출판사 소유주

해설 보도자료의 두 번째 단락에서 알덴 씨를 롤로 스포츠웨어를 창립
한 후 18년간 최고경영자직을 맡았던 인물(Shirley Alden, who
founded Lolo Sportswear and then served as its CEO for
eighteen years)로 소개했으므로, (A)가 정답이다.

> ▸▸ Paraphrasing 지문의 who founded Lolo Sportwear
> → 정답의 founder of a ~ company

200 연계

번역 알덴 씨에 대해 암시된 것은?

(A) 동아시아에서의 은퇴 생활을 즐기고 있다.
(B) 그녀의 신규 사업은 그녀가 처음 경험하는 업계의 일이다.
(C) 이전에 컬러스프라이트 주식회사에 투자한 적이 있다.
(D) 차카타 씨에게 조언을 구했다.

해설 이메일의 초반부에서 차카타 씨는 알덴 씨가 '이번에는' 가구 업계
(this time in the furniture industry)에서 회사를 시작할 준비가
되었다(you are ready to begin another commercial venture)
는 소식을 들었다고 했다. 보도자료의 두 번째 단락을 보면, 알덴 씨
가 롤로 스포츠웨어(=의류 업계)를 창립한 이래 18년간 최고경영자직
을 맡았다(Shirley Alden, who founded Lolo Sportswear and
then served as its CEO for eighteen years)고 나와 있으므로,
가구 업계는 알덴 씨에게 새로운 사업 분야라고 추론할 수 있다. 따라
서 (B)가 정답이다.

어휘 retirement 은퇴, 은퇴 생활 invest 투자하다

101 (C)	**102** (D)	**103** (A)	**104** (D)	**105** (B)
106 (A)	**107** (D)	**108** (A)	**109** (C)	**110** (A)
111 (B)	**112** (C)	**113** (D)	**114** (B)	**115** (D)
116 (A)	**117** (D)	**118** (C)	**119** (D)	**120** (A)
121 (B)	**122** (B)	**123** (B)	**124** (A)	**125** (C)
126 (B)	**127** (D)	**128** (C)	**129** (D)	**130** (B)
131 (D)	**132** (A)	**133** (A)	**134** (C)	**135** (C)
136 (A)	**137** (D)	**138** (A)	**139** (D)	**140** (C)
141 (C)	**142** (A)	**143** (D)	**144** (B)	**145** (B)
146 (C)	**147** (D)	**148** (B)	**149** (C)	**150** (D)
151 (A)	**152** (B)	**153** (D)	**154** (A)	**155** (C)
156 (B)	**157** (D)	**158** (D)	**159** (D)	**160** (A)
161 (A)	**162** (C)	**163** (D)	**164** (A)	**165** (C)
166 (B)	**167** (D)	**168** (A)	**169** (C)	**170** (B)
171 (B)	**172** (D)	**173** (A)	**174** (C)	**175** (B)
176 (B)	**177** (A)	**178** (A)	**179** (C)	**180** (B)
181 (C)	**182** (C)	**183** (A)	**184** (B)	**185** (D)
186 (B)	**187** (B)	**188** (D)	**189** (A)	**190** (C)
191 (B)	**192** (A)	**193** (C)	**194** (B)	**195** (B)
196 (C)	**197** (A)	**198** (B)	**199** (C)	**200** (D)

PART 5

101 형용사 자리 _ 명사 수식

해설 부정관사 A와 명사 salesperson 사이에서 salesperson을 수식하는 형용사 자리로, 판매원의 특성을 나타내는 단어가 들어가야 한다. 따라서 (C) helpful(도움을 주는, 유용한)이 정답이다.

번역 도움이 되는 판매원 한 씨가 새 컴퓨터를 고르는 것을 도왔다.

어휘 salesperson 판매원 assist 돕다

102 부사 어휘

해설 반복되는 일을 나타내는 현재시제 동사 gives와 어울리는 부사를 선택해야 한다. 따라서 '정기적으로, 규칙적으로'라는 의미의 (D) regularly가 정답이다.

번역 작가 다니엘 아이덕은 전국 글쓰기 회의에서 정기적으로 강연을 한다.

어휘 give a talk 강연하다 conference 회의, 회담 gradually 점차, 서서히 longer 더 오래 together 함께

103 명사 자리 _ 동사의 목적어 _ 어휘

해설 동사 has의 목적어 역할을 하는 자리로, 양을 나타내는 표현인 a great deal of의 수식을 받을 수 있는 명사가 들어가야 한다. 따라서 보기 중 불가산명사인 (A) experience(경험)가 정답이다. 참고로, 빈칸과 performing 사이에는 전치사 in이 생략되어 있는데, 이는 experience, difficulty, problem 등의 일부 명사만 가능하다.

(D) experiencer는 가산명사로 a great deal of의 수식을 받을 수 없고 의미상으로도 어울리지 않으므로 오답이다. (B) experienced는 동사/과거분사, (C) experiencing은 동명사/현재분사로 품사상 빈칸에 들어갈 수 없다.

번역 콜 씨는 비용 분석 업무 수행에 경험이 많다.

어휘 a great deal of 많은 perform 수행하다 analysis 분석 task 업무, 임무

104 명사 어휘

해설 빈칸을 포함한 to부정사구는 고객이 "일정(Schedule)"을 클릭해야 하는 목적을 나타낸다. 따라서 make와 함께 '예약하다'라는 의미를 완성하는 (D) appointment가 정답이다.

번역 고객은 예약을 하려면 홈페이지의 오른쪽 상단에 있는 "일정"을 클릭하면 된다.

어휘 make an appointment 예약을 하다 example 예시 option 선택권 individual 개인

105 한정사 자리 _ 어휘

해설 전치사 of의 목적어 역할을 하는 복합명사 business day를 수식하는 자리이다. 매 영업일이 끝날 때마다 커피 찌꺼기를 처리해야 한다는 내용이므로, '각각'이라는 의미의 (B) each가 정답이다. 나머지 보기는 구조상으로도 빈칸에 들어갈 수 없다.

번역 사용한 커피 찌꺼기는 매 영업일 종료 시 처리해야 한다.

어휘 grounds 찌꺼기 be disposed of 처리되다

106 접속사 자리 _ 어휘

해설 완전한 두 절을 이어주는 접속사 자리이므로, 보기에서 접속사인 (A) because, (B) although, (D) unless 중 하나를 선택해야 한다. 최근 많은 직원들이 퇴직한 것(so many employees have recently retired)은 새 직원을 채용하기 위한(to hire new workers) 노력이 강화된 원인이라고 볼 수 있다. 따라서 '~ 때문에'라는 의미의 (A) because가 정답이다. (C) instead는 부사로 절을 이끌 수 없다.

번역 최근 아주 많은 직원들이 퇴직했기 때문에 새 직원을 채용하려는 우리 회사의 노력이 강화됐다.

어휘 intensify 강화하다 recently 최근 retire 퇴직하다, 은퇴하다 instead 대신

107 형용사 자리 _ 주격 보어 _ 어휘

해설 빈칸은 be동사 is의 주격 보어 자리로, 부사 fairly의 수식을 받는다. 따라서 빈칸에는 형용사가 들어가야 하므로, '예측 가능한'이라는 의미의 (D) predictable이 정답이다. (A) predict와 (B) predicts는 동사로서 주격 보어 역할을 할 수 없으며, (C) predicting은 타동사의 현재분사/동명사이므로 구조상 빈칸에 들어갈 수 없다.

번역 5월 중 폭우 발생은 상당히 예측이 가능하다.

어휘 occurrence 발생 fairly 상당히, 꽤 predict 예측하다

108 전치사 어휘

해설 return their rental car와 a full tank of fuel을 적절히 연결해주는 전치사를 선택해야 한다. 연료 탱크는 렌터카에 있는 것인데, 이를 가득 채워서 반납해 달라는 내용이므로, '~와 함께, ~한 채'라는 의미의 (A) with가 정답이다.

번역 고객에게 렌터카 연료 탱크를 가득 채워서 반납해 달라고 상기시키십시오.

어휘 remind 상기시키다 fuel 연료 except ~를 제외하고

109 전치사 자리

해설 명사구 the winter season을 목적어로 취하는 전치사 자리로, 문맥상 시기를 나타내는 단어가 들어가야 자연스럽다. 따라서 '~ 후에'라는 의미의 (C) After가 정답이다. (A) Such as는 '~와 같이'라는 뜻으로 어색하며, (B) Moreover은 부사, (D) Whereas는 부사절 접속사로 품사상 빈칸에 들어갈 수 없다.

번역 세리나 빌더스는 겨울 이후 지붕 설치 및 수리를 한번 더 제공할 것이다.

어휘 installation 설치 repair 수리 moreover 게다가 whereas 반면에

110 동사 자리 _ 수 일치

해설 복수주어인 The lights의 동사 자리이므로, 복수동사인 (A) dim이 정답이다. (D) dims는 3인칭 단수동사로 lights와 수가 일치하지 않고, (B) dimming은 현재분사/동명사, (C) dimmer는 비교급 형용사로 구조상 빈칸에 들어갈 수 없다.

번역 영화가 시작되기 전, 극장 조명이 어두워진다.

어휘 dim 어둑해지다, 낮아지다; 어두운

111 형용사 어휘

해설 회의 일정을 잡을 때(When scheduling a meeting) 주의해야 할 것을 당부하는 문장이므로, 다른 표준 시간대에 있는 동료(colleagues in other time zones)를 고려하라는 내용이 되어야 자연스럽다. 따라서 '~를 염두에 두는, 유념하는'이라는 의미의 (B) mindful이 정답이다. 참고로, mindful은 「전치사 of + 명사」, 혹은 that절과 자주 쓰인다.

번역 회의 일정을 잡을 때 다른 표준 시간대의 동료들을 염두에 두십시오.

어휘 colleague 동료 significant 중요한 exclusive 배타적인, 독점적인 serious 심각한, 진지한

112 부사 자리 _ 동사 수식

해설 자동사 rose를 수식하는 부사 자리이므로, (C) sharply(급격히)가 정답이다. 참고로, (A) sharp도 부사로 쓰일 수 있는데, 시간 표현 뒤에서 '정각에'(eg. ten o'clock sharp), 방향 표현과 쓰여 '급히'(eg. turn sharp left), 음악과 관련된 표현 뒤에 '원래 음보다 높이'(eg. sing sharp)라는 뜻을 나타내므로 빈칸에는 적절하지 않다.

번역 새로운 배송 정책을 도입한 후 그린트림의 제품 판매량은 급격히 증가했다.

어휘 introduction 소개, 도입 policy 정책

113 동사 어휘

해설 가정용 전자제품이 필요하면(for all your home appliance needs) Hearnshaw에서 구매하라고 독려하는 내용이므로, '고려하다'라는 의미의 (D) consider가 정답이다.

번역 가정용 전자제품 일체가 필요할 때 헌쇼를 고려해 주십시오.

어휘 home appliance 가정용 전자제품 assemble 모으다, 조립하다 balance 균형을 맞추다 share 공유하다

114 인칭대명사의 격 _ 목적격

해설 전치사 for의 목적어 역할을 하는 자리로, (B) us, (C) ours, (D) ourselves 중 하나를 선택해야 한다. 빈칸은 to부정사구 to clean the carpet in the lobby의 "의미상" 주어 역할을 하는데, 카펫 청소의 주체가 될만한 대상은 '우리'이므로 (B) us가 정답이 된다. (C) ours는 '우리의 것[사람]'을 뜻하는 소유대명사, (D) ourselves는 '우리 자신'을 뜻하는 재귀대명사로 앞에 가리키는 대상이 있어야 하므로 빈칸에는 적절치 않다.

번역 월요일은 우리가 로비 카펫 청소를 하기에 가장 좋은 요일일 것이다.

115 형용사 어휘

해설 사람 명사 Hikers를 보충 설명하는 형용사 자리로, 새로 연 산길을 탐방하려고 하는(to explore the newly opened trails) 등산객들의 성향을 적절히 묘사하는 형용사가 들어가야 한다. 따라서 '간절히 바라는, 열심인'이라는 의미의 (D) eager가 정답이다. 참고로, 빈칸 앞에는 「관계대명사(who) + be동사(are)」가 생략된 것으로 볼 수 있으며, eager는 to부정사와 자주 어울려 쓰인다.

번역 새로 연 산길을 탐방하고 싶어 하는 등산객들이 기록적인 수치로 밀라 자연보호구역을 방문하고 있다.

어휘 explore 탐험하다 nature reserve 자연보호구역 tender 부드러운, 연한 bright 밝은 vast 방대한, 막대한

116 명사 자리 _ 동사의 주어 _ 동격

해설 KOHW부터 Jenae Johnson까지가 주어, will be promoted to news anchor가 본동사구인 문장이다. 따라서 빈칸에는 뉴스 앵커로 승진할 만한 직책이 들어가서 주어인 Jenae Johnson을 수식해 주어야 하므로, '기자'라는 뜻의 (A) reporter가 정답이다. 참고로, 조직 내 직책을 나타내는 명사는 사람 이름 앞에 자주 쓰여 이처럼 수식어 역할을 하기도 하며(reporter), 관사가 생략되기도 한다(news anchor). (B) reporting과 (C) to report의 경우 구조상으로는 빈칸에 들어갈 수 있지만, '지나 존슨을 보고하는 KOHW는 승진할 것이다'라는 내용이 되므로 적절하지 않다.

번역 KOHW 기자인 지나 존슨은 다나 와그너가 은퇴하면 뉴스 앵커로 승진할 것이다.

117 부사 자리 _ 어휘

해설 동사구 raised concerns를 수식하는 부사 자리로, 보기에서
(C) densely와 (D) primarily 중 하나를 선택해야 한다. 주민
들(Residents)이 특정 문제(the project's impact on traffic
congestion)에 대한 우려를 제기했다는 내용이므로, '주로'라
는 의미의 (D) primarily가 빈칸에 들어가야 자연스럽다. 참고로,
(A) extremely는 형용사/부사를 강조하는 부사이고, (B) unlikely
는 형용사로 빈칸에 들어갈 수 없다.

번역 주민들은 프로젝트가 교통 혼잡에 미치는 영향에 대한 우려를 주로 제
기했다.

어휘 resident 거주자 raise concerns 우려를 제기하다 impact
영향 congestion 혼잡 extremely 극도로, 매우 unlikely
~할 것 같지 않은 densely 빽빽이, 밀집하여

118 부사절 접속사

해설 완전한 절(your Fromo grocery order is placed before 10:00
A.M.)을 이끄는 접속사 자리로, 빈칸이 이끄는 절이 콤마 뒤 주절을 수
식하는 역할을 한다. 따라서 부사절 접속사인 (C) As long as(~하
기만 하면)가 정답이다. (A) That은 완전한 절을 이끄는 경우 명사절
접속사로 쓰이므로 빈칸에 들어갈 수 없고, (B) Such는 한정사/대명
사/부사, (D) In spite of는 전치사로 절을 이끌 수 없다.

번역 프로모에서 오전 10시 전에 식료품 주문이 완료되기만 하면, 당일에
배송됩니다.

어휘 place an order 주문을 넣다 in spite of ~에도 불구하고

119 동사 어휘 _ 현재분사

해설 a lunch-and-learn session을 목적어로 취하는 동사의 현재분사
자리이다. 점심 식사 강의 세션은 일종의 행사이므로, '개최하다'라는
의미의 (D) holding이 빈칸에 들어가야 자연스럽다.

번역 재무 부서는 수요일에 점심 식사 강의 세션을 열 예정이다.

어휘 finance 재무, 금융 session 세션, 시간 contact 연락하다
collect 모으다, 수집하다

120 형용사 자리 _ 명사 수식 _ 어휘

해설 주어인 명사 clothing을 수식하는 형용사 자리로, 의복의 특성을 나
타내는 단어가 들어가야 자연스럽다. 따라서 '보호용의'라는 의미
의 (A) Protective가 정답이다. (B) Protecting을 동명사로 볼 경
우 구조상으로는 빈칸에 들어갈 수 있으나, '의류를 보호하는 것이
입혀져야 한다'라는 의미가 되므로 적절하지 않다. (C) Protect와
(D) Protects는 동사로 품사상 빈칸에 들어갈 수 없다.

번역 공사구역에 들어가는 모든 직원은 방호복을 착용해야 한다.

어휘 personnel 인원, 직원들 construction 공사, 건설 protect
보호하다

121 전치사 어휘

해설 동명사구 incurring a rebooking fee를 목적어로 취하는 전치사
자리로, 항공편 변경 시 재예약 수수료의 발생 여부를 나타내는 단어
가 들어가야 자연스럽다. 따라서 '~ 없이'라는 의미의 (B) without이
정답이다.

번역 스타 엘리트 회원 등급에서는 대다수의 항공편 변경이 재예약 수수료
발생 없이 이뤄질 수 있다.

어휘 incur 발생시키다

122 현재분사 _ 명사 수식

해설 Any부터 information까지가 주어, should be sent가 동사인 문
장이다. 따라서 빈칸에는 명사구 sensitive information을 목적어
로 취하면서 letter를 수식하는 준동사가 들어가야 하므로, 현재분사
인 (B) containing이 정답이다. (A) contains, (C) will contain,
(D) has contained는 모두 본동사이므로 빈칸에 들어갈 수 없다.

번역 민감한 정보를 담고 있는 모든 편지는 택배업체 서비스를 이용해 발송
되어야 한다.

어휘 sensitive 민감한 courier 택배 회사 contain ~이 들어 있다

123 부사절 접속사 자리 _ 어휘

해설 빈칸이 완전한 절과 형용사 possible 사이에 있으므로, 이 둘
을 연결해 줄 수 있는 요소가 들어가야 한다. 따라서 접속사인
(B) whenever와 (C) once 중 하나를 선택해야 하는데, 주절의 현재
시제 동사 sources가 반복되는 상황을 나타내므로, '~ 할 때마다'라
는 뜻의 (B) whenever가 빈칸에 들어가야 자연스럽다. 참고로, 일부
부사절 접속사 뒤에는 「주어+be동사」가 생략된 채 형용사나 분사구
가 올 수 있다.

번역 아벨로스 카페는 가능할 때마다 지역 농장들로부터 채소와 과일을 구
한다.

어휘 source 얻다, 공급자를 찾다

124 명사 어휘

해설 「so+형용사(high)+that절」 구조의 문장으로, 빈칸이 포함된 부
분은 운동화에 대한 수요가 너무 높아져(Demand for the ~
running shoes was so high) 생긴 결과, 즉 가게 주인이 취한 조
치를 나타낸다. 고객 1인당 2켤레씩만 사게 하는 것은 구매에 제한
을 두는 것이므로, (A) limit가 정답이다. 참고로, limit은 set 이외에
put, impose와 같은 동사와도 자주 쓰인다.

번역 워터레이스 운동화에 대한 수요가 매우 높아서 매장 주인은 고객 1인
당 2켤레로 제한을 두었다.

어휘 demand 수요 supply 공급 procedure 절차

125 재귀대명사

해설 주어인 The new security camera를 가리키는 재귀대명사를 선택
해야 한다. 따라서 (C) itself가 정답이다.

번역 새로운 보안 카메라는 야간에 화질 좋은 동영상을 녹화할 수 있는 방식으로 스스로 조정한다.

어휘 security 보안 adjust 조정하다, 적응하다

126 동사 어휘 _ 과거분사

해설 명사구 the budget analysis를 뒤에서 수식하는 과거분사 자리이다. 예산 분석은 발표 도중(during the president's presentation) 다뤄지는 내용이라고 볼 수 있으므로, '언급된'이라는 의미의 (B) mentioned가 정답이다. 참고로, (A) occurred는 자동사의 과거분사로 수동의 의미를 나타내지 않으므로 구조상으로도 빈칸에 들어갈 수 없다.

번역 회장님의 발표 중 언급된 예산 분석을 출력본으로 원하시면 마이어 씨에게 연락하세요.

어휘 budget 예산 analysis 분석 presentation 발표 occur 발생하다 learn 알다, 배우다 serve 서비스를 제공하다

127 부사 자리 _ 형용사 수식

해설 동명사 receiving의 목적어 역할을 하는 「형용사(negative)+복합명사(customer feedback)」 앞에서 negative를 수식하는 부사 자리이다. 따라서 (D) increasingly(점점, 더욱더)가 정답이다. (A) increase와 (B) increases는 명사/동사, (C) to increase는 준동사로 구조상 빈칸에 들어갈 수 없다.

번역 솔 피자리아는 점점 더 부정적인 고객 의견을 받게 된 후 메뉴를 변경했다.

어휘 receive 받다 negative 부정적인 increase 증가하다, 증가시키다; 증가, 인상

128 형용사 어휘

해설 빈칸에는 기기 생산(produces devices) 시 고려할 만한 사진가(photographers)의 능력이나 수준을 묘사하는 단어가 들어가야 자연스럽다. 따라서 '아마추어의, 취미로 하는'이라는 의미의 (C) amateur이 정답이다.

번역 탑티컬러는 아마추어 사진가들이 사용할 만한 기기를 생산한다.

어휘 produce 생산하다 intended 대상으로 하는, 의도된 visible 눈에 보이는 eventual 궁극적인 necessary 필요한

129 명사 자리 _ to부정사의 목적어

해설 to부정사 to ensure의 목적어 역할을 하는 명사 자리로, 정관사 the 및 전치사구 of the results의 수식을 받는다. 따라서 (D) reliability(신뢰성, 믿음직함)가 정답이다. (A) rely와 (B) relies는 동사, (C) reliable은 형용사로 품사상 빈칸에 들어갈 수 없다.

번역 결과의 신뢰성을 보장하기 위해 소비자 행동 연구가 반복될 예정이다.

어휘 behavior 행동 ensure 보장하다 rely 의지하다 reliable 믿을 만한

130 부사 어휘

해설 고객과의 중요한 커뮤니케이션을 놓치지 말라고 당부하는 내용으로, 하루 종일(throughout the day) 이메일을 확인하는(Check e-mail) 빈도를 나타내는 부사가 빈칸에 들어가야 자연스럽다. 따라서 '주기적으로'라는 의미의 (B) periodically가 정답이다. 참고로, check는 빈도(always, daily, regularly, periodically)를 나타내거나 방식(carefully, thoroughly)을 나타내는 부사와 자주 쓰인다.

번역 고객과의 중요한 커뮤니케이션을 놓치지 않도록 종일 주기적으로 이메일을 확인하세요.

어휘 overlook 못 보고 넘어가다, 간과하다 artificially 인위적으로 reluctantly 마지못해 simultaneously 동시에

PART 6

131-134 공지

> 헤멜 서점에서는 다가오는 휴가 시즌[131]을 위해 임시로 일할 매장 직원을 찾습니다. 직무에는 고객을 맞이하고 문의사항에 응답하는 일이 포함됩니다. [132]또한 이 직무에는 매매 거래 처리도 수반됩니다. 아울러 상품을 선반에 채우거나 닦고 정리해야할 것입니다. 친절하고 [133]활기찬 지원자를 채용하고자 합니다. 지원하시려면 www.hemelbookstore.com/application에서 온라인 구직 지원서를 작성하세요. [134]기한은 10월 21일입니다.

> 어휘 seek 찾다 temporary 임시의 store associate 매장 직원 upcoming 다가오는, 곧 있을 include 포함하다 greet 맞이하다 in addition 게다가 merchandise 상품 candidate 지원자, 후보자 apply 지원하다 fill out 작성하다, 적어 넣다 job application 구직 지원서

131 전치사 어휘

해설 다가오는 휴가 시즌(the upcoming holiday season)은 임시직 매장 직원을 구하는 이유이므로, '~을 위해'라는 의미의 (D) for가 정답이다.

132 문맥에 맞는 문장 고르기

번역 (A) 또한 이 직무에는 매매 거래 처리도 수반됩니다.
   (B) 휴일에는 자정까지 문을 엽니다.
   (C) 저희 서점은 미술용품도 취급합니다.
   (D) 카페는 매장 1층에 있습니다.

해설 빈칸 앞뒤 문장에서 임시직 매장 직원의 직무(greeting customers and answering questions/shelve, clean, and organize merchandise)를 설명하고 있으므로, 빈칸에도 관련 업무에 대한 내용이 들어가야 자연스럽다. 따라서 (A)가 정답이다.

어휘 involve 수반하다 transaction 매매 거래 supply 용품

133 형용사 자리 _ 명사 수식

해설 형용사 friendly와 함께 명사 candidates를 수식하는 형용사 자리 이므로, (A) energetic(활동적인, 활기찬)이 정답이다. (B) energy와 (D) energizer는 명사, (C) energize는 동사로 품사상 빈칸에 들어갈 수 없다.

어휘 energize 활기를 북돋우다

134 명사 어휘

해설 앞 문장에서 일자리에 지원하고 싶으면 온라인 구직 지원서를 작성하라(To apply, please fill out an online job application)고 했으므로, 해당 문장의 10월 21일은 지원 일정과 관련된 날짜라고 보아야 한다. 따라서 '기한'이라는 의미의 (C) deadline이 빈칸에 들어가야 자연스럽다.

어휘 celebration 기념 행사 release 발표, 공개

135-138 기사

> **어촌, 분주한 항구가 되다**
>
> 도도마 (4월 14일)—탄자니아 해안의 '키콜레'라는 소박한 마을이 지역 내 135투자 증가 이후 각종 시설을 갖춘 항구가 될 예정이다. 정부는 최근 이 지역을 업무 지구로 지정했다. 이는 신규 업체들을 유치하고 더 나아가 경제 성장에 박차를 가하기 136위함이다. 마리나 인터내셔널 해운이라는 회사는 이곳에 거점을 열 계획을 이미 발표했다. 137이것으로 이 해운회사는 동아프리카에 처음으로 주요 입지를 구축하게 될 것이다.
>
> 많은 공무원들은 최근 해당 계획에 반대 의사를 표시했다. 138그렇기는 해도, 필요 자금이 이미 확보된 게 있으니, 프로젝트가 추진될 것이 확실해 보인다.
>
> ---
>
> 어휘 bustling 부산한 unassuming 겸손한, 소박한 region 지역 designate 지정하다 business district 업무 지구 further 더 나아가 spur 원동력이 되다, 박차를 가하다 announce 발표하다 hub 중심, 거점 government official 정부 관료, 공무원 express opposition 반대 의사를 표하다 secure 확보하다, 획득하다

135 명사 어휘

해설 빈칸이 포함된 부분은 소박한 마을이 각종 시설을 갖춘 항구가 되는 데(The unassuming town ~ is set to become a fully equipped port) 영향을 미친 요인을 나타낸다. 뒤 문장에서 정부가 최근 이 지역을 업무지구로 지정했다(The government has recently designated the area as a business district)고 했으므로, 경제와 관련된 부분의 증가(increase)로 인한 것임을 알 수 있다. 따라서 '투자'라는 의미의 (C) investment가 정답이다. 참고로, 마지막 문장에서 필요 자금이 이미 확보된 게 있다(with the needed finances already secured)고 했으므로 투자가 증가했음을 한번 더 확인할 수 있다.

어휘 security 보안 tourism 관광(업) fishing 어업

136 동사 어형 _ 태

해설 주어 This와 동사 attract의 수가 일치하지 않으므로, 빈칸이 This의 동사 자리임을 알 수 있다. 따라서 빈칸에는 This와 수가 일치하면서 attract와 to부정사를 이루는 to가 포함된 본동사가 들어가야 한다. 앞 문장 전체를 대신하는 This는 신규 업체들을 유치하고 경제 성장에 박차를 가하기 위해 '의도된' 것이므로, 수동태 동사인 (A) is meant to가 정답이 된다. (B) means to는 능동태로 '~할 셈이다'라는 뜻을 나타내므로 적절하지 않고, 준동사인 (C) meaning to와 for가 포함된 (D) is meant for는 구조상 빈칸에 들어갈 수 없다.

137 문맥에 맞는 문장 고르기

번역 (A) 일부는 다른 항구를 개선하는 편이 낫다고 확신한다.
       (B) 탄자니아 정부는 새 항구를 위한 자금을 대겠다고 약속했다.
       (C) 개발자들은 10년 이내에 키콜레의 변화를 완료하기를 바란다.
       (D) 이것으로 이 해운회사는 동아프리카에 처음으로 주요 입지를 구축하게 될 것이다.

해설 앞 문장에서 마리나 인터내셔널 해운이라는 회사가 키콜레 항구에 거점을 열 계획을 발표했다(One firm, Marina International Shipping, has already announced plans to open a hub there)고 했으므로, 빈칸에는 유사한 사례나 이 회사와 관련된 내용이 들어가야 자연스럽다. 따라서 회사가 항구에 거점을 연 의의를 설명한 (D)가 정답이다.

어휘 improvement 개선, 향상 fund 자금을 대다 complete 완료하다 transformation 변화, 변신 presence 입지, 진출

138 접속부사 자리 _ 어휘

해설 빈칸 앞 문장에서는 많은 공무원들이 최근 해당 계획에 반대 의사를 표시했다(A number of government officials have recently expressed opposition to the plan)고 했는데, 빈칸 뒤에서는 프로젝트가 추진될 것이 확실해 보인다(with the needed finances already secured, it seems certain that the project will move forward)며 대조되는 결과를 예측했다. 따라서 '그렇기는 하지만, 그렇더라도'라는 의미의 (A) Nonetheless가 정답이다. 참고로, (C) In case는 접속사, (D) Equally as는 부사에 접속사/전치사가 결합한 형태이므로 구조상으로도 빈칸에 들어갈 수 없다.

어휘 therefore 그러므로 in case ~할 경우 equally as ~와 똑같이

139-142 광고

> 올해 델레이에서 있을 패밀리 유원지 축제를 달력에 표시해 두세요! 6월 20일부터 6월 26일까지 7일 동안의 여름 활동을 함께해 주세요. 환상적인 음식, 놀이기구, 게임뿐 아니라 전 연령대를 위한 흥미진진한 공연들139도 있습니다. 그리고 저희의 최신 140명물도 절대 놓치지 마세요. 크레이지 카우보이 기차는 와일드 웨스트를 통과하는 흥미진진한 여정이에요!
>
> 올해의 공연에는 자전거 서커스, 공룡쇼, 마법사 월터가 포함됩니다. 기본 입장권 소지자는 모두 공연 입장을 위해 추가 요금을 지불해야 함을

알려드립니다. ¹⁴¹**공연 시간 및 가격은 엔터테인먼트 일정표를 참조하세요.**

저희는 또한 VIP 패밀리 펀 이용권을 95달러에 ¹⁴²**제공합니다.** 이 입장권은 모든 공연 무료 입장 및 놀이기구 무제한 무료 이용 혜택을 제공합니다.

어휘 **fun fair** 이동식 유원지, 축제 **ride** 놀이기구 **magician** 마법사 **admission ticket** 입장권 **additional** 추가의 **entrance** 입장 **admission** 입장 **unlimited** 무제한의

139 상관접속사

해설 not only와 함께 상관접속사를 이루어 두 명사구 fantastic food, rides, and games와 exciting shows를 연결하는 자리이다. 따라서 (D) but also가 정답이다. 'not only A but (also) B'는 'A뿐만 아니라 B도'라는 의미로 쓰인다.

140 명사 어휘

해설 빈칸은 패밀리 유원지 축제에서 놓치지 말아야(not to miss) 할 대상으로, 바로 뒤 문장에 나오는 크레이지 카우보이가 기차를 가리킨다. 따라서 '명물'이라는 의미의 (C) attraction이 정답이다.

어휘 **attraction** 명소, 명물 **refreshment** 가벼운 식사, 음료

141 문맥에 맞는 문장 고르기

번역 (A) 유원지에는 20개 이상의 다양한 먹거리 노점이 있습니다.
(B) 유원지의 놀이기구 대부분은 나이 제한이 있습니다.
(C) 공연 시간 및 가격은 엔터테인먼트 일정표를 참조하세요.
(D) 자격이 있는지 여부를 확인하시려면 저희 웹사이트를 방문하세요.

해설 해당 단락은 축제에서 열리는 공연과 관련된 내용을 설명하고 있다. 바로 앞 문장에서 기본 입장권 소지자는 공연 입장을 위해 추가 요금을 지불해야 한다(all basic admission ticket holders will need to pay additional fees to gain entrance to shows)며 입장료에 대해 언급했으므로, 공연 시간 및 가격 확인 방법을 안내한 (C)가 빈칸에 들어가야 자연스럽다.

어휘 **vendor** 노점상, 행상인 **fair** 유원지 **age requirement** 연령 제한 **refer to** ~를 참조하다 **eligible** 자격이 있는

142 동사 어형 _ 태 _ 시제

해설 주어 We의 동사 자리로, 명사구 a VIP Family Fun pass를 목적어로 취한다. 따라서 능동태 동사 중 하나를 선택해야 하는데, 표에 대한 일반적인 사항을 설명하는 문장이므로 현재 동사인 (A) offer가 정답이 된다.

143-146 편지

브라이트만 냉난방
프림로즈 길 16번지

시드니 뉴사우스웨일스 2146
(02) 5550 8899
www.brightmanheatingandcooling.com.au

5월 15일

알리아 바즈파
허드슨 가 422번지
시드니 뉴사우스웨일스 2000

바즈파 씨께,

알려드릴 중요한 소식이 있습니다. 저희가 업계에서 40년간의 영업 끝에 철수하고 회사를 닫기로 ¹⁴³**결정했습니다.** ¹⁴⁴**그러나** 귀하가 서비스 중단을 겪지 않도록 해 드리고 싶습니다. 이러한 이유로 콘도 난방 공조가 6월 1일부터 귀하에게 서비스 제공을 시작할 수 있도록 처리했습니다. ¹⁴⁵**그들의** 서비스에 만족하시리라고 확신합니다.

콘도는 능숙하고 매우 숙련된 기술자들을 갖춘 훌륭한 업체입니다. ¹⁴⁶**곧 그들에게서 편지를 받으실 것입니다.** 문의사항이 있으시면 언제든 전화 주십시오.

나다니엘과 콘스턴스 브라이트만

어휘 **retire** 퇴직하다, 철수하다 **disruption** 중단, 혼란 **arrange** 주선하다, 처리하다 **effective** (~부로) 시행되는, 발효되는 **experienced** 경험이 풍부한, 능숙한 **highly skilled** 고도로 숙련된 **hesitate** 주저하다

143 동사 어형 _ 시제

해설 앞 문장에서 바즈파 씨에게 알릴 중요한 소식이 있다(We have some important news to share with you)고 했으므로, 업계에서 철수하기로 한 것(to retire and close the company)이 이미 결정된 사항임을 알 수 있다. 따라서 현재완료시제 동사인 (D) have decided가 정답이다.

어휘 **decide** 결정하다

144 접속부사

해설 빈칸 앞 문장에서 회사를 닫기로 결정했다(We have decided to ~ close the company)고 했는데, 뒤 문장에서는 서비스 중단을 겪지 않도록 하겠다(make sure that you do not experience any disruption to your service)며 결정과는 상반되는 조치를 언급했다. 따라서 '그러나, 하지만'이라는 의미의 (B) However이 정답이다.

어휘 **similarly** 마찬가지로 **in general** 대개, 보통 **at that time** 그 당시에는

145 소유격 인칭대명사

해설 앞 문장에서 콘도 난방 공조가 6월 1일부터 서비스 제공을 시작할 수 있도록 처리했다(we have arranged for Kondo's Heating and Air to begin providing service to you effective on 1 June)고 했으므로, 빈칸에는 콘도 난방 공조를 가리키는 소유격 대명사가 들어가야 한다. 회사는 3인칭 단수 it, 혹은 복수 대명사 they로 대신할 수

TEST 10

있으므로, 보기 중 (B) their가 정답이다.

146 문맥에 맞는 문장 고르기

번역 (A) 탄탄한 고객층을 구축하는 일은 몇 년이 걸릴 수 있습니다.
(B) 재개점식 행사를 개최할 예정입니다.
(C) 곧 그들에게서 편지를 받으실 것입니다.
(D) 난방 및 공조에 많은 일자리가 있습니다.

해설 빈칸 앞 부분에서 콘도 난방 공조가 바즈파 씨에게 서비스 제공을 시작할 수 있도록 처리했다(we have arranged for Kondo's Heating and Air to begin providing service to you)고 한 후, 회사에 대한 설명을 덧붙이며 바즈파 씨를 안심시켰다. 뒤 문장에서는 문의사항이 있으면 언제든 전화하라(If you have any questions, please do not hesitate to call)고 했으므로, 빈칸에도 콘도 난방 공조를 주선해준 것과 관련된 내용이 들어가야 자연스럽다. 따라서 그쪽에서 곧 편지를 받을 거라고 한 (C)가 정답이다.

어휘 customer base 고객층   available 이용 가능한

PART 7

147-148 문자 메시지

브라이슨 보딘 [오후 1시 7분]
안녕하세요, 아비차이. 레빈 씨의 소파와 의자에 커버 씌우기를 끝마쳤습니다. 멋져 보여요! 아주 좋은 직물이더군요. [147]다음으로 어떤 주문 건을 작업해야 하죠?

아비차이 로젠 [오후 1시 14분]
잘됐군요. [147]첸 씨 부부에게 그들의 식탁 의자를 토요일까지 해주기로 약속했어요. [148]그건 그렇고, 6월 14일 메트로폴리탄 디자인쇼가 7월 7일로 연기됐어요.

브라이슨 보딘 [오후 1시 19분]
아, 그럼 저는 못 가겠군요.

아비차이 로젠 [오후 1시 22분]
안타깝네요. 와서 도와줄 직원이 적어도 두 명은 필요해요. 사무용 책상과 책꽂이를 전시할 거거든요.

브라이슨 보딘 [오후 1시 24분]
리타와 톰에게 그날 시간이 되는지 물어볼게요. [148]안타깝게도 저는 그날 가족 모임으로 여기 없어요. [147]첸 씨 부부의 주문은 지금 시작하겠습니다.

아비차이 로젠 [오후 1시 25분]
좋아요. 고맙습니다!

어휘 upholstery 덮개(를 씌우는 일)   postpone 연기하다   make it 참석하다, 시간 맞춰 가다   available 시간이 되는   commitment 약속

147 추론 / 암시

번역 보딘 씨는 다음으로 어떤 작업을 할 것인가?
(A) 소파
(B) 사무용 책상
(C) 책꽂이
(D) 의자 세트

해설 보딘 씨가 오후 1시 7분 메시지에서 자신의 다음 작업(Which order should I work on next?)을 물어봤는데, 이에 대해 로젠 씨가 첸 씨 부부의 식탁 의자를 토요일까지 해주기로 약속했다(I promised the Chens their dining chairs by Saturday)고 응답했다. 보딘 씨의 1시 24분 메시지를 보면 그가 다음에 첸 씨 부부의 주문을 작업할 것임(I'll get started on the Chens' order now)을 확인할 수 있으므로, (D)가 정답이다.

148 의도 파악

번역 오후 1시 19분에 보딘 씨가 "저는 못 가겠군요"라고 쓸 때, 그 의도는 무엇인가?
(A) 리타나 톰을 보지 않을 것이다.
(B) 행사에 참석하지 못할 것이다.
(C) 기한을 맞추지 못할 것이다.
(D) 가구 만드는 방법을 모른다.

해설 로젠 씨가 오후 1시 14분 메시지에서 6월 14일 메트로폴리탄 디자인쇼가 7월 7일로 연기됐다(the Metropolitan Design Show on June 14 has been postponed to July 7)는 소식을 전했는데, 이에 대해 보딘 씨가 '저는 못 가겠군요(I can't make it)'라고 응답한 것이다. 1시 24분 메시지에서 가족 약속이 있어 못 간다는 것을 다시 한번 드러냈으므로, (B)가 정답이다.

어휘 attend 참석하다   meet a deadline 기한을 맞추다

149-150 공지

스푸모니 휴대전화 앱을 다운로드해 주셔서 감사합니다!
[149]귀하의 현재 기본 회원 자격으로는 조리법 저장이 하루당 5개로 제한됩니다. 매일 조리법을 무제한으로 저장하고 쇼핑 목록을 자동 생성하며 매주 식단을 작성하고 영양 데이터를 추적하는 자유를 누리고 싶다면, [149]한 달 요금 2.99달러만으로 프리미엄 회원이 되어 보십시오.

많은 사용자들은 이 적은 비용이 유익하게 쓰인다고 생각합니다. 프리미엄 기능은 시간을 절약해주고 더욱 건강한 식단을 선택하게 해주니까요. [150]저희 "PM 커뮤니티" 웹페이지를 방문하셔서 프리미엄 회원들의 실제 추천 글을 살펴보세요.

어휘 current 현재의   limit 제한하다   unlimited 무제한의   automatically 자동으로   generate 생성하다   track 추적하다   nutritional 영양상의   feature 기능, 특징   enable 가능하게 하다   testimonial 추천의 글, 추천서

149 세부 사항

번역 공지는 사용자들에게 무엇을 하라고 권하는가?

(A) 자신의 레시피 공유
(B) 자신이 쓴 추천글 제출
(C) 회원 자격 업그레이드
(D) 최근 소프트웨어 업데이트 다운로드

해설 두 번째 단락에서 기본 회원 자격의 제한 사항(At your current basic membership level, your ability to save recipes is limited to five per day)을 언급한 후, 한달 요금 2.99달러로 프리미엄 회원이 되어 보라(you can become a premium member for just $2.99 a month)고 했다. 즉, 회원 자격의 업그레이드를 권하는 것이므로, (C)가 정답이다.

어휘 submit 제출하다 status 자격, 지위

▸▸ Paraphrasing 지문의 become a premium member
→ 정답의 Upgrade their membership status

150 세부 사항

번역 공지에 따르면, 사용자들은 왜 웹페이지를 방문해야 하는가?

(A) 가상 투어를 하기 위해
(B) 식단 견본을 보기 위해
(C) 유사한 조리법들의 재료를 비교하기 위해
(D) 사람들의 경험에 대해 알아보기 위해

해설 마지막 단락에서 웹페이지를 방문해 프리미엄 회원들의 실제 추천글을 살펴보라(Visit our ~ Web page to view real testimonials from our premium members)고 권했으므로, (D)가 정답이다.

어휘 virtual 가상의 compare 비교하다 ingredient 성분, 재료 similar 유사한, 비슷한

▸▸ Paraphrasing 지문의 Visit → 질문의 go to
지문의 view real testimonials from our premium members
→ 정답의 find out about people's experiences

151-152 이메일

수신: 마타 프리가리나 〈mprigarina@ymw.co.za〉
발신: 배리 윈터스 〈bwinters@kerwinecs.co.za〉
날짜: 10월 23일
제목: 사무실 청소

프리가리나 씨께,

사무실 청소를 위해 커와인 청소 서비스를 선택해 주셔서 기쁘게 생각합니다. 저희 미화원들이 모든 청소 업무를 빠르고 효율적으로 완료하는 데 필요한 상용등급의 장비, 도구, 제품을 가지고 귀하의 시설에 도착할 예정입니다. 시작일자를 10월 30일로 이미 확정하셨습니다만, ¹⁵¹서비스를 매주 이용하실지, 아니면 격주로 이용하실지는 아직 확정하지 않으셨어요. 알려주시는 대로 계약서를 작성해 드리겠습니다. 현재 특별 프로모션을 진행하고 있습니다. ¹⁵²10월 31일까지 6개월 계약을

체결하실 경우 첫 2회 청소가 무료입니다.

배리 윈터스
커와인 청소 서비스

어휘 janitor 수위, 청소부, 잡역부 facility 시설 commercial-grade 상용등급, 일반규격 equipment 장비 complete 완료하다 effectively 효과적으로 biweekly 격주로 draw up a contract 계약서를 작성하다 currently 현재

151 세부 사항

번역 윈터스 씨는 프리가리나 씨에게 무엇을 확정해 달라고 요청하는가?

(A) 사무실 청소 빈도
(B) 시설에 도착해야 하는 시간
(C) 사무실 위치
(D) 선호하는 제품

해설 이메일 중반부에서 윈터스 씨는 프리가리나 씨가 서비스를 매주 이용할지 아니면 격주로 이용할지 확정해 주지 않았다(you have not yet confirmed whether you will use our services weekly or biweekly)고 한 후, 알려주는 대로(As soon as you let us know) 계약서를 작성하겠다고 했다. 이는 서비스 이용 빈도를 알려달라고 우회적으로 요청하는 것이므로, (A)가 정답이다.

어휘 prefer 선호하다

▸▸ Paraphrasing 지문의 whether you will use our services weekly or biweekly
→ 정답의 How often to clean her office

152 세부 사항

번역 프리가리나 씨는 어떻게 2회 무료 청소 서비스를 받을 수 있는가?

(A) 서비스 대금을 미리 지불해서
(B) 6개월 계약을 체결해서
(C) 시작일자를 변경해서
(D) 할인 코드를 사용해서

해설 후반부에서 10월 31일까지 6개월 계약을 체결할 경우 첫 2회 청소가 무료(If you sign up for six months of service ~ your first two cleanings are free)라고 했으므로, (B)가 정답이다.

어휘 prepay 선불하다, 미리 치르다 discount 할인

▸▸ Paraphrasing 지문의 sign up for six months of service
→ 정답의 signing a contract for six months

153-154 이메일

수신: 안젤라 젠킨스
발신: 마커스 켈러
날짜: 11월 2일 금요일
제목: 통화 연기

안젤라,

¹⁵³안타깝게도 계획되어 있던 오후 통화를 막바지에 취소해야겠군요. 이 이메일을 제때 보셨으면 합니다. 일정을 변경할 수 있을까요? 제 실수입니다. ¹⁵³어쩌다 보니 약속 시간을 이중으로 잡았거든요. 사실 지금 다른 약속을 지키러 문을 나서는 중입니다. 최우선순위에 있는 고객과의 회의예요. 죄송합니다.

월요일 정오에 원격 회의 하는 것 괜찮으실까요? ¹⁵⁴아울러 회의에 앞서 현재 프로젝트에 사용할 수 있는 보조금 기회를 좀 더 살펴봐 주실 수 있나요? 그동안 저는 레오나에게 자금이 필요한 향후 계획들의 예산을 더 정확히 계산해 달라고 부탁할게요. 그러면 다음 주에 만날 때 더욱 생산적일 겁니다.

마커스 켈러
오코너 소기업 재단

어휘 postpone 연기하다, 미루다 at the last minute 마지막 순간에 reschedule 일정을 변경하다 appointment 약속 high-priority 최우선순위 apologize 사과하다 teleconferencing 원격 회의 grant 보조금 meanwhile 그동안에, 당분간 accurate 정확한 budget 예산 initiative 계획 productive 생산적인

153 세부 사항

번역 켈러 씨는 왜 계획대로 회의할 수 없다고 말하는가?

(A) 출장에서 늦게 돌아올 것으로 예상한다.
(B) 보고할 새 정보가 없다.
(C) 오후에 휴가를 쓰기로 결정했다.
(D) 일정이 겹쳤다는 사실을 알았다.

해설 첫 번째 단락에서 계획되어 있던 오후 통화를 취소해야 한다(I have to cancel our planned afternoon phone call)고 한 후, 어쩌다 보니 약속 시간을 이중으로 잡았다(I somehow double-booked our appointment time)며 이유를 덧붙였다. 따라서 (D)가 정답이다.

어휘 anticipate 예상하다, 기대하다 discover 발견하다, 찾다 scheduling conflict 겹치는 일정

▸▸ Paraphrasing 지문의 cancel our planned afternoon phone call
→ 질문의 cannot meet as planned
지문의 double-booked our appointment time → 정답의 a scheduling conflict

154 추론 / 암시

번역 회의 전에 무엇이 이루어지겠는가?

(A) 재정 관련 정보가 더 모일 것이다.
(B) 회의 장소가 변경될 것이다.
(C) 다른 사람이 참석하라고 초대받을 것이다.
(D) 마케팅 계획이 수정될 것이다.

해설 두 번째 단락에서 켈러 씨는 젠킨스 씨에게 회의 전에 프로젝트에 사용할 수 있는 보조금 기회를 좀 더 살펴봐 달라(prior to our meeting, could you look further into any grant

opportunities)고 요청했다. 따라서 젠킨스 씨가 회의 전에 재정 관련 정보를 더 모을 것이라고 추론할 수 있으므로, (A)가 정답이다.

어휘 financial 금융의, 재정적인 gather 모으다 modify 수정하다

▸▸ Paraphrasing 지문의 prior to our meeting
→ 질문의 before the meeting
지문의 look further into any grant opportunities → 정답의 More financial information will be gathered.

155-157 의견 카드

그라치오 스토어 의견 카드

그라치오 스토어는 저희 매장 방문이 더 좋은 경험이 될 수 있게 만들어 드리고자 합니다. ¹⁵⁵고객님들을 모시는 방식을 개선할 수 있도록 오늘 저희 매장 방문 경험에 대해 말씀해 주세요. 그리고 매주, 제출된 의견 카드 중에서 한 장을 ¹⁵⁶뽑아 50달러의 매장 쿠폰을 드립니다!

고객명: 후이 응우옌
이메일 연락처: hnguyen@brightmail.co.nz
날짜: 5월 4일
오늘 방문 이유: 선물 구입

의견: 친구 생일 선물을 구입하고 있었습니다. 액세서리 부문의 판매사원 데이비 씨가 저를 맞이했고, 선물을 찾는 데 선택의 폭을 좁힐 수 있도록 제게 질문을 하셨습니다. 제가 더 쉽게 쇼핑할 수 있게 제 가방들을 맡아 주기까지 해 주셨습니다. 다채로운 실크 스카프 진열대로 안내하고 스카프들이 생산된 다양한 장소에 대해 이야기해 주셨습니다. ¹⁵⁷제가 선택한 제품은 결국 계획했던 가격대에도 맞았습니다.

어휘 seek 구하다, 추구하다 improve 향상시키다, 개선하다 submit 제출하다 earn 얻다, 받다 sales associate 판매사원 narrow down (선택의 폭을) 좁히다, 줄이다 various 다양한 end up in 결국 ~로 끝나다

155 사실 관계 확인

번역 그라치오 스토어에 대해 알 수 있는 것은?

(A) 최근 문을 열었다.
(B) 신입 판매사원들을 교육하고 있다.
(C) 고객 서비스를 개선하고 싶어 한다.
(D) 대회를 조직했다.

해설 첫 번째 단락에서 고객을 응대하는 방식을 개선할 수 있도록 매장 방문 경험에 대해 말해 달라(Tell us about your visit to our store today so we can improve the way we serve you)고 요청했으므로, 그라치오 스토어가 고객 서비스를 개선하고 싶어 한다는 것을 알 수 있다. 따라서 (C)가 정답이다.

어휘 recently 최근 organize 조직하다, 준비하다 competition 대회, 시합

▸▸ Paraphrasing 지문의 the way we serve you
→ 정답의 its customer service

156 동의어 찾기

번역 첫 번째 단락, 세 번째 줄에 쓰인 "drawn"과 의미가 가장 가까운 단어는?

(A) 스케치된
(B) 선택된
(C) 매료된
(D) 묘사된

해설 'drawn'을 포함한 부분은 '제출된 의견 카드 중에서 한 장이 뽑혀진다 (one comment card will be drawn from those submitted)'라는 의미로 해석되는데, 여기서 drawn은 '뽑혀진'이라는 뜻으로 쓰였다. 따라서 '선택된, 뽑혀진'이라는 의미의 (B) picked가 정답이다.

157 세부 사항

번역 응우옌 씨는 자신의 경험에 대해 무엇이라고 썼는가?

(A) 여러 개의 다양한 액세서리를 샀다.
(B) 선물을 찾는 데 시간이 오래 걸렸다.
(C) 관리자가 자신의 질문에 대답했다.
(D) 선물 구입 예산 범위 내에서 할 수 있었다.

해설 의견(Comment)란의 마지막 문장에서 자신이 선택한 제품이 결국 계획했던 가격대에도 맞았다(The one I chose ended up in my planned price range)고 했으므로, (D)가 정답이다.

어휘 budget 예산

> ▶▶ Paraphrasing   지문의 in my planned price range
> → 정답의 within his gift budget

158-160 이메일

발신: lcho@cuvacorporatetraining.com
수신: all_staff@cuvacorporatetraining.com
날짜: 4월 12일 월요일 오전 10시 53분
제목: 특별 공지

동료 여러분,

¹⁵⁸여러분의 컴퓨터에 설치된 고객 보안 시스템(CSS)이 이번 주말 자동으로 업데이트될 예정임을 알려드립니다. ^{159/160}구체적으로 말씀 드리면, 업데이트는 4월 17일 토요일 자정부터 4월 18일 일요일 자정까지 진행될 것입니다. 해당 기간 동안 일부 기능이 제한되거나 이용 불가합니다. 여러분의 기기는 업데이트가 완료된 후 재시작됩니다.

본 업데이트의 목적은 두 가지입니다. 첫째, 고객 정보의 보안을 향상할 것입니다. 아울러 시스템 전체 성능도 높일 것입니다. 그 결과, 여러분은 향상된 처리 속도 및 계획에 없던 시스템 중단의 감소를 느끼게 될 것입니다.

¹⁵⁹업데이트 이후 CSS 로그인 화면 모습에 변화가 있겠지만, 해당 변화는 로그인 절차에 영향을 주지 않습니다.

기술지원팀에서는 업데이트 전후로 있을 수 있는 문의사항에 응답해 드릴 수 있습니다. 목요일까지 업데이트로 이용 가능해질 새 기능에 대한 설명을 담은 교육용 비디오 링크를 받으시게 될 겁니다.

리나 조
관리자, 기술지원팀

어휘 colleague 동료   install 설치하다   automatically 자동으로   specifically 구체적으로, 특별히   take place 일어나다   complete 완료하다   twofold 두 부분으로 된, 이중적인   moreover 게다가   overall 전체의   downtime 작동 정지 시간   appearance 모습, 외관   affect 영향을 미치다   procedure 절차   feature 기능, 특색

158 주제 / 목적

번역 이메일이 발송된 이유는?

(A) 직원들에게 실적 향상을 위한 동기를 부여하기 위해
(B) 직원들에게 컴퓨터 프로그램 업데이트 설치 방법을 알려주기 위해
(C) 새로운 보안 절차에 관한 피드백을 받기 위해
(D) 직원들에게 곧 있을 소프트웨어 변경사항을 알리기 위해

해설 첫 번째 단락에서 컴퓨터에 설치된 고객 보안 시스템(CSS)이 이번 주말 자동으로 업데이트될 예정임을 알린다(Please be advised that the Customer Security System (CSS) installed on your computer will be automatically updated this weekend)고 한 후, 업데이트에 대한 설명을 이어가고 있다. 따라서 (D)가 정답이다.

어휘 motivate 동기를 부여하다   instruct 알려주다, 가르치다   alert 알리다

> ▶▶ Paraphrasing   지문의 be advised → 정답의 alert
> 지문의 will be automatically updated
> → 정답의 upcoming changes

159 세부 사항

번역 이메일에 따르면, 직원들은 4월 18일 이후 무엇을 경험할 것인가?

(A) 더 나아진 웹 카메라 화질
(B) 달라진 CSS 로그인 화면
(C) 더 빨라진 기술지원 서비스
(D) 쓰기 더 편해진 키보드

해설 4월 18일은 CSS 업데이트가 종료되는 날(the update will be taking place from midnight, Saturday, April 17, to midnight, Sunday, April 18)인데, 이후 직원들이 겪게 될 상황은 두 번째 및 세 번째 단락에 나와 있다. 세 번째 단락에서 업데이트 이후 CSS 로그인 화면 모습에 변화가 있을 것(following the update there will be a change in the appearance of the CSS log-in screen)이라고 했으므로, (B)가 정답이다. 참고로, 빨라지는 것은 업무 처리 속도(improved processing speeds)이지 기술 지원 서비스가 아니므로 (C)는 정답이 될 수 없다.

> ▶▶ Paraphrasing   지문의 following → 질문의 after
> 지문의 a change in the appearance of the CSS log-in screen
> → 정답의 A different CSS log-in screen

160 문장 삽입

번역 [1], [2], [3], [4]로 표시된 곳 중에서 다음 문장이 가장 적합한 곳은?

"해당 기간 동안 일부 기능이 제한되거나 이용 불가합니다."

(A) [1]
(B) [2]
(C) [3]
(D) [4]

해설 주어진 문장에 this period가 있으므로, 앞에서 먼저 일부 기능이 제한되거나 이용 불가한 기간이 언제인지 구체적으로 명시되어야 한다. [1] 앞에서 업데이트가 4월 17일 토요일 자정부터 4월 18일 일요일 자정까지 진행될 예정(the update will be taking place from midnight, Saturday, April 17, to midnight, Sunday, April 18)이라며 특정 기간을 언급했으므로, 이 뒤에 주어진 문장이 들어가야 자연스럽다. 따라서 (A)가 정답이다.

어휘 function 기능 limited 제한된, 한정된

161-163 웹페이지 정보

---

https://www.electronicsplusexpress.com/returns

일렉트로닉스 플러스 익스프레스 ¹⁶¹ 반품 정책

¹⁶²모든 반품은 사전 승인이 필요합니다. ¹⁶¹/¹⁶²영업시간(월-금요일 오전 9시-오후 7시, 주말 오전 10시-오후 5시) 내 전화하시거나 고객 서비스 부서에 반품 요청서를 포함한 이메일을 보내셔서 반품 승인 코드를 받으십시오.

결함이 있는 상품은 구입일 30일 이내에 반품될 수 있습니다. 신상품은 구입일 14일 이내에 반품될 수 있습니다. 원래 상자 및 포장재가 포함되어야 합니다. ¹⁶³물품을 우편으로 반품해야 할 경우, 집에서 출력해 소포에 붙일 수 있는 우편 요금 지급필의 반송용 라벨을 매장에서 발행하여 이메일로 보내 드립니다. 제품이 수령되면 물품 대금을 환불해 드립니다.

고객 서비스 연락처는 다음과 같습니다.
전화번호: 1-800-555-0176
이메일: cs@electronicsplusexpress.com

어휘 require 요구하다, 필요로 하다 prior 사전의 authorization 허가, 승인 defective 결함이 있는 merchandise 상품, 물품 purchase 구입 material 자재, 재료 postage-paid 우편 요금 지급필, 우편 요금 결제가 완료된 attach 부착하다 refund 환불해 주다 as follows 다음과 같이

161 추론 / 암시

번역 정보는 누구를 대상으로 하겠는가?

(A) 일렉트로닉스 플러스 익스프레스 고객
(B) 고객 서비스 상담원
(C) 수리 기사
(D) 운송부서 직원

해설 제목이 '반품 정책(Return Policy)'이며 첫 번째, 두 번째 단락에서

구매한 물품을 반품하는 방법을 안내하고 있으므로, (A)가 정답이다.

162 사실 관계 확인

번역 모든 반품 건에 대해 알 수 있는 것은?

(A) 매장에서만 수령한다.
(B) 주말에는 처리가 안 된다.
(C) 승인 코드가 필요하다.
(D) 14일 후에는 받지 않는다.

해설 첫 번째 단락에서 모든 반품은 사전 승인이 필요하다(All returns require prior authorization)고 한 후, 영업시간 내 전화하거나 고객 서비스 부서에 반품 요청서를 포함한 이메일을 보내서 반품 승인 코드를 받으라(Please call during business hours ~ or e-mail Customer Service with your return request to receive a return authorization code)고 안내했다. 따라서 (C)가 정답이다.

어휘 accept 받아 주다, 수락하다

163 사실 관계 확인

번역 반품 배송비에 대해 언급된 것은?

(A) 소포 무게에 따라 계산된다.
(B) 회사 웹사이트에 올라와 있다.
(C) 30일 이내에 고객에게 환불이 이뤄진다.
(D) 회사에서 지불한다.

해설 두 번째 단락을 보면, 물품을 우편으로 반품해야 할 경우 매장에서 우편 요금 지급필의 반송용 라벨을 발행하여 이메일로 보내준다(If you need to return the item by post, the store will issue and e-mail a postage-paid shipping label)고 되어 있다. 그리고 제품을 받고 나서 물품 대금을 환불해 준다(The cost of your item will be refunded)고 한 것으로 보아, 반품 배송비를 차감하지 않고 회사측에서 지불한다는 것을 알 수 있다. 따라서 (D)가 정답이다.

어휘 calculate 계산하다 based on ~에 기반하여

> ▸ Paraphrasing 지문의 a postage-paid shipping label
> → 정답의 paid for by the company

164-167 온라인 채팅

켈리 웨더스 [오후 2시 15분] 안녕하세요, 이스턴 씨. ¹⁶⁴오늘 저녁 매그놀리아 그릴에서 당신의 고객인 카사이 씨와 저녁 회의가 있다는 것을 알려드리려고요. 카사이 씨는 공항에서 바로 오실 겁니다. 마케팅 부서의 안나 권이 두 분과 함께할 겁니다.

애덤 이스턴 [오후 2시 31분] 고맙습니다, 웨더스 씨. 공항에서 바로 오시면 짐은 어떻게 하실까 생각이 드는데요.

켈리 웨더스 [오후 2시 33분] 걱정 마세요. ¹⁶⁵카일 프리드먼이 카사이 씨를 공항에서 픽업하고 가방을 호텔에 내려드릴 겁니다. 두 분이 얘기를 나눠야 할 경우를 대비해 카일을 이 메시지에 지금 추가할게요.

애덤 이스턴 [오후 2시 34분] 좋아요. **166/167**회의 후 제가 카사이 씨를 호텔로 태워드릴 수 있습니다. 그런 주요 고객에게는 좋은 성의 표시가 될 겁니다.

카일 프리드먼 [오후 2시 36분] 공항으로 곧 출발해요, 웨더스 씨. 제가 더 알아야 할 사항이 있으면 나중에 문자 주세요.

켈리 웨더스 [오후 2시 40분] 좋은 생각입니다, 이스턴 씨. 그럼 저녁 식사 후 택시가 필요하지 않겠군요.

어휘 remind 상기시키다 directly 바로 occur to ~에게 생각이 떠오르다 luggage 짐, 수하물 in case ~할 경우를 대비하여 following ~후에 gesture 제스처, (의도의) 표시 head to ~로 가다, 향하다

164 주제 / 목적

번역 온라인 채팅의 목적은?
(A) 고객 방문을 위한 준비를 검토하려고
(B) 회사 기념 행사를 위한 장소를 선정하려고
(C) 저녁 식사 행사 초청장을 주려고
(D) 이동하는 동료들을 위해 택시를 준비해 주려고

해설 웨더스 씨가 오후 2시 15분 메시지에서 이스턴 씨에게 고객인 카사이 씨와 저녁 회의가 있다는 것을 다시 한번 알려주고 싶다(I want to remind you about dinner meeting with your client, Mr. Kasai)고 한 후, 관련 준비 사항을 다시 한번 검토하고 있다. 따라서 (A)가 정답이다.

어휘 arrangements 준비 invitation 초대, 초대장 colleague 동료

▸▸ Paraphrasing 지문의 **the dinner meeting with your client**
→ 정답의 **a client visit**

165 세부 사항

번역 누가 공항으로 갈 것인가?
(A) 웨더스 씨
(B) 이스턴 씨
(C) 프리드먼 씨
(D) 권 씨

해설 웨더스 씨가 오후 2시 33분 메시지에서 카일 프리드먼이 카사이 씨를 공항에서 픽업할 것(Kyle Friedman is picking Mr. Kasai up at the airport)이라고 했으므로, (C)가 정답이다.

166 사실 관계 확인

번역 카사이 씨에 대해 알 수 있는 것은?
(A) 매그놀리아 그릴에서 식사하는 것을 선호한다.
(B) 중요한 고객이다.
(C) 호텔에 제때 도착하고 싶어한다.
(D) 운전 경로 정보에 대해 헷갈려 한다.

해설 이스턴 씨가 오후 2시 34분 메시지에서 회의 후 카사이 씨를 호텔로

태워주겠다(I can drive Mr. Kasai back to his hotel following our meeting)고 한 후, 그런 주요 고객에게는 좋은 성의 표시가 될 것(It would be a nice gesture for such a key client)이라고 했다. 따라서 카사이 씨가 중요한 고객임을 알 수 있으므로, (B)가 정답이다.

어휘 prefer 선호하다 on time 시간을 어기지 않고 confused 혼란스러워하는

▸▸ Paraphrasing 지문의 **a key client**
→ 정답의 **an important customer**

167 의도 파악

번역 오후 2시 40분에 웨더스 씨가 "좋은 생각입니다, 이스턴 씨"라고 쓸 때, 그 의도는 무엇이겠는가?
(A) 저녁 식사 자리가 격식 없이 편해야 한다고 생각한다.
(B) 호텔 선정이 적절했다고 확신한다.
(C) 고객이 운전면허증을 가지고 있다고 생각하지 않는다.
(D) 고객이 호텔까지 교통편을 제공받아야 한다는 데 동의한다.

해설 이스턴 씨가 오후 2시 34분 메시지에서 회의 후 카사이 씨를 호텔로 태워주겠다(I can drive Mr. Kasai back to his hotel following our meeting)고 한 후, 그런 주요 고객에게는 좋은 성의 표시가 될 것(It would be a nice gesture for such a key client)이라고 했다. 이에 대해 웨더스 씨가 이스턴 씨에게 좋은 생각이라며 동의하는 응답을 한 것이므로, (D)가 정답이다.

어휘 informal 격식에 얽매이지 않는, 편안한 appropriate 적절한

▸▸ Paraphrasing 지문의 **drive ~ back to his hotel**
→ 정답의 **be offered a ride to a hotel**

168-171 이메일

수신: staff@rindersbusiness.co.ke
발신: dcloeten@rindersbusiness.co.ke
제목: 정보
날짜: 10월 25일

린더스 직원 여러분께,

168우리 회사는 성장하고 있으며, 새로운 직원들을 맞게 되어 기쁩니다. 우리 나이로비 사무소 직원들은 메리 기추키 씨에 대해 매우 잘 알게 될 것입니다. 그녀가 11월 1일부터 그곳의 신임 사무소 관리자가 될 예정이거든요. 여러분 중 일부는 지난주 그녀가 사무실을 방문했을 때 만나셨을 겁니다. 그녀는 데이비드 알버츠를 대체하게 됩니다.

169아닐라 필라이 씨도 나이로비 사무소의 새 직원이 될 겁니다. 필라이 씨는 행정 비서로 일할 예정이며 방문객 맞이, 전화 응대, 사무 업무 수행 등을 할 것입니다. **169**매주 수, 목, 금요일 오전 10시부터 오후 3시까지 근무하게 됩니다.

170지난 15년간 나이로비 사무소에서 일해 온 마크 카룽가 씨는 상급 회계사로 승진하여 11월 15일부터 새로 생긴 몸바사 사무소에서 근무할 예정입니다.

TEST 10

171 몸바사 사무소 직원들을 아직 채용하고 있으므로, 더 많은 신입사원들을 여러분께 알려드리는 이메일을 곧 보내겠습니다. 11월 개소식 이전에 모든 충원이 이뤄지길 바랍니다.

데보라 클로에텐
부회장
린더스 비즈니스 시스템

어휘 replace 대체하다, 후임이 되다 administrative 행정상의, 관리상의 perform 행하다 promote 승진시키다 accountant 회계사 alert 알리다 personnel 직원들 have all positions filled 충원하다

168 주제 / 목적

번역 이메일을 쓴 주요 목적은?
(A) 일부 직원 변동사항을 이야기하려고
(B) 새 사무소 절차를 논의하려고
(C) 두 회사 위치를 대조해 보려고
(D) 최근 사무소 방문자에 관해 보고하려고

해설 첫 번째 단락에서 새로운 직원들을 맞게 되어 기쁘다(I am pleased to welcome new staff members)고 한 후, 새로 입사하거나 전근하는 직원들을 소개하고 있다. 따라서 (A)가 정답이다.

어휘 describe 말하다, 묘사하다 procedure 절차 contrast 대조하다

▸▸ Paraphrasing 지문의 new staff members
→ 정답의 some staff changes

169 세부 사항

번역 린더스 비즈니스 시스템에서 시간제로 근무하게 될 사람은?
(A) 기추키 씨
(B) 알버츠 씨
(C) 필라이 씨
(D) 클로에텐 씨

해설 두 번째 단락에서 필라이 씨가 매주 수, 목, 금요일 오전 10시부터 오후 3시까지 근무할 예정(She will work on Wednesdays, Thursdays, and Fridays from 10:00 A.M. to 3:00 P.M.)이라고 했으므로, (C)가 정답이다.

▸▸ Paraphrasing 지문의 work on Wednesdays, Thursdays, and Fridays from 10:00 A.M. to 3:00 P.M.
→ 질문의 working part-time

170 사실 관계 확인

번역 카룽가 씨에 대해 명시되지 않은 것은?
(A) 회계사이다.
(B) 최근 채용한 직원이다.
(C) 승진할 것이다.
(D) 전근을 갈 것이다.

해설 세 번째 단락에서 나이로비 사무소에서 일해 온 마크 카룽가 씨가 상급 회계사로 승진하여 새로 생긴 몸바사 사무소에서 근무할 예정(Mark Karunga, who has worked in the Nairobi office ~ is being promoted to senior accountant and will work in our new Mombasa office)이라고 했으므로, (A), (C), (D)가 사실임을 확인할 수 있다. 하지만 그는 지난 15년간 나이로비 사무소에서 근무한 사람(who has worked in the Nairobi office for the past fifteen years)이므로, 사실이 아닌 (B)가 정답이다.

어휘 hire 채용자 transfer 전근 가다, 전근시키다

▸▸ Paraphrasing 지문의 will work in our new Mombasa office → 보기의 is being transferred

171 사실 관계 확인

번역 클로에텐 씨가 몸바사 사무소에 대해 명시한 것은?
(A) 자신의 새 일터이다.
(B) 아직 개소 전이다.
(C) 충원이 다 됐다.
(D) 나이로비 사무소보다 크다.

해설 네 번째 단락에서 몸바사 사무소 직원들을 아직 채용하고 있다(we are still hiring personnel for the Mombasa location)고 한 후, 11월 개소식 이전에 충원이 모두 이뤄지길 바란다(We hope to have all positions filled there before the grand opening in November)고 했다. 따라서 아직 개소 전이라는 사실을 확인할 수 있으므로, (B)가 정답이다.

어휘 fully staffed 충원이 다 된

172-175 웹페이지

http://www.finnertontheater.com/aboutus

피너튼 극장

172/173 피너튼 극장은 독립 영화, 다큐멘터리, 고전 영화 등을 위한 그렌빌 최고의 극장입니다. 50여 년간 지역에서 소유하고 운영해 온 이 극장은 시와 강한 연대를 유지하고 있습니다. **175** 한때 최고의 엔터테인먼트 장소였던 이 극장은 수 년간의 경기 침체와 도시 쇠퇴를 거치면서도 계속 유지되어 왔습니다. 변화하는 도시 경관 가운데서도, 그것은 주변 지역들과 함께 계속 진화했습니다. **175** 인근 지역 활성화 및 성장을 위한 기반인 피너튼 극장은 이제 시의 번화한 리버사이드 예술지구의 중추 역할을 하고 있습니다.

피너튼 극장은 지난 50년간 지역 전체의 영화 애호가들이 찾아오는 곳이 되었습니다. 네스터포트와 벨미어만큼이나 먼 도시에서 오는 방문자들은 극장의 독특한 분위기를 즐기기 위해 정기적으로 옵니다. 극장의 역사에 걸쳐, 천 편 이상의 영화가 상영되었으며 그 중 수십 편은 초연이었습니다. 피너튼 극장은 비평가들의 찬사를 받는 감독들과 함께 행사를 개최했고 유명한 대중 연설가들을 위한 무대 역할을 했습니다. **174** 지난 10년 동안 그레이터 신시내티 영화제, 미드웨스트 다큐멘터리 축제 및 시 최대 규모의 업체인 클리어에이커 테크에서 후원하는 연례 클리어에이커 회의 등을 주최한 바 있습니다. 5년 전에는 극장이 주의 역사적 장소 명부에 추가되었습니다.

지금까지 영화팬들은 영화 개봉작이 상영될 때마다 피너튼 극장을 자주 찾고 있습니다. 온라인 영화 스트리밍 서비스의 계속 늘어나는 인기에도 불구하고 피너튼 극장의 표 판매량은 주의 역사적 장소 명부에 오른 이래 계속해서 증가했습니다. 극장은 진정한 문화적 보배이며, 지역 주민들에게는 시민으로서 갖는 자긍심의 원천입니다.

어휘 premier 최고의, 가장 중요한; 초연되다 independent 독립적인 retain 유지하다 destination 목적지, 찾는 곳 persist 계속되다 stagnation 불경기, 침체 decline 감소, 하락 anchor 기반, 닻 revitalization 활성화 serve as ~의 역할을 하다 backbone 중추, 척추 thriving 번화한, 번성하는 attendee 참석자 regularly 정기적으로 ambience 분위기 critically acclaimed 비평가들의 찬사를 받는 renowned 유명한 register 명부, 기록[등기부] to this day 지금까지도 frequent 자주 다니다 release 개봉작 continuously 계속해서, 끊임없이 gem 보배 civic 시의

172 주제 / 목적

번역 웹페이지의 목적은?

(A) 다가오는 영화제 공표
(B) 새 극장 개장 논의
(C) 최근 영화 개봉작 홍보
(D) 지역 영화관 소개

해설 첫 번째 단락에서 피너튼 극장을 독립 영화, 다큐멘터리, 고전 영화 등을 위한 그렌빌 최고의 극장(The Finnerton Theater is Grenville's premier cinema for independent movies, documentaries, and film classics)이라고 소개한 후, 극장의 역사와 의의에 대한 설명을 이어가고 있다. 따라서 (D)가 정답이다.

어휘 upcoming 다가오는, 곧 있을 promote 홍보하다 profile 소개하다, 개요를 알려주다

173 세부 사항

번역 피너튼 극장은 어떤 도시에 있는가?

(A) 그렌빌
(B) 네스터포트
(C) 벨미어
(D) 신시내티

해설 첫 번째 단락에서 피너튼 극장은 그렌빌 최고의 극장(The Finnerton Theater is Grenville's premier cinema)이며 50여 년간 지역에서 소유하고 운영해 왔다(Locally owned and operated for over 50 years)고 했다. 따라서 피너튼 극장이 그렌빌에 있음을 알 수 있으므로, (A)가 정답이다.

174 사실 관계 확인

번역 피너튼 극장에 대해 알 수 있는 것은?

(A) 곧 새 건물로 이전할 예정이다.
(B) 구내 매점 메뉴를 확대했다.
(C) 연례 회의가 개최되는 장소이다.
(D) 시에서 직원이 가장 많은 회사이다.

해설 두 번째 단락에서 지난 10년 동안 연례 클리어에이커 회의 등을 주최한 바 있다(In the past decade, it has served as the host for ~ the annual Clearacre Conference, which is sponsored by the city's largest employer, Clearacre Tech)고 했으므로, (C)가 정답이다.

어휘 expand 확대하다 concession 구내 매점

▶▶ Paraphrasing 지문의 has served as the host for ~ the annual Clearacre Conference
→ 정답의 a yearly conference is held

175 문장 삽입

번역 [1], [2], [3], [4]로 표시된 곳 중에서 다음 문장이 가장 적합한 곳은?

"변화하는 도시 경관 가운데서도, 그것은 주변 지역들과 함께 계속 진화했습니다."

(A) [1]
(B) [2]
(C) [3]
(D) [4]

해설 주어진 문장에서 '변화하는 도시 경관 가운데서도, 그것은 주변 지역들과 함께 진화했다(Amid a changing cityscape, it continued to evolve with the neighborhood around it)'고 했으므로, 앞에서 먼저 그것이 무엇인지, 도시 경관이 어땠는지가 설명되어야 한다. [2] 앞에서 피너튼 극장이 수 년간의 경기 침체와 도시 쇠퇴를 거치면서도 계속 유지되어 왔다(it later persisted through years of economic stagnation and urban decline)고 했고, 뒤에서는 현재 시의 번화한 리버사이드 예술지구의 중추 역할을 하고 있다(the Finnerton Theater now serves as the backbone of the city's thriving Riverside Arts District)고 했다. 따라서 이 사이에 주어진 문장이 들어가야 도시 및 극장이 변화한 흐름이 자연스럽게 연결되므로, (B)가 정답이다.

어휘 amid ~중에서 cityscape 도시 경관 evolve 발달하다, 진화하다

176-180 안내책자 + 이메일

이곳 하플러 조경회사에서는 조경 설계가 어려울 필요가 없다고 생각합니다. **176 저희 목표는 고객이 원하는 사양에 부합하면서, 설치되고 나서 최소한으로만 돌보면 되는 독특하고 아름다운 정원을 설계하는 것입니다.** **177 저희는 또한 공기, 토양, 수질 오염 감소에 상당히 신경을 쓰고 있습니다.** 이를 성취하는 방법에 대한 더 자세한 정보를 원하시면 haplers.co.uk를 방문하세요.

절차는 네 단계로 실행됩니다. 방식은 아래와 같습니다.

1단계 - 저희 상담원 중 한 명이 전화를 드려서 귀하의 부지에 대한 목표와 비전에 대해 논의합니다.

2단계 - 수위, 고도, 토양 종류, 일조 패턴에 관한 정보를 수집하기 위해, 귀하의 토지에 대해 철저한 조사를 시행합니다. **178 다수의 프로젝트를 동시에 진행하고 있어 최초 상담 전화 이후 한 달까지 조사를 완료하지 못할 수도 있음을 알려드립니다.**

¹⁷⁹**3단계** - 저희 설계 전문가들이 기존 조경에 어울리는 설계 제안을 제시해 드립니다. 설계도의 모든 측면에 만족하실 때까지 조정 사항을 논의할 것입니다.

4단계 - 승인된 프로젝트 사양대로 설계를 시행합니다.

해당 과정을 시작하고 눈 앞에서 토지가 변화하는 모습을 지켜볼 준비가 되셨나요? 하플러에 01632 960255로 전화 주십시오.

어휘 landscape 조경 challenging 어려운, 힘든 unique 독특한 specifications 사양 require 요구하다, 필요로 하다 minimal 최소의, 아주 적은 reduce 감소시키다 pollution 오염 achieve 성취하다, 달성하다 implement 시행하다 phase 단계 property 부동산, 부지, 구내 conduct 시행하다, 실시하다 thorough 철저한, 꼼꼼한 elevation 해발, 고도 at once 동시에 complete 완료하다 survey 조사 initial 처음의 consultation 상담 present 제시하다, 보여주다 existing 기존의 adjustment 조정 (사항) approved 승인된 process 과정, 절차

수신: melinda_grotenhuis@charmail.net.uk
발신: martin.sampsell@haplers.co.uk
날짜: 2월 22일
제목: 제안
첨부: 🔗 하플러-초안1.org

그로텐후이스 씨께,

¹⁷⁹조경 설계 초안을 첨부했으니 생각해 보셨으면 합니다. 저희가 부지를 답사했을 때, 주차장에서 사무실까지의 통로를 어디에 만들고 싶은지 말씀하셨었죠. ¹⁸⁰하지만 고려해 보실만한 약간 다른 내용을 제안합니다. 경험상 상업용 환경에서는 통로를 가능한 한 직행으로 만들어야 하더군요. 그렇지 않으면 어쨌든 사람들이 종종 잔디로 걸어가거든요. 또한 일년 내내 꽃이 있었으면 한다고 말씀하셔서, 개화기가 각기 다른 다양한 자생식물을 설계에 포함시켰습니다.

이 설계를 보게 되시면 전화 주십시오. 세부사항을 설명해 드리겠습니다.

마틴 샘셀

어휘 proposal 제안 attach 첨부하다 walk-through 답사, 설명 indicate 내비치다, 시사하다 slightly 약간 commercial 상업적인 setting 환경, 배경 otherwise 그렇지 않으면 incorporate 포함하다 a variety of 다양한 walk A through B A에게 B를 자세히 설명하다, 보여주며 설명하다

176 사실 관계 확인

번역 안내책자에서 회사의 설계에 대해 명시한 것은?
(A) 다채롭다.
(B) 관리하기가 쉽다.
(C) 비어 있는 공간을 활용한다.
(D) 예전 구조물을 포함한다.

해설 안내책자의 첫 번째 단락에서 회사의 목표는 설치하고 나서 최소한으로만 돌보면 되는 독특하고 아름다운 정원을 설계하는 것(Our goal is to design unique, beautiful gardens that ~ require minimal care once they have been planted)이라고 했으므로, 관리하기 쉬운 설계를 한다는 사실을 알 수 있다. 따라서 (B)가 정답이다.

어휘 maintain 유지하다, 관리하다 vacant 비어 있는 structure 구조, 구조물

▸▸ Paraphrasing   지문의 **require minimal care**
→ 정답의 **easy to maintain**

177 세부 사항

번역 독자들을 하플러의 웹사이트로 안내하는 이유는?
(A) 회사의 환경 보호 관행을 알 수 있도록
(B) 직원의 자격증을 볼 수 있도록
(C) 설계 아이디어를 탐구해 볼 수 있도록
(D) 이전 고객이 쓴 추천의 글을 볼 수 있도록

해설 안내책자의 첫 번째 단락에서 공기, 토양, 수질 오염 감소에 상당히 신경을 쓰고 있다(We also care deeply about reducing air, soil, and water pollution)고 한 후, 이를 성취하는 방법에 대해 더 자세한 정보(more information about how we achieve this)를 원하면 haplers.co.uk를 방문하라고 안내했다. 따라서 웹사이트에 회사의 환경 관리 방안에 대한 정보가 있다는 것을 알 수 있으므로, (A)가 정답이다.

어휘 environmental 환경적인, 환경(보호)의 practice 관행, 관리 방안 credentials 자격증, 자격 testimonial 추천의 글, 추천서

▸▸ Paraphrasing   지문의 **haplers.co.uk**
→ 질문의 **Hapler's Web site**
지문의 **reducing air, soil, and water pollution** → 정답의 **environmental practices**

178 사실 관계 확인

번역 하플러에 대해 알 수 있는 것은?
(A) 다수의 고객에게 동시에 서비스를 제공한다.
(B) 고객들에게 시간 단위로 청구한다.
(C) 주거용 고객과만 작업한다.
(D) 고객 대다수가 추천한다.

해설 안내책자의 2단계(Phase 2) 절차가 설명된 부분을 보면, 하플러가 다수의 프로젝트를 동시에 진행한다(we work on many projects at once)고 쓰여 있다. 따라서 (A)가 정답이다.

어휘 bill 청구서를 보내다 on an hourly basis 시간제로, 시간당으로 residential 주택의, 거주지의

▸▸ Paraphrasing   지문의 **work on many projects at once**
→ 정답의 **provides services to multiple clients at the same time**

179 연계

번역 그로텐후이스 씨의 프로젝트는 절차상의 어느 단계에 있는가?

(A) 1단계
(B) 2단계
(C) 3단계
(D) 4단계

해설 이메일의 첫 번째 단락에서 그로텐후이스 씨가 생각해 볼 수 있도록 조경 설계 초안을 첨부했다(I have attached an initial draft of a landscape design for you to consider)고 했다. 안내책자의 절차(process)를 보면, 이는 설계 전문가들이 기존 조경에 어울리는 설계 제안을 제시(Our design specialists will present you with a proposed design to suit your existing landscape)하는 3단계에 해당하므로, (C)가 정답이다.

180 세부 사항

번역 샘셀 씨가 통로 위치를 바꾸자고 제안한 이유는?

(A) 잠재적인 위험을 방지하기 위해
(B) 가장 효율적인 선택사항을 제공하기 위해
(C) 쓸 수 있는 그늘을 이용하기 위해
(D) 건물의 가장 매력적인 부분을 보여주기 위해

해설 이메일의 첫 번째 단락에서 샘셀 씨는 그로텐후이스 씨가 원했던 것과는 약간 다른 내용을 제안한다(we are proposing something slightly different)고 한 후, 경험상 상업용 환경에서는 통로를 가능한 한 직행으로 만들어야 한다(make pathways in commercial settings as direct as possible)며 그렇지 않을 경우 사람들이 종종 잔디로 걸어간다(Otherwise, people often walk through the grass anyway)고 덧붙였다. 즉 그로텐후이스 씨가 희망하는 안의 부작용을 알려주며 더 효율적인 방안을 제시하는 것이므로, (B)가 정답이다.

어휘 avoid 방지하다, 막다   potential 잠재적인   efficient 효율적인   take advantage of ~을 이용하다

▸▸ Paraphrasing   지문의 proposing something slightly different → 질문의 suggest changing

181-185 공지 + 이메일

메렌빌 지역 버스 당국
공지

181 메렌빌 지역 버스 당국(MRBA)에서는 최근 시행된 승객 설문조사에 대응하여, 메렌빌 중앙역(MCS)과 루버그를 오가는 토요일, 일요일 서비스를 조정할 예정입니다. 다음의 일정 변경은 5월 1일부로 시행됩니다.

• 183 매주 토요일에만 운행되는 36번 버스는 매시 정각 MCS를 출발하며, 첫 출발 차량은 오전 6시, 막차는 자정입니다. 본 조정사항은 승객들에게 선택 가능한 출발편을 더 많이 제공하고자 하는 것입니다.

• 182 양일 모두 운행하는 47번 버스는 오후 12시 15분과 오후 6시 15분의 정기 출발 시간 외에 이제 오전 7시에도 MCS에서 출발합니다.

• 양일 모두 운행하는 51번 버스는 계속 MCS에서 3회 출발합니다. 단, 이제 오전 7시 30분, 오후 1시 30분, 오후 4시 30분으로 예정되어 있습니다.

• 매주 일요일에만 운행되는 65번 버스는 오전 8시 대신 오전 10시에 MCS를 출발합니다. 오후 1시, 오후 3시, 오후 5시로 예정된 출발편은 변경 없이 그대로입니다.

어휘 regional 지역의   authority 당국   in response to ~에 대한 응답으로, ~에 대응하여   recently 최근에   conducted 시행된, 실시된   passenger 승객   survey 설문조사   adjust 조정하다   be in effect 시행되다   as of ~부로   departure 출발   intend 의도하다   in addition to ~에 더하여, ~ 외에도   regularly 정기적으로   be scheduled to ~할 예정이다   take place 일어나다   remain ~한 채로 있다

수신: 아드리아노 마르티네즈 〈amartinez@mrba.com〉
발신: 클레어 브룬크호스트 〈cbrunkhorst@mrba.com〉
날짜: 5월 14일
제목: 교대 근무 전환 요청

안녕하세요, 아드리아노.

183 당신의 요청에 관해 말씀 드리면, 저는 5월 22일 토요일 야간 버스 운행조를 맡을 수 있습니다. 정신이 맑아야 한다는 사실을 184 인지하고 있으니 휴식을 많이 취해 두도록 할게요.

185 대신 5월 25일 화요일 제 주간조를 대신해 주실 수 있나요? 전에 일했던 같은 시카고 기반 회사에서 일하는 친구 한 명이 그날 저를 방문할 예정이라서요.

도움에 미리 감사 드립니다.

클레어 브룬크호스트, MRBA 동료

어휘 switch 바꾸다   request 요청   regarding ~에 관해   realize 알아차리다, 인지하고 있다   alert 정신이 초롱초롱한   in return 대신에, 보답으로   take over ~을 대신 맡다   in advance 미리   assistance 도움

181 주제 / 목적

번역 공지의 목적은?

(A) 새로운 버스 노선 소개
(B) 버스 정류장 폐쇄 대해 보고
(C) 교통 서비스 개선 공표
(D) 제안된 일정 변경에 대한 의견 요청

해설 공지의 첫 번째 단락을 보면, 승객 설문조사 결과에 대응해(In response to ~ passenger survey) 메렌빌 지역 버스 당국(MRBA)에서 메렌빌 중앙역과 루버그를 오가는 토요일, 일요일 서비스를 조정할 예정(will be adjusting its Saturday and Sunday service between Merenville Central Station (MCS) and Louberg)이라고 한 후, 관련 내용을 설명하고 있다, 따라서 (C)가 정답이다.

어휘 improvement 개선, 향상

182 추론 / 암시

번역 공지에서 47번 버스에 대해 암시된 것은?

(A) 노선상에 새로운 정류장이 있다.
(B) 가장 이른 출발 시간을 가지고 있다.
(C) 오후에만 출발했었다.
(D) 1주일에 하루만 운행한다.

해설 공지의 세 번째 단락을 보면, 47번 버스가 오후 12시 15분과 오후 6시 15분의 정기 출발 시간 외에 오전 7시에도 MCS에서 출발하게 된다(Bus 47 ~ will now be departing MCS at 7:00 A.M. in addition to its regularly scheduled departure times of 12:15 P.M. and 6:15 P.M.)고 나와 있다. 따라서 일정 조정 전에는 오후에만 출발했다고 추론할 수 있으므로, (C)가 정답이다.

> ▸ Paraphrasing 지문의 **regularly scheduled departure times of 12:15 P.M. and 6:15 P.M.**
> → 정답의 **depart only in the afternoon**

183 연계

번역 브룬크호스트 씨는 5월 22일에 어떤 버스를 운행하겠는가?

(A) 36번 버스
(B) 47번 버스
(C) 51번 버스
(D) 65번 버스

해설 이메일의 첫 번째 단락에서 브룬크호스트 씨는 5월 22일 토요일에 마르티네즈 씨 대신 야간 버스 운행조를 맡을 수 있다(I can take over your late-night bus driving shift on Saturday, May 22)고 했다. 공지에 나온 4대의 버스 중 토요일 늦은 시간에 운행하는 버스는 막차 출발 시간이 자정(with ~ the last (departure) to take place at midnight)인 36번이므로, (A)가 정답이다.

184 동의어 찾기

번역 이메일의 첫 번째 단락, 두 번째 줄에 쓰인 "realize"와 의미가 가장 가까운 단어는?

(A) 벌다
(B) 이해하다
(C) 교환하다
(D) 성취하다

해설 'realize'를 포함한 부분은 '정신이 맑아야 한다는 사실을 인지하고 있다(I realize that I'll have to be alert)'라는 의미로 해석되는데, 여기서 realize는 '알아차리다, 인지하고 있다'라는 뜻으로 쓰였다. 따라서 '이해하다, 알다'라는 의미의 (B) comprehend가 정답이다.

185 사실 관계 확인

번역 브룬크호스트 씨가 이메일에서 시사한 것은?

(A) 시카고에서 새 일자리를 얻을 계획이다.
(B) 마르티네즈 씨를 방문할 시간이 없다.
(C) 화요일에 이른 교대조로 일하는 것을 선호한다.
(D) 옛 친구와 시간을 보내고 싶다.

해설 이메일의 두 번째 단락에서 브룬크호스트 씨는 마르티네즈 씨에게 5월 25일 화요일에 자신의 주간조를 대신해 달라고(could you possibly take over my day shift on Tuesday, May 25?) 요청한 후, 예전에 일했던 회사의 친구가 그날 방문할 예정(A friend of mine, who works for the same ~ company that I used to work for, will be visiting me that day)이라고 덧붙였다. 따라서 옛 친구와 시간을 보내고 싶어 한다는 것을 알 수 있으므로, (D)가 정답이다.

어휘 prefer 선호하다

186-190 전단 + 안내책자 + 이메일

퀵 픽스 워크숍

1월 15일 커뮤니티 센터에서 헤이거스타운 주민들과 함께 퀵 픽스 워크숍에 참여하세요. 당신의 흥미를 불러일으킬 주제가 최소 한 가지는 확실히 있을 것입니다. **186예를 들면, 생활 방식을 억제하지 않고 재정적으로 절약하는 법이나 현명한 생활로 환경에 미치는 영향을 감소하는 방식을 찾는 법을 배울 수 있습니다.** 아니면, 워크숍에 참석함으로써 가족의 건강이나 웰빙을 향상시킬 영감을 얻을 수도 있습니다. **187저명한 헤이거스타운 장기 거주자 그랜트 카드웰이 주택 단열에 관한 강의를 진행합니다.** 해당 강의의 좌석을 확보하시려면 일찍 도착해 주세요. 거의 모두가 냉난방 비용을 삭감하는 방법을 배우고 싶어하니까요.

등록하실 필요는 없지만 참석자 수를 기록할 예정입니다. 문의사항은 마이크 그린리에게 m.greenly@hagerstown.gov로 연락 주십시오.

어휘 resident 거주자 at least 최소 economize 절약하다 financially 재정적으로, 재정상 inhibit 억제하다 discover 찾다 reduce 줄이다, 감소시키다 impact 영향 environment 환경 alternatively 그 대신에, 아니면 inspiration 영감 prominent 저명한, 중요한 weatherize 단열하다 be eager to ~하고 싶어 하다 trim (불필요한 부분을) 잘라내다 registration 등록 required 필수인 record 기록하다 attendance 참석자 수, 참석률

퀵 픽스 워크숍 - 일정표	
오전 10시	**187단열** - 마리온 카운티 지역 단열 계획(MCRWI)에서 나온 전문가로부터 배워서 집의 에너지 효율성을 높여 보세요. **물과 돈을 아끼세요** - 헤이거스타운의 물 공급에 대해 알아보고, 소비를 제한하고 월 수도요금 줄이는 요령을 얻으세요.

오전 11시	DIY 개인 미용 용품 - 데오도란트, 비누, 피부 수분로션 등 매일 쓰는 개인 미용 용품을 직접 만들어보세요.
오후 1시	190자연 공간 조성 - 자생식물을 기르고 지역 생태계 돌보기에 대해 알아보세요. 당신의 정원이나 뜰에 자연적으로 지속 가능한 서식지를 만들도록 도와주세요.
188오후 2시	새해를 맞이하여 더욱 건강한 당신 - 가족을 위해 맛있고 건강에 좋은 식사를 만드는 시연을 지켜보세요. 시식이 제공됩니다. 188필수 유지보수 - 당신의 차량을 매서운 겨울 날씨 속에서도 최상의 주행 상태로 유지하세요.

어휘 efficient 효율적인 expert 전문가 supply 공급 consumption 소비, 소모 utility bill 공과금 native plant 자생식물 nurture 보살피다, 양육하다 ecosystem 생태계 sustainable 지속 가능한 habitat 서식지 demonstration 시연 essential 필수적인 despite ~에도 불구하고 harsh 가혹한, 혹독한

수신: 마이크 그린리
발신: 안토니오 퍼킨스
날짜: 1월 12일
제목: 문의

그린리 씨께,

최근 헤이거스타운으로 이사했는데 지역 내 고유식생에 대해 배우고 싶습니다. 이전 고향에서 나무와 식물을 많이 기른 경험이 있지만 여기서 자라는 품종들은 완전히 다르더군요. 이웃이 말하길, 원예와 관련된 강의가 있을 거라고 하던데요. 189/190워크숍 중에 지역 고유의 동식물에 대해 배우고 싶은 저의 특정 관심사를 다루는 것이 있을까요?

안토니오 퍼킨스

어휘 native vegetation 고유식생 former 이전의 variety 품종 completely 완전히 related to ~에 관련된 address 다루다 specific 특정한, 구체적인 flora and fauna (특정 지역의) 동식물

186 세부 사항

번역 전단에 따르면, 워크숍에서는 어떤 주제를 다룰 것인가?
(A) 집 꾸미기
(B) 돈 절약하기
(C) 반려동물 돌보기
(D) 시 재활용 서비스 이용하기

해설 전단의 첫 번째 단락에 언급된 워크숍의 주제는 크게 네 가지(생활 방식을 억제하지 않고 재정적으로 절약하는 법, 현명한 생활로 환경에 미치는 영향을 감소하는 방식을 찾는 법, 가족의 건강이나 웰빙을 향상시키는 법, 주택 단열 방법)인데, 이 중 첫 번째(how to economize financially without inhibiting your lifestyle)에 해당하는 (B)가 정답이다.

▸▸ Paraphrasing 지문의 economize financially
→ 정답의 Saving money

187 연계

번역 카드웰 씨에 대해 가장 사실에 가까운 것은?
(A) 전문 일기예보관이다.
(B) MCRWI 단체의 구성원이다.
(C) 대학 교수이다.
(D) 퀵 픽스 워크숍 준비를 담당한다.

해설 전단의 첫 번째 단락에서 그랜트 카드웰이 주택 단열에 관한 강의를 진행한다(Our own Grant Cardwell ~ will be leading a session on weatherizing your home)고 했는데, 안내책자를 보면 '단열(Weatherization)' 강의를 하는 사람은 마리온 카운티 지역 단열 계획(MCRWI)에서 나온 전문가(an expert from the Marion County Regional Weatherization Initiative)라고 소개되어 있다. 따라서 단열 강의를 진행하는 카드웰 씨가 MCRWI 단체 소속이라고 추론할 수 있으므로, (B)가 정답이다.

어휘 in charge of ~를 맡아서, 담당해서

▸▸ Paraphrasing 지문의 an expert from ~ MCRWI
→ 정답의 a member of the MCRWI organization

188 세부 사항

번역 차량 관리에 대한 강의는 몇 시인가?
(A) 오전 10시
(B) 오전 11시
(C) 오후 1시
(D) 오후 2시

해설 안내책자의 일정표에 나온 워크숍 중 차량 관리에 대한 것은 추운 날씨에도 차량을 최상의 주행 상태로 유지(Keep your vehicle in top driving condition)하는 방법을 다루는 '필수 유지보수(Essential Maintenance)' 워크숍이다. 해당 워크숍은 오후 2시에 진행될 예정이므로, (D)가 정답이다.

189 세부 사항

번역 퍼킨스 씨는 무엇에 관한 정보를 원하는가?
(A) 행사 주제
(B) 행사 등록
(C) 행사 장소
(D) 행사 일정

해설 이메일의 후반부에서 퍼킨스 씨는 지역 고유의 동식물에 대해 배우고 싶은 자신의 관심사를 다루는 워크숍이 있는지(do any of the workshops address my specific interest in learning about the native flora and fauna?) 문의했다. 따라서 워크숍의 주제에 대한 정보를 원한다고 볼 수 있으므로, (A)가 정답이다.

190 연계

번역 퍼킨스 씨는 어떤 워크숍에 참석하겠는가?

(A) 단열
(B) DIY 개인 미용 용품
(C) 자연 공간 조성
(D) 필수 유지보수

해설 이메일의 후반부에서 퍼킨스 씨는 지역 고유의 동식물에 대해 배울 수 있는(learning about the native flora and fauna) 워크숍에 참석하고 싶다는 의사를 밝혔다. 안내책자의 일정표(Schedule)에 따르면, 자생식물을 기르고 지역 생태계 돌보기에 대해 알아보는(Grow native plants and learn about nurturing the local ecosystem) '자연 공간 조성(Creating Natural Spaces)' 워크숍이 퍼킨스 씨의 관심사에 부합하므로, (C)가 정답이다.

191-195 이메일 + 도표 + 온라인 후기

수신: 로완 플레이랜드 경영진
발신: 헨리 루이스
날짜: 4월 12일
제목: 업데이트

여러분,

어제 경영진 회의에서 모두를 뵐 수 있어 좋았습니다. **191제가 이곳에 없어서 다음 2주간 월요일에 회의를 할 수 없음을 알려드립니다.** 다음 달까지 뵐 수 없다는 뜻이지요. 그동안 신경 써야 할 긴급 사안이 있을 경우 리디아 창에게 연락해 주세요.

192/193이제 곧 런어바웃 룸에 인공 암벽을 설치할 계획을 추진할 예정입니다. 193켈리 멀그루가 해당 작업을 수행할 수 있는 업체들 이름을 작업 가능 시간 및 비용과 함께 보내주기로 했습니다.

톰 홀덴이 리틀 엔지니어 카페에서 판매하는 샌드위치와 간식의 새 판매업체를 찾아볼 것입니다.

감사합니다.

헨리 루이스
로완 플레이랜드

어휘 management 경영진, 간부 urgent 긴급한 attention 주의, 주목 in the meantime 그동안에, 당분간 availability 이용 가능성, 작업 가능 시간

193인공 암벽 옵션		
193업체	193총 비용	193가장 빠른 설치일자
릭 월 오브 펀	1450달러	5월 29일
클라이밍 월 갤로어	1300달러	5월 18일
프루 클라이밍 월	1350달러	6월 3일
웨더스필드 월 앤 플레이 그라운드	1450달러	6월 10일

비고: 릭, 프루, 웨더필드는 녹색과 검은색으로 이뤄진 인공 암벽 제공. 195클라이밍 월 갤로어는 다양한 색상 및 혼합색상 옵션 제공

★★★★★
5월 22일

어제 자녀 두 명과 로완 플레이랜드에 다시 갔습니다. 항상 그렇듯이 즐거운 시간을 보냈지만 이번에는 더더욱 특별했습니다. 195아이들은 런어바웃 룸에 있는 새 인공 암벽에서 대부분의 시간을 보냈어요. 많은 곳에 인공 암벽이 있긴 해도, 이 인공 암벽은 전에 본 것들보다 더 많은 색상이 들어가 있었죠. 194리틀 엔지니어 카페의 새 메뉴도 역시 맛있었습니다. 원래 있던 어린이들이 먹기 좋은 음식 외에, 이제 어른들을 위한 새 메뉴도 제공하고 있어요. 로완 플레이랜드를 강력 추천합니다. 실망하지 않을 거예요.

존 로울스톤
이스트 린드스트롬 빌리지

어휘 in addition to ~에 더하여, ~외에도 usual 평상시의, 기존의 recommend 추천하다 disappointed 실망한

191 세부 사항

번역 이메일에 따르면, 경영진 회의는 보통 얼마나 자주 열리는가?

(A) 주 2회
(B) 주 1회
(C) 월 2회
(D) 월 1회

해설 이메일의 첫 번째 단락에서 다음 2주간 월요일에 회의를 할 수 없다(Please note that we will not be able to meet the next two Mondays)고 했는데, 여기서 경영진 회의가 주 1회 월요일마다 열린다는 것을 알 수 있다. 따라서 (B)가 정답이다.

192 사실 관계 확인

번역 이메일에서 런어바웃 룸에 대해 명시한 것은?

(A) 변화를 겪을 것이다.
(B) 특별 행사가 열릴 것이다.
(C) 최근에 열었다.
(D) 최근 출판물에 다뤄졌다.

해설 이메일의 두 번째 단락에서 런어바웃 룸에 인공 암벽을 설치하는 계획을 추진할 예정(we will move forward with plans for installing a climbing wall in the Runabout Room)이라고 했으므로, 변화가 있을 것임을 알 수 있다. 따라서 (A)가 정답이다.

어휘 undergo 겪다 feature 특별히 포함하다, 특집으로 다루다 publication 출판물

▸▸ Paraphrasing 지문의 installing a climbing wall
→ 정답의 some changes

193 연계

번역 도표는 누가 만들었겠는가?

(A) 루이스 씨
(B) 창 씨
(C) 멀그루 씨
(D) 홀덴 씨

해설 도표는 인공 암벽 옵션(CLIMIBING WALL OPTIONS)에 관한 것으로, 각 업체(Company)의 총 비용(Total Cost) 및 가장 빠른 설치일자(Earliest Installation Date)를 비교해 보여주고 있다. 이메일의 두 번째 단락을 보면, 켈리 멀그루가 인공 암벽 설치 작업을 수행할 수 있는 업체들 이름을 작업 가능 시간 및 비용과 함께 보내주기로 했다(Kelly Mulgrew has agreed to send us the names of some companies that can do the work, along with their availability and prices)고 쓰여 있으므로, 멀그루 씨가 이 도표를 작성했다고 추론할 수 있다. 따라서 (C)가 정답이다.

194 사실 관계 확인

번역 온라인 후기에 따르면, 카페에 대해 사실인 것은?

(A) 가격을 내렸다.
(B) 영업시간이 연장됐다.
(C) 메뉴에 새 항목이 포함됐다.
(D) 내부 장식을 다시 했다.

해설 온라인 후기의 중반부에서 리틀 엔지니어 카페의 새 메뉴도 맛있었다(The new menu at the Little Engineer Café is also nice)고 했으므로, (C)가 정답이다.

어휘 reduce 줄이다, 낮추다 extend 연장하다, 늘리다 decorate 장식하다

195 연계

번역 로완 플레이랜드의 인공 암벽은 어떤 업체가 설치했겠는가?

(A) 릭 월 오브 펀
(B) 클라이밍 월 갤로어
(C) 프루 클라이밍 월
(D) 웨더스필드 월 앤 플레이그라운드

해설 온라인 후기의 중반부에서 로울스톤 씨는 아이들이 런어바웃 룸에 있는 새 인공 암벽에서 대부분의 시간을 보냈다(They spent most the time on the new climbing wall in the Runabout Room)고 한 후, 이 인공 암벽은 전에 본 것들보다 더 많은 색상이 들어가 있었다(this one included many more colors than any we had seen before)고 덧붙였다. 도표의 비고란(Note)을 보면, 클라이밍 월 갤로어가 다양한 색상 및 혼합색상 옵션을 제공한다(Climbing Walls Galore offers many colors and mix-and-match options)고 되어 있으므로, 이 업체가 인공 암벽을 설치했다고 추론할 수 있다. 따라서 (B)가 정답이다.

196-200 안내책자 + 도표 + 이메일

더블린 인 더 선
도노반 투어 운영사

[196]다음 투어들은 4월 1일부터 8월 30일까지 진행됩니다. 각 날짜의 투어 시삭 시간을 알아보시려면 저희 본사를 방문하시거나 +353 22 455 0827로 전화하십시오.

더블린 캐슬—3시간, 1인당 15유로
더블린의 13세기 성을 해당 역사 전문가의 진행으로 돌아보는 가이드 투어입니다. 가격에 성 입장료가 포함됩니다. 성의 방문객용 정문에서 시작 및 종료됩니다.

시크릿 오브 더블린—2시간, 1인당 12유로
더블린 도보 투어입니다. 더블린의 숨은 이야기를 찾아보세요. 도노반 본사에서 시작 및 종료됩니다.

[198]**가든 오브 아일랜드**—5시간, 1인당 30유로
[198]더블린 남쪽 산과 옛 도시 킬케니로 떠나는 반일 여행입니다. 가디너 가 버스 정류장에서 시작 및 종료됩니다.

[200]**골웨이 미니 크루즈**—9시간, 1인당 70유로
[200]대서양으로 나가서 웅장한 모허 절벽 옆을 둘러보는 미니 크루즈 전일 여행입니다. 점심 식사가 포함됩니다. 가디너 가 버스 정류장에서 시작 및 종료합니다.

어휘 headquarters 본부 expert 전문가 entry 입장 entrance 입구 excursion (짧게 하는) 여행 magnificent 대단히 아름다운, 웅장한

도노반 투어 운영사: 7월 요약

투어명	1일 투어 횟수	투어당 평균 수익 (유로)	1일 평균 수익 (유로)	고객 후기 평점 (/5)
[197]더블린 캐슬	8	41	328	[197]4.8
시크릿 오브 더블린	6	58	348	3.3
[198]가든 오브 아일랜드	[198]2	124	248	4.5
골웨이 미니 크루즈	1	-297	-297	4.6

수신: agupta@donovantouroperators.ie
발신: somalley@donovantouroperators.ie
날짜: 8월 13일
제목: 투어 상품

굽타 씨께,

아시는 바와 같이 관광업계 비수기로 접어드니, 우리의 투어 상품을 줄일 예정입니다. [200]모허 절벽 투어에서는 수익을 얻지 못했기 때문에 이를 중단해야 한다고 생각하고 있어요. 하지만 새로운 안내책자 디자이너들에게 이러한 결정사항을 알리기 전, 당신에게 확인을 받고 싶어요.

이번 주는 새로운 옥토버 매직 투어를 위한 투어 가이드를 모집하느라 바쁘신 걸로 압니다. 그러니 월요일에 만나면 될 것 같아요. 오후 2시 괜찮으신가요?

사라 오말리

어휘 offering 내놓은 것, 제공하는 상품 reduce 줄이다, 낮추다 discontinue 중단하다 confirmation 확인 brochure 안내책자 recruitment 모집

196 세부 사항

번역 안내책자에 따르면, 모든 투어의 공통점은?
(A) 동일한 시간 동안 이어진다.
(B) 같은 장소에서 출발한다.
(C) 같은 달 동안 제공된다.
(D) 1인당 비용이 같다.

해설 안내책자의 첫 번째 단락에서 '다음 투어들은 4월 1일부터 8월 30일까지 진행된다(The following tours run from 1 April to 30 August)'라고 했으므로, 모든 투어가 같은 기간에 제공된다는 것을 알 수 있다. 따라서 (C)가 정답이다. 진행 시간 및 1인당 비용이 각기 다르고, 세 개의 다른 장소에서 출발하므로 나머지는 오답이다.

197 사실 관계 확인

번역 도표에서 더블린 캐슬 투어에 대해 명시한 것은?
(A) 가장 높은 평가를 받았다.
(B) 시크릿 오브 더블린보다 덜 자주 진행된다.
(C) 모든 투어 중에서 1일 수익이 가장 높다.
(D) 가든 오브 아일랜드 투어보다 투어당 수익이 많다.

해설 도표에서 더블린 캐슬 투어의 고객 후기 평점(Average customer review)이 4.8로 가장 높다는 것을 확인할 수 있다. 따라서 (A)가 정답이다. 시크릿 오브 더블린보다 2회 더 진행되며, 1일당 수익은 두 번째로 높고, 가든 오브 아일랜드 투어보다 투어당 수익이 적으므로 나머지는 오답이다.

어휘 highly rated 높은 평가를 받은

198 연계

번역 도노반 투어 운영사는 킬케니 투어를 하루 몇 회 진행하는가?
(A) 1회
(B) 2회
(C) 6회
(D) 8회

해설 안내책자를 보면, 킬케니로 가는 여행이 '가든 오브 아일랜드(Garden of Island: Half-day excursion to the mountains south of Dublin and the old city of Kilkenny)'임을 확인할 수 있다. 도표에 나온 '가든 오브 아일랜드'의 1일 투어 횟수(Tours per day)는 2회이므로, (B)가 정답이다.

199 주제 / 목적

번역 이메일을 쓴 목적은?
(A) 안내책자를 주문하려고
(B) 신입 투어 가이드에게 정책을 설명해 주려고
(C) 동료와의 회의 일정을 잡으려고
(D) 고객 불만사항에 응대하려고

해설 이메일의 첫 번째 단락에서 오말리 씨는 굽타 씨에게 의논할 것이 있다고 한 후, 두 번째 단락에서 월요일에 만나면 될 것 같다(so we can meet on Monday)며 시간(Would 2 P.M. work?)을 제시했다. 따라서 동료와 회의 일정을 잡기 위해 쓴 이메일이라고 볼 수 있으므로, (C)가 정답이다.

어휘 place an order 주문을 넣다 policy 정책 colleague 동료 respond 응하다, 답하다

200 연계

번역 오말리 씨에 따르면, 어떤 투어가 중단되겠는가?
(A) 더블린 캐슬
(B) 시크릿 오브 더블린
(C) 가든 오브 아일랜드
(D) 골웨이 미니 크루즈

해설 이메일의 첫 번째 단락에서 오말리 씨는 모허 절벽 투어를 중단해야 할 것 같다(I was thinking we should discontinue the tour to the Cliffs of Moher)며 자신의 의사를 밝혔다. 안내책자를 보면, 오말리 씨가 중단을 제안한 모허 절벽 투어는 골웨이 미니 크루즈(Galway Mini Cruise: Full-day excursion to the Atlantic coast for a mini cruise beside magnificent Cliffs of Moher)에 해당하므로, (D)가 정답이다.

<ETS 기출문제집 1000 Vol.1 1위> LC: 교보문고 19년 8월 13일, RC: 11월 03일 발표 기준
<ETS 기출문제집 1000 Vol.2 1위> LC: 교보문고 21년 8월 31일, RC: 10월 25일 발표 기준

'토익 베스트 1위'에
빛나는 1,2탄에 이어
3탄 전격 출시!

국내 유일 정기시험 성우 음원 제공
기출 포인트에 초점을 맞춘 명쾌한 해설
"ETS 토익기출 수험서" App 채점으로 취약점 진단

각권 17,800원

**ETS가 독점
제공하는**
진짜 기출문제 7회

+

동일 스펙의
예상문제 3회
전격 공개!

공식홈페이지 www.ybmbooks.com | ETS 공식카페 www.etstoeicbook.co.kr